POLITICAL IDEOLOGIES

May 24 - Midter Question
May 31 - Return
June 7 - Class Essay
June 14 - Final Exam
Questions
June 21 - Return
Exam

To Becky and Laura

Political Ideologies

EDITED BY
PAUL WETHERLY

OXFORD
UNIVERSITY PRESS

OXFORD
UNIVERSITY PRESS

Great Clarendon Street, Oxford, OX2 6DP,
United Kingdom

Oxford University Press is a department of the University of Oxford.
It furthers the University's objective of excellence in research, scholarship,
and education by publishing worldwide. Oxford is a registered trade mark of
Oxford University Press in the UK and in certain other countries

Published in the United States of America by Oxford University Press
198 Madison Avenue, New York, NY 10016, United States of America

British Library Cataloguing in Publication Data

Data available

Library of Congress Control Number: 2017932605

ISBN 978-0-19-872785-9

Printed in Great Britain by
Bell & Bain Ltd., Glasgow

Preface

This book provides an introduction to the range of ideologies that frame the way political debates are conducted and political issues are decided. These debates and decisions are not the preserve of 'specialists' such as academics and politicians for, as argued in Chapter 1, we are all ideologists in the sense that we have understandings of the way the world works and values which guide our assessments of how it could be improved.

As the subtitle of the first chapter suggests, ideologies can be seen as contesting the nature of the 'good society'—advancing rival claims about how the world works and could be improved through political action—and this conception is used throughout the book to set out and analyse each ideology. However, it is important to understand that ideology is a contested concept which can be defined and used in different ways, and developing this understanding is one of the main objectives of the first chapter.

The approach to the study of ideologies in this book involves a number of aspects. We consider the origins and development of each ideology and, in doing so, we distinguish between 'classical' (Chapters 2–7) and 'new' ideologies (Chapters 9–12). However, we also note that this distinction should be treated with caution as some of the new ideologies go back quite a long way. We also examine how ideologies that may be characterized as Western and modern in their origins have subsequently become globalized, a process that has been driven largely by the expansion of the West and that has involved resistance and adaptation.

Ideologies are identified by familiar labels—liberalism, conservatism, socialism, etc.—and this can create the impression that each ideology is a distinct and self-contained set of ideas that can be placed in its own separate 'box'. Of course, each ideology must be substantially distinct, or ideological labels would have little meaning. In each chapter this distinctiveness is analysed in terms of the ideology's key concepts and vision of the good society. However, the book emphasizes the complex and messy nature of ideological debate, which has a number of aspects. Debate takes place *within* as well as *between* ideologies as they contain internal variants—there is more than one way to be say a liberal or a socialist. Ideologies may share some key concepts, such as liberty and equality, and contest their meanings. There may be blurred edges rather than sharp boundaries between some ideologies, such as versions of liberalism, socialism, and anarchism. And there are some ideological 'marriages', such as between liberalism and feminism or environmentalism and socialism.

In considering the development of ideologies we consider them not just as abstract sets of ideas but as action-oriented, and we therefore consider the connections between ideology and politics and the way ideologies are embodied in political movements and parties. This also leads us to consider the impact of ideologies in the world and how we can assess their influence. In this respect a key argument is around the status of liberalism as a dominant ideology, and contemporary claims that liberalism has triumphed in the ideological contest.

Most readers of this book will be using it as a textbook. I hope that it helps them to be successful in their studies. More than that, though, I hope they find the book a stimulating guide to political ideologies that helps them to develop their own thinking as critical ideologists.

There are many people who deserve my thanks for their help in making this book possible and with whom it has been a pleasure to work.

First, the contributors, without whom this book would literally not have been possible (or certainly would have taken a lot longer and not been as good). I am very grateful to colleagues from Leeds Beckett University and elsewhere who have very generously given their time and expertise to write chapters for the book. This collective approach means that the book draws on a stock of knowledge that is vastly greater than any single author could muster. It is also, I think, a strength that although there are common features in the chapters they benefit from the individual voice and approach of each author. As contributors, they have had to put up with my editorial suggestions and occasional pesterings, which I hope they have not found too irksome.

It has been a pleasure to work with the team at Oxford University Press, and I am particularly grateful to Sarah Iles who commissioned the book and, latterly, Emily Spicer. Both have been extremely helpful and supportive throughout.

Finally, the book has benefited from the thorough and constructive feedback given by a group of academic reviewers. Their assistance is greatly appreciated, and has helped to shape the book. In alphabetical order they are:

Robin Barklis, University of Oregon

Tom Bentley, University of Aberdeen

Simon Birnbaum, Stockholm University

Jacqueline Briggs, University of Lincoln

Michael L. Coulter, Grove City College

Ashley Dodsworth, University of Bristol

Paul Flenley, University of Portsmouth

Ian Fraser, Loughborough University

Antje Grebner, The Hague University of Applied Sciences

Mathew Humphrey, University of Nottingham

Robert Jackson, Manchester Metropolitan University

Malte Kaeding, University of Surrey

Rasmus Karlsson, Umeå University

Aynsley Kellow, University of Tasmania

Alia Middleton, University of Surrey

David S. Moon, University of Bath

Saul Newman, Goldsmiths University of London

Niklas Olsen, University of Copenhagen

Phil Parvin, Loughborough University

Andy Price, Sheffield Hallam University

Sam Raphael, University of Westminster

Paola Rivetti, Dublin City University

Geoffrey Robinson, Deakin University

Andrea Schapper, University of Stirling

Finally, it is one of the little privileges and pleasures of being editor that I get to dedi-
cate the book, as I do to my wonderful daughters, Laura and Becky.

Paul Wetherly

Guided tour of the book

Political Ideologies is a rich learning resource, enhanced with a range of features designed to support your learning and to help you get the most out of the book.

OBJECTIVES

- Provide an outline of the key ideas and concepts of 'classical' ana
- Show how anarchist views on human nature, the state, political a and religion vary, and where possible, what unites them
- Assess recent critical responses to anarchism, in particular 'post-a
- Assess specific historical examples of anarchism
- Examine the extent to which anarchism can be regarded as a col

Objectives—each chapter begins with a clear set of objectives to help you understand what you can expect to learn as you read the chapter.

Case Study 8.2 Political attitudes and the 'centre groun

The idea that elections are won in the 'centre ground' has become co all common sense it needs to be scrutinized. The strategy of occupyin ideological terrain, strongly advocated by former Labour Prime Min the assumption that this is where political attitudes are clustered, tha the end decide the result in a democracy— . . . are located more in t ise' (Blair, quoted in *The Herald* 2016). Thus parties that occupy eithe spectrum will find only minorities of voters gathered there.

Case studies—throughout chapters, you will find a number of Case studies that extend or apply your understanding by focusing on a particular aspect of an ideology or highlighting a relevant political event or issue.

Stop and Think

From this discussion of the basic concept of ideology, consider how a provide a framework of political ideas encompassing both understand ment or, in other words, both theory and action.

Variants of ideologies

Freeden refers to 'observed liberalisms' rather than liberalis

Stop and think boxes—the text is broken up at regular intervals by questions that encourage you to reflect critically on the text and provoke discussion.

---

he same difficulties arise in relation to attempts to disting atism' (e.g. **authoritarian**, **paternalistic**, **libertarian**, an nspection, usually turn out to be different ways of denoting litional' and 'modern' conservatism. Traditional conservati oth 'authoritarian' and 'paternalistic', since it portrayed the al stability through rigorous enforcement of the law and th c amenities to the poor. This is not to say, of course, that all ' y definition 'conservative'; for conservatives, authority is in

Glossary terms—important terms are highlighted on first use in each chapter and included in the glossary at the end of the book.

Summary

- Religion is a contested concept with no agreed defi
  many forms.
- Religion can be likened to an ideology, particularly
  code governing the conduct of human affairs.
- There is debate about whether religion is in declin

Summaries—each chapter finishes with a bulleted summary to help you to consolidate your understanding of key points.

Further reading

The obvious starting point for anyone who is interested in con
Burke's *Reflections on the Revolution in France* (1790: numerou
book includes detailed discussions of revolutionary events wi
but the magnificence of the writing should encourage enthusia

More recently, John Gray's essay 'The Undoing of Conservatism',
(1995), bears a strong resemblance to the argument in the p

Further reading—at the end of each chapter, suggestions for further reading help you to deepen your understanding of each ideology.

Review and discussion questions

1. What influence has a liberal ideology had on addressing ques
2. Given the threats to freedom, is the problem that the world is
3. Is a commitment to liberal rights enough to overcome gender
4. Is it inevitable that we face a trade-off between free economic equality?

Review and discussion questions and research exercises—questions and exercises designed to test and extend your understanding of each ideology will help you to put your learning into practice as the chapter comes to a close.

Guided tour of the online resources

Political Ideologies is accompanied by comprehensive online resources, which provide additional material for students and lecturers, to support political ideology courses.

www.oup.com/uk/wetherly/

For students:

- Further reading and resources for each chapter help you to undertake further research and deepen your understanding and critical thinking.
- Regular updates, in the form of links to blog posts, will help you keep up to date with ideologies as frameworks of understanding and political action in the real world.

For lecturers:

- Indicative answers to Review and discussion questions provide a framework for approaching the questions in the book.
- PowerPoint® slides support each chapter, providing an overview and key points to assist teaching.

Contents

Detailed contents

About the contributors

Dr Robin Redhead is a Senior Lecturer at Leeds Beckett University. She has been engaged in research-informed teaching for ten years. She publishes on human rights practices: specifically, how mobilising human rights does or does not empower those at risk. From a socio-political approach, her current work challenges the effectiveness of rights-based approaches in protecting human rights.

Dr Stephen Hood is a Lecturer in Political Theory at the University of Manchester. His main areas of interest are liberal theories of justice and their compatibility with different forms of socioeconomic institutions. Of particular focus within his work are questions relating to the ethics of competitive arrangements.

Dr Mark Garnett is a Senior Lecturer in Politics and International Relations at Lancaster University. He has written numerous books on articles relating to British politics, and his main research interest is the relationship between ideas and practice.

Dr John Gregson is a Senior Lecturer in Criminology at Leeds Beckett University. He teaches modules on crimes of the powerful and criminological theory and leads the MSc in Criminology. His research interests include Marxist theory, the philosophy and politics of Alasdair MacIntyre, and critical criminology.

Dr David Bates is a Principal Lecturer and Director of Politics and International Relations at Canterbury Christ Church University. His research is concerned with two key areas: first, contemporary social and political theory, with specific reference to the Marxist and anarchist 'traditions'; second, the theoretical underpinnings of contemporary social movements.

Dr Mark Langan is a Senior Lecturer in International Politics at Newcastle University. His research examines the 'pro-poor' impact of trade and development ties between countries of the Global North and Global South. In particular, he is interested in European trade and aid linkages with states in sub-Saharan Africa and the MENA region (Middle East and North Africa). He is also very interested in critical theories of African statehood, and nationalisms.

Dr Aristotle Kallis is Professor of Modern and Contemporary History at Keele University. His current research focuses on generic and transnational fascism, contemporary political extremism, and urban modernism. Amongst his publications are *The Third Rome* (2014), *The Fascism Reader* (2003), and (together with Antonio Costa Pinto) *Rethinking Fascism and Dictatorship* (2014).

Dr Sophia Price is the Head of Politics and International Relations at Leeds Beckett University and a Senior Fellow of the Higher Education Academy. Her research interests are feminist political economy, international political economy, global development, and the external relations of the European Union.

Dorron Otter teaches political economy at Leeds Beckett University. He co-edited *The Business Environment* with Paul Wetherly (Oxford University Press, 2014).

Dr Paul Wetherly is Reader in Politics at Leeds Beckett University. His teaching and research interests are political ideologies, governance and the state, and migration and diversity. Other books edited by him include *Islam in the West* (Palgrave 2012, with Farrar, Robinson and Valli) and *The Business Environment* (Oxford University Press 2014, with Otter).

1

Introduction to ideology
Contesting the nature of the 'good society'

Paul Wetherly

OBJECTIVES

- Explain why ideology is seen as a 'contested concept'
- Discuss the negative perceptions of ideology prevalent in political discourse, and the opposing view that we are all ideologists
- Analyse the components or building blocks of a basic conception of ideology, including the morphological approach
- Critically assess the Marxist understanding of 'ideology' as false or misleading ideas
- Consider whether there is an independent vantage point from which to assess the claims of rival ideologies, and the problem of relativism

---

Introduction

The names of the ideologies examined in this book—liberalism, conservatism, social-ism, nationalism, and so on—will already be familiar to many readers, either as a result of the previous study of politics or because they come up in the discussions of politics going on around us in society and in which we take part. However, people often have vague ideas idea of what terms like 'liberal' or 'conservative' mean, and may find that these are different to the ideas that other people have. It is quite common to find one set of supporters of an ideology claiming to be the defenders of its true principles and accusing other self-proclaimed supporters of compromise or betrayal. For example, the divisions in the British Labour Party following Jeremy Corbyn's election as leader in 2015 (and re-election in 2016) involved, in part, different ideas about what it means to be socialist (as well as different ideas about whether Labour should be a socialist party of any kind). A key aim of this book is to undertake a systematic examination of each ideology, not to elucidate the single authentic version but to show how different variants of an ideology can develop from a set of core principles or ideas.

Before we embark on that examination of particular ideologies we need to begin with an understanding of ideology in general terms: What is an ideology? What are the origins of ideology? How does ideology work? What roles does ideology play in politics and society? These are the questions that we will explore in this chapter. In answer to the first question, what is an ideology, it is easy enough to give an *example* of an ideology (liberalism, conservatism, etc.), and we might back that up by saying that we know liberalism is an ideology because that is the way it is commonly referred to. However, that is not the same as providing a *definition*, and giving a straight-forward definition of the term 'ideology' is not simple. Indeed, it has been argued that 'Ideology is the most elusive concept in the whole of social science . . . [I]t is an essentially contested concept, that is, a concept about the very definition (and there-fore application) of which there is acute controversy' (McLellan 1995: 1). According to Freeden, 'There has rarely been a word in political language that has attracted such misunderstanding and opprobrium [i.e. abuse or disapproval]' (Freeden 2003: 3).

'Nobody would claim that their own thinking was ideological'

We will return to the issue of contestability shortly, but to begin with we might look for some clarification of the nature of ideology in the way the term is used in political debate. However, in doing so we encounter a, perhaps surprising, problem in that politicians rarely use the term 'ideology'. When they do it is not usually with reference to their own **values** and beliefs but to those of their opponents, and their usage bears out Freeden's claim that 'ideology' is used as a term of abuse or to convey disapproval. It seems that, as Eagleton puts it,

> Nobody would claim that their own thinking was ideological, just as nobody would habitually refer to themselves as Fatso. Ideology, like halitosis, is in this sense what the other person has.

> (Eagleton 1991: 2)

For example, in 2009 the Labour Party leader and Prime Minister Gordon Brown, referring to the financial **crisis** which erupted during the previous year, argued that

> what let the world down last autumn was not just bankrupt institutions but a bankrupt ideology. What failed was the Conservative idea that markets always self-correct but never self-destruct. What failed was the right wing fundamentalism that says you just leave everything to the market and says that free markets should not just be free but values free.

> (Brown 2009)

Following the 2010 general election, Prime Minister David Cameron defended the coalition government's austerity programme of public spending cuts on the grounds that

> We are not doing this because we want to. We are not driven by some theory or some ideology. We are doing this as a government because we have to, driven by the urgent truth that unless we do so, people will suffer and our national interest will suffer too.
>
> (Cameron 2010a)

Crossing the Atlantic, we find a similar avoidance of the term 'ideology' in the speeches of Barack Obama. One of the rare examples is in a speech during the 2008 presidential contest (the so-called 'race speech' in which Obama responded to controversial comments on **racism** in America by his former pastor Reverend Wright) in which Obama referred in passing to the 'perverse and hateful ideologies of radical Islam' (Obama 2008).

It is not surprising that Obama did not use the term 'ideology' in his speeches since he described himself as 'not a particularly ideological person' (Rucker 2013) (see Case Study 1.1). Similarly, launching her bid to become Conservative Party leader and UK Prime Minister, Theresa May disavowed 'ideological fervour' and described her motivation in terms of 'public service', implicitly seen as non-ideological (conservativehome 2016).

From these examples we can see that the use of 'ideology' as a term of abuse takes a number of forms.

- First, 'ideology' is used to refer to ideas and policies that have 'failed' or are 'bankrupt'.

- Second, 'ideology' is equated with **fundamentalism** or **dogma**, terms which can be understood as referring to a belief that a person holds to be true regardless of whether there is any evidence to support it (see Chapter 13). This leads to the criticism of policies that are based on ideology ('ideologically-driven') rather than on evidence of what will lead to successful outcomes or is necessary in current circumstances.

- Third, 'ideology' is used to refer to ideas that are characterized as 'perverse', 'hateful', or **extremist**.

In other cases ideology is seen as unhealthy or pathological—something that people become 'obsessed' with or 'infected' by. The use of 'ideology' as a term of abuse or insult aimed at other people is also an aspect of conservative thought (see Chapter 3).

 Stop and Think

Do you accept Cameron's claim that austerity was a matter of necessity rather than of ideology? How might this denial of an ideological basis for the policy have been convenient for the government?

'We are all ideologists'?

Of course, just because politicians refrain from using the word 'ideology' does not mean that they do not have one. Even when politicians, such as Obama, say they are 'not particularly ideological' it might be that actually they are. Indeed it can be argued that everyone's thinking is inescapably ideological—that we are all **ideologists**.

Case Study 1.1 Obama—'Not particularly ideological'?

Does Barack Obama's claim to be 'not particularly ideological' bear close scrutiny? In elaboration of this claim, Obama stated that 'he is passionate about his values but is practical about how to achieve them' (Rucker 2013), thus contrasting being 'ideological' with being 'practical' (or **pragmatic**), and distinguishing ends ('values') from 'means' (how to achieve the values, i.e. specific policies). It appears that, for Obama, being ideological meant being committed to a specific set of policies regardless of pragmatic or practical considerations as to which policy would actually be most effective in achieving the desired values, while the values themselves are not regarded as matters of ideology. However, contrary to Obama, it can be argued that values are fundamental components of ideologies and a prime focus of ideological disputes. In other words, we can say without too much simplification that what basically distinguishes between, say, liberals and conservatives or republicans and democrats is that they cherish different values (though there may also be some values that they both cherish).

The values that Obama espoused included

- making sure that 'everybody gets a fair shake' (i.e. a fair chance or opportunity) and is treated with 'dignity or respect regardless of what they look like or who they are';

- providing a strong defence; and

- 'leaving a planet that is as spectacular as the one we inherited from our parents and our grandparents' (McCalmont 2013).

The first of these might be understood as expressing commitment to a liberal conception of equality in terms of opportunity ('a fair shake') and moral worth (dignity or respect), the second is about protecting the public from foreign threats, and the last may be seen as an expression of an environmentalist ethic of sustainability. The point here is that, in expressing his 'passion' concerning certain values, Obama was thereby setting out an ideological standpoint. While eschewing ideology in one breath he was effectively stating 'this is what I stand for ideologically speaking' in the next.

It can be argued that Obama's statement of values does not amount to very much since they were rather vague and ill-defined. This vagueness is a characteristic of politicians' speeches, and statements of 'values' often seem to be little more than 'warm words' that most people can be expected to identify with and that generate positive responses. Most people would endorse Obama's belief that 'everybody [should] get . . . a fair shake' (what reasonable person would say they believe some people should get an unfair shake?), but they might have very different ideas about what this means in practice and what a society of 'fair shakes' looks like.

Clearly we need to be wary of how politicians express their beliefs and values, but this does not mean we should dismiss them. Rather, we should investigate what Obama meant by a 'fair shake' and how this principle was embodied in policy decisions. In other words, the question is not whether Obama is ideological, but what that ideology is and how it is expressed and can be observed.

Stop and Think

Are you persuaded by Obama's self-description as 'not particularly ideological'?

The UK Labour peer Lord Hattersley asserts the necessity, and also desirability, of ideology in politics and has criticized claims that it is possible to conduct politics in a non-ideological fashion (see also Chapter 13). In Hattersley's view, politics cannot be reduced to a technical process of finding fixes for problems, and technicians 'are not notable for their ability to inspire'. In order to inspire, 'The Labour party has to have a vision of a different and better future' that is supplied by an ideology (Hattersley 2009; also see Hattersley 1997). Thus 'Politics is, or ought to be, about great issues— the rival definitions of the good societies that the contending parties hope to create' (Hattersley 2009a). Similarly, the economist Paul Krugman, in countering the notion of Obama as pragmatist, has argued that 'everyone has an ideology—which is another way of saying that everyone has (a) values and (b) some view about how the world works. And there's nothing wrong with that' (Krugman 2011). Everyone is, in other words, 'an ideologue' (Krugman 2011). This view is supported by Freeden:

> We produce, disseminate, and consume ideologies all our lives, whether we are aware of it or not . . . . We are all ideologists in that we have understandings of the political environment of which we are part, and have views about the merits and failings of that environment.
>
> (Freeden 2003: 1–2)

 Stop and Think

1. Do you agree that 'Everyone has an ideology'?
2. Do you see yourself as an 'ideologist'?
3. Lord Hattersley believes that 'The voters prefer politicians with firm principles' (Hattersley 2003)—do you agree?

In response to the use of 'ideology' as a term of abuse it can be argued.

- First, a person can have an 'unhealthy' approach to an ideology and become 'obsessed' by it or hold their ideological views as an inflexible 'dogma', just as religious or other ideas in society can be the basis of an obsession or dogma. But people can also reason about their ideological beliefs and be open-minded in the sense of being willing to revise their opinions in the face of convincing argument or evidence.
- Second, an ideology can promote ideas that are 'extremist'. Fascism (Chapter 7) and so-called 'Islamist extremism' (Chapter 12) may be characterized in these terms (even though their adherents might take a different view of them). We

have to be careful with terms such as 'extremism' because of the temptation to use them in a rather indiscriminate way in order to dismiss an opponent's views, and because there can be reasonable disagreement about the application of these terms. But the general point is that, however extremism is defined, it does not apply to all ideologies—ideology as such cannot be characterized as extremist.

- Third, the criticism that 'ideologically-driven' policies ignore evidence of what will lead to successful outcomes is rejected on the basis that it involves a false opposition. All policies are ideologically-driven in the sense that they are based on values, such as Obama's commitment to an environmentalist ethic of sustainability. Politicians might not always be very good at basing policy on evidence, but in principle there is no point in being passionate about values unless you are interested in implementing the policies that will realize those values. Similarly the negative association of ideology with policies that have 'failed' misdiagnoses the problem. For example, if, as Brown claims, policies based on free market ideology were to blame for the financial crisis, this was not because ideology as such is bankrupt but because this particular ideology was bankrupt—it needed to be replaced by a non-bankrupt ideology rather than by a non-ideology.

Ideology as a 'contested concept'

It is now time to move towards a definition of ideology, and this means we must examine the basis for the claim we came across at the start of this chapter: that ideology is an 'essentially contested concept' whose definition is controversial (see also Gerring 1997). Like other **contested concepts** or terms in politics, there is actually quite a high degree of agreement about the basic definition of ideology, and it is only when we try to develop the basic idea that disagreement gets going. We will see in subsequent chapters that this point also applies to the concepts that are the building blocks of particular ideologies and that are in dispute both within and between them.

Towards a basic definition of ideology

A basic definition of ideology is implicit in much of our previous discussion, most clearly in the arguments from Hattersley and Krugman. A good starting point, though, is Gordon Brown's speech to the 2009 Labour Party conference in which he attributed the financial crash to a 'bankrupt ideology' (see the quote in the opening section). He characterized this ideology in terms of a 'Conservative idea' (though it might be argued that it is actually a neo-liberal idea adopted by a conservative party—see Chapter 3) and 'right wing fundamentalism'. In the passage quoted earlier Brown identifies two components of this ideology, as follows:

1. the belief 'that markets always self-correct but never self-destruct';
2. the **prescription** to 'just leave everything to the market'.

The first component is a simple statement of belief or understanding about how the world works. More specifically, it claims that markets have a tendency to 'self-correct' or operate in a stable fashion, and not to 'self-destruct'. In other words, this is a claim to knowledge of how a market economy *actually works* which is, in principle, capable of being tested on the basis of empirical evidence. The second component is a statement of a different kind since it advocates a view about how society *should be* organized in terms of its economic life. It prescribes a 'free market' policy in which government should disengage from the market and leave economic life to be organized through a decentralized system of voluntary exchange between individuals. This prescription cannot be tested using empirical evidence since it is, in essence, a statement of **values**; that is, a description of a social arrangement that a person making that statement values or views as desirable. The two statements can be distinguished on the basis of 'is' and 'ought': the first makes a claim about what the world 'is' and how it works, while the second advocates a view of how the world 'ought' to or should be organized.

The two statements are apparently linked in the following way: free markets are advocated because they are believed to be self-correcting, and economic stability is seen as desirable for society. In other words economic stability can be seen as the value that lies behind the support for free markets. (Of course, other values could also be invoked in support of free markets, such as freedom or efficiency). Thus, if it is true that

a) economic stability (or liberty, or efficiency) is desirable for society, and

b) free markets are good ways of organizing economic life to ensure economic stability (or liberty, or efficiency)

then (a) and (b) together support the prescription

c) 'just leave everything to the market'.

So, we can see that an 'ought' always implies an 'is', since to have any chance of realizing your values in the world you have to have reliable knowledge of the way the world actually works. The prescription to leave things to the market in order to achieve the economic stability (or liberty, or efficiency) that you value relies on knowledge that the free market does actually self-correct.

It should be clear now on what grounds critics of this 'Conservative idea', like Brown, might launch their attacks.

- They might share the value of economic stability but argue that the theory of how markets work (the 'knowledge') is defective. This is Brown's line of attack—free markets in fact have a tendency to self-destruct, he claims.

- They might agree that markets do tend to self-correct but argue that there are more important values, such as equality, which are not compatible with free markets.

Krugman, in arguing that everyone has an ideology, also refers to the elements that we have teased from Brown's statement—an understanding of 'how the world works' (e.g. markets are self-correcting) and 'values' (e.g. economic stability is desirable for society). Hattersley refers to rival conceptions of the 'good society' (e.g. leaving everything to the market). These are elements of a basic definition of ideology, as stated by MacKenzie:

> all ideologies . . . embody an account of social and political reality and an account of how that reality could be bettered. On the one hand, then, ideologies help us to make sense of the complex social world in which we live. . . . On the other hand . . . ideologies also embody a set of political ideals aimed at detailing the best possible form of social organisation.
>
> (MacKenzie 2003: 2)

 Stop and Think

All ideologies involve a mix of 'is' and 'ought' statements or claims. How are these types of statements distinguished? Devise some 'is' and 'ought' statements of your own.

We can unpack this basic definition to allow us to identify a number of related components of ideology as a set or system of ideas: the good society; values; political action; and knowledge claims.

The good society

What fundamentally distinguishes one ideology from another is that they offer rival accounts of how 'social and political reality . . . could be bettered', and rival visions of the 'good society'—they 'stand for' different ideals about how we should live together. This is how we can distinguish between, say, liberals, socialists, and feminists. The kind of good society a feminist advocates differs in fundamental ways (though it may overlap in others) from the versions of the good society that socialists and liberals aspire to. In simple terms, feminists seek to establish a society in which there is sexual equality, whereas socialists strive for an equal society defined in terms of the narrowing or eradication of class differences in living standards, and liberals envision a good society in terms of individuals having equal opportunities to get on in life or a 'fair shake'. (Notice that each ideology advocates some notion of equality). The need for feminism arose, it can be argued, because the position of women was not addressed by socialism or liberalism or by the political parties and movements based on these ideologies. Yet feminism has also converged with socialism and liberalism through sexual equality being tied to the eradication of class differences (socialist feminism) or the realization of equal opportunities between men and women (liberal feminism). This has created different strands of feminism which define the good society of sexual equality in different ways. So, as we will see in later chapters, the vision of the good society differentiates ideologies from each other, but can also be the basis for convergence between ideologies as well as internal differences.

If rival visions of the good society are the basic currency of ideological debate then, in each case, the other side of the coin is a critique of existing society. For a view of how society could be bettered must be based on an identification of what's wrong with society as presently constituted. But ideologies also make an assessment of what's worth valuing and defending in the current society. Thus 'critique' involves weighing up the 'goods' and 'bads' of existing society. For example, if, like Obama, you want to ensure that everybody gets a fair shake, you need to evaluate which attitudes, rules, and behaviours currently support this goal and need to be maintained and defended, and what obstacles stand in the way of further progress and need to be overcome. The critique of existing society provides a way of differentiating between ideologies: the terms **'reactionary'**, 'conservative', **'reformist'**, **'radical'**, and **'revolutionary'** are commonly used to denote how limited or far-reaching are the changes that are required to bring about the good society.

Values

When we speak of ideals, how society could be bettered, and visions of the 'good society', we are invoking the language of values. Values can be seen as statements about things we 'believe in' or 'stand for'. In this vein we saw earlier that Obama was 'passionate about his values', including equality of opportunity. To say that this was one of Obama's values is to say that equality of opportunity is a condition to which he attaches value or which he believes to be right. We can also infer that Obama had, in his view, good reasons for believing that equality of opportunity is right.

Values can be an important element of individual identity and inform decisions about how individuals live their lives. In this sense values are powerful things: you can't easily believe in something but live your life in a way that contradicts that belief without inducing some psychological strain. More important from a political perspective, values are the basis for the emergence of shared identities, ideologies, and forms of collective decision-making to make society better in the light of those values. If Obama proclaimed equal opportunity as one of his values, we might reasonably have expected him to take actions in office to make opportunities more equal, and might have held him to account on this basis.

In guiding political action, values can be used for both descriptive and evaluative purposes. In descriptive terms, we can ask questions such as 'to what extent is a specific group of people in a particular society treated equally?' and devise measures to enable us to answer this question (e.g. the relative chances of African Americans being a victim of shooting by police compared with white people). And, in evaluative terms, if we find that the group is disadvantaged, we can condemn this situation as wrong, as an injustice, and demand effective action to rectify it (e.g. the 'Black Lives Matter' movement—see Day 2015).

Of course, for these purposes we need to know what Obama, or anyone else, means or meant by equality of opportunity or a fair shake. The meaning of equality of opportunity, like other values, is disputed—it is a contested concept. This is important because different critiques of existing society and visions of the good society, and different proposals for political action, may be expressed in rival definitions of equality of opportunity or other values.

Furthermore, since different definitions express deep differences about what we believe to be good, and which may be reasonable, an agreed definition may be unattainable. Indeed, ideological struggle or competition can be seen in terms of trying to win support for a particular idea of equality of opportunity and other values as a basis for political action.

Political action

As part of their basic definition, ideologies can be characterized as action-oriented. The point of providing an account of how society could be bettered is to carry out the actions needed to make it better, and to make the good society a reality. An ideology is, in other words, a cause to which its supporters can passionately commit themselves. However, this is not to say that support for an ideology necessarily involves being a committed activist, and there is a probably larger number of supporters who do very little or nothing to further the cause (such as so-called 'armchair socialists'). In all liberal democracies people who espouse a particular political ideology and/or engage in political action of some kind beyond voting are a fairly small minority of the population. Although most people would not define their political beliefs in terms of an ideological label, Krugman and Freeden can still be right to claim that everybody is an ideologist in the sense that they do have values and political beliefs.

Ideological commitment, especially as an activist, typically means involvement with a political party or movement of some kind, as a member or supporter. Thus ideologies are intrinsically connected with parties and movements, and these organizations can be seen as 'ideology containers', or 'carriers' (Berman 2006: 11). They are among the most important vehicles for expressing ideological beliefs and for engaging in political action in order to make progress towards the good society that the ideology stands for.

Knowledge claims

As we have seen, Hattersley (2009) disparages the 'technician's approach to politics' in favour of an ideological approach. However, if this is understood as a dichotomy it is a false one, for the ideologist cannot do without 'technical' knowledge. Hattersley's point is rather that this knowledge has to be connected to, or in the service of, 'a vision of a different and better future' (Hattersley 2009). More specifically, Hattersley argues that it is the ideological vision that is needed in order to inspire and win popular support.

In this view a political party will find it hard to get elected just on the basis of setting out a range of policies to deal with specific issues or problems, for it also has to show how these policies contribute to the greater purpose of moving towards the good society. But the relationship between the vision and technical knowledge can also be looked at the other way: it will be hard for a party to command support for a vision of a better future without a set of policies that will actually work and move society in the right direction.

As Brown's remarks in relation to the financial crash illustrated, an ideology embodies two distinct but related types of knowledge claims: 'is' and 'ought'. The former involves knowledge in the conventional sense: we can, in principle, 'know' whether 'is' statements are true or false because we can test them on the basis of empirical observations (though in practice this may be very difficult). On first glance we might not think of 'ought' statements as knowledge since they are not testable in this way and seem to be no more than preferences, but this is misleading. If someone says that they value equality between men and women we would expect them to be able to explain what they mean by equality and to give reasons why sexual equality as they conceive it should be valued (whereas we don't expect people to explain and justify their preference for strawberry ice cream).

The two types of knowledge are related because it is necessary to know how the world works in order to have a chance of changing it. At the most fundamental level all ideologies rest on a theory of **human nature** since humans are the 'raw ingredients' with which the better future is to be built. You cannot, for example, consistently maintain (a) that there ought to be far-reaching equality between men and women, and (b) that there are fixed biological differences between males and females that make some inequalities inevitable: either the 'is' or the 'ought' statement has to give.

Since ideologies embody an account of how society could be bettered, knowledge of how the world works must include not only how the current society works but also how society could work differently, and how to get from here to there. This involves understanding the relationship between means and ends, and this is where the role of the 'technician' comes into play. For example, equality (usually defined in terms of reducing or eliminating differences in income and wealth) is a key value in socialist ideology, meaning that it is the principal purpose or end of socialist politics. But if the good society is an equal society, a strategy is needed to guide political action to achieve it, and this involves two related dimensions. On the one hand, inequality is seen as a social problem in the current constitution of society to be remedied, and this requires an understanding of the underlying causes of inequality in order to devise effective solutions, whether 'reformist' or 'revolutionary' in character (see Chapter 4).

On the other hand, knowledge of how the world works includes an understanding of the disposition and operation of political **power**. Even mild redistribution is likely to provoke resistance and, more generally, all social change is likely to involve winners and losers. To put this another way, social problems may be understood in terms of the social and economic arrangements of society that generate them and the exercise of political power that sustains those arrangements. For example, if we follow the argument that the financial crash was due to a free market ideology which allowed banks to make reckless decisions, this leads to an argument for some form of government intervention to regulate markets, particularly the financial markets. But this is not just a 'technical' question of devising an effective regulatory framework, for it is also necessary to understand the banks and other organizations that may be opposed to regulation and how they may be able to influence or control the policy agenda. Thus political strategy is at least an implicit component of all ideologies, and tends to be most explicit in ideologies that conceive the task of achieving the good society in terms of overcoming an entrenched structure of power, such as some versions of socialism, feminism, and environmentalism.

System of ideas

It will be clear by now that an ideology comprises a set or system of ideas. For example, liberalism advocates freedom and this might be seen as liberalism's prime value, but the ideology cannot be reduced to a commitment to this single idea. Rather, as we will see (Chapter 2), freedom is connected in liberal ideology with a set of related values such as equality, **tolerance**, and **individualism**, that together make up the liberal vision of the good society. In addition, we have seen that an ideology links these values with knowledge claims about how the world works. It is useful to think of ideologies as comprising three inter-related components:

1. a *critique* of existing society—involving an assessment of its shortcomings in relation to certain cherished values, and an understanding of how the world works in terms of how current society operates to generate these defects;

2. a *vision* of the good society—again defined with reference to the cherished values, and combined with an understanding of how the world works reflected in proposals for how the good society would be organized;

3. a *strategy* to get from current society to the good society—involving an understanding of political power.

In this sense, an ideology is a coherent set of ideas: these three components fit together in a logical way. And an ideology may provide its adherents with a fairly comprehensive set of ideas, or a 'world view', which they can use to understand the world and navigate their way within it (or to change it). However ideologies may differ in the extent to which they attain this coherence, so the three components might best serve as an analytical framework which we can use to study and compare ideologies. Similarly, ideologies may differ in the extent to which they provide a comprehensive world view or look through a more restricted lens. So, again, this provides a criterion for comparing ideologies.

Another way of analysing ideologies as sets of ideas is by using what Freeden refers to as a 'morphological' approach, that is concerned with form and structure

(Freeden 1996, 2003, 2013). This approach 'sees the internal structure of ideologies as a vital aspect of their analysis' (Freeden 2003: 51). The idea of structure here is consistent with the critique–vision–strategy structure just outlined; indeed Freeden defines ideologies as 'systems of political thinking . . . through which individuals and groups construct an understanding of the political world they . . . inhabit, and then act on that understanding' (Freeden 1996: 3). However, for Freeden, structure refers to the ways ideologies 'assemble . . . political concepts', which are the 'basic units of political thought', 'in particular patterns' (Freeden 2003: 51). As already indicated, each ideology consists of a set of concepts, and within this set primacy is assigned to specific concepts, such as freedom in liberalism or equality in socialism. Taking this further, Freeden suggests that

> ideologies . . . are characterised by a morphology that displays core, adjacent, and peripheral concepts. For instance, an examination of observed liberalisms might establish that liberty is situated within their core, that human rights, democracy and equality are adjacent to liberty, and that nationalism is to be found on their periphery.
>
> (Freeden 1996: 77)

Crucial to understanding morphology is that ideologies are not merely assemblages of discrete concepts but that these concepts are 'mutually defining' (Freeden 2003: 52). This means, for example, that the meaning given to freedom in liberalism influences the meaning of equality, and the same is true in socialism. In liberalism an understanding of the core concept of freedom in terms of individual choice and freedom from coercion is bound up with a corresponding understanding of equality as equality of opportunity. In socialism an understanding of the core concept of equality in terms of equality of outcome is bound up with an understanding of freedom in terms of having sufficient resources to enable meaningful choices to be made. Thus within each ideology the two concepts are mutually defining, and each ideology seeks, in effect, to de-contest or fix the meanings of the concepts.

 Stop and Think

From this discussion of the basic concept of ideology, consider how an ideology can be said to provide a framework of political ideas encompassing both understanding and political commitment or, in other words, both theory and action.

Variants of ideologies

Freeden refers to 'observed liberalisms' rather than liberalism in the singular and so highlights that there are variants of each ideology. In fact there is both continuity, such as that liberty is a core concept in all forms of liberalism, and variation (e.g. 'classical liberalism', 'social liberalism', and 'neo-liberalism'—see Chapter 2). Liberalism, conservatism, socialism, and other ideologies can be seen as traditions that have developed over time and, as they have done so, given rise to variants in response to changing circumstances and to the ongoing dialogue between ideologies. At the same time, ideologies have developed within different societies and therefore different cultural contexts that have given rise to national variations.

Ideology, politics, and policy

The basic definition of ideology suggests a fairly clear understanding of how the relationship between ideology, politics, and policy does, or should, work. 'Politics' can be defined as the range of decisions that members of a group or community have to take together in order to create conditions for cooperation and for the community to function successfully; that is, collective decisions. For this purpose, 'community' can be understood at many levels—collective decisions are necessary within households, within nations, and at a global level. This involves a broad conception of politics that is not defined purely in terms of the role of government, and this is an important perspective for it enables us to understand how ideology operates in different settings within society. For example, some strains of feminism alert us to the way an ideology of sexism can operate within the household and pervade institutions throughout civil society that are distinct from government. However 'government' (understood in terms of multi-level governance, including local, state, national, and supra-national or inter-governmental levels) is clearly the most important mechanism for collective decision-making, in the form of law and public policy.

The basic political problem is that there are disagreements in society about these collective decisions and even about what issues should be decided collectively or left to individuals. As Stoker puts it, 'because we are human we disagree and seek different things and we need politics not only to express but also to manage those disagreements and if possible find ways to cooperate' (Stoker 2006: 5).

Stoker's claim raises some big questions about the sources of disagreement. It may be the case that, to some extent, political differences are 'hard-wired' in the sense of being attributable to genetic differences between individuals. Some people may be 'naturally' left- or right-oriented in their political thinking. For example, Pinker claims that 'Liberal and conservative attitudes are heritable [i.e. have genetic roots] . . . because they come naturally to people with different temperaments' (Pinker 2002: 283). However, it would be implausible to claim that political disagreements are all down to genetics since this would ignore the societal influences on political thinking, and the interaction between these influences and the capacity of individuals to exercise reason and to revise their views. The claim would also be refuted by the historical evidence of large-scale shifts of values and political ideas within societies. (See Case Study 1.2 for a discussion of 'Human nature, violence, and ideology'.)

However these questions are resolved, ideologies can be seen as the dominant way in which political disagreements are expressed and framed. Individuals' views normally draw on and express the sets of ideas that comprise the ideologies that are available within the society. This does not mean that all, or even most, individuals would usually express their political views in terms of adherence to a coherent ideology by declaring themselves to be, say, a socialist or a conservative—it is quite common, for example, for an individual to express socialist views on inequality and conservative views on crime. But on any issue of political controversy the terms of disagreement will normally be drawn from ideological perspectives. A person might not have a consistent or coherent set of ideological beliefs but they will still have a set of beliefs that are ideological.

If disagreements are expressed in ideological terms, we can also say that disagreement involves ideological competition which is won by one ideology attracting more adherents than others and, through this support, influencing or controlling political decisions in the form of law and public policy. More realistically, it is not ideologies as such that compete but the organizations that promote them, most notably (but not solely) political parties (see Chapter 8). Here we can recall Hattersley's view that the purpose (indeed the necessity) of ideology is to provide inspiration—to win support by showing how a set of 'technical' policy proposals are united by their contribution towards achieving an attractive vision of the good society. In this way ideologies frame political choices by setting out different views of political goals that are feasible and desirable.

It might be objected that this view of politics is somewhat 'rose-tinted', and contradicted by empirical evidence of how politics actually works in liberal democracies, particularly the evidence of low levels of trust and engagement in the political system (Stoker 2006; Hay 2007; Hansard Society 2016). However, the objection misses the mark insofar as Hattersley is not providing a description of the way politics works but a prescription of how it could be improved. Hattersley's argument, in summary form, is that citizens need to be invigorated by political parties setting out rival, ideological, visions of the good society to which they aspire.

 Stop and Think

What do you understand by the term 'politics'? Explain how the relationship between ideology, politics, and policy does, or should, work.

Case Study 1.2 Human nature, violence, and ideology

All ideologies contain explicit or implicit assumptions (or knowledge claims) about human nature. This is because humans are the raw materials with which the good society is to be created. Debates about human nature concern biological facts, and these facts have direct implications for the feasibility and desirability of proposals for social change—to be *feasible*, a vision of the good society has to be consistent with what we know about human nature, and to be *desirable* it must enable humans, with the nature they possess, to flourish.

Ideologies can be compared in terms of whether they see human nature as fixed or as mould-ed by changing social conditions ('nature versus nurture'), and whether they hold positive or negative conceptions of our nature ('good versus evil'). The important question then is: if we can understand what drives the way we are (nature or nurture) and can distinguish positive and nega-tive attributes, what can we do about it? And, what is the effect of ideology?

According to Pinker, human nature consists of specific attributes or 'psychological motives' that are the product of human evolution and are therefore essentially fixed within an historical timescale. These fixed motives do not make humans either innately good or innately evil. For example, they include motives that orient us towards violence and those that orient us towards peace—what Pinker refers to as our 'inner demons' and 'better angels' (Pinker 2011). This is a generalization about all humans—humans everywhere and throughout history should be seen as essentially the same in that they come 'equipped' with the same mix of motives. But people are not the same everywhere and throughout history in their behaviour. One immense transforma-tion in behaviour through history is the decline of violence, and the gap between fixed motives and changing behaviour is filled, according to Pinker, by 'the artifices of civilisation' (Pinker 2011: xx) or nurture. More specifically, the decline of violence is explained by 'changes in historical circumstances that engage a fixed human nature in different ways' (Pinker 2011: xxiv), that is 'changes in our cultural and material milieu that have given our peaceable motives the upper hand' (Pinker 2011: xxi).

THE ROLE OF IDEOLOGY IN THE DECLINE OF VIOLENCE

Pinker argues that through much of human history violence has been driven largely by ideology, and he even identifies ideology as one of our 'inner demons' (Pinker 2011: xxiv and 580–688). Pinker defines ideology as 'a shared belief system, usually involving a vision of utopia, that justi-fies unlimited violence in pursuit of unlimited goals' (Pinker 2011: xxiv) and sees it as 'the most consequential cause of violence' (Pinker 2011: 613). This seems to exemplify the opprobrious view of ideology. More specifically, Pinker argues that 'the most destructive eruptions [of vio-lence] of the past half millennium were fuelled . . . by ideologies, such as religion, revolution, nationalism, fascism, and communism' (Pinker 2011: 815).

It can be argued that this approach ignores the role of ideologies that have sought to reduce or eliminate violence. In fact, what would normally be recognized as ideology does figure in Pinker's discussion of the decline of violence. The five historical forces identified by Pinker as responsible for the decline in violence can be summarized as follows:

- The rise of the modern state (The 'Leviathan')
- Market economies ('Commerce')
- 'Feminization'
- 'Cosmopolitanism'
- The 'escalator of reason'

(Pinker 2011: xxiv–xxv and 822–35)

As we will see in later chapters, all of these historical forces have been, and continue to be, the focus of intense debate between ideologies. For example, all ideologies contain perspectives on the **state**, and the 'classical' ideologies of liberalism and socialism have been centrally concerned with the relationship between the state and the market. A 'cosmopolitan' society can be defined as one in which there is a mix of people from different backgrounds, and a cosmopolitan out-look suggests viewing other people's beliefs and lifestyles with an open mind. Managing cultural diversity is the central concern of multiculturalism. 'Feminization is the process in which cultures have increasingly respected the interests and values of women' (Pinker 2011: xxv) or embraced 'female-friendly values' (Pinker 2011: 828), and this is arguably a process that has been driven largely by feminism.

Reason is a psychological motive or faculty (one of our 'better angels'), but the concept of the 'escalator of reason' involves this faculty being engaged by exogenous forces such as literacy and education leading to progress in our thinking and behaviour, manifested in a reduction in violence. According to Pinker the escalator of reason takes us 'toward humanism, classical liberalism, autonomy, and human rights' (Pinker 2011: 835). In this way Pinker directly invokes ideology in the explanation of the decline of violence. For example, Pinker refers to **humanism** or human rights as 'a new ideology . . . that placed life and happiness at the center of values, and that used reason and evidence to motivate the design of institutions' (Pinker 2011: 160). This ideology emerged out of the **Enlightenment** and was at the centre of the 'humanitarian revolution' that has unfolded since the mid-eighteenth century. It can be argued that the related ideologies of humanism and liberalism have been dominant in the modern era, but they have not been uncontested (see Chapter 8). Thus the period since 1789 can be seen as 'a battle for influence among four forces—Enlightenment humanism, conservatism, nationalism, and utopian ideologies' (Pinker 2011: 287). In the twentieth century, although 'the enduring moral trend . . . was a violence-averse humanism' (Pinker 2011: 232) it was overshadowed for a time by counter-Enlightenment utopian ideologies of fascism and communism. The 'long peace' that began after the Second World War followed the defeat of these ideologies.

For Pinker, ideology, defined narrowly as one of our 'inner demons', has been the cause of the worst episodes of violence in history. But we can also see the decline of violence in terms of a struggle between ideologies, with those favouring peace gaining the upper hand.

 Stop and Think

What is human nature? How does an understanding of human nature influence ideological visions of the good society that are both desirable and feasible?

Beyond the basic definition—sources of controversy

The basic definition of ideology provides a conceptual basis and framework for the analysis of ideologies in this book. However, it is possible to agree that ideology has all the characteristics already discussed—that it is a system of ideas embodying a vision of the good society, values, and knowledge claims, and that is action-oriented—but disagree about how it works: why do people hold the ideological views that they do? and, how can we explain the prevalence in society of particular ideological beliefs and not others?

Let us return to Stoker's claim: because we are human we disagree (Stoker 2006). One way of interpreting this claim is in individualist terms, so that the claim is that individuals differ from one another in their beliefs, values, and lifestyles and that these differences arise on the basis of individual choice—we all make up our own minds and decide our political views for ourselves. This claim has strong intuitive appeal since 'making up our own minds' seems to make sense of a fundamental aspect of our experience and what it means to be human. However, as an explanation of why people hold the ideological views that they do, it encounters a number of difficulties. As we have seen, Pinker claims that our political views are in part heritable in the sense that they reflect our temperaments, and therefore whether a person is a liberal or a conservative is not simply a matter of choice. If we think of making up our minds on the basis of our capacity to exercise reason, the idea of the 'escalator of reason' suggests that our political beliefs may be thought of partly as being 'arrived at' rather than simply chosen. This is based on the idea that reason takes our beliefs in certain directions, so that some views are incompatible with reason and others are dictated by reason. For example, the decline of violence may in part be attributable to beliefs and practices that were once pervasive, such as a belief in the existence of 'witches', and the practice of burning them, becoming untenable once exposed to reason.

Thus, even if beliefs are conceived in individualistic terms, the claims that they are in part heritable and in part arrived at by the escalator of reason complicate the idea that they can be explained simply as expressions of individual choice. However, we will now turn to three related arguments about how ideology works that focus on societal influences. These are that:

- ideologies reflect the interests of different social groups based on the form of society (or social structure) and their positions within it;

- ideologies represent successful attempts by powerful groups to manipulate beliefs so as to conceal or mystify the true nature of social reality in order to maintain the status quo;

- ideologies are expressions of the dominant values and beliefs of particular societies and, as such, might not have universal validity.

In shorthand, these three views are that ideology reflects interests, the exercise of power, or cultural embeddedness. For example, a particular conception of freedom—as freedom to buy and sell in a market with minimal interference from government—may be valued by owners and senior managers of private sector businesses in a capitalist system because they believe that their *interests* are best served by a free market economy. Second, businesses, acting through business associations (such as the CBI in the UK), think-tanks, political parties, or media organizations, may be able to persuade other groups that a free market is in their interests even if they are in fact disadvantaged. This would involve an exercise of ideological *power*. Third, it might be argued that freedom is a distinctive value of Western societies reflecting their particular histories and cultures, but one which is not championed by non-Western societies due to their different histories. Thus the fact that individuals in Western societies tend to cherish freedom could reflect their *'embeddedness'* in Western culture. In each case, why individuals hold the ideological beliefs that they do is explained, in large part, in terms of societal influences.

Ideology and interests

Our discussion of the basic concept of ideology may support the idea that the different visions of the good society, with their associated values, knowledge claims, and commitments to certain forms of political action, are all put forward in good faith—as genuine attempts to combine understanding of how the world works with a vision of how it could be improved that can, in principle, appeal to everyone in the society. People may disagree, for example, about whether freedom or equality should be the most cherished value, how to define these values, and how to manage any trade-offs between them that may be necessary, but they debate these issues openly with a shared concern to decide on the basis of what is good for society. There are, in this view of ideological debate, no hidden agendas.

For example, David Cameron justified the austerity measures introduced by the UK government in 2010 on the grounds that 'we are all in this together' (Cameron 2010b), claiming that all members of society would benefit from the government's strategy of public spending cuts and tax increases. Politicians often use the language of the 'national interest' (or 'public interest' or 'common good') to justify their policies. However, quite often the appeal to the national interest may be criticized as little more than a rhetorical device to garner support for a policy that might otherwise be characterized as partisan or divisive, such as austerity policies. Critics argued that the 'sacrifices' necessitated by the programme were made disproportionately by certain groups in society, such as women, young people, the disabled, the 'squeezed middle', or ordinary working people. More pointedly, it has been argued that 'austerity is being used as a narrative to conduct class war' by redistributing wealth from the poor to the rich (Varoufakis in Stone 2015). The general point is that politics expresses competing or conflicting interests of different social groups. Thus, while we may disagree, as Stoker argues, simply 'because we are human', the more fundamental source of disagreements may lie in the form of organization or structure of society that gives rise to distinctive social groups with competing interests, such as the division between rich and poor.

If politics expresses competing interests, this gives us a way of understanding, at least in part, why people hold some of the ideological views that they do and the existence in Western societies of particular ideologies. These views and ideologies may reflect the structures of these societies, the social groups of which they are comprised, and their competing interests. The classical ideologies of liberalism, conservatism, and socialism can be interpreted as different responses to the social and economic transformations constitutive of **modernity**. More specifically, these ideologies can be seen as in some way representing the interests of the major social classes which experienced modernization as a disruptive force undermining traditional class relations and ways of life or whose very existence was largely a product of modernizing processes such as industrialization and urbanization: the aristocracy, the class of industrialists or capitalists, and the working class. For example, socialism has historically claimed to represent the interests of the working class. Nationalism claims to represent the interests of a particular nation, understood as a form of community with a distinctive culture and way of life that is worth preserving. While nationalism sees a nation as culturally homogeneous, multiculturalism starts from a recognition of modern societies as culturally diverse, characterized by the co-existence of a plurality of communities each with its own beliefs and lifestyle, often expressed in claims for respect and **recognition**. Finally, the essential purpose of feminism is to represent the distinct interests of women which are an expression of their collective experience of disadvantage or oppression in 'patriarchal' or sexist societies.

 Stop and Think

If society is made up of groups with competing interests can politicians ever convincingly claim to be acting in the public interest or that 'we're all in this together'?

The relationship between specific ideologies and sectional or group interests is often out in the open. Nationalists openly declare that they represent the interests of a 'nation' and that certain entitlements are due to members of the nation that are not due to foreigners or immigrants. Feminists openly declare that they represent the interests of women and that progress towards sexual equality requires some privileges unjustly enjoyed by men to be removed. However, sometimes the agenda is hidden and the purpose may be to mislead others as to the true nature of a person's or a group's interests. This is where recognition of the link between ideology and interests can lead to a consideration of ideological power.

Ideological power

The connection between ideology, interests, and power is not surprising. Once we have recognized that ideologies may express particular interests then ideological competition can be seen, to some extent, as an expression of competing interests. In that case, succeeding in getting other groups to accept or support an ideology that reflects your interests may be crucial for securing those interests. To use Varoufakis's argument about austerity, the rich will benefit if the poor, who are actually disadvantaged by austerity, can be persuaded that 'we are all in this together'. The capacity to manipulate others' beliefs can be described as ideological power. However, it is tricky to distinguish between deciding to change our beliefs of our own volition, in response to persuasive arguments, and those beliefs being changed by the exercise of power, as a result of manipulation. For in the latter case it will still *feel* like we have made up our own mind.

The concept of ideological power is most closely associated with the ideas of Karl Marx and the Marxist tradition, and it has come to exert a strong influence in the debate on the nature of ideology. There are scattered, and sometimes only brief, references to ideology in Marx's writings, and a range of approaches within the Marxist tradition after Marx. However, in perhaps his best known statement on ideology Marx claims that 'the ideas of the ruling class are in every epoch the ruling ideas: ie, the class, which is the ruling material force of society, is at the same time its ruling intellectual force' (Marx and Engels 1970). This statement can be unpacked and laid out as three related claims.

- Society is divided into classes. In Marx's theory there are essentially two classes in a capitalist society: the capitalist class which owns and controls the means of production (that is, the resources and tools used in production) and the working class which is property-less in the sense of lacking access to the means of production and is therefore dependent on working for a wage or salary.
- Ownership and control of the means of production makes the capitalist class 'the ruling material force of society'. Capitalists exercise power over members of the working class in the production process since working for a wage entails placing yourself under the **authority** of an employer.
- Ideology is specifically linked to class division. The ideas of the capitalist class rule within the society, meaning that ideas that reflect the interests of this class are prevalent or dominant.

So we can see that Marx makes a strong connection between interests and ideology—ideology is essentially a reflection of class interests. This can be described as a materialist approach, meaning that we can understand why certain ideologies are prevalent in any society by looking at the material aspects of the way that society is organized, particularly its mode of economic life. In a capitalist society ideas such as individualism, voluntary exchange, contract, and self-interest become common currency because they help to 'make sense' of that society and how to conduct ourselves within it, and they help to keep the society going. The upshot of this is that, for Marxists, it is not so much ideologies that drive social and economic transformations but more the other way around. The emphasis is on the rise of **capitalism** generating new ways of thinking rather than new ideas being responsible for capitalism's emergence. However, this does not mean that ideology is purely passive and has no impact in the 'real world'.

The basic purpose of economic power is to generate profit, but this entails a conflict of interest between workers and capitalists over wages, effort, skill, and working conditions. Ideological power figures in the theory as one of the mechanisms through which a system which is inherently conflictual is stabilized and the rule of the capitalist class is sustained. According to Miliband, the capitalist class constitutes

> a dominant [or ruling] class . . . by virtue of the effectiveness and cohesion it possesses in the control of *the three main sources of domination*: control over the main means of economic activity . . . ; control over the means of state administration and coercion; and control over what may broadly be called the means of communication and persuasion.

(Miliband 1969: 27)

Control over 'the means of communication and persuasion' tells us, in broad terms, the means by which the ideas of the ruling class prevail in society. More specifically, Miliband refers to a range of 'agencies of political persuasion' involved in the 'process of legitimation': conservative and pro-business political parties, organized religion, nationalism, business associations and promotional groups, corporate advertising and branding, the mass media, and the education system (Miliband 1969: 179–264). As to the nature of these ideas, they are not going to be simply a bald expression of capitalist interests (e.g. 'we demand a higher rate of profit and greater wealth for capitalists!') since, if that were the case, it could be expected that they would be opposed by members of the working class who would be intent on pressing their own interests (e.g. 'we demand shorter working hours and higher wages!' or even 'we demand the abolition of private ownership of the means of production!'). Clearly, that is no way to stabilize the system. So the trick is to get the workers to accept a distorted understanding of the world that conceals the true nature of the conflicting class interests. Thus the ideas of the ruling class consist of

> certain false or misleading ideas which help to sustain class-divided societies, typically by concealing or misrepresenting or justifying certain flaws in those societies, flaws which redound to the advantage of the economically dominant class.

(Leopold 2013: 23)

Central to these flaws is the exploitative and dehumanized nature of work which benefits capitalists through the creation of profit, and these flaws may be concealed or misrepresented by various ideas, such as: that workers and employers are engaged in a voluntary exchange in the labour market; that workers and employers are members of the same team with shared interests; that workers' wages involve 'a fair day's work for a fair day's pay'; that capitalist economies are efficient and there are no viable alternative economic systems, and so on. (Of course these ideas are only 'false or misleading' from the vantage point of the knowledge claims contained within the Marxist understanding of capitalism—that workers are exploited by capitalists, etc.)

Marx's theory takes the 'neutral' basic definition of ideology in a 'critical' direction (Leopold 2013: 21). In this sense the Marxist approach displays a clear affinity with the opprobrious view of ideology discussed earlier in the chapter, and specifically the notion of ideology as an 'infection', but an infection that we have without realizing it. Indeed, reinforcing this point, Miliband characterizes the process of legitimation in terms of 'indoctrination' (Miliband 1969: 182).

Ideology is not the only way of stabilizing the system, and not all political ideas count as ideology in the Marxist sense. Marx tended to put more emphasis on the coercive power of the state as the primary mechanism for sustaining the capitalist system, but ideology was given more emphasis in the work of subsequent Marxists as a way of explaining the, to them, remarkable stability and longevity of capitalism. The failure of working class revolution or, more especially, the failure of the working class to show much interest in revolution, could be explained by the successful inculcation of ruling class ideology. Gramsci's concept of **hegemony** or 'intellectual and moral leadership' suggests that this is achieved not just by overtly political ideas but also through many institutions and areas of life, such as the arts, film, and literature. This theory became a major influence on the development of Marxism in the twentieth century (Leopold 2013). Arguably, the history of that century, and especially its second half, is that of the strengthening of capitalist hegemony, to the extent that some declared the 'death of socialism' (see Chapters 4 and 13).

Historically an important ideology might be seen as conservatism in the UK (e.g. see Miliband 1969) or its equivalents in other societies, such as **republicanism** in the United States or Christian Democracy in Germany. Miliband also mentions the related ideology of nationalism. However, it can be argued that liberalism and, since the 1980s, neo-liberalism (or 'free market fundamentalism') has constituted the principal pro-capitalist ideology. The prescription to 'leave things to the market' and minimize the role of the public sector means emphasizing the virtues of a capitalist system and maximizing opportunities for profit-seeking capitalist enterprises.

But other ideologies can also play a part in helping to sustain capitalism, even those that appear to be critical of the system. For example, Marxists have criticized 'reformism' within the socialist tradition, such as 'labourism' or 'parliamentary socialism' in the UK, on the grounds that by accepting rather than seeking to challenge the constraints of a capitalist system reformism has effectively helped to keep capitalism going (Miliband 1973; Coates 1975).

 Stop and Think

1. In what way does Marx's approach to ideology introduce a 'critical' conception? How are the concepts of interests, power, and ideology related in the Marxist approach?

2. Are we imprisoned by ideology?

If it is true that the ruling ideas in society are the ideas of the ruling class, then we are in effect imprisoned by ideology. Because we have internalized ruling class ideas, our beliefs are false and misleading, and we cannot see the world as it really is. This is a disturbing thought. However, according to the Marxist approach there is a way out of the prison, and the way is revealed by . . . Marxism. At the most basic level, Marxism reveals that we are in a prison or that, to repeat an earlier metaphor, we do have an infection, and being armed with that knowledge is the first step towards release or cure. More generally, Marxism can be understood as a project of ideological demystification or debunking of false and misleading ideas. How can that be achieved?

Ideological power is assisted by the fact that the way the world works is not immediately obvious from experience and observation. Rather, an important aspect of Marx's theory is the claim that the way the world appears to us can be deceptive and conceal its true character. For example, the market system with voluntary exchange between workers and employers in the labour market makes it harder to see the reality that workers are exploited, compared to the situation of slaves or peasants. Therefore workers do not spontaneously know their own interests. Yet the facts, as Marxists see them, that work is dehumanizing and workers are exploited, provide the potential for working class consciousness to develop. Ideological domination requires constant effort and resources and is not always successful, and counter-hegemonic struggle is possible. Similar thinking is also found in other emancipation movements, such as feminism. The idea of 'consciousness-raising' in feminism has a close affinity with the idea of developing 'working class consciousness' in Marxism. In each case it is about an oppressed group coming to recognize their real situation and true interests, and throwing off false and misleading ideas that keep them in chains.

> ## ➲ Stop and Think
>
> Explain which of the following characterizations of ideological debate you feel is most persuasive.
>
> 1. Ideological debate involves testing rival values and knowledge claims in a disinterested way to determine which ideology is true.
> 2. Ideological debate involves a shared concern to formulate the public interest or common good.
> 3. Ideological debate is an expression of the interests of competing social groups.
> 4. Ideological debate involves unequal competition and the exercise of power.

Is Marxism itself an ideology?

Before we leave Marxism, an important challenge arises at this point. Marxism claims to provide an escape from ideological domination by providing a non-ideological vantage point that allows us to see the world as it really is. But it could be argued that there is no such vantage point. Perhaps Marxism is just another ideology? This idea is sometimes referred as the 'Mannheim paradox' after the sociologist Karl Mannheim with whom it is most associated (Mannheim 1960). On this understanding

> the paradox [is that] every time we uncover an opponent's political ideas and world-view as ideology [i.e. as a partial and distorted view], we achieve this only from the vantage point of another ideology, and so there is no vantage point outside of ideology to understand and criticize ideology.

> (Breiner 2013: 38)

Mannheim sought a way of avoiding this problem by relying on intellectuals, in an approach that contrasts with the Marxist tradition. For Marx, a scientific understanding was attained by *engagement* in the political struggle on the side of the working class. This looks like a recipe for a partial or one-sided view of the world, only seeing it from a working class standpoint (this would be Mannheim's view). However, for Marx the interests of the working class are universal, congruent with human interests in general, because they stand for human emancipation by bringing an end to exploitation. In contrast, Mannheim saw the crucial characteristic of intellectuals as being that they are *unattached* and not tied to particular interests, and therefore able to adopt a more impartial standpoint. The kinds of people who, in Marxist theory, might be seen as purveyors of ruling class ideas are seen by Mannheim as 'free-floating', capable of assessing rival ideological viewpoints and developing knowledge about the real world.

There is something to be said for the idea that the education and training of intellectuals may allow them to think more independently and take a many-sided view of things. However, Mannheim's approach can be criticized on two grounds, pointing in different directions. On the one hand, even if we don't see intellectuals as servants of a capitalist class, we might still doubt their capacity to detach themselves from social influences—it is not as though they do not occupy a particular position in the class structure with particular experiences, interests, and attitudes. On the other hand, perhaps Mannheim places too little confidence in the capacity for reason of the mass of people outside of the charmed circle of intellectuals. It could be argued that generally low levels of political knowledge and engagement belie any optimistic assessment in this respect, but the point may be to demand reforms that will develop in everyone the capacity for 'critical autonomy', meaning our ability not just to make choices about how we live within a culture but to stand back and take a critical view of that culture (Doyal and Gough 1992).

 Stop and Think

Can there be an independent vantage point outside of ideology?

The West, the rest, and globalization

The ideologies examined in this book, particularly the 'classical' ideologies, may be characterized as modern and 'Western' in the sense that they emerged in Western societies in the modern era in association with processes of modernization occurring in these societies (Gamble 1981; McLellan 1995: 2–8). Of course this is a simplification, and we should not homogenize either **the West** or 'the rest' and ignore diversity within each camp, or ignore the influence of traditions of thought inherited from the past (notably ancient—Greek and Roman—political thought and religion) or from beyond the West.

Nevertheless this historical and geographical contextualization suggests that we can explain the emergence of these ideologies in part in terms of the specific historical conditions to which they responded (and which they in turn helped to shape). Thus Western ideologies emerged because these societies developed along a distinctive modernizing path that differentiated them from the rest. 'Modernization' refers to the emergence of industrialized capitalist or market economic systems, based on advances in science and technology, and associated social and political changes including population growth, urbanization, distinctive patterns of class structure and inequality, and mass politics. Although these processes had earlier origins, the key process of industrialization can be dated to the late eighteenth century, with Britain as a pioneer. The societies that have emerged from these processes can be 'described by the acronym WEIRD: . . . Western, educated, industrialised, rich and democratic' (Diamond 2013: 8–9).

Ideologies that originated in the West have subsequently spread on a global scale. As Diamond notes, cultures can 'spread in either of two ways. One way is by people expanding and taking their cultures with them. . . . The other way is as the result of people adopting beliefs and practices of other cultures' (Diamond 2013: 22). These two processes have been involved in the spread of ideologies with the expansion of the West, through trade and other economic linkages, migration, settlement, and conquest. Today these forms of interconnection are often referred to as **globalization**.

As a consequence 'Western' ideologies now have a global reach. They have expanded from their European heartland to all other continents. They now partake of a global ideological debate and, it can be argued, are only Western in the sense of their contingent origins in Europe. Western expansion can be seen as having created a powerful homogenizing trend in the world, seen in terms of more countries developing WEIRD characteristics. As societies modernized they also adopted the modernist ideologies (Gamble 1981). However, homogenization or erosion of differences also faces counter-trends. Expansion of 'the West' has created encounters between previously unconnected cultures, specifically between Western ideologies and the pre-existing political ideas and traditions in 'the rest'. These encounters have played out differently in different places involving opposition and resistance to **Westernization** and defence of 'traditional', '**indigenous**', or non-Western values and cultures, as well as adoption of Western beliefs and practices. Thus the diffusion of Western ideologies has not been uniform but requires contextual analysis (Aguilar Rivera 2013; Bajpai and Bonura 2013; Hendrickson and Zaki 2013; Jenco 2013). Despite erosion of differences and diffusion of WEIRDness, the world is a long way from being (and might never become) uniformly 'Western'—it remains multicultural. Western societies have themselves also become, to varying degrees, multicultural, largely as the result of immigration from non-Western countries. Western expansion has led not to a one-way process of 'Westernization' but interconnectedness involving two-way (though asymmetrical) influences—sometimes referred to as reverse globalization. This has changed the terms of political debate within Western societies, particularly through the emergence of multiculturalism as a new ideology or field of debate. For example, it can be argued that African ideologies 'address the particular concerns of African peoples [not only] on the continent . . . [but also] in the African Diaspora . . . in Europe and the New World' (Hendrickson and Zaki 2013: 607). Thus African ideology can be seen to include the anti-slavery and **civil rights** movements in the USA.

Relativism, reason, and using this book

The encounter between 'the West' and 'the rest' raises the question of relativism: whether 'Western' political ideas and ideologies merely reflect the particular historical experiences and cultures of these societies so that they are relevant only in these contexts (**relativism**), or express human needs and aspirations that are relevant to people everywhere and all societies (**universalism**). In other words, does each culture have its own vision (or range of visions) of the good society, or can a vision of the good society claim to be valid for all cultures and peoples? This is essentially a restatement of the Mannheim paradox in terms of cultural embeddedness: in this case when we criticize other cultures and their conceptions of the good society, the question is whether we are really expressing a kind of parochialism, the particular values of our own culture.

For example, liberalism emerged in the specific historical circumstances of modernization in Europe, and may be seen as epitomizing 'the Western ideology' (Gamble 2009) and as an expression of Western values. But liberalism makes universalist claims on grounds of human dignity and rights. On these grounds it condemns certain practices such as forced marriage as universally wrong. Yet defenders of the practice may argue on relativist grounds that what is judged to be wrong from within a liberal or Western world view is judged to be worthy from a non-liberal, non-Western world view. Each judgement is 'correct' from the internal point of view of a particular ideology or culture, but neither is correct in absolute terms. The only judgements that are possible are internal ones. There are no absolute standards.

Relativism can be seen as safeguarding non-Western societies or cultures from imperialism by providing a way of rejecting clams that, say, a liberal form of **civilization** is superior, or it can be seen as blocking progress by preventing us from condemning certain practices as harmful to people everywhere. Which is it? The answer is that it can be both, depending on the beliefs and practices in question. In other words, there is a strong case for applying absolute standards (universalism) in some areas, while in other areas differing internal standards of judgement (relativism) are appropriate. This means that the controversy is not so much universalism *versus* relativism but how to decide which approach is appropriate for which issues. This can be seen in the distinction between 'forced' and 'arranged' marriage.

> A Forced Marriage . . . is a marriage conducted without the valid consent of one or both parties and where duress is a factor. . . . A person commits an offence under the law of England and Wales if he or she –
>
> a) uses violence, threats or any other form of coercion for the purpose of causing another person to enter into a marriage, and
>
> b) believes, or ought reasonably to believe, that the conduct may cause the other person to enter into the marriage without free and full consent.
>
> (Crown Prosecution Service, no date a)

> An arranged marriage is very different from a forced marriage. An arranged marriage is entered into freely by both people, although their families take a leading role in the choice of partner.
>
> (Crown Prosecution Service, no date b)

Forced marriage is a criminal offence in the UK under the Anti-Social Behaviour, Crime and Policing Act 2014. Criminalizing the practice can be justified on universalist grounds that it violates fundamental human rights and is therefore always wrong. If not justified in this way, the law would simply be imposing the values of the majority community on ethnic minorities in multicultural UK society. The ethnic minorities might argue that forced marriage is an integral and cherished aspect of their way of life. In contrast, it can be accepted that arranged marriage is a cultural practice in some ethnic minorities that is at variance with the practice of the majority community but which does not violate human rights and therefore should be tolerated on the grounds of differing internal standards of a good way of living (relativism).

But in adopting a universalist stance as a justification for outlawing forced marriage, how do we know that UK legislators are not embedded in their own culture and mistaking an internal standard for an absolute one? The only basis on which to make this judgement is reason, and the notion of an escalator of reason holds out the prospect of ascending to higher levels of knowledge and understanding. We have seen this idea applied in Pinker's analysis of the factors that have driven down levels of violence through history. It is reason that can provide an impartial vantage point on the basis of an understanding of human nature, needs, and interests. It is the capacity for reason that allows us to, in effect, dis-embed ourselves from our particular cultural influences and adopt a universalist standpoint.

In using a capacity for reason to critically engage with the rival ideologies set out in the chapters in this book, readers need, like the authors, to be aware that this capacity is affected by existing ideological influences or cultural biases. But those influences need not be so dominating that our minds are entirely closed. As McLellan puts it 'we are indeed all implicated in ideology which is both real and powerful; but an understanding of this fact can at least prevent us from becoming its unconscious victims' (McLellan 1995: 2).

Summary

- Ideology is a contested concept; that is, a term about whose meaning or definition there is disagreement.
- Nevertheless there is broad agreement on a basic conception of ideology as a system of ideas involving a vision of the good society, a critique of existing society, and a notion of political action. As systems of connected concepts, ideologies may also be studied using a morphological approach.
- Although politicians tend to abstain from using the term 'ideology' to refer to their own ideas and use it as a pejorative term for their opponents' ideas, it can be argued that ideology plays a necessary and positive role in politics—that we are all ideologists.
- Difficult questions about the nature of ideology and its role in political debate arise from consideration of its connections to conflicting interests, power, and cultural embeddedness.
- The capacity for reason provides the possibility of an independent vantage point from which to evaluate ideological arguments, and therefore of not being an 'unconscious victim' of ideology.

Review and discussion questions

1. Explain McLellan's statement that 'Ideology is the most elusive concept in the whole of social science'.
2. Compare and contrast the negative conception of ideology that is prevalent in politicians' speeches with a positive conception.
3. Examine the role played by assumptions about human nature in ideological debate.

4. Critically examine the Marxist theory of ideology. Is Marxism itself an ideology?

5. To what extent is ideological debate inescapably caught in a 'relativist trap'?

Research exercises

1. Using academic dictionaries and textbooks, compare and contrast definitions of 'ideology' from six separate sources.

2. Analyse three recent political speeches to identify the extent to which they can be read as statements of ideology.

3. Using media sources, examine the extent to which one of the following issues is framed in ideological terms.

   * immigration
   * climate change
   * terrorism

Further reading

For discussions of the concept of ideology see Eagleton (1991), Freeden (2003), Gerring (1997), and McLellan (1995). The morphological approach is set out in Freeden (2013) and at full length in Freeden (1996).

Freeden, Sargent, and Stears (eds) (2013) is an exhaustive 'handbook' on political ideologies. Gamble (1981) is an introduction to the origins of modern ideologies. Heywood (2000) is a useful guide to key concepts. Festenstein and Kenny (2005) introduces the main ideologies with the use of extensive extracts from primary sources.

See Fairclough (2015) for a study, using critical discourse analysis, of how language is used to reinforce power relationships in society.

References

AGUILAR RIVERA, J. A. (2013), 'Latin American Political Ideologies', in R. Eccleshall et al., *Political ideologies: An Introduction*, London: Routledge.

BAJPAI, R. AND BONURA, C. (2013), 'South Asian and Southeast Asian Ideologies', in M. Freeden, L. T. Sargent, and M. Stears (eds), *The Oxford Handbook of Political Ideologies*, Oxford: Oxford University Press.

BERMAN, S. (2006), *The Primacy of Politics: Social Democracy and the Making of Europe's Twentieth Century*, Cambridge: Cambridge University Press.

BREINER, P. (2013), 'Karl Mannheim and Political Ideology', in M. Freeden, L. T. Sargent, and M. Stears (eds), *The Oxford Handbook of Political Ideologies*, Oxford: Oxford University Press.

BROWN, G. (2009), Leader's speech, Labour Party Conference, Brighton, British Political Speech, http://www.britishpoliticalspeech.org/speech-archive.htm

CAMERON, D. (2010a), Prime Minister's speech on the economy, 7 June, https://www.gov.uk/government/speeches/prime-ministers-speech-on-the-economy

CAMERON, D. (2010b), Leader's speech, Conservative Party Conference, Birmingham, British Political Speech, http://www.britishpoliticalspeech.org/speech-archive.htm

COATES, D. (1975), *The Labour Party and the Struggle for Socialism*, Cambridge: Cambridge University Press.

CONSERVATIVEHOME (2016), Theresa May's launch statement: full text, http://www.conserva-tivehome.com/parliament/2016/06/theresa-mays-launch-statement-full-text.html

CROWN PROSECUTION SERVICE (no date a), *Honour Based Violence and Forced Marriage*, http://www.cps.gov.uk/legal/h_to_k/honour_based_violence_and_forced_marriage/#content

CROWN PROSECUTION SERVICE (no date b), *Honour Based Violence and Forced Marriage: Guidance on Identifying and Flagging Cases*, http://www.cps.gov.uk/legal/h_to_k/forced_marriage_and_honour_based_violence_cases_guidance_on_flagging_and_identifying_cases/

DAY, E. (2015), '#BlackLivesMatter: The Birth of a New Civil Rights Movement', *The Observer*, 19 July, https://www.theguardian.com/world/2015/jul/19/blacklivesmatter-birth-civil-rights-movement

DIAMOND, J. (2013), *The World Until Yesterday*, London: Penguin Books.

DOYAL, L. AND GOUGH, I. (1992), *A Theory of Human Needs*, Basingstoke: Macmillan.

EAGLETON, T. (1991), *Ideology: An Introduction*, London: Verso.

FAIRCLOUGH, N. (2015), *Language and Power*, London: Routledge.

FESTENSTEIN, M. AND KENNY, M. (2005), *Political Ideologies*, Oxford: Oxford University Press.

FREEDEN, M. (1996), *Ideologies and Political Theory: A Conceptual Approach*, Oxford: Clarendon Press.

FREEDEN, M. (2003), *Ideology: A Very Short Introduction*, Oxford: Oxford University Press.

FREEDEN, M. (2013), 'The Morphological Analysis of Ideology', in M. Freeden, L. T. Sargent, and M. Stears (eds), *The Oxford Handbook of Political Ideologies*, Oxford: Oxford University Press.

FREEDEN, M., SARGENT, L. T., AND STEARS, M. (eds) (2013), *The Oxford Handbook of Political Ideologies*, Oxford: Oxford University Press.

GAMBLE, A. (1981), *An Introduction to Modern Social and Political Thought*, London: Macmillan.

GAMBLE, A. (2009), 'The Western Ideology', *Government and Opposition*, Vol. 44, No. 1.

GUNNING, J. (1997), 'Ideology: A Definitional Analysis', *Political Research Quarterly*, Vol. 50, No. 4.

HANSARD SOCIETY (2016), *Audit of Political Engagement 13—The 2016 Report*, Hansard Society, https://assets.contentful.com/u1rlvvbs33ri/24aY1mkabGU0uEsoUOekGW/06380afa29a630 08e97fb41cdb8dcad0/Publication__Audit-of-Political-Engagement-13.pdf

HATTERSLEY, R. (1997), *In Praise of Ideology—The First Hansard Lecture*, Southampton: University of Southampton.

HATTERSLEY, R. (2003), 'Progressive Without the Progress', *The Guardian*, 14 July, http://www.theguardian.com/politics/2003/jul/14/labour.politicalcolumnists

HATTERSLEY, R. (2009), 'Labour must Regain its Reputation as a Party of Principle', *The Guardian*, 7 June, http://www.theguardian.com/commentisfree/2009/jun/07/roy-hattersley-labour-crisis

HATTERSLEY, R. (2009a), 'Ideology's our Life, Esther', *The Guardian*, 31 July, http://www.the-guardian.com/commentisfree/2009/jul/31/mp-ideology-constituents-esther-rantzen

HAY, C. (2007), *Why We Hate Politics*, Cambridge: Polity.

HENDRICKSON, J. AND ZAKI, H. (2013), 'Modern African Ideologies', in M. Freeden, L. T. Sargent, and M. Stears (eds), *The Oxford Handbook of Political Ideologies*, Oxford: Oxford University Press.

HEYWOOD, A. (2000), *Key Concepts in Politics*, Basingstoke: Palgrave-Macmillan.

JENCO, L. (2013), 'Chinese Political Ideologies', in M. Freeden, L. T. Sargent, and M. Stears (eds), *The Oxford Handbook of Political Ideologies*, Oxford: Oxford University Press.

KRUGMAN, P. (2011), 'Everyone has an Ideology', *New York Times*, 13 April, http://krugman.blogs.nytimes.com/2011/04/13/everyone-has-an-ideology/?_php=true&_type=blogs&module=Search&mabReward=relbias%3Aw%2C%7B%222%22%3A%22RI%3A15%22%7D&_r=0

LEOPOLD, D. (2013), 'Marxism and Ideology: From Marx to Althusser', in M. Freeden, L. T. Sargent, and M. Stears (eds), *The Oxford Handbook of Political Ideologies*, Oxford: Oxford University Press.

McCALMONT, L. (2013), 'Obama "Not Particularly Ideological"', *Politico*, 25 November, http://www.politico.com/story/2013/11/obama-ideology-100328.html

MACKENZIE, I. (2003), 'The Idea of Ideology', in R. Eccleshall et al., *Political Ideologies: An Introduction*, London: Routledge.

McLELLAN, D. (1995), *Ideology*, London: Open University Press.

MANNHEIM, K. (1960), *Ideology and Utopia*, London: Routledge and Kegan Paul.

MARX, K. AND ENGELS, F. (1967), *The Communist Manifesto*, London: Penguin.

MARX, K. AND ENGELS, F. (1970), *The German Ideology*, London: Lawrence and Wishart.

MILIBAND, R. (1969), *The State in Capitalist Society*, London: Weidenfeld and Nicolson.

MILIBAND, R. (1973), *Parliamentary Socialism: A Study in the Politics of Labour*, London: Merlin Press.

OBAMA, B. (2008), Speech: 'A More Perfect Union "The Race Speech"', Philadelphia, PA, March 18, 1980', http://obamaspeeches.com/E05-Barack-Obama-A-More-Perfect-Union-the-Race-Speech-Philadelphia-PA-March-18-2008.htm

OBAMA, B. (2014), 'Obama Address on Sweeping Immigration Executive Actions—Full Speech Text', *The Guardian*, 21 November, http://www.theguardian.com/us-news/2014/nov/20/obama-speech-on-immigration-in-full

PINKER, S. (2002), *The Blank Slate: The Modern Denial of Human Nature*, London: Penguin Books.

PINKER, S. (2011), *The Better Angels of Our Nature: A History of Violence and Humanity*, London: Penguin Books.

RUCKER, P. (2013), 'Obama: I'm "not a particularly ideological person"', *The Washington Post*, 25 November, http://www.washingtonpost.com/blogs/post-politics/wp/2013/11/25/obama-says-house-republicans-are-biggest-barrier-to-progress/

STOKER, G. (2006), *Why Politics Matters*, Basingstoke: Palgrave-Macmillan.

STONE, J. (2015), 'Austerity is being Used as a Cover-story for Class War against the Poor, Yanis Varoufakis says', *The Independent*, 25 September, http://www.independent.co.uk/news/uk/politics/austerity-is-being-used-as-a-cover-story-for-class-war-against-the-poor-yanis-varoufakis-says-10516247.html

2

Liberalism

Robin Redhead and Stephen Hood

OBJECTIVES

- Outline the basic features of liberal ideology
- Examine key contributions to the development of the ideology
- Discuss the key values of liberalism and distinguish different variants of liberalism
- Examine the influence of liberalism on social movements and political parties in the United Kingdom and beyond
- Illustrate the pervasiveness of liberalism and examine the relationship between liberalism and other ideologies

Introduction

Let us begin by imagining a way of life in which our lives are based, to the fullest extent possible, on our own choices. We can choose to shape our identity in any way we wish, no matter how different this makes us from others. We can choose where we want to go and to whom we want to talk. It is entirely up to us what we wish to talk about, or the conclusions our discussions reach. In fact, what we believe is just a matter for us. Political power is exercised in a way that respects the importance of our choices to us: there are strict limits on what a government may ask of us or expect us to do. They cannot—unless they are able to provide a very good reason for doing so—override our own choices. Equally, other people are expected to respect the equal standing of our choices and allow us to live our lives as we wish. This life we imagine is a life lived in freedom.

This is the basic ideal that animates liberalism: that the key task of politics and political institutions is to facilitate the free choices of individuals. Equally, liberalism strives to ensure that this freedom is respected by other individuals and by government power. So, there must be a recognition that each person's choice cannot be absolute and that there are some limits on what anyone is entitled to do to others. Thus, limits such as individual rights, government accountability and the separation of the legislative, executive, and judicial powers are often core features of liberal regimes. But liberals hold that the mutual acceptance of such limits is the basis for freedom at its fullest.

As this chapter will show, however, this initial commitment to free individual choice can result in a variety of different, even conflicting, political positions, depending upon the sorts of choice considered to be of particular value and the factors seen as forming the biggest obstacles to individual freedom. This means that liberal politics can take a wide variety of forms: from prizing economic liberty and seeking to restrict the scope of government activity, to advocating the use of government power in attempts to radically reshape societies. As a result, in most countries, politicians who adhere to liberal ideas will not just be found in Liberal parties, but in parties across the traditional political spectrum.

This chapter begins with a look at the origins of liberalism, establishing the historical, political, and philosophical roots of the ideology we see today. We then explore some key concepts and values of a liberal ideology: liberty, democracy, rights, and **tolerance**. While these values are closely associated with liberalism, their value may still be understood or weighted differently by different liberal positions. Two of the most important, yet contrasting, strands within liberalism will then be examined in more detail: economic liberalism, which gives support to policies of privatization and **laissez-faire** economics, and social liberalism, which couples its concern for individual freedom with a commitment to social equality. The chapter finishes by considering some key criticisms of liberal ideas. Throughout these sections the liberal vision of a just society will be defined and explored. We will see the initial **radical** force of liberal ideals and also how, in parts of the world today, this **radicalism** remains. And, throughout, we will see how liberalism seeks to advance its profound commitment to free choice and liberty for all human beings.

Origins of liberalism

In this section we will enquire into the origins of liberalism. We will see how, at their conception, liberal ideas were seen as radical, and how over time these ideas have evolved and withstood challenge, such that they came to play a defining role in Western democracies.

Liberalism first became a distinct political movement in the late seventeenth century, when it began gathering support from philosophers and economists in the Western world. Prior to this point, the political organization of society had reflected the idea of a divinely ordained order, expressed through principles such as hereditary privilege, state religion, absolute monarchy, and the Divine Right of Kings. A consequence of viewing the appropriate organization of society as being derived from religious ideas was that differences of belief between or within countries could often result in wars or civil strife. The period after the early-sixteenth-century Protestant Reformation in Europe, in particular, was marked by violent confrontation between Protestants and Catholics.

Yet the idea that society ought to be organized in accordance with patterns of faith and tradition began to come under increasing scrutiny. The period that became known as the Enlightenment saw advances in knowledge, gained through innovations such as the development of the scientific method, which started to undermine the religious view of the world. Instead, Enlightenment thinkers argued that individual reason had the potential to discover and understand the way the world worked. Yet it was not just the understanding of the natural world towards which they turned reasoned attention. Attempts were also made to understand human society according to a purely materialist world view, without the need for divine explanations.

One early such account was provided by Thomas Hobbes (1588–1679) in his work *Leviathan* (1651), which attempted to uncover rational principles for the ordering of a system of political government. Hobbes began by asking his readers to imagine what life would be like in a **state of nature**, without any government. Individuals would be perfectly free to choose how they wished to act. But famously, Hobbes thought life in this state would be 'solitary, poor, nasty, brutish, and short' (Hobbes 1994 [1651]: 76). This is because perfect freedom would inevitably lead to disputes between people when the free choices of one individual impacted upon the way another wished to live. But, with no authority, it would be hard for individuals to solve these disputes by themselves. As a result, the best course of action for individuals in a state of nature may be, rather than waiting for disputes to arise, to forcibly exert their own will whenever possible. If each person thinks like this, the competitive pressure that results could lead to a state of war, where everyone is battling to protect or advance their own personal interests. Hobbes thought that the desire to avoid a state of war such as this would give individuals good reasons to make an agreement, or contract, under which they would be bound by a strong authority, which would have absolute power to make and enforce laws.

This stark choice—that individuals either face a state of chaos and disorder or give up much of their liberty to live under the power of an absolute sovereign—has often been criticized as an unduly pessimistic result of Hobbes having lived through the tumult of the English Civil War (1642–51) and it means that Hobbes should not himself be considered as a liberal. But what is highly radical about his ideas, and proved influential with subsequent liberal thinkers, is the way Hobbes used the idea of a **social contract** between a government and its citizens as a means to think about the reasons that each individual could have to agree to be bound by a set of laws. In other words, it raises the idea that the way people are governed should be something that they could freely choose to endorse.

Similar ideas are also present in the work of John Locke (1632–1704), whose seminal *Two Treatises of Government* (1690) has seen him described as 'the father of liberalism'. Like Hobbes, Locke argued that people would consent to the authority of a government through a social contract because they would find this preferable to life in a state of nature. Where Locke's ideas differ from those of Hobbes is that he did not think people were totally free to act as they wanted in a state of nature. Instead, he thought that everyone was born with natural rights that protected their life, liberty, and personal property from incursion. The reason that individuals would enter into a social contract with government was that a government would be better able to protect and enforce these rights. Individuals would therefore be guaranteed a private space of liberty, in which they could live as they personally chose. A distinctively liberal feature of Locke's ideas is that he thought the rights individuals possess did not simply offer them protection against other people, but also against government. This means that he thought the power of government must have clear limits, defined in a constitution, in order to protect these rights. Any government that went beyond the specified limits and infringed the rights of its citizens would lose the legitimacy it had derived from their free consent. A government that does not respect rights can therefore be rightfully resisted by its citizens.

Locke was writing around the time of the Glorious Revolution of 1688, an upheaval in England that saw **parliamentary sovereignty** enshrined in English law and witnessed the birth of the first modern liberal state. Significant legislative milestones such as the 1679 Habeas Corpus Act, the 1689 Bill of Rights, and the 1680 Act of Toleration were achieved. Habeas Corpus, meaning 'produce the body' or 'you may have the body', required courts to have the accused present to hear the charges against them in a court of law. Before this act, it had been a common practice to detain people without them even knowing the charges made against them. The Act made this treatment of detainees illegal, thus comprehensively transforming the judicial system, and paving the way for increased individual rights. The 1689 Bill of Rights gave parliament sovereignty over law making, the electoral process, and taxes. Society would thereafter be governed by the rule of law, not the whims of the monarch. Freedom of worship for non-Protestants was provided for in the Act of Toleration 1680, while freedom of the press became possible through the refusal to renew the Licensing of the Press Act 1662. These milestones provided the initial basis for a commitment to liberal ideas in England.

> ### ➡ Stop and Think
>
> The Habeas Corpus Act of 1679 requires the court to have the accused present to hear the charges against them in a court of law. Since the attacks in the United States on 11 September 2001 (9/11), and those in London on 7 July 2005 (7/7), both the USA and the UK have passed anti-terrorism acts, which permit the detention of individuals without their being charged with a crime. Can governments justify suspending the rights of particular individuals suspected under anti-terrorism acts for the wider protection of the public?

Liberalism continued to evolve through the end of the seventeenth century and the beginning of the eighteenth. The assertion of individual political rights was gaining momentum outside of Europe, giving liberal values an early global reach. In 1765, the tensions between the British and their American colonies worsened as settlers were being asked to pay taxes to the crown without proper political representation in the British parliament. This stimulated colonial rebellion and the American War of Independence ensued. In drafting the Declaration of Independence (1776), Thomas Jefferson (1743–1826), echoing Locke, wrote: 'we hold these truths to be self-evident, that all men are created equal, that they are endowed by their Creator with certain unalienable Rights, that among these are Life, liberty and the pursuit of Happiness' (United States National Archives 2015). His words are quite possibly the most influential articulation of a commitment to liberal values. The new constitution of the United States of America (1787) established a strong national government and ensured the separation of the executive, the legislature, and the judiciary as a hedge against the concentration of power in one individual or group. The American Bill of Rights (the first 10 amendments) enshrines rights such as free exercise of religion (First Amendment) and protection from unreasonable search and seizures of one's person or property (Fourth Amendment).

While the USA was fighting for its republic, back in Europe the middle classes (**bourgeoisie**) in France were looking to increase their power and liberalize the state. The French Revolution, as examined in Case Study 2.1, is considered to be a 'triumph of liberalism' as it focused on the abolition of **feudalism** in France in favour of the Declaration of the Rights of Man and the Citizen (1789), which aimed to provide that every male citizen live under conditions defined by the values of liberty, equality, and fraternity.

Case Study 2.1 French Revolution: liberté, égalité, fraternité

The French Revolution is an historical period in France, spanning the years 1789–99, during which time the monarch, King Louis XVI, was overthrown in a popular rebellion motivated by ideological changes brought about by Enlightenment authors and thinkers. A sharp rise in taxes, owing to disarray in the country's finances, coupled with widespread famine, contributed significantly to the context for this revolt. Protesters gathered at Versailles demanding action from the King. When the King sent troops to disperse these protesters, people saw this as a provocation and the poor labourers of Paris stormed the Bastille Prison on 14 July 1789. This act of defiance became symbolic of the revolution and is still celebrated in France today.

The origins of the revolution can be traced to the legal debates between the monarchy and aristocracy over state finances and political authority. In 1787, an unsuccessful Assembly of Notables, comprised of the aristocracy, demanded political power and tax reform. The aristocracy wanted more power and political influence, but were not interested in extending this to any other tier of society.

At this time, the bourgeoisie (middle class) were the most noteworthy contributors to the French economy. They were professionals who generated significant wealth but had little status, as position within society was dictated by birth and land ownership. The revolution gave the bourgeoisie unprecedented political authority. Abolishing aristocratic privilege (birth rights), confiscating lands belonging to the church and the aristocracy, and removing internal obstacles to trade and commerce allowed the bourgeoisie greater economic and social mobility.

From the perspective of the middle classes, the French Revolution was a liberal revolution. Premised upon ideas that mankind is essentially rational and that the purpose of life is the 'pursuit of happiness', it swept away the old regime and secured a new state where individuals had the opportunity to freely pursue their own aims.

The most influential document to come out of the French Revolution was the *Déclaration des droits de l'homme et du citoyen*, the Declaration of the Rights of Man and the Citizen. Passed in the National Constituent Assembly in August 1789, influenced by the work of Rousseau, Montesquieu, Thomas Jefferson, and General Lafayette, this document became the basis for the vision of a nation of free individuals protected equally by law. The Declaration was a statement of the core values of the Revolution and had a fundamental impact on the development of democracy in Europe and worldwide. The concept that the rights of man are universal and inalienable is captured within it.

Even though many illiberal and **authoritarian** acts were committed during the French Revolution, the principles contained within the Declaration remained in some form in the Napoleonic Code (1804), which forbade privileges based on birth, allowed freedom of religion, and specified that government jobs should go to the most qualified rather than those of high social status.

Early liberal thinkers did not just focus their attention upon the relationship between government and its citizens. They also sought to understand the way trade and the economy functioned. Adam Smith (1723–90) was a Scottish philosopher and economist during the Enlightenment. His work *An Inquiry into the Nature and Causes of the Wealth of Nations* (1776) is one of the most influential books ever written. In Smith's day, a nation's wealth was understood as a country's stock of gold and silver. Importing goods from other countries was seen as damaging because it meant spending national wealth to pay for them. Exporting goods was seen as good because the gold and silver came back as payment. Much effort was put into taxes on imports and subsidies to exporters as controls that prevented draining gold and silver stocks. Within countries, tradesmen could only practise their trade in their own city, while manufacturers and merchants petitioned the king for protective monopolies. This system was called **mercantilism**.

Smith showed that mercantilism was a folly. He argued that free exchanges of goods leave both sides better off. He suggested that nobody would choose to trade if they expected to lose from it. The buyers would profit, just as the sellers would. In some ways, this is a very simple idea. Yet its implications are far-reaching. It means that leaving individuals free to pursue their own interests, and to make their own economic choices, might also be the best way to create prosperous outcomes. It also means that the way to judge a nation's wealth is not by the quantity of gold and silver in its vaults, but the total of its production and commerce. This concept today is called *gross national product* (GNP). These ideas were very influential on politicians and provided the conceptual foundation of the nineteenth-century era of free trade and economic expansion. Smith's ideas of free trade continue to have global influence. The wide scope of global trade that we see today is a result of the demise of mercantilist ideas.

Accompanying the development of processes of free trade, the period after the French Revolution saw the further development of liberalism in England. Pressure was applied in favour of parliamentary and electoral reform that would fully instantiate natural rights and popular **sovereignty**. Important works such as Thomas Paine's (1737–1809) *The Rights of Man* (1791) and Mary Wollstonecraft's (1759–97) *A Vindication of the Rights of Women* (1792) helped to encourage mass support for democratic reform.

In 1839, a group of members of the Whig Party, a political party committed to parliamentary sovereignty, were joined by a small number of parliamentary radicals, who together informally called themselves the Liberal Party (Bellamy 1992: 40). This party would go on to produce one of the most influential of all British Prime Ministers, William Gladstone (1809–98), who would be responsible for the compulsory education of all children until the age of 13, the disestablishment of the Church of Ireland, and the introduction of secret ballots for local and parliamentary elections (Bellamy 1992: 39)—policies that help to establish political and social rights for citizens.

It is worth noting that, while liberal ideas required an end to the privilege exemplified by institutions such as monarchy and aristocracy as a means to achieve fair and equal treatment for all citizens, early liberals were not always consistent or comprehensive in their advocacy of these ideas. Many of the reforms of this era, such as the British Reform Act of 1832, were primarily a success for propertied men, yet did nothing for **women's suffrage** or that of the lower classes. Equally, liberal states and thinkers were often blind to racial subjugation: the advance of liberal ideas and institutions occurred alongside practices of slavery and imperial domination. For excluded groups, further political struggle was required—and even today may still be required—in order to gain a truly secure share of liberal freedom.

Now, one thing we have seen so far is that there is a key challenge that liberal ideas must face. This is that liberalism holds that individuals have an interest in being able to make their own choices about how to live their own lives. But allowing free choice may give rise to disputes, as the freedom of one individual can come into conflict with that of another. So some form of coordination is going to be required. Yet, as can be seen starkly in the ideas of Hobbes, the coordinating authority can itself come to form a threat to the liberty of its citizens. This is even the case with a democratic form of government, as the choices of a majority may threaten the freedom of minority groups. This creates one of the biggest questions for liberal thinkers: that of establishing the relationship between liberty and authority. Perhaps the most influential of all attempts to address this question was provided by John Stuart Mill (1806–73) in his 1859 work *On Liberty*. Here, Mill offered a defence of certain basic and fundamental liberties: freedom of conscience and expression; liberty of tastes and pursuits, so that an individual can choose a plan of life that suits their own character; and freedom of association. The only grounds for an authority to interfere with these liberties would be to prevent harm being caused to others, which is known as the *harm principle*.

The harm principle is intended to offer strong protection for individual liberty from threats of interference by the state. It clearly rules out some common grounds that might be appealed to as reasons for restriction. An individual's choices should be respected even if they are perceived to be harmful to that individual's own interests—it is only when they threaten harm to others that interference is allowed. Equally, not every unpleasant consequence for others counts as genuine harm: Mill is clear to distinguish harm from mere offence, which means that an individual cannot have their liberty infringed simply because other people do not approve of their actions. Instead it must be demonstrated that these actions genuinely threaten the basic interests of others. What makes this idea so important in liberal thinking is that it provides a systematic defence of the liberal idea that there should be a protected area of activity in which an individual is not answerable to others. Certain areas of an individual's life should be regarded as being outside of the concern of state regulation.

Mill also made a point of analysing the economic inequality of women, its economic character and consequences and how greater equality between the sexes might change these conditions. Although he was not the first to engage with the plight of women, as Wollstonecraft preceded him, his prominence lent strength to the idea that women are also equal citizens, thus lending support for feminist ideologies (see Chapter 9 on feminism).

 Stop and Think

What common forms of government legislation would be judged to be impermissible according to Mill's harm principle?

In the latter half of the nineteenth century, while parts of Europe were experiencing political unrest and a shift towards socialism, in Britain, liberals maintained political control by conceding incremental employment and electoral reforms that helped to defuse political crises and led, eventually, to the acceptance of full democracy in the twentieth century.

This section has traced the emergence of liberalism from the Enlightenment to the twentieth century. We observed how strong demands for individual and political rights overthrew monarchical control in Europe and established governments that were to be limited in the way they dealt with their citizens. We traced the evolution of a commitment to liberal values, and saw how these ideas became law. With a better understanding of the origins of liberalism, we can begin to examine some of its central concepts.

Core values and concepts

In this section we will consider liberty, democracy, rights, and tolerance as some of the core values and concepts of liberal ideology. When we say 'core' concepts, this does not mean that all liberals adhere to all of these values or understand them in the same way, as we will see. For example, democracy has an uneasy relationship with liberalism, even if the two often go together. We will now start with the most fundamental value for liberals, which is a commitment to liberty.

Liberty

For liberals, liberty is the most important moral and political value. It was Locke who clearly articulated the primacy liberty plays in liberalism: humans are in 'a State of Perfect Freedom to order their Actions . . . as they see fit . . . without asking leave or depending on the Will of any other Man' as imagined in a state of nature (Locke 1988 [1690]: 269). Locke expresses a view of liberty that holds that a person should be free to act as they choose without the influence or permission of others. Locke establishes the basic foundation for liberalism with his idea that liberty means that one should not interfere in the lives of others, and that one is free to pursue ones' own goals as long as they do not limit the freedom of others.

Mill expanded on Locke's view of liberty by focusing on the consequences of ones' actions. He argued that: 'the burden of proof is supposed to be with those who are against liberty: who contend for only restriction or prohibition . . . . The a priori assumption is in favour of freedom' (Mill 1963: 262). Mill started from the position that all people are born free and equal, and as such every person has a natural right (birthright) to liberty. In his view, a person need not defend this liberty, but rather, only those who seek to override it need provide a justification. This has been called the *Fundamental Liberal Principle* (Gaus 1996: 162–6), asserting that freedom is the standard way of being for all humans. Only those who would limit freedom, especially through coercive means, must provide a rationale for their actions. This means then that political authority and law must be justified, as they limit the liberty of their citizens. But this requires having a clear understanding of what makes an individual free, and what sorts of condition will limit their liberty. There is, however, no single shared liberal understanding of what individual liberty means. Equally, because liberals hold different positions as to what liberty is, they also hold different positions as to what the task of government should be in protecting or promoting liberty. Let us now look at two competing ways of understanding liberty: *negative* and *positive* liberty.

This distinction is attributed to Isaiah Berlin (1909–97), a Latvian-British philosopher and political thinker who is well-known for defending the negative conception of liberty. Negative liberty can be thought of as a space free from any physical or legal obstacles, within which an individual may choose how they wish to act. Where others act to prevent us from doing something, this is a coercive infringement upon our freedom. A liberal government, on this account, should aim to avoid placing unnecessary barriers to its citizens' activity and should seek to prevent citizens from coercing others, so as to protect the widest possible space for individual choice. It does not matter whether citizens wish to exercise particular choices, or even that they have the personal capability to do so; what is important is that the choices remain open to them. This way of thinking about freedom is particularly associated with libertarians such as Steiner (1994) or Nozick (1974) and classical liberals such as Hayek (1960).

In contrast to this, Berlin describes positive liberty as being very much focused upon the choices people actually make and the way they make them. An early exponent of this way of thinking was Jean-Jacques Rousseau (1712–78). For Rousseau, people are naturally good—a state of nature would be characterized by free and happy individuals—but the shape of society can corrupt them. Living among others tends to make people become vain and competitive, striving to be seen as stronger, cleverer, or more talented than their fellows. This actually undermines the ability of people to live life as they would really wish; instead, they become too caught up in the desire to impress others or to further their own personal status. As a result, Rousseau thought true freedom could only exist if the political system allowed people to live together in an equal and cooperative manner.

Rousseau set out his idea of what this system might look like in *The Social Contract* (1762). Like Hobbes and Locke before him, he viewed this as requiring people to agree to be bound by the rule of a government. However, this government would not be other people ruling over them, but instead all citizens together making decisions about the laws that would govern them. Rousseau's ideal form of government would be a strong form of democracy. This differentiates his ideas from those of liberal thinkers who rely on a negative account of liberty: what Rousseau thinks people would get in return for agreeing to the social contract is not a private space in which they could choose individually how they wished to live, but instead he thinks they would gain true moral and civil freedom by coming together with others in a collective process to choose the rules they would then live their lives by.

But Berlin, and other critics of positive freedom, have noted a danger present in defining freedom as a component of the type and manner of choice made. This danger can be outlined by looking a bit more closely at the functioning of Rousseau's ideal democratic society. In this system, Rousseau thought all citizens should come together to directly vote upon the laws that would govern them. Each individual was supposed to vote not based upon what would most benefit themselves, but instead upon what would be in the best interests of all citizens. If they did this, he thought, then what would emerge from a majority vote would be the **general will**—the correct idea of what would be best for all. Since this would be the correct choice, then true freedom would involve complying with its demands, even for those who may have voted against it. This meant that Rousseau thought that people who refused to obey the general will could be compelled to do so without any loss of freedom—they could 'be forced to be free' (Rousseau 1993: 195).

Here we can see the problem that Berlin identified with positive freedom: if freedom consists in making the right sort of choices, or making choices in the right way, then it is possible for people to be mistaken in the choices they actually make. Positive freedom might therefore allow someone else to impose a decision upon an individual, all the while insisting that this is making them more free, which might seem to be quite an illiberal conclusion for a view based upon liberty to arrive at.

Now, defenders of positive liberty would argue that there are times when it is definitely possible to identify situations where an individual's choices are not in line with their best interests. For instance, Thomas Hill Green (1836–82), an English philosopher and political radical, argued that a person can be unfree if she is subjected to an impulse or craving that cannot be controlled. Such a person, he claimed, would be 'in a condition of a bondsman who is carrying out the will of another, not his own' (Green 1986 [1895]: 228). Consider the example of an alcoholic: an alcoholic is controlled by his craving to look for satisfaction in ways that, ultimately, will be harmful to his interests. In other words, a person will only be free if she is free from such compulsions and acts in a self-directed or autonomous way. One is free only to the degree that one has effectively determined oneself and the shape of one's life (Taylor 1979). Such a person takes time to critically reflect on her ideals and does not simply follow what others are doing. She does not flout long-term goals for short-term pleasures.

This understanding of a flourishing life as one in which an agent rationally reflects upon their choices and goals in a way that allows them to be understood as an autonomous self-author is one that has consistently been held to be attractive by some liberal thinkers. Indeed, for many, this account of flourishing is the key idea that justifies the liberal ideal. It is present in the work of Mill and also animates the thinking of contemporary liberals such as Ronald Dworkin (2002) and Will Kymlicka (1991). Yet some liberal thinkers go even further to argue that, if we view an autonomous life in which individuals make good choices as something of value, the state should act in ways that promote autonomy or make it more likely that individuals choose valuable options, as this will improve the lives of individual citizens. Key advocates of this idea, known as liberal perfectionism, include Joseph Raz (1986) and Steven Wall

(1998). Many liberals remain unpersuaded by these arguments, however, claiming that, in order for a liberal state to respect the free choice and equal standing of its citizens, it must remain neutral about the particular goals or forms of life its citizens should choose (Rawls 1996; Quong 2010).

We see, then, that although liberty is at the core of liberalism, there remain a variety of liberal positions about its true nature. Some hold liberty to take a negative form, consisting in a space of non-interference in which choices are open to people. Others hold that genuine freedom involves examining the sorts of choices people make and the way in which they make them, stressing that these choices should be autonomous and self-directed. The fact that liberty can be understood in different ways helps to explain why liberalism is such a varied ideology: different accounts of liberty will lead to different ideas as to how liberty might best be defended and advanced. One further thing that we began to see in the discussion of Rousseau's ideas is that there is some tension between liberalism and democracy, as democratic outcomes may go against some people's personal choices. We will now turn to examine this relationship in more detail.

Democracy

Although the practice of democracy varies greatly across different types of state, the common idea has been shared as a value among economically and politically advanced countries. Democracy is concerned with a system of rule that attempts to be responsive to the choices of individuals, which provides a liberal ideology with an approach to governing consistent with the protection of individual freedom. Democracy offers liberals a way of pulling individuals together and providing a system to coordinate their lives that is responsive to their choices.

We see, then, that underpinning both democracy and liberalism is an idea of individuals being in control of their own lives. Liberalism grew out of a rejection of the idea that God dictates what human actions *ought* to be, instead putting control in the hands of human beings. Hence, individuals need to be protected from the rule of any authority, whether religious or **secular**, which would seek to trample upon an individual's right to **self-determination**. It is this element of liberalism that makes it a target for religious fundamentalists, who believe that human beings are not autonomous and society should be organized according to the will of God (see Chapter 12). Liberals stress that democratic freedom is found by limiting the state and through the protection of individuals' rights, in documents such as the Bill of Rights and the Human Rights Act (see Case Study 2.3).

But sometimes, as we saw in the discussion of Rousseau in the previous subsection, if the outcomes of democratic decisions are not supported by everyone, this may lead to a scenario where a decision made by the majority ends up infringing the freedom of those who did not support the decision. This situation is referred to as the **tyranny of the majority**. One way of protecting individual freedom from such tyranny is to insist upon strong individual rights that cannot easily be overridden by democratic decisions. Yet here we see the tension between democracy and a liberal ideology: how much weight should be given to the choices made by the collective and how much weight should be given to the ability of an individual within the group to make their own choices? Many democratic systems will hold that the decisions of the collective should more often take precedence over individual interests, but this compromises the extent to which a system can be fully liberal. Alternatively, it is possible to imagine a liberal system in which many individual rights are fully respected even in the absence of democracy. So liberalism and democracy are not synonymous.

We can see this in religious states, which can imagine free and fair electoral processes or representative governments, but struggle with redefining the individual political citizen to include, for instance, women. This is because the religious beliefs already define the social relationships available to women and are not open for debate. It is the element of individual choice that non-democratic and illiberal states fundamentally cannot get past. It is also the desire for rights and freedoms that often leads to uprisings and the overthrow of authoritarian regimes. As in the Enlightenment, when liberalism was a radical idea, the recent uprisings in the Arab world echo this quest for choice and show, with their successes and failures, just how difficult transitions to free democratic societies can be, and the heavy price often paid by those caught in the struggle (see Case Study 2.2).

Case Study 2.2 Liberalism in the Arab world: the 2011 uprising

What came to be known as the Arab Spring was a sequence of protests in Arab countries against the authoritarian regimes across the Middle East and North Africa (MENA). Protesters, activists, and citizens demanded a better life where they were free from fear, from police corruption and brutality, free to express their views, and free to live in a democracy. A desire to adopt the rule of law and freedom of expression sparked clashes in many Arab countries, resulting in the dismissal of dictatorships and military regimes. It was an attempt to bring liberal and democratic principles, such as free and fair elections, to Islamist states.

Growing economic disparity, unemployment, and violent conflicts within countries in the region brought desperation to its people. On 17 December 2010, Mohamed Bouazizi, a young university graduate unable to find work other than as a fruit seller, set himself alight in a market square in Tunisia as a protest against police harassment and unemployment. This act was a catalyst for widespread protests in Tunisia, Algeria, Oman, Yemen, Egypt, Syria, and Morocco. Tunisian President Zine El Abidine Ben Ali's government was overthrown on 14 January 2011 and he was sentenced to life in prison in June of the following year. In Egypt, thousands of protesters took to the streets in Tahrir Square, which resulted in the resignation of President Hosni Mubarek on 11 February 2011. Mubarek was also sentenced to life in prison by an Egyptian court. In Libya, protests against Muammar Gaddafi's dictatorship began an uprising that led to a civil war resulting in Gaddafi's death on 20 October 2011. There was a failed assassination attempt on the

President of Yemen, Ali Abdullah Saleh, on 3 June 2011, which resulted in his eventual resignation. In Syria tensions ran high, as President Bashar Al-Assad delivered a speech blaming foreigners for the uprisings and requested the cooperation of all Syrians to stop the rebel forces. A civil war broke out.

The protests in Egypt became the focal point of the Arab Spring as the size of the crowds on the streets and squares across the country was in the hundreds of thousands. Inspired by the capacity of public outrage in Tunisia to effect change, Egyptians set up online communities that created surprisingly strong bonds among young people leading many to demonstrate for the first time. Satellite television (particularly al-Jazeera) broadcasts enabled Egyptians to see both the size of the crowds and the regime's brutal response. As a reaction to the military's violent methods of dissuading protesters, the youth movement developed new ways of outmanoeuvring Egypt's vast and plodding security apparatus (Rutherford 2008). The collective activism facilitated by social media and technologies was impressive.

These grassroots demonstrations were matched by the lobbying efforts of various political parties who sought to bring the rule of law and democracy to Egypt. The Western world watched in anticipation of a wave of democracy across the region. In Egypt, liberal candidates were on the ballot paper, but lost out to the Muslim Brotherhood candidate Mohammed Morsi.

The Arab Spring did not end with the spread of democracy across the Arab world. Instead, many were killed or imprisoned. In Egypt alone, 800 people lost their lives at the hands of state security forces. But the activism and determination of millions of people to change the oppressive regimes in which they are forced to live should not be explained away as a failure. These revolutions have exposed the effects of dictatorships, repression, and religious states. The quest for freedom from tyranny has always been a long and dangerous one, which has taken the West hundreds of years to accomplish. What is most important about the revolutions associated with the Arab Spring is to acknowledge the desire for a commitment to freedom, equality, liberty, and tolerance within the Arab world.

Rights

One really important component of liberal ideology is the idea that individuals possess certain protections that place limits upon the way that either government or other individuals may treat them. This is typically expressed through the idea of rights. Key areas where liberals think individuals should be offered the protection of rights are: the protection of their body and personal security; securing freedom of conscience, so that individuals can believe, think, and express themselves as they wish, or can associate with whomever they choose; due process rights, so that individuals cannot be punished without charges being assessed through fair procedures such as a criminal trial; political rights requiring that government be responsive and accountable to them, often outlined as democratic rights to vote or to run for office; secure access and control of particular objects, maintained through the idea of property rights. Often, these protections get written into the law of states in the form of a bill of rights.

We have already seen how Locke thought that people have these protections before any sort of government is formed. That is to say, he thought people possessed natural rights. There are religious features to Locke's account of natural rights—he thought they were bestowed upon people by God—that few thinkers would endorse today. However, the idea that people automatically have certain moral claims still remains influential, more usually expressed today in the idea of universal human rights. This is the idea that each individual is owed a certain type of treatment simply on account of being human and irrespective of what is specified by the law of the country they live in.

This forms one of the most influential moral and political commitments of the liberal ideology. In the aftermath of the Second World War, world leaders got together and composed a list of thirty rights that every human being is entitled to on the basis of their shared humanity. The Universal Declaration of Human Rights (1948) provided, for the first time, agreement on a common standard for all peoples and all nations. It set out fundamental human rights to be universally protected. Enshrined in the document is a commitment to liberty, equality, dignity, and freedom. The UDHR was a mechanism designed to hold states accountable to their citizens and to protect citizens from the state. Where a state infringes upon, or fails to protect, the human rights of its citizens, it can find itself subject to criticism or to sanctions. Universal human rights hold that every human being has the power of reason and conscience and entrench peace and justice as human values worth protecting and promoting.

In the West, the language of rights is commonplace. Governments and civil society organizations alike use this language to articulate pressing social, cultural, and political issues. In light of this, human rights are perhaps liberalism's most successful legacy. At the same time, though, attempts to protect human dignity can reveal the difference between the individualistic basis of liberalism and more collective cultural world views. For instance, the adherence to some cultural traditions, such as female genital cutting, goes against the assertion of rights—in this case, a young woman's right to decide what she does with her body. While practices that infringe rights in this way are widely criticized, some people call into question the idea that we should always prioritize the rights of the individual in cases where they come into conflict with cultural practices, arguing that groups should also possess rights that would allow them to protect their traditional ways of life.

Another rights debate that explores key liberal tenets is the debate around privacy. Consider for a moment the internet and the question of data privacy. Data privacy has become a global issue with the advent of the internet. In some ways, the internet seems highly congruent with liberal values, as it powerfully enables freedom of expression. Yet, at the same time, it makes it much easier for people's lives and activity to be recorded or tracked. How do we balance open access to information with concerns for personal protection? This problem can be seen in government requests for powers to observe people's online activity so as to prevent the growth of dangerous extremism, which is justified by appeal to the need to protect the liberty of citizens.

Yet, at the same time, there is a major worry that these measures themselves involve too great an infringement upon citizens' liberty. This raises the question: how liberal should one be? This is one of the inherent challenges of rights-based approaches to public policy.

 Stop and Think

Should we limit freedom of speech for the sake of preventing the growth of extreme views? If you were asked to write government policy on this issue how would you tackle it?

Protecting human rights is a tricky business. Although human rights are universal, those entrusted with their protection—sovereign states—often fail in this task. We prioritize human life, liberty, and the pursuit of happiness for all of humanity, but when threats to our way of life are encountered, we often empower states in ways that threaten ours and others' rights in the name of national security. In Western countries, rights language and provision shape the behaviour of healthcare workers, social services, public authorities, police and security services, because it forms part of the domestic law (see Case Study 2.3). This provision is admired and desired by many people around the world, as we see large migration flows to countries with better human rights records. For asylum seekers fleeing persecution, liberal states offer an attractive vision of the 'good' society.

Case Study 2.3 The UK Human Rights Act 1998

The Human Rights Act (HRA) was introduced in the UK in 1998 to 'bring rights home'. It came into force in 2000. Specifically, it allows for UK citizens to rely on the rights contained in the European Convention on Human Rights (ECHR) through the domestic courts. It also requires ministers who bring primary legislation before the House of Commons to produce a 'statement of compatibility' indicating whether or not the legislation is in conformity with the provisions of the ECHR. Parliament's Joint Committee on Human Rights is tasked with considering the human rights compatibility of legislation, although it does not have any ability to veto it (Parliament UK 2015). Some of the rights contained in the HRA are absolute, which means they cannot be restricted, such as Article 2, the right to life, while others can be restricted, such as Article 5, the right to liberty. Your liberty can be restricted if you commit a crime that warrants imprisonment.

In essence the Human Rights Act is about government, the state, power, and people. Governments often struggle with the protection of human rights precisely because human rights protect people from government. The controversy over the Conservative Party's pledge to withdraw from the ECHR and replace the HRA in favour of a British Bill of Rights stems from this frustration. The Conservatives (a.k.a. Tories) resent the influence the European Court of Human Rights (ECtHR), located in Strasbourg, has over UK laws as it challenges the power of government. The ECtHR, the court associated with the ECHR, adopts a principle of interpretation that regards the Convention as a 'living instrument', which means that the Convention can expand into new areas, areas that go beyond the original draft. This is seen as problematic for the Tories because it forces all UK legislation to be in compliance with the ECHR, even at the expense of a British interpretation of the issue. What a British Bill of Rights would do is repeal the HRA and replace it with a new bill that will keep the same rights, but regain power from Strasbourg, and return it to UK courts. For instance, the HRA provides that foreign people convicted of a crime in the UK and who have served their sentence can use Article 8 (the right to respect for your family and private life), to remain in the UK. The Tories see this as an infringement on the rights of British nationals and in contravention of the government's duty to provide a safe society for the British people.

The HRA, like all human rights legislation, is liberal in its provision of rights and freedoms to citizens and in its goal to hold the state accountable to its people. Under the HRA, public authorities must make sure they respect and protect human rights when they provide healthcare services. This means taking positive steps to ensure human rights are not breached. For instance, the cruel and inhumane treatment of elderly people in private care homes, as recently discovered to have taken place in the UK, is prohibited under Article 3 of the HRA, providing families with a mechanism to challenge public authorities for failing in their duty of care towards their loved ones.

A controversial ECtHR ruling was that the UK's policy of preventing all prisoners from voting in elections was unlawful under the HRA. This judgement was derided by some as 'perverse' and provoked Prime Minister David Cameron to say the idea of prisoners having the right to vote made him physically ill (BBC 2015).

The Conservative Party wants to disassemble the HRA in order to 'break the formal link' between domestic courts and the ECtHR. Part of their reasoning is to allow government more leeway in responses to security threats. There is nothing in the Act that prevents convicted criminals and terrorists from being imprisoned; instead, it requires serious offences, like murder, terrorism, and rape, to be investigated by the police, who can be held responsible for serious failures on their part. Amnesty International's position claims it is safer to prosecute these cases in the UK, and if found guilty, to imprison the perpetrators. Having a system of rights protected by a higher authority means countries cannot pick and choose at whim which rights they wish to protect. Scrapping the HRA could reduce the UK's authority to speak out about human rights abuses elsewhere.

➲ Stop and Think

Traditionally, the UK government has held the view that prisoners forfeit their right to vote as they have broken the laws of civil society. The Human Rights Act gives prisoners the right to vote as, even though they are prisoners, their human rights are still available to them. From a liberal perspective, prisoners are indeed entitled to vote. How would you resolve this political dilemma?

Tolerance

As we saw when we looked at the origins of liberalism, the liberal ideology was partly a response to religious wars and civil strife. If you have experienced such conflict, there is a pragmatic attraction to being able to live instead alongside people with whom you do not share common beliefs and customs, as this allows for a peaceful rather than an antagonistic society. This is much easier if the state does not seek to promote any particular way of life, instead leaving it up to individuals to make choices for themselves about how they want to live. While this may initially have been a pragmatic stance, liberals gradually became more committed to tolerance as an ideal in itself. This means acknowledging the right each individual has to make their own life choices, even if you personally disagree with how they want to live.

This idea of leaving individuals to determine their own lives is the motivation for many different strands of political action and evolution, leading to a whole range of legal measures, such as forbidding the denial of opportunities on criteria such as ethnicity, religion, and sexuality. Equally, legal systems have opened up the possibilities for free individual choice through measures like the decriminalization of homosexuality, the permission of same-sex marriage, and the growing incorporation of **transgender** people's rights.

For the many advances that a commitment to tolerance has achieved, there remain some big challenges. At what point does a commitment to tolerance undermine a commitment to other liberal values? For instance, should a liberal state permit schools to operate that are run on segregated grounds? Here we can see that the freedom of some to live according to their own personal beliefs may conflict with the wider liberal commitment to the idea that each individual should be valued and respected equally. The question is whether there are certain forms of organization that are so contrary to core liberal values that they should not be tolerated.

As a wider exploration of the challenges of governing a society characterized by distinct and separate groups living alongside each other, Canada is an interesting experiment in tolerance (see Case Study 2.4). Having developed from former French and British colonies, built on indigenous lands, Canada from the outset needed to find a way to embrace respect for liberal values while attempting to deal with the challenges of multiple cultures and linguistic groups (see Chapter 11). A return to a liberal ideology has seen success in Canada, whereas in Germany and the UK liberal parties have experienced poor electoral results. In Europe, the rise in **populist** right-wing movements sets nationalist narratives against liberal commitments to tolerance creating a debate around the extent to which widespread differences in cultural practice pose a threat to the maintenance of a liberal society.

Case Study 2.4 The return of the Canadian Liberal Party and the rise of Justin Trudeau

Canada has three major political parties that compete for national leadership: the right-of-centre Conservatives, the centrist Liberals, and the social democratic New Democratic Party. Of the three, the Liberals have been the most popular and also the most politically inconsistent, as over the years they have oscillated between centrist and social democratic policies. Since women got the vote in 1918, the Liberals have won 19 out of 29 elections, meaning they have governed Canada for roughly 70 per cent of the last century.

Justin Trudeau's landslide victory in October 2015 reinvigorated a liberal majority in Parliament after nine years of a Conservative government under Stephen Harper that had tarnished Canada's international reputation for being a nation of peacekeepers, neutral conciliators, and environmentally concerned moderates. Trudeau's acceptance speech offered Canadians 'real change . . . a government with a vision and an agenda for this country that is positive and ambitious and hopeful' (Liberal Party of Canada 2015).

Trudeau offers a platform of inclusion and tolerance. His cabinet is equally balanced, fifteen women and fifteen men. It is ethnically diverse and mostly aged under fifty years old. There are two aboriginal MPs and three Sikh politicians. Justin Trudeau says of his cabinet that it reflects the Canada it serves. His platform calls for electoral reform, moving away from first past the post to proportional representation. His party is calling for an open and transparent government, ensuring accountability by funnelling power away from the Prime Minister's office (Harper's legacy) and back to cabinet. As Harper's government took the Canadian economy into a recession, Justin Trudeau aimed to invoke Keynesian spending policies that invest in infrastructure, to get Canada working and out of the recession. The Liberal Party have made commitments to legalize marijuana. Further, they have made commitments to improve transgender rights as well as to investigate the murders of hundreds of aboriginal women. This mandate gives Justin Trudeau the opportunity to reclaim the liberal roots of Canadian politics by amending sections of the controversial anti-terror legislation and pulling Canadian forces out of the US-led coalition against so-called Islamic State (otherwise known as IS, ISIS, ISIL, or Daesh).

The re-election of the Liberal Party of Canada shows a reassertion of liberal values after a long period of neo-liberal reformism.

 Stop and Think

What kinds of practices or ideas should we not be tolerant of? For example: is it ever right to ban political rallies because of worries about the ideas being promoted?

Different liberalisms

As we have seen, regardless of the divergent concepts of liberty, all liberals hold free choice as a value of the highest importance. It is at the centre of both their political and their economic theories. In this section we will look at some of the different variants within liberalism. We will look at how classical liberalism leads to a major focus upon economic freedom, and forms the precursor to neo-liberalism. Then we will look at social liberalism, which includes a commitment to equality alongside its emphasis upon individual liberty.

Classical liberalism

From the liberal point of view, individuals are rational beings who are entitled to freedom to choose how they wish to live their own lives. Resulting from the breakdown of feudalism in Europe and the growth of a market capitalist society, *classical* liberalism relies on a belief in a limited state, where its role is primarily in ensuring the maintenance of property rights, domestic order, and personal security. This is because classical liberals believe that individual human beings are generally the best judges of what will make them truly happy. Therefore they think an economic system in which individuals are allowed to pursue their own interests will be most effective: if rewards are distributed in a **meritocratic** way, this will encourage people to develop their talents and work hard. So, as well as being good for individuals, a system of markets and free trade may also be the best way to a productive economic system. This idea is expressed in Adam Smith's image of the invisible hand of markets, guiding individuals to optimal social outcomes even though they are personally only focused on their own interests. It also forms a utilitarian defence of individual freedom, which is to say that it holds that free choice leads to the best outcomes for human welfare and happiness. As a whole, it forms an economic doctrine where the focus is the idea of a self-regulating market in which government intervention can be unnecessary and damaging. Classical liberals hail the virtue of laissez-faire capitalism and call into question economic and social intervention by governments.

Economic liberalism

The critique of **globalization**, a concept often equated with liberalism, is more specifically a critique of neo-liberalism and the unrestrained forces of free markets and capitalism. As this section will explore, elements within economic liberalism were crucial to the development of neo-liberalism. Key thinkers associated with economic liberalism include Adam Smith, John Maynard Keynes, F. A. Hayek, and Milton Friedman.

Economic liberalism is the ideological belief in organizing the economy so that the greatest possible number of economic choices are made by individuals and firms, not by government. It includes a range of different economic policies, such as freedom of movement of labour and goods, but it is always based on strong support for a market economy and private ownership of business. Economic liberalism is supportive of some government regulation, such as legal support for contracts, that provides a stable environment for trade, but it tends to favour open competition in the free market and free trade rather than government intervention. However, economic liberals argue that the state still has a role in providing public goods—things like national defence that are hard to supply through markets. As we have seen, historically, economic liberalism's roots were in its opposition to mercantilism and feudalism, arguing that free trade is the best route to national wealth. Today, it is generally considered to oppose non-capitalist economic orders, such as socialism and planned economies.

While free market economies grew in popularity for hundreds of years, much of the twentieth century saw economic activity begin to come under tighter government control. The First World War broke the liberal order and initiated an era of war, depression, and tyranny. Nationalist movements took over as old empires collapsed. Totalitarian regimes came to power in Germany, Italy, and Russia, stifling liberty across Europe, while aggressive, military authoritarian government prevailed in Japan. Marxist ideology presented the liberal epoch as but a phase in the historical passage to socialism, such that by the 1930s, the dominant opinion was critical of liberalism. Even in liberal democratic countries, governments were encouraged to take a more active role in their economies. Many states began to take a social democratic form, providing key goods and services to their citizens through the development of **welfare states**. Equally, due to the influence of the ideas of John Maynard Keynes (1883–1946), an English economist, governments began to believe that economies work best when steps are taken to actively manage them. Keynes held that a country's total or aggregate demand for goods and services at any one time was what determined the overall level of economic activity. Therefore, he argued, state intervention was needed to moderate 'boom and bust' cycles of economic activity and to promote and maintain full employment. To achieve this, he advocated that states seek to stimulate growth by increasing their spending in conditions of recession. His thinking developed into a school of thought called *Keynesian* economics. Keynesian economic policies that called for greater intervention in the economy held sway in macroeconomic policy until the 1970s.

In academic thought, classical liberalism was revived in the work of Austrian economist F. A. Hayek. His thesis in *The Road to Serfdom* (1944) was a return to classical liberalism, arguing that there is a danger in adopting collectivist policies, as attempts to plan and manage economies would always tend to be unsuccessful. In turn, this would be likely to prompt calls for further controls. As a result, government intervention in economies would eventually lead to totalitarianism. Through the Mont Pelerin Society, Hayek managed to keep classical liberal ideas—that economies run best when they are left free from government intervention allowing individual people to make their own choices—alive throughout the postwar period.

The 1970s were riddled with economic crises that destabilized the prosperity upon which social democratic ideologies had thrived in the developed nations. When oil prices were raised in 1973, the first of the 'oil shocks', the price of petrol quadrupled overnight, leading to runaway inflation and rising unemployment occurring at the same time. This combined negative effect, dubbed 'stagflation', undermined the postwar Keynesian consensus on economic management in social democracies. Corporate profits plummeted and political agitators moved against what they saw as the fundamental limitations of 'big government'. Thus, it was in this unstable economic environment that a new breed of liberals were born. They sought to revive classical liberalism under the new-found conditions of globalization. The awarding of Nobel Prizes to Hayek and Milton Friedman in 1974 and 1976 confirmed the rise to prominence of *neo-liberalism*.

Milton Friedman (1912–2006) was an American economist who challenged Keynesian economics by suggesting that there is a natural rate of unemployment, and argued that Keynesian attempts to keep unemployment below this natural rate would cause inflation to accelerate. His view, developed in *Capitalism and Freedom* (1962), came to be known as **monetarism**, which argued that governments should abandon attempts to promote full employment and instead focus on maintaining stable economic conditions free from such factors as high inflation. His ideas about monetary policy, taxation, privatization, and deregulation influenced many governments' policies in the 1980s. Friedman himself was advisor to US President Ronald Reagan and British Prime Minister Margaret Thatcher. His advice affirmed a commitment to the virtues of free market economic systems with minimal intervention. These became the tenets of neo-liberalism.

Neo-liberalism, like Marxism, sees the production and exchange of material goods as essential to the human experience. But whereas Marx claimed to show the immorality of capitalist production, neo-liberals declared its virtue. As a form of governance, neo-liberalism expounds entrepreneurial values such as competitiveness, self-interest, and decentralization, adopting the self-regulating free market as the primary model for proper government. It views individuals, in all areas of their lives, as being strategic in pursuit of their own interests. Therefore, the best schemes for organizing society and the provision of services are those that will provide people with the right incentives to take positive actions. For instance, a model of public administration known as 'new public management' infiltrated the world's state bureaucracies. This system sought to make public services more like private companies, managed with the goal of providing satisfaction to citizens, who were now viewed as customers or consumers. In regard to public policy, neo-liberalism is dedicated to deregulating the economy, liberalizing trade and industry and privatizing state-owned enterprises.

Neo-liberalism took at least some hold in most developed countries in the world, but was strongest in the English-speaking countries. What is most notable about neo-liberals is the force and open declaration of their belief in free markets. The pioneer neo-liberal leaders were Margaret Thatcher in the UK and Ronald Reagan in the USA, known for their strong leadership and determination to do away with traditional social and governmental institutions in favour of a smaller state, even if that meant greater inequality. Thatcher, known as the 'Iron Lady', was a vocal advocate of market freedoms and the necessity for reform, against much public consternation: 'To those waiting with bated breath for that favourite media catchphrase, the U-turn, I have only one thing to say. You turn if you want to. The lady's not for turning' (10 October 1980, Conservative Party conference). Perhaps because of the strong association with the Thatcher and Reagan governments, it is arguable whether

neo-liberalism should be considered more as a part of a liberal or a conservative ideology (however, Chapter 3 argues that neo-liberalism is a liberal ideology adopted by
a conservative party). Either way, both Thatcher and Reagan were strong opponents
of socialism in any form, and saw themselves as playing a key part in encouraging the
leader of the Soviet Union, Mikhail Gorbachev, to shift away from communism and
loosen the communists' grip on Eastern Europe.

The success of neo-liberalism can be found in its longevity after the Thatcher–
Reagan dominance of the 1980s. Thatcher famously declared that one of her greatest
achievements was the later Labour Prime Minister Tony Blair and his 'New Labour'
project. It is true that subsequent governments felt they had to accept the changed
reality and implement their own versions of neo-liberal policies. Hence, governments on the left, including that of UK Labour's Tony Blair and Gordon Brown, and
US Democratic Party's Bill Clinton, accepted the basic premise of neo-liberal ideas—
that economic success was best achieved by governments trying to reduce their role
in actively managing or regulating the economy. These governments did still try to
take some measures for social welfare, seeking to spend the increased tax revenue
they raised from improved economic performance on better public services such as
healthcare and education, while also introducing some measures such as the minimum wage to protect workers. This idea was termed the **Third Way**, as it aimed to
strike a balance between unchecked free market policies and state-oriented social
intervention in the economy. Many argue, however, that the Third Way should still be
seen as having a neo-liberal character, as it always tried to avoid putting an increased
tax or regulatory burden on business interests.

Neo-liberals set the world's economic and political agenda from the early 1980s
to 2008–09. In France, the socialist President François Mitterrand pursued an active
privatization strategy. Meanwhile, even in that bastion of social democracy, Sweden,
neo-liberalism has made some headway, although arguments persist as to whether
the 'Swedish model' has been truly displaced.

The global financial crisis of 2008 could have spelled the end for free-market fundamentalism, but this has not occurred. Neo-liberal economic policies, crucial to
overall economic management and therefore to many other public policies, remain
institutionalized in many states. Free trade agreements which would deepen neo-
liberalism across the globe are currently in negotiation between the major economic
powers, which would see a further weakening of the ability of government to take an
active role in the economy. Yet the future of the neo-liberal economic model remains
in question as, in the wake of the financial crisis, governments around the world have
struggled to recharge their economies and achieve previous levels of growth. Fiscal
austerity imposed by neo-liberal governments has been controversial and has generally failed to deliver the intended results.

Some critics, like French economist Thomas Piketty, predict the neo-liberal future
will be one of low growth and drastically increasing inequality, in which inherited

wealth becomes more and more important to national and global elites (Piketty 2014). Without an alternative economic model being put in place, he believes such inequality will become unsustainable and political instability will result, in a way returning us to the conditions of the late nineteenth century. As we will now turn to examine, Piketty's views—and many other criticisms of the neo-liberal account of the relationship between government, its citizens, and the economy—are actually endorsed by many liberals.

Social liberalism

While many socialist and Marxist critics of liberalism see it as being inseparable from capitalism, *social* liberalism is more favourable towards welfare reform and economic management than classical liberalism. This is because theorists in the late nineteenth and early twentieth centuries recognized that the conditions of industrial capitalism could themselves pose a threat to free individual choice, leaving the majority of the population at the mercy of the whims of those with greater economic power. In light of this, social liberals take a more sympathetic attitude towards the state. Social liberalism links freedom to personal development and self-realization, holding that options will only be valuable to individuals if they have some means of achieving them. Therefore, economic conditions that prevent individuals from achieving their aims can be a threat to the value of freedom.

Social liberalism's early development was in the ideas of Mill, who did not include protection of freedom of economic choice in his list of basic liberties, instead focusing on those freedoms essential to the development of individual identity. But its fullest theoretical account comes in American moral and political philosopher John Rawls' (1921–2002) great work *A Theory of Justice* (1971). He updated the idea of a social contract, by arguing that a truly just society would be one that would give every person a decisive reason to choose to live under its institutions. In order to work out what this would look like, Rawls asks us to imagine what organizing principles for society we would choose if we knew nothing about where within that society we would end up. If we did not know key features of our identity—our race, gender, beliefs, talents—he thinks we would therefore be impartial in the principles we would select.

There are three component parts to what Rawls thinks would come out of this decision. First, he thinks that individuals would want to ensure that their basic freedoms were protected. This would include many of the key rights that liberals have sought to defend: guarantees of freedom of conscience, association, and expression; protection of the physical and psychological integrity of the person (which includes freedom of occupation, freedom of movement, and access to some personal property); rights of due process under the rule of law; equal political liberties (rights to vote, to run for and hold office, to organize or join political parties). A second feature of a just society would be an account of equality of opportunity that ensures that individuals' life chances are not determined by their social background. This goes beyond the meritocratic account of equal opportunity that argues people should not be denied entry into social or political positions on account of their **ethnicity**, gender, or beliefs to also argue that wealth should not provide significant advantages in the competition for valuable positions. This would mean, for instance, that a just society would be one in which the poor had just as good access to education as the wealthy. Here we see a key distinction between classical and social liberalism: classical liberals think that the outcome of a free meritocratic competition for positions of influence is enough to guarantee individual freedom; social liberals argue that this competition must take place on a relatively level playing field, allowing each person a meaningful chance of success.

The third feature of Rawls' account of a just society is his famous *difference principle*, which argues that any social and economic inequalities should be organized so that they are to the greatest advantage of the least well off (Rawls 1999: 226). Rawls thinks that we may, ideally, want an equal distribution of income and wealth. However, if it can be demonstrated that arrangements—such as markets for goods, occupations, and services—that led to inequality still made everyone better off by increasing the general wealth of society, then this inequality could be justified. The idea is to try to find the economic system that best allows people the chance to exercise their freedom and live as they choose. Inequalities that benefit everyone, including the least well off, by increasing the general wealth of society aid this aim; inequalities that are so wide as to threaten people's chances of attaining their personal goals undermine freedom and so should be prevented. Here we can see the way that social liberal ideas hold there to be close ties between the values of freedom and equality.

Rawls' theory of social justice has been hugely influential in reinvigorating liberalism in moral and political thought, prompting a wide debate within liberalism about the proper account of a just society. Responses have included that of Robert Nozick (1938–2002), whose *Anarchy, State and Utopia* (1974) advanced a libertarian counter that Rawls' attempt to advance **egalitarian** aims would inevitably require infringements upon individual rights. Other important contributions to these debates about liberal justice have come from Ronald Dworkin (2002) and Amartya Sen (1999).

So far, these debates have had only limited influence upon political debate outside of academia. Yet they show that liberalism can itself prove a source of critique of unconstrained neo-liberal capitalism. As a result, they demonstrate the continued attractiveness and versatility of a moral ideal of individual freedom of choice, which can be used as the basis for a spectrum of liberal views that advance widely divergent accounts of what society should look like. Classical liberalism argues for little government involvement and a wide scope of economic freedom, while social liberalism sees a key role for the state in maintaining equality.

Stop and Think

Given that liberalism can be identified with such contradicting views, what does this tell us about ideology? Are ideologies fixed or must they always be open to very different interpretations?

Critics of liberalism

Liberalism, because of its pervasiveness, has many critics. In this section we will consider those of feminists, **communitarians**, and Marxists. These critics seek to establish that the limitations of liberalism are conceptual in nature: that there are flaws in the moral foundations of liberal individualism. All three positions are critical of the seeming lack of historical and social awareness the liberal individual has, and how this lack creates a blindness to 'reality', which is, in their view, insurmountable.

Even though the roots of feminism are found in liberalism (e.g. see the discussion of 'first wave' feminism in Chapter 9), prominent feminist scholars such as Alison Jaggar and Catharine MacKinnon have challenged liberal politics on the grounds that it is totally inadequate in addressing the needs of women because it neglects to recognize the asymmetry of power between men and women in the world. Feminists take issue with liberalism primarily for three reasons: (1) it is too individualistic, (2) its vision of persons is too abstract, and (3) its focus is reason (Nussbaum 1997: 5). The first criticism refers to the liberal individual: liberals err 'by thinking of individuals in ways that sever them from their historical and social context' (Nussbaum 1997: 19). Feminists argue that this atomized individual is unrepresentative of how people actually live their lives, it 'slights and unfairly subordinates the value to be attached to community and to collective social entities such as families, groups, classes' (Nussbaum 1997: 5). The second criticism concerns the liberal concept of equality, and how this concept lacks acknowledgement of 'the concrete realities of power in different social situations' (Nussbaum 1997: 5). This refers to an asymmetry of power that renders women structurally less equal to men in social, political, and economic realms. Finally, the third criticism relates to the emphasis on the idea of the rational liberal individual, which feminists argue leads liberalism to 'unfairly slight the role we should give to emotions and care in the moral political life' (Nussbaum 1997: 5). This failure has 'permitted men to denigrate women for their emotional natures, and to marginalize them on account of their alleged lack of reason' (Nussbaum 1997: 26). Feminists accept that personhood, autonomy, rights, dignity, and self-respect are all worthy pursuits; they simply take issue with how these are brought about in the world when the foundations from which these liberal politics spring do not recognize a fully formed and socially contextualized agent.

The communitarian critique is similar to the first feminist criticism outlined above, in which liberalism appears to view the individual as an asocial and atomized being. By contrast, communitarians emphasize that individuals are instead embedded within social contexts, shaped by the families, groups, and communities that surround them. Therefore, communitarians believe that you cannot separate the individual from her social context that gives her meaning. Communitarians such as Michael Sandel find it problematic that liberal claims of justice (à la Rawls) are absolute and universal. The argument is that our personal identity cannot be independent of our social context and so we may have to give particular attention to the local and particular values within which our thought is based. Communitarians claim the liberal individual is a person abstracted from class, ethnicity, gender, religion, race, etc. As a result, they think liberals disregard the extent to which people identify with their religious heritage, their ethnicity, etc., and the degree to which these social differences shape people. Sandel argues that, in these ways, liberalism rests on a series of mistaken claims. He suggest that we should avoid focusing our efforts on individual rights in favour of a 'politics of the common good' (Sandel 1984). Communitarians see the liberty of the liberal individual as a misguided myth and desire instead forms of justice that account for the rooted, collective nature of social life.

Marxists reject the notion of a common experience among all humans, instead believing that human societies progress through class struggle. This is a fundamentally different outlook to liberalism, as it sees classes as the defining feature of societies, rather than individuals. These classes are formed of collectives with common associations to one another in their relationship to the means of production. The liberal individual's lack of reference to productive dynamics, according to Marxists, renders liberalism ignorant of the social context that determines history. Marxists claim this blindness conceals the reality of unequal class power. They reject universal standards and forms of justice, charging liberalism with being an example of bourgeois ideology serving only to legitimize capitalist class relations (see Chapter 1). The freedom sought by liberals is a 'bogus liberation [that] produces a society of isolated, self-seeking individuals' (Femia, 1993: 27). True emancipation can only be achieved through a collective reshaping of productive relations (see also Chapter 4 for socialist criticisms of liberalism).

The main thrust of each of these critiques is that liberalism rests on an account of individuals that removes them from their proper social context. While debates between liberals and their critics are complex, we can identify three key strands within the liberal response to such criticisms. One is to argue that the world view advanced by these alternative ideologies could require people to make certain types of choice. For example, a Marxist would hold that those who do not contribute to the effort to overcome capitalist relations of production can never be free, while for communitarians each person has responsibilities to contribute to collective social goals. However, these demands would undermine the ability of individuals to fully choose how they personally wish to live. A second way liberals would respond would be to deny the accusation that they do not value collective social groups such as families or communities. However, for liberals these groups only have value to the extent that they are valued by their individual members, rather than possessing independent value. People are likely to choose to place value upon collective ties, but if they do not then there is no reason to insist that such ties must always matter. Finally, many liberals have sought to demonstrate the ways in which liberal ideas can tackle the injustices highlighted by critics (Rawls 2008: 319–72; Okin 1989). The liberal ideal is of free individual choice to determine your own life, so if structural inequalities based on gender or class truly present obstacles to this aim, then a fully effective liberal theory should seek to find ways to overcome them.

Conclusion

In the period after the end of the Cold War, liberalism came to have a predominant influence within global politics. There was a feeling that the global future would be marked by greater openness and scope for individuals to exercise free choice. Yet fresh challenges have emerged. Jihadists who reject Western liberal values have launched terrorist attacks in service of the idea of a world where individuals are not free to choose how they wish to live, but are instead expected to live according to a singular religious world view. Authoritarian states such as Russia and China have grown in importance on the global stage, making claims that closer state control over populations and economies is necessary to avoid instability. Populist politicians in Europe and North America have sought to characterize liberalism as the ideology of a failing order. These factors present a challenge to liberal politics and a test of liberal resolve to uphold a commitment to freedom, equality, peace, and tolerance around the world. It is, therefore, important to remember how radical the liberal demand is: 'the demand to see and to be seen as human, rather than as someone's lord, or someone's subject' (Nussbaum 1997: 38). This chapter has provided an insight into the liberal ideology, showing its pervasiveness, its accomplishments, and the challenges it faces for the future.

Summary

- The basic claim of liberalism is that each individual should be left free to make choices about how they wish to live their own lives.

- While there is an acknowledgement that free choice cannot be absolute, liberals seek to create a private space, defined by rights, in which an individual is free from outside constraint and interference, to make their own choices.

- One key debate within liberalism is where exactly the limits of this space should lie. This is a complex issue because sometimes people might object to the choices others make. In these instances, there is a need to decide whether those choices are genuinely harmful to others or simply perceived to be unattractive. If individual choices are not harmful, then liberal thinking holds that they should be tolerated. However, distinguishing between what is tolerable and what is actually harmful is not an easy task.

- It is often assumed that liberalism and democracy are synonymous. Instead, there are tensions between the two, as there is potential for democratic decisions to result in the infringement of individual rights.

- Although all liberals hold to an ideal of individual freedom, there are differences in the way this ideal can be interpreted and understood. The wide range of positions within a liberal ideology is a result of these differences.

- This variety means that there are areas where liberalism easily overlaps and influences other ideologies such as feminism, environmentalism, and multiculturalism.

- The pervasiveness of liberal ideas means they are often the focus of criticism. One major critique is that by prioritizing individual choice, underlying structures of domination, working through concentrations of economic power or cultural norms, will be left unchecked.

Review and discussion questions

1. What influence has a liberal ideology had on addressing questions of discrimination?

2. Given the threats to freedom, is the problem that the world is not liberal enough?

3. Is a commitment to liberal rights enough to overcome gender inequality?

4. Is it inevitable that we face a trade-off between free economic choices and a commitment to equality?

Research exercises

1. This chapter has noted the tension between liberalism and democracy. Can you find examples of a democratically enacted policy that infringes upon individual liberties?

2. If you look at the sort of reforms that neo-liberal governments implement, such as privatization, in what ways might these be thought of as increasing liberty and how might they come to threaten liberty?

Further reading

Bell (2014), Rawls (2008), and Gray (1986) provide clear and comprehensive overviews of the history and general content of liberal ideas. Jones (1994) introduces key philosophical debates about rights, while Hopgood (2000) tackles the question of individual rights in modern society.

Steiner (1994), meanwhile, uses rights as the basis for an interesting and complex, yet highly readable, account of justice. Some of the tensions between liberalism and democracy become evident in Bobbio (2005). Issues of tolerance and how liberalism deals with different world views are examined in Kymlicka (1991) and Rawls (1996).

The differences between economic and social liberalism can be explored more deeply by considering Steger and Roy (2010), Freeman (2001), and Van Parijs (1997). Okin (1989) develops a thorough liberal feminist account of the just society. Gutmann (1985) provides a good response to communitarian criticisms of liberalism, while Femia (1993: Chapter 2) offers an analysis of the main Marxist critiques of liberal ideas and of the liberal organization of society.

References

BBC (2015), http://www.bbc.co.uk/news/live/world-europe-30722098 (accessed 6 January 2015).

BELL, D. (2014), 'What is Liberalism', *Political Theory*, Vol. 42, No. 6, pp. 682–715.

BELLAMY, R. (1992), *Liberalism and Modern Society*, Cambridge: Polity Press.

BERLIN, I. (1969), 'Two Concepts of Liberty' in his *Four Essays on Liberty*, Oxford: Oxford University Press, pp. 118–72.

BOBBIO, N. (2005), *Liberalism and Democracy,* London: Verso.

DWORKIN, R. (2002), *Sovereign Virtue: The Theory and Practice of Equality*, Cambridge, MA: Harvard University Press.

FEMIA, J. V. (1993), *Marxism and Democracy*, Oxford: Clarendon Press.

FREEMAN, S. (2001), 'Illiberal Libertarians: Why Libertarianism is not a Liberal View', *Philosophy and Public Affairs*, Vol. 30, No. 2, pp. 105–51.

FRIEDMAN, M. (1962), *Capitalism and Freedom*, Chicago: University of Chicago Press.

GAUS, G. (1996), *Justificatory Liberalism: An Essay on Epistemology and Political Theory*, New York: Oxford University Press.

GRAY, J. (1986), *Liberalism*, Milton Keynes: Open University Press.

GREEN, T. H. (1986 [1895]), *Lectures on the Principles of Political Obligation and Other Essays*, ed. P. Harris and J. Morrow, Cambridge: Cambridge University Press.

GUTMANN, A. (1985), 'Communitarian Critics of Liberalism', *Philosophy and Public Affairs*, Vol. 14, No. 3, pp. 308–22.

HAYEK, F. A. (1960), *The Constitution of Liberty*, Chicago: University of Chicago Press.

HEYWOOD, A. (2004), *Political Theory: An Introduction*, 3rd edn, Basingstoke: Palgrave Macmillan.

HOBBES, T. (1994 [1651]), *Leviathan*, Cambridge: Hackett.

HOPGOOD, S. (2000), 'Reading the Small Print in Global Civil Society: The Inexorable Hegemony of the Liberal Self', *Millennium: Journal of International Studies*, Vol. 29, No. 1, pp. 1–25.

JONES, P. (1994), *Rights*, London: Palgrave Macmillan.

KYMLICKA, W. (1991), *Liberalism, Community, and Culture*, Oxford: Oxford University Press.

LIBERAL PARTY OF CANADA (2015), https://www.liberal.ca/#gf_1091 (accessed 4 December 2015).

LOCKE, J. (1988 [1690]), *Locke: Two Treatises of Government, Student Edition*, Cambridge: Cambridge University Press.

MILL, J. S. (1963), *Collected Works of John Stuart Mill*, ed. J. M. Robson, Toronto: University of Toronto Press.

MILL, J. S. (2014), *On Liberty*, USA: SMK Books.

NOZICK, R. (1974), *Anarchy, State and Utopia,* New York: Basic Books.

NUSSBAUM, M. C. (1997) *The Feminist Critique of Liberalism*, Lawrence, KS: University of Kansas Department of Philosophy.

OKIN, S. M. (1989), *Justice, Gender and the Family,* New York: Basic Books.

PIKETTY, T. (2014), *Capitalism in the Twenty-First Century*, Cambridge, MA: The President and Fellows of Harvard College.

QUONG, J. (2010), *Liberalism Without Perfection*, Oxford: Oxford University Press.

RAWLS, J. (1996), *Political Liberalism*, New York: Columbia University Press.

RAWLS, J. (1999), *A Theory of Justice*, rev edn, Cambridge, MA: Harvard University Press.

RAWLS, J. (2008), *Lectures on the History of Political Philosophy*, Cambridge, MA: Harvard University Press.

RAZ, J. (1986), *The Morality of Freedom*, Oxford: Clarendon Press.

ROUSSEAU, J.-J. (1993), *The Social Contract and Discourses*, London: Everyman.

RUTHERFORD, B. K. (2008), *Egypt After Mubarak: Liberalism, Islam, and Democracy in the Arab World*, Princeton, NJ: University of Princeton Press.

SANDEL, M. (1984), 'Morality and the Liberal Ideal', *New Republic*, Vol. 190, No. 19, pp. 15–17.

SEN, A. (1999), *Commodities and Capabilities*, Oxford: Oxford University Press.

SMITH, A. (1993 [1776]), *An Enquiry into the Nature and Causes of the Wealth of Nations,* Oxford: Oxford University Press.

STEGER, M. B. AND ROY, R. K. (2010), *Neoliberalism: A Very Short Introduction*, Oxford: Oxford University Press.

STEINER, H. (1994), *An Essay on Rights*, Oxford: Blackwell.

TAYLOR, C. (1979), 'What's Wrong with Negative Liberty', in A. Ryan (ed.), *The Idea of Freedom*, Oxford: Oxford University Press, 175–93.

UNITED STATES NATIONAL ARCHIVES (2015), Declaration of Independence, available at http://www.archives.gov/exhibits/charters/declaration.html#more (accessed 8 December 2015).

VAN PARIJS, P. (1997), *Real Freedom For All: What (if Anything) can Justify Capitalism?* Oxford: Clarendon.

WALL, S. (1998), *Liberalism, Perfectionism, and Restraint*, Cambridge: Cambridge University Press.

3

Conservatism

Mark Garnett

OBJECTIVES

- Outline the basic features of conservative ideology, explaining that its nature is strongly contested, focusing chiefly on the British example

- Examine the work of the Irish-born politician Edmund Burke, whose response to the French Revolution provided conservatism with its most eloquent expression

- Distinguish this ideology from varieties of liberalism, with which it is commonly confused

- Sketch the developments which have led to this confusion

- Examine some apparent manifestations of conservatism in political parties and movements outside the UK

Introduction

In the eyes of its critics, conservatism does not give rise to serious problems of definition. Depending on the strength of their feelings, they tend to depict it either as an unreflective acceptance of the currently existing socio-political order, or as a crude attempt to spread a veneer of principled respectability over glaring social and political inequalities, making it little more than a doctrine of selfishness (see especially Honderich 1990).

However, those who wish to *understand* conservatism rather than to condemn it will encounter considerable complexity. For example, some eminent authorities have denied that conservatism is an ideology at all. In addition, many writers on conservatism have argued that its core principles have changed over time, and that 'modern conservatism' shares many key ideas with liberalism. Thus students of conservatism have to wrestle with basic issues which are far less troublesome in relation to other ideologies.

Thanks to these (and other) considerations, there is a danger that brief discussions of conservatism will be dominated by *argument* instead of straight-forward *exposition*. The present chapter is an attempt to balance these two approaches. It begins by trying to address the two major questions mentioned above: is conservatism a distinctive ideology? and, have the core ideas of conservatism changed over time? While the nature of conservatism will continue to be contested, the chapter presents an interpretation which promises to eliminate much of the confusion surrounding the term. It argues that conservatism is a distinctive ideology and that any attempts to distinguish between 'traditional' and 'modern' (or any other) variants of conservatism are confusing rather than illuminating.

Is conservatism an ideology?

For understandable reasons, individuals who have tried to articulate and embody a distinctively conservative brand of politics have tended to be more precise in identifying the kind of thinking they *oppose* than in delineating any *positive* programme of their own. They have often lambasted their opponents as **ideologues** while denying that label to anyone within their own camp. In other words, conservatives tend to use 'ideology' as an insult, denoting rigid (and usually *radical*) thinking (Gilmour 1977: 132–43; see Chapter 1).

This partisan use of the term has rightly been rejected by academic observers, and even academics who sympathize with the conservative position now usually accept that ideology is ubiquitous among *anyone* who is sufficiently motivated to respond (whether by thought, word, or deed) to political developments on a principled basis—in short, that we are *all* ideologues to some degree (see Chapter 1). Whatever they might like to think, conservatives are no exception to this rule. The key point, for students of ideology, is to find the most plausible basis for classifying the ideologies of individuals, groups, or parties after a careful consideration of the available evidence. From this perspective, when self-proclaimed 'conservatives' identify 'ideology' with extremism they shed far more light on their own ideas than on those of their opponents. If, in their view, 'ideology' is the hateful hallmark of inflexible political radicals, it seems to follow that conservatives can only tolerate limited political changes—or no changes at all. For some observers, this is enough to condemn conservatives as blinkered adherents of the status quo; but for the student of ideology, after accepting the ideological nature of conservatism the next step should be to ask *why* conservatives have such a deep-rooted antipathy to rapid or wide-ranging change.

Can ideologies change? Can they share 'core' concepts?

If our initial problem arises chiefly from the work of conservatism's advocates, the second one presents a more powerful challenge for the present chapter because it features in a good deal of *academic* work on conservatism as well as developments among political practitioners. As such, it requires more lengthy treatment.

In recent decades there has been a marked tendency for individuals, parties, and groups who describe themselves as 'conservative'—particularly in the UK and the USA—to endorse policies which are usually held to be characteristic of *liberalism*, and to do so on grounds which reflect a distinctively liberal view of human nature (see Chapter 2). This tendency is most noticeable in relation to economic policy, where many self-styled contemporary 'conservatives' argue that individuals can be trusted to take 'rational' decisions in their own interest, so that significant state interference in the economic sphere is likely to be at best ill-informed and in most cases counter-productive. At the same time, many of these individuals identify themselves with long-established institutions, practices, and moral norms (such as 'family values'), thus apparently satisfying a common assumption about the conservative outlook.

However, those who accept this understanding of conservatism are faced with at least two serious problems. First, if so-called 'conservatives' and people generally agreed to be liberal tend to bring the same underlying principles to bear in relation to a key policy area such as economics, any attempt to characterize liberalism and conservatism as distinctive ideological viewpoints seems to invite confusion rather than clarity in discussions and analyses of political principles.

Second, if we accept that 'conservatives' share the liberal antipathy towards externally imposed restrictions on the operations of the free market, in practice (particularly in a 'globalized' economic context) this implies that 'conservatives' are prepared to accept the unpredictable developments, possibly involving radical socio-political changes and challenges to traditional institutions, practices, and values, that such an environment is likely to instigate. At best, this means that proponents of the free market who persist in calling themselves 'conservative' are confused, supporting policies in the economic sphere which have a definite tendency to undermine the political and social stability which they are supposed to crave.

It is hardly unprecedented for the self-proclaimed supporters of an ideology to support policies which conflict in practice with their stated values, but in this instance the source of the confusion seems quite easy to explain. These particular 'conservatives' are confused, one might say, because their views are a mixture of two ideological traditions, and their economic ideas (distinctively liberal) generate rapid and unpredictable changes which challenge their (conservative) preference for social stability. Many commentators on ideology try to reconcile this incoherent *mélange* with a continuous conservative tradition, often by giving it the name of 'modern conservatism'. However, even if one allows that people holding these views sometimes exhibit a genuine desire for stability, their continued adherence to free market ideas in the face of unsettling evidence shows that their true ideological allegiance lies with liberalism. Such individuals typically support a punitive approach to policing and criminal justice, in the hope of *enforcing* a superficial semblance of stability amidst the 'creative destruction' caused by liberal economics. In Britain during the 1980s, this approach was often described as the **new right** and was aptly characterized by Andrew Gamble as 'the free economy and the strong state'—in a less elegant phrase, a determination to defend a liberal economic order by the resort to illiberal methods (Gamble 1988). Rather than showing that 'conservatism' contains a strong strand of liberalism, on close inspection this evidence thus invites a conclusion about *liberalism* itself—that is, that those who try to implement political programmes derived from doctrinaire liberalism often find themselves having to adopt policies which depart from their stated principles.

'Traditional' and 'modern' conservatism?

Some scholars of ideology try to surmount (or, perhaps, evade) the problematic relationship between liberalism and contemporary 'conservative' parties and movements by distinguishing between 'traditional' and other variants of 'conservative' ideology, such as 'modern conservatism'. However well-intentioned, this terminology leaves the key questions unanswered. If the core principles of 'modern' conservatism are the same as those which informed 'traditional' conservatism, why should we differentiate between them? One explanation is that in the 'modern' context political actors confront dilemmas which were barely imagined when conservatism first emerged as a distinctive ideology; so while the basic principles have not changed, some elements of the creed are now more relevant than they were, while others have been discarded. Nevertheless, there must be a suspicion that the perceived need to distinguish between 'traditional' and 'modern' conservatism reflects *fundamental* differences between these ideological positions.

The same difficulties arise in relation to attempts to distinguish variants of 'conservatism' (e.g. **authoritarian**, **paternalistic**, 'libertarian', and 'new right'). These, on inspection, usually turn out to be different ways of denoting the contrast between 'traditional' and 'modern' conservatism. Traditional conservatism could be described as both 'authoritarian' and 'paternalistic', since it portrayed the state as an upholder of social stability through rigorous enforcement of the law and the provision of at least basic amenities to the poor. This is not to say, of course, that all 'authoritarian' regimes are by definition 'conservative'; for conservatives, authority is inherent in society itself and the state is thus 'natural', rather than the artificial entity envisaged by liberals.

By stark contrast, 'libertarians' believe that state activities should be kept to a minimum, and are thus clearly members of the broad 'liberal' family (indeed, they are closer to anarchists than to traditional conservatives—see Chapters 2 and 5). In the 1980s the term 'new right' was used by a number of academic commentators (particularly those analysing politics from a left-wing standpoint) to characterize an ideological shift on the right, exemplified by the UK Conservative Party in the guise of 'Thatcherism' but also occurring in right-wing parties in other capitalist societies, notably the USA. In an influential analysis, the 'new right' was seen as a novel synthesis between 'neo-liberalism' and 'neo-conservatism'—Gamble's 'free economy and strong state'. In effect, the new right could be seen as expounding ideas of 'classical' liberalism and 'traditional' conservatism, but revived and newly ascendant in a novel combination (Hall and Jacques 1983; Levitas 1986). Thus, according to Gamble

> The real innovation of Thatcherism is the way it has linked traditional Conservative concern with the basis of authority in social institutions and the importance of internal order and external security, with a new emphasis upon re-establishing free markets and extending market criteria into new fields.
>
> (Gamble 1983: 121)

As such, it is not unfair to describe representatives of the new right as people who see wide economic inequalities as inevitable (even desirable), and trust that any resulting social friction can be contained by the police and the courts. However, although the new right appears to involve the continuation of 'traditional' conservatism in combination with liberalism, this is a confused (if not self-contradictory) position because, as already argued, the liberal and conservative elements are in tension and the liberalism is dominant. Since proponents of the new right reject the traditional conservative belief in an inter-related, '**organic**' society (see the discussion of an organic view of society in the section 'What is conservatism?' below), they are best understood as confused liberals rather than conservatives of any kind.

In practice, academic commentators who adopt the terminology of 'traditional' and 'modern' conservatism are accepting the claims of self-ascribed 'modern conservatives' at face value. If a significant body of active political individuals choose to call themselves 'conservative', it seems, scholars of ideology have no reason (or right) to challenge their claim, and should merely try to bring ideological terminology into line with everyday assumptions about political positions. This accommodation is usually reached by means of the further claim that ideologies can *change* over time.

As we shall see, the nature of conservatism lends superficial support to this argument: if conservatives are 'pragmatic' rather than 'programmatic', they are more capable than other ideologues of adapting their ideas to changing circumstances. However, if the study of ideology is to illuminate (rather than to obfuscate) political disagreement, this argument cannot be sustained; there must come a point when the underlying principles of an individual—as opposed to tactical responses to new conditions—have 'adapted' to changed circumstances to such an extent that it no longer makes sense to understand him or her as an exponent of any kind of 'conservatism'. Conservatives may indeed be 'pragmatic' in their approach to political questions, but the crucial point is that their pragmatism arises from an ideological position which is clearly distinct from (if not directly antagonistic to) liberalism.

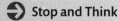 **Stop and Think**

Why does the distinction between 'traditional' and 'modern' conservatism cause so much confusion?

The nature of conservatism is warmly contested, and even the testimony of many so-called 'conservatives' makes it difficult to distinguish from liberalism. However, this confusion need not present an insuperable obstacle to careful students of ideology.

What is conservatism?

The basic premise of the present chapter is that conservatism is not a hybrid of different ideologies, but rather a distinctive world view which, like other ideologies, derives from a specific view of human nature and involves a set of core ideas.

Pessimistic view of human nature

Simply expressed, conservatives believe that human beings are flawed creatures, who are equipped with remarkable reasoning powers, but whose rationality is nevertheless all too often overborne by passion, and whose passionate attachments are often misplaced. The conservative readily accepts that human *knowledge* can increase; indeed, this is more likely than not, since even imperfectly rational beings can be expected to build on past discoveries to their further advantage. However, *wisdom* and *judgement*, particularly in political matters, are not susceptible to progress in the same sense; even though a close study of history is indispensable for the prudent decision-maker, new dilemmas cannot replicate historical examples in every last detail and the repercussions of even limited reforms of the past are no guide to the likely effects of similar measures in the present (this pessimistic view of human nature contrasts sharply with the optimistic views found in liberalism, socialism, and anarchism—see Chapters 2, 4, and 5).

Defence of the 'tried and trusted'–bias against change

This core principle of conservatism—which is apparent in the work of some ancient philosophers and a major theme in the writings of Plato (*c*.428–347 BC)—informs and explains the other ideas which are associated with the ideology. Most obviously, it explains the conservative tendency to defend the status quo; that is, things as they are. If even limited reforms are hazardous, radical change is almost unthinkable since even the very wisest politician cannot possibly anticipate the ultimate effects (because of the imperfection of his/her rational powers, as well as the fact that the human beings who will be subjected to the proposed radical changes are themselves highly unpredictable). For the conservative, the 'tried and trusted' is thus infinitely preferable to any projected improvement, however plausible the latter might appear on paper. Even if existing institutions and practices are clearly less than perfect, the conservative sees this as the inevitable lot of all human contrivances. As a result, prudent politicians should retain a prejudice in favour of the familiar unless and until there is unanswerable evidence in favour of reform.

Attacked by its critics as a stubborn attachment to things as they are, or a '**reactionary**' refusal to contemplate beneficial change and a desire to 'turn back the clock' to some imaginary golden age, this crucial element of conservatism can also be designated by the less value-laden term '**prescription**'. This term, indicating a respectful attitude towards policies and institutions created by previous generations, conveys more accurately the sense of a clear bias against change which nevertheless allows the possibility of a more flexible attitude when the status quo seems literally indefensible. There is a fascinating, albeit fictional, exposition of the conservative argument about change in J. K. Rowling's *Harry Potter and the Order of the Phoenix*. After her appointment as instructor in Defence against the Dark Arts, the repulsive Professor Dolores Umbridge tells the assembled students that

> Every headmaster and headmistress of Hogwarts has brought something new to the weighty task of governing this historic school, and that is as it should be, for without progress there will be stagnation and decay. There again, progress for progress's sake must be discouraged, for our tried and tested traditions often require no tinkering. A balance, then, between old and new, between permanence and change, between tradition and innovation . . .

> (Rowling 2003: 192)

Edmund Burke himself would have nodded with approval (even if he would not have endorsed Professor Umbridge's disciplinary methods) (see Case Study 3.1).

Benjamin Disraeli (1804–81) put the conservative view on change as follows:

> Change is inevitable in a progressive country. Change is constant; and the great question is, not whether you still resist change which is inevitable, but whether that change shall be carried out in deference to the manners, the customs, the laws and the traditions of a people, or … in deference to abstract principles and arbitrary and general doctrines.

> (Speech at Edinburgh, 29 October 1867, in Jay 2012)

Organic view of society

The perceived weakness of human reason also encourages conservatives to subscribe to an **organic** view of society—that is, they believe that individuals depend upon each other for mutual support, and that everyone within a social order performs a useful function (however humble it might appear). This contrasts strongly with the liberal view, which emphasizes the autonomy of the rational individual.

Necessity of hierarchy

At the same time, conservatives believe that this organic social order depends upon **hierarchy**. In theory, a conservative might concede that, ideally, society should be led by its most able members, selected on the basis of fair competition. However, the relevant abilities are very difficult to measure—a superficially clever individual might be wholly lacking in judgement, for example—and in any case from the conservative perspective even the cleverest human being is prone to error.

Duty

For want of a better alternative, British conservatives have usually taken inherited wealth as an adequate indication of a person's fitness to rule. Some conservative politicians have argued that their status creates an *obligation* to take part in government, rather than succumbing to the temptations of idle self-indulgence. This stern injunction is typical of the conservative emphasis on duty, in contrast to the liberal preoccupation with *rights*. In practice, privileged individuals did not always fulfil their duties in this respect—as indeed one might anticipate, if conservatives are right in emphasizing the frailties of human nature. However, the argument was underpinned by the more practical proposition that those who possess extensive property (especially in land) have the most to lose if social order collapses, and thus have a powerful incentive to govern in a fashion which keeps discontent to an unavoidable minimum.

Opposition to meritocracy

While conservatives regard a hierarchical society as both natural and desirable, their preference for stability does not necessarily entail a belief in a *static* social order, in which the 'haves' keep everything that they hold and the 'have-nots' are condemned to a life of subservience. In conservative Britain social mobility was not unknown, even if for the humbly-born the road to social and political advancement was difficult to navigate, and entailed acceptance of the values and outlook of the socio-political leaders whom they were hoping to join. In short, the conservative preference for hierarchy is strongly antipathetic to the liberal idea of 'meritocracy' (see Chapter 2).

Sceptical view of democracy and the free market

It follows that the conservative will take (at best) a **sceptical** view of democracy. If this is used as a means of choosing between elites of roughly equal ability, it can be acceptable if other forms of political rule are no longer realistic possibilities. Yet the conservative viewpoint finds it easy to envisage representative democracy as an open invitation for unprincipled demagogues, who try to beguile the irrational voting public. For the conservative, though, the devices of *direct* democracy (referendums, etc.) are even less palatable, throwing decisions which may have a crucial effect upon a whole political community into the hands of individuals who only imperfectly understand their own petty, personal interests, and are almost wholly lacking in the virtues of statesmanship. The decision by a Conservative government to hold a

referendum on the UK's membership of the European Union in 2016 is thus a significant indication of that party's distance from traditional conservatism.

From the conservative perspective, it is also difficult to make much sense of the
liberal notion of 'freedom', except as a more palatable synonym for irresponsibility
or 'licence'. Rather than thinking of life as a series of free choices, the conservative is
far more aware of unavoidable *constraints* on choice. Do we choose our parents? Can
we choose to be talented? For that matter, do we choose to be born? The key corol-
lary here is the conservative view of the economic sphere, and the notion of the 'free'
market which is so central to liberal thought. From the conservative viewpoint—
concerned as it is with stability in society, economics, and politics, and acutely conscious of their interconnections—the operations of the market since the advent of
industrialism constitute the socio-economic equivalent of government by referendum: the active encouragement of 'freedom' in this sphere is like handing the keys of
a high-performing sports car to a testosterone-fuelled adolescent. In the contemporary globalized economy, periods of frenzied optimism are as ominous as the more
sober moods which inevitably succeed them; whether the economy is 'booming' or
'busted', society is likely to be unstable and, as a result, life will be more unpredictable
and hazardous.

Judgement versus dogma

On this basis, conservatives could be expected to endorse any economic policy which
promises stability—or, at least, keeps instability to a minimum. Yet, in the increasingly complex economic conditions of modernity, their own theory of human nature
makes the idea of continuous and detailed government intervention seem highly
dubious: mistaken governmental decisions which can affect numerous individuals
could easily make a bad situation even worse. In such straits the conservative in a
responsible government position can only make a judgement call based on his or
her reading of the situation; a response dictated by dogma (whether in favour of
economic freedom or of state control) would have been alien to the conservative
approach before the industrial revolution, let alone in today's globalized economy.

Thus conservatives cannot subscribe to theories (like that of the German philosopher Hegel, 1770–1831) which indicate an uncritical view of the state. Nevertheless,
the state is different from other human institutions; it can (or should) to some degree
reflect and reinforce the sense of solidarity which should animate any healthy society.
The state, then, is not just a 'necessary evil', as it is even to moderate representatives
of the liberal tradition.

This account is necessarily brief, and represents a series of generalizations
derived from the work of authors who are associated with the conservative tradition. However, it can readily be seen that the ideas build into a relatively coherent
approach to political questions, and that this approach is clearly distinct from other

ideologies. Whether or not the presentation over-simplifies the conservative tradition, the ideas themselves, and their link with the core understanding of human
nature as radically imperfect and unamenable to significant improvement, really *are*
quite simple—certainly comparable to other ideologies which give rise to much less
confusion over basic terms of reference.

 Stop and Think

What are the main principles of conservative thought?

The ideas which underlie conservative ideology are that human beings are imperfect
and imperfectable; that such beings are interdependent and require an *organic* society
in which to flourish; and that order cannot be maintained within such a society without a *hierarchical* structure which is determined without reference to immeasurable
individual merit. From this perspective, the liberal values of meritocracy, democracy,
and freedom are at best dangerous, and potentially disastrous. At the same time,
the caricature of conservatism as merely a 'reactionary', backward-looking creed is
clearly mistaken; so that contemporary conservatives have no choice but to operate
within a framework of rules and assumptions which they find highly distasteful.

Sources of confusion

Why, then, is conservatism so often misunderstood? Three main reasons can be
suggested:

- the attitude of academic commentators;
- the nature of conservatism;
- socio-political developments, both domestic and international.

The attitude of academic commentators

It would not be unfair to claim that academics in general (but particularly those
based in Europe) have not been characterized by an overwhelming enthusiasm for
'conservatism' (however it is defined). The same people who are eager to explore
every nuance of liberalism or socialism seem happy to accept the definition of 'conservatism' currently in vogue, not least because it conforms to their own idea that
'conservatives' are apologists for inequality and other injustices. This tendency has
been reinforced in recent years by the fact that the most eloquent defenders of 'conservatism' have actually been ideological *liberals* (such as British Thatcherites and, in
the USA, supporters of right-wing Republican positions).

The nature of conservatism

However, academics are not entirely to blame for the failure to understand conservatism; as we have seen, the nature of conservatism itself is a potent factor. Apart from the ideologically loaded protest that their ideas are *not* ideological, most of the classic conservative texts have been written by individuals who sense that their approach to politics and society is under serious threat. This is not surprising; those with an inexhaustible enthusiasm for change have a perpetual incentive to pick up the pen, while those who feel fairly comfortable within the existing order are unlikely to experience the same impulse unless they sense that established institutions and practices are in urgent need of support (or, *in extremis*, extensive reforms). Even in those unusual circumstances (like, for example, Britain's 'Glorious Revolution' of 1688–89), conservatives are more likely to *act* than to write in justification of a reform programme. When conservatives do feel the need to write under pressure they have a tendency to extol the virtues of the existing order in a way which distorts their true opinion; in their anxiety to repel the prospect of radical change they often sound as if reform of any kind would lead to disaster. However, even if their writings misleadingly suggest an addiction to any established order it must be remembered that conservatives are sceptics, who deny that any socio-political dispensation can even approximate to a state of perfection. Thus, one might say, they are inveterate grumblers who would be uneasy in Paradise. As the philosopher Michael Oakeshott (1901–90) put it, the conservative 'disposition' thrives when 'there is much to be enjoyed'. On the surface this might look like a rather complacent remark, but it implies that the best a conservative can hope for is a time when the potential for enjoyment is plentiful, but by no means *complete* (Oakeshott 1962: 169).

While Oakeshott's depiction of a conservative 'disposition' is highly attractive, it is not very instructive for those who want to know about conservative *beliefs*. Oakeshott himself, while often hailed as a key conservative thinker, displayed a concern for individual freedom which is difficult to reconcile with the tradition of thought sketched here. A much more pertinent example, for our purposes, is Edmund Burke (1729–97: see Case Study 3.1), who emerged as an early opponent of the French Revolution for reasons which bear a close resemblance to our previous discussion of conservative ideas. In particular, Burke's *Reflections on the Revolution in France* (1790) showed a tendency to downplay the glaring flaws in the pre-revolutionary French constitution (despite allowing that there was scope for some reform). Burke used his remarkable rhetorical powers in the hope of inspiring sympathy for the French monarchy while showing scant compassion for the sufferings of French families who enjoyed less exalted status: as Burke's radical opponent Thomas Paine aptly put it, 'he pities the plumage, but forgets the dying bird' (Paine 1985 edn: 51). Yet Burke had adopted a task which all conservatives face in perilous times—the need to stimulate support for a status quo (whether at home or abroad) which is perceived to be preferable to any 'radical' alternative even if it shares in abundance the imperfections which are inseparable from human affairs.

Case Study 3.1 Edmund Burke (1729–97)

Widely regarded as the founder of modern conservatism, Edmund Burke was in fact a member of the Whig Party (which later formed the basis of the Liberal Party) rather than of the Tory Party (the forerunner of what became the Conservative Party). In itself, this fact illustrates the dangers of associating party labels with ideological positions without searching inquiry. His career also provides a concrete example of the conservative approach to social mobility. As he put it near the end of his life, 'At every step of my progress in life (for in every step I was traversed and opposed), and at every turnpike I met, I was obliged to shew my passport, and again and again to prove my sole title to the honour of being useful to my Country' (McDowell 1991: 160). In other words, Burke, who came from a prosperous but untitled Dublin family—and was thus a migrant who had adopted England as his country—had managed to attain high political rank within a system dominated by aristocrats, by dint of talent and tenacity: as he defiantly proclaimed in the same passage, 'I was not made for a minion or a tool'.

Burke's outspoken opposition to the French Revolution led to his retirement from the Whig Party (which initially welcomed the Revolution) in 1791. By that time (before the September Massacres of 1792) it looked as though Burke had exaggerated the potential effects of the Revolution; indeed, the Prime Minister, William Pitt the Younger, regarded Burke's writings on the subject as 'rhapsodies . . . [there is] much to admire and nothing to agree with' (Auckland 1862: Vol. III, 320). Burke was particularly vulnerable to criticism because in earlier years he had attacked British policy towards the American colonies, to the extent that he could be regarded as a supporter of the revolution which led to the formation of the United States. However, the contradiction was more apparent than real, since in America the states were essentially fighting to preserve their existing mode of governance, whereas the leading French revolutionaries were actuated by ideas which implied a radical breach from the established monarchical regime.

Burke's relevance to the current chapter extends to his views on economics—a subject where he earned applause from no less an authority than Adam Smith, founding father of economic liberalism. In his *Thoughts and Details on Scarcity* (1795), Burke included 'the laws of commerce' among 'the laws of nature, and consequently the laws of God'. Government should not interfere with the 'laws' of the market, even (indeed especially) at times of scarcity—it should confine itself 'to every thing that is *truly and properly* public, to the public peace, to the public safety, to the public order, to the public prosperity' (McDowell 1991: 143). The poor should be supported, if necessary, by individuals' acts of charity.

On the face of it, Burke seems to have suffered from the same inconsistency which afflicts so many so-called 'conservatives' today. Indeed, the last item on his list of 'truly public' functions suggests that his sufferings on the score of consistency were particularly acute, since if governments are allowed to concern themselves with 'public prosperity' it seems to follow that they have an economic role after all. His comments also conflict with two of his most famous utterances, which are particularly relevant to the argument of this chapter. In his *Reflections*, for example, he wrote that the state should be an object of 'reverence': it 'ought not to be considered as nothing better than a partnership agreement in a trade of pepper and coffee, calico or tobacco, or some other such low concern' (Mitchell 1989: 147); and that 'We are afraid to put men to live and trade each on his own private stock of reason; because we suspect that this stock in each man is small, and that the individuals would be better to avail themselves of the general bank and capital of nations, and of ages' (Mitchell 1989: 138). By belittling commercial activity and eulogising the state, the first quotation furnishes a plausible foundation for an argument in favour of government intervention in the economy, at least in times of dire public distress. The second quotation is even more unpalatable for ideological supporters of free market economics, since in stark contrast to the abstract models of 'rational actors' used by the latter, Burke deliberately employs commercial metaphors to emphasize human *irrationality*.

Burke's economic writing, in fact, is best understood as the product of a specific historical context. *Thoughts and Details on Scarcity* is concerned with the question of 'public' intervention in the operations of the *rural* economy which was still dominant at the time of his death. When confronted with evidence arising from a mainly *urban* society and a dehumanized manufacturing sector, writers in the Burkean tradition, such as the poet Samuel Taylor Coleridge (1772-1834), were far less laudatory of the so-called 'laws' of the free market. Also, the closing passages of *Thoughts and Details* show that Burke's own rational faculties had been unhinged by a succession of private and political misfortunes. Every socio-political question was now being seen in lurid colours, through the prism of the revolutionary threat, and Burke had convinced himself that government action to alleviate hunger would actually help to precipitate an insurrection. In other words, under the pressure of events, Burke had been forced from the sure conservative foundations which he had laid down in the *Reflections*, and was prepared to embrace an abstract economic doctrine even if that endangered social stability. Thankfully, in 1795 his own superficial researches revealed that there was very little hunger to alleviate—which leaves open the question of how he might have reacted in the face of truly devastating rural deprivation at a time when the revolutionary threat had receded.

 Stop and Think

After studying the social philosophy expounded in Burke's *Reflections*, do you think he would have stuck to his laissez-faire approach to economics if he had lived to witness the full impact of the 'manufacturing system' on British society?

Socio-political developments, both domestic and international

The third source of confusion is the hardest to shift, since its origins can be located long before the Second World War. As such, this issue demands lengthy historical explication.

The previous discussion of conservatism emphasised its opposition to models of humanity which stress the capacity for *rational* thought. Such ideas, essentially 'liberal' in nature, also challenged the concept of an organic society based on mutual dependence, promoting in its place a loose assemblage of individuals in which (for example) the free market should reign and every adult should have an equal right to a voice in the selection of political representatives. In other words, conservatives like Edmund Burke were chiefly concerned with the possible effects of essentially *liberal* revolutions, which were inspired by what they saw as a false and dangerously over-optimistic assessment of human capabilities.

Despite the initially mixed reception of his *Reflections*, Burke's writings were gradually accepted by the opponents of radical change in several European states. By
the early 1830s the 'Conservative' label was being adopted by former members of
the British Tory Party. However, this period saw changes, in political institutions
and economic policies, which champions of the established order in Britain either
deplored or regarded as regrettable necessities—notably the limited extension of the
franchise in the Great Reform Act of 1832, and the apparent ascendancy of free-
market ideas exemplified by the repeal of the protectionist Corn Laws (accepted and
finally enacted by the Conservative Prime Minister Robert Peel in 1846).

Despite these significant setbacks, and various splits in the party's ranks, the
'Conservative' label was not jettisoned by the erstwhile Tories. However, rather than
opposing socio-political change to the last ditch, the party increasingly directed its
appeal towards those who were uneasy about the supposedly inevitable trend of 'progress' which the passage of the 1832 Reform Act seemed to have endorsed. With
varying degrees of reluctance, Conservative Party leaders accepted that further social
and political change was inevitable, but they argued that the accompanying hazards
could safely be navigated only with a 'Conservative' ministry at the helm—a view
expressed with typical wit and cynicism by Benjamin Disraeli in the novel *Coningsby*
(1844), when one of his characters ('Taper') defines 'a sound Conservative government' as consisting of 'Tory men and Whig measures' (Disraeli 1989: 129). The tenacity and skill of Conservatives such as Disraeli helped to ensure that the Conservative
'brand' persisted as a considerable political force in Britain, even as the party presided over socio-economic developments which would have convinced acute observers
that their ideological rationale was weakening fast.

By the beginning of the twentieth century, it can be argued, the British Conservative
Party had ceased to be 'conservative' in any recognizable sense, and was now surviving merely on its *institutional* reserves. These, however, were still considerable in the
first decade of the century: to adapt Taper's words, although the ideological initiative
had clearly passed to ideological liberals there were still plenty of 'Tory men' who
were prepared to preside over the implementation of 'Whig measures' in the hope of
exercising some control over their effects.

Although circumstances cannot alter the fundamental principles of an ideology,
they can certainly have an effect on its fortunes; what seems entirely plausible in one
context can look hopelessly irrelevant at another time. Changing circumstances provide the key to understanding the eclipse of conservative ideology over the course of
the nineteenth century. A vital clue can be gleaned from Robert Peel's decision that
the Corn Laws should be scrapped. The Corn Laws, which protected home-grown
agricultural produce from cheaper foreign imports, was seen as a crucial bulwark for
British landowners—that is, the aristocracy and gentry. The powerful extra-parlia-
mentary movement to repeal the Corn Laws was funded and spearheaded by representatives of 'the manufacturing interest' and their political supporters, who saw

cheaper bread as a key weapon in their fight to repress the wages of their employees. Repeal of the Corn Laws did not spell the end of the British aristocracy—far from it—and it did not stop members of this class and their sympathizers from endorsing distinctively conservative views. But it did mean that the political initiative had passed decisively to a socio-economic force which had scant sympathy for the conservative outlook.

Even a cursory examination of the conservative principles sketched above should make clear their affinity with a society in which the possession of landed property was the main lever of political influence. An organic, hierarchal society in which things changed very gradually (in tandem with the seasons, perhaps) looks suspiciously like an idealized portrait of pre-industrial British society—which, indeed, is what it is. Conservatism can be seen as a means of providing principled backing for a social order of that kind—advanced sincerely or out of cynical self-interest, according to one's taste. Equally, the rise of liberal ideology in Britain reflected socio-economic changes which were antipathetic to conservatism, along with growing political influence and self-confidence among manufacturers and those who issued propaganda on their behalf.

From this perspective, the title of George Dangerfield's lively book *The Strange Death of Liberal England* (1935) is apt to mislead the unwary. In the years covered by Dangerfield (1910–14), even though the Liberal Party suffered serious setbacks, it was actually *conservative* England that finally lost its *raison d'être* and took its final breath. In domestic politics, the aristocracy was deliberately targeted by tax reforms, and by the Liberal Party's dogged attempts to reduce the political potency of the House of Lords, which conservatives rightly saw as the last defensive outpost against the ideological enemy. As a final, inadvertent 'mopping-up' operation, Asquith's Liberal Government committed Britain to the conflict now known as the First World War, in which aristocratic families suffered particularly devastating losses. Thanks to the slaughter in the fields of Flanders, the 'Tory men' were far fewer in number by the end of the war; and the survivors who continued to harbour political ambitions were even less likely to resist the populist appeal of 'Whig measures' after the introduction of universal manhood suffrage in 1918. After this, if they wanted to continue in politics, representatives of the conservative ideological tradition would at least have to pay lip-service to liberal ideas, such as democracy and meritocracy.

To make matters even more difficult for the remaining 'Tory men', the democratic system which conservative ideology strongly opposed arrived at a time when a Labour Party had emerged, with an obvious chance of taking the lion's share of votes from newly-enfranchised individuals whose livelihoods derived from manufacturing rather than rural economic activity. It was reasonable to assume that, under the new franchise which had been superimposed on Britain's first-past-the-post system (which was strongly biased towards two-party competition), the political contestants in future would be Labour plus 'one other'. Since the Liberal Party had already established an amicable working relationship with Labour—and because, unlike the Conservative Party, it could face the democratic dawn without any serious palpitations of principle—it seemed that the Conservative Party faced a long-overdue oblivion.

However, the Liberals chose this moment to hand the Conservative Party a gratuitous life-line after its ideological heart had stopped beating. They embarked on a protracted period of infighting, arising from clashes of personality rather than serious differences of principle. However, despite the dramatic impact of these events on the party-political battles at Westminster, in terms of ideological history it can be argued that the resulting eclipse of the Liberal *Party* was of marginal relevance. Whatever the party labels that emerged to contest elections in the era of universal suffrage, and the differences of emphasis which served in the place of real divisions of principle, the battle would henceforth lie between two teams composed of 'liberal men' purveying what were, for all their superficial differences, essentially 'liberal measures'.

The Russian Revolution and the Bolshevik threat

On the basis of the preceding argument, we can appreciate that (regardless of the fortunes of the Conservative *Party*) a 'conservative' ideology which was clearly distinguishable from liberalism gradually became less persuasive as a basis for political *action* during the nineteenth century—as one by one the conservative bastions were abandoned—and had little chance of exercising significant influence over political decisions after the First World War. But the survival of the British 'Conservative' Party as the main rival to Labour requires a little more explanation. Surely, if liberal ideology was so successful—and conservatism so archaic—the Liberal Party could have made a comeback, once its internal difficulties had been resolved?

The answer to this apparent problem lies in another piece of uncovenanted luck for the Conservative Party—which, by the same token, makes life much more difficult for scholars who persist in the view that conservative ideology is not just a confused variant of liberalism. In 1917, European politicians had to digest the implications of another ideologically inspired revolution. The opponents of both the French and Russian revolutions could claim that each episode resulted in crimes against humanity on an epic scale; but the principles involved were very different. Whereas the French Revolution had been inspired (at least in its early stages) by essentially *liberal* beliefs, appealing to the 'rational' individual, the perceived threat arising from the Soviet version related to *collectivist* ideas which portrayed historical change in terms of antagonistic classes rather than individuals.

In this new ideological battle-ground, the British Liberal Party, with its inveterate attachment to individualistic beliefs, could have been expected to take the lead in combating the **Bolshevik** menace. However, the crucial early years of the Revolution coincided neatly with the schism in Liberal ranks, leaving the Liberal Prime Minister, Lloyd George, increasingly dependent on Conservative support in parliament.

Liberal weakness meant that the Conservative Party now came to be regarded as the only effective option for those who sought to defend Britain against revolutionary forces abroad—and at home (since Labour's radical intentions were subjected to deliberate distortion at the time). If politics in the age of universal suffrage was going to boil down to Labour versus 'the Best of the Rest', a Conservative Party which had already exhibited considerable powers of institutional resilience was now handed the unexpected opportunity to don the latter mantle. The ensuing tactical decisions of senior Liberal politicians such as Winston Churchill (see Case Study 3.2) provide vivid practical testimony to the transformation of the Conservative Party from an anti-liberal to an anti-socialist organization, in response to the ideological threat apparently posed by Bolshevism, and the irresistible electoral opportunity provided by the Liberal Party.

Case Study 3.2 Winston Churchill (1874–1965)

Winston Churchill began his political career as a partisan Conservative—unsurprisingly, since his father had been a Conservative Chancellor of the Exchequer. However, Lord Randolph Churchill had been somewhat erratic in his political conduct even before the onset of illness which claimed his life in 1895, at the early age of 45; whatever motivations lay behind his drive to make the Conservative Party into a 'progressive' force, it seems reasonable to cite Churchill senior as an example of the dilemmas facing the party in the late nineteenth century, when the familiar landmarks of the past were receding from view.

After becoming a Conservative MP in 1900, Winston Churchill defected to the Liberals four years later, on the key economic issue of free trade (which he favoured, along with ideological liberals whether or not they were members of the Liberal Party). It seemed that he had found his true political home; not only did he serve as a Liberal minister (1908-15, 1917-22), but he also contributed through his ministerial decisions as well as his writings and speeches to a new style of interventionist liberalism as opposed to the laissez-faire version which had generally prevailed throughout the nineteenth century (see Chapter 2).

However, in 1911 Churchill was removed from domestic responsibilities and made First Lord of the Admiralty. In one sense, this was an agreeable move since, with his military training, Churchill was well suited to the preparation and prosecution of war. On the other hand, during the First World War his desire to break out of the stalemate on the Western Front led him to promote an ill-starred attack on Turkey (the Dardenelles campaign), and he was subsequently made the chief scapegoat for its failure. Although he returned to ministerial office before the end of the war, this episode was deeply scarring, and might have been expected to alienate him forever from former Conservative Party colleagues who had demanded his resignation with considerable relish.

Instead, by 1924 Churchill had not only rejoined the Conservative Party but had emulated his father by becoming a Conservative Chancellor of the Exchequer—without giving any sign that he had changed the domestic political views which had led him to leave the Conservatives and become a Liberal! In particular, he remained a very strident anti-communist—more so, indeed, than most politicians who had stuck to the Conservative Party throughout these years. As this chapter suggests, the explanation for this behaviour lay in the much-diminished prospects of the Liberal Party, to which Churchill (essentially a politician who wanted to exercise power rather than sit in parliamentary impotence) responded by changing his partisan allegiance for a second time. He remained with the Conservatives to the end, although he and his party retained a some-what equivocal relationship. As Prime Minister, Churchill voiced serious misgivings about both the proposals of the Beveridge Report (1942) and its author; but in ideological terms this hesita-tion (which he subsequently overcame by embracing 'cradle to grave' welfare) implies at most a struggle within Churchill's soul between two variants of *liberalism*—that is, 'classical' and 'social' liberalism (see Chapter 2)—rather than a belated twinge of residual 'conservatism'.

In ideological terms, then, the main lesson arising from Winston Churchill's illustrious politi-cal career is the danger of confusing party labels with coherent systems of political belief. The Conservative Party has every reason to acclaim him as one of its heroes, but it is far more prob-lematic to regard him as an exemplar of 'conservatism' in action.

➜ Stop and Think

Do you think that Winston Churchill's various changes of party make it impossible to regard him as a truly principled politician, such that he is best understood as an opportunist?

An argument can be made that, in establishing itself as the main political bulwark against 'socialism' after 1918, the Conservative Party was living up to its ideological heritage by acting *pragmatically*. On this view, the overriding conservative priority of defending the status quo necessitates tactical shifts if the nature of the enemy chang-es; but the change is one of emphasis rather than of underlying principle.

However, as we have seen, this argument is based on a misunderstanding of con-servative ideology. When Burke and others opposed the French Revolution, they based their argument on a world view which was strongly *anti*-liberal. When the British Conservative *Party* emerged as a principled antagonist of socialism, it read-ily deployed arguments which were characteristically *liberal* in nature: simplistic, question-begging slogans such as 'freedom' suddenly sounded far more effective in this context than the distinctively conservative case against communism, which was rooted in more sophisticated arguments about the imperfections of the human con-dition. Far from being a superficial tactical shift behind which a distinctively con-servative world view continued to hold sway, this move by the Conservative Party actually confirmed the new ideological identity which a range of irresistible practical developments had made compulsory for those who wanted to stay in the political game. Since the aristocratic social order which had underpinned ideological con-servatism had been fading away for several decades, the overwhelming majority of politicians who had chosen to build careers within the Conservative Party were now those who were already strongly sympathetic to *liberalism*: those who contin-ued to hold Burkean views tended to drop away to the fringes of public debate. The steady stream of new converts who joined the Conservatives from the ailing Liberal Party were not really 'converts' at all, in an ideological sense; like Churchill, they brought their liberalism with them and had no reason to modify their views in a party which welcomed them not just as important new recruits but also, increasingly, as fellow-believers.

 Stop and Think

Why did the Conservative Party emerge as the main electoral rival to Labour after 1918?

The survival of the 'Conservative Party' in Britain is a misleading (though very interesting) historical accident; the party of that name ceased to be 'conservative' in a distinctive ideological sense before the First World War, and despite its considerable institutional resources it only survived that conflict because the Liberal Party was in no position to defeat the Conservatives in the contest to emerge as the main political opponent of the rising Labour Party (or of Soviet 'Bolshevism').

'New' liberalism versus laissez-faire

At the risk of over-simplifying, then, one could argue that after the introduction of universal suffrage two *liberal* parties fought for the position of chief opponent to Labour in British politics—and the battle was lost by the institution which, decades earlier, had chosen to adopt the title of 'Liberal Party'. In this respect, at least, Humpty Dumpty (as portrayed by Lewis Carroll in *Through the Looking Glass*) was wrong when he claimed that a word 'means just what I choose it to mean'—the word, *liberal*, proved to be less important than the ideological *substance* which lay behind it.

However, if the Conservative Party had now embraced liberal ideology as well as winning the allegiance of many ex-supporters of the Liberal Party, it still had a choice. Liberal ideology, in the interwar period, offered alternative routes: the laissez-faire liberalism which had exercised such a profound influence on public policy in the nineteenth century, or the 'new' liberalism (associated particularly with the Balliol scholar and local politician Thomas Hill Green, 1036=02). (Also see the discussion in Chapter 2 which distinguishes 'laissez-faire' and 'new' liberalism using the terms 'economic' and 'social' liberalism respectively.) The latter, while remaining clearly distinct from conservative ideology, nevertheless had a few points of congruity, especially in its goal of social harmony rather than the constant struggle for individual aggrandisement suggested by laissez-faire. 'New' or social liberalism was duly established as the dominant ideology of the Conservative Party, at least after 1923, when Stanley Baldwin became leader. After the Second World War, this brand of Conservatism was given the name 'One Nation Conservatism', in recognition of its partial semblance to the ideas of the nineteenth century Conservative leader Benjamin Disraeli. Yet laissez-faire liberals remained as an active minority within the party, mainly because they had no realistic alternative if they wanted to influence government policy. In 1975, thanks to a conjunction of favourable circumstances, Margaret Thatcher seized the Conservative leadership, claiming that the party had always supported her own unusual brand of laissez-faire liberalism.

Thatcher's victory in the 1975 leadership election triggered an internal party debate about the nature of 'conservatism'. Even at this late hour, none of the protagonists were prepared to entertain the subversive thought that their sharply-contrasting versions of the true faith were in fact derived from different tendencies within the liberal tradition; even the more thoughtful of the 'One Nation' politicians within the Conservative Party managed to convince themselves that they must be the 'true' conservatives because they were opposed to radical change, failing to perceive that the postwar policy framework they sought to defend had been devised chiefly by the 'New' liberals, William Beveridge and John Maynard Keynes. For the purposes of practical politics, since there was no serious move on either side to reject the redundant 'Conservative' party label, the failure to explore the real ideological implications of Thatcher's victory was understandable.

In office after 1979, 'Thatcherites' adopted the mission of curbing the economic scope of state activity (thus helping to undermine its authority more generally), while insisting on the government's duty to regulate personal conduct (a task which would have been difficult enough in the first place, given the unmistakable trend in favour of liberal ideas in the personal sphere, but which was further undermined by the tendency of successive Conservative governments after 1979 to use 'freedom' as a key propaganda tool against Labour). Thus, rather than exposing the inherent contradictions of 'conservative' ideology, Thatcherism, properly understood, is best regarded as a combination of laissez-faire liberal ideology with 'reactionary' elements. Rather than embodying the spirit of Edmund Burke, it is like a mismarriage between Adam Smith and J. K. Rowling's (2003) Professor Umbridge.

Case Study 3.3 Conservatism and contemporary political issues

Since the nature of 'modern conservatism' tends to be accepted without adequate analysis, it is no surprise to find that conservative views on specific issues are assumed rather than being explored in a critical spirit. This discussion, while necessarily brief, suggests that such assumptions are often seriously misleading; it also illustrates a general theme of this chapter, that while conservative viewpoints might suggest interesting (even persuasive) approaches to topical issues, they are too idiosyncratic to form the basis of a practical political programme in today's Western democracies. Our examples are property, taxation, nationalism, and the environment.

• Property: 'conservatism' is commonly associated with strong support for the institution of private property. This is only natural if one assumes that ownership can often be a source of stability and familiarity, in terms of apparently trivial possessions as well as major investments like a house. In the UK, in particular, the Conservative Party is associated with the idea of 'a property-owning democracy'.

However, it would be a mistake to argue on this basis that conservative ideology is invariably supportive of the capitalist economic system in all of its forms. Home ownership, for example, is easily compatible with the conservative view of human nature when the property in question has been acquired as a dwelling for the owner and her family. But buying property as a piece of financial speculation (of one sort or another) is very difficult to square with conservative ideology; it is much more characteristic of the liberal view of the calculating, 'rational' individual. Thus the 'Thatcherite' interpretation of 'a property-owning democracy' is not one which a conservative could readily embrace. Similarly, while the British Conservative Party made much of a 'share-owning democracy' during the 1980s, the Thatcher government's privatization programme tacitly assumed that potential buyers would try to maximize their profits at the first opportunity rather than building a lasting relationship with the firms in question.

- Taxation: again, it is readily assumed that 'conservatives' hate taxation, especially when it is designed to redistribute economic resources from the rich to the poor. There is some warrant for this belief, since conservatives are bound to be sceptical of all such attempts at 'social engineering', and doubt that governments can be trusted to use tax revenues effectively. But this does not mean that they oppose taxation in principle, or indeed that they have any serious problem with a tax regime which falls much more heavily on the rich than on the poor. Rather, their belief that the possession of wealth and substantial property creates additional duties rather than new rights prompts a readiness to accept a heavier burden of taxation for specific purposes (e.g. to finance a National Health Service which is run fairly, so as to uphold social stability).

- Nationalism: the conservative preference for the familiar suggests a rooted preference for one's native land. Conservative thinkers such as Edmund Burke (see Case Study 3.1) have given eloquent expression to this view, seeing a love for one's country as an extension of other relationships, spreading outwards from one's immediate family.

However, the conservative preference for one's country does not entail knee-jerk negativity towards foreigners. The conservative outlook actually suggests a particular fondness for migrants who (like Burke himself) want to make a positive contribution in their adopted land. In short, conservatism is far more compatible with **patriotism**—a prejudice in favour of one's country which does not preclude criticism of a government's actions—as opposed to pugnacious nationalism or **xenophobia**. Nevertheless, for various good reasons, conservatives will feel serious misgivings about the European Union (EU), which even in its present form bears the hallmarks of **utopian** thinking more characteristic of liberals (see also the discussion of 'conservatism and nationalism' in Chapter 6).

- Environmentalism: in contemporary debate, 'conservatism' is often associated with opposition to 'Green' politics, and, in particular, a furious denial of the link between human activity and climate change. However, this is another excellent example of the confusion which surrounds the word 'conservative'.

True, a conservative should be sceptical of all proposals for radical change, even (or especially) when they seem to be supported by rigorous scientific research. Nevertheless, preservation of the natural environment is a key principle for conservatives, wherever the perceived threat might originate. In this case, the notion that the human (or rather, Western) obsession with consumption has imperilled the planet as a whole is certain to resonate with conservatives (see Chapter 10). Serious students of ideology will not find it surprising that the leading conservative thinker John Gray highlighted his concern for the environment in a book which announced his (rather belated) estrangement from Margaret Thatcher's neo-liberal project (Gray 1993).

'Conservatism' in the USA

On the basis of the preceding discussion, it can be concluded that, while conservatism is a distinctive ideology which individuals can still find appealing today, its plausibility as a spur to political *action* is strictly limited in any non-agrarian society—in other words, its message seems to be at odds with *modernity* (see Chapter 8 for further discussion of this point).

This analysis, a critic might complain, ignores the popularity of the 'conservative' ideological label in the USA, where many supporters of the Republican Party wear it with pride. Thanks to grass-roots movements like the 'Tea Party', it might even be claimed, 'conservatism' is an extremely potent force in the USA, and thus a major factor in global politics. Furthermore, the Tea Party movement can be seen as 'reactionary' to the extent that it wishes to reverse a long-established tradition of federal activism; and, far from being a movement of contemplative citizens in search of a quiet life, it is also unashamedly noisy and **populist**.

The argument appears to be all the more powerful since, whereas in the UK supporters of the Conservative *Party* are almost obliged to refer to themselves as 'conservatives' in the ideological sense, in the USA the badge has been chosen *voluntarily* by people, like members of the Tea Party, who tend to support the Republican Party. Yet if the overwhelming majority of Britons who continue to call themselves 'conservative' are using ideological terminology in a way which suits their 'tribal' sense of political identity rather than any 'objective' classification of beliefs, the same could easily be true of their self-ascribing counterparts in the USA. On closer inspection, this indeed turns out to be the case.

In the USA, the word 'conservative' was not widely encountered prior to the Second World War; more precisely, it has passed into common usage since the onset of the Cold War which ranged the USA against Soviet Russia. As we saw in the previous section, in the contest against communism/socialism, 'laissez-faire' *liberal* arguments had far more ideological purchase than the Burkean conservative position, which (among other things) was nowhere near so antipathetic towards the state and prioritized the need for social harmony over the ceaseless quest of rootless individuals for material acquisition. To the extent that 'new' liberalism emphasized the importance of social ties as well as individual self-improvement, it was equally disadvantaged as a source of ideological weapons against Soviet 'collectivism'.

Thus the advent of the Cold War provided laissez-faire liberals in the USA with an ideal opportunity to fight back against interventionist **New Deal** Democrats such as Franklin Roosevelt, and even moderate Republicans such as Dwight D. Eisenhower. In the Cold War polemical battle, it helped greatly if politicians such as Roosevelt and Eisenhower, who accepted an active role for the state in domestic matters, could be branded 'soft on Communism'. To denounce people who fought elections on the Republican ticket as 'insufficiently Republican' was far less effective than claiming that they were not 'conservative' enough. 'Conservatism', in this sense, denoted an adherence to the original terms of the US constitution, with its emphasis on the rights of individual states against the Federal government, etc. (see Case Study 3.3). The really brilliant aspect of this terminological trick was its ability, in the eyes of self-designated 'conservatives' at least, to confer a diabolical status on the word 'liberal'. In part, this tactic was enforced by the fact that there was no significant US counterpart to the British Labour Party, so that there could never be much mileage in the accusation that their opponents were 'socialists'. In political terms, the attack on 'liberals' has been (and continues to be) highly effective in the USA; but this should not deflect students of ideology from the abundant evidence which shows that the Tea Party and other supposedly 'conservative' movements in the USA are themselves best understood as members of the broad liberal family.

Case Study 3.4 Barry Goldwater, *The Conscience of a Conservative*

Barry Goldwater (1909–98) was a self-styled 'conservative' Republican who, after serving as a Senator for Arizona, secured his party's nomination for the 1964 presidential election. The result was a landslide victory for his opponent, Lyndon Johnson, and this example was frequently cited as evidence that the majority of American voters are alienated by any hint of ideological extremism.

In 1960, Senator Goldwater published *The Conscience of a Conservative*, which expounded his personal creed. It is a fascinating book, which provides ample (if unwitting) support for the argument of this chapter. For example, Goldwater argues that 'the Conservative looks upon politics as the art of achieving the maximum amount of freedom for individuals that is consistent with the maintenance of the social order' (Goldwater 1960: 13). The apparent priority allotted to 'social order' makes Goldwater seem like a conservative in the distinctive, Durkean sense. However, as his discussion proceeds, it becomes increasingly difficult to discern a limit beyond which 'freedom for individuals' really could become a hazard to social order. Goldwater clearly perceives the individual from the characteristic liberal perspective of rationality and self-interest. However, despite their splendid inheritance of autonomous existence, by 1960 American citizens had elected a succession of Presidents who allegedly spent their time thinking of ways of interfering with their otherwise-blissful existences. Roosevelt, Truman, and Eisenhower might have adopted different party labels, but in ideological terms, according to Goldwater, they were all 'liberals'— that is, in the confusing vocabulary of US politics, little better than Soviet communists.

As a practising politician with a polemical purpose (and considerable personal ambition), Goldwater felt no need to explain why these 'liberals' should have advocated increasing federal interference, at the risk of alienating the average American citizen (and thus, one would have presumed, inviting cataclysmic electoral defeats on the scale that he himself suffered in 1964). However, those who wish to *understand* the advance of governmental activity in the USA can find a useful clue by subjecting to critical scrutiny Goldwater's main claim to a distinctively 'conservative' viewpoint. Goldwater's text presents the initial US constitution (plus some of the early amendments) as something akin to holy writ, from which any deviation must, *ipso facto*, be a bad thing. Superficially, this might be accepted as a distinctively 'conservative' position, since the constitution was drafted by people who had plenty of wisdom of their own to add to the accumulated intelligence of previous generations. However, time did not exactly stand still after the constitution-makers stopped deliberating; and when Barry Goldwater was testifying to his 'Conservative conscience' American society was changing as never before, especially with regard to assumptions of racial superiority, leaving good grounds for even the most hidebound 'conservative' to wonder whether the constitution as it stood in (say) 1800 could really be regarded as an ideal instrument for what had subsequently become the government of the world's most powerful nation.

In reality, by appealing to the original terms of the US constitution, Barry Goldwater was hoping to lend a 'conservative' veneer to a case which he would have endorsed anyway—namely that the federal government should stop trying to prevent individual states from deciding political questions in their own way. This, of course, was an entirely reasonable argument to make; but to characterize it as 'conservative' was a polemical ruse which presumably owed much to the Cold War context and cannot be sustained even after a cursory review of the evidence. It is difficult to see how (or why) someone should be accepted as 'conservative' in a distinctively ideological sense because he or she subscribes to a document which was endorsed two centuries ago by people whose premises clearly derived from the *liberal* tradition.

➔ Stop and Think

After reading the US constitution drawn up in 1787, and reading this chapter, to what extent (if any) do you think that the US constitution reflects distinctively 'conservative' views?

The claim that American 'conservatives' are really liberals searching for a label to distinguish them from their opponents is not new; it was articulated eloquently, for example, by Louis Hartz, who argued that US politics was narrowly bounded within a Lockean liberal consensus (see Chapter 2), and that the country's success derived at least in part from its *avoidance* of the kind of feudal, organic stage of society which had given rise to conservative ideas in Britain (Hartz 1955). The argument is also supported by the testimony of eminent and committed liberals who refused to join the postwar stampede of anti-communists into the 'conservative' stable (see Case Study 3.4), and by the unsuccessful attempt by the political theorist Russell Kirk (1918–94) to import the European, Burkean interpretation of conservatism into the US context.

Kirk's critics characterized his views as anachronistic, and with good reason since the creed he expounded in his 1953 book *The Conservative Mind* bore no more than a distant relationship to the practical politics of the time in either Europe or the USA.

Case Study 3.5 Friedrich von Hayek (1899–1992): 'Why I am not a conservative'

If we want to understand why the subject of conservatism generates so much confusion, we could hardly do better than to consult Friedrich von Hayek's book *The Road to Serfdom* (1944), and take a measure of its impact among individuals who called themselves 'conservatives'. It was widely read and discussed in Britain, despite wartime restrictions on the publishing industry; Margaret Thatcher was among Hayek's enthusiastic audience. In the USA, the impact was even greater.

The popularity of *The Road to Serfdom* is not surprising, since even today it is a stimulating polemic. However, as a professional economist who had never studied history—and who had enough knowledge of totalitarian regimes to regard even a remote approach to their practices with horror—Hayek was never likely to address the prospects facing liberal democracies from a dispassionate perspective. *The Road to Serfdom* duly interprets any evidence of state encroachment on personal (especially economic) liberty as a significant stride towards the acceptance of totalitarian practices, even within states (such as the USA and the UK) whose long-established political cultures were inhospitable to any movement which might present an overt threat to individual freedom. In other words, Hayek's book was merely adding a bit of eloquent verbal ammunition to individuals who were already armed and ready for the defence of 'freedom'.

By 1960, with so many ideological liberals choosing to call themselves 'conservatives' and citing Hayek as their inspiration, the author himself decided to reassert his real position by including a short piece entitled 'Why I am Not a Conservative' in his book *The Constitution of Liberty*. Like so many hostile commentators on conservatism, Hayek presents the conservative approach as a timid, unimaginative (indeed 'unprincipled') attachment to the status quo. However, this clichéd and one-dimensional characterization of the conservative position does not prevent Hayek from making some pertinent points concerning the distance between conservatives and individuals of his own, strongly liberal, viewpoint. For instance, he emphasizes the incompatibility of the premises of so-called American 'conservatives' with the Burkean tradition. While Hayek's 'conservative' admirers on both sides of the Atlantic have focused on his claim that the operations of the free market result in a 'spontaneous' social order, his essay makes clear that this concept arises from the typical liberal view of the 'rational' individual, whose free and self-interested choices miraculously turn out to benefit 'society'. Another fascinating point made by Hayek (almost as an aside) is his claim that 'it seems much easier for the repentant socialist to find a new spiritual home in the conservative fold than in the liberal'. From Hayek's liberal perspective, this means that disillusioned socialists are more likely to embrace conservatism, for a variety of reasons including a more positive view of the state and a shared appreciation that individuals are embedded in a social context rather than autonomous creatures for whom, as Sartre put it, 'Hell is other people'.

Needless to say, Hayek's well-intentioned attempt to dissociate himself from 'conservatives' cut no ice with the liberals who had chosen to don 'conservative' clothing on both sides of the Atlantic. However, when read with due attention, the work of those who try to reclaim him for the 'conservative' cause merely lends weight to his own refusal to consider himself a conservative. In this unusual instance, in short, we have plenty of reasons to accept an individual's testament to ideological allegiance at face value.

> **⟳ Stop and Think**
>
> On what grounds is it permissible to challenge the testimony of a politician or author who claims
> to belong to a specific ideological tradition?

Conservatism and religion

According to some authorities, conservatism is inseparable from religion, and many conservatives, in Europe and elsewhere, have cited a religious inspiration for their ideas. Edmund Burke, for example, insisted that 'religion is the basis of civil society, and the source of all good and of all comfort' (Mitchell 1989: 141). In 1947 Quintin Hogg (a Conservative Party MP and later, as Lord Hailsham, a long-serving senior minister) claimed that 'There can be no genuine [c]onservatism which is not founded upon a religious view of the basis of civil obligation' (Hogg 1947: 16).

The link between religious views of various kinds and the interpretation of conservatism presented in this chapter is obvious: for example, a belief that the material world is transient and radically imperfect is likely to fuel strong political opposition to any scheme (whether radical or not) derived from an optimistic take on the human condition. However, there are many pious people who are anything but conservative, dreaming of the establishment of a Kingdom of Heaven on earth; and some notorious unbelievers (like the sceptical Scottish philosopher David Hume, 1711–76) can only be denied a berth in the conservative pantheon by people who regard religious faith as a *defining characteristic* of conservatism. Indeed, incidents (such as the First World War) which led people to question the existence of a benign deity might also inspire a more sceptical view of human nature. In other words, one can imagine circumstances which make sincere believers *less* religious and *more* conservative.

It can even be suggested that in many cases (like that of Burke) religious faith of a particular kind serves to underpin the confusion which afflicts contemporary 'conservatives'. Some religions (particularly the Protestant variants of Christianity) might suggest a combination of 'robust individualism' in economic matters and fairly inflexible standards in the moral sphere. This seems to be helpful in explaining the apparently contradictory attitudes of many so-called 'conservatives' in the USA.

Outside the Protestant tradition, a distinctively 'conservative' identity is sometimes claimed for Christian democratic parties across Europe (whose religious affiliation is overwhelmingly Catholic), and for the Hindu-dominated Bharatiya Janata Party (BJP) of India. However, the postwar emergence of Christian democracy reflected a (limited) acceptance by the Vatican of liberal ideological hegemony in western Europe; as such, Christian democrats are best understood within the liberal tradition, despite their preference for gradual, rather than radical, change. Meanwhile, despite the very different context, the BJP shows similarities to 'conservative' parties and movements elsewhere: it is 'socially conservative', but in office has presided over neo-liberal economic policies which reflect the potent effects of contemporary 'globalization'. The parallels to Thatcherism in the UK extend to a fairly aggressive brand of nationalism which is difficult to square with the sceptical conservative outlook presented in this chapter.

 Stop and Think

Would it be reasonable to argue that, while religious people are not necessarily conservative in outlook, their faith tends to promote conservatism whereas a more secular approach does not?

Many conservatives see the link between religion and politics in a positive light, citing their various faiths as a major inspiration for their outlook on life in general. Critics, however, have tended to regard the conservative appeal to religion more cynically, seeing it as a means to muster supernatural support for existing regimes. In reality, religious faith has very often been a motivational factor for radicals as well as supporters of the status quo; indeed, there have been numerous cases in which the same *form* of religious belief has served as an inspiration (and/or a pretext) either for radical change or for political passivity (see Chapter 12). The safest conclusion for the student of ideology is to treat understandings of human nature as the ultimate key to ideological identity, whether or not these understandings are related to specific religious views.

Conservatism beyond the Anglo-Saxon context

It would be tempting to argue on this basis that the conservative world view can only be a going concern in states which have contrived to insulate themselves to some extent from the unrelenting, transformative force of the globalized economy. Leaving aside eccentric examples like Bhutan—which itself made the radical decision to exchange 'absolute' for 'constitutional' monarchy in 2008—possible candidates for conservatism could include Cuba and North Korea, which (until recently, in the Cuban case) have tried to isolate themselves from global 'liberal hegemony'. It would be superbly ironic if the sole remaining bastions of conservatism turned out to be the products of postwar revolutions; and during the last years of the Cold War many commentators had no hesitation in describing opponents of change in the Soviet Union itself as 'conservatives'. In reality, though, none of these regimes would have been especially palatable to Edmund Burke.

A more interesting example is the way in which the Chinese state has adapted to globalization, which bears some of the hallmarks of conservatism—especially to the extent that Confucius, rather than Marx, has become the presiding spirit.

Conclusion

In 1995 the philosopher John Gray (a one-time enthusiast for Margaret Thatcher's brand of 'conservatism') argued that 'there is no historical possibility—political or intellectual—of a return to traditional conservatism. Western conservatism every-where, but especially in the USA, is now merely a variety of the Enlightenment pro-ject of universal emancipation and a universal civilisation' (Gray 1995: x). As we have seen, it is largely owing to a terminological accident that scholars have to concern themselves about US 'conservatism' at all. The UK is a better example of the phe-nomenon Gray describes; but even here the survival of 'conservatism' in the political lexicon is largely accidental, arising from the fact that the Conservative *Party* has managed to keep trading under the same name even though it has long since aban-doned its original line of business.

Gray's most effective argument against the Thatcher 'project' was that its pro-motion of decontextualized economic liberalism undermined the necessary foun-dations of a recognizably 'conservative' polity by fostering institutional instabil-ity and social insecurity. Apparent enough before her departure from office in 1990, the impact of Mrs Thatcher's approach continued to be registered even after her death in 2013; the referendum on Scottish independence held the following year showed the extent to which her period in office had endangered the survival of the UK itself, and her supporters were prominent in the campaign to with-draw Britain from the EU. Indeed, Gray argues that Mrs Thatcher's iconoclas-tic approach contrived to endanger the conditions in which liberalism itself can thrive, to the extent that it depends upon *some* elements of social and institutional stability (Gray 1995: 102).

The UK Conservative Party is thus an excellent example of an institution which continues to claim a label associated with stability, despite triggering off unexpected and undesirable effects in those areas where it sought radical change, and unwit-tingly transforming institutions and practices which it wanted to preserve. As such, the results of the Thatcherite episode would be no surprise for the attentive reader of Burke's *Reflections on the French Revolution*. This, however, is unlikely to console Burke's modern-day disciples. Gray's picture of their plight may be slightly over-drawn—in European states and further afield they can continue to adhere to the distinctive conservative world view, and on occasion they might even find individual candidates for office who suit their taste. However, at the level of the nation-state in a globalized economy Gray's pessimism seems justified. On the view presented here, conservatism as a distinctive ideological position (rather than a partisan label purloined by liberals) is of no more than marginal political relevance, and there are no foreseeable circumstances which could lead one to anticipate a significant revival in its fortunes.

Summary

- The nature of conservatism is sharply contested, and academic commentators have tended to add to the confusion.

- Nevertheless, conservatism is a very distinctive ideological position, arising from a sceptical view of human nature.

- This viewpoint informs the characteristic conservative opposition to radical change of any kind, but the main ideological antagonist of conservatism is liberalism, which is based on the view that human beings are inherently *rational*.

- Many contemporary political parties and movements claim to be 'conservative', but in the context of a globalized economy in which radical, undirected change is a constant factor, distinctive conservative ideology has nothing positive to say.

- As a result, although it is perfectly possible for private individuals to retain the conservative world view which remains entirely coherent, their views are of marginal relevance to the conduct of politics in the UK, the USA, and elsewhere.

Review and discussion questions

1. Critically evaluate the contention that conservatism is a body of ideas designed to legitimize economic, social, and political inequality.

2. Comment on the features of this fictional pen-portrait which could lead one to regard the central character as an idealized exemplar of conservatism:

   Sir Harry Hotspur of Humblethwaite was a mighty person in Cumberland, and one who well understood of what nature were the duties, and of what sort the magnificence, which his position as a great English commoner required of him. He had twenty thousand a year derived from land. His forefathers had owned the same property in Cumberland for nearly four centuries, and an estate nearly as large in Durham for more than a century and a half. He had married an earl's daughter, and had always lived among men and women not only of high rank, but also of high character. He had kept race-horses when he was young, as noblemen and gentlemen then did keep them, with no view to profit, calculating fairly their cost as a part of his annual outlay, and thinking that it was the proper thing to do for the improvement of horses and for the amusement of the people. He had been to Parliament, but had made no figure there, and had given it up. He still kept his house in Bruton Street, and always spent a month or two in London. But the life that he led was led at Humblethwaite, and there he was a great man, with a great domain around him—with many tenants, with a world of dependents among whom he spent his wealth freely, saving little, but lavishing nothing that was not his own to lavish—understanding that his enjoyment was to come from the comfort and respect of others, for whose welfare, as he understood it, the good things of this world had been bestowed upon him.

   (Anthony Trollope, *Sir Harry Hotspur of Humblethwaite*, 1871)

3. Critically evaluate the assertion that, of the leading contenders in the 2015 UK general election, the Green Party provided the closest approximation to the account of conservative ideology offered in this chapter.

4. What arguments (both 'for' and 'against') might occur to a conservative in relation to the following policy proposals?

   a) the legalization of same-sex marriage

   b) the relaxation of restrictions (except well-founded fears for national security) on the free movement of peoples across international boundaries

   c) revision of the US constitution to remove any wording which might be construed as granting a 'right' for citizens to possess firearms

   d) continued UK membership of the European Union (EU)

   e) armed intervention in civil conflicts taking place within other nation-states, or action to remove regimes guilty of flagrant violations of human rights

Research exercises

1. The argument of this chapter suggests that, between the later years of the nineteenth century and the interwar period, the Conservative Party ceased to be distinctively 'conservative' and instead adopted a distinctively 'liberal' ideology. Does the *Hansard* record of speeches on key ideological issues by Conservative politicians substantiate this claim, or can you find any evidence of distinctively conservative views in this material? (*Hansard* is available online, at http://www.hansard-archive.parliament.uk.)

2. The chapter claims that political movements of any significance which either claim to be 'conservative' or have that label stuck upon them turn out, on closer inspection, to have much more in common with the liberal tradition. Can you find any evidence to challenge this assertion?

Further reading

The obvious starting point for anyone who is interested in conservative ideology is Edmund Burke's *Reflections on the Revolution in France* (1790: numerous subsequent editions). Burke's book includes detailed discussions of revolutionary events which might now seem obscure, but the magnificence of the writing should encourage enthusiastic students to persevere.

More recently, John Gray's essay 'The Undoing of Conservatism', in his book *Enlightment's Wake* (1995), bears a strong resemblance to the argument in the present chapter, as does Kieron O'Hara's full-length discussion in his excellent book *Conservatism* (2011).

From the US perspective, Russell Kirk's *The Conservative Mind* (1953) represents the most serious attempt to implant the Burkean tradition of thought into an inhospitable climate. Barry

Goldwater's *The Conscience of a Conservative* (1960) presents a sharply contrasting viewpoint; outside academia, at least, Goldwater's polemical account has been far more influential.

At roughly the same time, British writers who were associated to varying degrees with the Conservative Party produced volumes which (inadvertently) shed light on the growing 'liberalization' of the party. Quintin Hogg's *The Case for Conservatism* (1947) is a key text in this respect, since the book combines a pretty clear exposition of distinctive conservative principles with a lengthy discussion of contemporary political issues which betrays unmistakable symptoms of ('new') liberal thinking. While Hogg seems like a conservative trying to adjust himself to a liberal context, Michael Oakeshott is best seen as a liberal masquerading as a 'conservative' in his deliberately opaque and playful essay 'On Being Conservative' (1956, published in *Rationalism in Politics,* 1962). A notable contribution to the debate on the nature of postwar 'conservatism' is Ian Gilmour's *Inside Right* (1977), written when the author was a member of Margaret Thatcher's shadow cabinet. Peppered with 'coded' warnings against Thatcher's brand of 'dogmatic' laissez-faire liberalism, the book is best seen as an impassioned plea for the Conservative Party to retain a more pragmatic form of politics which, in essence, derives from the interventionist (**Keynes/Beveridge**) school of liberalism rather than any distinctive 'conservative' tradition.

However, the real jewel amid this battle for the 'conservative' soul is Lord Coleraine's little-read book *For Conservatives Only* (1970), which is a thinly concealed ideological attack on the party leadership of the time. While it is freely conceded that the leader in 1970, Edward Heath, was a 'new' liberal rather than a conservative, Coleraine's argument is heavily dependent on the work of Friedrich von Hayek, who, as we have seen, hotly denied the allegation that he was a closet conservative.

References

AUCKLAND, LORD (1862), *The Journal and Correspondence of William, Lord Auckland*, Volume III, London: R. Bentley.

BURKE, E. (1986), *Reflections on the Revolution in France*, London: Penguin.

COLERAINE, LORD (1970), *For Conservatives Only*, London: Tom Stacey Ltd.

DANGERFIELD, G. (1935), *The Strange Death of Liberal England,* New York: Harrison Smith and Robert Haas.

DISRAELI, B. (1989), *Coningsby: Or the New Generation*, London: Penguin.

GAMBLE, A. (1903), 'Thatcherism and Conservative Politics', in S. Halland and M. Jacques (eds), *The Politics of Thatcherism*, London: Lawrence & Wishart.

GAMBLE, A. (1988), *The Free Economy and the Strong State: Politics of Thatcherism*, Basingstoke: Palgrave Macmillan.

GILMOUR, I. (1977), *Inside Right: A Study of Conservatism*, London: Hutchinson.

GOLDWATER, B. (1960), *The Conscience of a Conservative*, Shepherdsville, KY: Victor Publishing.

GRAY, J. (1993), *Beyond the New Right: Markets, Government and the Common Environment*, London: Routledge.

GRAY, J. (1995), *Enlightenment's Wake: Politics and Culture at the Close of the Modern Age*, London: Routledge.

HALL, S. AND JACQUES, M. (eds) (1983), *The Politics of Thatcherism*, London: Lawrence & Wishart.

HARTZ, L. (1955), *The Liberal Tradition in America: An Interpretation of American Political Thought since the Revolution*, New York: Harcourt, Brace.

HAYEK, F. VON (1944), *The Road to Serfdom*, London: Routledge.

HAYEK, F. VON (1960), *The Constitution of Liberty*, London: Routledge & Kegan Paul.

HOGG, Q. (1947), *The Case for Conservatism*, West Drayton: Penguin.

HONDERICH, T. (1990), *Conservatism*, London: Hamish Hamilton.

JAY, A. (2012), *Oxford Dictionary of Political Quotations*, Oxford: Oxford University Press.

KIRK, R. (1953), *The Conservative Mind*, Chicago: Henry Regnery.

LEVITAS, R. (ed.) (1986), *The Ideology of the New Right*, Cambridge: Polity.

McDOWELL, R. B. (ed.) (1991), *The Writings and Speeches of Edmund Burke: Vol. IX*, Oxford: Oxford University Press.

MITCHELL, L. G. (ed) (1989), *The Writings and Speeches of Edmund Burke: Vol. VIII*, Oxford: Oxford University Press.

OAKESHOTT, M. (1962), *Rationalism in Politics and Other Essays*, London: Methuen.

O'HARA, K. (2011), *Conservatism*, London: Reaktion.

PAINE, T. (1985), *The Rights of Man*, Harmondsworth: Penguin.

ROWLING, J. K. (2003), *Harry Potter and the Order of the Phoenix*, London: Bloomsbury.

TROLLOPE, A. (1871), *Sir Harry Hotspur of Humblethwaite,* London: Hurst and Blackett.

4

Socialism and communism

John Gregson

OBJECTIVES

- Examine the history of socialism and some of its key theorists and practitioners
- Explain the key concepts and beliefs of socialism and illuminate the socialist understanding of human nature
- Explain and examine the variants of socialism, particularly communism and social democracy
- Examine the overlap between socialism and other ideologies, notably liberalism
- Outline the historical, contemporary, and future impact of socialism

---

Introduction

Of all the 'classical' ideologies, socialism is perhaps the most complex. Socialism's variants are numerous and broad, often strongly opposed to each other on one or more central questions or issues. Variants of socialism have converged with other classical ideologies (such as liberalism) in their beliefs and values, yet other variants have remained vehemently opposed to much within liberalism. These complexities have resulted in rival factions, movements, systems, and values. None more so than in the deep divide seen between communism and social democracy which, certainly at times, have seemed to share little with each other. Yet it is still possible, whilst recognizing these often profound differences, to draw out shared beliefs, critiques, and visions of the good society within the ideology of socialism. After sketching a brief history of socialism, this chapter will attempt to illuminate the central beliefs, values, and assumptions of socialism before discussing their significant variants. It is important to look not only to the past but also to the future, so a discussion of the future prospects for socialism will also be provided.

A history of socialism

Although there were predecessors to socialism, such as the political movements of the **Levellers** and the **Diggers** in the English Civil War, socialism emerged as an ideology and movement in the early nineteenth century. Socialism is perhaps best understood as a specifically modern phenomenon and as a reaction to the perceived injustices and inequalities associated with modern industrial society and capitalism. Key figures in early socialism—what later became known as **utopian socialism**—included the British social reformer and founder of the cooperative movement, Robert Owen, and French thinkers Henri de Saint-Simon and Charles Fourier. Whilst none of these early socialists developed either a thorough analysis of capitalism or even, necessarily, an outright rejection of capitalism, the effects of industrial capitalism on the working class were largely what they were concerned with. Owen, from a prosperous family and a factory manager from an early age, was appalled by the working conditions that were prevalent for the majority of the working classes. He set up a number of community experiments, so everyone could share in the fruits of their labours, where people would live and work together in relatively small groups, avoiding the misery and drudgery of typical work under capitalism. Saint-Simon developed a political ideology known as industrialism, which suggested that the needs of workers must be taken into consideration in order to develop a more effective workplace and society. Saint-Simon was not fundamentally opposed to capitalism, rather he was concerned with reforming it and making it more efficient and beneficial for all. Fourier also believed that a society based on cooperation was necessary to improve productivity and efficiency, along with the key utopian idea that labour should be transformed into pleasure—and pleasure was something which was a far cry from the experiences of the vast majority under capitalism. The early socialists were therefore chiefly concerned with remedying the ill effects of industrial capitalism, often through espousing visions of ideal societies based on community, cooperation, and fairness, whilst addressing the problems of inequality and poverty which were closely associated with capitalism. The label 'utopian' was actually given to them by other socialists who were critical of what they saw as their unrealistic demands and unobtainable goals. Later socialists, such as Marx and Engels, thought that these early socialists lacked any kind of political programme for achieving their goals.

The early socialist ideas of cooperation arguably provided the first coherent sets of beliefs for socialism (Vincent 2009: 90), and were an influence on key figures in the socialist movement that followed, particularly in the work of Karl Marx and his lifelong collaborator, Friedrich Engels. Published in 1848, on the eve of the revolutions that swept through Europe, Marx and Engels' *Communist Manifesto* asserted that 'A spectre is haunting Europe—the spectre of Communism', and provided an analysis of society which proclaimed that 'the history of all hitherto existing society is the history of class struggles' (Marx and Engels 2002: xviii, xix). The *Communist Manifesto* embodied a number of key differences from the earlier utopian socialists and represented, so Engels would claim, a move from utopian to **scientific socialism**.

From a Marxist perspective, an important difference between utopian and scientific socialism was that the former was simply a reflection of personal opinions and ideas about what society should be like. In contrast to this, scientific socialism claimed to be based on an analysis of history and social conditions, having a 'scientific' knowledge of its developments and the causes of societal change. This was what became known as **historical materialism**. The key distinction that therefore emerged between the utopian socialists and the scientific socialists such as Marx and Engels was not so much about what was wrong with society but how it would be possible to change it. This would form a question that was to remain central to socialist ideology and practice throughout the nineteenth and twentieth centuries—reform or revolution? Using this new scientific method Marx predicted that capitalism would be replaced by communism through a revolutionary struggle by the agency of change in society—the working class. Capitalism could only be abolished by these 'gravediggers' in a revolutionary struggle that would see the overthrow of the ruling class, the **bourgeoisie**.

Following the bourgeois revolutions of 1848 that swept through Europe, with demands for democracy, workers' rights, and other freedoms, the eventual failure of these revolutions and the reestablishment of the old order signalled a period of relative calm and a decrease in the influence of socialism. In 1864, however, the establishment of the **International Workingmen's Association**, with its millions of members and attempt to unify the radical left, saw an upsurge in the support for socialism (although the organization itself split largely due to political and organizational differences between Marxists and anarchists—see Chapter 5). The **Second International** (1889–1916) formed as an organization of socialist and labour parties that campaigned for workers' rights and whose members included Vladimir Lenin. This organization was also not to last as it eventually rejected international socialism in favour of nationalism, with many of its members supporting their respective governments in the First World War (1914–18). However, if this was seen as a failure, it did at least lay the foundations for possibly the most significant event of the twentieth century, the **Russian Revolution**.

Marx and Engels had predicted that revolutions were most likely to occur in the advanced Western countries with a large working class. Yet it was in the much more backward Russia, first in 1905, and then much more significantly in 1917, that revolution first occurred. The (communist) **Bolsheviks** swept to power, defeating all other socialists and counter-revolutionaries internally, as well as the external opposition led by Western countries. Led by Vladimir Lenin, leader of the Bolsheviks, the revolution of 1917 signalled the beginning of the great rise of communism in the twentieth century and one of the most significant movements in modern history (see also the discussion of the 'short twentieth century' in Chapter 8). The Union of Soviet Socialist Republics (USSR), established in 1922 and based on the doctrine of **Marxism–Leninism**, lasted nearly seventy years, covered vast swathes of territory, played a pivotal role in the outcome of the Second World War, and contributed significantly to a Cold War with the West that brought the world to the brink of nuclear war.

Yet there was more to socialism than just being revolutionary. Social democracy provided a reformist understanding of socialism that aimed to work within the parameters of capitalism and parliamentary democracy. Whilst Eastern Europe was under the grip of communism, many Western nations developed a form of socialism that espoused socialist principles combined with democracy and a reformist approach. Social democracy's focus on welfare, social justice, and redistribution of wealth had success in places as diverse as India, Israel, Mexico, West Germany, and most of Scandinavia, as well as in the UK with the Labour Party. By the middle of the twentieth century, socialism, in either its revolutionary or reformist variant, was undoubtedly a hugely significant political and ideological force. Yet if socialism had seemingly reached its zenith, the latter decades of the twentieth century saw the gradual erosion of social democracy through the growth of more neo-liberal, individualist governments that were actively hostile to socialism. Ronald Reagan in the USA and Margaret Thatcher in the UK kick-started a trend that pushed socialism off the political agenda for many previously social-democratic countries in the West (and beyond) and the influence of neo-liberalism continues, seemingly unabated, today. As for communism, the collapse of the Soviet Union in 1989, and the demise of communist regimes in the rest of Eastern Europe shortly after, seemed to signal the end for communism as a political movement and the influence of Marxism more generally (see Chapter 13).

What is socialism?—critique, vision, and strategy

Critique of industrial capitalism

The early 'Utopian' socialists as well as the 'scientific' socialists such as Marx and Engels were appalled by the living and working conditions of the working classes in industrialized western Europe. Engels wrote passionately about the 'starving workmen' of northern England and about the 'excessive mortality', the 'progressive deterioration' in physique, and the 'unbroken series of epidemics' that were their fate (Engels 2009: 121, 129). Socialism was, from the very start, rooted in its critique of industrial capitalism and focused squarely on improving the conditions of the working class. John Dunn has argued that socialism's greatest achievement was its 'understanding of the intrinsic defects of a capitalist mode of production' (Dunn 1984: 37). Most socialists would agree that capitalism, unchecked, creates vast inequalities of wealth as well as unacceptable conditions for many in society. Socialism aims to mitigate these effects through the redistribution of wealth, trade unions, or the creation of institutions of welfare designed to reduce inequality or improve working and life conditions. The British socialist G. D. H. Cole in the early twentieth century argued:

> The crowning indictment of capitalism is that it destroys freedom and individuality in the worker, that it reduces man to a machine, and that it treats human beings as means to production instead of subordinating production to the well-being of the producer.
>
> (Cole in Masquelier and Dawson 2016: 9–10).

The socialist understanding of capitalism is that it restricts the life chances of the majority and subjects them to mind-numbing and repetitive labour. Some people at the top can do very well out of this economic system, yet there is little opportunity for the majority to flourish. The good society would be one where no individual was trapped within such restrictive and dehumanizing work and the labour process instead would be stimulating and creative. In the 'plain Marxian argument' (Cohen 1988: 228), Marxists argue that the relationship between the two main classes within capitalism is one where the ruling class dominate society and exploit the working class systematically in the labour process. Exploitation, in this sense, simply means that the working class do not receive the full value of their labour as a portion of it is expropriated by the bourgeoisie.

Vision of the good society

Capitalism tends to be regarded by socialists as being an exploitative economic system—one that either needs to be controlled and made fairer through reforms and redistribution, or needs to be abolished and replaced with a non-exploitative, class-less system such as communism. These two alternatives represent one of the key differences between social democracy and communism. The former aims to work within the parameters of the capitalist system whilst the latter argues that capitalism itself must be abolished and replaced with the good society. In echoing Marx's rather unsubstantiated vision of what this good society might look like, Booth argues that the 'shape of the future can best be seen in the criticism, the exposure of the faults, of the present' (Booth 1989: 207). For Marxists, the good society would amount to an inversion of capitalism—non-exploitative, classless, and based on communal ownership of the means of production. For other socialists, the good society might broadly be one that only reduces the ill effects of capitalism such as inequality, poverty, or lack of opportunity.

Strategy—reform or revolution?

One of the key debates within socialism is closely related to this vision of the good society—the question of reform or revolution. It is this issue of conflict that fundamentally distinguishes revolutionary socialists, or communists, from other socialists (Stanckiewicz 1993: 132). Revolutionary socialists argue that revolution is fundamental to achieving the socialist vision of a good society. It is necessary because the capitalist class would not give up their position of class dominance willingly, nor would they allow the kind of radical reforms that socialism deems necessary to bring into fruition their vision of a good society. From this perspective, reformist socialism, such as contemporary social democracy, is doomed in trying to implement the good society within the parameters of capitalism—genuine socialism is simply not possible within capitalism. Alternatively, reformist socialists argue that any kind of violent revolution is both undesirable and unnecessary. Violence and conflict contradict socialist ideas about community and fraternity and cannot be justified in any transition towards socialism (Geoghegan 1984). Indeed, it can be argued that revolution can provide and has provided the foundations for authoritarian and oppressive states. Furthermore, reformist socialists argue that socialism can be achieved peacefully through constitutional means and the institutions of liberal democracy.

The core concepts and beliefs of socialism

As with many ideologies, the vast number of variants and strands within socialism make it difficult—though not impossible—to identify concepts or values that are fundamental to all forms of socialism. Values which might once have been intrinsic to socialism have been jettisoned by one variant or another. Nineteenth-century revolutionary socialism would have seen a classless society as a key aim of socialism, yet late twentieth-century socialism might not even see the concept of class itself as important any more. Similarly, the whole idea of conflict would be integral to revolutionary forms of socialism yet this would be actively opposed by more moderate, reformist perspectives. Some go so far as to argue that 'there is no such thing as socialism, rather there are socialisms, which overlap with other ideologies' (Vincent 2009: 90) and there is clearly logic here. Whilst the interpretation and practical meaning of certain concepts and values within socialist ideology remain contested, these concepts nevertheless remain central to all forms of socialism.

Human nature

At the basis of most political ideologies is a view as to what human beings are like, should be like, or could be like. Socialism is no different. There are several interrelated features of the socialist view of human nature that set it apart from both liberalism and conservatism. First, in opposition to the egoistic, individualistic view of human beings characteristic of liberalism (e.g. see 'classical liberalism' and the self-interest involved in the idea of the 'social contract' in Chapter 2), socialism conceptualizes human beings as fundamentally social in their nature. Human beings can only be properly understood when they are recognized as being essentially constituted through their relations with others—as part of a society. Karl Marx ridiculed the essentially liberal idea of man abstracted from his social relations by, in reference to Robinson Crusoe, calling its proponents 'Robinsades' for conceptualizing human beings as solitary and individualistic beings (Marx in Tucker 1978: 222). What liberalism had done was to generalize the atomized, bourgeois view of human nature, characteristic of life under capitalism, into a view of human nature in all forms of society. This is the second, related feature of the socialist view of human nature—the belief that human nature is not purely static but that aspects of it can and do change from society to society. This gives socialism a uniquely optimistic edge, in that it can characterize what many see as the negative aspects of human nature under capitalism (self-interest, greed, and such like, the 'nasty, brutish, and short' existence characterized by Hobbes) as being characteristic only of a particular type of society and not necessarily all societies.

An obvious potential problem with this view of human nature is that such optimistic assertions of our social nature are themselves 'largely untested' (Freeden 1996: 419). Socialism developed within capitalist society, and since we have not moved beyond capitalism in the 200 years or so of socialist thought, the claim that capitalism provides an essentially distorted development of human nature is conjecture. Whilst, as a species, we have some knowledge of pre-capitalist societies, it is highly debatable whether this can offer any kind of accurate picture of a post-capitalist society. Similarly, whilst there are communal relationships within capitalist society, it is hard to say how much such relationships are influenced and shaped by the capitalist system. This means that socialist ideology displays a 'massive leap of faith' to claim that what has never been is intrinsic to human beings (Freeden 1996: 419).

Socialists do not believe that *all* aspects of human nature are changeable. As we saw, there is a debate as to whether or not socialism is too optimistic in its assertions about human nature being changeable. Yet what remains constant to the socialist view of human nature is the belief that human beings are inherently social in nature or essence. Socialists maintain that this social nature is integral, indeed essential to human beings, and this is integral to the foundations of socialist ideology. The socialist emphasis on the social nature of human beings provides the basis for other values of socialism, such as those of community and cooperation. These values are therefore regarded as the ideals of socialism, not simply because they are abstractly appealing, but because they are based on real human needs and desires. As Kain succinctly puts it: 'since need indicates essence, the fact that human's need each other indicates that their essence is social' (Kain 1991: 55).

Another important aspect of the socialist view of human nature links closely with the socialist critique of capitalism—in particular the nature of labour under capitalism. Certainly, not all socialists would agree with Marx's view that creative labour is integral to human beings, yet socialists would agree that the often dehumanizing, repetitive, and spirit-crushing nature of work for many under capitalism means that humans cannot fully develop their potential. Capitalism has brought with it the **division of labour** in the quest for efficiency and profit. The effects of such menial tasks on the worker are such that they are unable to develop to their full mental capacities and their potential is left unrealized. Socialism therefore provides a critique of capitalism based on the assertion that humans could develop their capacities much better within an economic system that did not permanently consign the majority within the labour process to boredom and dehumanizing tasks.

The socialist view of human nature as both social and partially changeable allows for expansive possibilities with regards to social and political change. Accusations of utopianism can be levelled at socialism, as critics might argue that an overly-optimistic view of human nature means that socialism tends to set itself unrealistic political and social goals. The idea of a cooperative, community-based society, free from self-interest, would be viewed by both liberals and conservatives as certainly unrealistic if not dangerous. For if the socialist vision of utopia was not going to plan then the temptation might be for political leaders to force the issue, and in doing so commit all manner of unsavoury acts in the name of the greater good. Historically, one might look to the Soviet Union as a key example of this. In this view, socialism may be a nice idea but its implementation is unworkable and the means used to try to bring socialism into fruition are far worse than those of the current society that they are trying to improve upon.

 Stop and Think

Consider this quote from Robert Owen:

> By my own experience and reflection I had ascertained that human nature is radically good and is capable of being trained, educated and placed from birth in such manner that all ultimately (that is as soon as the gross errors and corruptions of the present false and wicked system are overcome and destroyed) must become united, good, wise, wealthy and happy. (Podmore 2013)

Robert Owen believed that human nature was changeable and, ultimately, could be 'good' and 'wise'. What do you think of this view of human nature? (Compare rival views of human nature that emphasize the individualistic, self-interested nature of human beings).

Equality

It is important to recognize that the concept of equality cannot be applied as an all-encompassing value that socialists advocate regardless of context and circumstances. Equality, from a socialist perspective, is not even understood as a desirable goal in some circumstances, as to treat people in an objectively equal way has the practical result of treating them unequally. Socialists might argue that one person's needs may be greater than another's—perhaps they have more children or a disability and therefore they require more resources than another childless or more able-bodied person. If these differences were not taken into account, then society would become less equal. Karl Marx argued that a communist society would be characterized by the slogan 'From each according to his ability, to each according to his needs!' This recognized both the inherent inequalities in peoples' abilities and also the differential needs that characterized society. What Marx was getting at was the idea that a Communist society would not, contrary to what many critics argue of Marxism, treat everybody the same, but recognize that the differences between people necessitated a rejection of absolute equality; as Terry Eagleton argues: 'Genuine equality means not treating everyone the same, but attending equally to everyone's different needs' (Eagleton 2011: 104).

Certain types of socialism might embrace different types of equality from others, yet all socialists would surely reject the current levels of inequality prevalent on a global scale. Capitalism is an undeniably revolutionary, progressive, and expansive economic system that has developed the world beyond recognition in just a few hundred years—Marx and Engels were quick to recognize this in the *Communist Manifesto*. Yet socialists, in contrast with the often celebratory tone of liberals, were also quick to recognize the injustices capitalism created—the vast inequalities between rich and poor and the terrible conditions for the majority it created. These problems have not gone away and equality remains central to socialism. The more radical the type of socialism is dictates the strength and form of the type of equality that is espoused. Revolutionary socialism argues for the necessity of revolution to end the inequality stemming from private property, profit, and the exploitation of labour. Social democrats might argue for a redistribution of wealth through a progressive tax system, whilst maintaining the current relations of ownership and rejecting a more radical conception of economic equality.

For socialists, equality also extends to how the individual is viewed or treated in society both by the state and by other members of that society. Indeed, it is equality in this sense that is less controversial within socialist ideology as it is difficult to imagine any form of socialism rejecting this view. Socialists tend to believe that every individual, whilst they could be very different in many ways, is of equal moral worth (a type of equality shared with liberalism) and therefore reject racism, sexism, and a conservative belief in a natural hierarchy. Many socialists would not reject the importance of universal suffrage and rights (although Marxists might argue these do not go far enough), yet socialists would differ from liberals in that equality would be framed not just in political terms, but also in economic terms.

Perhaps the clearest dividing line between socialists and liberals can be understood in terms of two types of equality—equality of opportunity and equality of outcome. Liberals and socialists would both embrace an equality of opportunity that would not discriminate against any individual or deny that individual the potential to acquire societal resources based on their ethnicity or gender for example (see discussion of liberal feminism and socialist feminism in Chapter 9).

However, adherence to a more substantive equality of opportunity, that recognizes the inequalities associated with wealth for example, can separate liberals from socialists. Socialists argue such privileges are unfair, advocating, perhaps, a redistributive tax system that alleviates some of these advantages in the first place. The idea here is to give everyone a more equal starting point and to mitigate the advantages enjoyed by the wealthy and privileged. The socialist goal is to increase social mobility so that the better jobs and higher incomes are not just the preserve of those from wealthy backgrounds. Liberals might argue that equality should be restricted to the removal of any arbitrary barriers that might have restricted such opportunity, yet economic factors do not fall within these boundaries and economic inequality is broadly acceptable. Other liberals might agree with the more substantive form of equality of opportunity, recognizing that greater disparities of wealth and privilege are unfair and need to be mitigated (see the discussion of equality of opportunity in the subsection 'Social liberalism' in Chapter 2).

Even if socialism dovetails with certain forms of liberalism regarding equality of opportunity, the idea of equality of outcome might serve to highlight more clearly the differences between them. Common to all forms of socialism is the belief that greater equality of outcome is necessary and desirable. Within capitalist society, social democrats recognize the gross inequalities created by capitalism and strive for a reduction in such inequality through redistributive taxation and a system of universal public services and social care. On a global level, no socialist would endorse a system where the world's eighty richest billionaires own assets equal to those of the bottom 50 per cent of the world's population (http://www.bbc.co.uk/news/business-30875633). Socialists therefore tend to believe that a more equal society is a more moral one. Liberals might agree with socialists on one level—perhaps that no human being should have to live in poverty. Yet, once poverty has been alleviated, inequality of *outcome* is not necessarily a bad thing from the perspective of liberalism. Liberals might argue that inequality is necessary, that large financial incentives encourage high achievement and contribute positively to society. Furthermore, equality of outcome is representative of an unwarranted level of state interference and contradicts the key liberal value of freedom. Socialism emphasizes that a greater equality of outcome is something that needs to be fought for in the context of the inequalities created by capitalism—although even the more radical forms of socialism have never advocated absolute equality.

Community

Stemming closely from its conception of human nature, socialism places paramount importance on both the necessity and desirability of some form of community— defined, perhaps most accurately, as a system of mutual care and cooperation. Socialists believe that humans are social animals and therefore the ideal form of social organization is one that emphasizes community and cooperation. This gives the emphasis on community both an explanatory and a normative element as it is based on assertions about what human beings are essentially like and goes on to suggest that this informs how life should be organized. Marx argues, in his early writings, that community is not simply something that human beings desire, it is integral to our human nature or 'essence' (Marx 2000: 8). Not all socialists would go this far, yet many, if not all, strands of socialism maintain a moral commitment to community and tend to resist those aspects of social life which threaten to destroy or damage such communal bonds.

Since its beginnings in the nineteenth century, socialists have railed against the isolation, marginalization, and individualized nature of life under capitalism. The importance of community, and the critique of capitalism, manifests itself practically in organizations such as trade unions. These can be seen to represent key socialist ideas such as cooperation and collectivism, centred on the belief that working conditions and pay are best improved and protected through common and collective action. Furthermore, each and every member of the organization is protected by the others, thus shunning isolationism and individualism in favour of communal bonds. Whilst liberals seem to celebrate the 'freedom' of the individual under capitalism, socialists lament the destruction of communal bonds and the rejection of cooperation in favour of competition. Socialists argue that a key problem with liberalism is its focus on the individual outside of any form of social relations. The failure of liberalism to place import on the social essence of man lays the foundation for a political ideology that—falsely—emphasizes and celebrates the individual and competitive nature of human beings. In essence, socialists would argue that liberalism fails to understand itself. Liberalism is regarded as a product of the emerging capitalist system—even the ideology of capitalism—and conceptualizes human beings, not as they are naturally, but as how they are, and indeed need to be, under capitalism.

 Stop and Think

Marx criticized liberalism for its 'Robinson Crusoe'-like view of human beings and human nature. What did Marx mean by this?

Freedom

Freedom is not a distinctly socialist concept or value. Indeed, freedom is most commonly recognized as a cornerstone of liberal ideology and, furthermore, critics argue that—at least in practice—socialism is actually the enemy of freedom. Stalin's Soviet Union or North Korea today would not be classified as 'free' except by the most dogmatic of their supporters. Socialists would respond here by arguing that these regimes had little or nothing to do with socialism—except in name—as their values and political practice share nothing with genuine socialism. The restriction of freedom in certain forms of practice does not preclude the fact that freedom remains central to socialist ideology and perhaps even at a deeper, more fundamental level than within liberalism.

Common to much socialist thought—particularly Marxism—is the assertion that freedom is not only something which human beings strive for, but it is a specifically human initiative that helps to define us as human beings. The pursuit of freedom is represented by concepts such as desire, intention, and choice, which only human beings are in possession of (MacIntyre 1960: 124). Freedom is not some abstract concept, but rather it is a 'historical activity' (Kosik 1976: 147) that constitutes a fundamental desire for human beings. It is therefore an essential aspect of mankind (part of our 'essence' or nature in the literal sense). The concept of freedom is closely linked with labour and the labour process because socialists—particularly Marxists—argue that labour (in the broad sense of creative and productive human activity) is a fundamental part of what makes us human beings—it is our human nature. This is an important claim made within socialist ideology. Some theorists, such as Freeden, argue that this view that work is the 'fundamental constitutive' (Freeden 2003: 82) aspect of human nature is one of socialism's core values. This is because Marx understood freedom, not as freedom *from* labour, but freedom *within* labour. Labour, when it is creative and productive, is freedom (Gould 1978: 102). It is this type of freedom that is clearly restricted for the majority within capitalism. It is logical, then, that socialists tend to advocate what might be understood as a more 'positive' form of freedom, rather than the 'negative' form of freedom espoused by liberalism. These two concepts are most closely associated with the work of British liberal philosopher Isaiah Berlin in his 1958 work, 'Two Concepts of Liberty', but can also be traced back further within the socialist tradition to Erich Fromm's 1941 work *The Fear of Freedom* as well as having roots in the work of the great nineteenth-century philosopher Hegel (see also Chapter 2 for discussion of Berlin's 'Two Concepts of Liberty'). Whilst negative freedom is primarily concerned with freedom from something—restraints, state interference, persecution, etc.—positive freedom is freedom to develop, to flourish, and to live a satisfying and fulfilling life. Freedom, from this perspective, is positive in the sense that it is not passive—it is concerned with providing members of a society with the ability to develop themselves and fulfil their own potential. Positive freedom extends to the belief that genuine freedom can only be achieved when an individual is able to actively partake in the democratic process as a citizen and an active member of the state or community. For socialists, this type of freedom might include a focus on economic freedom, in terms of a redistribution of wealth or resources, perhaps through taxation, to ensure that all members of a society can enjoy a certain standard of life. This type of freedom is not necessarily specific to socialism, also being found within social liberalism—in the philosophy of John Rawls or the economics of John Maynard Keynes, for example (see Chapter 2;

also referred to in Chapter 3 as 'new' liberalism). For communists, however, freedom might extend further to the view that genuine freedom can only be achieved within a classless society, where capitalism itself has been superseded by communism.

The liberal and the socialist conceptions of freedom are not always complementary; it is not necessarily simply a matter of accepting the liberal idea of negative liberty and extending it with a broader conception of positive liberty. From a liberal perspective, a more positive notion of freedom can actually restrict rather than extend freedom. Many liberal thinkers have suggested that there is a danger with positive freedom— and certainly as applied to socialist ideals of freedom more specifically—in that in practice it tends to restrict freedom through becoming oppressive and authoritarian. This is because, in the pursuit of positive liberty, the coercive methods used to gain such liberty can trample over the protections offered to the individual by negative liberty. Berlin was writing at the height of the Cold War, and it was not difficult to see authoritarian regimes that were doing just that. Alternatively, for socialists, the narrow, liberal conception of freedom is not real freedom at all as it does not guarantee economic freedom, fulfilment, choice, agency, or societal participation.

 Stop and Think

Consider these quotes from Isaiah Berlin:

'Everything is what it is: liberty is liberty, not equality or fairness or justice or culture, or human happiness or a quiet conscience.' (Berlin 1969: 4)

'But to manipulate men, to propel them towards goals which you—the social reformer—see, but they may not, is to deny their human essence, to treat them as objects without wills of their own, and therefore to degrade them.' (Berlin 1969: 11)

The above quotes are from Berlin's famous discussion of positive and negative liberty. How can one form of liberty contradict another? Think of some examples of how negative liberty (freedom from) could be damaged by positive liberty.

Variants of socialism

Communism

It has been argued that during the nineteenth century there was no clear distinction between communism and social democracy, yet by the twentieth century there were certainly fundamental differences between the two (Newman 2005). Communism can be understood as part of the tradition of revolutionary socialism and the most significant starting point can be traced back to Marx and Engels' *Communist Manifesto*. These ideas have come to be known as Marxism and are so closely linked to the concept of communism that some have argued that Marxism is the theory and communism is the practice (Eatwell and Wright 1999: 104, 116). It is hard for many political commentators to even discuss communism without descending into moral indignation or political caricature. Nevertheless, there are certain commonalities that can be brought together under the still relatively broad banner of communism.

One of these would be how communism tends to view the role of the state. Communist societies often feature a high level of control by the state, such as state ownership or control over the means of production, or even intellectual or ideological control through ownership or censorship of the media. The state, in Stalin's Russia, became monolithic and hugely bureaucratic and, in some ways, conservative (Freeden 2003: 91)—its whole point being to conserve the status quo and maintain the regime at all costs. It could be argued that communism refers to the institutionalization of Marxism (Eatwell and Wright 1999: 104, 166). Yet Engels' (and Marx and Lenin's) conception of the state was theoretically very different to this. Engels argued that with the coming of socialism the state is not 'abolished', it withers away. There seems to be a huge gap here between the theory of communism and the practice of communism. Engels seems to be suggesting that far from growing in power and size, a communist state would shrink, becoming no more than a tool of administration. This has led many commentators to question whether or not, in practice, a communist society can be genuinely implemented.

Communism undoubtedly posits the most radical form of equality within socialism in that genuine equality can only be achieved within a society where all class divisions have been abolished. Marx understood class as being defined by your position in relation to the means of production—essentially if you owned the means of production you were a member of the ruling class whilst the vast majority, who had to sell their labour power to survive, were part of the working class. On this definition, a classless society had never actually existed since primitive hunter-gatherer societies; it was only with the vast wealth and ever-expanding technological breakthroughs that capitalism created that it had finally become possible for a classless society to come into existence. Yet only a small minority of socialists would now argue that a classless society is both possible and desirable, and this relates to perhaps the biggest internal question of socialism—reform or revolution?

 Stop and Think

Is Marx's idea of two key classes in capitalism still relevant today?

Since the beginnings of socialism, the question that has separated socialists is how best to achieve its aims. Should socialism be brought about through gradual reform and working within the confines of the current parliamentary system? Or can only a radical overhaul of society bring about any genuine social change? It is the latter position that distinguishes communism from other forms of socialism. Social democrats tend to accept that it is both desirable and realistic to aim to implement socialist values within the confines of the capitalist system. Communism distinguishes itself from other forms of socialism through the way it views society as being irreconcilably in conflict between the two main classes of capitalism. This means that communists tend to believe that socialism cannot be implemented peaceably, or through reform, as the capitalist class will necessarily oppose the implementation of a system that runs directly counter to its own interests (see Case Study 4.1). In order to bring about real, meaningful social change, a working class revolution was necessary that would suppress the capitalist class and bring about a new phase of human society—communism.

Case Study 4.1 Allende's Chile: The possibility of communism in a capitalist world

In Chile in 1973, Salvador Allende became the first democratically elected Marxist President of any Latin American country. On 11 September 1973, Allende was overthrown in a military coup, resulting in the rise to power of General Augusto Pinochet, ushering in a period of seventeen years of dictatorship before democracy was finally restored. Pinochet was notorious for his political repression, human rights abuses, as well as being a close ally of British Prime Minister Margaret Thatcher. Most interestingly in the case of Chile was the reaction to Allende's election from the West, particularly from the USA, bringing into focus the difficulties faced by radical socialist regimes in the modern world. There is some debate on the issue, yet the CIA has been implicated as being directly involved in the overthrow of Allende. What is not in doubt is that the USA, wary of the spread of communism, at the very least, helped to create the conditions for the coup, through economic and political pressure and sanctions, and actively supporting and encouraging the coup. Once Pinochet's dictatorship was in place, a group of Chilean economists, known as the 'Chicago Boys' because they studied neo-liberal economics at Chicago University, implemented aggressive neo-liberal policies of free market deregulation and privatization, thus immediately stamping out the socialism that had threatened to take hold in Chile. Whilst more recent American Presidents and officials have admitted this was 'not something they were proud of', President Obama stopped short of apologizing, saying that people needed to learn from the past but move on to the future.

The case of Allende's Chile brings into sharp focus the kinds of problems envisaged by the likes of Marx and Trotsky in implementing a socialist society within the confines of a capitalist world. In opposition to the Stalinist idea of 'socialism in one country', Trotsky argued that socialism could not sustain itself in isolation, surrounded by capitalist states, unless other countries quickly followed with socialist revolutions. And although the situation in Chile was different in that this was a democratically elected government, the world context was strikingly similar, with the key capitalist powers ensuring that what they regarded as a threat to their interests—communism—could not take hold in Latin America.

⤴ Stop and Think

1. Does the case of Chile suggest that the only genuinely implementable form of socialism is a moderate one?

2. Why might socialism (particularly in its Marxist form) be seen as such a threat by world powers such as America?

Some theorists have argued that it is only after we add Lenin to Marx that we get communism (Reija 1994: 82). The Russian revolutionary and head of the Soviet Union from 1917 until his death in 1924, Vladimir Lenin, developed Marx's theory of proletarian revolution by arguing that a successful revolution must be led by an organized, 'vanguard' party, consisting of the most politically advanced and class-conscious sections of the working class. This vanguard party in Russia took the form of the Bolshevik Party and provided the organization and the political leadership necessary to defeat the counter-revolutionaries in Russia. Revolution, as Marx had also argued, must come from 'below', from the working classes, as not only were they the only genuinely revolutionary class that could succeed, but the process of revolutionary activity itself would make them 'fit' to rule. Many critics have argued that Leninism amounts to an undemocratic and elitist, theoretically rigid, organizational form (MacIntyre 2010: 177) where a small number of revolutionaries control the masses from above. This view traces a direct line from Marxism to Leninism and finally to Stalinism. Others, though, argue that revolution from below is integral to Marxism and particularly Leninism, as the party should be understood as being the organization through which genuine democracy and peoples' power could best be expressed and realized (Rabinowitch 2007: 4).

Whatever the merits or otherwise of communism and Leninism, most would agree that, to a large extent, they have been buried by their own history. Numerous regimes, from Stalin's Russia to Mao's China, the **Khmer Rouge** in Cambodia to North Korea, have claimed allegiance to communism but have committed terrible atrocities in its name. Freedom, democracy, equality, and other socialist values have all been discarded in the name of the greater good. It is a pressing question as to whether such distortions of communism amount to just that, distortions, or whether they mean that communism simply does not and cannot work.

The 'new' communism

In recent years, there has been an attempt to rediscover or 'rescue' the idea of communism from its association with the Soviet Union. High-profile academics such as Slavoj Zizek, Alain Badiou, Jodi Dean, and Gianni Vattimo—sometimes collectively called the 'new' communists—have attempted to outline a much more positive notion of communism, free from its associations with such authoritarian regimes. The dominant tendency, they argue, is to dismiss communism from any discussion of serious alternatives to neo-liberal capitalism and this only serves to strengthen the neo-liberal consensus. All these theorists argue that the pressing problems of capitalism, such as inequality, financial and ecological turmoil, and political mistrust, need a revolutionary solution such as communism. Vattimo and Zabala have identified the strengthening, not weakening, of neo-liberal political and military agendas post 9/11 and the 2008 financial crisis (see Case Study 4.2) and, dishearteningly, the subsequent 'lack of emergency that reigns over the world now' (Vattimo and Zabala 2011: 7) in trying to find an alternative to neo-liberalism. New communists argue that it is communism, free from its association with oppressive regimes, which can provide such an alternative.

There are significant disagreements and debates amongst such new communists—one label cannot apply easily to all. Zizek and Dean, for example, argue for the continued necessity of the organizational, Leninist form of the party in developing such an alternative, without which we have a 'politics without politics' and no means with which to achieve communism (Dean 2012: 19). Alternatively, Hardt and Negri and Badiou see such forms of political organization as defunct and look to new forms of organization more suited to the modern world. Perhaps the key question from a communist—and indeed a more broadly socialist—perspective is whether such ideas can become entwined with more mainstream politics and the broader public consciousness, or whether they remain in the realms of academia.

 Stop and Think

Has the history of communism proven that it is unworkable?

Social democracy

The other great tradition within socialism falls under the broad banner of social democracy. Modern social democracy has become strongly associated with reformist socialism (Vincent 2009: 87). Reformism indicates where a key difference lies between the two major variants of socialism. As Gerassimos Moschonas points out (Moschonas in Lavelle 2008: 7), all modern social democrats are reformist so this must be regarded as a fundamental characteristic of social democracy. Whilst revolutionary socialism advocates the necessity of revolution (this can be either a violent overthrow or a more peaceful, but still radical, transformation), social democrats believe either that socialism can be brought about through peaceful methods or that there can be some kind of middle ground between capitalism and socialism. This latter belief has become dominant within the vast majority of social democratic thought. This initially leads to a sharp division between revolutionary socialism and social democracy regarding the nature and role of the state. Marxists tend to regard the state as being a specifically capitalist state, serving only the interests of capital. From this perspective, the state can play no part in building a socialist society and must be dismantled or smashed in order for socialism to take hold. The social democratic view is very different in that it regards the state as being able to be used as a vehicle for social reform. The creation of the welfare state is testament to the social democratic belief that the state can be and has been used to put into practice socialist values and beliefs (see also Chapter 8). The broader social democratic view that can be developed from this is that capitalism itself can be made more humane and more socialistic; therefore social democrats aim to work within the parameters of the capitalist system. This includes, as the name suggests, a commitment to liberal democracy and a desire to strengthen and extend democracy, and the use of constitutional means to achieve socialism or find a middle ground between capitalism and socialism. Indeed, it has been argued that social democrats, particularly within the Labour Party, came to regard capitalism and socialism as no longer fundamentally distinct from each other, as the former had been reformed beyond recognition from earlier, nineteenth-century industrial capitalism (see Geoghegan 1984: 88).

With the acceptance of the parameters of capitalism, there comes from social democracy a rejection of the revolutionary socialist notion of class conflict and the ultimate aim of a classless, communist society. Social democracy does not aim to overthrow the ruling class, it has no fundamental objection to the existence of classes, and it perceives society in terms of relative harmony rather than conflict. It also rejects the revolutionary socialist belief in the common ownership of the means of production and instead advocates a more measured combination of public and private ownership, or a 'mixed' economy. Social democracy is concerned with mitigating the detrimental effects of free-market capitalism, therefore it advocates the redistribution of wealth through the mechanism of the liberal democratic state. This involves state intervention in the economy to deal with the excesses of capitalism and a strong welfare state to provide support for those who are worse off within society. Private property and private ownership of the means of production are not eschewed, so long as the excesses of inequality and poverty that they might potentially contribute to are kept in check by a relatively strong state, together with a robust system of workers' rights and protections. Consequently, social democracy places a strong emphasis on institutions that provide education, health care, and welfare for its citizens which aim to extend and implement the key socialist value of equality whilst ensuring a more communal approach to politics to combat the ill effects of capitalism.

Fabian socialism, ethical socialism, and the third way

There are a number of variants of socialism which broadly share social democracy's commitment to a reformist approach. A key twentieth-century variant of socialism is Fabian socialism. Closely associated with the Labour Party in Britain, the Fabian Society formed in 1884 with the aim of implementing socialist values within democratic societies through reformist and gradualist methods. Fabian socialism is an excellent example of a debate within socialism concerning just how socialism can be brought about and how it operates; whether this be from an enlightened group of intellectuals introducing socialism to the masses from 'above'; or whether socialism must be a democratic movement from 'below' and brought about by the workers themselves. The Fabian Society is an academic society, historically associated with many high-profile public figures such as H. G. Wells, George Bernhard Shaw, and the co-founder of the London School of Economics, Sidney Webb. Webb, like the Fabian Society more generally, had little faith in the working class being able to see the benefits of socialism for themselves. Webb himself said that the working class were only interested in 'horse racing odds' (quoted in Chomsky 1995), meaning that socialism must be something introduced and developed from above. On the one side, this socialism from 'above' can be seen as a representation of the dominant social democratic approach in the west and, on the other, it is used to characterize the authoritarian, top-down Stalinist regimes prevalent in Eastern Europe in the twentieth century. The Fabians did not endorse the building of any mass movement of socialism and, as Draper puts it:

> they thought of themselves as a small elite of brain-trusters who would permeate the existing institutions of society, influence the real leaders in all spheres Tory or Liberal, and guide social development toward its collectivist goal with the 'inevitability of gradualness'.

> (Draper 1966)

In opposition to this, Marx argued that socialism must be the emancipation of the working class by and for themselves. Socialism could not be introduced from outside the working class movement—any conception of socialism as being forced upon an essentially passive working class was not actually socialism at all. A key problem with socialism from 'above', on Draper's interpretation, is that it amounts to domination, elitism, and manipulation of those below. What is interesting about Draper's analysis is that he recognizes that socialism from 'below' has historically and contemporarily had very few practitioners or supporters—whereas socialism from 'above' has a long and prominent role within the history of socialism.

Ethical socialism has been influential within social democrat circles, particularly in Britain in the twentieth century. This variant of socialism develops a moral critique of capitalism akin to utopian socialism. This ethical critique of capitalism extends to attempting to combat the morally corrosive values of capitalism, whilst advocating a more morally and ethically conscious variant of capitalism that promotes typically socialist values such as community and cooperation and maintaining the liberal focus on liberty and rights. Key figures in ethical socialism include R. H. Tawney, who wrote the influential book *The Acquisitive Society* which criticizes the selfishness and individualism characteristic of capitalist society. Important figures in British politics, such as the Labour Prime Minister Clement Atlee, were advocates and the ideology played a key role in Labour Party policy during the 1940s. More recently, British Prime Minister Tony Blair claimed to be influenced by ethical socialism and displayed many of its key values in this excerpt from a speech made at the Labour Party Conference in 1994:

> Working together, solidarity, co-operation, partnership. These are our words. This is my socialism. And we should stop apologising for using the word. It is not the socialism

of Marx or state control. It is rooted in a straightforward view of society, in the understanding that the individual does best in a strong and decent community of people with
principles and standards, and common aims and values.

(Blair, quoted in White 1994)

Critics might argue that it is paradoxical to continue to have faith in an economic
system—capitalism—whilst simultaneously arguing that it is that same system which
tends to create the type of values that ethical socialism opposes. So capitalism is simultaneously both accepted by such variants of liberal socialism and also something
which needs to be opposed—or at least the values that it creates need to be. Perhaps
more controversial still in socialist ideology is the contemporary variant known as the
'third way'. The third way represents an attempt by contemporary social democrats to
find a desirable political and economic position between socialism and capitalism,
or left- and right-wing politics. Taken from the 'right' is the belief in the necessity of
free-market economics over state socialism, whilst the 'left' provides the social justice
and the need to make capitalism more egalitarian and less unjust. The key theoretical proponent of the third way is Anthony Giddens (1998) and third way politics has
been hugely influential in Britain and America. British Prime Minister Tony Blair was
a keen advocate of third way ideology whilst in America Bill Clinton was a proponent,
as was German Chancellor Gerhard Schroeder. The third way is controversial within
socialism as many traditional socialists condemn it for leaning too much to the right
and supporting the interests of capital, whilst those on the right condemn the third
way for being nothing more than socialism (Sargent 2009: 123). Politically, third way
politics has undoubtedly been very effective. In Britain, 'New Labour' under Tony
Blair won three consecutive elections after eighteen years of the Labour Party being
out of power. This could be seen as a result of Blair's rejection of less electable, traditional social democracy, in favour of a more centrist approach with a broader electoral
appeal. Yet many socialists despised New Labour and what they saw as a betrayal of
socialist values, while more nuanced critics argued that third way politics lacked substance (Hattersley in Lavelle 2008: 87) and a clear ideological vision.

Ideological crossovers

As with many political ideologies there are areas where socialism overlaps
and converges with other political ideologies. Various political thinkers, leaders,
and movements have tried to combine aspects of differing ideologies into what they
view as a more palatable and effective political ideology or philosophy. In particular, numerous political leaders and organizations have attempted to draw together
what they see as the best aspects of socialism with the best aspects of liberalism.
Whilst many theorists draw a definite distinction between socialism and liberalism,

others have emphasized that such a distinction is false. On this interpretation, social-ism is understood as the ideology that can actually put into practice the liberty and rights that liberalism holds dear but that it ultimately fails to deliver (Rooksby 2012). Socialism is understood to be the 'radicalization and transcendence' (Rooksby 2012: 495) of liberalism through the implementation of its values in political practice. This does not set socialism and liberalism in opposition to one another, but conceptual-izes socialism as fulfilling the unfinished business that liberalism cannot.

Social liberalism can be seen as a significant merger of liberal and socialist values and beliefs. Social liberalism can be viewed as a more socialistic version of liberal-ism—perhaps chiefly in opposition to neo-liberalism (or 'economic liberalism'—see Chapter 2). Historical figures such as John Maynard Keynes, David Lloyd George, even Franklin D. Roosevelt would come into this category of social liberals. More recently, the great liberal philosopher John Rawls expressed this ideology in his hugely influential work, *A Theory of Justice* (1981), in which he argued that inequality was only acceptable if the accumulation of wealth ultimately lead to the least well off in society becoming as well off as is realistically possible. Rawls's version of social liberalism argues that whilst economic inequalities of wealth and income are accept-able, they are only acceptable if they are beneficial to the poorest in society. Rawls advocates some kind of essentially socialist principle of redistribution of wealth, which meant that his theories created much interest and admiration from socialists (Alexander 2015). This can perhaps be understood as a liberal attempt to address the socialist critique of liberalism, in that liberalism tends to drive towards political equality whilst simultaneously fostering economic inequality (MacIntyre 2003: 133). So, whilst there are clear elements of socialist thought here, the liberal framework of the pursuit of self-interest and private enterprise tends to remain intact. Socialism and liberalism have also merged in developing and bringing into being the contem-porary institutions of social welfare in the twentieth century. The welfare state is strongly social-democratic in its logic, yet Freeden argues that it was brought into the world as a 'liberal construct' and 'most of the liberal ideologists of the welfare state were hybrid social-liberals' (Freeden 2003: 86). Whilst the welfare state was a social-ist idea or claim, it was only when 'social-liberals' incorporated this belief that the welfare state became reality through a combination of liberal and socialist ideology.

There are also ideological crossovers between socialism and anarchism, yet this time the relationship is usually (though not exclusively) between the revolutionary form of socialism rather than the reformist brand. It has been—controversially—argued that anarchism is a kind of synthesis between liberalism and socialism in that it combines the liberal critique of state domination and the socialist critique of capitalist exploi-tation (see McLaughlin 2007: 52). This suggests that anarchism and socialism both share a critique of existing social relations and a view of capitalism as fundamentally exploitative. On this interpretation, anarchism has elements of three ideologies, combining a radical liberal critique of authority with a socialist critique of capitalism along with an anarchist rejection of the state. An important strand of anarchism is anarchist communism which argues that 'property in land, natural resources, and the means of production should be held in mutual control by local communities' (Ward 2004: 2), echoing the radical socialist belief in the common ownership of production. Indeed, Chomsky has argued that the 'consistent' anarchist will be a socialist, though a socialist of a particular kind—a libertarian socialist (Chomsky 1970: xv, xviii). This conception of libertarian socialism points towards the key disagreements between socialism and anarchism, despite the common ground. The libertarian element suggests a form of socialism that is a 'decentralized social order of authentically democratic, autonomous, and federated "communes" or communities of free and equal individuals' (McLaughlin 2007: 158). The realization of anarchism therefore involves the negation of the state which is viewed as oppressive and authoritarian. Whilst anarchism is the 'enemy' of the state, socialism's key failure in this view is that, despite claiming that the capitalist state must be smashed, it merely replaces the capitalist state with another form of oppressive state which, in turn, remains the enemy of freedom.

Contemporary socialism

The impact of socialist ideology on world politics and political movements has lessened considerably since the latter part of the twentieth century. The revolutions of 1989 signalled, for many, not just the collapse of the communist regimes in the East, but also the unworkability of socialism and the triumph of global capitalism. Liberalism had won the ideological war with socialism and the decisive rejection of the latter seemed to confirm this. Socialism, even in its social democratic form, tended to be supplanted by more neo-liberal approaches to economics that focused on privatization, deregulation, free trade, and reduced government spending and which generally viewed the welfare state with suspicion. Particularly in the USA and the UK in the 1980s, under Reagan and Thatcher respectively, neo-liberal leaders celebrated business and private enterprise whilst, in the case of Thatcher, attacking the unions and privatizing public industries. Socialism, at least for much of Europe and the West, had seemed to have lost both its ideological magnetism and its political and economic power.

The huge influence of international organizations such as the World Bank, the International Monetary Fund (IMF), and the World Trade Organization (WTO) are often seen as testament to the dominance of neo-liberalism in the contemporary world. Critics argue that such institutions tend to increase inequality between richer and poorer countries. They tend to impose conditions of development that favour neo-liberal policies of privatization and deregulation (Harvey 2005). Statistics suggest that, on a global level, the gap between rich and poor is growing (Reuben 2015) wider than ever, with a select few at the very top controlling vast swathes of the world's wealth. None of this suggests that socialism is the dominant force it was one hundred years ago.

Case Study 4.2 The financial crisis of 2008: causes

The financial crisis of 2008, the worst of modern times, provides an excellent example of the explanatory claims and understanding of world events, and the responses to such events, interpreted through the lens of socialist ideology. The 'mainstream' explanation for the crisis tended to involve blaming simple greed, bad decision-making, lack of financial regulation, or some other form of economic and financial mismanagement. The thrust of this argument is that the tightening of regulations can prevent the reoccurrence of such economic disasters in the future. A socialist explanation, particularly from the more radical elements, interprets the causes of the crisis as lying much deeper—in the nature of the capitalist system itself. Marxists, in particular, argue that as long as there is capitalism—an economic system that necessitates constant expansion, competition with other capitalists, and a free market—then the world will always be prone to these types of crises as capitalism continues its never-ending search for profit. Sub-prime mortgages and high-risk lending are not so much bad decisions as they are a logical consequence of constant competition and the search for new markets and profits. The Marxist Chris Harman argued:

> The runaway world is, in fact, the economic system as Marx described it, the Frankenstein's monster that has escaped from human control; the vampire that saps the lifeblood of the living bodies it feeds off. Its self-expansion has indeed led it to encompass the whole globe, drawing all of humanity into its cycles of competing in order to accumulate and accumulating in order to compete.

(Harman 2008: 325)

It is easy to link the theoretical explanation of the financial crisis with the political solution from those on the revolutionary left. For the consequences of the financial crisis were devastating, causing vast economic destruction, unemployment, and destitution. Not only this, but the economic responses to the crisis, widely known now simply by the word 'austerity', reinforced the idea that it was the most vulnerable sections of society that tended to have to pay for these crises. From the perspective of the anti-capitalist left, the logical political solution is to attempt to tackle the causal factor—the capitalist system itself. Anything less and the result will be that such crises will reoccur. Beginning with Marx's analysis of capitalism, Marxists therefore argue that a reformist strategy is unworkable and that only a radical, revolutionary overhaul can bring about the type of genuine change necessary to bring into fruition any real interpretation of socialist values such as equality, freedom, and community.

⮎ Stop and Think

1. Capitalism is a truly global economic system, uncontrolled by any one state, institution, or governing body. Is the revolutionary-socialist strategy of trying to overthrow capitalism realistic?

2. Has the anti-capitalist movement gained momentum from the financial crisis and the responses to it? Try and think of some examples in your answers.

Even those that were closely associated with socialism and indeed inseparable from it at one time (such as the British Labour Party) incorporated a fundamentally neo-liberal approach into their policies, embracing 'third way' politics and trying to reconcile capitalism with a new form of market socialism. This resulted in policies that did not really seem to share much with traditional socialist ideology, such as New Labour's continuation and development of PFIs (Private Finance Initiatives) which involved using private capital to fund public projects such as the National Health Service (BBC News 2002). Perhaps New Labour's most significant break with its socialist roots was its rewording of Clause Four of the Labour Party constitution. This clause originally advocated the 'common ownership of the means of production, distribution and exchange' for the workers, yet Tony Blair argued, successfully, that this needed to be changed in order to modernize the party. Whilst many commentators maintained that this signalled the decisive move from Old to New Labour, it is of interest to note that the new Clause Four still contained reference to cornerstones of socialist ideology such as common endeavour, community, and greater equality. Other European countries, such as Denmark, Sweden, Finland, and Norway, whilst not always being run by socialist parties, remain more socialistic in their general approach to the management of society. Finland and Norway are both well known for their comprehensive welfare systems, whilst Denmark ranks consistently high for workers' rights and a high minimum wage—suggesting some credence is still given to key socialist values such as equality and community and that social democracy can still flourish within a global capitalist world.

Looking beyond Europe and the West, there are still a small number of examples of socialist regimes (again, often in wildly varying forms) that have either continued late into the twentieth century and beyond, or emerged as new socialist regimes in this period. Undoubtedly, the most powerful and long-lasting of these countries is China. China has been governed by the Communist Party of China since 1949 yet, although officially socialist, its practical manifestation of socialism seems to diverge greatly from communism and indeed from the core values of socialism more generally. China is still run by single-party rule in the form of the Communist Party and is highly centralized. Many aspects of Chinese society, such as the media, are state-owned and this centralization and common ownership arguably fit in more with communist ideology and practice. Yet there is also a strong private sector and a general liberalization of the economy, pointing towards the adoption of a capitalist model. China is a recent member of the WTO, opening up to economic liberalization and foreign investment as a result, and is a key player in the global market. The global trend towards inequality is particularly noticeable in China, with huge disparities of wealth and income, suggesting any attempt to genuinely build socialism is probably long gone—certainly the communist vision of a classless society seems a long way off. Furthermore, China's record on human rights has long been a target of humanitarian groups and international pressure, suggesting freedom and community are not central to China's distorted socialist vision.

Other current socialist states include Vietnam and Cuba, both of which have adopted single-party rule by their respective communist parties. Cuba perhaps seems more committed to socialism than other countries. It consistently ranks highly for the universal provision of healthcare and education and it has strong regulations in place to resist the private sale of property and the ownership of the means of production. However, as with China, allegations of political and human rights abuses have dogged Cuba, with organizations such as Human Rights Watch and the EU being enormously critical of what is viewed as Cuba's very poor record in these areas (Human Rights Watch 2014), despite the recent end of US sanctions on Cuba. Other countries influenced by socialism, beyond those that claim adherence to a Marxist–Leninist model of socialism, include Venezuela under the leadership of the colourful yet controversial figure Hugo Chavez (see Case Study 4.3). Beyond these relatively isolated examples, early twenty-first century socialism seems to be at its lowest ebb for a long time. Western democracies have embraced neo-liberalism and have seemingly dismantled, or begun to dismantle, any hold that socialism once had—with a few notable exceptions. Beyond Western liberal democracies, those countries that still maintain an adherence to socialism have continued to open themselves up to capitalist investment and the globalized world. The collapse of communism in the East was seen, by many, as the final confirmation of the death of socialism and the triumph of liberalism. Yet this is not necessarily to say that socialism has run its ideological course and needs to be cast aside as a defunct ideology, now part of history.

Case Study 4.3 Hugo Chavez's Venezuela

The modern political history of Venezuela is a prime example of the often contradictory nature of socialism and the difficulties faced by a leader of a country who swept to power on a radical socialist programme. Hugo Chavez was the President of Venezuela from 1999 until his death in 2013, coming to power on a strong anti-imperialist stance and with support based largely in the poorer classes. Many of Chavez's policies and achievements had a strong socialist element to them—he decreased illiteracy and infant mortality rates, also lowering unemployment rates and reducing poverty. His social programmes, financed through high oil prices, resonated with the poor and helped cement his support amongst these sections of society. Chavez increased funding for health, education, and social security programmes, reducing inequalities, nationalizing industry, and implementing land reforms and worker-owned cooperatives.

Yet commentators have noted that after the 2007 general election, and Chavez's announcement of a new party—the United Socialist Party of Venezuela—Chavez had become a 'prisoner of power' (Gonzalez 2014: 120), displaying some distinctly un-socialist values. This new party was regarded as undemocratic in that it was not formed organically from the working classes (therefore not tying in with the concept of 'socialism from below' associated with the radical left), being controlled by a political elite largely focused on Chavez himself. It also lacked freedom and there seemed no possibility of dissent from the party line (Gonzalez 2014: 114–15). It seemed that, at least on this interpretation, power had turned the regime into an authoritarian one and that the radical agenda of Chavez and the multitudes that supported him, ended in the old adage that 'power corrupts and absolute power corrupts absolutely'. It is, of course, important to recognize that such a politically divisive leader as Chavez, with his anti-Western and anti-imperialist senti-ment, is bound to conjure up wildly contrasting sentiments. The neo-liberal weekly newspaper, *The Economist*, called his regime 'corrupt, cynical and incompetent' (9 March 2013) whilst many on the left continue to view him as a hero of Venezuela.

 Stop and Think

1. Does socialism always lead to authoritarianism?

2. Does political power always eventually corrupt and therefore warp socialist values such as freedom?

Does socialism have a future?

If we split socialism into two distinct forms, socialism from above and socialism from below, there is some evidence that both have had some recent resurgence. Movements such as **Occupy** (though strongly influenced by anarchism) have had notable support in a great number of countries and have arguably succeeded in put-ting pressure on governments, raising public awareness, and altering the parameters of political debate so as to focus on addressing the gross inequalities of wealth that they campaign against (see also Chapter 5). Similarly, the so-called anti-globaliza-tion movement has increased, with high profile figures such as Naomi Klein, Noam Chomsky, and Joseph Stiglitz coming under this broad umbrella movement and campaigning for, and raising awareness of, restrictions on the free market, free trade, and the unfair power distribution that so often defines the relationship between the developed and the developing world. Although not necessarily socialist in name, such movements suggest a concern for equality, human freedom, and community, carrying some of the key values of socialist ideology with them into new forms of political activity.

In terms of more traditional forms of top-down politics, there have been some interesting developments recently. In the UK in 2015, the election of the left-winger and self-proclaimed socialist Jeremy Corbyn to the Labour leadership in Britain has signalled a rejection of New Labour, whilst the shadow chancellor, John McDonnell, vowed in his 2016 party conference speech to bring social-ism back to the mainstream. Membership of the Labour Party has risen to over half a million—the highest for decades. In the USA, another self-proclaimed socialist Bernie Sanders enjoyed unprecedented popularity in the Democratic presidential race before the 2016 election—and this in a country where socialism is usually regarded as an alien concept. Although both these developments have been in traditional forms of politics, the campaigns that have pushed Corbyn and Sanders to the forefront of politics have been from strong grass-roots movements, such as **Momentum** in the UK, suggesting strong 'bottom-up' support for socialist ideology in both countries. Greece, in the wake of the 2008 financial crisis, elected Syriza, led by Alexis Tsipras, a radical, left-wing socialist party, to government (see Case Study 4.4).

Case Study 4.4 Syriza

Many socialists characterized austerity measures taken by governments and institutions in response to the 2008 financial crisis as 'socialism for the rich'. The poor were being made to pay for the mistakes made by the rich in the form of cuts to welfare, wages, and a generally decreasing standard of living whilst the rich—the banks for instance—were bailed out by the state. The socialist value of equality was being eroded as the rich got richer and the poor, poorer. In Greece, a coalition of left-wing parties, known as Syriza, were becoming increasingly popular with their radical anti-austerity programme that had been developed in response to the austerity measures forced upon Greece by the EU. Syriza was becoming an increasing concern to the countries of the Eurozone and its institutions that were continuing to implement austerity measures. Syriza's political programme included advocating a substantial increase to the minimum wage, the promotion of 'tax justice', the deepening of democracy, and, crucially, a renegotiation of the (neo-liberal, austerity-heavy) terms of the $270 billion debt with the European Union and International Monetary Fund.

Led by Alexis Tsipras, in the January elections of 2015, Syriza became the largest party and formed a coalition government, with Tsipras becoming the Prime Minister of Greece. This was generally regarded as a huge victory for socialism and the left and a potentially significant victory in the battle against austerity. Yet things did not run smoothly. Greece's debt levels were critical and Tsipras came under increasing pressure to strike a deal with the European Union and International Monetary Fund regarding a bailout fund. A deal was eventually done, yet it angered many on the left as, from their perspective, Tsipras had accepted many of the austerity and neo-liberal measures he had originally claimed to oppose. These included public spending cuts, the modernization of the labour market and reform of the pension system. Tsipras's position was that if he had not accepted then the consequences would have been far, far worse for Greece.

➡ Stop and Think

1. Does the failure of Syriza to strike a bailout deal on its own terms suggest that radicalism—or socialism—cannot be implemented within the confines of a globalized, neo-liberal world and the financial institutions that dominate within it?

2. Do you agree the election of a left-wing socialist government in Greece suggests that, on a global level, the future of socialism looks bright in the twenty-first century?

The death of socialism has been announced many times; and if this is too premature and triumphalist for many, there is a kernel of truth here. Socialism, in certain
forms, did die in the twentieth century, yet this is not to say that it cannot be reborn
anew. For the death of a political system and the death of an ideology are not the
same. Social democracy continues to work in a number of European countries and
beyond and there is some evidence of more radical conceptions of socialism taking
hold elsewhere, both in traditional and non-traditional forms. The financial crisis of
2008 and the austerity measures that followed it seemed to create an awareness of and
opposition to the dominant neo-liberal framework. Many would agree with Anthony
Giddens' argument that traditional forms of socialism were 'obsolete', yet, in practical
terms, it can still be argued that socialism still has an important (if currently more
oppositional) role to play in the contemporary world.

Summary

- Socialism emerged largely as a reaction to the injustices and exploitation
  associated with industrialization and capitalist practices.
- The key ideological battleground between socialists has traditionally been
  over the question of reform or revolution—a belief in the necessity of the
  latter is encapsulated in and definitive of communism.
- Historically, socialism was enormously influential as a political practice and
  shaped the course of the twentieth century.
- Perhaps the most contested of all ideologies, and the most complex,
  socialism encompasses a wide range of ideological variants and crossovers
  with other ideologies such as liberalism.
- Since the collapse of the Soviet Union, the influence of socialism has
  decreased dramatically, with new variants of liberalism providing the
  dominant ideological framework.

Review and discussion questions

1. Critically discuss the idea that revolution is necessary to bring about socialism.
2. What are the prospects for socialism in the twenty-first century?
3. Does the concept of class still matter today?
4. Discuss the key differences between socialist and liberal forms of equality.

Research exercises

1. Think about the ideological framework of socialism—particularly the critique and the vision. Look at the 2015 Labour Party General Election Manifesto—can any of these elements be seen in the manifesto? Do you think the British Labour Party is a socialist party from what you have examined?

2. There are currently four self-identified socialist states that claim adherence to Marxism–Leninism (China, Cuba, Laos, and Vietnam). Use the internet to do some preliminary research. Do they share anything in common—such as values, government and politics, or economic policy? Can they accurately be described as socialist? If not, why not?

Further reading

A good place to start (being a relatively easy read) is Marx and Engels' *Communist Manifesto* (2002). This can be supplemented with any good edition of Marx and Engels' collected writings such as Tucker's (1978) before moving onto the more difficult work of Marx's three volumes of *Das Kapital*.

There are a number of good, recent introductory texts on socialism and Marxism such as Singer (2000) and Newman (2005).

Any work by G. A. Cohen (e.g. 1988) is interesting and thought-provoking, whilst Giddens (1998) is the definitive modern text on social democracy and the third way. G. D. H. Cole's seven volume history of socialist thought remains an important and comprehensive history of socialism. More recently, David Harvey (2015) and Terry Eagleton (2011) have applied Marx's ideas to the modern world and defended their continued relevance.

References

ALEXANDER, J. (2015), 'The Major Ideologies of Liberalism, Socialism and Conservatism', *Political Studies*, Vol. 63, pp. 980–94.

BADIOU, A. (2010), *The Communist Hypothesis*, London: Verso.

BBC NEWS (2002), Q & A: What is PFI? http://news.bbc.co.uk/1/hi/business/2284758.stm

BBC NEWS (2015), Richest 1 per cent to Own More than Rest of World, Oxfam says, http://www.bbc.co.uk/news/business-30875633

BERLIN, I. (1969), 'Two Concepts of Liberty', in: *Four Essays on Liberty*, Oxford: Oxford University Press.

BOOTH, W. J. (1989), 'Gone Fishing: Making Sense of Marx's Concept of Communism', *Political Theory*, Vol. 17, No. 2, pp. 205–22.

CHOMSKY, N. (1970), 'Introduction' in D. Guerin, *Anarchism*, London: Monthly Press.

Chomsky, N. (1995), 'Interview with Noam Chomsky', *Red and Black Revolution*, Issue 2.

Cohen, G. A. (1988), *History, Labour and Freedom: Themes from Marx*, Oxford: Oxford University Press.

Cole, G. D. H. (1953–60), *A History of Socialist Thought*, London and New York: St. Martins Press.

Dean, J. (2012), *The Communist Horizon*, London: Verso.

Draper, H. (1966), 'The Two Souls of Socialism', *New Politics*, Vol. 5, No. 1, pp. 57–84.

Dunn, J. (1984), *The Politics of Socialism: An Essay in Political Theory*, Cambridge: Cambridge University Press.

Eagleton, T. (2011), *Why Marx Was Right*, New Haven, CT: Yale University Press.

Eatwell, R. and Wright, A. (eds) (1999), *Contemporary Political Ideologies*, 2nd edn, London: Pinter.

Engels, F. (2009), *The Condition of the Working Class in England*, London: Penguin.

Freeden, M. (1996), *Ideologies and Political Theory: A Conceptual Approach*, Oxford: Clarendon Press.

Freeden, M. (2003), *Ideology: A Very Short Introduction*, Oxford: Oxford University Press.

Fukuyama, F. (2006), *The End of History and the Last Man*, New York: Simon & Schuster.

Geoghegan, V. (1984), 'Socialism' in R. Eccleshall et al. (eds), *Political Ideologies: An Introduction*, 3rd edn, London: Routledge.

Giddens, A. (1998), *The Third Way: The Renewal of Social Democracy*, Cambridge: Polity Press.

Gonzalez, M. (2014), *Hugo Chavez: Socialist for the Twenty-First Century*, London: Pluto Press.

Gould, C. (1978), *Marx's Social Ontology*, Cambridge, MA: MIT Press.

Hardt, M. and Negri, A. (2000), *Empire*, Cambridge, MA: Harvard University Press.

Harman, C. (2009), *Zombie Capitalism: Global Crisis and the Relevance of Marx*, Chicago: Bookmarks.

Harvey, D. (2005), *A Brief History of Neoliberalism*, Oxford: Oxford University Press.

Harvey, D. (2015), *Seventeen Contradictions and the End of Capital*, London: Profile Books.

'Hugo Chavez's Rotten Legacy' (2013), *The Economist*, 9 March 2013, available at http://www.economist.com/news/leaders/21573106-appeal-populist-autocracy-has-been-weakened-not-extinguished-hugo-ch%C3%A1vezs-rotten

Human Rights Watch (2014), World Report 2014: Cuba, https://www.hrw.org/world-report/2014/country-chapters/cuba

Kain, P. J. (1991), *Marx and Ethics*, Oxford: Clarendon Press.

Kosik, K. (1976), *Dialectics of the Concrete*, Boston: D. Reidel.

Lavelle, A. (2008), *The Death of Social Democracy*, Aldershot: Ashgate.

Lenin, V. I. (1973), 'To the Rural Poor', in *Collected Works*, Vol. 6, Moscow: Progress Publishers.

MacIntyre, A. (1958), 'Notes from the Moral Wilderness—I', *The New Reasoner*, No. 7, Winter 1958–59, pp. 90–100; also available at http://www.amielandmelburn.org.uk/collections/nr/index_frame.htm

MacIntyre, A. (1960), 'Freedom and Revolution', originally published in *Labour Review*, Vol. 5, No. 1, February–March, pp. 19–24, also published in P. Blackledge and N. Davidson (eds), *Alasdair MacIntyre's Engagement with Marxism: Selected Writings 1953–1974*, Boston: Brill, pp. 123–34.

MacIntyre, A. (2003), *Marxism and Christianity*, London: Duckworth.

MacIntyre, A. (2010), 'Where We Were, Where We Are, Where We Need to Be', in P. Blackledge and K. Knight (eds), *Virtue and Politics: Alasdair MacIntyre's Revolutionary Aristotelianism*, Notre Dame, IN: University of Notre Dame Press, pp. 170–84.

McLaughlin, P. (2007), *Anarchism and Authority*, Aldershot: Ashgate.

Marx, K. (2000), Marx's notebook comments on James Mill, available at http://www.marxists.org/archive/marx/works/1844-mil/index

Marx, K. and Engels, F. (2002), *The Communist Manifesto*, London: Penguin.

Marx, K. and Engels, F. (2004), *The German Ideology*, New York: International Publishers.

Masquelier, C. and Dawson, M. (2016), 'Beyond Capitalism and Liberal Democracy: On the Relevance of GDH Cole's Sociological Critique and Alternative', *Current Sociology*, Vol. 64, No. 1, pp. 3–21.

Newman, M. (2005), *Socialism: A Very Short Introduction*, Oxford: Oxford University Press.

Podmore, F. (2013), *Robert Owen: A Biography*, Vol. 1, London: Forgotten Books.

Rabinowitch, A. (2007), *The Bolsheviks: The First Year of Rule in Soviet Petrograd*, Bloomington: Indiana University Press.

Rejai, M. (1994), *Political Ideologies: A Comparative Approach*, 2nd edn, London: Routledge.

Reuben, A. (2015), Gap Between Rich and Poor 'Keeps Growing', http://www.bbc.co.uk/news/business-32824770

Rooksby, E. (2012), 'The Relationship between Liberalism and Socialism', *Science and Society*, Vol. 76, No. 4, pp. 495–520.

Sargent, L. T. (2009), *Contemporary Political Ideologies: A Comparative Analysis*, Belmont, CA: Wadsworth.

Simon, L. (ed.) (1994), *Karl Marx: Selected Writings*, Cambridge: Hackett.

Singer, P. (2000), *Marx: A Very Short Introduction*, Oxford: Oxford University Press.

Stankiewicz, W. J. (1993), *In Search of a Political Philosophy: Ideology at the Close of the Twentieth Century*, New York: Routledge.

Tucker, R. C. (ed.) (1978), *The Marx-Engels Reader*, New York: W. W. Norton & Company, Inc.

Vattimo, G. and Zabala, S. (2011), *Hermeneutic Communism: From Heidegger to Marx*, New York: Columbia University Press.

Vincent, A. (2009), *Modern Political Ideologies*, 2nd edn, London: Blackwell.

Ward, C. (2004), *Anarchism: A Very Short Introduction*, Oxford: Oxford University Press.

White, M. (1994), 'Blair Defines the New Labour', *The Guardian*, 5 October, http://www.theguardian.com/politics/1994/oct/05/labour.uk

5

Anarchism

David Bates

OBJECTIVES

- Provide an outline of the key ideas and concepts of 'classical' anarchist thinkers
- Show how anarchist views on human nature, the state, political action, private property, and religion vary, and where possible, what unites them
- Assess recent critical responses to anarchism, in particular 'post-anarchism'
- Assess specific historical examples of anarchism
- Examine the extent to which anarchism can be regarded as a cohesive political ideology

---

Introduction

What is anarchism? To attempt an answer to this question, we must begin with etymology. 'Anarchy' is a word of Greek origin, derived from ἀν (without) and ἀρχή (authority). The suffix 'ism' gives at least the appearance of its 'ideological' status. Like all basic definitions, however, this conceals much complexity.

Michael Freeden (2003) suggests that we can differentiate ideologies into a range of core, adjacent, and peripheral concepts (see also Chapter 1 and Levy 2010). But even to identify the core concepts of anarchism is a challenge; for there is no clear answer we can give to the question 'what does it mean to be an anarchist?' Perhaps we might venture the following:

- a belief in the potential of human nature, and a corresponding critique of arbitrary authority;
- a **refusal** of state authority;
- a rejection of the institution of private property;

- militant **atheism**;
- a stress on the importance of revolutionary politics.

Yet all of these are contentious. Some anarchists challenge the idea of human nature, others are anti-revolutionary. Some support the institution of private property. Some are deeply religious. We might be led therefore to conclude that the term anarchism is a 'floating signifier'—that is, its meaning is entirely open. Or we might think of anarchism not in terms of a core essence, but rather of what the philosopher Ludwig Wittgenstein refers to as a 'family resemblance' (see Wittgenstein 1953, Aphorism 67; the idea of family resemblances is also used in relation to religious fundamentalism in Chapter 12). As demonstrated elsewhere in this book, the core concepts of 'liberalism', Marxism, and even conservatism may be frequently difficult to pin down; but we tend in a way to know what these features are when we see them. Yet I am also making a special claim for anarchism. Perhaps somewhat playfully, we might say that a common feature of anarchists is their refusal to be pinned down, their refusal to be defined.

If we say that anarchism can be characterized by a type of familial diversity, we can perhaps also extend the analogy a little further. Take a family gathering. In many families, there are overbearing fathers, unruly children, and the uncle no one wants to mention. Often such gatherings are fractious affairs, in which politics is best not brought up as a subject for discussion. Yet, beneath the argument, there is often a degree of unity which is difficult to pin down. Such unity is not reducible to biology, but may be best explained by common emotional histories, celebrations, and shared grief. It might also be claimed that any definition of what it is to be an anarchist will be the result of a not always free and open conversation—certain voices will be more powerful than others.

We start this chapter with only one definition of anarchism, taken from the Russian anarchist Peter Kropotkin. For Kropotkin, anarchism is

> the name given to a principle or theory of life and conduct under which society is conceived without government—harmony in such a society being obtained, not by submission to law, or by obedience to any authority, but by free agreements concluded between the various groups, territorial and professional . . .

(Kropotkin 1910)

As we explore the different thinkers in this chapter, we will see that this definition does not go very far towards capturing the complexity of anarchist thought.

Anarchism may be a complex political ideology; it is also an ideology embedded in real world politics and history. Whilst, as stated, this involves a shared history, the realities of political struggle led to the production of a wider range of anarchist politics. There are '**anarcho-syndicalists**' who argue that trade unions can become a basis of solidarity and radical political action. Key thinkers who influenced anarcho-syndicalism include Pierre-Joseph Proudhon (1809–1865). There are '**anarcho-communists**' who argue for the abolition of the state and private property.

Key anarcho-communists include Carlo Cafiero (1846–1892), Errico Malatesta (1853–1932), and Peter Kropotkin (1842–1921). Mikhail Bakunin (1814–1876) is better described as a '**collectivist anarchist**', though his work does have many affinities with the type of position adopted by anarcho-communists. Bakunin is a strong critic of the state and all forms of capitalist exploitation. Yet, partly because of the strongly critical position Bakunin adopted in relation to Marx's vision of communism, we must be careful to differentiate between collectivist and communist strands of this ideology. There are '**ecological anarchists**' who place a specific stress on environmental issues and a critique of the exploitative relations not only between humans, but between human beings and the natural environment of which they are a part. The social ecology approach of Murray Bookchin is a particular variant of this type of approach (see Chapter 10). There are **anarcha-feminists** who critique the patriarchal character of state exploitation and oppression. We will also see that there is an approach which might be typified as '**anarcho-capitalism**'. Anarcho-capitalism, as one would expect, is quite different to anarcho-communism. It considers private property not as a barrier to freedom, but rather as a necessary condition for it.

The approach in what follows is to set out some of the contestable 'key beliefs' of the anarchist 'family' through a discussion of the following themes: human nature, the critique of state power, property, religion, and political action.

Human nature

It has been maintained that anarchists hold to a view of human nature as at its core social and good. This basic human goodness means that the type of social cooperation demanded by an anarchist society—that is social cooperation without state compulsion—is possible. Indeed, anarchists oppose states because they make human beings perform terrible acts which they would not otherwise perform. But the reality of anarchist ideology is more complex. Most anarchists are not **essentialists**; for they tend not to consider that there is a core and immutable character to human nature, external to socialization. Socialization is a key theme in much anarchist thought.

As with other themes in this chapter, the task of identifying the core anarchist view of human nature is a challenging one. William Godwin (1756–1836) might be regarded as the great-grandfather of classical anarchism. Godwin argued that human characteristics are almost entirely the result of social factors. For Godwin, 'if man is corrupt . . . it is because he has been corrupted . . . place him under other circumstances . . . and he would be altogether a different creature' (Godwin 1793).

The good society in this view can produce the good human, just as the bad society can produce the bad one (see Case Study 5.1 on anarchist views of education). The implications Godwin drew from this argument appear challenging even to the contemporary reader. On the issue of moral responsibility, for example, if 'criminal' activity is simply a response to circumstance, then it makes little sense to punish the action of the 'criminal', any more than it does to praise the activity of the 'good man'. Godwin was a **utilitarian** philosopher; a just society for him was one where social circumstances were structured in such a fashion that they allowed individuals to make decisions which maximized the happiness of the greatest number. Thus, the good human being—and the good society to which this corresponds—was very much a product of circumstance.

The views of the **individualist anarchist** Max Stirner (1806–1856—real name Johann Kaspar Schmidt) make an interesting point of contrast with Godwin. In the *Essence of Christianity* (1841), the 'Young Hegelian' Ludwig Feuerbach had come to invert the Christian view of creation. For Feuerbach, God was a creation of Man, not vice versa. But in making this move, Feuerbach had argued that there was a human essence that was by its nature creative and social. In rejecting God, we should embrace this essence. For Stirner, the very idea of a human essence—and the notion of society in which it is based—is a tyranny, a 'spook'. The term 'spook' is central to Stirner's argument; he uses this to refer to all those 'higher beings' and ideas to which humans sacrifice themselves, and hence by which they are dominated. Even social morality comes to be regarded as a 'spook'. It is also worth noting that there seems to be something of a contradiction in Stirner's argument, for on the one hand he regards the idea of human essence as a 'spook', but on the other thinks of human beings as at their core egoistic and selfish. Surely he cannot have it both ways.

If extreme individualism was Stirner's response to Feuerbach, the responses of Proudhon and Bakunin were more socially inclined. Although coming to have the same opinion of Marx, Proudhon and Bakunin did differ on other issues including how they understood human nature. Proudhon initially suggests an argument which is closer to the 'essentialist' account of human nature; Bakunin is more socially minded. For Proudhon, human nature seems mostly constant. Human beings are individuals. Society is not a simple cause of individual behaviour. Rather, individuals have an existence prior to society. Taken in isolation, this claim might be regarded as more 'libertarian' than 'anarchist'. For the libertarian, society is regarded largely as an annoying obstacle to the realization of individual freedom. However, Proudhon introduces an argument which seems to contradict this idea of the asocial character of human nature, and thus human nature's static character. For he also maintains that individuals are 'an integral part of collective existence' (Marshall 1993: 248). Society has a will and force of its own. Thus human nature is best understood as a product of individuals operating in given social contexts. If Proudhon suggests a form of essentialism he pretty quickly challenges his own view.

We can now return to the work of another bitter rival of Marx—Bakunin (see Case Study 5.2). Despite this rivalry, there are clear similarities between the arguments put forward by Marx and Bakunin. Both were influenced by Hegel's dialectical philosophy in which mind and body, nature and humanity, were regarded as having important internal connections. Bakunin indeed stated that 'Man forms with Nature a single entity' (Bakunin, in Maximoff 1953: 83). Consequently, the idea that we can view human nature as detached from the animal kingdom is to be challenged. We share many drives, such as the drive to overcome hunger. But to state that we share such drives with members of the animal kingdom is not the same as maintaining that we are *mere* animals. We are higher animals, with more complex powers and capacities. It is here that the Enlightenment and anarchistic aspects of Bakunin's thought become clear.

Like key **Enlightenment** thinkers, Bakunin regarded freedom as a core value. But such freedom could not be understood in a purely negative fashion. Bakunin wrote: 'Society, far from decreasing his freedom, on the contrary creates the individual freedom of all human beings' (Bakunin 1871). But there is also a rebellious aspect to Bakunin's thought, for 'The passion for destruction is a creative passion, too!' (Bakunin 1842). It is this combination of reason and rebellious desire which has led one writer to label Bakunin a 'fanatic of freedom' (Marshall 1993).

Before going on to explore the work of the most systematic writer on human nature in the anarchist tradition—Kropotkin—we first need to make some remarks on the work of Tolstoy. All of the authors we have discussed so far might be regarded as radical. However, Tolstoy was a radical Christian thinker of the most unorthodox kind. Whereas for Stirner the idea of God was a 'spook' which restricted human freedom, for Tolstoy the notion of freedom was entirely bound up with the idea of the 'Kingdom of God'. Tolstoy argued that humans had an inbuilt desire not for rebellion, but for happiness; true happiness was the basis of real human freedom. Such happiness could be satisfied in a range of ways.

First, egotistically, humans may seek to satisfy cravings for wealth, fame, material goods, or love. This, for Tolstoy, was a shallow and illegitimate way of seeking happiness. It was also a form of happiness pursued by the priestly classes. Second, Tolstoy maintained that happiness could be achieved in a non-egoistic fashion, through pursuing a life in the service of the Kingdom of God. Only in embracing this Kingdom were human beings truly free. Yet Tolstoy did believe that the passions could be directed in the service of God. Lest we consider him a humbug, it is also important to note that Tolstoy did not think—nor indeed live as though—a life of complete abstention was possible, or desirable.

Despite his atheism, Kropotkin held Tolstoy's work in high regard; however, he brings the analysis of human nature back down to earth. The Victorian thinker Herbert Spencer came up with the term the 'survival of the fittest' through an 'application' of Charles Darwin's theory to social life. Kropotkin challenged the basis of such an approach. Kropotkin argued that human beings had proved so adaptable to their natural environment not because of the way in which they pursue egoistic self-interest, but because of their cooperative capacities. Individual egoism undermines the possibility of survival. Social cooperation for the purpose of survival, Kropotkin terms '**mutual aid**'.

For the social ecologist Murray Bookchin, cooperation is important. Human beings should not seek to dominate and exploit one another, Moreover, Bookchin draws attention to how in those societies structured through the domination by one individual or group of individuals, there is a tendency also to exploit the natural world—to the detriment of humanity and nature.

The **anarcha-feminist** Emma Goldman challenged liberal conceptions of human nature. She wrote: 'Poor human nature, what horrible crimes have been committed in thy name! Every fool, from king to policeman, from the flatheaded parson to the visionless dabbler in science, presumes to speak authoritatively of human nature' (Goldman 1910). Contemporary anarcha-feminists have continued to challenge the way in which theories of universal human nature serve to mask the underlying patriarchal character of contemporary exploitative and hierarchical societies. As such, they refuse the sexism of the classical anarchist canon (see also Chapter 9 for discussion of anarcha-feminism).

Contemporary post-anarchist thought has made a type of return to Stirner, preferring not to write of concepts such as human nature (or nature more widely). For Todd May (1994) and Saul Newman (2010) 'human nature' is nothing but a field of multiple possibilities, a project of becoming. The advantage of such an approach is that it allows us to become who we want to be. Perhaps the problem is that these possibilities are constrained by the very factors which thinkers such as Bakunin and Bookchin have done so much to identify—for example, environmental destruction, poverty, and human exploitation.

Anarchist views on human nature can be summarized as follows:

- Most anarchists understand human nature as the result of interaction between individual and social factors. Pernicious structures of authority prevent the realization of our human potential.

- Stirner and the post-anarchists reject all talk of human nature. But where, for Stirner, this rejection is connected to a strong egoism, the post-anarchists are concerned to stress how the rejection of human nature means that what we can become is entirely open.

- Most anarchists develop arguments regarding human nature which are premised on atheism. Tolstoy is a key exception. For Tolstoy we only recognize our higher human potential when we live in accordance with the 'Kingdom of God'.

⊃ **Stop and Think**

1. To what extent are concepts of good and evil objective, or rather products of our imagination?

2. Are human beings egoistic or social? (Support your response with examples.)

Case Study 5.1 Anarchism, human nature, and education

CONTEXT

Anarchists' understandings of human nature have a particular significance for how they approach the purpose of education. As with other areas of anarchist thought and action, the anarchist view of education is characterized by significant diversity. Yet beyond this diversity there is a widely held view: education founded on coercion and arbitrary authority should be challenged. Such a challenge is in part necessary because of the socially oriented commitment which many—though not all—anarchists have to an idea of human flourishing. Many anarchists would consider abhorrent a selective education system based on the 'survival of the fittest'.

So-called classical anarchist views of education must be considered as anti-statist (see the section 'Property' below). Yet at the time these writers were at their prime, state education as such was only just starting to be developed, and in the case of Godwin, on the distant horizon. The public school system had taught the British ruling classes how to carry out their 'duty', at least from the fifteenth century when Eton was founded.

Universal education in Britain was only introduced in 1870 (applying to children aged from 5 to 13). A centralized system of state education was also developed in Germany in the 1870s. The Reform Act of 1867 gave the vote to working men in Britain. Germany followed in 1871. This process was clearly a result of the pressures placed on European states by workers' mobilization. Effective civic participation requires a certain level of literacy. But it is also the case that those with privilege across Europe were concerned about how working men would use this vote. Clearly an idea of state funded education for social control assumed a certain importance—an importance which it no doubt continues to have to this day.

The idea off education for the purpose of social control was considered objectionable by anarchists.

IDEOLOGY

The typical conservative view of education is shaped significantly by the conservative view of human nature. Human beings cannot live together without strong mechanisms of social control of which education is one. Most anarchists—for all of their differences—have a stronger belief in the potentiality of human nature, combined with a critique of arbitrary authority.

William Godwin held to a 'dissenting' view of education. Just as an education system stressing conformity would produce the conforming human being, an education based on dissent would produce a creative one. Godwin argued that a key purpose of education ought not to be discipline, but the promotion of human happiness—which for him was intimately connected with freedom and creativity. Proudhon, Bakunin, and Kropotkin each argued for an 'enlightened' approach to education which opposed all forms of authoritarianism. The purpose of education was not authority and discipline, but rather the promotion of free thought.

For Kropotkin in particular, education ought to challenge the social division of mental and manual labour. This is so for two reasons: first, because this division leads to authoritarianism—from Plato onwards, the body was to be led by the intellect; second, because a fulfilled human existence was only possible with a unity of the mental and physical.

As with other anarchists, Tolstoy set out to challenge authoritarianism in education. For Tolstoy, education for conformity should be refused, and education for freedom supported. Importantly,

Tolstoy put these ideas into practice. In 1859 he set up a school in his house in Yasnaya Polyana which provided free education for peasant children on his family estate.

Max Stirner, unlike the other thinkers discussed here, was a school teacher. He worked in a private school for girls. In his text *The False Principles of Our Education*, he suggests that the idea of the 'learner as object' should be challenged. Pedagogy should not be a matter of cultural indoctrination; its 'civilizing' function should be challenged. Indeed, education could not be concerned with such an abstract idea as 'human flourishing', given that Stirner believed that all ideas of human nature were 'spooks'. Rather, education should be concerned with 'the development of free men, sovereign characters' (Stirner 1842), that is, with supporting the ego.

In his 1971 text *Deschooling Society*, Ivan Illich argues that the formal school curriculum is instrumental in reproducing a distortion of human nature. Society should move away from the authoritarianism of schooling and instead stress informal education—that is the learning resulting from real life experience. Illich's ideas have been taken up by British anarchists such as Colin Ward (1973).

Somewhat watered down versions of Illich's arguments can be found in much day to day educational practice, with ideas such as 'experiential learning' and 'life-long learning'. More radical applications of anarchist views of education can be found in the 'free school' movement—not to be confused with the Free School policy of the UK Conservative Government—which has its origin in Spanish anarchism.

Stop and Think

1. Should education encourage human free expression, or a respect for authority and hierarchy?

2. What alternatives to formal education might society adopt in order to facilitate the development of skills and knowledge?

The state

This discussion of human nature in classical anarchism brings us to what is perhaps the key component of anarchist ideology: the refusal of the state.

The German sociologist Max Weber characterized the modern state as a 'human community that successfully claims the monopoly of the legitimate use of physical force within a given territory' (Weber 1919: 78). Government on the other hand can be viewed as the agency through which such a territory comes to be organized and administered. Anarchists would agree that states claim the 'monopoly' of 'physical force' within a given territory. However, they would question the view that such force could in any sense be 'legitimate'.

To a significant extent, classical anarchism was born almost in two worlds. Bakunin, Kropotkin, and Tolstoy were Russian nobles born into the final period of a feudal world, where states were absolutist, brutal regimes which claimed to be justified by the authority of God. However, at this very moment a new world was coming into being—the period of what the historian Eric Hobsbawm (1991) has termed 'classical modernity' (a period running roughly from 1789 to 1900). It was in this period that the nation-state came to be consolidated. Accordingly, these anarchists witnessed—often at first hand—the brutality of states in feudal and modern capitalist forms.

Yet the views of the grandfather of anarchism, William Godwin, were developed not in feudal eastern Europe, but in Anglican England. Godwin does not often refer to the state as such, but rather to government. This was in part a function of the time he was writing, where the idea of the modern state was at best in its infancy. Yet we can read into Godwin's critique of government, a critique of the state. There is an extent to which Godwin builds on typical British arguments for minimal government, which we have seen within Enlightenment liberalism. However, he takes this argument further, rejecting government outright as 'nothing but regulated force' (Godwin 1793). Legitimate authority could only be based on consent. Godwin was critical of how government was instituted to defend the exploitative character of private property. This was a key concern of Proudhon and Bakunin in particular, but a departure from the British liberal tradition where the legitimacy of private property is rarely questioned.

Proudhon and Bakunin bring together a critique of government with a direct attack on the idea of state authority. For Proudhon:

> To be governed is to be . . . fined, despised, harassed, tracked, abused, clubbed, disarmed, choked, imprisoned, judged, condemned, shot, deported, sacrificed, sold, betrayed; and, to crown all, mocked, ridiculed, outraged, dishonored.
>
> (Proudhon, cited in Joll 1979: 78)

It is true that Proudhon tends to conflate the category of the state with that of government—both of which he finds objectionable. Proudhon argues that the growth of modern society had turned the state into a monster capable of untold repression of its subjects. In contrast to the state, he advocated the continual growth of individual liberty.

Bakunin's opposition to state power was shaped not only by his views of those imperialist nations as they emerged in the nineteenth century, but by a growing 'statism' in the communist movement—particularly as embodied in the work of Marx. Marshall has insisted that 'Bakunin's philosophy consists largely of Proudhonian politics and Marxian economics' (Marshall 1993: 270). Engaging, at times positively, with Marx's ideas, he was also critical. At one point he wrote of Marx: 'The cult of the State is . . . the principal characteristic of German Socialism' (Bakunin 1990: 38–9). No doubt also influenced by his personal experiences of the violence of the Russian state of Tsar Alexander II, Bakunin declared all states to be 'evil'.

First, Bakunin considers that states are always structured to protect the powerful against the powerless. Second, Bakunin does not think that the state can be captured and put to the services of freedom; states always consolidate their own power. In contrast, for Marx, the state was the 'ruling committee of the bourgeoisie' (Marx and Engels 1848); however, state power could be captured and transformed so as to establish the 'dictatorship of the proletariat'.

In some ways Tolstoy came to oppose the state on even more profound grounds than was the case with the atheist anarchists. For not only were states founded on violence; they also made claims to authority which conflicted with the scope of the Kingdom of God. Thus, states were structures for the violent imposition of false authority. The solution which Tolstoy posed to the oppressive power of the state was not one of violent resistance, but rather one of radical love (Christoyannopoulos 2010). For, if violence begets violence, love begets love. In an 1881 letter to the Tsar, Tolstoy wrote: 'Return good for evil, resist not evil, forgive everyone' (Marshall 1993: 370).

Kropotkin's critique of the state, in contrast, is firmly grounded in the material realm. He provides a detailed historical and geographical account of the development of modern European states. States were not solutions to what Hobbes characterized as the brutality of human nature; rather, they have always supported the power of privileged minorities. On the other hand, small-scale forms of social cooperation typical of Kropotkin's 'anarcho-communism' were best able to support equality and human progress.

It is worth returning briefly to the voice of Stirner. For Stirner, states did not serve as supports for individual egoism. Egoism was *the* human condition; or perhaps more accurately, the reality of egoism denied the 'spooky' idea that there was a human condition. The idea of the state was grounded in the opposite of egoism. At one point, Stirner wrote:

> . . . we two, the State and I, are enemies. I, the egoist, have not at heart the welfare of this 'human society', I sacrifice nothing to it, I only utilize it; but to be able to utilize it completely I transform it rather into my property and my creature . . .
>
> (Stirner 1845)

We might remark that, if for Stirner, the state was the enemy of the egoist ideal, for our other anarchists, such an 'ideal' was far from idyllic!

Contemporary anarchist thinking tends to continue the focus on the relationship between state power and exploitation, whilst considering the state as the key loci of pernicious power. Colin Ward insists that 'Every state protects the privileges of the wealthy' (Ward 2004: 2). And Murray Bookchin is clear about this when he writes: 'Almost anyone . . . can call himself or herself an anarchist, if he or she believed that the society could be managed without the state' (Bookchin 1986). Contemporary post-anarchists such as Todd May (1994) and Saul Newman (2010) aim to go beyond such a 'state-centric' focus. The exercise of power for post-anarchists is not so simple. Invoking writers such as Michel Foucault, post-anarchists argue that power must rather be understood as diffuse, as embedded in 'networks', rather than a function only of the apparatuses of the state.

Anarchist views on the state can be summarized as follows:

- All anarchist thinkers are critical of the state, and want it to be abolished.

- Most anarchists extend their critique of the state to a critique of government, and more widely to the realm of human exploitation.

- Post-anarchists are concerned to insist that power is so diffuse and all-encompassing that a focus on state power—though important—can be a distraction. We need to understand the various complex hierarchies and personal relationships in which power is embedded in contemporary society.

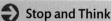 **Stop and Think**

1. What would a society without the state be like? (Would life be 'nasty, brutish, and short', or peaceful and harmonious?)

2. How do our understandings of human nature shape our views of state authority?

Property

It is often claimed that a factor uniting anarchist political ideology is an opposition to private property. In reality, anarchist views on private property are more disparate. For example, some anarchists wish to refuse the institution of private property in its entirety. Others think of private property as the best bulwark for the defence of freedom against the state.

A distinction can be drawn between **individualist** and **collectivist** forms of anarchism. Individualist anarchism has clearer affinities with liberal and libertarian ideologies, and tends to support the institution of private property. Collectivist anarchism (which includes the work of Proudhon, Bakunin, and the communist anarchism of Kropotkin) not only has affinities with socialist ideology, it in part emerged from this ideology. It also takes a more critical stance to private property.

But to start with, what is the difference between liberalism and libertarianism? It will be useful first to differentiate between negative and positive liberty. Here we follow a distinction made by Isaiah Berlin (1958). Negative liberty is understood primarily as 'freedom from' restrictions imposed from the outside—particularly by the state. Positive liberty on the other hand is concerned with self-mastery, that is the capacity to exercise control over one's life in order to achieve a fundamental purpose. Berlin considers positive liberty problematic because it can lead to collectives—including states—imposing forms of control judged to be necessary for self-mastery. That is, states and groups come to tell people what they should desire. For Berlin, this could lead to totalitarianism (see also Chapter 2).

In the British context, liberal ideology is more closely aligned with the idea of supporting negative liberty and refusing positive liberty. In the US context, liberal ideology is usually considered to be more socially minded—as in the work of John Rawls. Strong supporters of negative liberty and property rights would be characterized as 'libertarians'. A key libertarian thinker in the US context is Robert Nozick (for further discussion of Rawls and Nozick see Chapter 2). Nozick is a libertarian and not an anarchist for one main reason—states are regarded by him as legitimate and necessary, though only in a 'minimal' sense.

For private property cannot be sustained without the functions of law and order. However, states should not go beyond these functions to provide social welfare. The views of anarcho-capitalists such as Murray Rothbard (1973) align with Nozick's premises—radical individual rights and negative freedoms—but they do not accept his conclusions. As they see it, minimal states do not stay minimal for long! They tend always to violate the principles of individual sovereignty, private property, and open markets.

The American anarchist Benjamin Tucker (1854–1939) influenced anarcho-capitalist thinking, and was himself influenced by Max Stirner's egoism. Stirner defends 'egoistic property'—supporting the removal of those moral restrictions on how individuals can use the world and others—but the institution of property itself he considered as a 'spook'. Tucker recognizes the need for a contractual basis to property—but not that such contracts would be enforced by the state. For all states undermine property which is the foundation of liberty. Tucker goes so far as to claim that: 'Whoever denies private property is of necessity an Archist [a supporter of elite rule]' (Tucker 1913).

To return to classical anarchism—we have noted Stirner's influence above. But what about other classical anarchists? Godwin's views on private property at times seem ambiguous—some regarding him as a defender of property, and others (including Kropotkin) as a proto-communist. In his *Enquiry Concerning Political Justice* (1793), Godwin provides a limited defence of the right to property. He distinguishes between three types of property: first, the property which a person uses for their individual satisfaction, second, the property resulting from an individual's own labour, and third, the property which results from the exploitation of others. It was this third form of property to which Godwin objected. But given the time in which he was writing, this itself was a radical stance to take.

Proudhon's critique of property appears to be much less nuanced and more overtly radical. In *What is Property?* (1840), Proudhon provided a simple answer: 'It is robbery!' Proudhon's claim is clearly rhetorical; but it is also regarded by some as oxymoronic. For, as many commentators have remarked (including Stirner), to have an idea of 'robbery', we must also think that property is somehow legitimate.

It is also the case that Proudhon's objections seemed to be focused more on large-scale than small-scale property. He did not particularly oppose the ownership of personal possessions through which individuals met their day to day needs—say through small-scale agricultural production; indeed, such property could be virtuous. Rather, he opposed property where it came to comprise a basis of misery and inequality. Indeed, Proudhon came to support a form of organization that would bring together the best aspects of 'private property and collective ownership', uniting moral virtues of historical small-scale ownership with the present realities of industrial society. To this extent, Marx considered his outlook to be 'petty-bourgeois'. For his part, Proudhon considered Marx a 'fanatic of State power' (Proudhon 1846, cited in Marshall 1993: 242).

In Proudhon's anarchism, society comes to be viewed as a free association between autonomous producers—this is what he meant by '**mutualism**'. Such association was necessary to ensure that no one individual or group enjoyed a monopoly of economic power.

Authors such as Bakunin and Kropotkin were critical of Proudhon's individualism and (ambiguous) support for private property. Yet—at least with Bakunin—property continues to have an ambiguous status. For example, he is not at all clear whether he supports small-scale peasant property. However, like Proudhon, Bakunin's main objection is to large-scale industrial property—that is, capitalism. The critique of industrial capitalism which both thinkers provide comes from anti-statist principles. Capitalism and the state are bound together in an (un)holy alliance in which the state is the dominant partner. Thus, in understanding property, we need to understand the will to power of the state.

This 'will to power' of the state led it to drive into new territories to acquire riches, and hence to war. If Bakunin's opposition to Tsarism stimulated his initial thought, then his encounter with Marx in the First International led him to think that 'statism' was a danger not only of feudal and capitalist class society, but also of the communist project.

Tolstoy's critique of private property—like others of his views—took quite a different line to other classical anarchists. Yet it is worth mentioning not least because like Bakunin he had witnessed the violence of large-scale aristocratic private property on which the Russian class system was based. As might be expected from his religious convictions, Tolstoy opposed the idea of individuals holding property to the exclusion of others; for the earth was a common resource of the Kingdom of God (Tolstoy 1893). The dominant ideology of the Tsarist state into which Bakunin, Tolstoy, and Kropotkin were born was based on the 'divine right of kings', where the earth was passed directly from Adam and Eve to monarchs, monarchs who were answerable only to God.

Tolstoy—like Locke in the seventeenth century—showed great bravery in rejecting this idea. Yet Tolstoy went further than Locke. For Locke, the earth was given to human kind in common; yet God commanded humans to labour and thus to take this common resource into private ownership. Tolstoy rejected any such idea. The communality of property was a Christian principle. Thus landed property in this sense is an evil comparable with that of government—comprising as it does a false authority. Tolstoy was only too well aware of the violence of large-scale landed property, excluding as it did in his own time the masses from the means of their basic subsistence. This did not lead him in any way to adopt a communist position however. He did not, for example, oppose the idea of small-scale peasant property.

We have seen already how Kropotkin challenged the 'survival of the fittest' ethos central to the capitalist conception of human nature. Indeed, most of Kropotkin's critique of capitalism is made at the level of the critique of capitalist conceptions of human nature. And it is difficult to think of an anarchist writer who challenges more the central assumptions which characterize the work of an anarcho-capitalist such as Murray Rothbard, or indeed individualist anarchists such as Stirner and Tucker.

Kropotkin's belief in the social character of human nature led him to adopt an anarchist-communist ethic. For Kropotkin 'All belongs to all. All things are for all men, since all men have need of them, since all men have worked in the measure of their strength to produce them' (Kropotkin 1907). Whilst critiquing the institution of private property and defending a form of communism, Kropotkin, like Bakunin, rejected the tendency towards absolute power characteristic of statist variants of this ideology, criticizing directly the Russian communist Lenin.

The contemporary anarchist Murray Bookchin sees property as a function of social hierarchy. Hierarchy in all its forms should be challenged by radical politics. Moreover, and importantly, he argues directly against those who maintain that capitalism and the protection of the environment are compatible. Contemporary post-anarchists such as Saul Newman have challenged the way in which capitalism attempts to subject the whole of social and natural life to exploitation and the rule of the market, as have **autonomist** thinkers such as Hardt and Negri.

Anarchist views on property can be summarized as follows:

- On balance it is possible (with some qualifications) to regard Bakunin, Kropotkin, and Tolstoy and contemporary post-anarchism as opposing private property.

- Proudhon's position is perhaps not so clear. Proudhon is less critical of petty-bourgeois property as he is of large-scale capitalist property (which for him was robbery).

- Stirner influenced anarcho-capitalist thinking. He was an egoist who believed that restrictions on how individuals could use the world and others should be removed. Yet he believed that private property rights and contracts were 'spooks'—entirely fictitious ideas with no basis.

⤵ Stop and Think

1. Is private property 'robbery' (Proudhon)?
2. Is there a moral difference between the property acquired through our own labour, and that acquired through using the labour of others?

Case Study 5.2 The International Workingmen's Association (IWA) and the division between anarchism and communism

CONTEXT

The International Workingmen's Association (IWA) was founded in 1864, and came to an acrimonious end in 1876. Referred to now as the First International, the IWA brought together a wide range of left wing groupings, from anarchists to socialists, from trade unionists to communists. The founding meeting was in St Martin's Hall, London, and its first congress was held in Geneva in 1866. At the founding meeting there were followers of the anarchist Pierre-Joseph Proudhon, of the social reformer Robert Owen (known as 'Owenites'), and of the radical socialist Blanqui. Karl Marx was also present at this meeting, and was to become more important as the association developed. One estimate is that at its peak the IWA had five million members.

The Owenite movement—named after its founder Robert Owen (1771–1858)—developed from the experience of widespread poverty in Britain after the Napoleonic Wars (1803–1815). Often characterized as 'utopian socialism', Owenism stressed the importance of 'a fair day's work for a fair day's labour'. To put its principles into practice, it helped in the development of utopian communities which stressed not the principle of competition characteristic of laissez-faire capitalism, but of cooperation. Although radical, it believed in the importance of social reform, not revolution. In contrast, Blanqui stressed the importance of violent revolution led by a small group of revolutionaries.

It was in this context of a battle between reformism and revolution that the revolutionary ideas of Marx and Bakunin were to be developed, and indeed an ideological break between anarchism and communism established, a break resulting in a split in the IWA in 1872.

It should also be pointed out that Marx and Bakuniun really did not get on. Bakunin was an anti-Semite (a prejudice he shared with Proudhon), who considered Marx's vision of communism to be a part of a Jewish conspiracy. And Marx, in a secret letter which was circulated to leaders in the German Social-Democratic Workers' Party, had raised the prospect that Bakunin may be a 'Russian suspect'—that is a spy working for the Russian state. And the express value Marx placed on Bakunin's work can be summed up in one word: 'drivel'.

IDEOLOGY

It is worth contrasting the specific ideological differences between Marx and Bakunin, in order to shed more light on the key themes of the chapter. Both Marx and Bakunin considered human nature to be the product of social circumstance. It has been argued that in his early work, Marx thought of human nature as a good which had come to be 'alienated' by the worst excesses of the capitalist system. By his later work, human nature was considered to be entirely the result of social forces. Human beings are simply different, depending on the period of history. Accordingly, Marx spoke less of human nature and 'freedom' than he did of the specific interests of social classes. The IWA for Marx should focus on overcoming class oppression; and this necessitated communism. Bakunin in contrast thought that a key function of the IWA should be to release the destructive and anti-authoritarian passions—through the promotion of the 'propaganda of the deed'.

Concerning the state, the differences between Marx and Bakunin were more pronounced. Marx clearly wanted to contribute to the development of the IWA partly because he considered that it could be regarded as a precursor to a workers' party. And as far back as the *Communist*

Manifesto in 1848, Marx and Engels had considered that the workers' party would comprise a key component in the 'dictatorship of the proletariat'. For Bakunin, these were 'Statist' aspirations. Marx was, he claimed, a proponent of the 'out and out cult of the State'. He thought that Marx 'saw no salvation for the workers except in the power of the State' (Bakunin 1867–1872).

The communists and anarchists adopted a rhetoric of opposition to the institution of private property. Marx wanted a society based on the common ownership of the means of production', in which social class relations would be abolished. This was also the case with Bakunin, although his views of peasant property were ambiguous. Yet the express position of the IWA never asserted the opposition to private property with such strength. This is in part because such a statement might well have alienated those members who were focused more on social reform than revolution.

We will look at anarchist approaches to political action and religion in the next section. For the moment, it should be noted that religion was not of overt political significance in the IWA. It does, however, have a particular significance in Spanish anarchism (see Case Study 5.3). On the theme of political action, Marx thought that Bakunin was not committed to the idea of the self-emancipation of the working classes; Bakunin was for Marx a 'Blanquist'. Indeed, Bakunin wrote of the need for the revolutionary cause to be developed through the 'organ' of the 'secret and worldwide association of the international brethren' (Bakunin, cited in Draper 1986: 57). Clearly such words led Marx to consider that Bakunin wished to take over the IWA for less than desirable purposes. It is also the case that during this period Marx had stressed the importance of agitating politics through parliamentary involvement. The supporters of Bakunin would have no truck with parliamentary politics in any form.

 Stop and Think

1. Will revolutionary movements always produce leadership elites?
2. Is it inevitable that revolutionary movements must engage with state power to achieve their objectives?

Religion

In his essay *What is Enlightenment?* (1784), Kant answered that it was having 'the courage to use one's own reason'. Yet Kant, like other classical liberal thinkers such as Locke, was no atheist. Both Kant and Locke were radical Protestants who believed in the right of the individual to pursue their own road to salvation. Both challenged the 'divine right of kings', and in particular the use this idea had been put to by authoritarian Catholic governments throughout Europe. Accordingly, both believed in the need to separate state and religious authority—but neither religion nor the institution of the state itself is rejected (though the view of its institution as based on Godly command is).

With the exception of Tolstoy, the classical anarchists in this chapter start with liberalism's Enlightenment stress on reason and turn it to radical purposes; that is they turn the critical tool of reason into an attack on religion and the state as institutions. Not only must religion and state be separated, both should be abolished, if real human freedom is to be possible. As such, they were atheists.

Before addressing the complexity of Tolstoy's thought, we can start this section with some remarks about Godwin. Godwin's position was far removed from that of the simple atheist. Godwin had been a strongly committed Calvinist in his youth (Marshall 1993: 79), going so far as training to become a minister. His views on religion seemed to take various turns throughout his life. At the time he wrote the *Enquiry Concerning Political Justice* in 1793, he had come under the influence of the atheist Baron d'Holbach and the view that not only was morality possible without religion, but that religion was a barrier to morality.

If Godwin's relationship to Christianity is complex, this would seem to be less so with Proudhon. What for example could be clearer than the statement 'God is evil, man is free', or 'Each step in our progress represents one more victory in which we annihilate the Deity'? (Proudhon 1846).

Proudhon's ideas can be compared with those of the journalist Christopher Hitchens. (Hitchens, it should be pointed out, was not an anarchist.) For Hitchens 'religion is our first . . . version of the truth . . . but because it is our first it is our worst ... it has become a really great peril to our ability to live as a civilised species' (Hitchens 2009; see also Hitchens 2007). Proudhon follows a similar narrative. The idea of God is initially necessary as a pre-scientific explanation of our origins, and indeed of the wider meaning of life. Yet it becomes a corrupting idea, an excuse not to think, a barrier to enlightenment. Moreover, for Proudhon—as for Hitchens after him—it is not only the idea of God which is problematic; criticism ought to be turned on the institutions of organized religion which perpetuate bigotry and unreason. This focus on the corrupting influence of religious institutions, we shall see later in this section, takes on an interesting form in the work of Tolstoy.

Stirner was a member of the Young Hegelian movement which had a significant impact on the work of Marx and Engels, as well as Proudhon and Bakunin. Stirner's thoughts on religion are perhaps some of his most uncompromising. Religious ideas are 'spooks', barriers to egoism. As Stirner put it:

> My concern is neither the divine nor the human, not the true, good, just, free, etc., but solely what is mine. . . . Nothing is more to me than myself!

> (Stirner, 1844)

Stirner is being playful here—however, the point is a variation of the one he frequently makes. On one level, he might be asking that we should think and act as though we can set aside all those ideas which operate as external constraints to our ego. Put crudely, embrace the ego and run with it! However, there is a further aspect to his argument. For it seems clear that there is no social or political aspect whatsoever to Stirner's critique of religion. It does not concern him at all whether others adopt his cause. As an egoist, Stirner will do what *he* wishes!

This is quite different to the work of Bakunin to whom we must now turn. For Bakunin really does care what others think. His thought on religion is political to the core.

Like Stirner and the other Young Hegelians, religious ideas were for Bakunin considered as alienated abstractions, that is, human creations which had come to dominate us. So, for example, Feuerbach had argued that human beings had come to place a range of attributes in the idea of God—truth, justice, beauty—which then came to shape principles of conduct. Of course, humans are not 'perfect'. We are flawed. In attempting to live up to a range of principles which we have created, we become—to put it simply—miserable, repressed hypocrites. But we also crucially become subservient to the 'guardians' of these principles.

Bakunin's argument follows such an approach. There is also a faith in reason which is comparable to Proudhon, but absent in Stirner. Bakunin wrote: 'All religions, with their gods, their demigods, and their prophets, their messiahs and their saints, were created by the credulous fancy of men who had not attained the full development and full possession of their faculties' (Bakunin 1871).

Religion again is viewed as a pre-rational form of thinking which humans should grow out of. Yet they were prevented from doing so by those with a vested interest in maintaining the status quo: the church and the state. Of course, Bakunin had been brought up in the context of Tsarist Russia where an orthodox religion was wedded to an absolutist state. And he was acutely aware of the violence which this coupling could bring. Accordingly, he called for the abolition of the church and state, by violent means if necessary. Indeed, it has been suggested that Bakunin was in part responsible for the position taken by the Spanish anarchists towards Catholicism in the Spanish Civil War, one which led to the burning of churches and the execution of priests.

We turn now to another Russian anarchist and aristocrat—Tolstoy. Tolstoy is a 'Christian anarchist'.

Tolstoy was such an unorthodox Christian that he challenges the assumptions of deism and theism. Both deism and theism hold to a view of the 'oneness' of God, which in Christian theology is supported by the idea of the Holy Trinity. Christ for Tolstoy was a man—a man who did not perform miracles. The stories of such miracles were for him more than simply superstitions; they also gave to someone who was a mere man a form of authority which could be held only by God. This idea of godlike authority was used time and again in history to justify the oppressive power of states. It should also be pointed out that deism is more directly political than theism—to the extent that in not intervening, God leaves politics to human beings.

Tolstoy wished to refuse the power of established religion and its relationship to state power. For Tolstoy, all governments must be considered as illegitimate. The idea of human allegiance to government was challenged. Tolstoy emphasized the word of the Gospels of Matthew—specifically Christ's Sermon on the Mount. Here the very idea of binding oaths is challenged. Thus: 'Do not take an oath at all, either by heaven. . . . Let what you say be simply "Yes" or "No"; anything more than this comes from evil' (The Bible, Matthew 5: 37).

Yet Tolstoy's denial of state authority did not lead him to adopt a revolutionary politics. In contrast, particularly to Bakunin, Tolstoy adopted a radical politics of non-resistance which many consider to be quite alien to the anarchist tradition. Again, Tolstoy grounds this in the words of Christ in Matthew 5–7: 'You have heard that it was said, "An eye for an eye and a tooth for a tooth". But I say to you, Do not resist the one who is evil. But if anyone slaps you on the right cheek, turn to him the other also.'

Kropotkin continued the anarchist critique of organized religion; and although he was sympathetic to much of Tolstoy's thought, he rejected religion in theory and practice. He was also not a pacifist, having supported the cause of the Allies in the First World War. There were no religious views holding back his desire to see revolution. He equated religious practices with other forms of exploitation, and saw the need to overcome such exploitation through revolutionary activity (see Kropotkin 1898).

Contemporary anarchist thinkers continue the critique of religion which we find, for example, in the work of Bakunin and Kropotkin. Bookchin sees religious authority as yet another hierarchical relation to be refused. For post-anarchists, religion is yet another meta-narrative to be refused. Organized religion is typically condemned because it is embedded in sets of oppressive social practices, which are frequently directed by the state, and is also used to justify discriminatory practices such as sexism and homophobia.

Anarchist views on religion can be summarized as follows:

- All the thinkers in this chapter—with the exception of Tolstoy—can be regarded as atheists. Stirner regarded religious ideas and practices as 'spooks'. Again he poses egoism as the way to exorcise these 'spooks'.

- Proudhon hopes that we will grow out of religion, but thinks too that—primarily because of its relation to state authority—religion should be abolished. Bakunin makes this claim in an even more radical form. Religion should be abolished, by violence where necessary.

- The odd one out in this chapter is Tolstoy. Like states, organized religion has no authority over human beings. We should deny their authority, but importantly we should not act to refuse it. Organized religion and states may together embody violence. But in response we should 'turn the other cheek'.

⮕ Stop and Think

1. Are anarchists correct to claim that organized religion supports practices of subordination, exploitation, and domination?

2. To what extent is religion compatible with anarchist ideas of human freedom?

Case Study 5.3 Anarchism in Spain

CONTEXT

In 1868, Bakunin himself had made an attempt to bring anarchism to Spain, through his follower Giuseppi Fanelli. It had been Bakunin's aim to engage with Spain in order to recruit members for the IWA, and therefore offset what he considered to be the disproportionate power of Marx and his followers. This plan was in part successful, to the extent that an active Barcelona section of the IWA was founded in 1869, and by 1870, the Madrid chapter had approximately 2,000 members.

Proudhon also had a significant number of followers in Spain; these followers were known as 'federalists'. The most prominent amongst them was Francesc Pi i Margall (1824–1901), who was also for a brief period President of the First Spanish Republic in 1873. During his time as President, Pi i Margall had tried to put his ideas into practice, with an attempt—in the words of the *Encyclopaedia Britannica*—to establish a 'decentralized, or "cantonalist," political system on Proudhonian lines' (*Encyclopaedia Britannica* 2014).

Throughout the remainder of the nineteenth century, anarchist ideas remained popular, although this was particularly with those in rural rather than industrial areas. Indeed, after 1872, Spanish anarchism became more firmly decentralizing in its aspirations. In the 1870s, peasant communities were involved in a number of rebellions which were brutally repressed by the state. Accordingly, Spanish anarchism for some time came to adopt an approach based on the Bakuninist idea of the 'propaganda of the deed', that is secretive, **sectarian**, and violent tactics. This in turn led the state to renew its violence against the anarchists.

Anarchist collectives in Spain were also vibrant and successful examples of anarchism in action. Rural collectives combined communal organization with popular forms of self-management. Spanish anarchists also attempted to use the lessons from the rural context to refuse the forms of technological rationalization which enabled the exploitation of Spanish workers in the cities (see Bookchin 1974).

At the beginning of the twentieth century, Spain also saw a rise in **anarcho-syndicalism**. Anarcho-syndicalism considers that revolutionary trade unions could become a mechanism via which workers can gain control of the economy in a capitalist society. As such, anarcho-syndicalism is a variant of collectivist anarchism. The Confederacion Nacional de Trabajo (CNT) (founded in 1910) adopted such an approach, with the general strike being its key weapon. In its policy, it met strong opposition from the state.

Anarchism in its various forms did find a common enemy in the Nationalist forces of General Franco who had, in July 1936, attempted a coup against the Popular Front government, resulting in the Spanish Civil War which was won by the Nationalists against the Republicans in 1939. During the Civil War the anarchist struggle simultaneously became an anti-fascist struggle. The anti-fascist cause was far from a united one, with serious hostilities particularly between the Soviet communist aspects of the Popular Front, and the anarchists.

IDEOLOGY

It is true to say that the Spanish anarchists had a more optimistic view of human nature than their nationalist enemies. As with all anarchists, their opposition to the state was strong. Spanish anarchists on the whole—perhaps again because of the influence of Proudhon and Bakunin—were critical of the institution of private property. Indeed, private property—possibly more so than in many European nations—was an institution bound together with state and religious power. Accordingly, the critique of private property simultaneously came to be a critique of state and religious authority. Not surprisingly, therefore, Spanish anarchism was deeply anti-clerical.

Though anti-clerical, it is difficult to imagine a form of anarchism further removed from Tolstoy than in Spain; for the orientation Spanish anarchism adopted to the state was one of violence.

The period from 1936 to the end of the Spanish Civil War has been characterized as the period of 'red terror'. During this period, churches and monasteries were burned, and nearly 7,000 members of the Catholic clergy were killed. But this was also a period of 'white terror'. Franco's forces used extreme forms of violence including targeting civilian populations, an example of which was the Nazi facilitated aerial bombing of the Basque town of Guernica. In contrast to the red terror, the period of white terror continued after the end of the civil war. From 1936 to 1975, the historian Antony Beevor (2006) estimates that 200,000 people were murdered by Franco's forces. Moreover, Franco's state frequently imposed different methods of terror on its population, including rape and other forms of torture.

⮑ Stop and Think

1. Why do you think the refusal of clerical authority, particularly by anarchists in Spain, became so violent?
2. Why were Nationalist forces ultimately victorious over Republican ones in the Spanish Civil War?

Political action

Anarchists tend to be characterized as adopting **pre-figurative** politics. Such politics, in the words of Carl Boggs, should embody 'within the ongoing political practice of a movement . . . those forms of social relations, decision making, culture, and human experience that are the ultimate goal' (see Boggs 1977). At its core, pre-figurative politics is social; it is concerned with generating the form of collective arrangement beyond the state through which a better society can become possible.

Anarchists have a range of views on the issues of politics and political action. Regarding the issue of political agency—that is, who are to be considered the agents of radical political activity—anarchists have adopted a range of complex positions. Regarding the goal of political activity, anarchists have been clear about at least one thing—the goal of political activity should not be the capture of state power.

For Godwin, the practice of government produced citizens who were incapable of using their own private reason to reach intelligent conclusions. As such, the seizure of government power could not be regarded as a sensible objective. Yet Godwin rejected the idea of revolution as a means to overthrow government authority. In a way that chimes with the thought of Tolstoy. Godwin wrote that 'Revolution is engendered by an indignation with tyranny, yet is itself pregnant with tyranny' (Godwin 1793).

Godwin's critical stance is largely negative. Whereas political agency—that is who is to bring about political change, how, and with what knowledge—is a key concern of many classical anarchist thinkers, this is not an issue that concerns Godwin. This is perhaps because it was not until the second half of the nineteenth century, with the growth of working class demands for political representation, that these issues really came to the fore.

We have seen how for Stirner, collective concepts are 'spooks'. Most radical political ideologies have a utopian vision (that is a vision of future society through which they aim to motivate action). For pre-figurative politics, the social and political means must embody this end. For Stirner, there is no such vision, in either means or end. This is because the ideas of society and politics are things which egoism seeks to dispel. Stirner's 'union of egoists' is little more than an arrangement of individuals acting together only where this is in their own interests.

We might consider Tolstoy to be an anti-political thinker too, though in a way quite different to Stirner. For where Stirner's **anti-politics** was based on atheism, Tolstoy's had a clear theological basis. We have seen already how Tolstoy refused the idea of the state—in all its forms—on theological grounds. It is also the case, as with Godwin, that Tolstoy was critical of revolutionary approaches to politics. This is partly because Tolstoy was an advocate of non-violence. It was this aspect of his work that had a profound impact on the work of Ghandi. Yet Tolstoy's argument went further than a simple assertion of non-violence. For example, while many of the anarchists discussed in this chapter advocated that the poor should rise up and overthrow their oppressors, Tolstoy was clear that we should not resist evil, a 'lesson' he took from the Gospel of Matthew.

Tolstoy does not have a substantive view of political agency. Moreover, his view of prefiguration is not political. Our moral life should not be directed at changing the state, but rather as embodying the 'Kingdom of God' which is 'within us'. As such, this is a personal rather than political or social goal. Tolstoy's fiction does document the troubling living conditions of the Russian masses in the nineteenth and early twentieth centuries. In doing so it troubles its readers morally, but makes no demands politically.

Let us move on to explore the work of two classical anarchist thinkers with a far more engaged view of political action and agency—Proudhon and Bakunin. Proudhon, as we have noted, explicitly refused the idea of engaging with the state, in so doing, he advocated a form of pre-figurative politics. Put simply, where Tolstoy instructed us not to resist evil, Proudhon instructed us to refuse evil by seeking to create a new and better world. Whereas it is often considered that for Marxists, revolutions should be tightly organized events, Proudhon thought revolutions are best when entirely spontaneous. Importantly, Proudhon also entertained the possibility—something which Bakunin seemed to refuse—that revolutions could be non-violent.

Who are the agents best situated to bring about such revolution? While Stirner and Tolstoy for different reasons do not answer this, Proudhon's stance is complex.

Marx and his followers had regarded Proudhon as a theorist of the 'petty bourgeoi-sie'. Yet he also seems to have considered that the 'proletariat' would be an important force of change, mainly because it had an interest in overthrowing the division of labour, and hence the status quo.

Two remarks need to be made in relation to this view. First, Proudhon also seems to wish to roll back industrialization, and return to a society of small-scale producers; second, his views were contaminated with serious prejudice. If he had a commit-ment to the emancipation of the proletariat, it was based on a rather limited view of what comprises this class. Proudhon was a sexist. He wished to exclude women from public life, writing 'society does no injustice to woman by refusing her equality before the law .... Woman really has no place in the world of politics and economics' (Proudhon cited in Marshall 1993: 256). Proudhon was also an extreme racist. He had a paranoid hatred of Jews, even calling for their 'extermination' (see Marshall 1993: 257). We can only conclude that the proletariat for whom Proudhon supported emancipation was white and male; his anarchist society would presumably be prem-ised on **segregation**, even genocide.

It is worth pointing out that Bakunin too was a sexist and anti-Semite (see Bakunin 1990 [1873]). If we can suspend our disapproval of these abhorrent views for a moment, we can explore some other aspects of Bakunin's politics. Marshall (1993) characterizes Bakunin as a 'fanatic' of freedom. His fanaticism meant that he was a person of action. He believed in the power of revolution. And he considered that violence was often—probably always—an aspect of such revolution.

It could be suggested that Bakunin's almost enthusiastic acceptance of violence must lead us to challenge the interpretation of Bakunin as a pre-figurative thinker. For Bakunin seems to suggest that violent means can produce a non-violent end. Yet this is not so clear cut; for in a way there is no end towards which Bakunin's politics aims. As we have noted, the 'urge to destroy was a creative urge'. He did not believe—in contrast to Marx—in a communist society which would restore harmony and peace to human kind. Bakunin's politics was a politics of the continual fight.

Bakunin also argued that revolutions should not be led by elites, but through the spontaneous activity of the masses. He wrote that: 'The peoples' revolution ... will arrange its revolutionary organisation from the bottom up and from the periphery to the centre' (Bakunin 1869). Bakunin's placed his faith in the 'lumpenproletariat'—the marginal, the excluded, the unemployed, the poor. For Bakunin, the lumpenproletariat were the 'flower', the truly revolutionary class. They were not interested in bargaining up their wage levels to a position of relative comfort. Theirs was a real urge to destroy!

We turn now to Kropotkin. First, we might note that racism and sexism were not an aspect of Kropotkin's thought; second, nor was the anti-communism which we see in the work of Proudhon and Bakunin. His anarchism was firmly of a collectivist, indeed communist, character. Could one imagine an argument more different to Stirner's than when Kropotkin writes: 'All belongs to all. All things are for all men' (Kropotkin

1907: 14)? Yet perhaps what sets this vision of communal life apart from Marx is the strength of Kropotkin's opposition to the state—which we have seen above in the section on 'The state'. As with Proudhon and Bakunin, Kropotkin expressed support for federalism, although within a wider structure of 'communist economics'. The extent to which this was achievable was questioned by many.

In contrast to his fellow Russian, Tolstoy, Kropotkin was no pacifist. He had stressed what he considered to be the militaristic threat of Germany at the start of the twentieth century, and had called for conscription. He also voiced his support of the Allies when war broke out in 1914. Interestingly, the concern about whether to support the war divided the left in a way from which it never really recovered. Kropotkin's position resulted in him being criticized both by fellow anarchists and Marxists.

Kropotkin retained a belief in the revolutionary potential of the working classes. This, he thought, was particularly the case with French, British, and—later in his life—American workers. Moreover, strikes and other forms of industrial action could educate workers in order to move in a revolutionary direction; as such, political action is the best way to generate further political action. Therefore, Kropotkin's politics is clearly pre-figurative, with the end never being predetermined, but rather emerging from the adoption of particular means. Consequently, Kropotkin's political views were opposed to the idea of vanguards; that is, he did not think that revolution was best brought about through the leadership of small elites with 'real' historical knowledge. Indeed, he thought that this was a sure way of defeating revolutions. This was because elites tend to govern in their own interests.

Contemporary anarchists such as Bookchin and Ward have argued for the importance of pre-figurative politics. Bookchin has stressed the significance of citizens' assemblies; Ward argues for non-hierarchical organization based on what he terms 'cybernetics'. Post-anarchist thinkers have maintained that political action cannot be exclusively state focused. Given that power and exploitation is everywhere, so must be its refusal. For a thinker such as Holloway (2002, 2010)—who has certain affinities with anarchism and Marxism—we subvert the power of the employer through 'bunking off' from the office and reading a book in the park. We subvert the commodification of knowledge ('intellectual property') by attempting to create new sites of 'the common'. And, yes, perhaps we subvert the power of the state not by voting—and therefore consenting but by turning away from 'representative democracy', and shaping new forms of decision-making, grounded in types of direct action (see Case Studies 5.4 and 5.5).

Anarchist views on political action may be summarized as follows:

- Stirner and Tolstoy might be regarded as anti-political thinkers, but in quite different ways. Stirner's anti-politics comes from his refusal of 'spooks'. Tolstoy considers that God commands us to refuse politics.
- Most other anarchist thinkers are committed to some idea of political action, though its forms vary. For Proudhon, Bakunin, and Kropotkin, political action

ought to focus on the overthrow of the state and of capitalism and the formation of a new society.

- None of our thinkers agree about what future society should look like.

➔ Stop and Think

1. Is political action the best way to bring about change? (What would happen if we simply 'turned the other cheek'?)

2. Is non-violent revolution possible?

Case Study 5.4 The Zapatistas

CONTEXT

The Zapatistas are a left-wing 'army of national liberation' (Ejército Zapatista de Liberación Nacional, EZLN), based in Chiapas in Southern Mexico. They get their name from Emiliano Zapata, a Mexican revolutionary who in 1910 formed an army aiming at the liberation of the land of indigenous people from the Mexican state.

On 1 January 1994—the day that the North American Free Trade Agreement (NAFTA) came into effect—the EZLN declared both a defensive war against the Mexican state, and what was to become a wider stance of resistance to the global neo-liberal project of which NAFTA is a key part. For the Zapatistas, signing up to NAFTA in effect was an example of the state signing over national assets to imperial aggressors.

Zapatista 'insurgents' took control of towns and cities in Chiapas, freeing prisoners and setting fire to state buildings. The initial success was short lived, when Mexican forces counterattacked, delivering serious casualties to the Zapatistas. Despite such defeats, the Zapatistas have continued to fight for their cause. In 2001, they marched on Mexico City to present their cause to the Mexican Congress. However, no agreement was reached. Instead the EZLN established thirty-two autonomous municipalities in Chiapas. Accordingly, they sidestepped government in order to deliver their demands.

The Zapatistas have also been broadly sympathetic to the alter-globalization movement, which aims to establish an alternative form of globalization based not on the tyranny of 'free trade', but on cooperation and solidarity. It has also been noted that Zapatistas have had a significant influence on Occupy. Indeed, it can be argued that there are significant rhetorical similarities between Occupy demands and the Zapatistas (see Case Study 5.5).

IDEOLOGY

The 'ideology' of the Zapatistas involves a complex combination of Mayan practices with libertarian socialism, Marxism, and anarchism. The Zapatistas do not advance a substantive account of human nature. Rather, the human condition is bound in a singular struggle for freedom. Human nature, if it is anything, is a project of becoming.

The Zapatistas developed a radical critique of state power. It has been argued (see Greebon 2008) that as an organic development from civil society, it represents a form of 'bottom up' governance—a governance by the people, for the people—which challenges the very legitimacy of state power. The movement challenges traditional representative politics, supporting instead a radical form of participatory democracy. The Zapatistas in this sense do not pursue political or

state power. The Zapatistas have provided an active critique of the neo-liberal project of property accumulation, particularly through the mobilization against NAFTA. To this extent, they at
least oppose the violence of large-scale property ownership.

The Zapatista's view of religion is complex. They combine practices of Christianity with substantive indigenous beliefs. What seems important is that the Zapatistas draw on the strongly
political aspects of different belief systems, in a way which might be characterized as truly post-
colonial. Catholic liberation theology is invoked, as are those indigenous beliefs which enable a
challenge to state power and to capitalist globalization.

Regarding political action, there is a definite pre-figurative aspect to their politics. As Hardt
and Negri note in their book *Multitude* (2004): 'The goal has never been to defeat the state and
claim sovereign authority but rather to change the world without taking power' (Hardt and Negri
2004: 85). If the Zapatistas are anarchists in any sense, they are not so in the sense with which
Tolstoy would sympathize; for they are not pacifists. The people should arm themselves against
the violence of the state. The movement is not traditional 'left revolutionary'. Its social basis is
not the 'industrial proletariat', but, as we have noted, indigenous people. However, the Zapatistas
have support from urban areas, and globally. The movement has a mythical pipe-smoking and
always masked spokesperson—Subcomandante Marcos. He has been described as 'anonymous'
and 'mysterious'. Indeed, some have maintained that his figure represents something of a post-
modern take on the idea of political leader.

In short, we might therefore say that the Zapatistas have been particularly successful at bringing
together a range of complex ideological positions—some, though by no means all, of which have
particular affinities with anarchism—to mobilize against the power of the neo-liberal project.

⬌ Stop and Think

1. Is it possible to 'change the world without taking power'?

2. To what extent is political and societal change more effective if it comes from the 'bottom up',
   rather than the 'top down'?

Case Study 5.5 The Occupy Movement

CONTEXT

The Occupy Movement emerged in late 2011, and appeared to be a global phenomenon. Some of
its members considered themselves 'anarchists'; others were not so overtly ideological. Yet it is clear
that there are many affinities between the ideals of Occupy and those of classical and post-anarchism.

In July 2011, the Canadian-based online magazine, *Adbusters*, circulated a call to 'flood into
lower Manhattan, set up tents, kitchens, peaceful barricades and occupy Wall Street' (*Adbusters*,
2011). The date set by the *Adbusters*' call of 17 September 2011 was the start of a sixty-day
encampment at Zucotti Park in New York City. By February 2012, there had been an estimated
1,517 occupations globally—in, for example, Armenia, Cyprus, Israel, Malaysia, Nepal, South
Korea, Turkey, the United Kingdom, and the USA.

The influences on Occupy were global. A group of long-term New York activists came together with
activists from Tunisia, Egypt, and Spain in August 2011, to discuss how the lessons of movements such

as the Arab Spring (the wave of violent and non-violent protests across the Middle East and North Africa which started with the Tunisian revolution of 18 December 2010) and Los Indignados (the popular movement in Spain against cuts to social welfare provision) could inform the practice of this movement. Although the Arab Spring and Los Indignados were very different, they did share certain features. First, they *seemed* to come from nowhere, without presenting an overall strategy or plan, and, second, they made extensive use of social media, including Facebook and Twitter.

IDEOLOGY

The *Adbusters* call had cited 'one demand': '#Occupy Wall Street'. To what extent was Occupy an anarchist movement? Some key 'Occupiers' (for example, David Graeber 2011) did identify themselves as anarchists. Yet it has been suggested that publicly they chose not to declare this for fear that it would get in the way of the attempt to develop a broad based movement. (For a further discussion of this issue, see Bates et al. 2016.)

To return to the philosophical themes of this chapter, the Occupiers hold rather disparate views concerning human nature. For some, the 'political classes' or the bankers represent the 'worst excesses' of human nature. Others regard human nature as ultimately cooperative, meaning that another world is indeed possible. And others avoid any talk of human nature which they consider an Enlightenment racist imposition.

Concerning the state, there is no one position adopted. Take for example Occupy Wall Street and Occupy London. Occupy Wall Street does not really engage with the issue of state power. Occupy London demands more extensive state regulation of banks, an end to the privatization of the welfare state, etc. In contrast, Occupy Wall Street's demands were largely ethical and pre-figurative—along the lines of 'another world is possible', an approach which in part can be explained by the sceptical attitude to government typical of American political life (see Bates et al. 2016).

On the theme of private property, arguments are again disparate. Some Occupiers are clearly motivated by an anti-capitalist ethos—challenging the institution of private property as a whole. Perhaps because of a wish to gain public support, such anti-capitalism was by no means the mainstream of Occupy. Others demand the reform of the worst excesses of private property, arguing for a society where the 99 per cent have a much larger share of global wealth. Those occupations in authoritarian countries often simply demanded an end to members of the government using national resources for their own private gain.

On the topic of religion, Occupy very much characterised itself as a movement of 'all faiths and none'. The extent to which this approach was designed not to alienate the public is an interesting one to debate (see Bates et al. 2016).

Regarding the issue of political action, this is perhaps where the affinities with anarchism are at their clearest. We have noted how anarchism typically favours horizontal structures of organization, in which the roles of leadership elites are challenged. And the General Assembly model favoured by Occupy is an example of this. Small groups come together in order to achieve a consensus on a particular policy. The consensus decision is then taken to the General Assembly with the wider aim of achieving consensus across the occupation. Note that without consensus, no further action can be taken.

There is no official 'leader' within this structure, although most often 'facilitators' are used. A key point of this model is that any programme has to be the result of such deliberation—rather than the adoption of a pre-planned strategy. Some have criticized Occupy, arguing that the lack of such a strategy means that they are not 'serious'. Others have questioned the extent to which Occupy really did operate without 'leaders'. Put another way, Occupy may not have had—at least initially—official 'leaders'—but it definitely had key 'opinion formers', although these individuals were often not out in the open.

 Stop and Think

1. To what extent was the Occupy 'movement' an example of anarchist ideology in action?
2. What are the strengths and weaknesses of the General Assembly as a form of decision making?

Summary

- Anarchism is a complex and often contradictory ideology—as such, its underlying principles are difficult to identify.
- Anarchism has developed crucially as a result of real historical struggle—to this extent it is a practical ideology, in which consistency is not necessarily its key concern.
- Given the complexity of anarchist thought, we are led perhaps to ask 'is there really such a thing as an anarchist ideology'?

Review and discussion questions

1. Compare and contrast the anarchist understanding of the state with that of any other ideology in this book.
2. To what extent is anarchism a coherent ideology?
3. Explain the difference between collectivist visions of anarchism and individualist ones.
4. To what extent are anarchism and religion compatible?

Research exercises

1. Use the internet to research the Occupy movement. Outline the key 'demands' of this movement. To what extent did these demands differ across national contexts? To what extent are these demands realistic? Are these demands anarchist ones?
2. This chapter provides five case studies which provide examples of anarchism in practice. But there are many more such examples. Using the internet as a key research tool, identify at least two others. Do your examples show the ideological coherence of anarchism? If yes, how? If not, why not?

Further reading

For introductions to anarchism by anarchists, see Kinna (2005) and Ward (2004). For an
excellent and extensive overview of the history of anarchism, see Marshall (1993). For 'all
you ever wanted to know about anarchism, but were afraid to ask', see McKay (2012). For
a historical account of the Spanish Civil War, see Beevor (2001). For a discussion of the
Spanish Civil War by a leading contemporary anarchist thinker, see Bookchin (2001). For a
compelling contemporary account of Christian anarchism, see Christoyannopoulos (2010).
For a seminal account of the debate between Karl Marx and his anarchist contemporaries, see Thomas (1980). For post-anarchism, see May (1994) and Newman (2010). See also
Hardt and Negri (2000). An online resource of anarchist literature can be found at: http://
www.spunk.org/

References

ADBUSTERS (2011), https://www.adbusters.org/blogs/adbusters-blog/occupywallstreet.html

BAKUNIN, M. (1842), *The Reaction in Germany*, https://www.marxists.org/reference/archive/
bakunin/works/1842/reaction-germany.htm

BAKUNIN, M. (1867), *Rousseau's Theory of the State*, https://www.marxists.org/reference/archive/
bakunin/works/various/rousseau.htm

BAKUNIN, M. (1867–72), *Marxism, Freedom and the State*, https://www.marxists.org/reference/
archive/bakunin/works/mf-state/ch03.htm

BAKUNIN, M. (1869), *The Program of the International Brotherhood*, https://www.marxists.org/
reference/archive/bakunin/works/1869/program.htm

BAKUNIN, M. (1871), *God and the State*, https://www.marxists.org/reference/archive/bakunin/
works/godstate/ch02.htm

BAKUNIN, M. (1990), *Marxism, Freedom and the State*, K. J. Kenafick (ed. and trans.), London:
Freedom Press.

BATES, D., OGILVIE, M., AND POLE, E. (2016), 'Occupy: In Theory and Practice', *Critical Discourse
Studies*, Vol. 13, No. 3, pp. 341–55.

BEEVOR, A. (2006), *The Battle for Spain: The Spanish Civil War 1936–1939*, Harmondsworth:
Penguin.

BERLIN, I. (1958), 'Two Concepts of Liberty', in I. Berlin (1969), *Four Essays on Liberty*, Oxford:
Oxford University Press.

BOGGS, C. (1977), 'Marxism, Prefigurative Communism, and the Problem of Workers' Control',
Radical America (November), Vol. 11, pp. 99–122. See also: https://libcom.org/library/marx-
ism-prefigurative-communism-problem-workers-control-carl-boggs

BOOKCHIN, M. (1974), 'Introduction', in S. Dolgoff (ed.), *The Anarchist Collectives: Workers' Self-
Management in the Spanish Revolution (1936–1939)*, New York: Free Life Editions. See https://
theanarchistlibrary.org/library/sam-dolgoff-editor-the-anarchist-collectives

BOOKCHIN, M. (1986), *Post-Scarcity Anarchism*, Chico, CA: AK Press.

BOOKCHIN, M. (1990), *Remaking Society*, Chico, CA: AK Press.

BOOKCHIN, M. (1997), *The Politics of Social Ecology*, Montreal: Black Rose Books.

BOOKCHIN, M. (2001), *The Spanish Anarchists: The Heroic Years 1868–1936*, Montreal: Black Rose Books.

CARTER, I. (2012), 'Positive and Negative Liberty', http://plato.stanford.edu/entries/liberty-positive-negative/

CHAPPEL, R. H. (1978), 'Anarchy Revisited: An Inquiry into the Public Education Dilemma', *Journal of Libertarian Studies*, Vol. 2, No. 4, pp. 357–72.

CHRISTOYANNOPOULOS, A. (2011), *Christian Anarchism*. Exeter: Imprint Academic.

DRAPER, H. (1986), *Karl Marx's Theory of Revolution*, Vol. III. New York: Monthly Review Press.

ENCYCLOPAEDIA BRITANNICA (2016), 'Anarchism', http://www.britannica.com/topic/anarchism

FEUERBACH, L. (1841), *The Essence of Christianity*, https://www.marxists.org/reference/archive/feuerbach/works/essence/

FREEDEN, M. (2003), *Ideology: A Very Short Introduction*, Oxford: Oxford University Press.

GODWIN, W. (1793), *Inquiry Concerning Political Justice*, http://oll.libertyfund.org/titles/90

GOLDMAN, E. (1910), 'Anarchism: What it Really Stands For', https://www.marxists.org/reference/archive/goldman/works/1910s/anarchism.htm

GRAEBER, D. (2011), 'Occupy and Anarchism's Gift for Democracy', http://www.theguardian.com/commentisfree/cifamerica/2011/nov/15/occupy-anarchism-gift-democracy

GREEBON, D. A. (2008), 'Civil Society's Challenge to the State: A Case Study of the Zapatistas and their Global Significance', *The Journal of Development and Social Transformation*, Vol. 5, No. 71, https://www.maxwell.syr.edu/uploadedFiles/moynihan/dst/Greebon.pdf?n=4980

HARDT, M. AND NEGRI, A. (2000), *Empire*, Cambridge, MA: Harvard University Press.

HARDT, M. AND NEGRI, A. (2004), *Multitude*, Harmondsworth: Penguin.

HARDT, M. AND NEGRI, A. (2010), *Commonwealth*, Cambridge, MA: Harvard University Press.

HARDT, M. AND NEGRI, A. (2011), *Declaration*, available as an ebook only, http://www.amazon.com/Declaration-Michael-Hardt-ebook/dp/B00816QAFY

HERN, M. (2003), 'The Emergence of Compulsory Schooling and Anarchist Resistance', http://theanarchistlibrary.org/library/matt-hern-the-emergence-of-compulsory-schooling-and-anarchist-resistance#fn13

HITCHENS, C. (2007), *Why God is Not Great—How Religion Poisons Everything*, New York: Twelve Books.

HITCHENS, C. (2009), 'God is Our First and Worst Attempt at the Truth', https://www.youtube.com/watch?v=LeV17JI-KVA

HOBSBAWM, E. (1991), *Nations and Nationalism*, Cambridge: Cambridge University Press.

HOLLOWAY, J. (2002), *Changing the World Without Taking Power*, see http://libcom.org/library/change-world-without-taking-power-john-holloway.

HOLLOWAY, J. (2010), *Crack Capitalism*, see http://libcom.org/files/Holloway%20-%20Crack%20Capitalism.pdf.

ILLICH, I. (1971), *Deschooling Society*, New York: Harper & Row.

INTERNATIONAL WORKINGMEN'S ASSOCIATION (1864), 'General Rules', https://www.marxists.org/history/international/iwma/documents/1864/rules.htm

Joll, J. (1979), *The Anarchists*, London: Routledge.

Kant, I. (1991 [1784]), 'What is Enlightenment?' in *Kant: Political Writings*, ed. H. S. Reiss and trans. H. B. Nisbet, Cambridge: Cambridge University Press.

Kinna, R. (2005), *Anarchism: A Beginner's Guide*, Oxford: One World.

Kropotkin, P. (1898), *Fields, Factories and Workshops: or Industry Combined with Agriculture and Brain Work with Manual Work,* https://theanarchistlibrary.org/library/petr-kropotkin-fields-factories-and-workshops-or-industry-combined-with-agriculture-and-brain-w

Kropotkin, P. (2002 [1898]), 'Anarchist Morality', in R. N. Baldwin (ed.), *Anarchism: A Collection of Revolutionary Writings*, New York: Dover Publications

Kropotkin, P. (1902), *Mutual Aid*, https://www.marxists.org/reference/archive/kropotkin-peter/1902/mutual-aid/

Kropotkin, P. (1907), *The Conquest of Bread*, https://libcom.org/library/the-conquest-of-bread-peter-kropotkin

Kropotkin, P. (1910), 'Anarchism', https://www.marxists.org/reference/archive/kropotkin-peter/1910/britannica.htm

Kropotkin, P. (1920), Letter to Lenin 4 March 1920, http://dwardmac.pitzer.edu/Anarchist_Archives/kropotkin/kropotlenindec203.html

Levy, C. (2010), 'Social Histories of Anarchism', *Journal for the Study of Radicalism*, Vol. 4, No. 2, pp. 1–44.

McKay, I. (2012), *An Anarchist FAQ*—2 Vols, Chico, CA: AK Press.

Marx, K. and Engels, F. (2015 [1848]), *The Communist Manifesto*, Harmondsworth: Penguin.

Marx, K. and Engels, F. (1879), 'Circular Letter', https://www.marxists.org/archive/marx/works/1879/letters/79_09_15.htm

Marshall, P. (1993), *Demanding the Impossible*, London: Fontana.

Maximoff, G. P. (ed.) (1953), *The Political Philosophy of Bakunin*, Chicago: The University of Chicago.

May, T. (1994), *The Political Philosophy of Post-Structuralist Anarchism*, University Park, PA: Pennsylvania State University Press.

Neal, A. (2004), 'Cutting Off the King's Head: Foucault's Society Must Be Defended and the Problem of Sovereignty', *Alternatives*, Vol. 29, pp. 373–98.

Newman, S. (2010), *The Politics of Post-Anarchism*, https://theanarchistlibrary.org/library/saul-newman-the-politics-of-postanarchism

Nozick, R. (1974), *Anarchy, State and Utopia*, Cambridge, MA: Harvard University Press.

Proudhon, P.-J., cited in P. Marshall (1993), *Demanding the Impossible: A History of Anarchism*, London: Fontana Press, p. 242.

Proudhon, P.-J. (1849), 'Resistance to the Revolution', in I. McKay (ed.), *Property is Theft! A Pierre-Joseph Proudhon Anthology*, Chico, CA: AK Press.

Rothbard, M. (1973), *For a New Liberty: The Libertarian Manifesto*, https://mises.org/library/new-liberty-libertarian-manifesto.

ucation, https://theanarchistlibrary.org/
ation

anarchistlibrary.org/library/max-stirner-

don: Routledge and Keegan Paul.
_u_, https://theanarchistlibrary.org/library/

tarian-labyrinth.org/items/show/318
m Press.
_on_, Oxford: Oxford University Press.
ploding School, London: Routledge.
H. H. Gerth and C. Wright Mills (eds), _From
ge_, pp. 77–128.
. Runciman (ed.) and E. Matthews (trans.),

WITTGENSTEIN, L. (2001) [1953]), _Philosophical Investigations_, Oxford: Blackwell Publishing.

WOLLSTONECRAFT, M. (2004 [1792]), _A Vindication of the Rights of Women_, Harmondsworth: Penguin.

ŽIŽEK, S. (2012), 'Occupy Wall Street: What is to be Done Next?', http://www.theguardian.com/commentisfree/cifamerica/2012/apr/24/occupy-wall-street-what-is-to-be-done-next

6

Nationalism

Mark Langan

OBJECTIVES

- Explore key concepts such as the 'nation', the 'nation-state', and the 'imagined community'
- Demonstrate how the nation is socially constructed, with reference to case studies
- Show how nationalist ideology is expressed within the institutions of the 'nation-state', with particular focus on political parties espousing nationalist views
- Draw distinctions between differing forms of rational-civic and irrational-ethnic nationalisms
- Explore nationalism as a 'sticky' ideology which combines with other forms of political thought i.e. liberalism, socialism, fascism, and conservatism

Introduction

This chapter examines nationalism as ideology. It first defines nationalism and examines how the nation is **socially constructed** as an **imagined community**. Second, the chapter examines the practical implications of nationalist ideology in terms of the functioning of the nation-state (and of nationalist political parties). Third, the chapter considers in more detail the 'rational' form of nationalism (that is the civic variety) and its 'sticky' connections to liberalism and socialism. The chapter then contrasts this rational and somewhat pragmatic nationalism with the 'irrational' and emotional variant found within both conservatism and fascism. The chapter concludes with a summary of key lessons regarding nationalism as ideology.

Defining nationalism

Nationalism as ideology entails a paramount commitment to the well-being of the 'imagined community' (that is, the nation). Nationalism seeks to galvanize individuals to work together for a common purpose within the nation-state (that is, a geographical entity combined with political and economic institutions through which the nation governs itself). Importantly, there is a distinction between differing forms of nationalist thought in terms of 'rational' and 'irrational' modes. The rational form of nationalism is associated with two main ideologies—socialism and liberalism. Nationalism as a creed is thereby 'sticky' in that it can combine with other modes of political thought (Halikiopoulou et al. 2012: 509). Importantly, rational nationalism bases membership of the 'nation' upon civic grounds—largely in terms of residency within the geographical confines of the nation-state. Irrational nationalism, on the other hand, privileges ethnic affiliation and imagines the 'nation' on the grounds of a shared ethno-cultural kinship. This form of nationalism is also deemed 'sticky' in the sense of combining with fascism and conservatism (see Table 6.1 for more information on 'sticky' nationalisms). In the fascist case, there is an extreme form of ethnic nationalism in which those deemed 'other' are often victimized. In conservative nationalism, strong emotional attachment to the idea of the nation is seen to draw upon historical narratives and cultural mythology to bolster allegiance to long-standing political institutions.

It is important to recognize that engagement with nationalism is crucial within an overall understanding of political ideologies. Indeed, nationalism is often viewed with deep suspicion in modern liberal societies. Many critics invoke imagery of the twentieth-century fascist regimes to illustrate the possible dangers of nationalist sentiment when (apparently) taken to its conclusion. Others such as *The Independent* (2015) obliquely 'consider nationalism guilty until proven innocent'. Nationalism as ideology, however, is a multi-faceted entity that has long historical roots. As a modern entity, nationalism arguably dates to the establishment of the **Westphalian** system in Europe in 1648. European powers began under the Treaty of Westphalia to recognize the legal sovereignty (that is, the legitimate power and right of self-rule) of neighbouring territories. This gave national rulers the ultimate 'sovereign' power to set the religion of their subjects without foreign interference. This helped to put an end to the European Wars of Religion that had dogged the continent since the Reformation. In the eighteenth and nineteenth centuries, nationalism—still a largely Western phenomenon—demonstrated certain 'progressive' credentials. American colonists involved in the eighteenth century Revolutionary War (against British King George III), for example, combined nationalism with republican and democratic ideals. In the nineteenth century, the key liberal philosopher, John Stuart Mill, himself saw that a specific type of *civic nationalism* is an important ingredient of a healthy functioning democracy (Tyndal 2013; Varouxakis 2002).

In the twentieth century the excesses of Nazi Germany saw genocidal actions committed in the name of nationalist ideology. Nevertheless, the spread of nationalism in this century to other parts of the non-Western world did witness certain 'progressive' advances. Many anti-colonial movements in sub-Saharan Africa, for example, incorporated a left liberation nationalist discourse into their calls for independence. Kwame Nkrumah, the first President of an independent Ghana, called for an African patriotic socialism that would bring dignity to once colonized peoples. Nationalism in an Indian context, moreover, helped to build a unified federal state after decades of British human rights abuses and misrule. More recently in the twenty-first century, certain democratic socialist leaders—such as Alexis Tsipras, the Prime Minister of Greece—have incorporated a left nationalist discourse into their calls for a more equal society, condemning ethnic forms of nationalism in the process.

It is also important to state from the outset that nationalism should be defined as a system of thought that prioritizes the well-being of *the nation*. It seeks to make sense of individual action in terms of the greater good. Benedict Anderson (1991) explains that the nation can be understood as an 'imagined community'. It is imagined in that it is socially constructed in relation to geography, myths, symbols, and historical narratives. It is a community in that the people existing within the nation are deemed to have common cause. Moreover, Anderson describes the *imagined community* as being limited—in the sense that no nation imagines itself as extending across the whole of humanity. Further, the nation is imagined mostly in terms of common residency within given geographical boundaries when a *civic nationalism* is expressed. In the case of *ethnic nationalism*, the nation is imagined in terms of ethnic identity and is limited in terms of a shared ancestry. Modern day Israel, for instance, is defined as a Jewish nation-state, and is therein somewhat *limited* to people sharing this religio-ethnic background (often with deleterious consequences for the rights of Arabs residing within Israel's borders). Anderson (1991) also usefully explains that the *imagined community* is sovereign. By this he means that the nation is understood in terms of the self-determination of the people. And indeed, this is one of the key objectives of nationalism—to maintain the sovereignty of the people and to ensure that their freedom is not made subordinate to that of another. This is perhaps most apparent in the liberation nationalisms that swept African countries. In terms of human nature, moreover, nationalism perceives the individual as a social creature that gains meaning from interaction with others. Ethnic nationalism also understands the human person as an emotional entity that may gain comfort from feelings of patriotism and sentimental attachment to political structures. Nationalism in this sense also assumes that the human individual is capable of comprehending issues surrounding **inter-generational justice** (De Schutter 2005; Castellano 2011). Nationalism also contends that a sense of national belonging is important for the practical functioning of state institutions.

Interestingly, some scholars such as Freeden (1998) question whether nationalism should be defined as an ideology per se. Some maintain that it instead constitutes a *doctrine*—a commitment to the nation—but without a systematic thought system. This line of argument does have certain merit. It is true that nationalism appears to morph according to territory and timeframe. However, its focus upon preservation of the nation, and therein of the principles of self-determination, cultural belonging, and sovereignty, does entail an *ideological* character. Halikiopoulou et al. (2012) provide a succinct defence of the characterization of nationalism *as ideology*:

> The key premise of any nationalism is the right of the nation to act as independent, free and sovereign. It is a coherent ideology in as much as it refers to the pursuit of autonomy, unity and identity of a nation. . . . What nationalism lacks is systematic answers to key social questions such as justice and welfare (Freeden 1998: 751). This leaves it as a thin ideology, granting it the ability to attach itself to other ideologies that do provide such answers. Hall (2011) emphasises the chameleon-like nature of nationalism, describing it as sticky, attaching itself to different situations according to the political forces with which it interacts.
>
> (Halikiopoulou et al. 2012: 509)

Nationalism is thereby seen as ideology, albeit one subject to many cross-fertilizations.

Constructing the imagined community

Imagining the nation

Benedict Anderson's (1991) aforementioned work on the *imagined community* is one of the seminal works on nationalism. His perspective emphasizes that the nation is a *social construct*. That is, the nation is not some 'natural' or 'God-given' entity. Rather it is something that is consciously created (that is, constructed) by human agents across historical contexts and epochs. The way in which individuals talk about their communities in certain geographical confines, and time periods, gives birth to the idea of the nation. It is something that is therefore *imagined* in a collective sense.

Anderson (1991: 49) elaborates that the national community 'is imagined in that the members of even the smallest nation will never know most of their fellow-members, meet them, or even hear of them, yet in the minds of each lives the image of their communion'. The nation is thus a human artifice. Moreover, it is (re)created on a day to day basis through the ways in which contemporary media, politicians, and citizens talk about national status. And by extension, it is something which is contested at given historical moments through competing 'national' narratives. This is important, according to Anderson (1991), not only in terms of our understanding of the workings of the modern nation-state but also in terms of individual identity construction (see Chapter 11 on multiculturalism for more detail on debates about such identity construction). Individuals not only help to construct the nation, but individual identities are themselves (re)made through perceptions of connectedness to a greater whole. Individuals help to construct the nation, and are themselves constructed by national imaginaries.

A community of individuals

This leads on to another important point in terms of the understanding of the *imagined community*. That is, that all nations are founded upon certain national archetypes or self-images. No nation is deemed to be identical to another. Each nation collectively imagines itself to have an innate personality that is commensurate with its historical experiences. For example, the archetypal English citizen may pride herself on self-restraint and refined good manners. A Scot on the contrary may associate her national identity with an outspokenness that might discomfit her southern counterpart (Kelly and Husaini 2012; see Case Study 6.1). Similarly, the Russian imagination of their menfolk as bold and physically strong contrasts with neighbouring China where the national imagination focuses more closely on an ideal of menfolk as balancing *wen* (the philosophical arts) with *wu* (the martial arts) (Louie 2002: 13; Foxall 2013). Such divergent national self-images can be traced to culture. In the case of the Chinese, the archetype of the industrious civil servant can be traced to a **Confucian** culture that historically privileges *wen* over *wu* (Louie 2002: 13). Parallels to this can perhaps be seen in Europe in the apparent 'Protestant work ethic' embodied in certain Northern European countries. Notably, German industriousness (as part of their imagined national self-image) is often ascribed to a culture of Protestantism that encourages hard work and self-sacrifice (Weber 2002).

 Stop and Think

Is ethnic nationalist sentiment on the rise in Europe?

The national community as 'limited': civic versus ethnic nationalism

Nation and culture are thus interwoven, with a national community giving birth to a distinct cultural ethos which in turn shapes self-identities to which the 'ideal' citizen ought to aspire (although certainly some individuals may rebel against such archetypes). Anderson's (1991) view of the 'limited' nature of the nation can be understood in terms of this cultural dimension, particularly in terms of civic forms of nationalism. Indeed, within certain civic forms of nationalism, a belonging to the 'nation' can be seen in terms of alignment to the preponderant culture of the national community, rather than in terms of a shared blood heritage. This implies a process of **assimilation** for those joining the nation from outside its borders, to adopt the preponderant culture, and to integrate into the national society. Gellner (2005) makes clear that civic nationalism operates on an assumption that

> People can be changed. They can acquire the culture—including the self-image fostered by that culture, and the capacity to project that image and to have it accepted—even if they had started from some other culture, some other set of internalised and projected images . . . the process may be largely spontaneous and even barely conscious, or it may be accompanied by directions from political and educational authority.

(Gellner 2005: 156)

Table 6.1 Ideological combinations resulting from the 'sticky' and 'thin' qualities of nationalism

Rational/civic forms	Irrational/ethnic forms
Liberal civic nationalism associated with key theorists such as John Stuart Mill	Conservative nationalism associated with Edmund Burke in which an 'irrational' and emotional attachment to the nation and its institutions can be observed
Left nationalism associated with socialism, and with political parties such as Syriza in Greece	Fascist nationalism in which an extreme form of ethnic nationalism prevails and where those deemed 'other' are often victimised e.g. Jews in Nazi Germany

It should be noted, however, that certain proponents of civic nationalism eschew this cultural element of *assimilation* altogether in favour of multicultural under-standings of the nation-state. This prioritizes geographical residency com-bined with adherence to certain political concepts such as democracy, without assuming that individuals should adhere to homogenizing cultural values. This multicultural variant of civic nationalism is suspicious about an emphasis upon common adherence to one particular culture, since this might privilege a certain 'way of doing things' as envisaged by a dominant ethnic group within the nation.

Critique

Nationalism in all forms critiques extreme individualism and egotism (as arguably witnessed in certain forms of liberalism and anarchism). It also critiques certain cosmopolitan ideals—by defending the continuing importance of nation-states and national 'we-feeling' in an era of globalization.

Vision

Nationalist ideology calls for common purpose and solidarity within the nation-state. It calls for the sovereignty and well-being of 'the people'. Ethnic nationalism imagines the people as a nation-race. Civic nationalism imagines the people as a community resident in a particular geography. The nationalist vision is particularly important for a 'rally round the flag' in times of national crises.

Strategy

Nationalism calls for political institutions and parties to inculcate patriotism and common cause among the citizenry. Likewise, it calls for the citizenry to mobilize within the bodies of the nation-state. Active citizens will take pride in the building of the nation, if nationalism compels them to it. Ethnic nationalism would additionally seek to 'purify' the nation by victimizing those deemed 'other' (and by waging war in the international system).

Figure 6.1 Making sense of nationalism

Civic nationalism, however, clearly conflicts with the ethnic form of national-ism which demands not merely assimilation into a preponderant national cul-ture, but also pre-qualification in the form of an 'ethnic' belonging; these differ-ences can be seen in Table 6.1. As mentioned, this form of ethnic nationalism can arguably be seen in modern day Israel where the idea of a secular Israeli national-ity is denied in preference for a *Jewish* ethnic construct of what constitutes this 'imagined community' (Tal 2013). Again, this can have negative consequences for Arabs within the nation's borders since they are not always imagined as being part of the nation proper. Figure 6.1 summarizes how nationalism can be made sense of.

Case Study 6.1 Constructing Scottish national identity

Scottish national identity is a particularly interesting phenomenon. Scotland narrowly rejected independence in September 2014 by a margin of 55 per cent to 45 per cent. The independ-ence referendum was said to be a 'once in a generation' event, but now appears as a first step towards a second and conclusive referendum (at least according to supporters of the Scottish National Party—SNP). This raises the question of Scottish national identity and why it is that a significant proportion of Scots seek political autonomy from the rest of the United Kingdom. Often the SNP and members of the 'Yes' movement emphasize a democratic argument—that those living in Scotland are best placed to run its affairs. This implies that a smaller popula-tion of 5 million people would be better able to achieve a more equal democratic society than possible within a political construct (the UK) comprising over 60 million citizens (Scottish Government 2013).

However, the civic nationalism embodied within the SNP also indicates that many 'Yes' supporters do see Scots as sharing a common identity which is distinct from that existing in other parts of Great Britain. In many cases, there is an emphasis on the egalitarian spirit of the Scots, seen, for instance, in terms of the poetry of Robert Burns, and more recently in the riots against the Thatcher government and its regressive taxation policies (the poll-tax) (Beland and Lecours 2008). This egalitarian spirit is portrayed—or imagined—as a distinctive feature of a Scottish 'personality' that helps to define the national community, and (impor-tantly) to make its politics distinctively more 'progressive' than that in the remainder of the British Isles.

Moreover, there is often an assumption that Scots possess a more 'European' personality as witnessed in the strong support there for the Remain camp in the 2016 'Brexit' referendum (Hassan 2009; see Case Study 6.2). This is sometimes explained in terms of historical experience, for instance, the 'Auld Alliance' forged between Scotland's medieval monarchs and their French counterparts. In addition, it is often explained in terms of the Scottish Enlightenment and a cul-ture that privileges education and the welfare state, with similarities to continental European countries, notably those of Scandinavia. Importantly, this construction of 'Scottishness' aligns to a civic nationalism. This means that the Scottish personality is explicitly *not* defined in terms of ethnicity. This can be seen in terms of the SNP and its efforts to consciously court ethnic minori-ties in Scotland for their support.

Accordingly, it can be seen that the Scottish nation is, even now, in the process of (re)construction, with participants in the independence debate imagining Scotland in certain ways—thus helping to legitimize certain political projects in the process. The 'imagined community' is brought into being in the context of statements, and strongly held beliefs, surrounding the apparent elements that make up the Scottish national personality. Interestingly, social media (notably Twitter), newspapers (such as *The National*, first published in 2014), and popular political figures (such as First Minister Nicola Sturgeon) play a role in shaping the norms and assumptions about the Scottish personality. This draws upon historical elements, such as the Battle of George Square, which remain in collective memory (Wings Over Scotland 2012). But it also involves a re-inventing of the Scottish persona—and therein what is understood as the nation.

This is something which, perhaps naturally, is contested by Unionist opponents of the cause of independence. Namely, the suggestion that Scots somehow possess a more egalitarian spirit (and that this somehow justifies political separation) is contested by those who point to the election of a Scottish member of UKIP to the European Parliament as evidence that Scotland has no special claim to a progressive politics. Indeed, the Better Together campaign often cited the plight of fellow progressives in cities such as Liverpool and Newcastle as a reason for Scotland to remain in the UK—namely that Scotland does not possess a political identity that is radically distinct from others in the British Isles—and that Scots should form common cause with like-minded individuals to achieve a more egalitarian British state (Nash 2014). Interestingly, Jackson (2014: 54) argues here that 'solidarity with the other residents of the United Kingdom who are not Conservatives, or who do not want to live in a country governed by neo-liberal nostrums, is one element of the British Labour tradition that Scottish nationalists do not want to make their own'. Of course, however, the SNP leader, Nicola Sturgeon, in the 2015 British election campaign focused squarely on the idea of an anti-Tory alliance, speaking the language of common cause, while retaining her commitment to an ultimate goal of Scottish independence (*The Independent* 2015).

The (re)construction of Scottish national identity is therein heavily politicized at the current time, given the sensitivities of the recent independence referendum, and the prospect of a second vote. Narratives, vocabularies, and imagery construct the idea of the nation—with real political consequences for those living within the geographical contours of the would-be Scottish state.

 Stop and Think

Would Scotland be better off within the European Union than within the United Kingdom?

Case Study 6.2 Brexit as ethnic and/or civic nationalism?

The decision of UK voters (or more accurately, those of England and Wales) to leave the European Union (EU) has been interpreted in a number of ways. Many leading 'Brexiteers' such as Boris Johnson and Liam Fox emphasize that Brexit represents a vote for sovereignty (*The Telegraph* 2016). The UK electorate, in this interpretation, voted to assert the sovereignty of the Westminster parliament over that of a Brussels bureaucracy. Voters therefore demonstrated a degree of civic nationalism—namely, a concern for the self-determination of people resident within the UK's borders. These influential Brexiteer politicians thus empha-size that the Leave vote does not represent a rejection of a multi-racial Britain. Many point to the fact that persons of non-white backgrounds voted for Brexit (*Washington Post* 2016). 'Britishness' as national identity—according to this narrative—is not defined in terms of an ethnic nationalism.

However, there are those—on both the Leave side and the Remain side—who argue that the Brexit vote does in fact represent a reassertion of a white British ethno-cultural identity. The 'Leave' side in the Brexit campaign itself was fuelled by racialized imagery—such as the 'Breaking Point' poster unveiled by the UKIP leader with its visual insinuation that Britain was under siege by (Muslim) immigrants. Meanwhile, far-right groups in the UK such as 'Britain First' have welcomed Brexit as a victory for a white English identity (Britain First 2016). Racially motivated attacks on ethnic minority communities in the UK have also been emboldened by the Brexit vote. In 2016, a Polish man was murdered by English youths, apparently for the fact that he spoke Polish to a friend in their earshot (*New York Times* 2016).

In this context, there is much argument that Brexit does represent the political victory of an ethnic form of nationalism within the UK—or at least, within England and Wales. Brexit in this vein is understood as an anti-immigration vote, one designed to preserve the UK nation-state (or at least the English/Welsh nations) for 'indigenous' white Britons. It is perhaps unsurprising there-fore that other far-right movements—such as the Front National in France—have hailed Brexit as a victory for a 'common sense' return to ethnic nationalism in Europe. Meanwhile, in the UK, the new Theresa May government pledges to undertake Brexit from the EU while emphasizing that racial attacks on minorities will not be tolerated. It remains to be seen, however, whether such incidents will die down—or whether ethnic nationalism (and racial violence) will remain at the forefront of politics in England and Wales.

Interestingly, however, the Brexit vote has emboldened a civic form of nationalism in Scotland—which voted very clearly for the UK to remain a European nation within the EU project. Nicola Sturgeon (the SNP leader) has now initiated a nation-wide listening campaign to learn the les-sons of the 2014 'indyref' defeat. Scottish independence, in the aftermath of the decision of the voters of England and Wales to leave the EU, appears again on the horizon. A vote in 2018/19 (if held) might allow Scottish nationalists to achieve their long held ambition of an independent Scottish state, removed from the racialized politics south of the border.

 Stop and Think

How might a Polish national resident in London or Cardiff view the decision of the English and Welsh electorates to leave the European Union?

Nationalism and politics

Justifying state authority

At a fundamental level, nationalist sentiment—and rhetoric—forms an important component in justifying the exercise of state authority (for example, see Case Study 6.3). That is, the role of government within the *nation-state* is legitimized in terms of the self-government of the people themselves. For example, in the United States, the role of the President and the Congress are routinely explained to citizens in terms of their role in supporting the nation, and in pursuing objectives that are within the national interest. Moreover, these institutions are viewed as a key part of the USA and its national identity. This is particularly framed in terms of the US constitution and the role of the founding fathers in creating institutions that would safeguard the rights of life, liberty, and the pursuit of happiness of the citizenry (Goldstein 2014).

Norms associated with the Westphalian system (that is an international society based on recognition of the sovereignty of nation-states) are thereby embedded within political communities—with citizens recognizing the role of the state, and government, as central to order and the provision of basic services for the national well-being. This of course stands quite at odds with *anarchist* ideology (see Chapter 5 on anarchism for more detail) that calls for the abolition of the state altogether. Accordingly, anarchism, in particular, is hostile towards nationalism and to nationalist rhetoric, viewing such narratives as part of the legitimation of *oppressive* state institutions (Woodcock 1963).

Nationalism is therefore important in ensuring citizen's respect for, and obedience to, state authority. Citizens view their own identity in terms of nationality and in so doing associate their own well-being with the successful administration of government, and the flourishing of the nation-state (although some, for instance, Marxists claim that this unified national sentiment is created by elites in order to veil social inequalities). Importantly, politicians can utilize this nationalist sentiment to call for civic order and for respect for state institutions such as the police, civil service, and army. This can be especially crucial in times of national crisis where politicians can attempt to instigate a 'rally round the flag' to call for citizens to heed the instructions of government (Chatagnier 2012). Non-conformity and disobedience in these circumstances can be deemed as disloyalty to the nation-state itself, and thus citizens can be pressured into acquiescence to state authority.

Political mobilization and nationalism

Nationalism can also provide a coherent ideology upon which certain political movements—and political parties—may choose to mobilize as part of a democratic framework within the state. There is a key distinction to be made, however, between those political movements that coalesce around an ethnic form of nationalism that bases belonging upon certain ethnic characteristics, and those political movements that instead coalesce upon civic nationalist lines, defining membership of the imagined community in terms of geographical residence and (often) cultural affiliation/assimilation.

The former type of (ethnic) nationalist party often seeks to 'redeem' the nation in the face of appparent threats such as immigration. This can be seen in the case of the Front National in France, currently led by Marine Le Pen, who has attempted to bring her party—often abbreviated as 'FN'—into the mainstream. In this process she has been vocal about the need for trade protectionism to assist French industry and workers. Nevertheless, even with her modernizing platform, the FN retains its central goal of reducing immigration and leaving the EU. Moreover, the party frames its ambitions in terms of a French patriotism which—when combined to an anti-immigration stance—is deemed by many commentators to retain an ethnic form of nationalism. This form of nationalism apparently views white, Catholic French citizens as the norm, and non-white, often Muslim, citizens as an alien 'other' to be feared (Le Monde Diplo 2011; Shields 2014). Indeed, the FN has been highly supportive of the ban of the burqa and has agitated about the terrorist threat allegedly deriving from the Islamic community in France. The party has also been accused of deliberately provoking the Muslim population with, for instance, opposition to halal meals within town canteens (Al Jazeera 2014).

 Stop and Think

What other European political parties might fit this ethno-nationalist archetype?

The *civic nationalist* type of party can perhaps best be seen in the modern Scottish National Party (SNP). As discussed in Case Study 6.1, the SNP leadership and grassroots emphasize that they embrace a civic form of nationalism that welcomes Scots from any ethnic background. Nationalism in this sense is geared towards the achievement of self-determination for people living within Scotland. This is often justified in terms of the need for people living in Scotland to have full powers to realize a different kind of society to that offered by the Westminster system. As Leith (2008) explains, recent SNP manifestos have:

> highlighted the inclusive nature of SNP policy. This stance was clear with statements such as no one country and no one human being is worth more or less than any other . . . continual reinforcement of Scotland as a place, rather than any ethnic or exclusive-based belonging, was clearly the message.

(Leith 2008: 89)

The SNP thus largely avoid any sense of ethnic antagonism towards the people of England, Wales, or Northern Ireland, but argue their case in terms of democratic self-government. It is interesting to note, however, that there have historically been fringe movements within Scotland that have articulated an ethnic form of nationalism. In particular, certain groups such as Seed of the Gael have apparently articulated hostility towards England and towards Anglo-Saxons more generally (*The Telegraph* 2014). In terms of the SNP itself, moreover, certain Unionist politicians accuse it of 'dog whistle' politics in which negative references to 'Westminster' and 'London' become synonyms for England or Englishness (*The Guardian* 2014). It is important to restate, however, that the modern SNP explicitly rejects any form of racism and is a party that extends its membership to all sections of Scottish society, regardless of gender, sexual orientation, or ethnic background.

Case Study 6.3 Chinese nationalism and civic (dis)order

China provides interesting insight into the working of nationalism and patriotic sentiment in a non-democratic setting. The Chinese Communist Party—which comprises the government of this de facto one party state—makes explicit appeal to the patriotism of the citizenry in order to maintain civic order and to dispel popular protests. Perhaps most interestingly, the Chinese Communist Party has appealed to nationalist sentiment on mainland China to ask for civic order and restraint in the wake of air pollution crises in a number of major metropolises, including Beijing and Shanghai. In 2014 Premier Li Keqiang of the National People's Congress declared a *war* against pollution and called upon citizens' patriotic pride to assist the government in this quest (*China Daily* 2014). In addition, the government has actively utilized social media sites to advise people how best to combat pollution, drawing upon a love for the motherland in order to inspire citizens to take personal responsibility and to tackle the problems of air quality.

Additionally, the Communist Party has drawn upon nationalist discourse in response to recent protests in Hong Kong about lack of democratic choice in the selection of the city's Chief Executive. The party has called for Hong Kongers to respect Chinese sovereignty, and to take pride in their own identity as citizens of a rising China. Those who protest Beijing's rule are seen as trouble-makers who border on treason against the nation. This brings to light what might be seen, in fact, as a conflict of competing nationalisms. The actions of protestors within the 'umbrella' movement in Hong Kong might equally be described in terms of a nationalist political movement. Many within Hong Kong struggle with their dual identity—and some in fact reject the label 'Chinese' altogether. While few advocate outright independence from Beijing, many adhere to a form of Hong Konger nationalism that makes them hostile to the imposition of decisions emanating from the mainland. This is something which the Chinese Communist Party has sought to draw attention to—attempting to delegitimize the umbrella movement as a separatist spasm that ought not to win support from loyal Hong Kong Chinese (Comparativist.org).

It is important to note, however, that the government has also used nationalist discourse to deliberately stoke protests within Chinese mainland cities—namely against the Japanese 'other'. Most notably, in September 2012, the government stoked riots against Japanese 'imperialism' in response to that nation's plans to develop disputed islands in the South China Sea. Lane (2012) reported at the time of the events that 'bloggers in China have posted accounts, with accompanying photos, of what they say are plain-clothes police instigating and leading the protest activity (in one photo a man appears to have a policeman's bullet-proof vest under his commoner's T-shirt)'. This was seen to serve as a useful tool not only to pressure Japan to reverse its decision, but also to distract the citizenry at a time of power transition within the Chinese Communist Party itself.

However, the exercise of a Han Chinese nationalism (that is a nationalism focused upon the majority ethnic group, the Han) has also provoked backlash in Xinjiang province from the indigenous Uighur community. This ethnic group is predominantly Muslim and has historically resented Han Chinese 'colonialism' in the province, particularly in terms of settler movements that seek to (apparently) displace Uighur communities as the dominant ethnicity. Moreover, many Uighur citizens resent the government's hard-line stance against any form of Uighur nationalism. Indeed, nationalist sentiment—expressed in terms of an independence movement for 'East Turkestan'—had gained political traction, only to face severe repression from the authorities in Beijing. As Heyer (2006: 76) makes clear, the Chinese Communist Party is intolerant of any form of nationalism, other than its own: 'The PRC [People's Republic of China] regards itself as a unified multi-ethnic country, denying the national identity of the minority nationalities, regarding them as Chinese ethnic groups within the Chinese state. . . . Any aspirations for independent statehood on the part of such groups are considered seditious.' Nationalism—although often a useful tool deployed by the Chinese Communist Party—can also pose a challenge to Beijing authority when deployed by possible 'separatist' groups, such as those in Xinjiang and Hong Kong. It is important to recognize, however, that such intolerant forms of nationalism are not confined to non-democratic contexts, such as that of present day China. Indeed, the previous section on the Front National in France reminds us that intolerant 'ethnic' nationalisms can flourish in a democratic, multi-party context too.

 Stop and Think

On what grounds do Chinese nationalists argue that the territorial integrity of the nation-state is vital for citizens' well-being?

'Rational' nationalism

'Sticky', 'thin' nationalism

The cross-fertilization which occurs between 'sticky', 'thin' nationalism and other ideologies can be understood in terms of *rational* and *irrational* variants. As noted, there is the possibility for a (so-called) liberal nationalism as well as a left nationalism, in relation to civic definitions of the 'imagined community'. This can be termed *rational* in the sense that it draws upon pragmatic, constitutional, and democratic arguments in order to justify the usefulness of patriotism in the governance of a polity. It eschews what can be deemed *irrational* commitment to the nation in the form of an instinctive or spontaneous emotional attachment to the imagined community (Kecmanovic 2005).

Notably, the work of John Stuart Mill is interesting to explore in more detail, in terms of his own justification of a rational, civic nationalism. Mill argues that the citizenry need to be bound together by a collective consciousness and 'common sympathies' in order to facilitate effective governance. Tyndal (2013) explains that, according to Mill, the development of common sympathies among the population

> encourages three impulses: (1) the desire to cooperate; (2) the desire to come together under a single government; and (3) the desire for that government to be a government by the people, or by a portion of the people. . . . [And when taken together] these three impulses constitute a 'feeling of nationality'.

(Tyndal 2013: 98)

Thus while Mill famously advocates for maximum liberty for the individual, his focus on civic nationalism allows scope for that individual to raise his/her sights beyond the personal. Mill intends that the polity can avoid competing narrow egotisms based on individual preference, and, on key issues (such as education or the environment), establish a politics that can comprehend the well-being of others, and of society. Just as Mill places a limit on individual liberty in his articulation of the harm principle, his focus on civic nationalism imposes what might be deemed as a *voluntary* and *moral* restraint upon the individual.

Mill's nationalism in this sense is a functional ingredient of a healthy democratic society. It is not a nationalism born of myth or emotionalism, but rather one in which individuals can imagine themselves to be bound together with the fate of their fellows. Moreover, it is a (civic) nationalism which can enable a single generation of individuals to perhaps comprehend the well-being of those yet to be born. Importantly, a healthy dose of civic nationalism is also arguably important in terms of ensuring that individual Members of Parliament (MPs) not only maintain sight of their narrow party or constituency interests (and therein their hopes of re-election), but also can conceive of the wider national interest and so, perhaps, on occasion, disavow the immediate interests of the constituency in favour of the longer term interests of the country. This at times reflects Mill's own utilitarian upbringing, and indeed, aligns somewhat to the work of Edmund Burke—who equally stresses that the individual MP must not always be beholden to the constituents.

Moreover, Mill articulates cosmopolitan attitudes in the sense of the need to respect people outside of the nation. He therefore argues for a form of civic nationalism in which a national citizenry should detest a government that inflicts misery upon another people (Varouxakis 2008). In so doing, he calls for an enlightened patriotism and maintains a high contempt for 'barbarism' or for extreme forms of ethnic/xenophobic nationalism. Notably, Mill includes the following explicit disavowal of petty nationalism in order to contextualize his endorsement of a limited civic variety of patriotism:

> No one disapproves more, or is in the habit of expressing his disapprobation more strongly than I do of the narrow, exclusive patriotism of former ages which made the good of the whole human race a subordinate consideration to the good, or worse still, to the mere power and external importance, of the country of one's birth. I believe that the good of no country can be obtained by any means but such as tend to that of all countries, nor ought to be sought otherwise, even if obtainable.

> (Varouxakis 2008)

It is a historical paradox therefore that Mill commended certain British imperial adventures on the grounds of their alleged 'civilizing' qualities.

 Stop and Think

In what ways does the history of Empire still impact upon nationalism(s) in the UK today?

Tensions between liberalism and nationalism

Mill's writings do raise questions about tensions between nationalism on the one hand and liberalism on the other. Many contemporary liberals would point to the possible negative repercussions of patriotic sentiment even within limited, representative democracies. For instance, there was much discussion of the US Patriot Act under the George W. Bush administration and how civic nationalism, in this context, did much to silence dissent to what is widely considered an illiberal counter-terrorism platform. Moreover, there is concern that civic nationalism can easily degenerate into ethnic or xenophobic varieties when democracies come under pressure. For example, the recent emergence of the anti-Muslim Pegida movement in Germany proves for many modern-day liberals that a functional patriotism can quickly descend into a hatred of the perceived 'other'. Accordingly, many liberals remain sceptical as to the merits of nationalism per se. Dzur (2002) provides a good exemplar of a cosmopolitan liberal who opposes the arguments of the liberal nationalists (such as J. S. Mill) when he states that:

> The argument that nationality is necessary for the functioning of liberal democratic states because it provides a social framework for democratic institutions, and because it explains and justifies boundaries and special obligations may be, at first glance, the strongest pillar of support for the theory of liberal nationalism. . . . Yet liberal nationalists ignore the normative and practical drawbacks of national affiliation as a justificatory device and social framework. There are other and better ways to justify borders and obligations, and other and better ways to interpret the meaning, sources, and content of communicative competence, trust, and collective sentiment.
>
> (Dzur 2002: 204)

Dzur hints here at the ways in which nationalism, even in a liberal democratic framework, may divide the citizenry—for instance, along ethnic lines in contemporary France. He implies that justifications of political authority and of common action among individuals should rest not upon national affiliation but instead upon a strictly rationalist conception of institutions as delivering certain common goods. Individuals thereby enter into a 'social contract' with institutions based on a rational conception of what common bodies might deliver for them (e.g. security under a police force and an army) rather than out of a nationalist attachment to an 'imagined community' (see Chapter 2 on liberalism for further explanation of the concept of the 'social contract').

Additionally, Dzur (2002) outlines how liberal nationalism maintains the perspective that co-nationals bear a higher moral significance to the individual, due to a collective sense of belonging, purpose, and mutual reliance:

> Liberal nationalists maintain that conationals have a greater moral significance because they have contributed to and participated in collective projects—public goods like defense, economic infrastructure, disaster relief—from which all benefit. We place the preservation of their basic rights and the satisfaction of their basic needs at a higher

priority than those of members of other countries. Though we have general humanistic duties by virtue of our bare existence, we have political obligations by virtue of our social boundedness and territorial rootedness.

(Dzur 2002: 203)

Even with cosmopolitan caveats, as expressed by John Stuart Mill, this privileging is deemed highly questionable by many liberals such as Dzur. The tendency—innate with nationalism—to prefer one's own co-national is deemed problematic in terms of implications for the rights of the 'other' (in this case, the non-citizen or foreign national). The potential for **jingoism**—or the use of nationalist rhetoric to induce unthinking loyalty to the state and government actions—is a major concern for many liberals (given their preference for the limited night-watchman state that respects individual liberty).

Left nationalism and the 'imagined community'

Tensions can also be found between socialism and left nationalism—albeit within a separate debate surrounding class consciousness and internationalism. Certain proponents of socialism argue that it is compatible with nationalist thinking. In the case of *liberation nationalism* (which can be described as a particular brand of left nationalism), African socialists in the 1950s and 1960s argued that it was important not merely to educate the masses about the exploitative nature of capitalism and of colonial economics, but also to inculcate nationalist pride among a citizenry that had been made to feel inferior to Western colonizers. Interestingly, this African socialist thought often took a pan-African perspective—seeking to unite all Africans within a federal state (the United States of Africa). Nevertheless, this was a form of 'imagined community' that limited itself to Africans, to African culture and to the geographical confines of the continent. In many cases it was combined with a nationally bound patriotism such as that in Julius Nyerere's Tanzania, where a specific Tanzanian identity was encouraged in order to unite different tribal affiliations. Nyerere maintained a pan-African vision, alongside his fellow African socialists, while at the same time he sought to (successfully) develop a Tanzanian personhood. Ryan and Worth (2010) comment here that

> Whether as specific liberation movements or as national political parties in every possible guise of socialism, all [left nationalists] sought to defend their own national strategies as a means of managing the universal principles of socialism. The positive aspect of this form of socialist strategy is that the socialist state acts as a sovereign nation and promotes peaceful co-existence with like-minded states, which serves to promote nationalism and internationalism at the same time.

(Ryan and Worth 2010: 54)

More recently, Alexis Tsipras—the democratic socialist Prime Minister of Greece—has combined a socialist economic vision with a left nationalist appeal to the well-being of Greeks. This has borne particular significance due to the fact that the Greek citizenry feel that they have been imposed upon by foreign creditors, notably Angela Merkel of Germany. Moreover, there is nationalist sentiment in the country that Germany has been guilty of historical crimes against the Greek nation. Accordingly, Tsipras and his socialist government have made certain nationalist appeals to the people, and have articulated a sense of national grievance against Germany as part of a strategy aimed at debt forgiveness. In the case of the SNP, moreover, this modern nationalist party often seeks to present socialist (or at least social democratic) arguments about the need for a 'progressive' egalitarian politics against austerity, while at the same time maintaining a nationalist programme for an independent Scottish state. Furthermore, in the case of certain Latin American countries—perhaps most memorably Hugo Chavez's Venezuela—a nationalist programme of economic autonomy (against US multinational interference) has been combined with a socialist outlook. Interestingly, this Latin American *twenty-first century socialism* has (akin to African socialism) taken a pan-continental perspective described in terms of a *Bolivarian revolution* (after Simon Bolivar who liberated many Latin American territories from Spain). This seeks to unite the Latin American countries to collectively combat poverty, and, crucially, to counteract perceived US interference in the Southern hemisphere.

Socialism with a national face?

As with liberalism, however, there are many within this school of thought who remain highly sceptical of socialism with a national face. While certain leftist politicians may utilize nationalism to safeguard the citizenry from imperialist interventions, nevertheless, other socialists (particularly Marxists) maintain that *internationalism* among the working classes is the true goal of that ideology. In this view, narrow nationalisms are a symptom of false consciousness inculcated by the bourgeois elite, which infects working people to divide them from their brothers and sisters. Indeed, Rosa Luxembourg, the heroine of the German Left, maintained that the nation-state was a bourgeois and liberal creation. As Ryan and Worth (2010: 54) explain, for Luxembourg, nation-states 'were thus defined as historical entities that were ultimately structural conventions [that is, structures created for pragmatic elite governance purposes], and nationalism was the ideology of such an expression, used entirely for the purpose of capitalist exploitation'. Many Marxists therefore emphasize that solidarity demands international working class action, and that socialists ought to therefore eschew nationalist programmes. Moreover, there is fear among certain anti-nationalist Marxists that patriotism more often than not lends itself to imperialist projects, rather than the obverse. Eric Hobsbawm, for example, noted the Thatcher government's patriotic appeal during the Falklands Crisis in 1982, and how this helped to cement neo-liberalism and a regressive British nationalism. With regard to nationalism itself, Hobsbawm memorably states that

> The dangers are obvious, not least because it is enormously vulnerable to anti-foreign nationalism and racism. These dangers are particularly great where patriotism can be separated from the other sentiments and aspirations of the working class, or even where it can be counter-posed to them; where nationalism can be counter-posed to social liberation.
>
> (Hobsbawm, cited in Perryman 2009: 41)

In particular, there is a certain fear among socialists in Europe that petty nationalisms can be used as a means of dividing the working peoples of the continent. In particular, many are concerned about the apparent nationalist overlap between populist Left parties such as Syriza led by Alexis Tsipras, and those of the centre-right and far right. In the Greek case, a coalition struck between Syriza and the populist right group, the Independent Greeks, proved for some Marxists that Syriza is in fact a bourgeois entity that departs from genuine socialist objectives. This is the line of argument maintained against Syriza by the Greek Communist Party, undoubtedly intensified by personal disputes between Tsipras (a former member of the Communists) and his ex-comrades. This leads us to a discussion, in fact, of *irrational nationalisms* associated with parties of both the centre-right and the far right. Whereas Syriza may coalesce with groups such as the Independent Greeks in terms of a nationalist outlook, the varieties of nationalism that these centre-right (and far-right) groups entail are quite distinct, as the next section demonstrates.

 Stop and Think

Should socialist leaders, such as the UK Labour Party's Jeremy Corbyn, embrace cultural aspects of nationalism to win popular support (for instance, the singing of the UK national anthem despite the song's anti-democratic credentials)?

'Irrational' nationalism

The right and irrational nationalism

The nationalism of the centre-right and the far right can be seen to entail an 'irrational' aspect that is quite distinct from the rational and pragmatic stance of certain liberal and left nationalists. This 'irrational' nationalism is one borne through an instinctive and immediate emotional attachment to the imagined community, which exists arguably at a more fundamental level of identity than that of practical politics (Kecmanovic 2005). That is, this form of nationalism is often held much dearer to the individual as part of his/her identity construction. It can often be deemed a *romantic nationalism* in the sense of a deep emotional attachment to the history and mythology of the nation in question (Nairn 1968: 7). In some cases it can also take the form of a fully formed *ethnic nationalism*, in which there is a strong feeling of connectedness to people of the same ethnic heritage. In this case the nation itself may in fact be imagined in such a way as to exclude certain individuals from the national community, irrespective of whether they live within the borders of the nation-state.

Conservatism and nationalism

It is important to make a distinction, however, even within this branch of 'irrational' nationalism(s), between what can be discerned as *conservative nationalism* and *fascist nationalism*. The former is often identified in the work of the chief philosopher of conservatism, Edmund Burke. In Burke's writings there is often a deep attachment to the English nation at a fundamental level of emotion and identity (despite the fact that he himself was born an Irishman). Burke speaks of the English parliamentary system, for example, with a deep degree of reverence, which takes into account the historical journey of the English nation in painfully putting together a constitutional firmament that maintains 'civilization'. Moreover, Burke's writings about the need for the preservation of traditional authorities is aimed ultimately at the well-being of the English as a 'people'. Memorably he states that the nation is 'not a blank sheet in which each goes his own way'—there must be a degree of cultural assimilation, and cultural preservation (cited in Aughey 2007: 140). His concerns about the excesses of the regicides in the French Revolution, and his warning to his English compatriots not to emulate the example of this continental upheaval, bears the mark of patriotic commitment (see Chapter 3 on conservatism for more detail). Moreover, he is keen that the nation should maintain its sovereignty and not undertake revolutionary action that would leave it vulnerable to foreign interference. There is also (arguably) a degree of pride in the writings of Edmund Burke, in that he positively identifies with the apparent cultural persona of the English—notably, in terms of the idea of English restraint—which he compares favourably (at times) to the rash behaviour of other nations.

It is perhaps clear from the outset why this form of instinctive, emotional nationalism is often found at the heart of conservatism. An emotional commitment to the nation helps to cement the citizens' acceptance of the status quo in terms of the existing constitution and preponderant institutions of governance. For example, an emotional attachment to the English monarchy helps to cement the maintenance of that institution. Moreover, a nationalist appreciation of the historical movement towards parliamentary democracy—as embodied in England within the House of Lords and House of Commons—helps to ensure these institutions' survival. Namely, a nationalist sentiment of reverence for Magna Carta, for the parliamentary struggle of the English Civil War, as well as the (alleged) gains of the (so-called) Glorious Revolution of 1688–89, helps to maintain the citizens' acceptance of these parliamentary institutions. This is in fact part of Burke's own argument—that the citizenry are an emotional entity and obey authorities out of attachment rather than due to a pure-ly rational acceptance of power structures. Thus Burke argues that it is dangerous to jettison existing institutions—given the (arguably nationalist) emotional appeal that these bodies maintain in terms of the exercise of power.

This 'irrational' nationalism can be found within parties of the centre-right that (at times) abide with conservatism in terms of their ideological outlook (recently in com-bination with an economic neo-liberalism). For example, the British Conservative Party often invokes the symbolism and mythology of the English nation itself (again, see Chapter 3 on conservatism for further detail and debate). For instance, the recent change of the Conservative Party branding from a torch of liberty to the English oak tree reflects, in part, an appeal to English identity. Moreover, the Conservative Party has sought to appeal to an instinctive, romantic Englishness—recently embod-ied in the self-effacing 'gentlemanly' David Cameron (publishing an England-only manifesto in the 2015 general election, the first time that such a venture had been undertaken). This is mirrored in other parties of the centre-right, notably the US Republican Party. Whereas the US Democratic Party itself makes emotional appeals to the importance of the US constitution in the make-up of an American national identity, this is taken much further by many Republicans (most evidently within the Tea Party associated with figures such as Rand Paul). Republican politicians appeal to an instinctive personal commitment to the idea of an American nationality, constitu-tionalism, and value system in order to win support for their policies. As Skocpol and Williamson (2012: 52) explain, this can at times approach a 'religious understanding of the Constitution'. This is important for the party in differentiating itself from the Democrats who are often said to lack patriotic appeal (for instance in terms of the Democrats' more lenient approach to the question of immigration and amnesty programmes).

Importantly, however, this emotional nationalism does not necessarily bear an exclusionary *ethnic* characteristic. As mentioned, there is often scope—and focus on—the idea of cultural assimilation within the nation. For example, note the (in)famous dictum from a UK Conservative politician that the British could discern the loyalties of South Asian heritage British citizens based upon their sporting affili-ations (namely, whether these citizens support Pakistan/India or England in crick-et games—see Chapter 11 on multiculturalism for further discussion of Norman Tebbit's 'cricket test') (*New Statesman* 2006). Moreover, recent emphasis on citizen-ship tests aligns with a conservative ideal that people of ethnic minority backgrounds can imbibe the preponderant 'way of life' of the nation: that through historical educa-tion as to the past trials of the national community (for instance, the bravery of the English in the Second World War) they too can begin to emotionally identify with their adopted nation. This is seen as important in terms of assimilation and national self-preservation—namely, that citizens respect political authorities and positively contribute to the well-being of others within the society (as fellow co-nationals).

Fascism and ethnic nationalism

The latter variant of 'irrational' nationalism, however, does include an ethnic variety of nationality, as well as the romantic emotionalism described in the previous section in relation to conservatism. It is here that we can observe the emergence of what can be described as a *fascist nationalism*, in which there is a political impetus to preserve the ethnic 'purity' of the nation. In this context, there is an emphasis on self-determination in opposition to 'rival' peoples outside of the geographical confines of the fascist state, but there is also a suspicion of ethnic minorities existing within the nation. This can be expressed in terms of outright persecution of those who are deemed 'other'. So-called 'aliens' have been the subject of historical abuse and murder at the hands of fascists—notably, in the case of Nazi Germany and the Holocaust— and more recently within present day Greece in which neo-Nazi party supporters (Golden Dawn) stand accused of 'disappearing' migrants (Debating Europe 2014).

This fascist nationalism fits into the broader totalitarian perspective of this particular ideology. The emotional appeal to an ethnic definition of the 'imagined community' is seen as part of the mobilization of the citizenry under a fascist leader. Members of the nation will be obedient and will be willing to die for the cause of national aggrandisement (and territorial expansion) as a result of the inculcation of this emotional, ethnic form of expansionist nationalism. The fascist leader, moreover, will seek to personify the apparent attributes of the nation—in terms of his ethnicity and personal characteristics—and will thereby gain the devotion of the nation at large. A political focus on internal and external threats allegedly posed by peoples of a different ethnic background also serves a useful purpose for the fascist party in the sense of distracting the population from other issues, for instance, economic dislocation or loss of civil liberties.

As mentioned, this fascist variety of ethnic nationalism is not confined to the twentieth century (see Chapter 7 on fascism for more detail on this ideology). Indeed, this form of 'irrational' nationalism is very much a contemporary phenomenon, not only in the case of Greece and Golden Dawn, but arguably also in the case of France and the Front National. Notably, the Front National is optimistic that their candidate, Marine Le Pen, will be able to reach the final round of the next presidential elections in 2017. This would repeat the 'success' of her father, Jean Marie Le Pen, who (in)famously reached a head-off with the conservative candidate, Jacques Chirac, in 2002. At that time, an anti-fascist coalition coalesced around Chirac, with socialists voting for him under the banner 'vote for a crook, not a fascist' (Workers' Liberty 2002). Marine Le Pen's attempt to detoxify the brand and (arguably) to redefine the 'other' as Muslims rather than Jews (distancing the party from her father's anti-Semitic statements), however, make the Front National more confident that they could perhaps win the Presidency outright. As opinion polls stand at time of writing, this is unlikely, but given Marine Le Pen's success to date, it would be complacent of the anti-fascists in France to underestimate her electoral appeal. Interestingly, there is also much discussion now of whether the Russian state under Vladimir Putin is moving towards a fascist political programme—characterized by an ethnic form of nationalism (explored in more detail in Case Study 6.4). However, it is important to contextualize this apparent contemporary success of fascist nationalism in light of an anti-globalization sentiment. This is discussed in more detail in the next section.

Case Study 6.4 Ethnic nationalism in a Russian proto-fascist state?

An ethnic variety of nationalism has gained increasing appeal among Russian citizens in the timeframe of Vladimir Putin's Presiden(cies) from 2000 onwards. A study by Chebankova (2007) underscores the rise of ethnic nationalism in the country, which she explains in terms of Kremlin pressure to resist a 'Colour Revolution' (that is a popular uprising as witnessed in neighbouring states such as Georgia); suspicion of international interference; and judicial reluctance to adequately deal with race-hate crimes. She also explains that 'apart from the Kremlin's experiments with ultra-nationalist organizations, there has been an alarming lack of a fair judicial review for racial crimes. The federal centre has clearly failed to send a message to the legal enforcement and judicial structures to adopt an uncompromising stance towards nationalistic activities . . . in 2004, with its 259 registered racial crimes and 47 murders, only nine custodial sentences were passed' (Chebankova 2007: 449).

This is combined with a recent foreign policy orientation which has espoused ethno-territorial claims about the well-being of the Russian people. The Russian annexation of the Crimea from Ukraine was justified in terms of the Kremlin's anxiety to protect a Russian-speaking population from the predations of alleged 'fascists' in Kiev. Similarly, the Russian state under Putin has made known its concerns about the safety of Russian ethnic people in the south-east of Ukraine, and has stated that it will protect their human rights (*Washington Post* 2014). Alarmingly, Putin has invoked the concept of a 'new Russia' in his references to south-eastern Ukraine where the ethnic Russians reside. Aron (2014: 19) explains that 'in a four-hour call-in show televised across Russia, Vladimir Putin assigned the name New Russia—Novorossiya—to the lands in Southeastern Ukraine he claimed were and are historically part of Russia . . . Putin said his lands of Novorossiya—Kharkov, Luhansk, Donetsk, Kherson, Nikolaev and Odessa—had *never* been part of Ukraine. The contention is nonsensical'. Moreover, there is evidence that the Russian Federation is actively assisting military operations conducted by separatist groups near to the Ukrainian border with Russia.

The use of an ethno-territorial discourse to justify Russian interventions has further heightened the appeal of ethnic nationalism within Russia's own borders. The approval ratings of Vladimir Putin increased in the aftermath of the Crimean episode, with the President viewed as a courageous patriot able to defend the interests of the ethnic nation. In particular, the foreign policy adventures undertaken by Putin appear to have cemented ethnic nationalist sentiment among Russian youth. Interestingly, Peregudov (2014) explains that 'the scale and radicalism of Russian ethnic nationalism among young people have promoted some researchers to place it in a special category of "youth nationalism"'. It is important to acknowledge that the Nashi youth movement affiliated to Putin's Presidency itself decries ethnic chauvinism. It in fact condemns fascist youth movements that attack ethnic minorities and states that 'cultural diversity is Russia's greatest asset in the modern world. Religious and ethnic cooperation empowers our country to develop further . . . our generation's task is to prevent the spread of fascist ideas, aggressive nationalism . . . and separatism that threatens the unity and territorial integrity of Russia' (cited in Atwal and Bacon 2012: 261). Nevertheless, this organization is characterized by its loyalty to the figure of Vladimir Putin, and his recent ethno-territorial interventions in the former Soviet sphere bodes ill for the eradication of 'ethnic nationalism' among Russian youth.

Furthermore, Putin's ethno-territorial interpretation of his recent foreign policy episodes has caused concern to other neighbouring countries, such as Estonia, which are also home to significant proportions of Russian ethnic citizens. There are fears that Putin's apparent irredentism (that is, his apparent quest to reclaim 'lost' parts of Imperial Russia) could be furthered by an ethno-nationalist appeal to possible separatist movements in countries such as Estonia. Indeed, this has not only been witnessed in the aforementioned case of Ukraine, but also in Georgia, where breakaway provinces have been supported by the Kremlin in order to claim their own sovereignty.

Given the rise of ethnic nationalism in Russia—combined with Putin's increasingly authoritarian behaviour in the domestic sphere—there are fears that the country is in fact a proto-fascist state (that is, one in the foothills of a fully-fledged fascism). One notable critic of the regime, Evgeny Gontmakher, claims that 'we are witnessing an open attempt by the regime's political technologists to play on prejudices, myths and other dark sides of human values. We are seeing a conscious attempt to counter a fairly large and open protest sensibility with the state's encouragement of nationalism and xenophobia, isolationism and imperial mentality, Stalinism, religion and other hideboundness' (cited in Aron 2014: 21). The cultivation of ethnic nationalism, in particular, as a response to economic dislocation as well as to international hostility towards Russia (real or imagined), is a worrying feature of the current Putin Presidency. Statements about proto-fascism may prove to be unfounded—nevertheless, the phenomenon of ethnic nationalism among the youth will have long lasting repercussions for the character of the Russian Federation.

 Stop and Think

Can you think of any other countries that might be characterized as 'proto-fascist'? See, for example, media coverage of the Presidency of Recep Erdogan, the current head of state of Turkey.

Nationalism and globalization

It is perhaps a paradox that many scholars view nationalism as one of the most important ideologies in an era of globalization. Indeed, nationalism as ideology is often associated (in historical terms) with the Treaty of Westphalia in 1648 (which gave birth to the aforementioned 'Westphalian system'), the French Revolution of 1789, and the subsequent arousing of French nationalism in response to external interventions, and/or the civic nationalist uprisings of the 1848 'events' where liberal elites sought to gain greater democratic freedoms in territories including the

German principalities (Hobsbawm 2012). Nevertheless, as a so-called 'global village' is constructed in terms of free markets, media, and consumer culture, there are many who view nationalism as increasing in strength, rather than abating. Indeed, while there are cosmopolitan individuals who now may feel little or no national affiliation, nevertheless, there is much evidence that processes of 'globalization'—particularly in terms of free market liberalization and increased migration flows—have re-energized nationalist sentiment, particularly in Western contexts (Kaldor 2004).

Moreover, there are arguments that the emergence of supranational bodies such as the European Union or African Union do not lead to a diminution of the importance of nationalism as ideology. Instead, they apparently give birth to new forms of pan-nationalism that perhaps retain ethnic features or, at the very least, a cultural nationalism (Shore 1996). In addition, there is discussion that the emergence of bodies such as the European Union in fact makes certain small nation nationalisms more viable. For instance, nationalist sentiment in Scotland, Catalonia, and Flanders can be partly explained in terms of movements which aspire to join the ranks of European nations within the auspices of the wider EU project. The existence of the common market with free movement of people apparently makes these small nation nationalisms more appealing—removing much of the economic uncertainty that might otherwise arise from these 'regional' claims. Moreover, such nationalisms—particularly in the case of the Scottish 'Yes' movement—can somewhat rid themselves of labels of xenophobia or ethnic chauvinism if they align themselves to a positive case for membership of the European family of nations (albeit as sovereign independent states) (Preston 2008).

As already discussed in the case of the centre and the far right, moreover, there is much discussion that, even within existing large nations such as England and France, processes of globalization galvanize nationalist movements. The success of the Leave campaign in the UK 'Brexit' referendum, for example, can arguably be traced to ethnic nationalist sentiment against immigration originating from new EU member states, particularly from Romania (which the UKIP leader Nigel Farage cited in his statements). Moreover, the apparent loss of sovereignty from long established states such as the United Kingdom to the European Commission (as part of the European project) was seen to heighten nationalist sentiment, as English nationals became resentful as to the diminution of traditional authorities—in this case the privileges of the House of Commons (Wellings 2010). Many cite this factor for the success of the UK Leave campaign, much to the wider detriment of the European supranational project and its unity.

It is important to recognize, however, that nationalism in the context of globalization is not purely a Western phenomenon. In Africa, a number of movements have grown in opposition to Chinese investments, often taking a nationalist form. In Zambia, for example, a recent Presidential candidate consciously drew upon nationalist and anti-Chinese rhetoric, blaming Chinese investors for mistreatment of local workers and for causing environmental degradation (Negi 2008). This was mirrored in Uganda where activists attacked and killed Indian nationals who were blamed for investments that threatened environmental integrity in Mabira Forest Reserve (Rights and Resources 2007). Perhaps most interestingly, the Mugabe regime's authoritarian shift in the late 1990s is explained by some in terms of the dislocation caused by the International Monetary Fund's structural adjustment programmes (SAPs). The consolidation of central power by Mugabe—and his use of nationalist rhetoric and seizure of white-owned farms—is interpreted as a power strategy used to counteract the hardship experienced as a result of economic drawbacks under SAPs (Bracking 1999). Just as African nationalism once emerged in response to anti-colonial struggles in the 1950s and 1960s, so too can modern brands of 'nationalism' be seen in the context of Chinese, Indian, and Western influences in the cases of Zambia, Uganda, and Zimbabwe (respectively).

Interestingly, the growth of Islamic fundamentalism is also often described as a form of Muslim 'nationalism' in relation to the umma—the world-wide nation of Islam (Halliday 2002). Jihadi rhetoric often juxtaposes the values of the Muslim community with those of an apparently godless and secular Western consumer culture. This has been interpreted in some quarters as a backlash against cultural globalization or perhaps more properly, against Westernization. The attempts of groups such as so-called Islamic State (otherwise known as IS, ISIS, ISIL, or Daesh) to establish 'Islamic' nations is deemed in part a response to the apparent immoral globalization imposed by Western countries in the Middle East. This chimes somewhat with the (in)famous work of Samuel Huntington (1993) and his prediction of a 'clash of civilizations'. Rather than bringing about a tranquil and cosmopolitan 'global village', Huntington predicted that the forces of globalization would provoke new cultural nationalisms—often organized on a regional or civilizational basis (for example, European culture as represented by the European Union). His thesis, however, remains highly controversial and many would dispute his (somewhat sensationalist) views as to the cultural fragmentation of the globe.

Nationalism—understood in terms of a belonging to the 'imagined community' within the nation-state—is therefore not necessarily a 'victim' of globalization, but something which will remain a potent force in the twenty-first century. What will be particularly interesting to examine will be the extent to which nationalism can perhaps be blended with other forms of affiliation and identity: for instance, to what extent a sense of 'Englishness' can co-exist with Britishness and a European identity; and to what extent global media will solidify global awareness and **transnational** bonds of solidarity (for instance, in terms of the 2015 refugee crisis). Whether individuals can successfully manage a multi-level system of identity—and in fact combine this with cosmopolitan forms of belonging in terms of participation in non-governmental organizations such as international refugee solidarity movements—will be keenly observed by the media and by the academic community alike.

Stop and Think

To what extent do you balance multiple identities in your own self-conception? How important is national identity for you?

Conclusion

It is clear from the above discussion of nationalism that it is too simplistic to think of this ideology as a monolithic, singular entity. Instead the phenomenon of nationalism can best be analysed in terms of rational and irrational schools. Within the rational camp we can observe both a liberal variant of nationalism which seeks to (pragmatically) balance individual freedom with a wider commitment to the good of the society; and a left nationalism, which seeks to balance a quest for egalitarian politics with a belonging to the imagined community. These forms of nationalism can also be defined in terms of their 'civic' quality—that is, defining membership of the nation on the basis of geographical and/or political values rather than on a shared ethnic affiliation. Importantly, this brand of civic nationalism often implies a process of assimilation whereby newcomers to the imagined community gain a sense of belonging upon inculcation of a dominant culture. This feeds into wider discussion about national traits and the 'spirit' of the nation—in terms of the self-image of the archetypal 'Englishman', for instance.

The irrational brand of nationalism, as discussed in the sections of this chapter, can meanwhile be associated with a conservative and fascist variant. What connects these brands of nationalism is a sense of 'gut', instinctive belonging to the nation, often involving emotionalism and romanticism. This is not the 'hard-headed' pragmatism of the socialist or liberal—but is a strong sense of identity on the part of the conservative and/or fascist with the nation-state. In the case of the conservative form, emotional attachment to the well-being of the nation and its political institutions is seen as a means of preserving a culture and polity that has served generations of citizenry. A patriotic attachment to political authorities ensures that radical experimentation with the constitution is avoided, and that evolutionary change is undertaken instead. This safeguards the populace from unnecessary upheaval—as memorably detailed by Edmund Burke in his *Reflections on the Revolution in France*. The fascist form also entails an emotional attachment to the nation that draws upon mythology and historical episodes—most often historical grievances against those deemed 'other'. This raises an important feature of the fascist form of nationalism which in many cases delineates it from conservatism. Thus the fascist form of nationalism is 'ethnic' in character. This means that membership of the imagined community is not solely based on shared geography or culture—but is explicitly defined in terms of a shared blood heritage. In many cases within the fascist state, this is expressed in terms of the alleged superiority of the nation race, and its subsequent duty to bring 'order' to the international system in terms of territorial expansion and conquest.

Finally, it is important to recognize that globalization has not dealt a death blow to nationalism. While **cosmopolitanism** has gained traction in certain quarters, nevertheless, nationalism as an attachment to the imagined community has gained strength in many countries as part of a resistance to homogenizing forces—notably those of the free market, consumerism, and global media. In many instances this has taken an ethnic form of nationalism with fascist features in countries such as France (the Front National), Greece (Golden Dawn), and arguably Russia under Vladimir Putin. In other cases it has energized civic nationalist movements such as that embodied by the Scottish National Party. Again, what differentiates these forms of nationalism is the means by which the imagined community is defined. And it is perhaps needless to (re)state that the ethnic variant is particularly troubling to observe in Europe given the history of the twentieth century.

 Stop and Think

Do you think that social media such as Twitter and Facebook can help to challenge ethnic nationalism in the twenty-first century? In what ways might social media in fact help to reinforce exclusionary forms of nationalism?

Summary

- Nationalism is characterized by its concern for the well-being of the imagined community, that is 'the nation'.

- Nationalism can be defined as a 'sticky' ideology in that it often finds itself co-joined with other ideological perspectives.

- Civic nationalism defines the nation in terms of geographical residency within the territorial confines of the state.

- Ethnic nationalism defines the nation in terms of blood heritage and 'race'.

- Nationalism is regularly seen as a regressive ideological phenomenon, yet it has been responsible for certain liberations—notably in sub-Saharan Africa against imperialism.

Review and discussion questions

This chapter has explored key concepts such as the 'nation', the 'nation-state', and the 'imagined community'. It has considered varying ethnic and civic forms of nationalism, as well as 'sticky' connections to liberalism, socialism, fascism, and conservatism.

Demonstrate your knowledge by answering the four key questions below.

1. Benedict Anderson states that the nation is 'imagined'. What does he mean, though, when he says that it is also 'limited', 'sovereign', and a 'community'?

2. Why do certain Marxists raise concerns about the use of nationalist language within campaigns for socialism?

3. Why is Dzur sceptical as to the ability to successfully marry nationalism to liberal precepts?

4. On what grounds might critics identify a fascist form of ethnic nationalism in Putin's Russia?

Research exercises

1. Search the www.gov.scot website for official publications issued by the SNP-formed Scottish Government (Scottish Executive) in the year 2014 in the lead up to the Scottish independence referendum held in September of that year. To what extent, from your reading of these documents, can we describe the Scottish Government as promoting a civic form of nationalism?

   (Hint: *Scotland's Future* was a main document issued in this timeframe).

2. Search for examples where Alex Tsipras or other leading figures of the radical left Syriza movement have combined a socialist outlook with nationalist rhetoric and/or nationalist appeals to 'the people'.

   (Hint: a number of newspapers and journals have covered this topic, often in condemnation of the apparent marriage between socialism and nationalism undertaken by Syriza).

Further reading

For a seminal work on this topic see Anderson (1991); you might want to read the opening chapter and determine how convincing you find his definition of the 'nation'.

The 'clash of the civilizations' journal article from Huntington (1993) is controversial. As you read it, think about whether or not you agree that we are now witnessing a global fragmentation based on pan-nationalism (i.e. Europe vs Islam vs China!).

As you read *The New Statesman* (2006) think about whether or not you agree that the Tebbit test is dead. It will help you to think about whether the UK should seek to impose a degree of cultural assimilation upon newcomers to the 'nation'.

For an account of Putin's defence of his actions in the Ukraine, read *Washington Post* (2014). As you read, think about whether you agree with his critics that he is advancing an ethnic form of expansionist nationalism.

References

AL JAZEERA (2014), 'French Mayor Calls for Halal Ban in Town Canteens', Al Jazeera, 8 April 2014, http://stream.aljazeera.com/story/201404080050-0023628 (accessed 1 May 2015).

ANDERSON, B. (1991), *Imagined Communities: Reflections on the Origin and Spread of Nationalism*, London: Verso.

ARON, A. (2014), 'Novorossiya', *Commentary Magazine*, 12 January 2014, https://www.commentarymagazine.com/article/novorossiya/ (accessed 1 May 2015).

ATWAL, M. AND BACON, E. (2012), 'The Youth Movement Nashi: Contentious Politics, Civil Society, and Party Politics', *East European Politics*, Vol. 28, No. 3, pp. 252–66.

AUGHEY, A. (2007), *The Politics of Englishness*, Manchester: Manchester University Press.

BELAND, D. AND LECOURS, A. (2008), *Nationalism and Social Policy: The Politics of Territorial Solidarity*, Oxford: Oxford University Press.

BRACKING, S. (1999), 'Structural Adjustment: Why it Wasn't Necessary and Why it Did Work', *Review of African Political Economy*, Vol. 26, No. 80, pp. 207–26.

BRUBAKER, R. (1992), *Citizenship and Nationhood in France and Germany*, Boston: Harvard University Press.

CASTELLANO, K. (2011), 'Romantic Conservatism in Burke, Wordsworth and Wendall Berry', *SubStance*, Vol. 40, No. 2, online pages.

CHATAGNIER, J. (2012), 'The Effect of Trust in Government on Rallies "Round the Flag"', *Journal of Peace Research*, Vol. 49, No. 5, pp. 631–45.

CHEBANKOVA, E. (2007), 'Implications of Putin's Regional and Demographic Policies on the Evolution of Inter-ethnic Relations in Russia', *Perspectives on European Politics and Society*, Vol. 8, No. 4, pp. 439–59.

CHINA DAILY (2014), 'China to "declare war" on pollution, cut energy use', *China Daily*, 14 March 2014, http://www.chinadaily.com.cn/china/2014npcandcppcc/2014-03/14/content_17346330.htm (accessed 1 May 2015).

COMPARATIVIST (2015), *The Coming Storm of Hong Kong Nationalism*, http://www.comparativist.org/the-coming-storm-of-hong-kong-nationalism/ (accessed 1 May 2015).

DEBATING EUROPE (2014), 'Why is Support in Greece for Golden Dawn still Growing?', *Debating Europe*, 19 June 2014, http://www.debatingeurope.eu/2014/06/19/support-greece-golden-dawn-still-growing/ (accessed 1 May 2015).

DE SCHUTTER, S. (2005), 'Nations, Boundaries and Ethics: On Will Kymlicka's Theory of Multinationalism', *Ethical Perspectives: Journal of the European Ethics Network*, Vol. 11, No. 1, pp. 17–40.

DZUR, A. (2002), 'Nationalism, Liberalism and Democracy', *Political Research Quarterly*, Vol. 55, No. 1, pp.191–211.

FOXALL, A. (2013), 'Photographing Vladimir Putin: Masculinity, Nationalism and Visuality in Russian Political Culture', *Geopolitics*, Vol. 18, No. 1, pp. 132–56.

FREEDEN, M. (1998), 'Is Nationalism a Distinct Ideology?' *Political Studies*, Vol. 46, pp. 748–65.

GELLNER, E. (2005), 'The Coming of Nationalism, and its Interpretation: The Myths of Nation and Class', in S. Bowles, M. Franzini, and U. Pagano (eds), *The Politics and Economics of Power*, London: Routledge.

GOLDSTEIN, J. (2014), 'The American Liberty League and the Rise of Constitutional Nationalism', *Temple Law Review*, Vol. 86, No. 2, pp. 287–330.

THE GUARDIAN (2014), 'The SNP's Negative Response to the Smith Commission Could Set it Adrift from Scottish People', *The Guardian*, 27 November 2014, http://www.theguardian.com/commentisfree/2014/nov/27/snp-smith-commission-scottish-people-devolution (accessed 1 May 2015).

HALIKIOPOULOU, D., NANOU, K., AND VASILOPOULOU, S. (2012), 'The Paradox of Nationalism: the Common Denominator of Radical Right and Radical Left Euroscepticism', *European Journal of Political Research*, Vol. 51, No. 4, pp. 504–39.

HALLIDAY, F. (2002), 'The Politics of the Umma: States and Community in Islamic Movements', *Mediterranean Politics*, Vol. 7, No. 3, pp. 20–41.

HASSAN, G. (2009), *The Modern SNP: From Protest to Power*, Edinburgh: Edinburgh University Press.

HEYER, E. (2006), 'China's Policy towards Uighur Nationalism', *Journal of Muslim Minority Affairs*, Vol. 26, No. 1, pp. 75–86.

HOBSBAWM, E. (2012), *Nations and Nationalism since 1780: Programme, Myth and Reality*, Cambridge: Cambridge University Press.

HUNTINGTON, S. (1993), 'The Clash of Civilizations?', *Foreign Affairs*, Vol. 72, No. 3, pp. 22–49.

HUFFINGTON POST (2016), 'EU Referendum Celebrated by Far Right Groups Like Britain First', *Huffington Post*, 24 July 2016.

THE INDEPENDENT (1993), 'The Warnings that Scotland's Patient Nationalism Could Turn Nasty', *The Independent*, 21 November 1993, http://www.independent.co.uk/voices/the-warnings-that-scotlands-patient-nationalism-could-turn-nasty-1505824.html (accessed 1 May 2015).

THE INDEPENDENT (2015), 'General Election 2015: Nicola Sturgeon to Use TV Debates to Deliver "Progressive Alliance" against Austerity', *The Independent*, 1 April 2015, http://www.independent.co.uk/news/uk/politics/generalelection/general-election-2015-nicola-sturgeon-to-use-tv-debates-to-deliver-progressive-alliance-against-austerity-10150363.html (accessed 1 May 2015).

JACKSON, B. (2014), 'The Progressive Thought of Scottish Nationalism', *The Political Quarterly*, Vol. 85, No. 1, pp. 50–6.

KALDOR, M. (2004), 'Nationalism and Globalisation', *Nations and Nationalism*, Vol. 10, Nos 1–2, pp. 161–77.

KECMANOVIC, D. (2005), 'The Rational and the Irrational in Nationalism', *Studies in Ethnicity and Nationalism*, Vol. 5, No. 1, pp. 2–26.

KELLY, J. AND HUSAINI, H. (2012), 'London 2012: A 12 Part Guide to the British in 212 Words Each', BBC News, 27 July 2012. http://www.bbc.co.uk/news/magazine-18983558 (accessed 1 May 2015).

LANE, P. (2012), 'Beijing's Dangerous Game', *The New York Review of Books*, http://www.nybooks.com/blogs/nyrblog/2012/sep/20/beijings-dangerous-game/ (accessed 1 May 2015).

LEITH, M. (2008), 'Scottish National Party Representations of Scottishness and Scotland', *Politics*, Vol. 28, No. 2, pp. 83–92.

LE MONDE DIPLO (2011), 'UK and France: Far Right's Opposing Fortunes', *Le Monde Diplo*, 9 July 2011, http://mondediplo.com/2011/09/07farright (accessed 1 May 2015).

LOUIE, K. (2002), *Theorising Chinese Masculinity: Society and Gender in China*, Cambridge: Cambridge University Press.

NAIRN, T. (1968), 'The Three Dreams of Scottish Nationalism', *New Left Review*, Vol. 1, No. 49, May–June 1968, pp. 3–18, http://newleftreview.org/static/assets/archive/pdf/NLR04801.pdf (accessed 1 May 2015).

NASH, P. (2014), *Better Together*, http://pamelanash.com/2014/08/better-together/ (accessed 1 May 2015).

NEGI, R. (2008), 'Beyond the "Chinese Scramble": The Political Economy of Anti-China Sentiment in Zambia', *African Geographical Review*, Vol. 27, No. 1, pp. 41–63.

THE NEW STATESMAN (2006), 'Tebbit's Loyalty Test is Dead', *The New Statesman*, 3 July 2006, http://www.newstatesman.com/node/153619 (accessed 1 May 2015).

THE NEW YORKER (2015), 'Le Pen's Moment', *The New Yorker*, 10 January 2015, http://www.newyorker.com/news/news-desk/le-pens-moment (accessed 1 May 2015).

NEW YORK TIMES (2015), 'To Call this Threat by its Name: Marine Le Pen—France was Attacked by Islamic Fundamentalism', *New York Times*, 18 January 2015, http://www.nytimes.com/2015/01/19/opinion/marine-le-pen-france-was-attacked-by-islamic-fundamentalism.html?_r=0 (accessed 1 May 2015)

NEW YORK TIMES (2016), 'Fatal Beating of Polish Man Fuels Debate over Xenophobia in Britain', *New York Times*, 1 September 2016.

PEREGUDOV, S. (2014), 'The "Question of the Ethnic Russians" in the Context of Ethnic Relations in the Russian Federation', *Russian Politics and Law*, Vol. 52, No. 1, pp. 6–20.

PERRYMAN, M. (2009), 'The Patriot's Game: The English Left Needs a Model of Civic Nationalism if England is to Have a Progressive Future', *Soundings*, Vol. 43, pp. 35–46.

PRESTON, P. (2008), 'Cutting Scotland Loose: Soft Nationalism and Independence-in-Europe', *The British Journal of Politics and International Relations*, Vol. 10, No. 4, pp. 717–28.

RIGHTS AND RESOURCES (2007), 'Uganda: Forest Riots Spark New Racial Unrest', *Rightsandresources.org*, 18 April 2007, http://www.rightsandresources.org/news/uganda-forest-riots-spark-new-racial-unrest/ (accessed 1 May 2015).

RYAN, B. AND WORTH, O. (2010), 'On the Contemporary Relevance of Left Nationalism', *Capital and Class*, Vol. 34, No. 1, pp. 54–9.

SCHEHR, R. (2005), 'The Marginalizing Rhetoric of Nationalism: How Patriotic is the Patriot Act? Freedom versus Security in the Age of Terrorism, by Amitai Etzioni', *Contemporary Sociology*, Vol. 34, No. 6, pp. 602–4.

SCOTTISH GOVERNMENT (2013), *Bringing the Powers Home to Build a Better Nation—Nicola Sturgeon, Strathclyde University, 3rd December 2013*, http://www.gov.scot/News/Speeches/better-nation-031212 (accessed 1 May 2015).

SHIELDS, J. (2014), 'The Front National: From Systematic Opposition to Systemic Integration?', *Modern and Contemporary France*, Vol. 22, No. 4, pp. 491–511.

SHORE, C. (1996), 'Transcending the Nation-state? The European Commission and the (Re-) discovery of Europe', *Journal of Historical Sociology*, Vol. 9, No. 4, pp. 473–96.

SKOCPOL, T. AND WILLIAMSON, V. (2012) *The Tea Party and the Remaking of Republican Conservatism*, Oxford: Oxford University Press.

TAL, D. (2013), *Israeli Identity: Between Occident and Orient*, London: Routledge.

THE TELEGRAPH (2014), 'Anti-English Racists Terrorising the No Campaign in Scotland', *The Telegraph*, 7 September 2014, http://www.telegraph.co.uk/news/uknews/scottish-independence/11079296/Anti-English-racists-terrorising-the-No-campaign-in-Scotland.html (accessed 1 May 2015).

THE TELEGRAPH (2016), 'Liam Fox Calls for Britain to Leave EU and Become "An Independent Sovereign Nation" Again', *The Telegraph*, 23 January 2016.

TYNDAL, J. (2013), 'Culture and Diversity in John Stuart Mill's Civic Nation', *Utilitas*, Vol. 25, No. 1, pp. 96–120.

VAROUXAKIS, G. (2002), *Mill on Nationality*, London: Routledge.

VAROUXAKIS, G. (2008), 'Cosmopolitan Patriotism in JS Mill's Political Thought and Activism', *Revue d'Etudes Benthamiennes*, 4, 2008, online OpenEdition, http://etudes-benthamiennes.revues.org/188 (accessed 1 May 2015).

WASHINGTON POST (2014), *Transcript: Putin Defends Russian Intervention in the Ukraine*, 4 March 2014, https://www.washingtonpost.com/world/transcript-putin-defends-russian-intervention-in-ukraine/2014/03/04/9cadcd1a-a3a9-11e3-a5fa-55f0c77bf39c_story.html (accessed 21 September 2015).

WASHINGTON POST (2016), 'The Uncomfortable Question: Was the Brexit Vote Based on Racism?', *The Washington Post*, 25 June 2016.

WEBER, M. (2002), *The Protestant Ethic and the 'Spirit' of Capitalism*, London: Penguin Books.

WELLINGS, B. (2010), 'Losing the Peace: Euroscepticism and the Foundations of Contemporary English Nationalism', *Nations and Nationalism*, Vol. 16, No. 3, pp. 488–505.

WINGS OVER SCOTLAND (2012), *When Push Comes to Shove*, http://wingsoverscotland.com/when-push-comes-to-shove/ (accessed 1 May 2015).

WOODCOCK (1963), *Anarchism: A History of Libertarian Ideas and Movements*, Harmondsworth: Penguin Books.

WORKERS' LIBERTY (2002), 'Should the French Left have Voted Chirac?', *Workers' Liberty*, 14 May 2002, http://www.workersliberty.org/node/96 (accessed 1 May 2015).

7

Fascism and the radical right

Aristotle Kallis

OBJECTIVES

- Map fascism onto the field of modern political ideologies, discussing aspects of continuity/discontinuity and the significance of the 1945 watershed

- Discuss the various terminologies and classifications that have been used in order to analyse fascism and the radical right

- Analyse the historical context in which fascism emerged as a radical ideology in twentieth-century Europe, seeking a 'third way' beyond liberalism and socialism

- Scrutinize fascism's overlaps with other established ideologies (e.g. conservatism, authoritarianism, liberalism, revolutionary socialism) and the ensuing hybrids that it has created, in terms of both movements and regimes

- Explore continuities and discontinuities between 'historic' (interwar) fascism and the postwar/contemporary radical right

---

Introduction

For decades fascism had been parodied as a non-ideology, empty of any intellectual substance, derided as simple nihilism or overused as a synonym for authoritarianism. Even if nowadays fascism is widely taken seriously as an ideology, questions remain about its intellectual sources and distinct attributes; about how far it travelled and whether it is over; about how to distinguish it from other related ideologies (e.g. nationalism) and concepts (e.g. authoritarianism or populism). In this chapter we will look at fascism as a distinct form of **ultra-nationalism**, combining glorification of the nation with aggressive exclusion of those perceived as outsiders and even more enemies (see also the discussion of 'fascist nationalism' in Chapter 6). Fascism can be defined as much through its rejections (socialism, liberalism, international-ism, cosmopolitanism, individualism, materialism) as through its vision of change (regeneration of the national community, a new state, and a new human being at the service of the eternal nation). Although fascism began its political life in Italy, it exercised a strong influence across interwar Europe and beyond. Due to the pri-mary significance of nationalism in the fascist world-view, inevitably fascism took on diverse forms in different countries—and sometimes within the same country too—that make generalizations about the ideological nature of fascism always very difficult. What is more, its political appeal in the interwar years reached much fur-ther than the constituency of the radical right, gaining qualified supporters from conservatives, authoritarians, and even some liberals. Finally, we explore whether fascism disappeared in 1945 or remains relevant as a concept beyond that watershed and even until our days. We explore two different genealogies that seek to relate the postwar radical right to 'classic' fascism: one based on the idea of ideological and political continuity with interwar fascism (what we may call **neo-fascism**); the other derived from a critical re-interpretation and updating of populist, redemptive ultra-nationalism for a very different world consumed by perceptions of crisis and insecu-rity. But we also ask the question whether fascism, as a concept, has become either a redundant or a potentially misleading tool of analysis for contemporary phenomena.

The 'era of fascism'

The word 'fascism' entered the realm of history just after the end of the First World War. On 23 March 1919, on the square of San Sepolcro in central Milan, Benito Mussolini announced to a small gathering of supporters the founding of the Fasci of Combat (Fasci di Combattimento), the precursor to the National Fascist Party that he also established two years later. From the early days of its existence, the movement made its mark with a novel blend of fervent ultra-nationalist rhetoric, a powerful faith in a sense of historical mission, aggressive hostility to perceived enemies, and a striking brand of radical, very often violent activism that took precedence over doctrine and ideas. Less than four years from the founding meeting in Milan, fas-cism had become a spectacular success story, with its **charismatic** leader in charge of the political fortunes of Italy as appointed Prime Minister. The 'fascist revolution' that Mussolini had audaciously proclaimed in 1922 was the first, critical step towards what one of the most eminent early historians of fascism, Ernst Nolte (1965: 20–2), has described as the 'era of fascism'.

Yet this 'fascism' remained a mystery. For more than a decade after its founding, it lacked any programmatic text or official expression of its ideology. Even the 'Doctrine of Fascism', the most authoritative ideological exposition penned by the philosopher

Giovanni Gentile together with Mussolini and published in 1932, a full ten years after the dictator had come to power, stated that

> Fascism is action and it is thought; action in which doctrine is immanent, and doctrine arising from a given system of historical forces in which it is inserted, and working on them from within. It has therefore a form correlated to contingencies of time and space; but it has also an ideal content which makes it an expression of truth in the higher region of the history of thought.

> (Mussolini 1932/2000: 46)

It was this 'immanent' nature of fascist ideology, its production from 'contingencies of time and space', its emphasis on action as a constitutive element of doctrine rather than the other way round, that gave fascism its ideological and political elasticity. George L. Mosse (1999: 28), the historian credited with being the first to approach fascism systematically as a distinct ideological phenomenon, likened it to an 'amoeba' that absorbed the most disparate ideas from the mainstream of political thought, only to re-synthesize them as instruments of a revolutionary programme. Some postwar historians were less forgiving of fascism's capacity for synthesis and adaptation. A. J. P. Taylor suggested that Italian Fascism was a 'fraud' (Taylor 1961). The British historian Denis Mack Smith (1992) dismissed Italian Fascism as an exercise in political deception and branded Mussolini a 'buffoon'!

It is a poignant irony that the first observers who were willing to treat 'fascism' as a dangerous force with a potentially global reach came from the communist/revolutionary left. The dramatic events of October 1922 that brought Mussolini to power in the wake of the 'March on Rome' unfolded a few weeks before the fourth **Comintern** congress. Although events took the delegates by surprise, in its final resolution, the Comintern congress noted that 'international fascism attempt[ed] through social demagogy to achieve a base among the masses—in the peasantry, the petty bourgeoisie, and even sectors of the working class' (Passmore 2002: 7). From the perspective of the communist left, there was a sense that an ominous fascist wind was now blowing across the continent.

In hindsight, they were right to be so alarmed. It was not just revolutionaries of the right who were attracted to fascism. Authoritarians from an otherwise conservative (typically patrician and/or military) background came to admire fascism's approach to maintaining order, crushing the left, and dismantling the liberal-parliamentary system. Within two decades of Mussolini's appointment as Italian Prime Minister, democracy and liberalism had all but disappeared from large parts of central, eastern, and southern Europe. Overlaps between fascism and authoritarianism, between the so-called 'old' (conservative) European right and the 'new' (fascist) radical right, presented postwar analysts with real difficulties in determining whether a movement or a regime was 'fascist', 'authoritarian', somewhere in-between or something else.

The basic tenets of fascist ideology

The intellectual origins of fascism as a distinct ideological and political alternative to the established ideologies of liberalism and socialism can be traced back to the late nineteenth century. It was then that a new brand of radicalism started to emerge in opposition to the perceived inefficiency of liberalism and the threat of international socialism, based on what Zeev Sternhell (1994: 1–5) described as a rogue synthesis of components from both the right and the left. These radicals were fiercely nationalist but at the same time appreciated how techniques of mass organization, protest, and agitation pioneered by the socialist left could be repurposed to serve a very different revolutionary platform for the right, based on the primacy of the nation instead of social class. But the critical incubation period for fascism coincided with the years just before and after the First World War. This period was marked by a pervasive perception of crisis—a crisis with political, social, and cultural tributaries that, coupled with the cataclysmic experience of the military conflict, eroded old certainties and generated a powerful desire for a radical new beginning (Overy 2007).

Fascism responded to this atmosphere of crisis with a unique blend of aggressive rejection of the past and intoxicating optimism for a new kind of future. Although it was born and shaped in Italy, where it also achieved its first seismic political success with the 'March on Rome' and the appointment of Benito Mussolini as Prime Minister in October 1922, its ideological and political paradigm exercised a strong influence on international constituencies of the ultra-nationalist, authoritarian, and anti-liberal right across Europe and beyond. In 1926, Giuseppe Bottai, one of the most prominent leaders and ideologues of the fascist regime in Italy, maintained that 'Fascism creates the new ideals, opens up new frontiers of political thought . . . makes history with its own programme and supplies civilised nations a sum of ideas and works' (Landauer and Honegger 1928: 17–18).

Mussolini also spoke about Fascism as a universal political phenomenon:

> Italian in its particular institutions, but universal in the spirit ... [A]nyone may foresee a Fascist Europe that draws inspiration for her institutions from the doctrine and practice of Fascism; Europe, in other words, giving a Fascist turn to the solution of problems which beset the modern State.

> (Mussolini 1932/2000: 62)

The myth of the nation

But what did fascism have to offer to its growing international audience of enthusiastic disciples and interested outsiders? The 1932 Doctrine of Fascism sketched the profile of fascist ideology, describing it more as a 'spiritual attitude' than as a coherent and fixed set of ideas. Fascism rejected the major established ideologies of the nineteenth century—liberalism and socialism. It opposed liberalism and the institutions of parliamentary democracy that equated 'a nation to the majority' and privileged the individual over the community, favouring instead an 'organic' conception of the nation, united on the basis of profound common ties that transcended class, political affiliation, or narrow self-interest. Fascism was also viscerally opposed to socialism because of its belief in materialism, its embrace of internationalism, and its emphasis on the idea of class struggle as the main engine of historical change (Payne 1997: 487–95). Yet rejection of existing ideologies did not mean that fascism was an **anti-ideology**, lacking its own vision for the future transformation of society. The violent destruction of the old order was the necessary stepping stone towards the pursuit of a radical new conception of life based on the absolute primacy of the nation (Griffin 2000a: 192–4). Mussolini claimed that:

> We have created our myth. The myth is a faith, it is passion. It is not necessary that it shall be a reality. It is a reality by the fact that it is a good, a hope, a faith, that it is courage. Our myth is the Nation, our myth is the greatness of the Nation! And to this myth, to this grandeur, that we wish to translate into a complete reality, we subordinate all the rest.
>
> (Scritti and Discorsi, II, 345)

The fundamental, uncompromising belief in the 'myth of the nation' placed fascism within the ideological genus of radical nationalism (see also Chapter 6). In his now classic definition of generic fascism, Roger Griffin (1991: 38–9) described it as an ideology of 'palingenetic populist ultra-nationalism'. Neither of the individual components contained in Griffin's definition were original or particular to fascism; in fact, as George L. Mosse (1999: 178, 195) argued, fascism was 'a scavenger, moulding bits of old ideologies into a new whole'. Thus fascism's ideological novelty lay in the radical and **palingenetic** re-combination and then radicalization of existing ideas, a process that involved both unique synthesis and aggressive rejection.

What set fascism apart from other—earlier as well as contemporary—expressions of this genus of ultra-nationalism was the fanatical determination to subordinate all other considerations to the pursuit of the greatness of the nation, even if this involved breaking of all sorts of taboos. Fascism saw its own place in history as the heroic force that would regenerate and glorify the nation through constant radical action that recognized no barriers or compromises on the road to its 'complete realization'. The language that fascists used to describe this new conception of the nation was steeped in quasi-religious references: the nation was a 'faith', a 'passion', a 'total' condition of truth and vision of salvation, supported by powerful rituals and functions that took on the characteristics of a political religion. As a 'total' condition, the fascist 'myth of the nation' achieved a quasi-sacred status in the fascist ideological universe. It came to resemble a religious cult, with its own charismatic figurehead and distinct rituals, dedicated to the worship of the nation as a mystical and timeless entity (Gentile 2006: 16–44).

 Stop and Think

In what ways and how much did fascism differ from nationalism?

New man, new community, new state

The negative (fundamental rejection of 'decadent' established ideologies) and the positive (the myth of the nation) aspects of fascist ideology combined to produce a programme of constant struggle to re-make the nation. The fierce attack on the old order was the prerequisite for the realization of an optimal alternative future; it was an act of creative destruction necessary to purge the nation from the harmful legacies of the past. It was only after this stage that the rebirth of the nation could begin and reach its full potential, working its way up from the individual and the family unit to the national community.

Guiding and safeguarding the entire fascist project of national regeneration, the institution of the fascist state would be elevated to an ethical category that encompassed all aspects of individual and communal life. The Mussolinian slogan 'all within the state; nothing but the state; nothing against the state' captured the totalitarian horizon of fascist ideology. This state

> embodies a spiritual force encompassing all manifestations of the moral and intellectual life of man. . . . It is no mere mechanical device for delimiting the sphere within which the individual may exercise their supposed rights. . . . It represents an inwardly accepted standard and rule of conduct ... that inspires every man who is a member of civilised society, penetrating deep into his personality and dwelling in the heart of the man of action and of the thinker, of the artist and of the man of science.
>
> (Mussolini 1932/2000: 50)

The fascist state, as a total and ethical conception, was the nation's primary constructive force. It was more than authority and hierarchy, acting instead as the single authentic expression of the collective will of the nation, 'the synthesis and unity of all values'. It was also more than a rational political and institutional unit, functioning instead as a spiritual and ethical expression of the totality and timelessness of the nation. Through its institutions, rituals, and actions, the fascist state intended to 'refashion not only the forms of life but their content—man, his character, and his faith' (Mussolini 1932/2000: 50–1). Its 'total' functions extended well beyond the public sphere—politics, economic organization, citizenship, education, mass culture, public works, housing—reaching deep into a wide range of private matters such as sexuality, reproduction, family life, gender roles, and leisure. Everyone and everything, everywhere and all the time, had to be constantly mobilized in the service of the national community.

 Stop and Think

Mussolini (1932) claimed that (Italian) fascism was a 'totalitarian' ideology. What do you think he meant?

Redemption

Through active re-education and re-socialization, as well as a process of 'weeding out' the remnants of old, corrosive mentalities from the past, a new kind of superior human being would emerge: a genuine 'new fascist man' (uomo novo) that would be part committed citizen and part soldier ready to sacrifice themselves for the defence of the nation, part individual and part a valuable cell in the organism of the national community (Ponzio 2015: 12–13). It was then this regenerated 'new man' who would spearhead the rebirth of the nation and at the same time flourish within the reborn national community. The national community would be an organic whole—the whole nation—purged from divisive influences of the past such as competitive political parties and fragmented parliaments, antagonistic social classes or even centrifugal regional and local affiliations. Redemption, however, also involved a vision of the national community encompassing nothing but the nation; in other words, not just total unity but also homogeneity that led to aggressive exclusion and removal of others, especially those perceived as threatening. The more fascist ideology exalted the unqualified unity and purity of the national community, the more it embraced a utopian vision of holistic national integration as the fundamental prerequisite of its ideal regenerative vision, the more it foregrounded difference and 'otherness'.

This process could easily lead to the denigration and persecution of those who were perceived as enemies of, or otherwise threats to, the national community, whether because they were seen as irreconcilably different (in ethnic, cultural, or even 'racial' terms) or because they were considered to have excluded themselves from it with their behaviour and had come to be perceived as obstacles to national rebirth. It was a duty of the individual and the national community as a whole to protect the nation from these threatening 'others' at all cost. From this point of view, redemptive violence was elevated by fascist ideology to a critical instrument of making history (Kallis 2009: 108–12). Violence was at the heart of the fascist history-making project. It was destructive of the status quo and generative of a 'new order'. Fascist ideology awarded violence a dramatic redemptive function—in the short term used against the perceived enemies of the national community that fascism was fighting against; in the long term as the vehicle for creative destruction that would pave the way for a new domestic and eventually global order.

Fascist ideology: an interim summary

Thus, fascism came about as a distinct ideology through a unique, innovative synthesis of existing ideas, not through new ideas themselves. At its core was a distinct form of ultra-nationalism that combined a vision of national regeneration with an extreme and violent quest for redemption directed at the alleged enemies of the nation. Fascism borrowed from both the left and the right of the political spectrum: if nationalism, authoritarianism, militarism, and belief in order were typical of the right, the embrace of techniques of mass mobilization and of central economic planning were more related to the modern revolutionary left (Sternhell 1986). It sought a revolutionary break with the recent past but at the same time did not remove traditional institutions (e.g. church, monarchy) or effect fundamental social and economic change. It advocated a violent rejection of established ideologies but was much more than simple anti-ideology or nihilism. It glorified the nation—but invoked a narrow, exclusive notion of national community, excluding all those it considered alien or harmful. It sought the creation of a new order but only after the relentless dismantling of the status quo and the destruction of 'decadent' forces. Redemption—getting rid of enemies and 'decadent' forces—was celebrated as the necessary step towards the regeneration of the nation—a process aiming to produce a 'new man', in a reborn society and national community, spearheaded by the ethical guidance of the fascist 'new state' that would encompass everyone and everything.

 Stop and Think

Can fascism be considered a revolutionary ideology?

Varieties of fascism

When fascists from twelve countries met at Montreux, Switzerland in December 1934, under the aegis of the Italian Fascist regime, there was a pervasive, deeper sense of affinity among them, as well as a joint recognition of the pioneering role of Mussolini's movement in the direction of changing European politics forever. At the same time, however, the delegates were also at pains to emphasize that their movements drew ideological inspiration from the traditions of their respective nations rather than mimicking foreign prototypes. Rather predictably then, the participants failed to agree on most matters of ideological substance discussed at Montreux. Anti-Semitism divided them down the middle, with some supporting an aggressive policy against the Jews while others rejected it as incompatible with the values of fascism. Similar divisions emerged in relation to the other major fascist innovation, the **corporatist** organization of political and economic life, even the role of the established religion and church in national life. In short, a 'fascist international' along the lines of its socialist namesake seemed doomed from the beginning.

It has proven similarly difficult for scholars of fascism to agree on which movement or regime, if at all, should be considered 'paradigmatic' or 'mainstream' fascism; and how far the concept itself should be stretched to include different manifestations. One of the most distinguished early scholars of interwar fascism, Eugen Weber, identified at least six main varieties of fascism. Beyond the paradigmatic and highly influential Italian Fascism, Weber distinguished National Socialism as an extreme version of racial fanaticism and state totalitarianism that also shaped radical ideologies in other European countries during the 1930s; the Spanish Falange for being more traditionalist, not least because of its adherence to Catholicism; the mystical variant of the Romanian Iron Guard, notable for its fusion of radical politics, religious mysticism, and fervent adherence to the Orthodox creed; the Hungarian Arrow Cross for its unique translation of both fascist and National Socialist elements into the language of Hungarian ultra-nationalism; and finally a range of other abortive fascist experiments in other countries that failed to develop a distinct ideological profile or their unique institutions (Weber 1964). Other typologies have emerged since then. Michael Mann identified five paradigmatic case studies of interwar fascism (Italy, Germany, Austria, Hungary, Romania), which he described as 'a family of fascists, . . . each [member] unique, yet all sharing some features' (Mann 2004: 10). Other scholars have broadly echoed the distinction made by Oswald Mosley, the leader of the British Union of Fascists (BUF), between a southern and a northern fascism, the former Mediterranean, mostly corporatist (see below) and steeped in Catholic culture, the other Protestant and Germanic/Anglo-Saxon (Gottlieb and Linehan 2004: 155–6).

Corporatism is a primary example of an ideological component that was central to some national variants of fascism and absent from others. An idea already rooted in traditional Catholic thought, it was identified by many fascist movements and indeed regimes as a 'third-way' alternative to liberalism and socialism. Corporatism was based on the idea of a reorganization of society according to economic functions (e.g. agriculture, different kinds of crafts and industry) and interests. This new system was in theory based on shared management of economic activity by workers and employers alike, under the aegis of the all-encompassing corporatist state. In addition, corporatist organization offered the basis for a new type of regional and national representation of interests on the political level that would replace the factious liberal-parliamentary system of the past. As an economic and social system, its main purpose was to realize a system of state-controlled labour relations within each category of professional activity that enforced mediation of competing interests and promoted an organic ideal of social unity. As a political alternative, it proposed a radically different, 'organicist' basis for the political representation of the interests, replacing the party fragmentation that was the trademark of the competitive liberal parliamentary system (Costa Pinto 2014: 89). Corporatism offered fascism the backbone of a fundamentally new relation between the state, society, and the individual: by embedding the economy into politics, the state would regain its authority over society and promote the primary goal of national unity.

Unsurprisingly, it was in the first years of Fascist Italy that the fascist doctrine of corporatism acquired its first paradigmatic formulation. The legislation of the corporatist Labour Charter (Carta del Lavoro) by Mussolini's government in 1927 marked the beginning of corporatism's fascinating trajectory as a transnational fascist idea. The political star of fascist corporatism shone the strongest during the 1930s, a time that has been described as a veritable corporatist turn in authoritarian politics. The scope of corporatist diffusion in interwar Europe was impressive but also surprising. Next to Portugal, Spain, and Austria, countries with strong Catholic traditions and historical depth in corporatist thinking, one finds corporatist outliers such as Yugoslavia and Estonia. Even more strikingly, the European corporatist experiences offered the basis for the 1934 constitution of Brazil, at the time a democracy headed by Getulio Vargas (see Case Study 7.3). When Vargas declared a dictatorship in 1937, his tribute to corporatism became even more pronounced: the re-written constitution of 1937 announced the establishment of the 'New State' (Estado Novo), a new regime that borrowed from Portugal's corporatist precedent with the same name introduced by the dictator António Salazar in 1933; and the 1935 Polish constitution that implemented a significant strengthening of executive powers at the expense of the legislature.

Still, corporatism in itself cannot be regarded as a core or essential ideological feature of interwar fascism, let alone of fascist ideology as a whole. On the one hand, fascist movements and regimes (among them, National Socialism and the Third Reich) showed little or inconsistent interest in the vision of a corporatist reorganization of national economy, society, and politics. On the other hand, sections of the wider European authoritarian right were attracted to fascist corporatism because of its promise of crushing the trade unions and the socialist left while promoting the power of the executive at the expense of the parliaments. Two of the three dictatorial regimes most associated with interwar corporatism, Salazar's 'New State' in Portugal and the Austrian 'Corporatist State' (Ständestaat) implemented by chancellors Engelbert Dollfuß and Kurt Schuschnigg, have not been widely or unequivocally described as 'fascist' in conventional typologies of interwar regimes. This highlights how corporatism became the ideological and institutional domain of fascinating intersections between different strands of the authoritarian right in the interwar period, fascist and not.

⊃ Stop and Think

Can you identify other ideas that were central to the ideology of some fascist movements but largely absent from other fascist movements?

Meanwhile, even within the same country, fascism could take on very different ideological forms. Interwar Belgium, for example, witnessed the emergence of potentially three 'fascist' parties. The Rex, derived from dissident Catholic youth circles, was not originally anti-Semitic (though it subscribed to it in the second half of the 1930s) and promoted a vision of national regeneration that involved the entire population of Belgium. The Verdinaso was from the outset vehemently anti-Semitic and envisioned the territorial reconstitution of the medieval kingdom of Burgundy that involved lands far beyond the then official country frontiers. Meanwhile, the Flemish National Union (VNV) started as a nationalist party for the country's distinct Flanders region but during the 1930s developed into an increasingly 'fascistized' political force, with a strong (and racial) ideological layer of anti-Semitism and a vision of national regeneration that looked towards the Netherlands and Germany rather than Belgium. In a similar vein, the fledgling Austrian republic witnessed the emergence of one fascist movement with strong ties to Italian Fascism (Stahlhelm) prioritizing Austrian independence from Germany and another (the Austrian NSDAP) aggressively pursuing the goal of territorial and political union with the German Third Reich.

National Socialism: German variety or unique?

However, it was National Socialism that presented the biggest challenge to the theories of generic fascism. For long historians have suggested that there was something 'unique' and unprecedented in the National Socialist blend of fierce biological racism, virulent anti-Semitism, and genocidal violent momentum (see Case Study 7.1). National Socialism's biological perception of individual, social, and national 'health', as well as its grotesque identification of nationality with racial heredity, invested the Nazi anti-Semitic project with a brutal violent dynamic that moved rapidly from legal disenfranchising of the German Jews to measures of persecution and eventually to a horrific genocidal campaign across the vast lands occupied by the Third Reich during the Second World War. In addition, the circle of perceived enemies in the National Socialist world view was grotesquely larger: beyond the Jews who were identified as the primary target of the Nazi project of 'cleansing', other groups such as the Sinti/Roma, the disabled (targets of the 1939–41 Nazi 'euthanasia' campaign that bore Hitler's personal authorization), homosexuals, Jehovah's Witnesses, as well as a wider range of people with non-conformist lifestyles (branded 'asocials') suffered immensely at different stages under National Socialist rule. From 1941 until the very last weeks before its collapse, the National Socialist regime oversaw an unprecedented, chillingly modern and devastatingly efficient 'industry of mass murder' and left behind millions of exterminated victims in the death camps of Poland, in addition to the millions of murdered Jews, Soviet prisoners of war, and Roma during the invasion of the Soviet Union.

Case Study 7.1 The 'uniqueness' of National Socialism and generic fascism

The 1970s witnessed a historiographical questioning of the idea of fascism as a generic concept. In an article published in 1979, Gilbert Allardyce denounced the term 'fascism' as a generic concept, arguing that its use and abuse by postwar historiography had deprived it of any meaning or analytical value. Under the eloquent title 'What fascism is not' the author called for the concept to be 'de-flated . . . de-modelled, de-ideologized, de-mystified'. In so doing, he argued, the unique dynamism of Hitler's regime could no longer be analysed in the same intellectual and political context with Italian Fascism or any other interwar radical phenomenon. Nazism, in his view, possessed unique characteristics and dynamics that set it clearly apart from any other extreme phenomenon of the interwar period, including Italian Fascism. Put simply, racial extremism and genocidal barbarism set the NS regime way apart from any other political ideology and interwar dictatorship, throwing at the same time the whole postwar edifice of generic 'fascism' into disarray.

Allardyce was by no means the first to argue this point. Ever since the end of the Second World War, the National Socialist regime had attracted special attention for the unprecedented scale and ferocity of its use of terror. The revelations about the functioning of the National Socialist totalitarian system and the horrific details surrounding the 'Final Solution' deepened the sense that there was something uniquely extreme and brutal about Hitler's regime and its underlying ideology. A. J. P. Taylor's suggestion that Italian Fascism was a 'fraud' by comparison (Taylor 1961), albeit exaggerated, reflected the mood of a wide section of historiography which tended to view Italian Fascism as less serious and extreme than German National Socialism. Within Germany, the emphasis had been placed on the key question of a troubling authoritarian and militaristic continuity between the Wilhelminian, Weimar, and National Socialist periods, with Fritz Fischer provocatively putting forward a narrative of uninterrupted authoritarian tendencies that survived the two watersheds of 1918 and 1933. The idea of a German 'special [historical] path' (Sonderweg) had already developed substantial pedigree amongst historians since the 1960s (Wehler 1973). But Allardyce did not simply reiterate this thesis. He also struck at the heart of the belief that 'fascism' was an appropriate or helpful term for analysing multiple movements, regimes, and ideologies that had made their appearance in interwar Europe.

In different formats, all these arguments pointed strongly towards the 'uniqueness' of National Socialism. Zeev Sternhell (1994: 6–7) published an account of the long-term evolution of what he perceived as 'generic fascist ideology'. In his introduction, he stated boldly that '(f)ascism can in no way be identified with Nazism' because the latter had biological racism and anti-Semitism at the heart of its world view and as its primary purpose. Two years later, in the conclusions of their authoritative analysis of the National Socialist regime as an ideologically driven 'racial state', Michael Burleigh and Wolfgang Wippermann provided one of the most categorical statements of the 'uniqueness' thesis when they argued that

> (i)n the eyes of the regime's racial politicians, the Second World War was above all a racial war. [This] points to the specific and singular character of the Third Reich. . . . The Third Reich was intended to be a racial rather than a class society. This fact in itself makes existing theories, whether based upon modernisation, totalitarianism, or global theories of Fascism, poor heuristic devices for a greater understanding of what was a singular regime without precedent or parallel.
>
> (Burleigh and Wippermann 1991: 306–7)

The most contested chapter of this 'uniqueness' perspective came with the publication of Daniel Jonah Goldhagen's *Hitler's Willing Executioners* in 1996. For Goldhagen, the Final Solution made sense as the product of a different kind of uniqueness—not of National Socialism's ferocious anti-Semitism or Hitler's ideological fixations but of a very particular German long-term ideological-cultural tradition which had been bent on the idea of Jewish annihilation long before Hitler assumed power and pursued his own racial utopia. Goldhagen therefore shifted the focus of interpretation from the debate on fascism's general ideological traits to Germany's specific development in the nineteenth and twentieth centuries—a development which, in his view, rendered a genocidal form of anti-Semitism more acceptable to extremely wide sections of the German population. Hitler's 'willing executioners', he argued, were not just the race-maniacs of the SS, the Nazi Party, or the traditional anti-Semitic right; in fact, as Goldhagen boldly asserted, the majority of the German population were culturally conditioned towards accepting and justifying the goal of annihilating the Jews without Nazi instigation or indoctrination. In this respect, he concluded, Germany presented a unique model of malicious anti-Semitism, capable of envisaging genocide as a radical but reasonable solution to what was widely perceived as a 'problem' by conventional wisdom.

 Stop and Think

What are the main arguments in favour of the idea that National Socialism was 'unique' in ideological terms? How convincing do they appear to you?

Whether all this talk of 'uniqueness' involving one movement/party or regime or ideological statement or country or political culture has contributed much to the understanding of interwar fascism is doubtful. Robert Paxton (2004: 20–1) has rejected the tendency to exaggerate differences between national varieties of fascism. He even argued that, all its variations notwithstanding, fascism is far less confusing as a concept than liberalism or communism! Proponents of 'generic fascism' have argued that fascism was distinctive enough as an ideology to deserve its own place in the spectrum of political 'isms'. As Roger Eatwell (2003) has noted, fascist ideology should be understood as a 'matrix' that features a number of different syntheses between core values, on the one hand, and national traditions or particular political priorities, on the other. Similarly, Roger Griffin (1991) has attempted to address the alleged 'uniqueness' of National Socialist biological racism by arguing that fascist ideology was at its core 'racist' but not necessarily anti-Semitic. Thus, while the anti-Semitism of only some movements/regimes—and the extreme biological variant put forward by National Socialism—were not common or so central to all allegedly 'fascist' groups in interwar Europe, they could be analysed as distinct expressions of a peculiar fascist resolve to promote national regeneration at any cost, without compromise, even with extreme violent methods in attacking perceived enemies and eliminating 'threats' to the national community (Kershaw 2000: 40–6).

From ideas to making history: the fascist regime

Fascism was peculiar in the sense that it came to power so soon after its emergence as an ideological force and political movement. During this short period of time, it had not produced a key ideological text, prioritizing instead action over doctrine and presenting ideology as a dynamic process determined through radical action. Indeed, so much of what we know about 'fascism' has come from its experience as a political regime, in Italy and Germany and to a lesser extent in other countries. It was only in these two countries that a movement identified by most as 'fascist' achieved and exercised power over a considerable period of time, leaving behind unique institutions and traces of its experiments with mass politics. Short-lived regimes headed by fascist movements were also observed in a number of European countries during the war but in most cases these regimes were installed as 'puppets' of National Socialist Germany and did not last long enough to develop their own political profile.

Many experts on fascism have cautioned against deriving ideological features from the practice of these two regimes—or any regimes for that matter. The reasons for this warning are manifold. Both regimes came about through an act of political compromise with parts of the existing order (both Mussolini and Hitler originally achieved power as heads of coalition governments with the support of parts of the conservative and liberal establishment) and never truly rid themselves of its institutional legacies. What is more, on their road to political victory, both Mussolini and Hitler made political compromises, diluting or in some cases abandoning their earlier radicalism in relation to key issues such as religion, economic policy, and constitutional rule.

In purely ideological terms, both Benito Mussolini and Adolf Hitler headed far more radical movements than regimes. Mussolini, a maverick socialist until 1914, had already made a colossal ideological U-turn in founding fascism as an ultra-nationalist radical movement. But the ideology of the early fascist movement was toned down or allowed to change in the 1920s. For example, early fascism was strongly anti-capitalist and anti-clerical. Mussolini consistently toned down both of these aspects in order to assuage elite fears on his way to gaining power. Nevertheless, it was his role in bringing about the resolution of the 'Roman Question'—a dispute about the sovereignty of the Pope over Rome and other territories of central Italy dating back to the birth of the modern Italian state in 1861—that produced the biggest ideological U-turn in the history of Italian Fascism. The signing of the Lateran Pacts in 1929 put an end to the dispute, enhanced Mussolini's prestige as a statesman, but also came with significant concessions to the Catholic Church. No wonder that quite a few fascist heavyweights resented the initiative and criticized Mussolini privately or in meetings behind closed doors (Pollard 2005: 62).

Similarly, the early ideology of National Socialism contained a number of radical propositions that all but disappeared in subsequent party manifestos and regime policy. The 1920 Twenty-Five Point Program of the Nazi Party contained the following demands: total confiscation of all war profits (Point 12); nationalization of all associated industries (Point 13); division of profits of all heavy industries (Point 14); free expropriation of land for the purpose of public utility [and] abolition of taxes on land (Point 17). Years later, and following on from the Nazis' electoral defeat at the 1928 elections, Hitler decided to transform the party's political message in order to appeal to the middle classes, both urban and rural, while also attempting to allay the fears of the political and economic elites of Weimar Germany about the intentions of National Socialism (Childers 2010: 128–32).

There is a further complication to the history of fascism as a form of political rule. The—perceived at the time—success of the Italian and the German regimes attracted attention from well beyond the fringe of radical nationalists and self-proclaimed fascists in other countries. Figures from conservative and authoritarian backgrounds appreciated the fascist regimes' approach to order, efficiency, hierarchy, as well as their ruthless capacity for problem-solving. These unlikely fascist sympathizers perceived fascism as a set of solutions that, deployed selectively and flexibly, would pave the way for the destruction of the left and the dismantling of the liberal-parliamentary system without endangering the status quo. In the 1920s and especially in the 1930s, the majority of southern, central, and eastern European countries witnessed their parliamentary systems replaced by a new brand of authoritarian dictatorships that, while usually headed by traditional figures of the conservative or military establishment, borrowed (and adapted) ideological, political, and institutional ideas from either Fascist Italy or National Socialist Germany (see Case Study 7.2).

These dictatorial regimes are notoriously difficult to classify. While they lacked the revolutionary horizon and radical edge of the Italian and especially German examples, they were notably more radical than earlier forms of authoritarian rule, in ways that clearly demonstrated the influence of the contemporary fascist experience. The first hybrid dictatorship was headed by General Miguel Primo de Rivera in Spain (1923–30), who openly admired Mussolini and saw in the Italian Fascist regime a novel political and constitutional arrangement, freed from the limits of liberal-democratic rule, and controlled tightly by a single figurehead from above. Following Hitler's appointment as German chancellor in January 1933, an authoritarian domino effect swept away most remaining democracies in southern, central, and eastern Europe, typically led by figures with conservative backgrounds who were nevertheless to learn from the fascist precedents and introduce a series of radical experiments in their dictatorial regimes (Mann 2004: 39–43).

Case Study 7.2 Unlikely fascists? The case of Ioannis Metaxas

The fledgling Greek Second Republic came to a crushing end on the morning of 4 August 1936. The interim Prime Minister, Ioannis Metaxas, with the full backing of the Greek monarchy, suspended the parliamentary system and established a dictatorial regime that lasted until Greece's defeat by the Axis powers in the spring of 1941. His regime displayed—from the beginning or developed over time—a lot of the ideological, political, institutional, and stylistic elements that we nowadays conventionally associate with fascism: ultranationalism, leadership cult, para-militarism, invasive state surveillance and secret police, all-encompassing youth organizations, state propaganda, quasi-religious mass public rituals.

And yet, Metaxas was no fascist by either conviction or political provenance. The former general-cum-politician was a staunch royalist and a social conservative, the leader of what to all intents and purposes was a failed, insignificant by the mid-1930s, political party (the 'Free Opinion' Party). His ideological profile was much closer to conventional authoritarian nationalism than to mass-mobilizing, anti-establishment radical populism. He was an admirer of the German imperial military tradition but otherwise far more willing to pursue alliances with Britain than with Italy or Germany. He was deeply impressed, however, by the dynamism of the regimes in Italy and Germany. He seemed to appreciate how fascist dictatorships had experimented with new conceptions of state, defeating with one single blow both liberalism and the left, and were now intent on shaping a new society.

Metaxas was particularly impressed by the constitutional and social experiments introduced by Antonio Salazar in Portugal during the 1930s—especially the concept of the 'New State' (*Estado Novo*), which constituted one of the central ideological discourses of his own regime. In 1937 he communicated to the Portuguese dictator his admiration for, and interest in, his political ideas. He also authorized detailed study of the Portuguese New State as a template for future revision of the Greek constitution. The two official ideologues of the '4th of August', Georgios Mantzoufas and Nikolaos Koumaros, outlined the principles of Metaxist *Neon Kratos* ('New State'), which was also the name given to one of the regime's official periodicals. Mantzoufas drafted a concise programmatic statement for the '4th of August' dictatorship, in which he identified family, nation, Christian-Orthodox religion and church, and Greek culture as the founding principles of the 'national transformation' pursued by the new regime. Like many other authoritarian dictators in the 1930s, Metaxas now saw Greece aligned with the other 'totalitarian' (in his own words) regimes in Germany, Italy, but also, interestingly, the Soviet Union against the international bloc of liberal democrats. In his view, the world was approaching a moment of historical reckoning between liberalism and its powerful enemies; and the outcome of this battle would define the ideological and political landscape for generations to come. His deep-seated disdain of the liberal-parliamentary system had convinced him that the new political model of fascism represented a viable alternative that could be absorbed into his vision of a 'third Hellenic civilisation' (Kallis 2010).

Metaxas often appeared ambivalent or circumscribed towards the two 'fascist' regimes in the late 1930s, this was because he was guided by a highly pragmatic political instinct, aware of the complex and delicate geopolitical context in which Greece—and his regime—operated. Even so, there was a lot of evidence that he also viewed what other fascist regimes represented politically as a source of inspiration in the campaign to re-structure Greece's allegedly broken political system and to revive its national spirit. He seemed in no hurry to turn ideas into concrete institutional shape. It was only in 1940 that Metaxas discussed with his closest advisers the first, sketchy draft for a new 'constitution'. But the surprise Italian attack on Greece in October 1940, his equally sudden death in January 1941, and the German occupation of the country in the spring of 1941 put an end to the 4th of August regime.

Meanwhile, fascism's influence travelled much further, reaching as far as Africa, Latin America, and east Asia. This influence resulted in the emergence of local radical ultra-nationalist cells (such as the Brazilian Integralist Action and the Young Egypt Party) that sought to adapt and impute 'fascist' innovations in their countries. The case of Japan remains one of the most fascinating—and still acrimoniously debated among scholars—cases in which fascist influences emanating from Europe merged with, and cross-fertilized, singularly Japanese long-term ideological, cultural, and geopolitical radical currents (Payne 1997: 328–36). Japan, of course, had been casually branded 'fascist' by the Allies immediately after its defeat in 1945. But the concept reached further, producing or at least influencing a range of political authoritarian syntheses. We can now talk of 'fascism' well outside its conventional confines of national historiography and a predominantly European focus—as international (Mallett and Sorensen 2002), trans-national, and indeed trans-Atlantic phenomenon (Finchelstein 2010).

Case Study 7.3 Transatlantic fascism: The case of Brazil

In early January 1931, the Italian minister of aviation Italo Balbo headed four squadrons of Italian S55 airplanes during the final legs of their record-breaking expedition to South America. Having left Italy on 17 December 1930—the twenty-seventh anniversary of the first flight by the Wright brothers—the fourteen-plane formation flew over the western Mediterranean, then skirted the west coast of Africa before crossing the Atlantic Ocean on 4 January, landing in Rio de Janeiro on the 15th. Balbo arrived in Brazil in the wake of seismic political change. On 24 October 1930, Getulio Vargas, an army officer who had been elected governor of the state of Rio del Sul but had unsuccessfully stood for election as president in the previous March, had seized power in a bloodless coup supported by an alliance of the liberal bourgeoisie, the regional periphery, and the armed forces. He ruled until 1945, the period divided between a first, nominally democratic phase (1930–37) and a second, based on the authoritarian and corporatist New State constitution.

Like many politicians who embraced authoritarianism in the 1930s, Vargas was no fascist. In the 1920s he had built his reputation as a political outsider ready to take on the Brazilian political establishment. His ideology was a mixture of modernizing nationalism, fervent anti-communism, and paternalistic authoritarianism. He headed a nationwide campaign for the spiritual, cultural, and physical 'renovation' (renovação) of modern Brazil, introducing a series of reforms with the principal aim to both 'educate and sanitise' the country. His regime also promoted a unifying collective feeling of 'Brazilian-ness' (brasilidade) that rejected the racial theories that were emanating from Europe at the time. Vargas, however, was also a staunch corporatist who studied and was influenced by the contemporary European experience in this domain. It is no coincidence that the 1937 constitution bore the name 'New State', referencing the Portuguese corporatist precedent masterminded by Antonio Salazar.

When the Italian embassy in Rio de Janeiro reported the emergence of a new radical movement in Brazil that bore striking similarities to Italian Fascism, the Brazilian Integralist Action (Ação Integralista Brasileira, AIB), the Fascist regime followed that lead, dispatching a special emissary in early 1937 to establish direct channels of communications with, and influence over, the AIB. The leader of the movement, Plinio Salgado, had visited Rome in 1930, in a form of political pilgrimage that was very common among right-wing radical nationalists and authoritarians in interwar Europe. Salgado's experience from the visit to the city and his meeting with Mussolini had a transformative effect upon his subsequent ideological development and political action (Gonçalves 2014: 84–5). Subsequent fears that Nazism was gaining ground—in Brazil as a whole, and inside the ranks of the AIB in particular—were taken very seriously by the fascist leadership, especially since South America (with Brazil as its largest country) occupied a special place in the fascist imaginary, as part of the 'Latin' sphere that had to be defended as a privileged space of Italian 'primacy' at all costs. In parallel, Italy was also cultivating stronger political and cultural ties with the government (and, from 1937, formal dictatorship) of Getúlio Vargas, whose corporatist experiments also shared common ideological reference points with Fascist Italy. The trans-Atlantic gaze offered some relief from the impression that the Italian influence in Europe, including the 'Mediterranean' and 'Latin' countries, was rapidly waning.

Fascism, neo-fascism, and the postwar radical right

The fascist project of destructive creation came to its terrifying climax with the Second World War. Starting in September 1939, Nazi Germany led a formidable intercontinental bloc of allies against liberal democracies and, eventually, against the communist Soviet Union. Hitler described this war as one of 'annihilation'—and, in hindsight, gazing at the tens of millions of soldiers and civilians killed, as well as at the horrifying death toll of millions of Jews, Roma, and other targeted groups brutally murdered at the hands of the Nazis and their allies, it certainly was. Between 1941 and 1945, the project of a fascist 'new order', in Europe and on a global scale, went from near-certainty to obliteration. This was an outcome that was decided on the battlefields of the Second World War but was marked symbolically by the execution of Benito Mussolini by Italian partisans and the suicide of Adolf Hitler on 29 and 30 April 1945 respectively.

1945: year zero for fascism and the rise of neo-fascism

Thus the year 1945 was greeted as the end of the era of 'historic' fascism. The military defeat of the Axis powers in 1945 was immediately invested with an unprecedented aura of moral authority derived from the claim that liberalism eventually triumphed against fascism. In the first decades after the war, the historical place of fascism in European history was explained away as 'just a bad moment we had to go through, a sort of historical error' (Guattari 2008) or alternatively as a 'malaise', a lapse into barbarism and 'discivilization' (Elias 1994) that, it was claimed, corrupted and denied everything that the liberal world stood for. Even in the case of right-wing, pro-fascist dictatorships that survived the 1945 watershed, such as Portugal (where the regime headed by Antonio Salazar lasted until 1974) and Spain (where General Francisco Franco ruled from the end of the Civil War in 1939 until his own death in 1975), their resilience was largely based on their ability to distance themselves from the fascism of Hitler and Mussolini (Payne 1997: 380–2). With very few exceptions, the words 'fascist' or 'national socialist' were dropped from party names and manifestos, replaced by less charged alternatives (e.g. the Union Movement that replaced the British Union of Fascists in the UK—Macklin 2007).

Still, even if, in hindsight, 1945 marked the definite end of the era of 'historic fascism', did it also signify an 'endgame' for fascism as a radical ideology (Griffin 2000b)? Not so. The example of the Italian Social Movement (Movimento Sociale Italiano, MSI) in Italy underlined how forces previously hosted within the fascist movement sought to refashion their radical agenda and become accommodated in a very different political system (see Case Study 7.5). The party was founded in December 1946 by a group of veteran fascist leaders who had followed Mussolini to his short-lived Italian Social Republic (RSI) in the north of Italy (1943–45). Among its founding members were Giorgio Almirante, last minister of propaganda in the RSI and also twice elected to the MSI's leadership; and Arturo Michelini, the former secretary of the PNF in Rome and a veteran of the Spanish Civil war fighting on the side of Franco's Nationalist forces.

The MSI was a primary driver of an attempt to establish a transnational network of radical right-wing parties with the aim of recasting themselves as 'European nationalists' and proponents of an independent, powerful European continent. The European Social Movement (Mouvement Social Europeen, MSE), founded in 1951, also involved Oswald Mosley's Union Movement, the Falange Party from Francoist Spain, and the Socialist Reich Party from Germany. While playing down any previous associations with fascism, the members of the MSE restated their commitment to fundamental values underpinning historic fascism—fierce opposition to liberalism and parliamentary democracy, vehement anti-communism, strong commitment to corporatism and third-way doctrines, and racism underpinning a sense of mission to defend Europe (Mammone 2015).

Nevertheless, beyond the narrow circle of nostalgic neo-fascists, the links of the postwar radical right to 'historic' fascism became less and less obvious as the years went by. In hindsight, the years from 1945 to the early 1970s can indeed by described as a period of 'interregnum', with radical intellectuals trying to come to terms with the shattering defeat of 1945 but also seeking ways to relaunch parts of fascism's radical project for a very different world in which 'extremism' held diminishing political and social currency. Ideological experimentation ensued, with a wide range of relatively small formations of the radical right operating in many European countries, typically on the fringes of the political system and lacking a coherent ideological agenda with which to launch a viable challenge on the postwar liberal-democratic consensus in the West.

From the Nouvelle Droite to the New Radical Right and the Golden Dawn

One of these new ideological currents that appeared in France in the late 1960s came to bear the name Nouvelle Droite (ND). Literally meaning New Right, it was shaped by France's turbulent postwar political context—especially the Algerian crisis and the 1968 student mobilization—but exercised an influence on the radical right across Europe and beyond. Alain de Benoist, the ND's most influential ideologue, was convinced that the radical-revolutionary right could only be successful in postwar Europe if it vied for political respectability by reclaiming the ideological mainstream (Bar-On 2007). While many of his views were typical of the first generation of post-1945 ideologies of the radical right (with an emphasis on European unity as an antidote to communism and American capitalism; third-way thinking that professes to be 'both right and left'; fierce critique of liberalism and egalitarianism), De Benoist's thought marked a shift in some key areas. In particular, his critique of racism, anti-Semitism, and ideas of a 'clash of civilizations' resulted in the formulation of the doctrine of **cultural differentialism** or ethno-pluralism. According to this idea, global cultures should be understood as different but not superior or inferior to each other. Each represents a set of values shared by a community that is also bound by a specific geographical location. Thus cultural diversity is a positive phenomenon only if these diverse cultures remain delimited; mass migration and liberal multiculturalism, by contrast, are fiercely opposed.

Although the ND proved politically inconsequential at the time, it did shape the ideological profile of a new generation of radical right-wing movements and parties. The so-called New (Radical) Right (NRR) emerged from the 1980s as a more successful ideological platform, relaunching some fundamental themes that had always formed part of the radical right's ideological DNA in a new, less objectionable, more coherent and appealing political attire. Filip Dewinter's Flemish Block in the Flanders region of Belgium, Jean-Marie Le Pen's National Front in France, and Jörg Haider's Freedom Party of Austria became the ideological-political pioneers of a new wave of radical right politics. They have all used populist arguments and techniques to normalize divisive themes and break into mainstream public opinion, having articulated a convincing ideological break with the 'fascist' past (Prowe 1994; Minkelberg 2000). The success of the experiment became evident in the late 1980s and 1990s, with immigration becoming an increasingly central aspect of the mainstream political discourse and a steady rise in the electoral support for

Case Study 7.4 Fascism with a new guise? Golden Dawn and Jobbik

It is hard to remember that, until 2010, Golden Dawn, a party movement that had been officially founded in 1980 by Nikos Michaloliakos, was still a fringe party without parliamentary representation and a diminutive share of the national vote (<0.5 per cent in all elections until 2010), albeit with signs of rapidly increasing support in municipal elections (e.g. 5.3 per cent in Athens in the 2010 municipal elections) and a burgeoning repertoire of visible populist activism (Hainsworth 2008: 65).

The recent electoral success of Golden Dawn (climbing to 6.9–6.97 per cent of the national vote in the two 2012 parliamentary elections; peaking at 9.4 per cent in the 2014 elections for the European Parliament; and becoming the third largest party in the September 2015 elections with 7 per cent) is even more surprising given the extremism of its ideological profile and political praxis. The party has a strong activist, paramilitary character, sporting ideas about an alleged biological superiority of the Greeks and demonizing a wide spectrum of 'others', from 'immigrants' to Jews and Muslims to homosexuals. But more troubling is the party's association with street violence, including accusations that its members lie behind a rapid rise in physical attacks against immigrants in urban centres and the murder of an anti-fascist rap musician in 2013. Many of the party's leaders, including Michaloliakos himself, are currently (2016) on trial accused of operating a 'criminal organization'.

The story of the rise of Golden Dawn shares crucial similarities with that of Jobbik (Movement for a Better Hungary). Jobbik was founded only in 2003 but achieved its first electoral breakthrough within six years in the 2009 elections for the European Parliament, reaching 14.77 per cent, before climbing to over 20 per cent in the 2014 Hungarian parliamentary elections. The party's ideology is a peculiar mix of social conservatism and nostalgia for allegedly traditional Hungarian values and with national megalomania, a distinct brand of para-militarism (Jobbik's leader, Gábor Vona, was the founder of what gradually became the party's paramilitary wing, the Magyar Guard) and an extreme form of ethno-nationalism that brands Roma, Jews, and Muslim immigrants as enemies of Hungary.

The Golden Dawn and Jobbik represent a distinct subset of the contemporary European radical right. They share an extreme form of ethno-nationalism with a demonization of perceived national enemies (immigrants, Muslims, Jews, Roma), a visceral opposition to globalization and internationalism, an aggressive anti-establishment rhetoric, and a belief in a strong state. In addition, they have manifested distinct ideological links and stylistic tributes to their respective country's historic fascism. Unsurprisingly, both parties have taken exception to the accusations that they are 'fascist' or 'far right' groups. But Golden Dawn has been widely accused of a neo-Nazi ideological orientation: in addition to its symbol and use of the 'Roman salute' in party gatherings, leading members have made numerous references to race and white supremism, occasionally praising Hitler and his regime. Similarly, Jobbik has consistently spoken in favour of the dictatorship of Admiral Horthy, a regime that remained an ally of Nazi Germany until 1944.

Recently, the leader of Jobbik has begun a campaign to moderate the ideology and improve the image of his party. This strategy, aimed at more centrist voters, appears to be paying off, even if the party's moderation seems so far to apply only to the top echelon, with local party branches and politicians continuing to pursue its earlier extreme policies and use the same inflammatory language (Budapest Times 2015).

these and other kindred parties that appeared afterwards (such as the Northern League in Italy, the Republicans in Germany, and the Swedish Democrats).

In the wake of more recent post-Cold War insecurities, a new breed of populist movements and parties of the radical right made their appearance in a number of European countries. Among them were the Dutch Pim Fortuyn List (from which the current Party for Freedom, led by Geert Wilders, emerged in 2005), the Danish People's Party, the Finns Party, as well as more recently the UK Independence Party (UKIP) and the English Defence League in Britain, the Platform for Catalunya, the Hungarian Jobbik, and Golden Dawn in Greece (see Case Studies 7.4 and 7.5).

'Designer fascism' or something new?

Whether the use of the term 'fascism' in relation to contemporary phenomena of the radical right is justified or useful remains open to debate. It is true that parties of the NRR have expended considerable effort in distancing themselves from certain aspects of the ideological radicalism of historic fascism or their own past legacies. The overwhelming majority of today's supporters of the radical right do not wear paramilitary uniforms. They do not roam the streets in pursuit of their perceived opponents. They do not endorse violence or call for authoritarian rule. They vociferously deny any allusion to 'fascism'. The new breed of radical/populist right-wing parties, with their slick presentation, tech-savvy strategists, and modern 'charismatic' leaders, have re-invented themselves for a different world. Their most successful politicians have correctly diagnosed that the demand for old-fashioned extremist politics has long run dry and have adapted accordingly. Their language continues to break taboos; but it does so largely without attacking or even questioning the fundamental values of mainstream liberal society. They have accepted, however strategically, democracy and the principle of human equality, campaigning instead on a platform of alleged cultural incompatibility against immigration. Most of them have formally jettisoned racism and a declared belief in human inequality in favour of arguments about 'absorption capacity' and 'cultural incompatibility'. They have swapped old-style nationalism with appeals to identity and sovereignty. They have learnt to use the language of freedom and human rights to launch a staunch, aggressive, and deeply exclusive defence of **nativism** against all sorts of 'others'. Not surprisingly then, many of them have been rewarded with levels of electoral support that would have been unimaginable only a few years ago and is still showing considerable potential for further growth. For decades, the Front National (FN) in France has been implicated in public and legal spats about its character as a 'fascist' (or not) party. The founder and first leader of the party, Jean-Marie Le Pen, has faced many convictions for his anti-Semitic and, more recently, anti-Muslim views. When he was succeeded by his daughter, Marine, in 2011, there was a clear sense that the new leader of the FN would 'de-toxify' the image of the party in order to make it easier for it to appeal to mainstream voters. Yet accusations

Stop and Think

Do you think it is justifiable to call Marine Le Pen and her party 'fascist'? Is it helpful to do so, given how much she has 'de-toxified' the image and rhetoric of her party since 2011?

that this strategy is intended to mislead the public and that the FN remains 'fascist' in its ideological core have not ceased. Marine Le Pen has repeatedly threatened to sue anyone who calls the party 'fascist' or even 'extremist'. However, on two occasions in 2014–15, French courts have ruled that it is not a criminal offence to use the term 'fascist' to refer to the party and its leader. In its rationale, the court argued that

> if the term 'fascist' can have insulting connotations when used outside of any political context or if accompanied by other demeaning terms, it has, on the other hand, no insulting character when employed between political opponents on a political subject.
>
> (RFI 2014)

But is this distance enough to shake off the use of the term 'fascist' altogether? Is the ideology of the new wave of radical right parties different in kind or just degree or even simply presentation from the core ideological themes of 'historic' fascism? On this question, scholars have been divided. Some argue that, in spite of the shift of focus away from anti-Semitism, biological racism, violence, and anti-parliamentarism, the parties of the NRR remain linked to the ideological paradigm of interwar fascism. Their transformation, they argue, is largely cosmetic and opportunistic—resembling a 'designer fascism' whereby old ideas have been dressed up in modern, more subtle garb (Wolin 2006: 256–77). Other scholars, however, have argued that the new wave of right-wing radicalism is sufficiently removed in ideological terms from 'historic' fascism to require a different interpretive framework—and the abandonment of the emotive language of 'fascism' altogether. They may detect a degree of continuity between interwar fascism and certain nostalgic 'neo-fascist' revivals but point to a fundamental rupture when it comes to the genealogy of the new radical right, from the 1970s all the way to the contemporary populist anti-immigration parties in Europe (Ignazi 2006).

Case Study 7.5 'Post-fascism'?

'I was born in 1952. I am a post-fascist and I hope that Italy stops talking about fascism and anti-fascism'. This is how Gianfranco Fini, then leader of the Italian Social Movement (MSI), described his ideological profile. Fini was leading a party that for decades had taken pride in its ideological and political links with Mussolinian fascism (Fini himself had declared that his party represented 'the heirs of fascism', a fascism that he had no problem proclaiming 'alive in terms of its ideas, after half a century').

Fini was about to make the most spectacular ideological U-turn in recent Italian political history. In January 1995, he announced the formation of a new political party, the National Alliance

(Alleanza Nazionale, AN), as the successor to the MSI, paving the way for the party's ideological and political normalization. In subsequent years, Fini and the AN were repeatedly co-opted by the coalition of Silvio Berlusconi, with Fini serving as Foreign Minister and President of the Italian Chamber of Deputies.

When Fini's AN launched its bid for social respectability, the use of the terminology of 'post-fascism' appeared to many to suggest a new attitude to the past. Fini used every opportunity to explain that the new party

> represents not only an evolution of the right, but a new identity, based on an unequivocal condemnation of all forms of totalitarianism, including that of the fascist period. . . . The new party is not a new face for the MSI; it is something substantially new.
>
> (Raffone 1998)

'Post-fascism' thus emerged as a strategy of 'by-passing' the MSI's fascist past and the historical polarizations that lay at the heart of the pre-1992 Italian Republic. This strategy has paid off—Fini and his AN have grown electorally and moved decidedly to the mainstream of the Italian political system.

 Stop and Think

Was Fini right when he professed that 'Like all Italians, we too are post-fascists. Not neo-fascists'?

Nearly a century after the emergence of fascism in Italy, one would expect that the intervening time would have effected deep changes on the ideas themselves, their overall framing and their operationalization, as well as their presentation techniques. For example, Piero Ignazi identified 'post-industrial' society as a fundamental differentiating factor between 'classic' fascism and the 'new' radical right (Ignazi 1997: 300). Meanwhile, Pierre-André Taguieff has questioned whether the 'new' postwar right can even be considered part of the revolutionary tradition of the right, given its anti-traditional stance and ideological debts to the left (Taguieff 1994).

On closer inspection, however, it is still possible to identify a number of key ideological themes shared across the majority of the parties that form the loose family of the contemporary radical right which remain linked to similar defining ideas of interwar fascism. More specifically:

- Ultra-nationalism and nativism. Parties of the radical right base their ideology on an ultra-nationalist position with an extreme nativist foundation, from which they attack modern phenomena such as liberal multiculturalism, cosmopolitanism, and international co-operation (Rydgren 2004).

- Populism. The discourse of radical right-wing parties is based on simple, highly emotive language that echoes an either–or, Manichaean view of the world and claims to represent the interests of the 'common people' against alleged elite indifference and corruption.

- Restricted 'circle of empathy'/demonization of 'others'. Parties of the radical right either restrict their 'circle of empathy' to a narrow in-group or give priority to the rights of native groups at the expense of others. This exclusionary perspective contributes to these parties' strong xenophobic and occasionally racist tendencies.

- Leadership and charisma. From Mussolini and Hitler to Joerg Haider, Pim Fortuyn, and Jean-Marie Le Pen, the radical right has been linked to the charismatic appeal of political leaders (Eatwell 2005). As in interwar Europe, parties of the radical right tend to be strongly hierarchical and dependent on the personality of their leading figures.

- Attack on 'decadence' and 'establishment' values. Contemporary radical right parties project a grotesque vision of current 'decadence' in the cultural and social sphere that is allegedly threatening the very existence of the nation. The diagnosis for the causes of such a decadence points the finger at a number of targets: political and economic elites, urban values, cosmopolitanism, liberal values, sometimes democracy.

- Ethno-pluralism/cultural differentialism. Even when, nowadays, parties of the radical right seem to accept (however strategically or cynically) the notion of human equality—in contrast to historic fascism's emphasis on inequality—they reject the co-existence of different cultural/religious groups and maintain that 'indigenous European culture(s)' are threatened existentially by increasing levels of immigration as well as 'liberal' multiculturalism (Fennema 2005: 4–5).

Continuities in the above key ideas do not of course prove that the contemporary radical right is directly or significantly linked to interwar fascism. What it does, however, is cast in a different light the attempt of parties of the new radical right to over-emphasize their differences from either interwar fascism or neo-fascist/extremist groups. Like the history of interwar fascism, the trajectory of the postwar radical right is full of intersections, entanglements, and hybrids with the more extreme forces of the right. As Nigel Copsey (2013) reminded us, the transformation of the new radical right owed a lot to the intellectual work of neo-fascist ideologues. It is obviously easier to integrate the ideological genealogies of interwar fascism, neo-fascism, and particular sectors of the contemporary extreme right. But there is an alternative genealogy, one based on redemptive and populist ultra-nationalism, where the histories of interwar fascism and the new radical right continue to intersect, even in the face of efforts to deny or disguise them.

Fascism and the radical right in the twenty-first century

Like every other term with significant moral baggage, 'fascism' has been deployed in contemporary discourse in relation to a variety of targets. Perhaps the most questionable usage concerns 'Islamofascism'—a term that has been in circulation for more than two decades and has been used in relation to Hizbollah, al Qaeda, and more recently so-called Islamic State (otherwise known as IS, ISIS, ISIL, or Daesh) (Hitchens 2007). Using the adjective 'fascist' or 'Nazi' to vilify Islam has also become a discursive technique for as motley a crowd as Geert Wilders, the late Italian journalist Oriana Fallaci, and the former US secretary of defence Donald Rumsfeld. More recently, the word has been widely deployed by both Ukrainians and Russians to discredit each other during their bloody conflict over the control of eastern Ukraine (see also the case study 'Ethnic nationalism in a Russian proto-fascist state?' in Chapter 6 in which the characterization of the Putin regime as 'proto-fascist' is considered). The Russian President Vladimir Putin went as far as accusing Ukraine of being 'overrun by fascists' (Motyl 2007). The former Greek finance minister, Yanis Varoufakis, referred to Golden Dawn as a clear and unadulterated revival of historic fascism. During a public news conference in February 2015, and in the presence of the German finance minister, Wolfgang Schäuble, Varoufakis stated that 'When I go home today, I will go home to a country where the third-biggest party is not a neo-Nazi but a Nazi party' (Lower 2015). In the USA, the rise of Donald Trump has provoked a heated discussion as to whether he can be described as a 'fascist' or not (Jacobin 2015). In fact, one comment went as far as suggesting that the rise of Trump is symptomatic of a much wider 'fascist mood' that reaches deep into mainstream American political culture (Steigmann-Gall 2016).

One of the most eminent historians of fascism, Walther Laqueur, prefaced an international discussion on the concept with the phrase 'fascism has had its time'. Laqueur's statement divulged scepticism about the utility of the term beyond 1945 and about its relevance to contemporary phenomena of radicalism and extremism (Laqueur 2006). If we invoke the term 'fascist' or 'Nazi' in order to indicate the danger of a revival of 'historic' fascism, as ideology or as political movement, then this use is deeply problematic and misleading beyond a relatively small number of nostalgic or mimetic new-fascist/new-Nazi groups in operation today. There was something very particular in the historical circumstances of interwar Europe in which this novel political ideology and praxis emerged, spread, and motivated so many different groups and regimes to join a trans-national alliance (partly political and partly based on something deeper, often experienced in quasi-religious terms as faith) that sought to remake the individual, reconceptualize the nation, and recast the future in unprecedented, previously unfathomable ways. Umberto Eco described a diachronic form of fascism that he called 'Ur-Fascism', not tied to any particular historical or cultural context, that remained at the heart of a threatening ideological continuity between 'historic' fascism and the new forms of right-wing radicalism. But he cautioned that

> Ur-Fascism is still around us, sometimes in plainclothes. It would be so much easier, for us, if there appeared on the world scene somebody saying, 'I want to reopen Auschwitz, I want the Black Shirts to parade again in the Italian squares.' Life is not that simple. Ur-Fascism can come back under the most innocent of disguises. Our duty is to uncover it and to point our finger at any of its new instances—every day, in every part of the world.
>
> (Eco 1995)

Thus, if we use the term 'fascism' to indicate common radical sources of ideological and political inspiration, taking into account re-calibrations that are necessary for a vastly different contemporary political context, then this 'fascism' becomes a useful marker that makes continuities easier to spot and casts a far more interesting light on disconti-nuities and (very important) differences. As noted earlier, on the ideological level, key elements of the 'fascist synthesis' had been around long before 1918 and survived in different forms after 1945. If we approach the fascism of the interwar years as a series of particular expressions of ultra-nationalism with a Janus-faced action-oriented vision of destructive creation (regeneration of the nation; fight against 'decadence'; redemption of its perceived enemies), then the concept of 'fascism' remains relevant to the postwar and contemporary world beyond the obvious cases of nostalgic/mimetic neo-fascism. In fact, far more than race or anti-Semitism or military uniforms or street fights, fas-cism can be fruitfully analysed as a historical, extreme expression of the broader genus of ultra-nationalism (see also Chapter 6 in which fascism is described as a 'severe form of ethnic nationalism'). This was an ultra-nationalism so uncompromising in its glori-fication of the national community and so extreme and violent in the demonization of its perceived foes that it saw fit to break all sorts of taboos—linguistic, cultural, ethical, political—in the pursuit of its goal of regenerating the nation and the world. Therefore, 'fascism' can still be useful—if not to brand contemporary politicians, regimes, ideolo-gies, or religions, then at least to remind us that some of them could still be members of that same burgeoning, troubled, and troublesome family of populist ultra-nationalism.

Summary

- Fascism's originality in ideological terms lay more in its capacity for absorp-tion and unique synthesis of popular themes than in the novelty of its core ideas themselves.
- As an ideology, fascism belongs to the genus of radical populist ultra-nation-alism but also possesses unique characteristics that set it apart from other related ideologies, such as authoritarianism.
- Fascist ultra-nationalism combined a singular vision of national regenera-tion with an extreme and violent quest for redemption directed at the alleged enemies of the nation. In this respect, it represented a rather unique, fanati-cally pursued, action-oriented vision of destructive creation.
- Historians have debated how far the concept of fascism can be stretched in space and time. Consensus has been steadily moving towards an understanding of fascism as a generic phenomenon—transcending national, state, and regional

boundaries, as well as the 1945 watershed. Even so, historic fascism, that is the fascism of the interwar years, was primarily a European phenomenon.

- Post-1945 movements of the extreme right can be broadly divided into those openly nostalgic of 'historic' fascism (generally referred to as neo-fascist) and those that have driven a wedge between themselves and this legacy (anything from the Nouvelle Droite to the parties of the contemporary radical/populist right). Nevertheless, even taking into account ideological shifts (e.g. acceptance of liberal democracy, rejection of racism and anti-Semitism), the parties of the contemporary radical right still share key ideological similarities with 'historic' fascism.

Review and discussion questions

1. Discuss to what extent and in what ways fascism was the product of a profound, multiple crisis in the first three decades of the twentieth century.

2. Did Italian Fascism and German National Socialism have more (and more important) ideological similarities or differences?

3. Explain the arguments (a) in favour of and (b) against ideological continuity between the contemporary radical right parties and 'historic' fascism. Where do you stand on this debate?

4. Reflect on whether and to what extent the history of fascism has been inextricably linked with charismatic personalities.

Research exercises

1. Search a reputable news archive for articles that attempt to compare the post-2008 period with the 1930s (economic crisis, rise of extremism, crisis of establishment politics, spike in hatred against particular groups, etc.). Identify how these articles describe any links/similarities between the 2010s and the 1930s—do they consider such a comparison legitimate, instructive, or not?

2. Research online news and newspaper resources to identify four recent uses (and abuses) of the term 'fascism' and/or 'Nazi'. Identify the context in which the term is used in each case and summarize the ways in which the author(s) justify the appropriateness of the term.

Further reading

In addition to Hitler's *Mein Kampf* (e.g. Vincent Murphy's classic 1939 translation, London / New York / Melbourne: Horst and Blackett) and Mussolini's 'Doctrine of Fascism' (originally published 1932; see Mussolini (1932) in the References below for information on a translated edition), Griffin's reader (1995) offers a selection of translated excerpts from key documents that capture the fascinating diversity of ideas among fascists in the interwar period.

Griffin (1991), Payne (1997), Paxton (2004), and Mann (2004) provide excellent, conceptually sophisticated survey studies of fascism, sometimes extending to the postwar period. For the postwar radical and extreme right, you may consult the monograph of Bar-On (2007) on the Nouvelle Droite, Rydgren (2004) and his edited collection *Movements of Exclusion: Radical Right-Wing Populism in the Western World* (New York: Nova Science, 2005); Paul Hainsworth's *The Extreme Right in Western Europe* (London and New York: Routledge, 2008) and *The Politics of the Extreme Right: From the Margins to the Mainstream* (London: Pinter, 2000).

An always useful survey of the radical right throughout the twentieth century, straddling the 1945 watershed, is P. Davies and D. Lynch, *The Routledge Companion to Fascism and the Far Right* (London and New York: Routledge, 2005).

References

ALLARDYCE, G. (1979), 'What Fascism Is Not: Notes on the Deflation of a Concept', *American Historical Review*, Vol. 84, No. 2, pp. 367–98.

BAR-ON, T. (2007), *Where Have All the Fascists Gone?* Aldershot: Ashgate.

BAUERKÄMPER, A. AND ROSSOLIŃSKI-LIEBE, G. , EDS (2017) *Fascism Without Borders. Transnational Connections and Cooperation between Movements and Regimes in Europe from 1918 to 1945*, Oxford and New York: Berghahn.

BUDAPEST TIMES (2015), '"Clean, moderate" image outweighs far-right taboos', *Budapest Times*, 17 April 2015, http://budapesttimes.hu/2015/04/17/clean-moderate-image-outweighs-far-right-taboos/.

BURLEIGH, M. AND WIPPERMANN, W. (1991), *The Racial State: Germany, 1933–1945*, New York and Cambridge: Cambridge University Press.

CHILDERS, T. (2010), *The Nazi Voter: The Social Foundations of Fascism in Germany, 1919–1933*, Chapel Hill, NC: University of North Carolina Press.

CODREANU, C. Z. (1936), *Pentru Legionari*, Sibiu: Tipografia Vestemean; English online translation by G. van der Heide at https://ia700501.us.archive.org/10/items/ForMyLegionariesTheIronGuard/ForMyLegionaries.pdf.

COLE, A. (2005), 'Old Right or New Right? The Ideological Positioning of Parties on the Far Right', *European Journal of Political Research*, Vol. 44, No. 2, pp. 203–30.

COPSEY, N. (2013), '" Fascism . . . but with an open mind". Reflections on the Contemporary Far Right in (Western) Europe', *Fascism*, Vol. 2, No. 1, pp. 1–17.

COSTA PINTO, A. (2014), 'Fascism, Corporatism and the Crafting of Authoritarian Institutions in Inter-War European Dictatorships', in A. Costa Pinto and A. Kallis (eds), *Rethinking Fascism and Dictatorship*, Basingstoke: Palgrave, 87–118.

EATWELL, R. (2003), 'The Nature of "Generic Fascism": The "Fascist Minimum" and the "Fascist Matrix"', in U. Backes (ed.), *Rechtsextreme Ideologien in Geschichte und Gegenwart*, Cologne: Bohlau Verlag, 93–137.

Eatwell, R. (2005), 'Charisma and the Revival of the European Extreme Right', in J. Rydgren (ed.), *Movements of Exclusion: Radical Right-Wing Populism in the Western World*, New York: Nova Science, 101–20.

Eco, U. (1995), 'Ur-Fascism', *New York Review of Books*, 22 June 1995, http://www.nybooks.com/articles/1995/06/22/ur-fascism/

Elias, N. (1994), *The Civilizing Process*, Oxford: Blackwell.

Fennema, M. (2005), 'Populist Parties of the Right', in J. Rydgren (ed.), *Movements of Exclusion: Radical Right-wing Populism in the Western World*, Hauppauge, NY: Nova Science, 1–25.

Finchelstein, F. (2010), *Transatlantic Fascism: Ideology, Violence and the Sacred in Argentina and Italy, 1919–1945*, Durham, NC: Duke University Press.

Gentile, E. (2004), 'A Provisional Dwelling: The Origin and Development of the Concept of Fascism in Mosse's Historiography', in S. G. Payne and D. J. Sorkin (eds), *What History Tells: George L. Mosse and the Culture of Modern Europe*, Madison, WI: Wisconsin University Press, 41–108.

Gentile, E. (2006), *Politics as Religion*, Princeton, NJ: Princeton University Press.

Goldhagen, D. J. (1996), *Hitler's Willing Executioners: Ordinary Germans and the Holocaust*, New York: Knopf.

Gonçalves, L. P. (2014), 'The Integralism of Plínio Salgado: Luso-Brazilian Relations', *Portuguese Studies*, Vol. 30, No. 1, pp. 84–5.

Gottlieb, J. V. and Linehan, T. P. (2004), *The Culture of Fascism: Visions of the Far Right in Britain*, London: I. B. Tauris.

Griffin, R. (1991), *The Nature of Fascism*, London and New York: Routledge.

Griffin, R. (ed.) (1995), *Fascism*, Oxford: Oxford University Press.

Griffin, R. (2000a), 'Revolution from the Right: Fascism', in D. Parker (ed.), *Revolutions and the Revolutionary Tradition in the West 1560–1991*, New York and London: Routledge, 192–4.

Griffin, R. (2000b), 'Interregnum or Endgame? The Radical Right in the "Post-fascist" Era', *Journal of Political Ideologies*, Vol. 5, No. 2, available at http://www.tandfonline.com/doi/citedby/10.1080/713682938#tabModule

Griffin, R. (2002), 'The Primacy of Culture: The Current Growth (Or Manufacture) of Consensus within Fascist Studies', *Journal of Contemporary History*, Vol. 37, No. 1, pp. 21–43.

Guattari, F. (2008), *Chaosophy*, Cambridge, MA: MIT Press.

Hainsworth, P. (2008), *The Extreme Right in Western Europe*, New York: Routledge.

Hitchens, C. (2007), 'Defending Islamofascism', *Slate*, 22 October 2007, http://www.slate.com/articles/news_and_politics/fighting_words/2007/10/defending_islamofascism.html.

Ignazi, P. (1997), 'New Challenges: Postmaterialism and the Extreme Right', in M. Rhodes, P. Heywood, and V. Wright (eds), *Developments in West European Politics*, Basingstoke: Macmillan, 300–19.

Ignazi, P. (2006), *Extreme Right Parties in Western Europe*, Oxford: Oxford University Press.

Jacobin (2015), 'Is Donald Trump a Fascist', *Jacobin*, 15 December 2015, https://www.jacobinmag.com/2015/12/donald-trump-fascism-islamophobia-nativism/

KALLIS, A. (2009), *Genocide and Fascism*. New York and London: Routledge.

KALLIS, A. (2010), 'Neither Fascist nor Authoritarian: The 4th of August Regime in Greece (1936–1941) and the Dynamics of Fascistisation in 1930s Europe', *East Central Europe*, Vol. 37, Nos 2–3, pp. 303–30.

KERSHAW, I. (2000), *The Nazi Dictatorship: Problems and Perspectives of Interpretation*, 4th edn, London: Bloomsbury.

KERSHAW, I. (2004), 'The Essence of Nazism: Form of Fascism, Brand of Totalitarianism or Unique Phenomenon?' in: R. Griffin and M. Feldman (eds), *Fascism. Critical Concepts in Political Science*. Vol IV: *The 'Fascist Epoch'*, London and New York: Routledge, 47–74.

KODAK, R. (2015), *The Politics of Fear: What Right-Wing Populist Discourses Mean*, London: Sage.

LANDAUER, C. AND HONEGGER, H. (eds) (1928), *Internationaler Faschismus*, Karlsruhe: G Braun.

LAQUEUR, W. (2006), 'Introduction', in R. Griffin, W. Loh, and A. Umland (eds), *Fascism: Past and Present, West and East. An International Debate on Concepts and Cases in the Comparative Study of the Extreme Right*, Stuttgart: Ibidem.

LOWER, M. (2015), 'Why did Greece's Varoufakis bring up Nazis in Berlin?', BBC News, 6 February 2015, http://www.bbc.co.uk/news/world-europe-31170591

MACKLIN, G. (2007), *Very Deeply Dyed in Black: Sir Oswald Mosley and the Resurrection of British Fascism After 1945*, London: I. B. Tauris.

MACK SMITH, D. (1992), *Mussolini: A Biography*, New York: Knopf.

MALLETT, R. AND SORENSEN, G. (eds) (2002), *International Fascism, 1919–1945*, London and New York: Routledge.

MAMMONE, A. (2015), *Transnational Neofascism in France and Italy*, Cambridge: Cambridge University Press.

MANN, M. (2004), *Fascism*, Cambridge: Cambridge University Press.

MINKENBERG, M. (2000), 'The Renewal of the Radical Right: Between Modernity and Anti-modernity', *Government and Opposition*, Vol. 35, No. 2, pp. 170–88.

MOSLEY, O. (1932), *The Greater Britain*, London: BUF Publications.

MOSSE, G. L. (1980), *Masses and Man: Nationalist and Fascist Perceptions of Reality*, New York: Howard Fertig.

MOSSE, G. L. (1999), *The Fascist Revolution: Toward a General Theory of Fascism*, New York: Howard Fertig.

MOTYL, A. (2007), 'Is Putin's Russia Fascist?', *The National Interest Online*, 3 December 2007, http://www.nationalinterest.org/Article.aspx?id=16258

MUDDE, C. (2000), *The Ideology of the Extreme Right*, Manchester: Manchester University Press.

MUDDE, C. (2007), *Populist Radical Right Parties in Europe*, Cambridge: Cambridge University Press.

MUSSOLINI, B. (1932/2000), 'The Doctrine of Fascism', in Jeffrey T. Schnapps, Olivia E. Sears, and Maria G. Stampino, eds., *A Primer of Italian Fascism: European Horizons*, Lincoln, NE: University of Nebraska Press, pp. 46–74.

NOLTE, E. (1965), *Three Faces of Fascism*, London: Weidenfeld & Nicolson.

OVERY, R. J. (2007), *The Interwar Crisis, 1919–1939*, 2nd edn, Harlow: Pearson.

PASSMORE, K. (2002), *Fascism. A Very Short History*, Oxford: Oxford University Press.

PAXTON, R. O. (2004), *The Anatomy of Fascism*, New York: Knopf.

PAYNE, S. G. (1997), *A History of Fascism, 1914–1945*, London: UCL Press.

PAYNE, S. G. (1999), *Fascism in Spain, 1923–1977*, Madison, WI: University of Wisconsin Press.

POLLARD, J. F. (2005), *The Vatican and Italian Fascism, 1929–32. A Study in Conflict*, Cambridge: Cambridge University Press.

PONZIO, A. (2015), *Shaping the New Man. Youth Training Regimes in Fascist Italy and Nazi Germany*, Madison, WI: University of Wisconsin Press.

PROWE, D. (1994), '"Classic" Fascism and the New Radical Right in Western Europe: Comparisons and Contrasts', *Contemporary European History*, Vol. 3, No. 3, pp. 289–314.

RAFFONE, P. (1998), 'Italy's Post-fascists Bid for Respectability', *Le Monde Editions*, May 1998, https://mondediplo.com/1998/05/09raff

RFI (2014), 'Front National's Le Pen Can be Called Fascist, Court Rules', *RFI English*, 10 April 2014, http://www.english.rfi.fr/france/20140410-front-nationals-le-pen-can-be-called-fascist-court-rules

ROBERTS, D. (2005), *The Totalitarian Experiment*, New York: Routledge.

RYDGREN, J. (2004), *The Populist Challenge. Political Protest and Ethno-National Mobilization in France*, New York and Oxford: Berghahn.

SCRITTI AND DISCORSI DI BENITO MUSSOLINI (1934). *La Rivoluzione Fascista*, Vol. 2, Milan: Hoepli.

STEIGMANN-GALL, R. (2016), 'One Expert Says, Yes, Donald Trump is a Fascist. And It's Not Just Trump', *Tikkun*, 5 January 2016, http://www.tikkun.org/nextgen/one-expert-says-yes-donald-trump-is-a-fascist-and-its-not-just-trump-2

STERNHELL, Z. (1986), *Neither Right nor Left: Fascist Ideology in France*, Berkeley, CA: University of California Press.

STERNHELL, Z. (1994), *The Birth of Fascist Ideology. From Cultural Rebellion to Political Revolution*, Princeton, NJ: Princeton University Press.

TAGUIEFF, P.-A. (1994), 'From Race to Culture: The New Right's View of European Identity', *Telos*, Vols 98–99, pp. 99–125.

TAYLOR, A. J. P. (1961), *The Origins of the Second World War*, Harmondsworth: Penguin Books.

WEBER, E. (1964), *Varieties of Fascism*, New York: Van Nostrand.

WEHLER, H.-U. (1973), *Das deutsche Kaiserreich, 1871–1918*, Göttingen: Vandenhoeck.

WODAK, R. (2015), *The Politics of Fear. What Right-Wing Populist Discourses Mean*, London: Sage.

WOLIN, R. (2006), *The Seduction of Unreason. The Intellectual Romance with Fascism from Nietzsche to Postmodernism*, Princeton, NJ: Princeton University Press.

8

Reviewing the 'classical' legacy
Left-right politics in the age of ideology

Paul Wetherly

OBJECTIVES

- Review the legacy of the 'classical' ideologies in terms of their European origins, expansion, and dominance
- Examine the idea that liberalism, in particular, constitutes a dominant ideology
- Examine the relationship between ideological principles, party politics, and statecraft
- Explore the relationship between the classical ideologies in terms of the Enlightenment and the left–right conception of ideological debate
- Introduce the conception of 'new' ideologies

Introduction

The preceding chapters have examined what are often seen as six 'classical' ideologies, so distinguishing them from a set of 'new' ideologies that are examined in the following chapters. However, we should note that this distinction is problematic. In the first part of this chapter we will consider in what way the ideologies we have examined so far can be thought of as 'classical', and examine how far these ideologies have been successful or dominant in the modern era. We will then look at the relationship between ideology and political parties. A conventional way of thinking about ideologies uses the left–right distinction, and discussion of this approach will be a key focus of the chapter. We will finish with a note about the 'new' ideologies that are the focus of the chapters to follow.

Revisiting the 'classical' ideologies

One way of understanding the classical–new distinction is in *chronological* terms; in this sense classical ideologies can be seen as the oldest ideologies, or the first generation of ideologies. We can draw a rough analogy with 'classical' music which can also be defined in chronological terms, for example as 'music written in the European tradition during a period lasting approximately from 1750 to 1830' (http://www.oxforddictionaries.com/definition/english/classical-music). Coincidentally, this is also roughly the period in which 'classical' ideologies took shape. Thus classical ideologies can be defined as 'forms of political thought created in the European or Western tradition mainly during the eighteenth and nineteenth centuries'.

Classical ideologies—particularly liberalism, conservatism, and socialism—can be understood as contrasting responses to the intellectual, social, and economic transformations referred to as the 'Enlightenment' and **modernization**, especially industrialization and the rise of capitalism in the eighteenth and nineteenth centuries (Gamble 1981). They are European or *Western* ideologies in the sense that these developments first took place in **the West**.

We can think of this as a complicated relationship of interaction between the realm of political thought and ideas on the one hand and the material realm of social and economic life on the other. Ideologies are both responses to and attempts to influence social and economic life, frameworks both of understanding (of how the world works and its good and bad points) and commitment (how to change it) (see Chapter 1). Thus the classical ideologies provide conflicting interpretations of and responses to this experience and so can be seen as rival understandings of the West.

'The West' can be understood essentially as the emergence and consolidation of a liberal civilization during this period, so that ideas of the West and liberalism can seem almost synonymous. However, if we think of the rise of capitalism as an essential characteristic of modernity and the West, then socialism, as an ideological opponent of capitalism, can be seen as contesting this liberal understanding. Conservatism, anarchism, and fascism also, from different standpoints, provide critiques of the liberal conception of modernity and the West.

The dominance of the classical ideologies

A second, related, sense of classical ideologies is that they have *dominated political debate* in Western societies over the last two hundred years. These ideologies have, to varying degrees, been successful in influencing public opinion, providing the basis for exercising government authority and guiding public policy, and spreading to other societies. However, correctly portraying the outcome of this ideological struggle involves some historical debate.

Gamble (2000: 20) states that 'the great Enlightenment ideologies of the modern era' are socialism, liberalism, and communism. Gamble omits conservatism because of its character as an essentially anti-Enlightenment ideology. He includes 'communism' together with 'socialism' in recognition of the great ideological division and rivalry of the last century between the revolutionary ideology of the Bolshevik Party (though we should be careful not to equate communism with the Soviet experience) and the reformist and constitutional brand of socialism that was dominant in Western European parties (often referred to as 'social democracy'). Gamble has also stated that liberalism and socialism were 'the two central doctrines of the Western ideology' that emerged 'out of the Enlightenment and the revolutionary era at the end of the eighteenth century' (Gamble 1981: 15).

Thompson identifies the 'four dominant political ideologies' of what, following Hobsbawm (1994), he refers to as 'the short twentieth century'—from the start of the First World War in 1914 to the collapse of communism in 1989–91—as liberalism, conservatism, communism, and fascism (Thompson 2011: 1). Again, it is worth noting that fascism is an anti-Enlightenment ideology and therefore is excluded by Gamble, but included by Thompson because his interest lies in identifying the ideologies that left their stamp on twentieth-century history, as fascism undoubtedly did. It is also worth pointing out that Thompson's inclusion of conservatism as one of the dominant ideologies of the twentieth century is contested by Garnett's argument in this book that conservatism withered as an ideological force during the last century (see Chapter 3).

What about socialism (or social democracy), as distinct from communism? Thompson (2011: 3) argues that 'social democracy . . . evolved . . . into a species of liberalism and formed the liberal ideology's left-wing', thus it is subsumed within the liberal tradition. This is a somewhat controversial view which abolishes the distinction between social democracy and social liberalism, but it does highlight the problematic and contested relationship between liberalism and socialism at the edge (see the discussion of left and right later in this chapter; see also the discussion of the relationship between social democracy and liberalism in Chapter 4 as shown by their understandings of equality and freedom). In contrast with Thompson, Berman (2006: 6) argues that social democracy was 'something quite different' from liberalism.

So far we have not mentioned nationalism, even though 'it can be regarded as the most powerful and pervasive modern ideology of them all' (Thompson 2011: 2). Thompson argues that nationalism does not require 'a separate categorisation [because] it permeates all the others' (2011: 2). In effect, this recognizes that nationalism is a 'thin' ideology, which has been expressed and made an impact through the other ideologies—notably fascism and conservatism but also, to a lesser extent, liberalism and socialism.

Of the six ideologies, anarchism has the weakest claim to be seen as a dominant ideology. On the left, it was overshadowed by socialism and communism. Most obviously it never became the ideological basis for successful revolution (in contrast to the revolutions inspired by communism which, though, ultimately unsuccessful, did achieve state power), never succeeded in creating an anarchist society, and never constituted an ideological challenge to liberal capitalism on a global scale. However, in parts of Europe anarchism did have more appeal than socialism or communism, notably in the struggle against fascism in the Spanish civil war. Anarchism gets only a few passing references in Thompson's (2011) history of ideologies in the twentieth century. Hobsbawm states that

> in the generations after 1917, Bolshevism [i.e. communism] absorbed all other social-revolutionary traditions, or pushed them on to the margin of radical movements. Before 1914 anarchism had been far more of a driving ideology of revolutionary activists than Marxism over large parts of the world. . . . By the 1930s anarchism had ceased to exist as a significant political force outside Spain.

> (Hobsbawm 1994: 74)

Even in Spain, anarchism was effectively destroyed by its defeat in the civil war (Hobsbawm 1994: 74). However, anarchism did not disappear altogether, and has continued, though on the political margin, as an element in post–short-post twentieth-century anti-capitalist protests (see Chapter 5).

 Stop and Think

Do you think it makes sense to refer to all the ideologies we have encountered in the first part of this book as 'classical' ideologies?

The triumph of liberalism as the dominant ideology?

It can be argued that the ideology that has emerged from the twentieth century as pre-eminent is liberalism. On a global scale it faced two main challengers in the form of communism (following the Russian Revolution in 1917) and fascism (particularly in the form of Nazi Germany after Hitler gained power in 1933). Both of these ideologies threatened to overturn liberal civilization, offering ostensibly very different alternative visions of society from the left and from the right—the communist vision of 'dictatorship of the proletariat' and the creation of a classless society, and the fascist vision of an authoritarian state and racial/national purity. (Although both have been characterized as '**authoritarian**' or '**totalitarian**' ideological projects, it can be argued that this was a perversion of the democratic aspirations of communism, whereas fascism is intrinsically authoritarian and totalitarian).

Liberalism triumphed over communism in the 'short twentieth century' (1917–89) which culminated in the collapse of communism in 1989. During this century, liberalism was in crisis and retreat in the second quarter of the twentieth century—what Hobsbawm (1994) calls the 'age of catastrophe'—but ultimately defeated fascism in the Second World War (1939–45) and recovered economically in the 'long boom' of the postwar decades. Thus liberalism has survived the challenge from these two rival ideologies and, it can be argued, has become the dominant ideology insofar as liberal ideas are widely accepted and taken for granted and define the Western way of life.

But if liberalism has triumphed this has involved two variants of the ideology. The secret of liberalism's success in the postwar decades was arguably a shift to its 'left wing' variant (Thompson), or 'social liberalism', as manifested in the **New Deal** USA of the 1930s and the **Keynes–Beveridge welfare consensus** of the postwar decades in the UK. This shift can be interpreted as a strategy to 'save capitalism from itself'. According to Hobsbawm, postwar capitalism was 'deliberately reformed' by political and economic elites because of a desire to prevent a return to the 'Great Slump' of the interwar period and because of the 'political risks of not doing so' (i.e. the risk of political unrest). These elites concluded that 'the Great Slump had been due to the failure of the unrestricted free market . . . [and that], for social and political reasons, mass unemployment must not be allowed to return'. There was a consensus that the market had to be managed by government through economic planning and social reform—that the free market had to give way to what was referred to as a mixed economy. 'The Golden Age of capitalism would have been impossible without this consensus that the economy of private enterprise . . . needed to be saved from itself to survive' (Hobsbawm 1994: 271–3). The prospect of a 'new Jerusalem' after the Second World War, epitomized by the 1942 Beveridge report setting out proposals for a 'cradle to grave' **welfare state**, was also important to sustain morale in the war with fascism. The success of capitalism in its Golden Years and the better life it provided for its citizens was also key to the eventual collapse of communism.

The Golden Years of prosperity came to an end in the 1970s with recession and the return of mass unemployment. The problems created by capitalism had returned. As the welfare state depended on tax revenues generated by a buoyant capitalist economy, recession triggered a 'fiscal crisis' of the state (i.e. a gap between tax revenues and state expenditure). As the mixed economy no longer seemed to be working, the consensus broke down giving way to a 'return of ideology'—a resurgence of left–right argument. But the argument that triumphed in the victory of the Conservative Party under Margaret Thatcher in 1979 was the neo-liberal one that the opposite remedy was required—'rolling back the state' through privatization, deregulation, and public spending cuts in order to restore the 'unrestricted free market'.

It was during the neo-liberal era, and in the aftermath of the collapse of communism, that the triumph of liberalism was proclaimed in Fukuyama's assertion that liberalism had prevailed over all ideological challengers, bringing the 'end of history'. (We will examine Fukuyama's argument in Chapter 13).

> **⊃ Stop and Think**
>
> To what extent can it be argued that liberalism succeeded in seeing off all its main ideological challengers in the twentieth century?

The expansion of the classical ideologies

The classical ideologies, though constituting the European or Western tradition, are also global ideologies, having spread on a global scale with the expansion of Europe. The expansion of Europe refers to the way in which 'Western ideas, techniques and political rule were spread around the world' (Gamble 1981: 2) in the modern era, particularly from the beginning of the nineteenth century. European expansion occurred through related processes of empire, settlement, and trade, and was based on the advantages enjoyed by European states and societies in terms of technology and organization, having been the first to be transformed by what Gamble refers to as the 'bourgeois revolution', the 'three pillars' of which were 'capitalist economy, democratic polity, and scientific rationalism' (Gamble 1981: 21).

The essence of the modern era can be summarized in terms of the transformation, first of Europe and then progressively of the rest of the world, by this revolution. This process is still working itself out in our own time, and is now often discussed using the term 'globalization'. Because the classical ideologies were essentially responses to the bourgeois revolution first occurring in Europe, they 'became the universal ideologies that spread across the world, because they could be utilised by all societies that embraced and were embraced by the new world civilisation' (Gamble 1981: 13). Further, Gamble argues that liberalism and socialism in particular, which he sees as the two central ideologies of the Western tradition, 'still provide the basic vocabulary and perspectives for responses to industrialism, and the challenge of economic and social development' (Gamble 1981: 13).

However, it should be recognized that the creation of a 'new world civilization' on Western lines is far from smooth but has been uneven and met with resistance. Thus Gamble notes that liberalism and socialism 'were . . . modified greatly in contact with other cultures' (Gamble 1981: 13) and that catch up has in some cases been attempted by nationalist movements embracing Western technology but combining this with 'strong hostility to dominant liberal ideas' and drawing on 'the symbols and values of the traditional culture' (Gamble 1981: 17).

The development of China as an 'emerging market economy' since the 1980s, transforming itself rapidly from a low income country to become the world's second largest economy after the United States by 2014, illustrates this simultaneous embrace of and hostility to the West. On one level the development of China epitomizes globalization as the creation of a 'new world civilization', for it has involved embracing Western technology and organization—economic liberalization and entry into world markets. However, the Chinese model has been described as 'socialism with Chinese characteristics' and this can be interpreted as the combination of a market economy with authoritarian one-party (communist) rule. In other words, the regime remains hostile to liberal ideology which it sees as a threat and has not adopted one of Gamble's 'three pillars' of the bourgeois revolution—a democratic polity.

Three arguments have been developed since the 1980s that challenge Gamble's conception of a 'new world civilization' in which liberalism and socialism continue to provide the central perspectives: the 'end of history', post-modernism, and the 'clash of civilizations'. The end of history thesis claims that, with the collapse of communism, liberalism has triumphed on a global scale and socialism has departed the scene. In effect, the 'new world civilization' is a liberal world order. Post-modernism presents a challenge to the 'universalist' aspirations of liberalism and socialism and, indeed, to the scientific rationalism pillar of the bourgeois revolution. Finally, the 'clash of civilizations' thesis contradicts the 'end of history' and the 'new world civilization' by asserting that there is no singular world civilization but a clash between 'the West' and, particularly, 'Islam' as rival civilizations. (We will return to some of these arguments in Chapter 13).

Dominant ideologies, dominant parties?

To what extent can the dominance of the classical ideologies be seen in the character of the political parties that have dominated Western democracies? We might expect a clear link on the basis that parties can be seen as vehicles for representing major societal groups or interests, embodying ideological beliefs and goals, and implementing them through the exercise of government or state power. For example, the two parties that dominated UK politics in the nineteenth century were Liberal (Whig) and Conservative (Tory), and these two parties can be seen as political expressions of the interests of two major social and economic classes—the manufacturing or capitalist class and class of landowners respectively. These parties and ideologies faced a growing challenge from the growth of the working class and labour movement as a consequence of industrialization. In the nineteenth century, trade unions aligned with the Liberals, but from the formation of the Labour Party (initially as the Labour Representation Committee) in 1900 this alignment broke down. Labour displaced the Liberal Party in the first half of the twentieth century so that, by the postwar period (i.e. post-1945), with Labour's sweeping victory in the 1945 general election, a two-party system had been established with Labour and the Conservatives as the dominant parties. Labour was largely a creation of the trade unions with a primary purpose to represent working class interests. Always a broad-church party containing some socialists rather than a pure socialist party, it can still be seen as a party with a real connection to socialist ideology. Hence it appears that the three dominant parties in the UK political system over this period have represented the three classical ideologies of liberalism, socialism, and conservatism.

However, we should be wary of giving a too-simple account. Despite the electoral success of the Conservative *Party* in the twentieth century, it is arguable that this involved the effective abandonment of conservative *ideology* and the adoption of liberal principles, particularly 'neo-liberalism' from the 1980s (see Chapter 3). Conversely, the electoral decline of the Liberal Party masks the ascendancy of liberal ideas during this period. As already noted, the relationship between the Labour Party and socialist ideology has always been contested, and it can be argued that its 'forward march' in the last century to the status of one of the two dominant parties involved a retreat from socialist principles and the dominance of the party by its social democratic right wing.

In the USA since the 1850s every President has been a Republican or Democrat, while in 2015 all members of the House of Representatives and all but two of the Senate were affiliated to these two parties. Here again, although the party labels differ for historical reasons, it looks as though these two parties have clear ideological identities, with the Republicans often referred to as 'conservative' and the Democrats as 'liberal' (but see Chapter 3 for critical discussion of the identification of Republicans as ideological conservatives). This suggests a, long-debated, peculiarity of the US system compared to Europe in the absence of a socialist party, although the support for Bernie Sanders, a self-proclaimed democratic socialist, in the 2016 contest for the Democratic presidential nomination may require a reassessment of this view. In both the USA and the UK, the classical ideologies appear to provide a starting point for understanding party identities and competition, but the relationship is complicated. The same could be said, while recognizing historically-based differences in party labels, of other European states.

 Stop and Think

To what extent is the dominance of the 'classical' ideologies reflected in the pattern of party competition in the UK?

The relationship between ideology, party, and policy

Figure 8.1 represents the relationship between ideology, party, and policy in a simple form. In this view politics is all about parties competing for power, and party competition is all about the clash of ideologies. Parties are seen as vehicles for implementing ideological beliefs. However, the relationship between ideology and party is not as straightforward as Figure 8.1 suggests, for the following reasons.

- Ideologies can be represented outside of the party arena by a range of other political actors such as 'think tanks', social movements, pressure groups, and

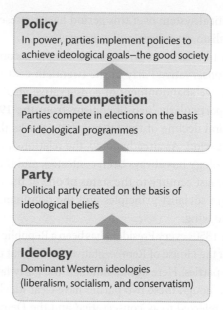

Figure 8.1 A simple model of the relationship between ideology, party, and policy

NGOs. Indeed, just as it can be argued that all individuals are 'ideologists' (see Chapter 1), it can be claimed that all organizations that are engaged in the political arena have some kind of ideological basis.

- Parties that engage in electoral competition tend to have the character of a 'broad church', containing diverse ideological strands represented by competing party factions and groups. The implication of this is that the translation of ideology into policy is mediated by factional struggles and the requirements of **'party management'**.

- Party labels can be misleading as guides to ideological beliefs (e.g. the UK Conservative Party).

- An ideology can be expressed through a plurality of parties where no single party is able to claim an ideological monopoly.

- Party politics is not just about ideology but also 'statecraft', which may be defined as 'the art of winning elections and, above all, achieving a necessary degree of governing competence in office' (Bulpitt 1986). The implication of this is that the translation of ideology into policy is mediated by the need to secure popular support ('populism') and by the demands and constraints of governing in practice ('pragmatism').

Figure 8.2 shows a more complex representation of the relationship between ideology, party, and policy, incorporating party management and statecraft.

Policy
In power, parties implement policies to achieve ideological goals, subject to the demands and constraints of governing in practice ('pragmatism')

Electoral competition
Parties compete in elections on the basis of programmes that reflect ideological beliefs mediated by party management and statecraft ('the art of winning elections')

Parties
Political parties are 'broad churches' reflecting variants of the ideology; ideology may be represented by competing parties rather than single 'monopoly' party

Non-party political actors e.g. pressure groups based on ideological beliefs

Ideology
Dominant Western ideologies (liberalism, socialism, and conservatism) are traditions of political understanding and commitment with variant forms

Figure 8.2 The relationship between ideology and policy, mediated by party management and statecraft

The notion of a party as a 'broad church' involves an analogy with religious organizations that may contain people with diverse religious beliefs who disagree strongly with each other on some matters of doctrine. There are, in other words, many ways to be a socialist (or liberal, conservative, etc.) just as there are many ways to be, say, a Christian or Muslim (although people may regard their own beliefs as the one true expression of the ideology or religion and deny the authenticity of others' beliefs). Given the 'broad church' character of political parties, effective party management to sustain unity can be seen as a precondition of statecraft. Disunity (or 'splits') can be damaging to the party's ability to practise 'the art of winning elections' because parties need to mobilize their members for electoral campaigning and, more important, because voters may be disinclined to support divided parties at the polls. Unity of the party in the legislature (i.e. party discipline) is essential either for effective opposition or 'achieving a necessary degree of governing competence in office'.

 Stop and Think

What is meant by the conception of a political party as a 'broad church'? What are the implications for party management?

Case Study 8.1 Ideology and 'statecraft'

Are parties vehicles for implementing ideological beliefs? Or are they motivated primarily by winning power? If the latter, it can be argued that ideology takes second place so that, rather than seeking power in order to put ideology into practice, parties may use (and abuse) ideology instrumentally in order to win power. At least, there can be a tension between ideological politics and statecraft because if the party's ideological beliefs are not popular among voters they militate against success in the art of winning elections. In Tony Blair's words, 'power without principle is barren. But principle without power is futile' (New York Times 1995).

Jeremy Corbyn's election as leader of the Labour Party (in 2015 and then again in 2016) highlighted this tension between ideological politics (principle) and the focus of statecraft on winning elections (power). Critics within the party, besides their ideological disagreements with Corbyn, argued that Labour would not be able to win the 2020 general election under his leadership (BBC 2015a; Smith 2016). This seemed to be supported by poor showing in opinion polls in the months following Corbyn's victory (O'Hara 2016). It was this combination of ideological differences and concern about electoral prospects that led to a no-confidence vote by Labour MPs and the leadership challenge in 2016. However, it could be argued that standing by ideological principles is more important than winning elections, and this seems to have been the view taken by many of Corbyn's grassroots supporters according to a poll in September 2015 which found

> 48% of Labour loyalists think the priority should be to win elections even if it means making compromises, while 52% think the priority should be to have the right principles even if it makes it more difficult to win elections.

> (Wintour 2015; see also Ashcroft 2015).

However the dilemma facing parties can be viewed in terms of '**preference accommodating**' versus '**preference shaping**' strategies. Blair, in repositioning the Labour Party as 'New Labour' after becoming leader in 1994, might be viewed as favouring the former: that is, adjusting the party's policies to align them with current voter preferences. However, this can mean allowing ideological opponents to shape voter preferences to their own advantage. In the context of New Labour, it can be argued that this involved adjusting to the ideological success of 'Thatcherism' and neo-liberalism in the 1980s. In addition a preference accommodating strategy might be inadvisable in its own terms since

> to massage one's beliefs for the sake of electoral gain can . . . be electorally counterproductive. It can be inexpedient to abandon principle for expediency, because it is hard to hide the fact that you are doing so.

> (Cohen 1994: 9)

and voters may lose trust in politicians whom they see as lacking conviction and not saying what they believe.

A plausible lesson of Thatcherism is that it demonstrates the potential for 'preference shaping' since the Conservatives set out ideological beliefs (neo-liberalism) that succeeded in shifting the consensus away from 'big government' in favour of 'rolling back the state'. Of course, it is very difficult to say how much scope there is for shaping voter preferences until the effort has been made. And parties' efforts in this direction, and their prospects for success, have to be considered in the context of the range of institutions, such as the media, that have a role in preference shaping. However, this approach leaves the answer to the electability of a party more open than would be suggested just by scrutiny of current preferences. It could even be argued that 'electoral success is to a large extent a by-product of commitment to something other than electoral success' (Cohen 1994: 6) such as politicians saying what they believe rather than what they believe is popular.

 Stop and Think

Which of the following statements do you agree with most?

a) A party should adopt policies that are more likely to make it electable even if this means compromising its ideological beliefs.

b) A party should champion policies that reflect its ideological beliefs even if this means compromising its electability.

Relationships between the classical ideologies

The relationship between ideologies is one of rivalry: they present us with *contrasting* frameworks of political understanding and commitment. However, we can also consider whether there are grounds on which ideologies can be seen as *comparable*; that is, whether there are commonalities as well as differences between them. First, classical ideologies can be classified in relationship to the Enlightenment—whether they are for or against, Enlightenment supporters or critics. The most familiar system for classifying ideologies is, second, in terms of a conception of politics as a left–right continuum or spectrum.

Contesting the Enlightenment: universalism versus particularism

We have seen that the classical ideologies offer contrasting responses to the intellectual, social, and economic transformations referred to as the 'Enlightenment' and modernization. More specifically, ideologies can be contrasted according to whether they are part of the Enlightenment 'project' or critical of it. In brief, the Enlightenment can be defined in terms of commitment to scientific knowledge and an optimistic view of the potential for progress in politics and other aspects of human affairs through reason.

> The revolutionary ideas . . . of the Enlightenment . . . harnessed science, democracy and capitalism in a heady mix to advance the idea that individuals could collectively improve their situation and create a society which was an advance on anything that had previously existed in terms of the promotion of human welfare and the prevention of human misery.
>
> (Gamble 2000: 13)

Table 8.1 Contesting the Enlightenment

	Enlightenment supporters	Enlightenment critics
Key ideas	Universalism	Particularism
	Universal human nature	Race / Nation
	Reason	Scepticism
	Progress	Tradition
Ideologies	Liberalism	Conservatism
	Socialism / Communism	Nationalism
	Anarchism	Fascism

These ideas are held to be universalist since scientific knowledge and reason are applicable everywhere and generate universal truths, and since the Enlightenment involves a universal conception of human nature in which what it means to promote welfare and prevent misery is the same for all humans.

Among the classical ideologies, liberalism, socialism, communism, and anarchism are part of the Enlightenment movement whereas, in contrast, conservatism, nationalism, and fascism adopt sceptical or critical standpoints. The first group are universalistic in the sense that political thinking and political projects are not tied to the peculiar histories and characters of specific nations or peoples—people are basically the same everywhere, they flourish or suffer harm in the same way, and therefore the vision of the good society is good for everyone. Liberalism, socialism, and anarchism can be said to share the same universalist aspirations based on the same Enlightenment values of freedom and equality, but they are different means to the same end. In contrast, fascism and some forms of nationalism (particularly in its ethnic variant) reject the notion of a universal human nature in favour of a **particularistic** conception of distinct races and nations, each with its own spirit, culture, or way of life. (Although note that, as we have seen, nationalism can also be found in the company of the Enlightenment ideologies of socialism and liberalism.) Conservatism is also tied to a particularist notion of national identity, and is sceptical of progress in defence of established institutions and tradition. This contrast is summarized in Table 8.1.

Left–right politics

The origin of the left–right distinction is customarily traced to the French Revolution in 1789 and the seating arrangements of aristocrats and radicals in the Estates General (i.e. the legislative assembly). Hence left versus right signifies revolution versus reaction, and the declaration of the rights of man versus the *ancien régime* (see also 'Origins of liberalism' in Chapter 2). Thus the concepts refer to the division between liberals and conservatives (e.g. see the discussion of Burke in Chapter 3), and map onto the Enlightenment versus anti-Enlightenment division identified in Table 8.1. However, the principle left–right axis has shifted so that it has largely become a debate *within* the Enlightenment tradition: that is, contesting the best way to realize the promise of the Enlightenment, particularly focused on capitalism and liberal democracy. Similarly, arguments that the left–right divide is no longer relevant are based on the claim that politics is no longer essentially a debate about capitalism. This claim can take the form that new ideologies have emerged or that the age of ideological politics has come to an end, as we will see (Chapter 13).

Notions of 'left' and 'right' provide a conventional and persistent way of framing political debate and understanding the relationships between ideologies, despite disagreements about the meanings of these terms and frequent claims that they have become less relevant or even redundant. As Giddens (1998: 37–8) notes, 'the distinction between left and right has remained ambiguous and difficult to pin down, yet obdurately refuses to disappear'.

On the face of it, 'left versus right' suggests a binary conception of politics, a simplification of political disagreements into two 'camps'. However, left–right debate is better understood as a spectrum or continuum, and this conception is familiar in everyday political discussion which often makes use of distinctions such as 'centre-left' or 'centre-right', contrasted with far (or extreme) left or right, or 'soft' versus 'hard' left or right.

This continuum means that although it can sometimes make sense for people to define themselves in broad terms as left or right, in other cases divisions within the left or right are more salient. For example, centre-left politicians committed to achieving gradual reform through electoral politics and within the basic structure of a capitalist economy typically strongly oppose socialists who are committed to change through revolution and the overthrow of capitalism (and vice versa), even though common cause might be found in relation to specific issues such as campaigning against public spending cuts or for higher taxation of corporations and the rich (see the distinction between 'communism' and 'social democracy' as variants of socialism in Chapter 4).

At the same time, the left-right division can be transcended where centre-left and centre-right find common cause in opposing an 'extreme' position. For example the recent rise of parties and movements in Europe that have been characterized as anti-immigration, extreme nationalist, or fascist (such as the English Defence League (EDL) or UK Independence Party (UKIP) in the UK, Norway's Progress Party, the Sweden Democrats, the Danish People's Party and Austria's Freedom Party, among many others) has been opposed by centre-right and centre-left parties and politicians, partly on grounds of principle (ideology) and partly on grounds of electoral expediency. On the other hand, electoral expediency sometimes favours coalition between 'centrist' and 'extremist' parties, as illustrated by the coalition between Norway's Conservatives and the Freedom Party in 2013 (*The Guardian* 2015).

How are 'left' and 'right' defined? What is the relationship between the classical ideologies and left–right politics? Where are these ideologies located on the spectrum? Although left and right are contested terms, a coherent idea of the left–right spectrum can be achieved based on the following related ideas:

- human nature and social change
- equality
- capitalism
- individualism
- role of the state

Human nature and social change

The Enlightenment ideologies of liberalism and socialism share a commitment to the idea of progress based on the human capacity for reason and the use of the scientific method to solve problems. This applies not only to the natural world but also to the possibility of social improvement through the application of reason in human affairs. But the two ideological traditions part company on the nature of the social change that is feasible and desirable, and this disagreement is expressed in left–right politics. The idea of equality is a good starting point to understand this disagreement.

Equality

According to Bobbio (1996: 60) 'the criterion most frequently used to distinguish between the left and the right is the attitude . . . to the ideal of equality'. In other words 'the left is egalitarian and the right is inegalitarian' (Bobbio 1996: 62). Similarly, Giddens (1998: 41) states that 'the idea of equality or social justice is basic to the outlook of the left'. As we have seen, commitment to equality is the essential or core value of socialist ideology (see Chapter 4). However, attitudes to equality always beg the question 'equality of what?', and some ideas of equality are supported by other ideological traditions, notably liberalism. Liberals and socialists may share some ideas of equality such as 'equality of moral worth' (that all human lives are equally valuable) and 'equality before the law' (though socialists may argue that this ideal is unattainable in a class-divided society). Where liberals and socialists part company is in relation to principles governing the distribution of resources in society: liberals argue that the distribution is fair if people have equal opportunities to acquire income and wealth (e.g. employment opportunities) whereas socialists favour equality of outcome (i.e. equal shares of resources such as income and wealth). Underlying these ideas of equality are conceptions of human nature. Although both ideologies emphasize the human capacity for reason, liberals tend to see humans as essentially egoistic and competitive so the type of equality they favour is to ensure individuals have an equal opportunity to compete for advantage, whereas socialists see humans as essentially cooperative and this makes equality of outcome feasible and desirable.

Still, it is easy to see that attitudes to equality constitute a continuum—the question is not 'for' or 'against' equality but the degree or extent of equality in the distribution of income that is favoured. A continuum on this issue can be constructed by asking people whether they agree or disagree that the gap in income and wealth between rich and poor is too large—a spectrum of opinion would be revealed from those who strongly agree (on the left) to those who strongly disagree (on the right). For example, according to the British Social Attitudes survey, in 2009 78 per cent of respondents believed that the gap between high and low incomes is too large, and this has been the view of a consistently large majority since the early 1980s, ranging from 72 per cent to 87 per cent (Orton and Rowlingson 2007). On this evidence there appears to be some support for the claim that a majority in Britain has left-wing sympathies, although it is notable that increased spending on benefits or redistribution of income are concrete measures to address inequality that are supported only by minorities.

 Stop and Think

1. 'The gap between rich and poor in our society today is too large'. Do you agree or disagree with this statement? Where would you place yourself on a scale of 1–10, where 1 = strongly disagree 10 = strongly agree?

2. Where are you on the left–right spectrum? A scale could be used to represent the left–right spectrum, e.g.
   9–10 = Left
   7–8 = Centre-left
   5–6 = Centre
   3–4 = Centre-right
   1–2 = Right

In order to decide whether the gap between rich and poor is too large we need to have some data on inequality. In the UK, the differential between high and low pay is monitored by the High Pay Centre. One way of illustrating this differential is to calculate the date by which chief executives earn as much as the 'typical worker' is paid in a year. If the typical chief executive earns twice as much as the typical worker this date would be around the end of June. In 2016 'Fat Cat Tuesday' was on 5 January (http://highpaycentre.org/blog/fat-cat-tuesday-2016).

The state and the market

Another way of defining the left–right distinction is in terms of positive or negative attitudes to capitalism or the market system, with the left being defined as critical of the market or anti-capitalist and the right as pro-market. This issue can also be framed in terms of attitudes to the state as the principle alternative mechanism to markets for allocating economic resources. Thus 'left versus right' can be expressed in 'state versus market' terms (Figure 8.3). Understood as a continuum, this involves a gradation of views of the desirable balance between the market and the state, ranging from state ownership and planning of economic activity on the left (socialism and, more particularly, communism) to a 'free market' or 'minimal state' position on the right (neo-liberalism). In between are various conceptions of a 'mixed economy' of public and private sectors. Because state action embodies a principle of collective choice and action and the market embodies a principle of voluntary exchange on the basis of individual choice, the state–market continuum can also be expressed in terms of **collectivism** versus **individualism** (or anti-collectivism).

The 'equality' and 'market' principles for defining left–right disagreement are closely related as they are both essentially economic principles (involving attitudes to economic equality and to the market or the state as mechanisms for allocating economic resources) and, more particularly, because the market–state argument has a primary focus on the question of equality. Advocacy of the market or the state is largely derived from attitudes to equality as a primary goal or value—they are judged as a means to an end. For example, 'Those on the left not only pursue social justice [equality], but believe that government has to play a key role in furthering that aim' (Giddens 1998: 41). In other words the left critique of the market is largely (though not exclusively) that, left to their own devices (i.e. without state intervention), markets are engines of inequality—there is a tendency for the gap between low and high incomes to widen. Conversely collective action is advocated as a mechanism for reducing inequality through state intervention.

For example, the UK National Health Service (NHS), a key component of the 'welfare state', can be seen as embodying left-wing values. This is because it was founded on the collectivist principle of 'equal treatment for equal need' wherein all citizens pay in to the service through a progressive tax system and receive treatment according to need and not on the basis of a contribution or payment principle. In effect, the NHS can be seen as a way of pooling the risks of ill-health and establishing a social right to healthcare on the part of those who need treatment, and a corresponding duty on the rest of society to make the resources for treatment available. It is, in other words, a collective response to health needs rather than leaving individuals to be responsible for meeting their own needs as they would be in a market for healthcare.

 Stop and Think

What other forms of collective action in the form of government policies can be used to promote equality?

Right-wing (neo-liberal) advocacy of markets involves support for inequality but in a more indirect way. The primary values—the ends towards which markets serve as means—are expressed in terms of freedom (liberty) and efficiency. In this view, the market is inherently individualistic in that it enables and encourages voluntary interaction among individuals (especially through voluntary exchange) using their own resources as they think best in pursuit of their own interests or goals, and competition in the market promotes innovation and efficiency. Inequality is justified as a result of a fair procedure of individual choices and as a system of incentives that encourages effort and efficient use of resources. In other words, the argument is that if you believe in freedom you must believe in the freedom of some people, on the basis of their choices and efforts, to make more of themselves than others do. This could include leaving healthcare to the market. Whereas the NHS commands a high level of public support in the UK, there is less support for the principle of collectivized healthcare in the more individualist culture of the United States as shown by the struggles over 'Obamacare'.

Figure 8.3 and Table 8.2 present the left–right spectrum based on attitudes to the related principles of equality and the market. Figure 8.3 sets out the ideas discussed so far as a simple spectrum showing the alignment between attitudes to equality, capitalism, the state, and collectivism. Thus movement along the spectrum in a left-ward direction involves a stronger commitment to egalitarian and anti-capitalist principles, whereas these principles are weakened with movement in a rightward direction and replaced by commitments to inegalitarian and pro-capitalist principles. In other words, on the 'extreme' right support for a pure or 'untamed' form of capitalism entails viewing the economic inequality spontaneously thrown up by the market as necessary and desirable, whereas on the 'extreme' left the aspiration to abolish capitalism is based on the desire to share resources in society in a planned way (something like cutting a cake into equal slices). In the centre both 'extremes' are rejected in favour of some form of compromise in between equal shares and leaving it to the market—neither too much equality nor too much inequality.

In Table 8.2 this spectrum is set out with ideological labels attached and some elaboration of those ideological positions. Here we can see that the market versus state conception of left–right politics involves a selective framing of ideological debate

Left	Centre-left	Centre	Centre-right	Right

←————————————————————————————→

Egalitarian	Inegalitarian
Anti-capitalism	Pro-capitalism
State	Market
Collectivism	Individualism
	(anti-collectivism)

Figure 8.3 The left–right spectrum

Table 8.2 The left–right spectrum

Left ◄──► Right

Anti-capitalism	Collectivism	Reluctant collectivism	Anti-collectivism
Marxism / Communism	Social democracy	Social liberalism / New liberalism ('One nation' conservatism might be included here)	Classical liberalism / Neo-liberalism
Replace capitalism with common ownership through revolution—'abolition of private property'	Humanize capitalism—achieve socialism through gradual reform	Remedy market failures—tackle 'five giant evils'—'save capitalism from itself'	Free market Minimal state
Capitalism is a class divided society—exploitation of workers by capitalists leads to class conflict and struggle	Labour is in weak bargaining position and needs a political voice; markets generate insecurity and inequality	Markets are desirable but cannot be left to their own devices; individuals cannot be left to sink or swim	Markets promote freedom (choice), innovation, efficiency
Egalitarian—'from each according to ability, to each according to need'	Redistribution—reduce gap between rich and poor	Reduce or eliminate poverty ('five giant evils')—social minimum model of welfare state	Inegalitarian—'rising tide lifts all boats'
With abolition of capitalism individualism will fade to be replaced by true human motives of cooperation and community	State embodies higher anti-market principles of need and community	Market where possible, state where necessary; state must leave room for individual initiative and not undermine incentives	Individualism—self-interest is basic human motivation, which is why markets exist

in terms of the contest between liberalism and socialism/communism. These two ideological traditions constitute the major rival interpretations of capitalism as an economic system and programmes of social and economic reform. Or, to put this differently, the two traditions constitute rival visions of the good society—capitalism versus socialism. Liberalism can be seen as providing ideological support for capitalism, and socialism provides an ideological critique of capitalism and support for an alternative economic system.

Contesting the 'centre ground'

The 'centre ground' (see Case Study 8.2) is messy and can be mapped using a variety of labels for ideological positions that have emerged historically through the process of ideological debate. Thus, in the socialist tradition, Marxism or communism have been distinguished from social democracy as major variants of the ideology, often encapsulated by the 'revolution versus reform' dichotomy. In Chapter 4 other reformist variants of socialism are identified as Fabian socialism, ethical socialism, and the third way. In the liberal tradition Chapter 2 distinguishes between economic liberalism (which embraces classical liberalism and neo-liberalism) and social liberalism. This distinction is also referred to in Chapter 3 in terms of 'laissez-faire' and new liberalism, and the latter is related to the idea of 'one nation' conservatism.

In Table 8.2 this messiness is reduced by identifying four main ideological positions: Marxism / communism, social democracy, social (new) liberalism, and classical liberalism / neo-liberalism. The table shows liberalism and socialism as ideological traditions with internal variants—what might be seen as 'moderate', 'compromise' variants of the 'full-blooded' versions, occupying the centre ground. Social democracy and social (new) liberalism reject the 'state versus market' dichotomy in favour of some combination of state and market. We might conceive of the four ideological positions shading into one another rather than there being sharp boundaries separating them, and this also suggests that each should be seen not as a single, unified 'position' but as encompassing a range of positions. There are, for example, debates within social liberalism as well as debates between social liberals and neo-liberals on the right and with social democrats on the left, and so on. Although there appears to be convergence between social liberalism and social democracy, each retains some core ideas and commitments which distinguish it from the other and attach it to its main ideological home.

For example, social liberalism advocates a 'reluctant collectivism' in the sense that the state is seen as a 'necessary evil' whose social and economic interventions are justified only in relation to specific and limited cases of **market failure**, meaning circumstances in which markets cannot be counted on to produce socially desirable outcomes (the term 'reluctant collectivism' is taken from George and Wilding 1976). The guideline is 'markets where possible, the state where necessary'. That is, as Keynes put it, 'the important thing for government is not to do things which individuals are doing already but to do those things which at present are not done at all' (Keynes, in Gamble and Wright 2004: 1). In identifying that markets are characterized by a cycle of boom and slump and therefore cannot be relied upon to sustain full employment, Keynes recognized that unemployment is not the responsibility of individuals but the result of a failure of the system. In a downturn in which rising unemployment is due to insufficient demand for goods and services, finding work is not something which individuals, in aggregate, can do for themselves. Keynes therefore identified that government could and should tackle unemployment by using macroeconomic (fiscal and monetary) policy to increase the level of demand. But in advocating this form of government intervention in the economy, Keynes was seeking to save capitalism from itself rather than to replace it, and to counter the demands to replace it that might otherwise become more clamorous (note that when Keynes was writing, during the 1930s, the socialist challenge to capitalism was taken very seriously). The point was that unemployment, and the social tensions and anti-capitalist sentiment which it was likely to cause, could be solved within the framework of a capitalist economy.

The problem of unemployment was also addressed by Beveridge, another liberal, in his 1942 report on *Social Insurance and Allied Services* (the so-called Beveridge Report) which is often seen as laying the foundations of the postwar UK welfare state (Beveridge 1942; Marquand 2008). The report advocated an expanded role for the state to tackle the 'five giants' of want, idleness, squalor, ignorance, and disease. Tackling want (poverty) involved a 'cradle to grave' system of benefits to address the main risks of poverty arising from not earning an income in the labour market: childhood, unemployment, sickness, and old age. The connection between want and 'idleness' (unemployment) was to be tackled through a system of social insurance involving flat-rate contributions and benefits. This contributory principle involved a contract between the individual and the state, and the level of benefits was to guard against poverty but leave room for individual initiative. The scheme complemented Keynesian economic management to sustain a high level of employment ('full employment') and, like Keynes, Beveridge can be seen as reforming capitalism to save it from itself.

Keynes and Beveridge were social liberals who believed in the market where possible and the state where necessary (i.e. the market as the rule, the state as exception), and Beveridge's proposals can be seen as extending the reforms introduced by the 'new' Liberal governments of 1906–14. Yet the blurred boundary between social liberalism and social democracy is shown by the claim of the postwar welfare state to be social democratic. In part this reflects the role of the postwar Labour government in implementing the programme of reforms, but it also reflects the claim that the welfare state embodies social democratic ideas and values. For example, Marquand (2008: 107) refers to the Beveridge proposals as a 'peculiarly British form of social democracy'. However, in principle, the 'reluctant collectivism' of social liberalism can be contrasted with the 'statist' approach of social democracy, involving a more pessimistic assessment of the market and more positive view of state action. Rather than saving capitalism from itself social democratic reforms may be seen as a gradualist strategy to replace capitalism with socialism. But even in terms of the more limited ambition to humanize capitalism rather than replace it, the social liberal default position of support for the market can be contrasted with social democratic default support for the state. In this view, the state is superior to the market in ethical terms for it embodies principles of need and community or solidarity which are preferable to the motives of self-interest and competition (sometimes characterized in terms of greed and fear) that characterize the market. The state's capacity to allocate resources on the basis of a rational plan is held to be superior to the instability and waste of the market. In contrast with Beveridge's 'social minimum' conception of the welfare state, leaving room for individual initiative, social democrats favour a more generous welfare system which is conceived as a redistributive mechanism. More generally, as a strand of the socialist ideology, social democracy sees the basic injustice of capitalism in terms of class inequality and sees its purpose as representing working class interests.

Case Study 8.2 Political attitudes and the 'centre ground'

The idea that elections are won in the 'centre ground' has become conventional wisdom, but like all common sense it needs to be scrutinized. The strategy of occupying the 'centre ground' of the ideological terrain, strongly advocated by former Labour Prime Minister Tony Blair, is based on the assumption that this is where political attitudes are clustered, that 'the broad public—who in the end decide the result in a democracy— . . . are located more in the centre than people realise' (Blair, quoted in *The Herald* 2016). Thus parties that occupy either the left or the right of the spectrum will find only minorities of voters gathered there.

There may be various reasons for this low satisfaction, but it can be argued that among them is disillusionment with a lack of meaningful choice among political parties all trying to occupy the centre ground and so diminishing the terms of political debate. In effect, the strategy erodes rather than enhances democracy. The disillusionment with mainstream parties is evidenced by the rise of what have been called 'insurgent' parties and candidates on both the right and left, including the election of Jeremy Corbyn as leader of the UK Labour Party in 2015 (and again in 2016), the rise of the UK Independence Party (UKIP), the rise of radical left-wing parties in Europe (e.g. Syriza in Greece, Podemos in Spain) and anti-immigration parties and movements (such as Pegida in Germany), and the support for insurgent candidates in the US 2016 contests for nomination as presidential candidates in both the Democrat and Republican parties (Bernie Sanders and Donald Trump). In the face of these phenomena the Blairite view might be defended by arguing that, although the insurgents are disruptive elements in the political system, their appeal is confined to minorities and so they do not fundamentally alter the fact that 'the broad public are . . . located . . . in the centre'. This view seems hard to sustain, though, in the face of Brexit and the election of Trump as US President (interpreted by some as Brexit 2.0 or, in Trump's words, 'Brexit plus').

There is other evidence that political attitudes can shift, and that political parties and ideological politics may play an important role in such shifts. The centrist thesis seems to apply quite well to the postwar Keynesian-welfare consensus which endured until the 1970s in the UK. However, as we have seen, this did not turn out to be a permanent settlement. In the 1970s the consensus broke down in circumstances of economic crisis, and it was the Conservative party that was able to redefine the terms of political debate in favour of a solution to the crisis involving 'rolling back the state'. It can be argued that 'Thatcherism' was a successful attempt to create a new neo-liberal ideological consensus. The Conservative Party succeeded electorally not by following the centrist playbook but by adopting a right-wing ideological stance, defining itself against the centre. And New Labour can be seen, in contrast with the avowed strategy of occupying the centre ground, in large part as adjusting to this new neo-liberal settlement. Thus it can be understood that:

> When Thatcher was asked about her greatest achievement, she promptly answered: 'New Labour.' And she was right: her triumph was that even her political enemies adopted her basic economic policies.
>
> (Zizek 2013)

This adjustment can be seen in the rhetoric and policies in relation to poverty and welfare. Neo-liberal ideology involves an individualist view of poverty—such as that it is caused by 'laziness or lack of willpower'—and a critical attitude to welfare, particularly on the basis that it creates dependence or a 'dependency culture' among benefit recipients. This individualist view can be contrasted with a left-wing 'societal' explanation that poverty is the result of 'injustice in our society', and a corresponding belief in a right to benefits. These and other statements have been used to measure public attitudes to poverty and welfare from 1983 to 2011 (Clery et al. 2013). The study found that

> the explanation that living in need is due to the individual's own characteristics and behaviour ('laziness or lack of willpower') has gained popularity at the expense of a societal explanation ('injustice in our society').
>
> (Clery et al. 2013: 12–13)

It is suggested that

> the more right-wing policies adopted by the Blair government led to the views of society in general, and Labour supporters in particular, becoming less left-wing during their term in office.
>
> (Clery et al. 2013: 13)

Thus, rather than occupying the centre ground in the company of the broad public, Labour adjusted to the neo-liberal ideology of the conservatives, and in doing so shifted political attitudes, particularly among its own supporters. The advent of Thatcherism and its 'greatest achievement' in New Labour offers clear evidence of preference shaping (see also Case Study 8.1).

However, the relationship between party ideology and political attitudes is complex, and there is evidence that attitudes shift in reaction to the ideology and policies of the party in power so as to act as a 'thermometer'. Whereas the ideology and policy direction of New Labour produced a shift in political attitudes on the issues of poverty and welfare, a long-term study of the 'policy mood' of the electorate, measured by averaging attitudes on a range of issues, finds that

> the electorate tended to move in the opposite direction to government policy. It is as if the policy mood was a thermostat: signalling the need to cool things when they get 'too hot' under Labour by supporting less government activity—less spending, less welfare and less regulation. The mood falls to the right. Equally, when things get 'too cold' under the Conservatives, the electorate signal their preference for warmer policy—more spending, more generous welfare and more regulation. The mood increases to the left.
>
> (Bartle 2015: 4; see also BBC 2015b)

The 'centre ground' refers to a position on the left–right ideological spectrum. The idea that the political attitudes of the broad public are located there is a piece of conventional wisdom that conceals a more complex picture.

 Stop and Think

What is meant by the centre ground in politics? Is it true that parties must occupy this ground in order to win elections?

Limitations of the left–right view of politics

The left–right spectrum as we have presented it has some important advantages: it allows us to understand the relationship between 'the great Enlightenment ideologies of the modern era'—liberalism, socialism, and communism (Gamble 2000); and it focuses attention on central questions in political debate about inequality and the market–state relationship. However, as a one-dimensional view of politics, it also has some limitations and fails to capture the 'complete picture' of ideological debate.

For and against the state?

In Figure 8.3, the left is associated with support for the state (contrasted with the right's anti-statism), and this association has been reinforced in the discussion of social democracy as a 'statist' approach. However, it is important to recognize the historical division within the left between the reform-minded social democratic variant and the Marxist commitment to revolutionary change involving the abolition of capitalism. Marxists argue that there are severe limits to how far a reform strategy within capitalism can go and reject the idea that the system can really be 'humanized'. A truly human society can be achieved only by the abolition of the class division between workers and capitalists and the creation of a classless society. Although social democratic reforms are sometimes seen as a long-haul socialist strategy, Marxists disparage this approach on the basis that the state in a capitalist society will always ultimately serve the interests of the capitalist class, because the rich are also powerful and the capitalist class is able to use its economic power to influence and control the state. Hence the state is not an instrument that can be used to transform capitalism but has itself to be overthrown. Thus Marxism is an anti-statist perspective which rejects the state in capitalist society and envisages the 'withering away' of the state in a classless communist society.

This understanding of Marxism raises interesting points in relation to communism and neo-liberalism. First, Marx's vision of communism is in stark contrast to the actual historical experience of the Soviet Union, which was supposed to be constructing a communist society. This has been the subject of an ongoing historical debate: liberal and conservative critics of Marxism have often either equated Stalinism with Marxism as an ideology or argued that authoritarianism is the inevitable, even if unintended, outcome of trying to put this ideology into practice. In contrast, Marxist critics of the Soviet Union saw it as a perversion of communist principles (in a similar way to Muslims today arguing that Islamist extremism has nothing to do with the true principles of Islam).

On the face of it, Marxism and neo-liberalism share an anti-statist perspective (so that the two opposite ends of the spectrum seem to converge on this point). However, this appearance masks fundamental differences. First, whereas neo-liberalism advocates a minimal state within capitalism (disengaging the state from the market) on the grounds that state intervention is damaging to the market and business, Marxism's critique of the state in capitalist society is on the contrasting grounds that it serves the interests of the capitalist class. Second, although Marxists tend to see welfare policies as integral to the capitalist state (e.g. supplying a healthy and educated workforce), the main point of Marx's critique of the state is that it is a coercive apparatus (police, prisons, etc.) used to repress working class struggle, and it is this coercive aspect that will become redundant in a classless communist society. In contrast, the minimalist state favoured by neo-liberalism certainly includes those institutions and capacities concerned with law and order. Hence neo-liberalism can be characterized in terms of 'the free economy plus the strong state' (Gamble 1988). Indeed the strong state is needed to deal with the social unrest that may ensue from rolling back the social protections afforded by the welfare state.

Varieties of liberalism

The left–right spectrum identifies the division between social liberalism and neo-liberalism but, in doing so, presents a partial view of the liberal tradition concerning its attitude to the state. The social liberal–neo-liberal division is focused specifically on the economic role of the state. However, this can be seen as one aspect of the liberal view of the state that can be traced back to its origins (e.g. in the writings of John Locke—see Chapter 2). The purpose of government in this view is to protect the 'natural rights' of its citizens—to 'life, liberty and property' in Locke's formulation, or to 'life, liberty and the pursuit of happiness' as in the American Declaration of Independence. Freedom, or liberty, is liberalism's core value. Fundamentally this requires checks on government, or 'limited' government, especially in the form of rights to protect individuals against interferences by the state that prevent them living as they choose (subject to laws that prevent harm to others). These 'negative' rights take the form of 'civil' rights or liberties, such as freedom of expression, freedom of association, and freedom of action. Alongside civil rights, political rights (to vote, stand for office, etc.) ensure government is accountable to the people, or government by consent.

We can see that the division between social liberalism and neo-liberalism is not one that concerns these central liberal ideas about the state. Rather the disagreement concerns Locke's right to property (i.e. private property) and, more generally, the distribution of property. Neo-liberals seek to protect property rights from interference by the state and argue that the distribution of income and wealth that results from voluntary exchanges in the market is justified. In contrast social liberals, while generally favouring liberty, private property, and the market system, are prepared to countenance some interference with property rights in order to tackle social problems such as Beveridge's 'five giant evils'. Such 'interference' takes the form of taxing people's income and wealth in order to finance welfare services provided by the state. The welfare state establishes a set of 'social rights' which ensures that all citizens enjoy 'positive freedom' in the sense of a modicum of resources that enable them to live a decent life, whereas neo-liberals favour a 'negative' conception of freedom which requires only that people are free from interference or coercion.

Hence criticisms of liberalism's view of the economic role of the state—whether social liberal or neo-liberal—need to be separated from the liberal view of civil and political rights. For example, social democrats do not generally differ from liberals in their attitudes to liberal democracy, while criticizing their views on capitalism and the market.

Locating anarchism—left or right?

Our left–right spectrum, focused on the market versus state debate, has not included anarchism. This seems odd since anarchism can be characterized as the most consistent anti-statist perspective—the meaning of anarchy being 'without rule'. This might suggest that anarchism should be located at the very end of the spectrum on the left, where there is a close affinity between anarchism and communism in that both visions of the good society conceive it as stateless. Both visions also rest on an 'optimistic' view of human nature as inherently social and cooperative. This location is reinforced by the association between anarchism and anti-capitalism, as exemplified by the contemporary global justice and Occupy movements (Graeber 2013).

On the other hand, anarchism can be characterized by its core value of freedom and autonomy, and this may seem to place it at the very end of the spectrum on the right in association with the individualist and anti-statist perspective of neo-liberalism.

It can be argued that the solution to this conundrum is to recognize that there are, broadly, two distinct forms of anarchism, one associated with socialism and one with liberalism. The former envisages personal autonomy in an egalitarian and cooperative context without private property. In contrast, the latter, which may be termed anarcho-capitalism, links personal autonomy to an inegalitarian conception of society based on individualism, private property, and markets. (See Chapter 5.)

Nationalism, conservatism, and fascism

As we have seen, the left–right spectrum focuses on the great Enlightenment ideologies, but it thereby leaves the anti-Enlightenment ideologies out of the picture. Yet this goes against a conventional view that conservatism and fascism are right-wing ideologies, as shown in Figure 8.4.

In this view liberalism has been moved to the centre to make room for conservatism and fascism on the right, but nationalism is still missing. As we have seen, it can be argued that nationalism is neither of the right nor the left since it can be married to any of the other ideologies (or all of the other ideologies at the same time!), hence it has no fixed location on the spectrum, even though it is mainly associated with the ideologies that are here shown on the right.

However, the problem with the expanded spectrum is that there is no organizing principle for differentiating left and right. The state–market (anti-capitalist–pro-capitalist) principle does not work since conservatism and fascism are not more pro-capitalist than neo-liberalism. Indeed it can be argued that conservatism involves a strain of 'market pessimism' rather than 'market optimism', on the basis that egoism or self-interest promoted by the market undermines social bonds, and individualism or '**permissiveness**' threatens valued traditions and ways of life.

Thus the expanded left–right spectrum, though familiar, is confused. This means that the only way we can retain the characterization of conservatism as a right-wing ideology is to accept that it involves a different conception of left–right politics, or a two-dimensional view of ideological debate. The conservative view of the role of government or the state is really concerned with a different issue to that which animates debate between liberals and socialists. Conservatism is more concerned with the role of government authority to maintain order and uphold morality than with its economic role. Liberalism and socialism are concerned with the economic outcomes generated by markets and the role of the state to correct these outcomes. This can be characterised as a debate about economic freedom. For liberals (especially neo-liberals) the market is a system of economic freedom in which individuals interact

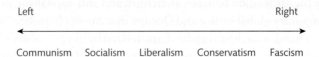

Left				Right
Communism	Socialism	Liberalism	Conservatism	Fascism

Figure 8.4 Conventional expanded left–right spectrum

through voluntary exchanges the results of which, if they take place on the basis of equal opportunity, are fair. For socialists the dependence of workers on wages in order to live and the greater bargaining power of employers in the labour market mean that the idea of a free and voluntary exchange is illusory and the inequalities that result are unjust. Conservatism is not really concerned with these issues except to lament the 'cash nexus' replacing the social bonds that supposedly tied the classes of pre-capitalist society together.

But there is another aspect to freedom on which liberalism and socialism take the same stance. This is freedom in relation to what might be called moral and social values, or questions of lifestyle. According to nineteenth-century liberal philosopher John Stuart Mill, freedom involves living your own life in your way, and the only justification for government interference in this freedom is to prevent harm to others. Living your own life in this way means not being bound by convention or tradition, and being free to engage in behaviours that others might not approve of or find offensive. But this is the kind of freedom that conservatism opposes in the name of upholding traditional modes of behaviour and moral codes. In this view, government has a responsibility to promote or even enforce desirable moral values, and shared values are seen as 'glue' which holds society together. This can incorporate a very wide range of concerns, including manners (civility, respect, deference), styles of dress, artistic expression (e.g. art, music, literature, film, theatre), sexuality, marriage, contraception, abortion, patriotism, and drug use. In the United States these issues have been at stake in the so-called culture wars, in which 'traditional' values and lifestyles have been championed by Republican politicians, notably in the Tea Party movement and often in association with evangelical Christianity. Homosexuality and the struggle for gay rights, one aspect of which has been the campaign for gay marriage, has been a prominent issue in the 'culture wars', not only in the USA but many other countries.

Thus we seem to need a second left–right dimension to capture the culture wars, as depicted in Figure 8.5. In this dimension, the spectrum concerns the balance between government authority and personal freedom across a range of social and moral values.

A similar approach is depicted in Figure 8.6, in which the left–right scale (economic dimension) is combined with a vertical scale (moral dimension) in a two-dimensional view of ideological debate. Libertarians adopt a permissive stance

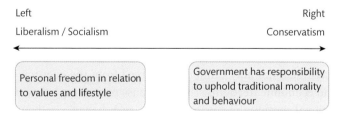

Left   Right

Liberalism / Socialism   Conservatism

Personal freedom in relation to values and lifestyle

Government has responsibility to uphold traditional morality and behaviour

Figure 8.5 The values and lifestyle left–right spectrum

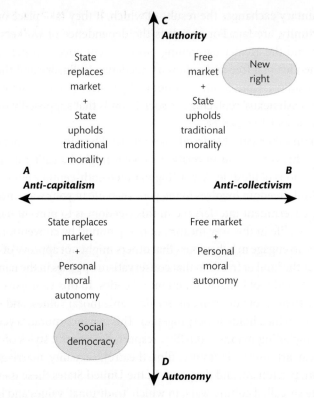

Figure 8.6 A two-dimensional view of ideological debate

AB = 'Economic' dimension (market vs state)
CD = 'Moral' dimension (autonomy vs authority)

allowing personal autonomy on social and moral issues, whereas this permissiveness is opposed by right-wing authoritarians. This approach generates four quadrants within which ideological positions can be located. For example, the new right combination of neo-liberalism and neo-conservatism could be located in the top right quadrant, combining the 'free market and strong state'. Social democracy is diagonally opposite combining permissiveness with state economic intervention. (For a similar approach see The Political Compass https://www.politicalcompass. org/analysis2.)

The market again

Although the first liberal-socialist left–right dimension is focused on economic issues while the second dimension highlights moral issues, it should be noted that upholding traditional morality cannot be divorced from the question of regulation of markets and economic freedoms. This is because preventing behaviours that contravene traditional morality means prohibiting such behaviours being engaged in through market transactions. For example, restricting abortion entails prohibiting or regulating abortion clinics operating in the market. The problem for conservatives is that markets are dynamic, innovative systems that, in the search for profit opportunities, are intrinsically corrosive of all conventional values and lifestyles. The difficulty is acute for conservative parties that embrace neo-liberal ideology in conjunction with conservative beliefs. Thus the issue of Sunday trading, allowing shops to open on Sundays, caused divisions in the British Conservative Party in the 1980s: between neo-liberals who wanted to remove restrictions on markets and conservatives who wanted to protect Sunday as a traditional day of worship and rest.

Of course, it would be wrong to think that conservatism has a monopoly on questions of morality or that socialism and liberalism are merely economic systems of thought, and the moral limits of markets (i.e. the question of what limits should be placed on market transactions on moral grounds) can be engaged by each ideological perspective (e.g. see Sandel 2012). But much of what conservatives see as moral questions liberals view as private matters, such as sexuality or attitudes to marriage. For liberals and socialists acceptance of homosexuality and gay rights constitute clear moral progress. The principle for liberals, following John Stuart Mill, is that people should be able to live their lives as they please so long as they do not cause harm to others.

Although the culture wars persist, especially in US politics, it can be argued that their noisiness conceals the fact that they have been (or are in the process of being) won by the 'progressives'. Conservatism is on a defensive footing in relation to these issues across the Western world. This reinforces the argument in Chapter 3 that the purchase of conservatism on the way we live now has weakened. For example, people can argue against gay marriage on conservative grounds but it seems that history is not on their side.

From 'classical' to 'new' ideologies

The following chapters examine a range of 'new' ideologies: feminism, environmentalism, multiculturalism, and religious fundamentalism. The 'new' label may seem questionable as, in chronological terms, some of these ideologies can be traced back as far as the 'classical' ideologies. For example, Mary Wollstonecraft's *A Vindication of the Rights of Women* was published in 1792. Environmentalist concerns accompanied industrialization from the beginning. Religious fundamentalism can be regarded as a pre-modern system of beliefs. On the other hand, multiculturalism is new, having developed as a response to contemporary conditions of ethnic and cultural diversity (although some of the forms of diversity, such as indigenous peoples, originate in European expansion and domination). However, all the ideologies can be considered new in the sense that they have become more prominent in the last fifty years or so, and have brought new issues to prominence. In identifying 'new' issues they can be seen as involved in a dialogue with the classical ideologies. On one hand, they provide critiques of these ideologies, particularly the left–right conception of politics focusing on economic issues and the state versus the market. In general terms they highlight issues and interests that are seen as being neglected or marginalized in these approaches. On the other hand, they have sought to extend these ideologies by attempting to incorporate new issues within them. For example, liberalism and socialism may be rejected on account of their focus on economic progress (growth) and neglect of environmental concerns, or environmental concerns may be incorporated within liberal or socialist ideologies and their visions of the good society. Taken together, the 'new' ideologies have extended the terms of political and ideological debate.

Summary

- The classical ideologies originated in Europe and can be seen as responses to the Enlightenment and the advent of 'modern' societies. Liberalism and socialism can be seen as the principal Enlightenment ideologies.
- These ideologies have dominated political debate and expanded beyond Europe with the spread of modernity.
- It can be argued that the twentieth century saw the dominance of liberalism above the other classical ideologies.
- Political parties can be viewed as vehicles for implementing ideological beliefs through controlling state power. However, the relationship between ideological beliefs and party policies is complex, mediated, in particular, by the demands of 'statecraft'.
- Ideological debate is conventionally framed in terms of a left–right spectrum. This approach offers important insights but also has limitations as it does not easily accommodate all the classical ideologies. A second left–right dimension can be used to incorporate conservatism.
- The ideological terrain is not populated only by classical ideologies. 'New' issues and ideologies have emerged to extend the terms of ideological debate.

Review and discussion questions

1. Consider whether 'classical' ideologies is a useful label or category.
2. Critically evaluate the view of political parties as vehicles for implementing ideological beliefs.
3. What is meant by the concepts of 'left' and 'right'? Do these concepts provide a useful way of framing ideological debate?
4. Critically assess the advice that political parties can only win elections by occupying the centre ground.

Research exercises

1. Choose one of the mainstream political parties in the UK (Labour, Conservative, Liberal Democrat). Carry out research to identify the principal internal factions within the party. Write a report summarizing the key ideological beliefs of each faction and showing the relationships between the factions in ideological terms.

2. Examine the websites of the following organizations. From inspection of their statements of 'aims', 'values', or 'mission' can you discern an ideological standpoint?

    Labour Party

    Liberty

    Oxfam

    TaxPayers' Alliance

Further reading

Gamble (1981) provides an account of the origins of the classical ideologies and their relationship to the Enlightenment and modernity. Thompson (2011) examines the role of the main ideologies in shaping the history of the 'short twentieth century'. The concept of the short twentieth century comes from Hobsbawm (1994). Marquand (2008) is a political history of Britain in the twentieth century framed in terms of four traditions of political thought (though these are not identified using the classical ideological labels). Marquand and Seldon (1996) examines the relationship between ideas and policy in postwar Britain.

A sustained discussion of the left–right distinction, focusing on equality, can be found in Bobbio (1996). Bartle (2015) analyses shifts in the 'policy mood' of the electorate in the UK (i.e. political attitudes) and suggests that the centre shifts in reaction to the party in power. Lee (2013) and Dommett (2014) examine the relationship between ideology and British party politics— whether parties are converging on the centre ground, and whether ideology is of decreasing relevance to party politics.

References

ASHCROFT, M. (2015), 'To Survive, Labour must Pick a Strong Leader who wants to be Prime Minister', *The Guardian*, 10 September, http://www.theguardian.com/commentisfree/2015/sep/10/labour-leader-prime-minister-voters-defectors

BBC (2015a), 'Tony Blair Warns against Moving Left as Jeremy Corbyn Leads Poll', 22 July, http://www.bbc.co.uk/news/uk-politics-33619645

BBC (2015b), 'Election 2015: How Close are You to the Political Centre?', 19 March, http://www.bbc.co.uk/news/uk-politics-31973051

BARTLE, J. (2015), 'The Policy Mood and the Moving Centre', NatCen / University of Essex, http://
www.natcen.ac.uk/our-research/research/the-policy-mood-and-the-moving-centre/

BERMAN, S. (2006), *The Primacy of Politics: Social Democracy and the Making of Europe's Twentieth Century*, Cambridge: Cambridge University Press.

BEVERIDGE, W. (1942), *Social Insurance and Allied Services* (the 'Beveridge Report'), http://www.
sochealth.co.uk/national-health-service/public-health-and-wellbeing/beveridge-report/

BOBBIO, N. (1996), *Left and Right: The Significance of a Political Distinction*, Cambridge: Polity
Press.

BULPITT, J. (1986), 'The Discipline of the New Democracy: Mrs Thatcher's Domestic Statecraft',
Political Studies, Vol. 34.

CLERY, E., LEE, L., AND KUNZ, S. (2013), *Public Attitudes to Poverty and Welfare, 1983–2011*, York:
Joseph Rowntree Foundation.

COHEN, G. A. (1994), 'Back To Socialist Basics', *New Left Review*, Vol. I, No. 207, September–
October.

DOMMETT, K. (2014), 'Ideological Quietism? Ideology and Party politics in Britain, Political
Studies', http://onlinelibrary.wiley.com/doi/10.1111/1467-9248.12160/abstract

GAMBLE, A. (1994), *The Free Economy and the Strong State: The Politics of Thatcherism*, London:
Macmillan.

GAMBLE, A. (1981), *An Introduction to Modern Social and Political Thought*, London: Macmillan.

GAMBLE, A. (1994), *The Free Economy and the Strong State: the politics of Thatcherism*, London:
Macmillan.

GAMBLE, A. (2000), *Politics and Fate*, Cambridge: Polity Press.

GAMBLE, A. AND WRIGHT, T. (2004), 'Introduction', in *Restating the State?*, *Political Quarterly*,
Vol. 75 (Special Issue), November.

GEORGE, V. AND WILDING, P. (1976), *Ideology and Social Welfare*, London: Routledge and Kegan
Paul.

GIDDENS, A. (1998), *The Third Way: The Renewal of Social Democracy*, Cambridge: Polity Press.

GRAEBER, D. (2013), *The Democracy Project*, Harmondsworth: Penguin.

THE GUARDIAN (2015), 'Norway's Conservatives to Form Coalition with Anti-immigration Party',
1 October, http://www.theguardian.com/world/2013/oct/01/norway-conservatives-coalition-
immigration

HANSARD SOCIETY (2015), *Audit of Political Engagement 12—The 2015 Report*, http://www.
auditofpoliticalengagement.org/media/reports/Audit-of-Political-Engagement-12-2015.pdf

THE HERALD (2016), 'Tony Blair: Centre Ground Key to Winning Elections', 22 January, http://
www.heraldscotland.com/news/14225296.Tony_Blair__Centre_ground_key_to_winning_
elections/

HOBSBAWM, E. J. (1994), *Age of Extremes: The Short Twentieth Century 1914–1991*, London:
Michael Joseph.

LEE, M. (2013), 'Are British Political Parties Converging at the Centre Ground?', *Journal of Politics
and International Studies*, Vol. 9.

MARQUAND, D. (2008), *Britain Since 1918: The Strange Career of British Democracy*, Jiangsu Sheng: Phoenix.

MARQUAND, D. AND SELDON, A. (eds) (1996), *The Ideas that Shaped Post-War Britain*, London: Fontana Press.

NEW YORK TIMES (1995), 'British Labor Drops Pledge on Nationalization', 30 April, http://www.nytimes.com/1995/04/30/world/british-labor-drops-pledge-on-nationalization.html

O'HARA, G. (2016), 'How is Jeremy Corbyn's Labour faring in Elections So Far?', *New Statesman*, 4 January, http://www.newstatesman.com/politics/elections/2016/01/how-jeremy-corbyns-labour-faring-elections-so-far

ORTON, M. AND ROWLINGSON, K. (2007), *Public Attitudes to Economic Inequality*, York: Joseph Rowntree Foundation.

SANDEL, M. (2012), *What Money Can't Buy: The Moral Limits of Markets*, Harmondsworth: Allen Lane.

SMITH, D. (2016), 'Tony Blair Admits he is Baffled by Rise of Bernie Sanders and Jeremy Corbyn', *The Guardian*, 23 February, http://www.theguardian.com/politics/2016/feb/23/tony-blair-bernie-sanders-jeremy-corbyn

THOMPSON, W. (2011), *Ideologies in the Age of Extremes*, London: Pluto Press.

WINTOUR, P. (2015), 'Labour Loyalists put Principles before Power—Ashcroft Poll', *The Guardian*, 10 September, http://www.theguardian.com/politics/2015/sep/10/labour-loyalists-put-principles-before-power-ashcroft-poll

ZIZEK, S. (2013), 'The Simple Courage of Decision: a Leftist Tribute to Thatcher', *New Statesman*, 17 April, http://www.newstatesman.com/politics/politics/2013/04/simple-courage-decision-leftist-tribute-thatcher

wmves : 259-278 — 4
convents : 278-285 16

9

Feminism

Sophia Price

OBJECTIVES

- Examine the rise and importance of gender awareness and gender equality by outlining the historical development of feminism
- Consider whether feminism is an ideology in its own right and identify variants of feminism
- Analyse the links between feminism and other ideological perspectives
- Explore linkages between the national and global dimensions of feminism
- Examine how feminist ideology has been expressed in political movements and shaped the policies of governments and international organizations
- Critically examine whether 'post-feminism' has rendered feminism obsolete

---

Introduction: What is feminism?

Feminism is an ideology that highlights societal inequality on the basis of gender, and as a movement aims to redress that imbalance. Radical feminist Fin Mackay states that feminism 'is a political response to a social structure where power and privilege is accorded to one half of humanity over another, based purely on their assigned sex and attached gender at birth' (Mackay 2015: 127). The language of this statement is important, as it denotes the difficulties in providing definitions, aims, and concepts within an ideology and movement that is riven with a variety of positions and approaches. Note that Mackay's statement does not explicitly refer to women, for as this chapter will show, even the definition of the movement and ideology in terms of gender and associated terminology is a cause for dispute. The choice of language and terminology reveals the multiplicity of positions within feminist ideology and movements, each charged with symbolism and meaning. Where there is agreement, however, is in the challenges feminism poses to the existing organization of societies and the relations of power that characterize and structure them.

Historical origins and development of the ideology: the waves of feminism

In order to explore the historical origins and evolution of feminism as an ideology, this chapter will use the analogy of 'waves'. This is a terminology used within the feminist movement and by feminist scholars to indicate how, throughout feminist history, there have been high points of debate and activism followed by more fallow periods. However, while the analogy of waves is recognized and utilized both within the movement and outside, it is important to note that this terminology is itself problematic and widely critiqued. First, as it underplays the progress within and between the waves, and prior to the initial 'first wave' and second, it is viewed as being reflective of the Western focus of feminist ideology. This critique is particularly strong within post-colonial and anti-imperialist feminism, that argues that while this depiction of a linear view of historic development might be reflective of feminism in western Europe and the USA, it fails to recognize the experience of women, feminist theorists, and activists from other parts of the world and in different forms of society to the Western liberal model. Many believe that this critique can also be applied to the feminist movement more generally (see the sections on 'Black feminism' and 'Post-colonial feminism' below). This chapter recognizes these critiques, and explores them in more detail in later sections; however it uses the terminology of waves as a tool, to first explore the development of the ideology and then to counter this narrative with the questions that arise from it.

First wave

The first wave of feminist ideology is often characterized as beginning in the late nineteenth and early twentieth centuries, however feminist theorists have pointed to the roots of feminist thought in ancient civilizations. For lesbian, bisexual, gay, and trans (LBGT) feminists, the ancient Greek lyric poet Sappho (approximately 630–570 BC) is particularly important. Sappho was born in Lesbos, and her poetry, which explores love and passion, gave rise to the terminology of female homosexuality: lesbian and Sapphic. These terms entered the lexicon in the nineteenth and twentieth century, following the translation of her work into English. Her importance within feminism points to the impact of lesbianism in the development of the movement. Other key figures include Hildegard of Bingen (*circa* 1098–1179), a German nun who challenged the stereotypical role of women in the Roman Catholic church by public preaching, criticizing the church, and calling for reform. Later the Italian French author Christine de Pizan (1364–1430) outlined the importance of women's contributions to society, and argued that their essential persuasive communicative abilities should be used within society in the brokering of peace. However, while history tends to prioritize the work of individual women from the higher social ranks, Federici, in her seminal work *The Caliban and the Witch* (2004) highlights how the heretic movement in medieval Europe depended on the participation and role of women from the serf classes that itself constituted a 'true woman's movement' (Federici 2004: 39).

The first wave of modern day feminism, however, is often attributed to the Enlightenment period and the development of liberal theory, most notably in the work of Olympes de Gouges (1748–1793) and Mary Wollstonecraft. These eighteenth-century feminists reflected the wave of revolutionary liberal theory, debate, and action sweeping across the Western world, which codified rights as 'inalienable' or 'natural'. Furthermore the Enlightenment and liberalism celebrated rationality and human reason over non-rationality, such as emotions. This translated into a division between the rational (male) public domain and the non-rational private sphere identified with women and the family, which reinforced unequal gender roles, rights, and privileges.

Olympes de Gouges, a French playwright who advocated for feminism and the abolition of slavery, wrote in response to the 'Declaration of the Rights of Man and the Citizen' passed by France's National Constituent Assembly in 1789, the 'Declaration of the Rights of Women and the Female Citizen' (1791) in which she challenged the idea of male authority and inequality in gender relations. Similarly the liberal conceptualization of male, property-owning heads of families as natural rights-bearers, prompted Wollstonecraft to write her revolutionary text *A Vindication of the Rights of Women*. She argued that the relegation of women as servants of men in the confines of the private, non-rational sphere was a result of a process of socialization that limits both the intellect and potential of women. For Wollstonecraft the education of women and the development of critical thinking would allow women to understand their own situation, to control their own lives and to develop their 'immortal souls', in turn bringing them closer to God. Women therefore should participate in the 'great enterprises' of public life, engage in professions and work, and not be confined to the private sphere and domination by men.

Enlightenment feminists who followed in Wollstonecraft's wake both developed and conflicted with her beliefs. While Sarah Grimké's 'Letters on Equality' (1838) presented a similar position to that of Wollstonecraft, she argued that men collectively subjugated womankind as it was in their interest to do so. Frances Wright, a Scots woman who embarked on a series of public lectures in the USA in 1829, agreed that critical thinking was key for women to understand their own subjugation, but as an atheist saw religion as a vehicle of women's subordination. She argued from a utilitarian position, that the progress of society is hindered by the subordination of women, a view shared by John Stuart Mill in his work *On the Subjection of Women*

(1869). Mill supported female suffrage and, like Grimké, argued that men subordinated women as it was in their interest to do so and because they could not abide the prospect of 'living with an equal'.

The women's movement in the late nineteenth and early twentieth centuries coalesced around the issue of rights, particularly political rights. This wave of feminist activism developed in the context of urban industrialization and focused on the achievement of equal rights for women. Its influences came from a range of other perspectives, including socialism, liberalism, and the temperance and abolitionist movements. The political, economic, legal, and social inequality facing women was the core focus of feminist ideology. Political inequality was apparent in the lack of women's right to vote. Economic inequality was evident in women's exclusion from certain types of work and of their employment on unequal terms to men. Legal inequality was evident in women's exclusion from areas of protection by the law, notably in relation to property rights and their loss of legal status through marriage. Social inequality was apparent through women's exclusion and/or relegation to a lower position within certain social institutions, such as colleges, universities, and private members' clubs and through marriage. While recognizing the relevance of the various elements of women's inequality, this first wave focused on political representation as the lever by which other forms of equality would be achieved.

In the USA the feminist movement led by Elizabeth Cady Stanton and Susan B. Anthony was greatly informed by the debates about legal and political rights in relation to the anti-slavery movement. The analogy of the slave was used to describe the general position of women in society due to their denial of property and political rights. The intersections of the abolition and women's movements converged around the situation of the black woman slave. However, Sojourner Truth, an ex-slave, highlighted how black women continued to face subordination despite the elimination of slavery, exposing the disparate experiences of white and black women in American society with her famous demand 'And ain't I a woman?' (see the section on 'Black feminism' below).

The 1848 Seneca Falls Convention marked the start of the American Women's Rights Movement. Inspired by the American Declaration of Independence, Elizabeth Cady Stanton drafted the Seneca Falls Declaration which outlined the new movement's ideology and political strategies, and demanded female suffrage. In Europe there followed the creation of similar movements, for example the French Union for Women's Suffrage in 1909, and the Women's Social and Political Union in England (see Case Study 9.1). The tactics and activism of the broader movement were hotly debated and challenged existing expectations of female behaviour, including public speaking, demonstration, and civil disobedience. In 1906, the movement was given particular impetus when, in Finland, the first European victory for unrestricted women's suffrage and eligibility for public office was realized.

Case Study 9.1　Suffragettes: votes for women

In the UK the campaign for the right for women to vote in elections began in 1897, with the National Union of Women's Suffrage Societies' call for the vote for middle class property owning women. Led by Millicent Fawcett, the movement used peaceful tactics such as demonstrations, petitions, and the lobbying of MPs, believing that such an approach would prove women responsible citizens worthy of the vote. Known as 'suffragists', their claims were represented in a number of bills that gained support from many Members of Parliament, although not enough to be passed into law.

Frustrated by the lack of success, Emmeline Pankhurst founded the Women's Social and Political Union (WPSU) in 1903. Pankhurst sought to go beyond the narrow concerns of middle class women to create a broader movement that encompassed working class women of all ages. While the focus of the movement was universal suffrage, it also campaigned on broader issues such as fighting prostitution and rape in marriage, and advocating for fair divorce, custody laws, raising the age of consent, and equal education. The movement spread across the country, with the Suffragette newspaper *Votes for Women* selling 20,000 copies a week by 1909. However, it was not universally popular, with organizations actively protesting against the cause, such as the National League for Opposing Woman Suffrage.

In the face of intransigence, the WPSU grew increasingly militant with suffragettes taking part in violent protests and demonstrations, including arson attacks, under the rallying cry of 'Deeds not words'. Those engaged in such protests were often imprisoned where many undertook hunger strikes to protest against their treatment as criminals rather than political prisoners, suffering the humiliation and violence of forced feeding. Marion Wallace-Dunlop was the first suffragette to go on hunger strike in 1909 while Emily Wilding Davison was the first person to die for the cause after stepping out in front of the King's horse at the Epsom Derby in 1913. The movement was suspended during the First World War with the prisoners released and efforts focused on the war effort.

While the WPSU appealed to women of all classes, the suffragettes were not a women-only movement. There was support from key male political figures such as Keir Hardie and George Lansbury, who was imprisoned in 1913 after publicly supporting the use of arson attacks. Frederick Pethick-Lawrence, Pankhurst's husband, was joint editor of *Votes for Women* and was imprisoned and went on hunger strike. Following the war, in 1918 the Representation of People Act gave the vote to women over 30 who either occupied property or were married to an occupier of property. It was finally the Equal Franchise Act of 1928 that gave women the same rights as men, with all women over 21 years of age being able to vote.

Stop and Think

1. Do you think that the ends of the suffragette movement justified its means?
2. Does formal political equality in the form of universal suffrage necessarily bring other forms of equality (social, economic, and cultural)?

Second wave

Second wave feminism has its roots in the post Second World War period. Although women had played crucial roles in both World Wars, in the aftermath of the Second

World War the expectations of the role of women in Western states returned largely to the domestic realm. In 1949 Simone de Beauvoir produced her celebrated text *Le Deuxième Sexe* (*The Second Sex*) which explored the lived experience of women. It reached the international best-seller list and was banned by the Catholic Church as immoral and godless.

'One is not born, but rather becomes, a woman'

De Beauvoir's starting point echoed Enlightenment feminists, that society squanders the abilities of women. However, rather than a focus on formal political rights, her analysis highlighted the construction of social forces that subordinate women. She argued that this subordination was not a natural phenomenon but was man-made. De Beauvoir argued that while biology determined a woman's identity, based on her capacity to reproduce, it is the construction of gender roles within society that determine her position. For De Beauvoir, the biological fact of a woman's body alone did not define her as a woman, rather her womanhood is a constructed experience. She argued that 'one is not born, but rather becomes, a woman'. The female character, therefore, is not unchangeable nor a biological destiny but rather a result of context and experience. From this perspective, while the gains of the first wave feminists in political and legal terms were real and tangible, the tyranny of society would continue to work in ways to ensure women's continued subordination.

De Beauvoir drew on the concepts of freedom of choice, enslavement, and transcendence in order to understand the oppression of women, and used the device of 'dualistic opposition' to explore the 'otherness' of woman. She argued that a woman is defined in relation to Man, that 'he is the subject. . . . She is the other'. Inequality in the relations between men and women are reflected in the way in which women's 'otherness' and difference are seen as inferior. This inequality is based on women's lack of freedom and their objectification by men. Through their exploitation, women are denied autonomy and freedom of choice, trapping them in a game of duplicity or complicity with men. Women therefore face constrained choices but not freedom.

In order to avoid this trap, De Beauvoir argued that women must gain independence and autonomy, and strive towards transcendence. For De Beauvoir, this salvation would be found through work outside the home and lived experience as an individual woman rather than collective action. De Beauvoir herself did not take part in the suffrage movement in her native France, which only gained the vote for women in 1944, and distanced herself from engagement with the feminist campaigns until the 1970s. Her position then changed and she wrote and signed Manifesto 343, a pro-abortion declaration, and joined the 'Mouvement de Libération des Femmes' (MLF).

Women's liberation

The focus on the lived experience of women and resistance to power relations (gendered and otherwise) defined a radical second wave of feminist ideology. While the

Western first wave was driven by middle class white women, the second wave drew in women from diverse social and cultural contexts, under the umbrella of sisterhood and solidarity. Federici (2012) argues that the first example of feminism in 1960s USA was activist 'welfare mothers', led by African American women inspired by the civil rights movement, who demanded a wage from the state for bringing up their children.

The radicalism of the second wave, which consolidated in the 1960s and 1970s, drew on a range of critical approaches, such as Marxism, and other social movements, such as the anti-Vietnam War, Black Power, and civil rights movements in the USA, and national liberation and anti-imperialist movements around the globe. Feminist demands shifted from equality to liberation. The rise of radical and revolutionary forms of feminism focused on the need to liberate women from subjugation, not least as female activists often experienced sexism and patronization within the new social movements they participated in. This further emphasized the need for an exclusively women's movement and political space to demand liberation from **patriarchy** and male domination. Feminist activist groups were often women-only, to enable women to collectivize without the constraints, social and otherwise, posed by male presence.

Germaine Greer was one of the foremost voices calling for liberation rather than equality. For Greer equality would mean women conforming to the actuality of men's lives, whereas liberation would mean women having the freedom to define their own values and priorities. Her seminal text, *The Female Eunuch*, published in 1970 argued that women were unaware of how much men hated them and how in turn they came to hate themselves. Greer argued that within modern society women had become like castrated beasts, to be fattened or made docile in the service of their master's needs. They had been separated from their capacity for action, their libido, desires, and sexuality. Central to this critique was a rejection of the nuclear family, the expectations and work of child rearing and modern-day consumerism that demeaned and confined women. Greer argued women had become eunuchs: powerless, isolated, and lacking joy and fulfilment, and that a revolution was needed to liberate and make them free.

Core demands

The emphasis on liberation was evidenced by the creation of Women's Liberation Movements (WLM). In the UK the Women's Liberation Movement held women-only conferences annually between 1971–1978 and articulated seven core demands which went beyond the achievement of political rights and into the economic, social, and cultural arenas. Mackay 2014 lists these as equal pay; equal education, and job opportunities; free contraception and abortion on demand; free 24 hour nurseries; financial and legal independence; an end to all discrimination against lesbians and a woman's right to define her own sexuality; freedom from intimidation by threat or use of violence or coercion, regardless of marital status and an end to all laws, assumptions, and practices which perpetuate male dominance and men's aggression towards women (Mackay 2014).

The WLM movement developed collective action and consciousness-raising activities, which highlighted and denounced cultures of oppression. This included the targeting of beauty pageants such as Miss World to publicly highlight the objectification of women and the construction of a particular representation of female beauty. The phrase 'burning the bra' reflected the radical protests against the parades, as feminists symbolically burned their clothing as artefacts of women's oppression. In parallel were debates about 'fat as a feminist issue' which sought to further highlight the social construction of the idealized form of female beauty and body, and how women adapt their lived experience in order to conform. The rejection of stereotypical and idealized forms of the female form and deviation from the perceived norms of beauty therefore could be revolutionary and liberating.

'The personal is political'

These critiques reflected a key concern of second wave feminism that 'the personal is political'. This phrase, coined by the American feminist activist Carol Hanisch, highlighted how gendered power relations operated within both the 'private' and the 'public' spheres of human activity and organization, and placed personal experience firmly in the collective political context. For feminism this was an important challenge to dominant frameworks as politics was traditionally thought of as being in the public realm, that of governments, institutions, political parties, and the like. In contrast, the family, the household, and the stereotyped realm of women was traditionally conceptualized as private and personal. Feminists both highlighted and challenged these delineations of public and private domains, in particular the construction of the family and home as private, 'female', and therefore inferior to the 'male' public domain. In doing so feminists challenged the societal division of labour that delineated roles as male/female and public/private, and the associated gendered expectations and societal positions which both subjugated and isolated women. In Western societies the stereotypical gendered division of labour rested on the housewife undertaking caring responsibilities for the household and family while the male breadwinner went to work and provided the financial resources to support the family.

This gendered division of labour was problematic. Betty Friedan's 1963 book *The Feminine Mystique* highlighted the disenchantment of middle class American women who had sacrificed their own careers in order to support their husbands as both wives and mothers. The work exposed the societal expectation of a choice between home and work, and the isolation that middle class women felt through that. In the USA this was exemplified via a rise in the use of personal therapy and prescription medication, euphemistically referred to as 'Mother's Little Helper'.

For those women in employment outside the home, feminism provided context and legitimized activism for equal pay and rights. One of the most famous of these was the strike by women machinists at Ford's Dagenham plant in the UK who demanded that their work be recognized as skilled labour and paid on equal terms to the skilled work of men. The campaign garnered political support and contributed to the formation of the National Joint Action Committee for Women's Equal Rights in 1969 and the passing of the Equal Pay Act in 1970. Other legislation was enacted, particularly within Western states, to guarantee social and economic equality regardless of gender. Pearson and Elson (2015) argue that this posed a challenge to the 'male breadwinner bias of post 1940s welfarism' and amounted to a 'reproductive bargain' that would allow women to combine their roles as wage earners and carers, and guarantee their financial autonomy. The state maintained this bargain via support for childcare costs, maternity pay and leave, social security support, and the provision of legislative protection for equality of pay and employment. These social provisions would later come under attack via the neo-liberal reforms undertaken from the late 1970s onwards.

The 'double burden'

Feminist authors highlighted that within the reproductive bargain women were required to carry a double burden of responsibility by combining paid employment with unpaid domestic labour. The concept of the double burden, or what Hochschild and Machung (1989) referred to as 'the second shift', highlights how in heterosexual couples women are more likely to undertake household chores and caring responsibilities, largely on account of traditional and stereotypical gender roles. Marxist feminists argued that such work is unpaid but central to the maintenance and (re)production of society and social relations within capitalism. Federici (2012: 6) explains that by locating the analysis of unwaged labour within the household the proletarian housewife is 'reconceptualised as the subject of the (re)production of the workforce'. Federici (2012) argued that unpaid household work was the major source of employment for American women, without providing them a wage, pension, or social security whilst limiting their ability to achieve economic independence.

The Wages for Housework Campaign and the Global Women's Strike Campaign, which operates as a grassroots network of national coordinators across the world, are both movements that have demanded payment and recognition of household and caring work. Perhaps the most effective national mobilization of women for pay equality and recognition of household and caring labour was seen in 1975 when Icelandic women undertook a one day strike. On 24 October 1975 an estimated 90 per cent of Icelandic women refused to go to work or to undertake domestic work at home, such as cooking and cleaning, effectively bringing society to a standstill for a day. The day of action had been called to celebrate the UN's declaration of 1975 as the Women's Year and to highlight both the inequality in wages and earnings between men and women and the expectations on women to carry the burden of undervalued domestic labour. A rally in Reykjavik drew an estimated

25,000 women from a total Icelandic population of 220,000. 'It was the real grass-roots. . . . It was in all seriousness, a quiet revolution' recalls Elin Olafsdottir (*The Guardian* 2005). Vigdis Finnbogadottir, who was later elected President of Iceland and the world's first democratically elected female president, attributed her election to office to the strike, 'After October 24, women thought it was time a woman became president. . . . The finger was pointed at me and I accepted the challenge' (*The Guardian* 2005).

 Stop and Think

1. Do you think that work in the household is valued by society and that it should be paid?
2. What is the gendered division of labour and is this equal?

Feminist analyses of women's position in the household and wider society also encompassed the issue of male violence. Highlighting the frequency of domestic abuse and the use of violence to subordinate women both inside and outside the home, feminists identified a variety of forms of violence against women, including rape, forced marriage, sexual assault, and sexual abuse of children. This focus provoked the proliferation of women's refuges, rape crisis centres, and organizations such as the Women's Aid Federation created in 1974. The identification of male violence against women extended to the analysis of sex work, pornography, and prostitution (Mackay 2015). The questioning of a woman's right to sell her sexual labour, however, contrasted with support for a woman's right to make choices in relation to her body and relationships, which came to the fore in the debates around sexuality, reproductive rights, and the right to abortion (see the section 'Choice and agency' below).

Feminist debates about which were the 'correct' choices for women evidenced the tensions between 'feminist factions', and highlighted the heterogeneity within both the ideology and the movement. The divisions within second wave feminism were exacerbated by widespread critiques, particularly by the mainstream media which often derided feminism and individual feminist activists. Susan Faludi in her 1991 book *Backlash: The Undeclared War Against American Women* argued that the media drove a backlash against feminism by blaming it for the social, economic, and political issues facing women. She claimed the media peddled the idea that although the feminist fight for equality had been won, women had never been so unhappy. She identified the use of unsubstantiated statistics and claims, to both support this idea and provoke a backlash against feminism that would halt and reverse the gains for female equality that had been won.

The question of homogeneity underpinned a wide-ranging critique of second wave feminism, notably that the attempt to unify all women around the cause of emancipation and liberation underplayed the variety of lived experiences of women in different societies and communities. The conceptualization of female collectivism and solidarity as a mobilizing force for a section of society negated the heterogeneity of womankind and their lived experiences, and the cross-cutting sectional identities of race, sexuality, and class that were not represented by white middle class feminism (see the section 'Intersectionality' below). For example bell hooks (2013) argued that black femininity was devalued and black women side-lined in the feminist movement, and she called instead for new and multiple feminisms (see the section 'Black feminism' below).

Third wave

The third wave reflected the debates about the intersections of oppression (see 'Intersectionality' below) and drew on black, queer, transgender, lesbian, anti-colonial, anti-imperialist, and anti-capitalist movements to question feminism's universalist claims. This wave was located in the challenges 'posed by women of colour regarding the whiteness of second wave feminism and the tendency of feminist theory and practice to purportedly speak for all women's experiences, while not acknowledging that these perspectives are based on those of white, privileged women, in the main' (O'Keefe 2014).

The third wave was heavily centred on the exploration of individual identities and subjectivities, and the construction of gender within these. It sought to challenge the representation of women, the language and stereotypes that construct identities, and to answer the critiques levied against second wave feminism by bringing to the fore a concern for gender, race, and sexuality. This new politics of identity prioritized the individualized woman, preferring women to define their own feminism away from the more rigid doctrines of the second wave. In this way the politics of gender shifted from a macro collectivized approach to an individualized micro approach. Mackay (2014) argues that in many ways this rested on a construction of feminism in opposition to a 'straw woman' imagined version of the second wave, writing it off as redundant. Within this critique the core concepts of feminism, such as patriarchy and women as a social category, were subject to criticism. This criticism centred on a rejection of universalizing ideas of what women are and particularly the dominance of white, Western feminist thinking.

Within the third wave there emerged a more ambiguous approach to sexual politics and freedom, in which sex work, pornography, and prostitution were represented as individual life choices and often disaggregated from the analysis of the structural forms of male violence and oppression. Advocates argued that the choices made about sex work could be viewed as empowering and sexually emancipating, whilst feminist activism highlighted the right to make individual choices, often via the utilization of the female body as a vehicle for protest (see Case Study 9.2).

Case Study 9.2 SlutWalks and Femen: the body as a site of protest

SlutWalking and Femen are what O'Keefe (2014) refers to as sexualized, gendered body protests, that is, 'protests that make explicit the use of the female body to call attention to issues that pertain to women's bodies, or simply protests where the gendered body is both subject and agent'. Femen is an international women's movement whose 'sextremism' protests are often topless or naked. Femen protestors paint their bodies with slogans that highlight the patriarchal control of women's bodies, the impact of pornography and patriarchy. Femen believes their sextremism mocks 'vulgar male extremism' and 'promotes new revolutionary female sexuality' (Femen no date).

The body as a political tool was also invoked in the global 'SlutWalk' movement. 'SlutWalks' emerged following an incident at Toronto's York University in 2011, when a male police officer advised female students to stay safe by avoiding 'dressing like sluts'. This 'victim blaming' suggested that 'there is a causal relationship between clothing and consent and that, ultimately, victims are themselves responsible when raped and sexually assaulted' (O'Keefe 2014). This provoked a call on women to flaunt their 'inner slut' and publicly denounce the comments, with the SlutWalk movement born as 3,500 protesters marched on Police Headquarters, with similar marches held across the world. The word 'Slut' was deliberately used in order to 'reclaim' it in a subversive, positive, and empowering way, with protestors often wearing revealing clothes and underwear and writing the word Slut on their bodies.

O'Keefe (2014) critiques this use of the gendered body in feminist struggles, arguing that it exemplifies 'the problematic interface between third wave and post feminism'. She argues that the subversive potential of protests involving scantily and provocatively dressed women is limited and simply reproduces patriarchal hegemonic norms. Moreover it marginalizes women from diverse backgrounds, particularly some women of colour for whom the terminology and significance is distant, whilst the class reference of the term 'slut' (referring to a dirty or unclean woman of a low order) is overlooked. She argues that the point of the protest as a subversive parody of 'sluttiness' is lost if the intended audience do not recognize the parody but rather just view (and enjoy) it as a spectacle of scantily clad and topless women.

Stop and Think

1. Are feminists right to use their bodies as political tools?
2. To what extent do Femen and SlutWalking reinforce or challenge gender norms and who is excluded from these forms of protest?

While the third wave aimed to broaden feminism, critics have argued that individual emancipation undermines the collectivity of the feminist struggle and the importance of the structural forces that oppress women. Many argue that this individualism reflects the neo-liberal context in which the third wave emerged. As such the radical critiques of capitalism and fights for collective social justice that conditioned second wave feminism have given way to the expression of individualized and atomized identities. Moreover, the third wave has given rise to 'post' feminism in which the identity politics of the individual has reduced the emancipatory project to a 'feminism-lite' movement reliant on consumer culture and mainstream identity expression.

Fourth wave? Feminism and the Twittersphere

It has been argued that the rapid development of ICTs and social media has given rise to a fourth wave of feminism as a digital movement, creating a global community of online activism and debate. One can question, however, whether this is an extension of the third wave, or a new wave in itself. Some feminists claim that the rise of social media has facilitated a wider culture of inclusion within feminism. Okolosie (2014) argues that 'social media, particularly Twitter and the feminist blogosphere, has revolutionised and, to some extent, democratised our movement, allowing women who once would have been assigned to the margins of debate a platform from which to speak. Through these mediums, black feminists have been able to seek redress when and where privileged voices within the movement have sought to speak on our behalf'. To counter the straight white middle class domination of feminism, online participants are often asked to 'Check their privilege' (i.e. to identify themselves and reflect on their own identity, particularly in relation to others) in internet discussions as a reminder of the subjective position of the speaker.

Within 'cyber feminism' there has emerged a 'call out' culture, that seeks to highlight and publicize the incidence of sexism and gendered oppression as well as to develop feminist debate. For example, the Everyday Sexism Project was created as a forum to discuss sexism, equality, and women's rights, and to record stories of sexism 'by ordinary women, in ordinary places'. It aims to demonstrate the frequency of sexism in the workplace, to encourage women to report their experiences and to challenge the status quo by calling out sexism. Moreover the project seeks to challenge the perception of women who object as 'complainers' or 'killjoys' (Everyday Sexism no date). However 'calling-out' sexism can be difficult. For example, Charlotte Proudman, a young human rights barrister, tweeted a screenshot of a message she regarded as sexist which she had received on the professional online network LinkedIn. The message, from 57-year-old male partner at another law firm, told Proudman that her profile picture was 'stunning'. A 'Twitterstorm' followed, with some suggesting that Proudman was at fault for the photo that provoked his attention, for misconstruing this as sexism, and for 'ruining' her own career by tweeting the screenshot. The media coined a new term 'Feminazi' to deride Proudman and this form of 'militant' cyber-action. Proudman replied that it 'isn't just about me. It is about sexism in our culture and the need for women to feel confident and call people up on it. . . . We need to collectively take a stand, not accept sexism on any level, support others in calling it out and make sure that professionals and websites are aware of how pervasive it is' (*Evening Standard* 2015).

The rise of ICTs has enabled the global spread of transnational feminist networks and sharing of ideas and debates. New terminologies have also accompanied the rise of online communities, reflecting the constraint of Twitter's 140-character limit. Terms such as **cis** (someone with gender identity that they were assigned at birth— i.e. non-transgender), WoC (women of colour), TERF (trans exclusionary radical feminism), or doxed have become mainstream. Doxing refers to the act of hacking and distributing the information of the account holder, with anti-trans activists accused of 'doxing' transpeople in order to 'out' them. This term reflects how the realm of cyberfeminism has been a site of conflict and often victim to extensive trolling, with prominent online feminists being subject to threats and malicious messaging and stalking. Moreover, the idea of inclusivity facilitated by online fora has been countered by criticism that ICTs can form an exclusionary social network, with the insiders being the relatively young and affluent. Older activists and those with limited access to ICTs are left as outsiders.

 Stop and Think

1. Are messages sent to colleagues and other professionals commenting on their appearance sexist?
2. Is the fourth wave a new and inclusive form of feminism?

Is feminism an ideology? Feminism as a framework or system of beliefs and concepts

In order to explore the extent to which feminism can be viewed as an ideology, we can review the discussion of ideology in Chapter 1, which developed a framework of three inter-related elements that constitute an ideology.

1. a *critique* of existing society—involving an assessment of its shortcomings in relation to certain cherished values, and an understanding of how the world works in terms of how current society operates to generate these defects

2. a *vision of the good society*—again defined with reference to the cherished values, and combined with an understanding of how the world works reflected in proposals for how the good society would be organized

3. a *strategy* to get from current society to the good society—involving an understanding of political power

All forms of feminism employ a critique of existing society rooted in an understanding of unequal gendered social relations. However, for some feminists the emphasis is not a concern for gender equality but for liberation. While this represents a degree of divergence, there is a common vision of the good society as one in which people are free from oppression—in other words a world of social justice. However, the variants of feminism differ in the way they imagine that good society and the strategies required to transform society to reach that ideal (for example, see Case Study 9.3).

Woman as a category

You will note from this discussion that the language of feminism has changed from one in which the concerns of women are at the forefront, to one in which the discussion is focused on the concept of gender. This change of discourse is indicative of the changes within and between the waves, most notably the shift between the second and third wave. The term 'Woman' as a category was relatively coherent within first wave and, to an extent, within second wave feminism. In the latter it was reclaimed in opposition to the term 'lady', which was rejected as it implies a construction of femininity, underpinned by an understanding of class and ethnicity (typically middle class and white). However the category of woman has come under scrutiny, particularly as the feminist movement incorporated transgender and non-binary people and those that self-identify as women. This widening of the feminist constituency is reflective both of the development within feminist ideology and also of wider changing societal understandings of sex and sexuality.

This raises key debates about 'nature' and 'nurture', the biological determination of sex and social construction of gender and the rigid dichotomies of male and female. Within these debates the binary definition and identities of male and female as identifiers of both biologically determined sex and of gender have been challenged and for many discarded. For example, the category of intersex has challenged the distinction between binaries of biologically assigned sex as either male or female. This binary distinction is also challenged in the identification of gender, not only in the variety of ways in which gender is expressed by people, but also by those that do not want to be defined by gender. From this position, therefore, gender is neither given nor fixed, but rather is a construction. This construction in turn structures relations within society as well as conditions our physical bodies (Mackay 2014). The manner by which we train and tend our bodies to fit gender roles is exemplified in a myriad of behaviours, such as dieting, going to the gym, shaving and waxing, applying make up, as well as how we walk, hold our bodies, talk, and communicate. Gender theorist Judith Butler argues that these acts, through which we define and construct our identities, are part of the 'performativity' of gender (Butler, cited in Mackay 2015). Through this 'performativity' gendered roles, characteristics, and appearances are played out, reinforced, and assumed to be natural. Butler argues gender is created, performed, and reproduced but not in a conscious, temporary, and voluntary way. Rather this 'performativity' of gender is subconscious, embedded, and ongoing (Mackay 2014).

This view of gender is in contrast to the view that male and female identities and roles are defined by biology. This is often the dominant view in society, related to reproductive function and capacity, perceptions of relative strength, weaknesses, and emotion. In this way the choices women make in relation to their career, family commitments, and sexuality are seen as natural and prescribed. In turn, certain characteristics and emotions are similarly viewed as 'essentially' female, such as being peaceful, caring, and non-violent, and as such are regarded as universal and a feature of all women everywhere. However, as we have seen from the discussion of De Beauvoir, this rigid distinction between nature versus nurture, essentialist versus constructivist arguments is often blurred.

The use of the term 'woman' as a category inherently implies a delineation of who can be included or excluded. For some the tendency of feminism to accept, use, and rely on pre-defined narrow gender categories means that it maintains and perpetuates those categories. This has led to the proposal that feminists should open up the category of women, in particular in relation to '**trans-inclusion**' (Mackay 2015). For others, however, this 'opening up' hits at the heart of the feminist movement, as it questions whether we can talk of women as a category of the oppressed and in turn whether there is a need for a women's movement at all (Mackay 2015). Some argue that trans-inclusion can negatively affect women-only spaces and political activism, with such a fluid self-definition of womanhood being dangerous for female activism and the visibility of women as a political class. It has prompted renewed calls for women-only space and separatism as trans-inclusion might give space to 'legacy male privilege' (Mackay 2015). For example, some radical feminist conferences have been closed to transwomen, and only open to those assigned as female at birth. Some have argued that trans-inclusion has led to the increasing marginalization of (cis) women from the movement, while others argue that transpeople have experienced more violence and discrimination than cis women who have had their (female) identity privileged from birth. The use of these identifiers therefore can convey hierarchy, and distinction. The politics of inclusion and exclusion has caused a storm within feminism, with many feminists being 'called out' as 'transphobic'. There have been angry exchanges in social media and 'no-platforming' protests in some universities, where prominent feminists such as Germaine Greer have been boycotted by students and student unions due to alleged 'anti-trans' sentiments.

In response there have been concerted attempts to overcome these divisions. Mackay (2015) argues for 'strategic essentialism' in which the stereotypical and patriarchal definitions of what a woman is and should be are rejected while at the same time the term woman is used strategically to challenge patriarchy and oppression. She argues that this position allows a consideration of the category of woman as varied and heterogeneous, but provides for unity through the shared experience of resisting and surviving sexism (Mackay 2015: 122).

Case Study 9.3 Women, peace, and Greenham Common

Women have been at the forefront of anti-militarist and peace movements internationally and nationally and played a long-standing role in the Campaign for Nuclear Disarmament (CND). The link between women and peace is often based on an understanding of womanhood as humane, collaborative, inclusive, peaceful, and nurturing. This is particularly evident in contemporary debates about the role of women in peace-building in former conflict zones. Such understandings are framed by essentialist views of what constitutes the 'essence' of womanhood.

In 1981 women protestors set up a peace camp at the United States Air Force base on Greenham Common, Berkshire, which was being used as a site for Cruise and Pershing missiles at the height of the Cold War. Their aim was to challenge the nuclear policies of the USA, the UK, and NATO and the dominant gender relations which underpinned them. In particular the women highlighted the perils of nuclear weapons, the threat to safety and human security they posed, and the need for peace through disarmament. In their protests they often emphasized their identities as mothers, grandmothers, daughters, and sisters by pinning pictures of their families to the fences along with other objects to reflect their lives. While the number of women who lived at the camp over the nineteen years of its existence was not large, at key events such as the 1982 'Embrace the Base' protest 30,000 women held hands around the six miles of the perimeter fence. Although initially the camp was mixed, it quickly became a women-only space with protestors derided by the tabloid press as 'burly lesbians'.

For Roseneil (1995) the Greenham women's opposition to US militarism was constructed into three main discourses: maternalism, with the moral and practical duty of mothers to protect life; materialism, highlighting the gendered nature of the material hardship of war falling on women and children; and feminism, highlighting the exclusion of women from the armed forces and from governmental decision-making, the cultural connections between militarism and masculinity, and the gendered and sexualized discourses of militarism and male violence. She argues that while the Greenham protest partially began from a maternal discourse, over time it became increasingly feminist (Roseneil 1995:171), with its ethos underpinned by radical feminism, anarchism and non-hierarchy, non-violence, and eco-feminism.

Stop and Think

1. Do women and men have essential characteristics and how do essentialist ideas frame gender roles?

2. What difficulties do we face in categorizing women as a group and how does this impact on feminist ideology?

Challenging patriarchy

Debate around the fluidity of identities and gender has challenged the concept of patriarchy as a central tenet of feminism. The term traditionally refers to the rule of the father and male leadership of the family: however within feminism it means more generally the all-pervasive dominance of male rule and/or superiority in the home, the community, and society as a whole. **Hegemonic masculinity** is a similar concept used to describe a form of social organization in which men hold, produce, and reproduce their power and dominance. Feminist theorists and historians have analysed and debated the extent to which male supremacy has defined social governance over time, with, for example, Gerda Lerner's (1988) arguing that there is no evidence of any alternative form of social organization existing. A hundred years earlier John Stuart Mill argued that male dominance was universal and a departure from this appears unnatural. For others this represents a simplistic view that overlooks the difference and heterogeneity in the ways various societies operate and are structured.

Within feminism the twin concepts of patriarchy and hegemonic masculinities are directly tied to male violence against women. Feminists argue women are disproportionally affected by physical, sexual, and/or psychological violence. Violence instils fear and operationalizes a hierarchy based on power and subordination. In response, feminist activists have created rape crisis lines and women's aid centres and refuges, and have lobbied for legislative changes such as the 1976 UK Domestic Violence Matrimonial Proceedings Act and changes to the Sexual Offences Act. In addition to physical acts of violence, feminists have argued that male violence includes sexual harassment in the workplace, exposure to pornography, and degrading and sexist advertising (Mackay 2015).

However, it can be argued that feminist concerns about male violence against women, particularly in the form of domestic violence, are reliant on essentialist and biological arguments. Gender studies, particularly within criminology, have emphasized how women can also be perpetrators of violence against men, other women, and children. In turn the discourse of violence has been adapted to reflect this, being generally referred to as gender-based violence (rather than male violence against women). In a similar vein the concept of patriarchy has been critiqued as attributing a fixed, fundamental, and biological essence to gender, and as such being simplistic and generalizing. In response, however, radical feminists such as Mackay (2015: 10) argue that this shift is significant and political as it suggests violence is neutral and un-sexed and therefore obscures the facts and reality of sexual violence. 'The focus is stealthily shifted away from the brutal fact that men are overwhelmingly the perpetrators of such crimes and that women are overwhelmingly the victims' (Mackay 2015: 10). She argues that by viewing male violence against women and more broadly patriarchy as political (rather than biological) it can be identified, challenged, and changed.

Intersectionality

The recognition that women's experiences vary according to their social context, in terms of their class, race, religious, sexual, and other identities, prompted the development of a new term—**intersectionality**. This term, coined by Kimberle Crenshaw, describes the multiple and overlapping identities and associated arenas of oppression and subordination that women, and those identifying as women, experience. It places a focus on the multiple identities that all people inhabit and the varied levels of power and privilege attached to them. Crenshaw (1991) developed the term in relation to her analysis of the experiences of black women in employment discrimination cases. She argued these women experienced discrimination in employment and within the legal system on account of both their gender and race. These identities intersect and combine within and between individuals and groups, with Crenshaw arguing that the failure to recognize and understand these intersections undermines social and political movements.

The term intersectionality highlights the longstanding critique of feminism that it is an overwhelmingly white, middle class, and **heteronormative** ideology and movement. Barrett and McIntosh (2005) highlighted two particular criticisms raised by black feminists in relation to the dominance of white middle class women within the movement and feminists' claims of universality.

> On the one hand it is argued that black groups are typecast, stereotyped and ghettoized; that the dominant racist ideologies, especially as they apply to black women, are reproduced rather than challenged in white feminist work. So black women appear as hospital ancillary workers, bus conductors or West Indian matriarchs, or as the docile 'victims' of arranged marriages, in white feminist work as well as in television sit-coms. On the other hand, and more likely in view of the fact that the dominant ideological construction of black women is to make them invisible, it is argued that they are invisible and unheard in white feminist work. Where crude stereotypes are not being aired, white feminists have simply assumed that whatever they say will apply to all women. White feminists do not bother to say how their arguments about pensions, or pornography, or poetry, would apply to women of different ethnic origin; they do not say whether, or how, a history of racism would give a different meaning to these things. In doing this, white feminists deny the importance of ethnic difference and racism. By ignoring these questions their work claims to be of relevance to all women but is in fact grounded in the specific experience of white women: it is ethnocentric.
>
> (Barrett and McIntosh 2005: 65)

While the concept of intersectionality highlights the heterogeneity within the lived experiences of women, for some it presents a challenge to feminism by encouraging division through the separation of identities and by moving away from collectivism in the movement.

Choice and agency

The recognition of the varied contexts and realities of women's lives in turn brings into focus their agency in making choices about their own lived experience.

This revolves around the ability of an individual to make free choices within the social structures that condition and frame those decisions. The extent to which the choices made by women within structures of patriarchy are free choices is a cause of debate and contestation. Feminism prioritizes the right of women to make choices in relation to their lives, to be emancipated, free, and in control of their own decisions. For example, reproductive choices, in terms of access to family planning, abortion, and whether or not to have children, have been central to feminist ideology and activism. However, this prioritization of individual choices can cause feminism to be repackaged in a liberal and/or libertarian form which authors such as hooks and McRobbie argue is a 'faux' form of feminism (hooks 2013).

The questions about choice and agency therefore are difficult. For some the prioritization of the individual and freedom of choice matters whatever the context or structure in which decisions are made. For example, the decision to wear high heels, make-up, or the burqa can be regarded as positive choices that women freely make for and by themselves (see also Chapter 11 for discussion of the debate about the veil). However, such choices can highlight the divergences or faultlines within feminist ideology. Debates surrounding prostitution and sex work exemplify this, with some arguing that these represent the free choices of women in relation to their body, labour, and sexuality. However, economic and social contexts structure these choices. For example, the English Collective of Prostitutes cite adverse economic conditions and declining social provision, such as benefit reductions and sanctions, as drivers of the choices sex workers make in relation to the generation of income. Some feminists argue that participation in these markets can be empowering, particularly if these markets are socially acceptable and regulated (Bell 2009). Critics, however, highlight how the sex industry is highly gendered, with those buying sex being predominantly male, and integrated with other illegal activities, particularly the marketing and use of drugs and the trafficking of women and children. They argue that those engaging in prostitution and sex work are trapped in the reproduction and enactment of hegemonic ideas of sex and women's sex roles. As such these are depoliticized, false notions of choice and agency, linked to consumption and the intensified sexualization of modern society. Those who problematize the sex industry include it in the definition of violence against women, arguing that rather than being about sex, these activities are about male power and the exploitation and denigration of women. These divisions are reflected in the debates about how to respond to the sex industry, whether to seek its abolition or to legislate to protect those involved. Some advocate a Nordic approach, which decriminalizes sex workers but criminalizes those who buy sex. Those in favour of pro market legislation argue that the sex industry is a legitimate business arena of lucrative private enterprise, in which sex workers should be protected and empowered.

Stop and Think

1. Is the market for sex like other areas of the labour market and should adults be free to sell their sexual labour without interference from the state?

2. Are sex work and pornography forms of violence against women?

Contested feminisms

As the previous sections have shown, there are a number of core issues that both define and divide feminists and feminist ideology. There are also a number of areas in which feminism overlaps with other ideologies and ideas. In this section we will explore a number of variants within feminism, and how the issues outlined in the previous section both shape and are represented within these variants. However, it is important to bear in mind that the labelling of these various forms can tend towards generalization and in reality many feminists tend not to fit easily into such categories.

Liberal feminism

This form of feminism is rooted in the liberal tradition with a focus on the individual woman and her ability to achieve equality and change discriminatory practices, with the explanation for female inequality regarded as unequal rights and barriers to participation in public life. Central to this approach are the concepts of personal and political autonomy and women's right to make their own choices. This is reliant on achieving certain conditions that enable women to exercise their freedom. In particular liberal feminists focus on political representation, both through suffrage and participation in government, as well as campaigns to ensure that women are treated on equal terms in the workplace, the labour market, and education. Liberal feminists utilize legal, judicial, and democratic processes to challenge gender stereotypes and the cultural, institutional, and legal barriers to women fully participating in all areas of life on equal terms with men. The state is central to this in delivering the conditions necessary to ensure and maintain equality. In this way liberal feminism contrasts with radical and revolutionary feminisms as it seeks to work within present systems to achieve reform, rather than wholesale societal change. A well publicized example of this form of feminism is Sheryl Sandberg and her book *Lean In: Women, Work and the Will to Lead*. In this text Sandberg, a Facebook Chief Operating Officer and one of Fortune Magazine's Most Powerful Women in Business, outlined strategies for individual women to help themselves by 'leaning in' and argued that through these personal development strategies women could achieve their ambitions. However, Sandberg's views have been critiqued as 'corporate feminism', neo-liberal feminism, or 'faux feminism' that does little to fundamentally alter the world or to build collective movements, but rather simply seeks to ensure equality within the existing system, without challenging 'the structures of imperialist white capitalist patriarchy' (hooks 2013). The emphasis is firmly on what individual women can do to change their position in society rather than changing the structures that limit and constrain women's lives.

Radical feminism

Radical feminism emerged in the late 1960s, challenging and rejecting male dominated social orders. Beasley (1999: 54) argues that it 'gives a positive value to womanhood' rather than supporting a liberal notion of assimilating women into male arenas (see also discussion of feminist criticisms of liberalism in Chapter 2). Mackay (2015: 61) has identified four main features of the movement.

1. a belief in the existence of patriarchy and determination to end it
2. the promotion of women-only space and political organization
3. the identification of male violence against women as a keystone of oppression
4. a maximal understanding of male violence against women to include institutions of pornography and prostitution

Radical feminism regards violence as both the foundation and the consequence of patriarchy, operating as a source of social control that affects all women, whether or not they are personally subject to it. For example, the rape and murder of a woman on a Delhi bus (Independent 2015) highlighted the reality of male violence and the position of women in that community, nation, and globally and sparked waves of protest and activism. Radical feminists aim to fundamentally change society by defeating patriarchy and ending all forms of male violence against women. Belief in the possibilities of change reflects a rejection of essentialist claims that men are naturally violent or abusive and the assumption of gender as being biologically determined. The radical feminist focus on women-only political organization and separatism provides links to political lesbianism/lesbian feminism.

Separatism and political lesbianism/lesbian feminism

Some areas of feminist activism are 'mixed' and welcome men into activist spaces, such as the He For She campaign, which is very publicly led by the actress Emma Watson and has deliberately targeted men to support women in their stand for equality. However, the inclusion of men in feminist activism is rejected by some who argue that the feminist movement must be organized around political autonomy and separate women-only spaces (a position that has informed debates around trans-inclusion). Ideas of political autonomy can extend to complete separatism, with women living in women-only communities and minimizing all contact with men—see, for example the Leeds Revolutionary Feminist Group paper published by Onlywomen Press in 1981—and to radical debates about forms of biological engineering and reproduction that exclude men. Political calls for separatism and the exclusion of men bring with them a focus on sexuality and lesbianism. They also reflect the place accorded to Queer Theory and politics within feminist ideology and their influence on feminist understandings of gender, sexed identities, and gender oppression.

Transfeminism

In 2001 Emi Koyama wrote 'The Transfeminist Manifesto', arguing for the inclusion of transwomen into the feminist revolution, as the liberation of all women was intrinsically linked. Amongst other things, the manifesto outlined two primary principles: first that every individual has the right to define their own identity and be respected by society; second that people have the sole right to make decisions in relation to their bodies without interference from political, medical, or religious authorities. **Transfeminism** rejects the gender binary of male oppression against women, but rather argues that there are multiple forms of sexism that intersect with each other and other forms of oppression. However, transfeminism has come into conflict with other forms of feminism, particularly radical feminism, as seen in relation to the debates about transinclusion/exclusion.

Revolutionary feminism

Revolutionary feminism (sometimes known as fundamental feminism) grew out of a fractious debate within feminism in the 1970s and the publication of a paper by Sheila Jeffreys entitled 'The Need for Revolutionary Feminism—Against the Liberal Takeover of the Women's Liberation Movement' (see Mackay 2014). This school of feminism shares many similarities with radical feminism, in particular the importance placed on women-only space and organization and the analysis of patriarchy and male oppression underpinned by male violence (Mackay 2014). Mackay (2014) argues that the main difference between radical and revolutionary feminism was the claim that radical feminism had become reliant on essentialism and a characterization of innate female superiority. Radical feminism had fallen into a form of cultural or lifestyle feminism, linked to New Age beliefs, environmentalism, and 'Goddess' worship that lacked revolutionary potential. Mackay (2014) argues that revolutionary feminism adopted a more practical course of action clearly aimed at wholesale societal change, but it too came into conflict with other forms of feminism. The critiques levelled at revolutionary feminism were that it had split the British feminist movement through a perceived insistence on political lesbianism and separatism, and was responsible for feminism and the women's liberation movement being derided as 'man-hating' (Mackay 2014).

Socialist and Marxist feminism

Socialist and Marxist forms of feminism share with revolutionary feminism the idea of wholesale social change; however these approaches focus on capitalism as the cornerstone of women's oppression. They argue that every form of society has a particular organization of gendered relations which structure the position of women within society, and it is necessary to understand this via an analysis of the interrelation of class, gender, and race. In this specific contemporary context, particular focus is placed on neo-liberal capitalism and on the way associated policies of austerity have been targeted at, and disproportionally affect, women. It is therefore important to understand how globalized neo-liberalism and patriarchy combine to structure society and condition the role, position, and behaviour of all people in society, but with particular impact on women. 'When neo-liberal politics and the world's financial institutions marginalise state welfare, as well as depriving women of support in the role as carers, they reconstitute women care workers as the precariat. . . . and they also reinstate patriarchal divisions of labour and redistribute incomes towards men' (Campbell 2014).

Marxist feminism emerged in the late 1960s and early 1970s in the context of revolutionary student movements and academic debate. In the face of resistance from some Marxist groups that disputed the analytical separation of class and gender, early Marxist feminists such as Mariarosa Dalla Costa and Selma James launched a campaign focused on the role of women in the reproduction of labour (**social reproduction**). They argued that 'the exploitation of women has played a central function in the process of capitalist accumulation, insofar as women have been the producers and reproducers of the most essential capitalist commodity: labor power' (Federici 2004: 8). The position of women as workers has been weakened by the idea of the male breadwinner 'establishing men's dominance and women's subordination in the home, and rendering single women with dependents very vulnerable. These theses can also be combined with the idea that women workers form a continuous supply of marginal and flexible labour and that some women workers (particularly married women) may form an industrial reserve army of dispensable labour to cushion the boom and slump of capitalist production' (Barrett and McIntosh 2005).

This analysis prompted campaigns for 'Wages for Housework' and the recognition that capitalist production and accumulation rested on the unpaid work undertaken in the home. This critique extended to the analysis of the commodification of the female body as an object of male desire though pornography and the sex industry, with Marxist feminists arguing that the eradication of all forms of gendered oppression and unequal gender relations should be integral to the socialist revolution (Tepe-Belfrage and Steans 2016: 1).

Socialist feminism differs from Marxist feminism by aiming for reform rather than revolution. It mounts a critique of the neo-liberal state, particularly in relation to the diminishing of welfare and social policies and how these contribute to the gendering of the labour market, the regulation of the supply of labour and unequal gender relations. However, in contrast to Marxist feminists, it argues that reform of existing structures is possible in order to deliver a more socially responsible and egalitarian society.

While socialist and Marxist feminisms can be located within broader political movements, proponents have often eschewed participation in these due to experiences of marginalization, repression, and stereotyping. Examples include the scandal that rocked the Socialist Workers Party in relation to allegations of sexual abuse of young female party members by an older and more senior male party member. The party was branded an 'unsafe space for young women' and its events boycotted (Platt 2014).

Anarchist feminism

Anarchist feminists share positions with socialist and Marxist feminists, in that they focus on the interrelationship between capitalism and patriarchy, and understand global systems of power as structural and pervasive (Mag 2014). Anarchist feminists view patriarchy as a coercive hierarchy, which needs to be opposed and replaced with a society based on the principles of equality and decentralized free association. The anti-authoritarian stance challenges all forms of domination, including racism, religious fundamentalism, and homophobia. Like Marxist feminism, anarchist feminism highlights the oppression of the individual and the manner in which people internalize subordination. For Mueller (2003: 129–30 cited in Maiguashca 2014) the realization of one's own voluntary servitude reveals how 'even a person who is oppressed on several counts (homosexuality, femininity) can be an oppressor on others (upper class, white)' (Mueller 2003: 129–30). Anarchist feminists therefore call for a comprehensive radical transformation of society on the principles of equality. It differs from socialist feminism in its analysis of the state as a progressive power, as anarchist feminists view the state and its institutions (such as the armed forces and education system) as the oppressor, that cannot be the vehicle of change (Mag 2014).

Eco-feminism

The term eco-feminism, first used by Françoise d'Eaubonne in 1974, argues that women are natural advocates of environmentalism. Some eco-feminists argue this is due to women's innate biological connection to earth and lunar cycles, for example through the female reproductive cycle. This specific relationship between women and nature is reflected in the idea of 'Mother Earth' and draws on essentialist 'female' elements such as nurturing, non-violence, and cooperation. This approach draws on Vandana Shiva's work which highlights the interconnection between women and nature, particularly in subsistence agricultural economies which rely on female stewardship of the land. Gaard and Gruen (1993) argue that through modernity the interconnectedness and relationship between nature and culture is under attack, while the oppression and exploitation of the environment reflects women's experience within patriarchal social relations. For eco-feminists, therefore, there is a crucial inter-relationship between the domination and degradation of nature and the exploitation and oppression of women which is intensified via contemporary patriarchal capitalism and forms of development. However, eco-feminism has come under critique as being reliant on essentialism and mysticism, and lacking in coherence in relation to its key claims (see also discussion of eco-feminism in Chapter 10).

Black feminism

Black feminism points out the intersections of race, gender, and class oppression and challenges the dominance of white, Western middle class women within the feminist movement. Key authors and activists such as bell hooks highlighted the lack of diverse voices within feminist theory and advocated for women to acknowledge and recognize difference. Lorde (1984) argued that 'Black Feminism is not white feminism in blackface. Black women have particular and legitimate issues which affect our lives as Black women'. Black feminism focused on how colonialism, post-colonialism, and imperialism condition contemporary societies and reproduce racialized, classed, and gendered hierarchies and societal divisions (Swaby 2014). This translated into analysis and activism around, for example, gendered and racialized immigration policies, the experience of marginalization in the workplace, the representation of women in the media, the lack of representation of black women, and the development of collective political strategies. Women of African, Asian, and mixed descent have collectively mobilized with prominent UK black feminist groups emerging, such as the Organisation of Women of Asian and African Descent (OWAAD) and the Southall Black Sisters (see Case Study 9.4), and similar groups forming internationally. In the USA in the 1970s these were often allied to the Black Panther and other radical movements.

Within black feminism, however, the definition of 'blackness' has been ambiguous. Guran argued that rather than being attributed to a geographical or biological origin, it referred to an excluded, racialized other. However, within and beyond feminism, as a categorization it has proved problematic and exclusionary. Anthias and Yuval-Davis (1983 cited in Barrett and McIntosh 2005) argued that the binary distinction of black and white women 'denies the existence of women who fit into neither category and denies the real complexity of the issues involved. Thus black as a category is both too narrow and too wide to be useful'. In order to overcome the potential divisiveness of identities, while at the same recognizing and challenging the gender and racial oppression of black women, the author Alice Walker coined the term 'womanism'.

Walker's (1983) definition of this all-embracing term was, among others, a black feminist or feminist of colour, a woman who loves other women (either sexually or non-sexually), and a universalist committed to the survival and wholeness of all. Womanism has therefore developed as an inclusive term to represent feminists of colour.

Case Study 9.4 Southall Black Sisters

The Southall Black Sisters (SBS) was established in West London in 1979 as a human rights group working locally and nationally to meet the needs of black, Asian, and African-Caribbean women. They support and advocate for women and families that have experienced violence, abuse, and other forms of inequality. Their aims are to 'highlight and challenge all forms of gender related violence against women, empower them to gain more control over their lives; live without fear of violence and assert their human rights to justice, equality and freedom'. SBS argue that race, culture, religion, language, and immigration status not only impact on women's experiences of domestic violence but also their ability and options for accessing support services. Issues highlighted by SBS include forced marriage, 'honour' based violence (HBV), female genital mutilation (FGM), the impact of immigration policies on women in abusive relationships, and the implications of fundamentalism for women.

In 2008 the SBS fought a decision by Ealing Council to withdraw their funding on the grounds that they contravened the Race Relations Act by excluding white women. The council argued that black and minority women did not need a specialist service and that all women should be provided for under a single body. SBS argued that this 'view failed to take account of the unequal social, economic and cultural context which makes it difficult, if not impossible, for black and minority women to access outside help or seek information about their rights'. In supporting their appeal, Lord Justice Moses argued that the council had failed to appreciate both the specific experience of domestic abuse amongst black and minority women and its under-reporting. Lord Justice Moses stated:

> An equal society protects and promotes equality, real freedom and substantive opportunity to live in the ways people value and would choose so that everyone can flourish. An equal society recognises people's different needs, situations and goals and removes the barriers that limit what people can do and can be.

> Lord Justice Moses quoting the Chairman of the Equalities Review in The Final Report Fairness and Freedom (2007) (*Kaur and Shah v London Borough of Ealing* [2008] EWHC 2062 (Admin) CO/3880/2008)

⮕ Stop and Think

1. What are the concerns of black feminists in relation to the wider feminist movement?
2. How do race, culture, religion, language, and immigration status impact on black and minority women's experience of violence and ability to access support?

Post-colonial feminism

The concerns of black feminism are shared by post-colonial feminism. Post-colonial feminists challenge the tendency of 'Western' feminists to regard their own societies as developmental models with norms that are to be aspired to. Post-colonial feminism emphasizes the need to understand and account for the ways in which racism and colonialism have affected and continue to affect non-white non-Western women across the world. In particular it highlights how the Euro-centric bias of feminism marginalizes and 'others' non-Western women. Mohanty (1991) argues that this constructs an idea of the 'third world woman' as victim, powerless and voiceless. Post-colonial feminists therefore work to highlight the agency of women in the developing world, particularly in relation to indigenous women's struggles and movements. This approach therefore prioritizes non-Western feminist thought and incorporates this into a more holistic understanding of feminism on an international scale.

The focus on non-Western women's movements has highlighted how these are often intertwined with nationalism and other representations of identity, such as Islam. For example, feminism in the Arab region emerged in the context of Arab nationalist and independence movements, with women leading and participating in the demonstrations against colonial rule and occupation. Islamic feminists advocated for women's rights, gender equality, and social justice within an Islamic framework. Treacher and Shukrallah (2005) argue that while nationalism and anti-Western feeling are a mobilizing factor in 'Islamic Feminism' and that feminists have been recognized in their fight against imperial and colonial powers, they can be overlooked in the struggle for their own gender-based demands. Conflicts emerge in the discourse and debates within Islamic feminism in relation to the expectations placed on women, such as dress and behaviour. While some feminists regard such expectations as repressive and systematic subordination, others utilize the discourse of rights to legitimize women's own choices to comply with cultural and religious codes.

Feminism as a global movement?

The analysis of feminism as an international or global movement brings together the various elements of the discussion of ideology and the differing feminist positions. The first International Women's Day was called at the second International Conference of Socialist Women in 1910. The date 8 March was chosen to commemorate a massive demonstration of women trade unionists in New York on that date in 1908, demanding political rights for working women. The event continues into the present day, drawing in activists and events across the world.

The concerns of the feminist movement have become ever more prominent at a global level, particularly in the work of organizations such as the United Nations. The impact of feminist ideology and movements is seen in the central place women and gender issues now occupy in development policy and debate, with international agreements and declarations which reflect and support the concerns of liberal feminists in particular. For example the Millennium Development Goals and Sustainable Development Goals have an explicit focus on gender, while the World Bank reports of 2012 and 2014 were entitled *Gender Equality and Development*, and *Voice and Agency: Empowering Women and Girls for Shared Prosperity*. Here gender equality and female empowerment are regarded as the 'smart economics' of socio-economic development (see Case Study 9.5). This liberal feminist approach links economic prosperity, rationality, and the role of the individual woman within an emancipatory project for gender. Karim (2013) argues that this depended on a stereotyped idea of the poor woman in the Global South as 'thrifty, hardworking, entrepreneurial, and a good manager of resources'.

The 2012 *World Development Report: Gender Equality and Development* argued that

> gender equality is a core development objective in its own right. But greater gender equality is also smart economics, enhancing productivity and improving other development outcomes, including prospects for the next generation and for the quality of societal policies and institutions. Economic development is not enough to shrink all gender disparities—corrective policies that focus on persisting gender gaps are essential.
>
> (World Bank 2012: xiii)

These corrective policies primarily focused on education, health promotion, and political representation.

This explicit focus on women has been characterized as the 'gendering' of development or an 'add women and stir' approach that both presents a stereotyped and universalized idea of women in the Global South and prescribes a solution to their poverty based on neo-liberal self-help principles. Critics argue that this is an opportunistic attempt to appropriate the language of feminism to justify the extension of a particularly Western form of capitalism to places that were formerly beyond its reach. Campbell (2014) argues this is the 'lie' of neo-liberalism. 'Beware the liberation language of global capitalism: it rules the world, and it deploys the language of freedom, choice and competition to oust solidarity, co-operative creativity and equality'.

Case Study 9.5 Microcredit and the empowered female entrepreneur

Microcredit, the provision of unsecured small loans (typically $10) to the poor, first came to prominence in the 1980s. Hailed as an innovative form of development financing, its novelty was that it provided access to financial provision to those normally excluded from traditional banking. Often the lending is provided and managed via community groups, where women jointly borrow and are collectively responsible for the loan and its repayment. The originators of this form of development finance in Bangladesh in the mid 1980s were awarded the Nobel Peace Prize in 2006.

Microcredit is often targeted at poor women, in the belief that by having access to their own source of credit they will create businesses and generate income, which in turn will empower them. While microcredit and microfinance (which encompasses a broader range of financial provision such as insurance) have been celebrated as innovative approaches to economic development and female empowerment, the results have been mixed. Although there has been some anecdotal evidence of success, there is also evidence of women and families experiencing extreme hardship in trying to meet the requirements of repaying their loans, often at high interest rates. There is debate about the extent to which accessing loans will create entrepreneurs and new enterprises and whether access to financial resources change gendered social relations and patriarchal cultures. There is an argument that microcredit is a cynical attempt to appropriate the feminist cause to justify the extension of banks and financial institutions into new markets.

 Stop and Think

1. What is meant by the term empowerment and can it be achieved by access to resources and market participation?
2. In what ways does microcredit represent liberal feminism?

Is feminism obsolete? Backlash and post-feminism

The mainstreaming of gender has brought into question the continued relevance of feminism. In a backlash against feminism, some argue that equality has already been achieved and the continuation of feminist activism is now pushing the advantage of women over men, with policies such as affirmative action and positive discrimination, for example all-women short-lists, disadvantaging white, middle class men. Faludi (1991), however, argues that while women have made political and economic headway which has brought them closer to equal representation and pay, this is a distorted form of feminism. She states that feminism has been co-opted by commercialism, and within this distortion economic independence has become reformulated as buying power; self-determination has become the commodified self-improvement of physical appearance; and public agency has been transformed to publicity. McRobbie (2008) similarly posits that backlash and **post-feminism** have resulted from the co-optation of radical and feminist approaches by neo-liberal consumer culture.

Depoliticized 'post-feminism' is represented in the way in which femininity and womanhood have been recast in 'sexualised and patriarchal notions of autonomy and agency' for example via 'stripper heels', pole dancing lessons, and designer breasts and vaginas (O'Keefe 2014). O'Keefe (2014) argues that post-feminism's emphasis on freedom of choice and ability to consume have created a 'raunch culture' and the pornification of dominant culture which is portrayed as liberating and empowering for women. The emphasis on individualized choice was echoed in hooks' (2013) critique of Sandberg's Corporate 'Faux Feminism'. Faludi (1991) argues that the work of feminism is not complete and we have yet to find our way to the 'more meaningful goals of social change, responsible citizenship, the advancement of human creativity, the building of a mature and vital public world'. Our societies have not been fundamentally changed; instead women have 'used our gains to gild our shackles, but not break them'. Hooks (2013) reminds us that the visionary feminist goal is not of a woman running the world as is, but of women changing the world 'so that freedom and justice, the opportunity to have optimal well-being, can be equally shared by everyone'.

Summary

- Feminism is an evolving and varied movement and ideology. We have seen from its historical development that there has been an identifiable expansion of focus.

- While the demands of the first wave feminists coalesced around the call for political representation and suffrage, the second wave moved beyond this to a more holistic concern to liberate women from the social forces that constrain them in a variety of different contexts and ways.

- However, the long-standing critique that the movement has been dominated by the universalist and generalizing ideas and concerns of heterosexual, white, middle class Western women has seen the development of a variety of different feminisms and particularly a recourse to the politics of identity that exemplify the post second wave movement.

- The methods of the movement have also developed to incorporate technological innovation to challenge sexism and inequality and to build cyberfeminist networks around the world.

- While the gains of the feminist movement are palpable and represented by reforms and recognition at a variety of different levels, from the family through to the global level, the notion that we have moved to a stage where feminism is no longer relevant is strongly contested.

- While the principles of freedom and equality might be formally recognized and represented in economic and political rights in some parts of world, women's lives remain structured and conditioned by the relations in which they are located.

Review and discussion questions

1. To what extent has the emergence of ICTs strengthened feminism and has this fundamentally changed the movement?

2. In what ways does neo-liberal capitalism shape gender relations and is there still a need for feminism?

3. Why is violence a key issue for feminism? What are the implied meanings of the terms 'gender-based violence' or 'male violence against women', and does it matter which term we use?

4. Why is trans-inclusion a key debate within feminism and what are the key issues related to this?

Research exercises

1. Access the World Bank's 2012 report *Gender Equality and Development,* and 2014 report *Voice and Agency: Empowering Women and Girls for Shared Prosperity.* Outline the key reasons why women are identified as central to economic development and the type of development policies that are particularly aimed at them. Evaluate the ways in which this

   a. relies on gendered stereotypes

   b. represents 'smart economics'

   c. is a representation of liberal feminism

   d. could empower women

2. In 2010 the French government made it illegal for anyone to cover their faces in public, in effect refusing women's right to wear the burqa. This was subsequently upheld by the European Court of Human Rights (ECtHR). Research both the decision by the French government and the decision by the ECtHR and answer the following.

   a. What is the justification for this decision?

   b. What has been the response by the Muslim community?

   c. What arguments do women use in relation to their choice to wear a burqa?

   d. To what extent can this decision and the response be understood from a post-colonial feminist perspective?

Further reading

Mackay (2015) gives an excellent historic and analytical account of the development of feminism, particularly in the UK, from a radical feminist perspective. Federici (2012) is a collection of essays, written between 1975 and 2010, by a leading Marxist feminist. The book is organized in three parts: 'Theorising Housework', 'Globalisation', and 'Social Reproduction and Reproducing the Commons'. This includes an exploration of the theorization of social reproduction, the wages for housework debate, and the International Women's Movement. Mohanty, Russo, and Torres (1991) provides a series of chapters that discusses of the post-colonial feminist and women of colour debates.

References

Amos, V. and Parmar, P. (1984), 'Challenging Imperial Feminism', *Feminist Review*, Vol. 17.

Barrett, M. and McIntosh, M. (2005), 'Ethnocentrism and Socialist-Feminist Theory', *Feminist Review*, Vol. 80.

BEASLEY, C. (1999), *What is Feminism?* St. Leonards: Allen and Unwin.

BEAUVOIR, S. DE (1989) [1952], *The Second Sex*, London: Vintage Books/Random House.

BELL, K. (2009), 'A Feminists Argument on How Sex Work Can Benefit Women', *Inquiries Journal*, Vol. 1, No. 11, http://www.inquiriesjournal.com/articles/28/a-feminists-argument-on-how-sex-work-can-benefit-women

CAMPBELL, B. (2014), 'After Neo-liberalism: The Need for a Gender Revolution', in S. Hall, D. Massey, and M. Rustin (eds), *After Neo-liberalism? The Kilburn Manifesto*, London: Lawrence Wishart.

CRENSHAW, K. (1991), 'Mapping the Margins: Intersectionality, Identity Politics, and Violence Against Women of Color', *Stanford Law Review*, Vol. 43, pp. 1241–99.

ELIAS, J. (2013), 'Davos Woman to the Rescue of Global Capitalism: Postfeminst Politics and Competitiveness Promotion at the World Economic Forum', *International Political Sociology*, No. 7.

EVENING STANDARD (2015), 'Charlotte Proudman: "I am Not a Man-Hating Feminazi." Barrister Explains Why she Exposed Lawyer's "Sexist" LinkedIn Message', *Evening Standard*, 10 September 2015.

EVERYDAY SEXISM (no date), *The Everyday Sexism Project*, http://everydaysexism.com

FALUDI, S. (1991), *Backlash: The Undeclared War Against American Women*, New York: Three Rivers Press.

FEDERICI, S. (2004), *The Caliban and the Witch*, Brooklyn: Autonomedia.

FEDERICI S. (2012), *Revolution at Point Zero: Housework. Reproduction and Feminist Struggle*, Oakland: PM Press.

FEMEN (no date), *About Us*, http://femen.org

FRIEDAN, B. (1963), *The Feminine Mystique*, New York: W. W. Norton.

GAARD, G. AND GRUEN, L. (1993), 'Ecofeminism: Toward Global Justice and Planetary Health', *Nature*, Vol. 2, pp. 1–35.

GREER, G. (1970), *The Female Eunuch*, London: MacGibbon and Kee.

THE GUARDIAN (2005), 'The Day the Women Went on Strike', 18 October 2005.

GUNARATNUM, Y. (2014), 'Black British Feminisms: Many Chants', *Feminist Review* 108, 1.

HOOKS, B (1982), *Ain't I a Woman? Black Women and Feminism,* Boston: South End Press.

HOCHSCHILD, A. and MACHUNG, A. (1989), *The Second Shift: Working Families and the Revolution at Home*, New York: Penguin Books.

HOOKS, B. (2013), *Dig Deep: Beyond Lean In*, http://www.thefeministwire.com/2013/10/17973/

THE INDEPENDENT (2015), 'Delhi Bus Rapist Blames Dead Victim for Attack because "Girls are Responsible for Rape"', 2 March 2015.

KARIM, L. (2013), 'NGOs, Neoliberalism, and Women in Bangladesh', *The Scholar and Feminist Online*, No. 11.1–11.2, http://sfonline.barnard.edu/gender-justice-and-neoliberal-transformations/ngos-neoliberalism-and-women-in-bangladesh/

KOYAMA, E. (2001), The Transfeminist Manifesto, http://eminism.org/readings/pdf-rdg/tfmanifesto.pdf

LEEDS REVOLUTIONARY FEMINIST GROUP (1981), *Love Your Enemy? The Debate between Heterosexual Feminism and Political Lesbianism*, London: Onlywomen Press.

LERNER, G. (1988), *The Creation of Patriarchy*, Oxford: Oxford University Press.

LORDE, A. (1984), *Sister Outsider,* Berkeley, CA: Crossing Press.

MACKAY, F. (2014), 'Reclaiming Revolutionary Feminism', *Feminist Review*, Vol. 106.

MACKAY, F. (2015), *Radical Feminism*, London: Palgrave.

MAIGUASHCA, B. (2014), '"They're Talkin' bout a Revolution": Feminism, Anarchism and the Politics of Social Change in the Global Justice Movement', *Feminist Review*, Vol. 106.

MCROBBIE, S. (2008), *The Aftermath of Feminism: Gender, Culture and Social Change*, London: Sage.

MOHANTY, C. (1991), 'Under Western Eyes: Feminist Scholarship and Colonial Discourses', in C. Mohanty, A. Russo, and L. Torres (eds), *Third World Women and the Politics of Feminism*, Bloomington: Indiana University Press.

MOORE, S. (2013), 'I Don't Care if you were Born a Woman or Became One', *The Guardian*, 9 January 2013.

MOSES, LORD JUSTICE (2008), EWHC 2062 (admin) in the High Court of Justice Queen's Bench Division the Administrative Court, CO/3880/2008, London: Royal Court of Justice.

MUNRO, E. (2013), 'Feminism: A Fourth Wave?' *Political Insight*, Vol. 4, No. 2, pp. 22–5, http://www.psa.ac.uk/insight-plus/feminism-fourth-wave

O'KEEFE, T. (2014), 'My Body is my Manifesto! SlutWalk, FEMEN and Femmenist Protest', *Feminist Review*, 107.

OKOLOSIE, L. (2014), 'Beyond "Talking" and "Owning" Intersectionality', *Feminist Review*, Vol. 108.

PEARSON, R. AND ELSON, D. (2015), 'Transcending the Impact of the Financial Crisis in the United Kingdom: Towards a Plan F—a Feminist Economic Strategy', *Feminist Review*, Vol. 109.

PLATT, E. (2014), 'Comrades at War: The Decline and Fall of the Socialist Workers Party', *The New Statesman*, 20 May.

ROSENEIL, S. (1995), *Disarming Patriarchy: Feminism and Political Action at Greenham*, Buckingham: Open University Press.

SANDBERG, S. (2013), *Lean In: Women, Work and the Will to Lead*, London: WH Allen.

SOUTHALL BLACK SISTERS (SBS) (nd) 'About Us', available at http://www.southallblacksisters.org.uk/about/about-us

SWABY, N. (2014), 'Disparate in Voice, Sympathetic in Direction: Gendered Political Blackness and the Politics of Solidarity', *Feminist Review*, Vol. 108.

TEPE-BELFRAGE, D. (2015), 'The New Materialism: Re-claiming a Debate from a Feminist Perspective', *Capital and Class.* Vol. 40, No. 2, pp. 305–26.

TREACHER, A. AND SHUKRALLAH, H. (2005), 'Editorial: The Realm of the Possible: Middle Eastern Women in Political and Social Spaces', *Feminist Review*, Vol. 80.

WALKER, A (1983) *In Search of Our Mothers' Gardens: Womanist Prose,* New York: Harcourt, Brace, Jovanovich.

WORLD BANK (2012), *World Development Report: Gender Equality and Development*, New York: World Bank.

10

Environmentalism

Dorron Otter

OBJECTIVES

- Explain the origins of modern environmental thinking
- Assess the degree to which there is a coherent and distinctive Green ideology
- Critically assess the likelihood of the transition of Green ideas into effective policy

Introduction

Green is the colour used to label environmental thinking but, as we shall see, there is a range of different shades of Green thinking. For some these variations mean that environmentalism has simply added a Green dimension to existing ideologies. This is denied by Green thinkers and activists who argue that there is now a new ideological position of 'ecologism' which doesn't treat environmental problems as mere side effects of rapid industrial development but which sees a focus on progress as defined by economic growth as the central human existential problem.

There are some difficult analytical questions to consider when assessing the impact of Green ideology. Meadowcroft argues that there are four chief challenges that confront us when judging the relevance of the Green political perspectives in the twenty-first century:

> first determining the point at which it gelled into an independent ideological approach; second, understanding how greens relate to the traditional left/right political continuum; third, assessing the place of the environmental critique within the green worldview; and fourth considering diversity within the family of green approaches
>
> (Meadowcroft 2001)

One critical question for Green thinking is itself an existential one. To what extent can we identify a distinctive ideological position emanating from concerns about the environment? The other key questions centre around the possible tensions that exist within Green political philosophy and action and the extent to which clear and credible practical policy proposals can be developed.

In order to address these questions we will first explore the origins of the rise of the environment as an issue in relation to global and national political systems and assess the point at which it might be possible to identify the emergence of a distinct new Green approach. The second section of the chapter will seek to explore if there is a distinctive core of Green thinking or the degree to which other ideologies have incorporated environmental issues into their conceptual and policy frameworks. We will do this by examining the range of environmental thinking and the degree to which there may be tensions within Green thinking. We will then seek to identify the embedded critique, ideal, and programme that defines Green thinking and assess the extent to which this new ideology is both distinctive and credible. In the final section we will explore the impact that Green policies have had in shaping the policy agenda and we will conclude by examining the main challenges that face the consolidation of Green thinking and action.

 Stop and Think

How central are environmental concerns to you in terms of ordering your political priorities?

Origins of environmental thinking

Thinking about the relationship between humans and the natural environment is as old as human life on earth itself. We can see evidence of this at the spiritual level in relation to ancient religions as well as in all modern global religions. One key area of theological debate is in defining the role that humans have in relation to the environment. Are we 'masters' of the environment implying that humans have the natural right to use the environment as an instrument to satisfy our needs or are we 'stewards' with the responsibility to 'safeguard' it?

The growth of 'industrial ideologies' and the pursuit of economic growth

As industrialization in Europe rapidly developed, concerns were expressed about the impact of industrialization but it was the possible adverse social effects or obstacles to economic progress and prosperity that were the main focus of attention.

In the eighteenth century Adam Smith laid the essential foundations of liberal political economy in arguing that the newly developing market economy would lead to boundless economic growth for the benefit of all. In the nineteenth century in

Britain it was clear that the 'opulence' that Smith predicted was not being spread widely across society as a whole. Malthus argued that the problem was that population growth would always rise at a faster rate than economic growth, so leading to rises in the costs of living and increasing the poverty especially of the 'lower classes' (Malthus 1798). As we shall see later this 'Malthusian pessimism' has been picked up by some in the environmental movement in the twentieth and twenty-first centuries. For Malthus the population problem would either be resolved through 'natural' checks and balances such as famine, disease, or war or it could be brought under control through people practising moral restraint to control family size. It was Malthus's friend but intellectual antagonist Ricardo who converted conservative pessimism to the view that universal free trade was the key to the ability to sustain economic growth and prosperity for all.

As the nineteenth century progressed it was clear to a wide range of social reformers that this growth was not being universally shared and was having a severe detrimental effect on the living conditions of the urban working classes, laying the basis for the birth of both the 'new liberalism' as well as the development of socialism. Throughout the nineteenth and twentieth centuries an underpinning core concern for all ideological positions was not only the means to achieve growth, especially in view of the relationship between markets and states, but also how best to distribute the rewards of such growth so that all could benefit, if not equally, at least in such a way that that poverty could be reduced.

Another side effect of industrialization emerged in the form of the pollution that it created, and from the nineteenth century onwards governments attempted to control this through anti-pollution agencies. In addition, even in countries such as the USA, Canada, and Australia—with extensive natural resources—there was an acknowledgement that there needed to be more rational planning to harvest these resources to maximize economic benefit and so a number of natural resource management agencies were developed. However, it was not until the 1970s that leading economic powers began to bring these piecemeal developments together into an integrated national environmental policy. Dryzek characterizes this approach as being one of 'administrative rationalism'. There was a recognition of the need for the state to control markets to ensure environmental problems were minimized but always the emphasis was on 'light touch' regulation. All too often attempts to control pollution or safeguard resources were undermined by powerful business lobbying, referred to as '**regulatory capture**' (Dyrzek 2013).

In the first half of the twentieth century, the mainstream ideologies of liberalism, conservatism, and nationalism appeared to have broken down and it was the lack of economic growth that was seen as the main problem in the heartlands of Western capitalism, especially when contrasted with the spectacular industrial growth and success of Soviet-style socialism and then with the rise of fascism in central and southern Europe (as well as right wing regimes in Latin America). Whatever the ideological standpoint people took, one common thread was that the economic goal of countries was to try to either restore or pursue economic growth.

 Stop and Think

What are the obstacles that might lie in the way of effective state control of environmental threats?

The rising critique of economic growth

After the Second World War the mass consumption/mass production model that was developed in the USA was adopted in Western Europe. At the national level this economic environment was underpinned by social welfare states and the development of more state interventionist approaches to macroeconomic management. National economies were integrated within a global economic environment underpinned by the three supranational global governance institutions of the International Monetary Fund, the World Bank, and the General Agreement on Tariffs and Trade.

For the rest of the world there were three choices:

- to try to replicate the 'first world' model of the West;
- to go down the route of the 'second world' model of communism and rapid industrialization directed and planned by a strong centralized government;
- to try and pursue distinctive 'third world' models which acknowledged the structural differences between 'advanced' (developed) and 'backward' (less developed) countries and therefore to pursue an industrial strategy aimed at developing markets but initially involving a more active state led industrial policy.

Common to all visions was the belief that it was industrialization that was the key to prosperity and in the postwar period the military arms and space race between the Soviet Union and the USA was mirrored by an economic race to see which system would prevail in terms of posting the highest rates of economic growth. By the end of the 1950s the 'American Dream' appeared well on the way to fulfilment whereas Soviet-style economic models of 'forced industrialization' through state planning were stagnating.

In Western Europe and the USA the 1960s saw the rise of modern feminism and a 'new left' approach which argued for greater social reform at home combined with support for the anti-imperial movements that had developed throughout the third word l and in the form of protests against the Vietnam War in particular. In the peace campaigns fuelled by the fears that Cold War would result in nuclear war was the explicit fear that the ability to harness the forces of nature was endangering life on the planet itself. Added to all these concerns was mounting evidence that economic growth was indeed in conflict with the environment, and people began to see the failure to consider this as 'ecocide'. There was a strong counter-cultural tendency amongst young people against the perceived rampant materialistic consumer culture of modern capitalism. This was accompanied by growing criticism of the rise of agribusiness in replacing traditional agriculture as well as the development of strong animal rights movements and the demand for vegetarian, vegan, and organic choices in relation to food.

In Eastern Europe there was a rise of dissident groups not only against the lack of political freedom generated by communist regimes, but also by the bitter irony of an economic system based on state-led industrialization that was failing to deliver prosperity while producing environmental catastrophes. From the developing world came the '**post-development**' school as a response to mounting evidence of the sacrifice of natural environments in the name of progress, pressure on indigenous tribal areas and traditional peasant agriculture, as well as the undoubted environmental problems caused by rapid urbanization.

Natural science and economics

Green thinking has been heavily influenced by the development of the natural sciences in relation to the environment and the concomitant response from within the social science community. In 1866 the German zoologist Ernst Haekel coined the term 'ecology' to describe the relationship between animals (including humans) and the natural environment. Ecology has since developed as the branch of biology that analyses this interrelationship between living organisms and the physical environment (including other living organisms). It is simple to outline the ecological problem. All living organisms need to extract the resources that we need for survival from the physical environment. Human beings have a distinctive role in that all other species use resources only for the purposes of survival and reproduction whereas we, in the pursuit of economic growth, place ever higher demands on resource extraction. Not all resources can be replaced, especially the fossil fuels on which so much of the industrial world's energy supplies currently depend. Many of our productive processes result in pollution or other forms of ecological damage and while nature itself can provide ways of neutralizing these harmful by-products in the form of 'sinks' such as the oceans, forests, and plants that can absorb the pollutants, the rising acidification of seas, deforestation, and loss of biodiversity are all undermining this.

Rachel Carson's *The Silent Spring* was published in 1962 and she 'quite self-consciously decided to write a book calling into question the paradigm of scientific progress that defined postwar American culture' (Lytle 2007). A biologist, Carson had worked for the US Fish and Wildlife Service and was well aware of the danger of regulatory capture and for many years had been concerned about the use of pesticides in agriculture and the effects on human beings through links with cancers, and on wildlife. This book had a huge influence on the grassroots environmental movement in the USA, resulting in the ban of the pesticide DDT (Dichlorodiphenyltrichloroethane).

Case Study 10.1 The tragedy of the commons

Garrett Hardin's article 'The Tragedy of the Commons' published in the journal *Nature* in 1968 is also widely seen as being important for the growing environmental movement. Hardin and Carson were biologists and in them we can see the beginnings of the transfer of the term 'ecologism' to its use as a term for a political ideology.

Hardin uses the analogy of common land which in medieval times was available to all as a source of additional land on which individual villagers could graze their animals. If this land was the individual property of one person that person would seek to preserve the fertility of the land and recognize that overuse or overgrazing would not be in their long-term individual interest and thus would be a responsible steward of the land. In the language of the economist there will be an 'optimal' point at which the farmer would cease to increase the amount of animals grazing on the land because s/he would not want to damage the long-run fertility of the land. However, 'The Tragedy of the Commons' is that, since no one owns the land, each individual will seek to maximize their own use of the land and they will do this by seeking to have all their own animals on the land. Collectively, in the long-run, the land will be become fundamentally degraded. This would not be a problem if wars and disease kept the numbers of humans and animals below the carrying capacity of the land but population growth will inevitably lead to this point being exceeded.

Hardin argued that this analogy can be generally applied to all the global natural resources available to humanity and that we face a long-term struggle to avoid overusing the earth's resources. Attempts to do so by enforcing private property rights, education, or regulation will all be doomed to failure unless we impose restrictions on individual freedoms, particularly in relation to reproduction.

Hardin echoes Malthus as his chief concern was population growth. He argued that its growth is exponential and will outstrip the 'carrying capacity' of the natural environment. For Hardin the proposition that self-interested individuals will promote the public interest in general is false and this is especially so in the specific case of sexual reproduction. Pollution of the environment is also a problem of the commons. It is cheaper for individuals to simply dump their wastes before paying for them to be cleaned and so we collectively foul our nests whilst pursuing individual self-interest.

 Stop and Think

How might we apply Hardin's 'Tragedy of the Commons' to other areas of environmental concern such as traffic congestion in urban areas?

Carson's popularity and public awareness of the fierce lobbying against her work led to a growing environmental movement in the USA (see Case Study 10.1) and recognition that piecemeal administrative rationalism with a focus simply on conservation would not be sufficient. In 1970 the US Environmental Protection Agency (EPA) was established. The role of the EPA was not only to try and undermine the lobbying of business interests: it was an explicitly anti-pollution body. Such anti-pollution agencies became common in many other advanced industrial countries.

In the last quarter of the twentieth century it is easy to identify across the developed first world a range of widely discussed threats. The main threats were seen to be:

- deforestation
- habitat destruction
- water insecurity
- overhunting
- overfishing
- the effects of introducing non-native species
- population
- global climate change

Whilst some today feel that there needs to be a primary or at least significant role attributed to population growth as the main source of environmental damage, for most people it is the pace of economic growth that is the problem.

It is perhaps not surprising that this shift in focus away from biology and population to resource use was occurring in the development of economic thinking and led to the formation of a distinct school of ecological economics. Georgescu-Roegen developed a synthesis of economics with the natural laws of physics and the first two laws of thermodynamics in particular. The first of these states that in closed physical systems energy is neither created nor destroyed but it simply changes its form and the second, or 'entropy law', states that as energy is used it is transformed but in such a way as to be degraded. If these laws are applied to production and consumption the implication of converting resources into products is clear. Using energy to produce goods does not create anything additional in terms of resources but simply transforms natural resources into things that are then consumed by people. In the process not only do we deplete these limited energy resources but we also degrade theme in the form of pollution and other forms of environmental damage (Georgescu-Roeden 1971).

Boulding (1966) evoked the image of 'Spaceship Earth' to argue that we had moved away from an open economy system, where resources could be seen as limitless, to a closed economy, where there was an urgent need to acknowledge the limits to resources. In pre-industrial societies human beings could always be secure in the knowledge that if resources became scarce they could move across frontiers to find new ones. However, in the modern age we face the problem of closed economic systems. Since our material prosperity relies on energy use and energy resources are limited there is thus a fundamental problem of economic growth (Boulding 1966). Since the 1970s these ideas have been most associated with Herman Daly's work on steady state economics and ideas of 'de-growth' and the journal *Ecological Economics* which was established in 1989 (Daly 1991).

Limits to growth and the rise of Green politics

The Club of Rome, a think tank formed in 1968 to find answers to global environmental problems, commissioned a group of scientists from Massachusetts Institute of Technology to use computer models to test a range of possible environmental scenarios. Led by Donella Meadows, the *Limits to Growth* report was published in 1972 (see http://www.clubofrome.org/?p=375).

The report made no specific predictions but its findings were simple: exponential growth in a finite closed system if unchecked would lead to collapse based on the simulations of estimates of resource use, agricultural productivity, and the ability of the planet to absorb pollution (Meadows et al. 1972). While the report came under sustained attack from many critics, both for what were seen to be the unrealistic assumptions made in the model and for its undue pessimism, it did have a large impact on global public opinion.

Reflecting back on the nature of this impact, Donella Meadows argued there were three broad conclusions from the report.

- If nothing is done now there will be a global environmental collapse.
- However, it would be possible to work towards a 'stationary state' in which 'the basic material needs of each person on earth are satisfied and each person has an equal opportunity to realise his or her human potential'.
- But that if we are to choose this course then we had better start building this world now! (Meadows et al. 1992).

It also appeared to be clear that not only would environmental policy need to be taken at the national level but that, given the '**trans-boundary**' nature of so many problems, a global environmental policy would be needed.

In Stockholm in 1972 the first ever global conference on the environment explored the phenomenon of 'acid rain' caused by the collective emissions of sulphur dioxide from a range of industrial and transport systems and its effects on lakes and forests in northern Europe. This led to the formation of the United Nations Environment Programme which in essence mirrored the US environment programme at the global level. It was acknowledged that if actions were to be taken to deal with 'global commons' issues then what was needed was effective global cooperation. In 1986 radioactivity from the Chernobyl nuclear explosion covered most of western Europe and the recognition of the role of chlorofluorocarbons (CFCs) in creating a thinning of the ozone layer reinforced the need for global action.

The World Commission for Economic Development (WCED) was established in 1983 by the United Nations to research the relationship between the global environment and economic development. Popularly referred to as the Brundtland Commission after its chair Gro Harlem Brundtland (Norway's Prime Minister in the 1980s and 1990s), it published *Our Common Future* in 1987. This report brought together the themes of limits to growth with the need for global cooperation to deal with the problems of growth (WCED 1987). This report also developed the most widely used definition of 'sustainable development', the most cited part of which is as follows:

> Sustainable Development is development that meets the needs of the present without compromising the ability of future generations to meet their own needs.
>
> (WCED 1987: 43)

This statement clearly shows the commitment that is made here to ensuring **inter-generational equity**—in other words that our actions today should not undermine the standards of living of the future. However the full statement continues as follows:

> it contains within it two key concepts: the concept of 'needs', in particular the essential needs of the world's poor, to which overriding priority should be given; and the idea of limitations imposed by the state of technology and social organization on the environment's ability to meet present and future needs.
>
> (WCED 1987: 43)

In this second statement we have then a call to consider **intra-generational equity** in a way that many of the left would argue is indeed the 'overriding priority'. However, in focusing on technology and social organization this raises the possibility that growth is not simply limited by resource use or pollution caused and that technology and political change could enable growth to continue in such a way as to have an eco-friendly but essentially 'business as usual' (**BAU**) model of capitalism.

Embedded within this definition, then, we can identify a tension between competing ideological perspectives as to the policy implications of sustainable development. The burgeoning environmental movement tended to focus on the first part of the definition and its emphasis on inter-generational equity. However, as we shall see later the nod in the direction of emphasizing the needs of the poor and the need to consider altering current forms of social organization (intra-generational equity) readily chimed with the primary concerns of socialism. Furthermore, the reference to the limitations of technology opens the door to the belief that environmental impacts could be minimized through technological fixes.

 Stop and Think

Is Brundtland saying that the problem is that resources are limited, are poorly distributed across social groups, or are limited only because of a lack of effective technology? How clear a definition of sustainable development do you think this is?

The Brundtland Report was also was highly influential in framing the context of the 1992 'Earth Summit', held for the first time in Rio de Janeiro, which developed 'Agenda 21'. It was hoped that Agenda 21 would be a comprehensive programme to deal with local, national, and global environmental problems (see https://sustainabledevelopment.un.org/content/documents/Agenda21.pdf).

Accompanying this rapidly evolving global political agenda was a growing environmental movement from below. A feature of this movement was frustration that central and indeed regional and local governments were not up to the task of dealing with environmental concerns and that new forms of decentralized political action were required. One example of such thinking can be seen in the publication of 'A Blueprint for Survival', originally a special edition of *The Ecologist* journal established by Edward Goldsmith in 1970. This book, co-edited by a range of prominent scientists, was produced in advance of the Stockholm conference in direct response to the Meadows et al. (1972) report. The book concludes that the only way to deal with the 'irreversible disruption' predicted by the *Limits to Growth* report is the development of small decentralized and post-industrial societies.

We can see here the transition from scientific evidence-based research into the fundamental problems of economic growth to a call for a distinctive new approach to organize people politically to challenge this system and recognize the need for a new philosophy.

> Such a movement cannot hope to succeed unless it has previously formulated a new philosophy of life, whose goals can be achieved without destroying the environment, and a precise and comprehensive programme for bringing about the sort of society in which it can be implemented
>
> (Goldsmith et al. 1972)

 Stop and Think

Why is it argued that dealing with environmental problems requires attention to be paid to the most appropriate spatial level of governance?

Small is Beautiful

Schumacher's *Small is Beautiful* (Schumacher 1974) perhaps best brings together the economic analysis of the dangers of ignoring the limits to growth and the need to develop a new philosophical way of thinking and a programme of action revolving around new forms of decentralized patterns of organization and ownership. For Schumacher the fateful error of the late twentieth century was to believe that the '*problem of production*' had been solved. Part of Schumacher's argument is simply contained within the limits to growth discourse. However, where Schumacher sows the seed for the development of Green thinking, is in his belief that a Western industrial model has been developed globally. In his view, this model is one that sets human beings in opposition to the natural world and indeed is phrased in the language of a battle against nature which in the long run will result in our loss as resources become depleted.

In the 1950s Schumacher had spent time as an economic consultant in Burma where he encountered economies underpinned by communal self-reliant villages and a way of life heavily influenced by Buddhism. This experience sparked a keen interest in village societies and economic organization in South Asia and across the third world. It also brought him into contact with other Eastern religious traditions and the ideas of Gandhi with his focus on political methods of non-violence and the need for strong local village-based societies. Schumacher concluded that the basis of these religious traditions was not simply material well-being but also spiritual health. Once well-being is expressed in these wider terms, it inevitably has major implications for the types of economic system that need to be developed in terms of organization and ownership.

While initially he was an atheist (at the time of writing *Small Is Beautiful* he had become a Catholic), Schumacher invited his readers to pursue the logic of seeing the purpose of economics in the context of Buddhism—but he was keen to argue that other religious faiths could equally be used in the same way.

A focus on increasing material well-being for a 'Buddhist economist' would be

> excessively irrational: since consumption is merely a means to human wellbeing the aim should be to obtain maximum wellbeing with the minimum of consumption

(Schumacher 1974: 47–8)

and ignoring the resource limits to growth would be 'parasitical' as we would be using up the natural capital on which our futures depend in the form of short-term income. For Schumacher any business that used up its capital as income will be sure to fail.

From this perspective human beings have become estranged from nature and the presumption that ultimately all human beings will attain universal prosperity and that there will be 'enough to go round' has to be questioned. This is a goal that can never be attained either in the long run, because no one will ever be able to define what constitutes enough, or in the short run, because we are already facing the problem of the limits to growth. Furthermore the reality of growth-orientated models is that they create vast gaps between poor and rich societies that undermine the prospects for peace by creating the potential for violence through competition for resources.

 Stop and Think

What might the link be between the alleged violence against nature and a corresponding violence between different social groups?

Is there a coherent and distinct form of Green ideology–the birth of ecologism?

Small is Beautiful is very much the work of an economist whose critique of industrialism takes him on a search for a deeper philosophy with which to challenge the ethics of materialism, but his conclusions in terms of solutions still place him within a reformist rather than a radical agenda. In this section we will investigate the claim that there has been the emergence of a more radical distinctive Green ideology.

Deep Ecology

Arne Naess was professor of philosophy at the University of Oslo and was influenced by the thinking of Spinoza and Gandhi. He lived his ideals as an 'ecological field worker' not only by immersing himself in the wilds of Norway as an avid mountaineer but also in his environmental activism, and he is most associated with developing the term 'Deep Ecology'.

At the core of his thinking is the belief in what he termed 'the universal right to self-unfolding and the correlative intrinsic value of every life form' and he used the term 'Ecosophy' to describe his philosophical approach. For Naess humans are defined by their relationship to the natural world or 'Ecosphere' and have no separate identity outside of this. Nature can be seen as a constant process of survival for all physical and biological systems and evolution does not stay still but creates a dynamic expansion and modification of these systems. He argued that all life on earth has the right to live but that there is a special responsibility for humans.

> The emergence of human ecological consciousness is a philosophically important idea: a life form has developed on Earth which is capable of understanding and appreciating its relations with all other life forms and to the Earth as a whole.
>
> (Naess 1989)

The implication of this is clear. If all forms of life have a 'universal right to bloom and blossom' then how do humans live out their relationships with nature?

Naess explicitly rejected the notion that it might be possible for us to devise rules to govern our use of nature on the basis of relative levels of intrinsic value as he asserts that all species have the same intrinsic value. When human beings are exploiting nature to ensure our survival we should not delude ourselves that we are doing this on the basis of our superiority over less intrinsically valuable species whether these be animals or plants. The guiding principle always has to be being able to justify our action in relation not to the satisfaction of our egotistical needs but to the needs of the ecosphere. The task is for human beings to form 'a togetherness with nature' that leads to the greatest benefit of the ecosphere. To do this he developed the term 'Deep Ecology' in contradistinction to the 'shallow ecology' of acknowledging environmental problems but still defining progress in terms of human material well-being.

For Naess there are seven principles that underpin the Deep Ecology Movement and form the basis of its distinctive 'Ecosophy' (Naess 1983). Taken as a whole these principles form a view that human beings are not apart from nature in the sense of standing above or outside of it but are intimately a part of the ecosphere. This implies that rather than seeing nature as something to be controlled and dominated, we need to live in partnership with nature. All animals and humans need to do some killing, exploitation, and suppression of the natural environment to survive but for humans this needs to be done in recognition of a deep respect for the diversity and symbiosis of all life forms. Naess explicitly argues for human social organization to be based on equal access to resources for all groups and in particular he argued that particular attention must be paid to the resource gaps between the developed and developing world. Deep Ecology is concerned with issues of pollution and depletion of resources but does not see these in isolation as single issues in the way that shallow Greens do. Given the complexity of our relationship to the ecosphere, we need to develop an ecological programme which is holistic rather than dissolving into action to deal with specific environmental issues and this also has implications for the spatial level at which action needs to be taken. Naess argued that there is a need for local self-government, self-sufficiency, and decentralization. Not only are there strong environmental efficiency arguments for local autonomy—as local sourcing of products and shorter supply chains are more resource efficient—but reducing layers of political decision-making can give greater voice to local communities.

 Stop and Think

In what ways does 'Deep Ecology' differ from 'shallow' environmental thinking?

Earth First! was established in 1979 (http://www.earthfirst.org/links.htm) and Dave Foreman, one of its co-founders, explicitly placed the natural diversity of the earth ahead of human interests and asserted that Deep Ecology was the guiding philosophy of the movement.

For Foreman, ecological activism is a necessity if the world is to change and therefore '**monkey wrenching**' or 'ecotage' (environmental sabotage) is a legitimate tactic. This involves active protest and resistance to potentially environmentally damaging developments and in that sense people need to act as eco-warriors (see Case Study 10.2). The term is drawn from Abbey's *The Monkey Wrench Gang*, a novel about a small gang of environmental activists in the south-western states of the USA (Abbey 1975).

This has led many critics to accuse such activist movements of having taken Deep Ecology in a fundamentally misanthropic direction and, certainly in Foreman's pronouncements that there are too many people on the earth or that in drought and famines the loss of biodiversity is even more tragic than human loss of life, there is a strong case to answer. Accusations have been made that, at the extremes, the environmental activism of groups such as Earth First! and animal rights groups has descended into what might even be described as eco-fascism.

As we shall see later there are many within the wider Green movement and outside it who see in Deep Ecology thinking a fundamentally hostile antagonism to any form of human action that impacts on the natural environment. Not only is this seen as an attack on basic human rights but that its forms of political protest and insistence (that the only true bearers of the Green flame must adopt radical forms of Green lifestyle) will do little to build the political support required to enact the reforms needed to safeguard Green values.

 Stop and Think

Do you think that environmental action as advocated by Foreman would be a help or a hindrance to advancing an ecological agenda?

Case Study 10.2 Monkey wrenching (or putting a spanner in the works)

There is a huge variety of forms of environmental campaigns and organizations. At one end, there are groups who derive their philosophy and approach from the idea of 'monkey wrenching' and the need for direct action based on decentralized modes of organization. At the other end of the spectrum, there are groups who have developed large environmental campaigning organizations with considerable public support and financial resources.

The Earth Liberation Front (ELF) and Earth First! Groups emphasize the need for direct action to promote environmental awareness (see http://www.earthfirst.org/ and http://earth-liberation-front.com/) and within such movements there is a clear ethical debate about what would constitute legitimate direct action and if there is ever a case to move beyond direct acts aimed at property to actions against people.

Dryzek argues that it was after the 2001 attacks on the World Trade Center and Pentagon in the USA that the FBI began to label radical environmentalists as being eco-terrorists. This was then used as the justification for the re-classification of some forms of direct action by the ELF as being terrorist acts rather than vandalism. However, there have been cases where the line between intended acts against property and people has been blurred. One widely reported tactic was 'tree-spiking' where metal spikes are hammered into trees to try and prevent logging by damaging the chainsaw blades. In 1987 there was a reported case of a logger who was seriously injured as a result of tree-spiking and such incidents have reinforced the view that Deep Green thinking inevitably leads to such extreme acts of terrorism. Critics from the right see this form of protest as deliberately involving violence towards people, but equally critics from the left can argue that at the very least it represents a fundamentally flawed view of the world which sees human beings as the fundamental threat to nature. For many within the wider environmental movement itself such extreme acts themselves are simply that. The actions of extremists that spill over into either intended or unintended violence against people are not to be confused with legitimate forms of direct and indirect protest to bring environmental issues to the fore.

A reaction to the rise in environmental action was the meting out of much longer jail sentences. One particular example Dryzek cites was a term of twenty-two years imprisonment for an activist who set fire to three sports utility vehicles (Dryzek 2013).

It is not only in the USA that the state takes such an interest in the activities of environmental movements. In the UK, environmental activist groups are under the surveillance of the police, the extent of which was brought to public attention with the revelation that undercover policemen had formed long-term relationships with female activists, in some cases fathering children, only to later vanish without trace (https://policespiesoutoflives.org.uk/the-case-overview/ and http://www.theguardian.com/uk-news/2015/nov/20/met-police-apologise-women-had-relationships-with-undercover-officers).

Where the line is drawn between legitimate environmental protest and illegal activity also became severely blurred with the sinking of Greenpeace's ship *Rainbow Warrior* in 1985. While at anchor in Auckland, New Zealand, and en route to protest against a French nuclear test in the Pacific the ship was sabotaged by the French secret services and sank. A photographer who had been on the vessel was drowned. Responsibility for this action was initially denied by the French government, but two French agents were arrested and convicted by the New Zealand authorities and sentenced to ten and seven years imprisonment for arson and manslaughter. They were released within two years having been placed under French custody under a UN brokered agreement. For Greenpeace

> [i]t was an instance when a government chose to respond to peaceful protest with deadly force. But peaceful protest has prevailed.
>
> (http://www.greenpeace.org/international/en/about/history/the-bombing-of-the-rainbow-war/)

 Stop and Think

Where would you draw the line between what constitutes legitimate and illegitimate forms of direct and indirect environmental protest?

Muddying the waters—the Greening of politics in general

Dobson argues that ecologism does indeed possess a distinctive core of central values and that these cannot be contested by other systems of thought (Dobson 1991).

While there is a clear belief that Deep Ecology is fundamentally different to single issue environmentalism, it is harder to reject the claim that far from being a universal new ideology, Green thinking as a separate ideological framework is not needed because its central values have been incorporated into existing ideological positions. One powerful critique of Green thinking is simply that Green ideas can be readily absorbed into existing ideological frameworks and that in fact there is not really any clear Green water separating Deep Green thinking from the shallow Green tinges that have now coloured traditional ideological positions.

Classical liberalism and neo-liberalism

While there are differences in emphasis between classical liberalism and neo-liberalism, at the heart of market liberalism there is an instinctive optimism that all economic problems can be solved by free markets and that the resulting growth will provide the resources to solve political problems (see Chapter 2). Dryzek labels this as a 'Promethean' approach. Prometheus, a god in ancient Greek mythology, stole fire from Zeus and in so doing freed human beings from being reliant on Zeus, giving them unlimited power over the earth.

Economists such as Beckerman, Simon, and Lomborg have mounted both an empirical and theoretical attack on the limits to growth approach and the ecological economics movement. They argue that if there were natural limits to resource exploitation then, as resources are increasingly used, prices would rise. However, empirically there is no evidence to support this, and the dire predictions of resources running out are not borne out in reality. The reason for this is that if resources do appear to be becoming exhausted then producers will respond in many ways: by seeking to discover new ones, developing substitutes by developing new technological solutions, improving resource efficiency, and developing new methods of disposing of pollution. Not only is ever-rising economic growth theoretically possible, in reality it is the necessary way of increasing human prosperity. Such views were given support by the development of the 'Environmental Kuznets Curve hypothesis' that sought to provide empirical evidence that as economies grew, while at first there would be environmental degradation, over time this would decrease as learning took place to use resources more efficiently and that greater wealth would enable resources to be deployed to rectify environmental damage. One movement that seeks to emphasize the ability of technology to 'fix' environmental problems is the eco-modernism movement (http://www.ecomodernism.org/).

Of course markets do fail but when they do there are a range of market solutions that can correct these failures. Taxes can be used to deter harmful environmental activities or subsidies to encourage environmentally favourable ones. There may well be a necessary role for governments in fostering scientific development and technological solutions and also in ensuring minimum environmental safeguards through environmental laws, regulations, and, where needed, environmental protection agencies. Here the fault lines lie between those liberals who will place their faith in the ability of bureaucratic agencies and regulations to address the harmful 'environmental side-effects' of growth (or what Dryzek refers to as 'Administrative Rationalism') and neo-liberals who have an inherent distaste of such interventions and have much greater faith that markets are only to be curtailed with care (what Dryzek labels as 'Economic Rationalism').

Green conservatism

Another attack on the claim for the need for a radical new Green distinctiveness comes from conservatism as exemplified by Scruton (2013). Scruton rejects the solution to environmental problems as lying in the hands of government through regulation as well as the neo-liberal faith in markets. He is also adamant that the answer does not lie in the radical solutions that emanate from the Green movement. It is conservatism that best diagnoses and treats these problems. Conservatism sees individuals loving their home environments and he describes this attachment as 'oikophilia' (from the Greek oiko which means house and from which we derive the word 'eco'). For Scruton, the left has been able to appropriate the claim to being oikophiles as the right has been too narrowly associated with free market liberalism. Scruton argues that while conservatives see markets and private property as a necessary condition to ensuring economic prosperity, this is not all they see. There is a need for representative government and to provide legal safeguards when markets do go wrong. There are strong historical and cultural traditions that underpin self-governing national and local communities which need to be respected and, above all, it is this local aspect of political organization that will be the best way to guarantee environmental security (see also the discussion of environmentalism in Chapter 3).

Eco-socialism

One of the biggest threats to the claim to the existence of a distinctive new Green ideology is that essentially the core of radical Green thinking is red. Greens are caricatured as being 'Watermelons' (green on the outside but red on the inside) (see Delingpole 2012). For Meadowcroft

> environmental issues are quintessentially distribution issues and this establishes a certain affinity with the left.
>
> (Meadowcroft 2001: 182)

There are many that would happily accept this and many members of the present day Green movement are indeed former socialists.

Eco-socialism and eco-Marxism emerged in western Europe from the counter-cultural revolutions of the 1960s and have been very influential in both France and Germany. Andre Gorz, who was born in Austria in 1923 but became a French citizen, is a good example of the fusion between Marxism and political ecology. Eco-socialists and eco-Marxists see the root cause of environmental crisis as being another manifestation of the inevitable crisis within capitalism. For Gorz, an irrational economic system has been created that keeps the majority of people working very long hours and yet at the same time excludes many from being able to do so. The lack of solidarity between those in regular full-time work and those relegated to the periphery undermines working class solidarity and the revolutionary potential of the working classes. At the top of society is a privileged elite who live on the profits that capitalism creates and who are forever wanting more and more to be produced. Capitalism then continues to pump out material possessions ultimately confronting the inevitable limits of resource capacity (Gorz 1989). For O'Connor, the ecological crisis will be the catalyst for revolutionary change (O'Connor 1988).

Gorz argues that this could come about in a more rationally organized society where work and material goods were shared more equally and where we demanded less material goods and shared the required working hours more equitably so that everyone had a better balance between leisure and work whilst maintaining ecological balance. Similarly Kovel and Lowy argue that eco-socialism can achieve the original goals of socialism in terms of emancipating people, not by pursuing the state bureaucratic methods of socialism as in the twentieth century, but by organizing production on the basis of needs predicated on 'ecological harmony' (Kovel and Lowy 2001).

Social ecology

In the 1980s one of the most vitriolic attacks on Deep Ecology came not from outside the Green movement but from inside. It came in the form of Social Ecology which is most closely associated with the American anarchist Murray Bookchin's Left Green movement and the Institute for Social Ecology he helped to establish in 1974. Bookchin himself acknowledges his influences as coming from radical decentralized thinkers such as Peter Kropotkin, William Morris, and Paul Goodman. The catalyst for Bookchin's (1987) attack on Deep Ecology was an article by Abbey arguing for the restriction of migration into the USA to preserve natural resources, and an article that appeared in the *Earth First!* journal (albeit without editorial support) that considered whether AIDS might not be a bad thing for the environment in helping reduce population pressures.

For Bookchin it is not human beings that are naturally antagonistic to nature but it is the way in which society has become unnaturally organized in patterns of domination derived from hierarchy that is the problem. He was scornful of what he saw as the neo-Malthusian origins of Deep Ecology. However, he reserved his real discontent for Deep Ecology's philosophy which he argued conceives of human beings in general as a form of cancer and which is based on a form of mysticism which he refers to as 'Eco-la-la'.

Bookchin argued that the exploitation of nature is the mirror image of exploitation in human society in general and here the common link is the organization of society in the form of hierarchies. He agreed that the view of nature as a hostile competitive environment is an unnatural reflection of the antagonistic and competitive way in which human society is organized but he saw the source of this in the hierarchical ordering of societies where exploitation of certain groups by others is the norm. The solution to the ecological crisis for social ecology lies in a radical restructuring of society in small-scale self-sufficient communities based on mutual cooperation and not domination of one group over another (Bookchin 1987).

Despite this seemingly hostile impasse between Deep Ecology and Social Ecology, which did indeed spark a bitter debate amongst the nascent Green movement in the USA in the 1980s (Spichen 1989), a rapprochement of sorts came in November 1989 with what was billed as 'The Great Debate', a meeting between Foreman and Bookchin out of which emerged a joint authored book (Bookchin and Foreman 1991) (for background see http://theanarchistlibrary.org/library/murray-bookchin-and-dave-foreman-defending-the-earth-a-debate).

Eco-feminism

Eco-feminism has developed into a strong current within radical Green thought. While it is the alleged anthropocentric dominance and behaviour that is the source of ecological stress for Deep Ecology, eco-feminism disaggregates anthropocentrism on the basis of gender and focuses on *androcentrism* (male-centred world view). Just as patriarchy dominates and shapes social relations, it is now extended into its relations with nature.

One strand in eco-feminist thinking is rooted in biological determinism and sees a dualism in cultural associations between the sexes in relation to nature. While men seek to entrench their dominance in society and over nature alike, women are the natural agents to recognize the impact of patriarchy on nature because they are intimately connected to it through their experience of childbirth and -rearing (see, for example, Daly 1978). (See also the discussion of eco-feminism in Chapter 9.)

For socialist feminists the source of this dualism is not naturally determined but it is socially determined through the impact of capitalism on the sexual division of labour. In the separation of work from the home, men come to dominate the social, economic, and political spheres with women being primarily orientated to the domestic sphere. In the pursuit of economic growth, men come to see nature as a force to be dominated, exploited, and controlled and this is the primary role for humanity with domestic issues being seen as secondary. Male cultural ideas about their dominant roles are thus socially determined.

Carolyn Merchant saw the male dominated view of nature as something that needed to be controlled occurring through the application of a mechanistic approach to science (Merchant 1980). In similar vein Vandana Shiva and Maria Mies seek to highlight the links between patriarchal science, the degradation of nature, and the oppression of women (Mies and Shiva 1993).

For Shiva (2014) the hope for a new world could be seen to lie in the struggle of the most marginalized women in the developing world who are now at the forefront of struggles against ecological destruction in the name of development. Shiva's environmental activism took her to the forests of Northern India where she saw women fighting to preserve their natural environment from the encroachment of industrialization. She contrasted a world in which women live in natural balance with the environment, which is now being undermined by a rapacious capitalist model of so-called development fundamentally shaped by partriarchy.

Stop and Think

Do you agree with the view that environmental issues are readily incorporated into other ideological frameworks and if so is this damaging to the claim by Greens that they have a distinctive approach to politics?

Case Study 10.3 Global climate change

The 21st Conference of the Parties of the United Nations Framework Convention on Climate Change (UNFCC) was seen as the last chance for the countries of the world to come together to agree a framework for global cooperation to combat global climate change and lay down the steps that each individual nation-state should take to curb the emissions of greenhouse gasses (GHGs), which are acknowledged to be the cause of global warming, as well as the collective actions that need to be taken.

Christiana Figueres, Executive Secretary of the UNFCCC, argued that:

> Successive generations will, I am sure, mark the 12 December 2015 as a date when cooperation, vision, responsibility, a shared humanity and a care for our world took centre-stage.
>
> (http://newsroom.unfccc.int/unfccc-newsroom/finale-cop21/)

Of course only history will tell us the extent to which the promises and commitments that have been made will be realized but to what extent does this apparent global concern for the environment mesh with the central concerns of a Green agenda for the future?

For many Green activists not only has the slow and protracted process to Paris shown how difficult it is to get policy makers to face up to the conflict between ever rising economic growth and sustainability, but many of the proposals for reducing GHGs have been too heavily influenced by BAU models and essentially a market liberal economic approach.

There is also a fear that the promises made will not in fact be delivered and, so far from showing that key environmental issues can be conventionally dealt with through normal political processes, that grassroots environmental pressure is still needed and indeed, if it were not for this action in the past two decades, the changes in public opinion that have brought politicians and businesses to Paris would not have happened.

The 350.org was established by Bill McKibben to campaign for progress on climate change and its response to the Paris agreement was that there was still much left to do:

> Paris isn't the end of the story, but a conclusion of a particular chapter. Now, it's up to us to strengthen these promises, make sure they are kept, and then accelerate the transition away from fossil fuels and toward 100% renewable energy.
>
> (http://350.org/paris/)

Furthermore there is a deep suspicion amongst Green activists and political parties that environmental policies are still being dealt with in a piecemeal manner and that if genuine environmental change is to occur there needs to be a more fundamental approach taken to developing a comprehensive Green agenda.

Clear Green water?

We have seen that Green thinking has emerged out of critique of the view that economic growth is the root of genuine well-being. It is argued that conventional approaches to growth are unsustainable and that sustainable development must be at the core of Green thinking. However, sustainable development is now widely used in many political traditions and there is the possibility that the concept can mean different things to different people. This 'fuzziness' of the concept therefore represents a problem for arguments that there is a distinct Green politics.

It can be said that while all other ideological positions take an anthropocentric approach to the end goals of political systems, ecologism is anchored in an eco-centric value system and that a green future will need the development of a Green consciousness.

However, the diversity of approaches within Green thinking is all too evident here. While it could be argued that most Green thinkers and activists see the ecological environment as being the determining factor which explains the totality of political, social, and economic problems, once Greens stray into issues of social injustice and inequity, discrimination, democracy, and political participation it can be difficult to distinguish their ideas from other radical ideological positions.

Finally those who argue that ecologism is indeed a radical form of Green thinking emphasize that at the heart of Green thinking is the belief that, while dealing with environmental challenges is complex, the solutions are not complicated if we approach these problems in a holistic way. However, attention then has to be paid to the extent to which there is a clear and viable programme for the delivery of a distinctively Green programme as well as the extent to which such a programme would win electoral support.

If we are to assess the viability of a distinctive new Green ideology and agenda in the twenty-first century, four key questions need to be considered.

1. Is a new Deep Green agenda based on a new ideology of ecologism needed to tackle the range of environmental problems confronting humanity or are shallow Green environmental approaches derived from existing ideological positions going to be sufficient?
2. Is there a new coherent Green agenda?
3. How would such an agenda be implemented and who or what will be the 'agents for change'?
4. What are the chances of such an agenda being accepted politically?

We have seen that while it was argued that the bleak pessimism of the limits to growth approaches has been overestimated, the seriousness of potential environmental collapse has not gone away and we do indeed need a stronger view of sustainable development. In economics there has been a plethora of books developing the ideas of steady state type economics or what has been characterized as the 'Economics of Enough' (see Jackson 2009; Coyle 2011; Dietz and O'Neill 2013; Skidelsky and Skidelsky 2013). In the natural sciences there is now the recognition that we do live in a world where bio-physical systems are inter-related and that if one part of the system is affected it, in turn, can undermine others. In this context the Gaia hypothesis of James Lovelock has been very influential as has the work on 'planetary boundaries' of Rockström et al. (see Lovelock 1979, 2014). The ecologist Paul Crutzen has argued that there is now incontrovertible evidence that 'human forcings' are irrevocably changing the environment and he characterizes our present times as 'The Age of the Anthropocene' (Rockström et al. 2009).

For Dobson environmentalism or campaigning on single green issues is to be distinguished from Green politics or ecologism, as

> there will always be a careful nurtured flame at the centre of Green doctrine where all its disciples can warm their hands.
>
> (Dobson 1991: 8)

Humphrey (2013) argues that while the central concepts in Green ideology are relatively few, it is still a 'thick' ideology in which there is the need for 'ecological restructuring' involving not only the need to have sustainable development as the central goal but a recognition that, if this to happen, there needs to be an inextricable co-development of a new Green consciousness recognizing the centrality of an ecocentric value system linked to the need for a holistic approach to policy. There is a strong core in Green thinking that sees humans as not above or outside of nature and sees the need to assert our relationship with nature as one based on symbiosis, cooperation, and non-hierarchical forms of social and political organization. This then implies the need for radical democratization based on self-sustaining local communities in which the principles of non-violence and ecological law are enshrined.

However, Goodin argues that there are fundamental problems in reconciling Green principles with their proposed theory of action and agency. We have seen previously that there is a problem in Deep Ecology because the emphasis on the intrinsic value of nature can lead to a fundamentally hostile conception of human activity. Goodin does assert that there is a clear Green theory of value and that it is logically indefensible that individual parts of Green policy can be picked off and stolen by other parties. However, to be a Green does not mean acceptance of the Deep Green ethical position. Goodin's 'moderately deep ecology' asserts that the value of nature lies in its relation to human beings, but that this does not imply that its only value lies in its instrumental use to us. Furthermore, it is not logically necessary that Green values necessitate idealized and decentralized methods of decision-making forms and an adoption of particular lifestyle recommendations. Indeed if there are real and present threats to the environment, then it is incumbent on Greens to enter into coalitions with other parties and seek to build support for wider environmental policies in the process (Goodin 1992).

Kenny (2001) asserts that there is clear Green water between ecologism and other ideologies, while he acknowledges that there is room for seepage in relation to some adjacent concepts. We have highlighted the claim that some aspects of Deep Ecology can flirt dangerously with authoritarian controls such as in fascism, and that democracy and sustainability can be incorporated comfortably into other traditions with the Green edge being blunted. Kenny thus sees a danger for ecologism being submerged in new developments in terms of identity politics, post-modernism (see Chapter 13), and post-materialism.

For Freeden Green ideology has emerged as a new ideology in its own right, but he argues that it is the 'thinness' in the core of Green thinking which results in the development of many strands of Green thinking (Freeden 1996). He sees Green ideology as a new 'ideational product' at first created by 'disaffected intellectuals' with a relatively thin core of central beliefs which have, however, been interpreted in sometimes fundamentally conflicting ways by the 'opinion formers, programmatic entrepreneurs and originators of new political messages'. Referring specifically to the German Greens, he argues:

> The fate of green ideology in Germany is a case in point, based as it is on diverse groups pulling in a number of disparate directions from an eclectic base of core beliefs.
>
> (Freeden 2001: 7)

 Stop and Think

What are the main arguments to undermine the claim that there is a new ideology of 'ecologism' or Deep Green thinking and how convincing do you think these arguments are?

Case Study 10.4 The German Green Party

While formal participation in government of Green political parties is not confined to Germany, nevertheless the experience of the German Greens, known as Bündnis 90/Die Grünen (Alliance 90/The Greens), since 1990 is instructive, allowing analysis of ideological tensions within Green thinking as well as the practicality of delivering a Green agenda.

Jachnow (2013) descibes how Die Grünen emerged in the 1970s and 1980s from a wide range of citizens' action groups concerned with the growing nuclear power programme and evidence of the acid rain that was polluting the rivers and forests of northern Europe. While many of these groups were drawn from the rising ecological movement, they were joined by feminists, students, and the counter-cultural groups that followed the civil unrest of 1968 (which at its extreme had created the Red Army Faction and the 'German Autumn' of 1977). However, conservative housewife groups as well as farmers were also involved in large-scale environmental protests. For

Jachnow what united this diverse group was a '[c]ritique of the industrial policy embraced by all three establishment parties', but the range of ideological views across these groups and 'the anti-authoritarian, decentralized nature of the local action group' meant that initial attempts to unite these groups as a single political movement were unsuccessful (Jachnow 2013).

And yet despite this Die Grünen did emerge as a formal party in 1980. While there were prominent spokespeople, the organization of the party was overtly non-hierarchical and from the outset sought to ensure equal gender balance.

In the federal system of the then West Germany, coupled with its electoral system built on strict proportional representation, minority parties always have a good chance of at least securing some formal political representation at regional and national level. In 1982 the more conservative elements of the party had left but, despite this, Die Grünen did begin to gain seats in many of the regional assemblies and by 1983 in the national parliament as well.

In these early days there was an ongoing interplay between the more overtly ecological elements of the party and those who had joined the party from the left and were influenced by eco-socialism and eco-Marxism. This was also accompanied by tension over the tactics of the party. The realists (or Realos) argued that, in order to achieve at least some of their programme, coalition and compromise would be necessay, whereas the fundamentalists (or Fundis) argued that to do so would be to renege on their essential founding principles. After the re-unification of the two Germanies Die Grünen came together with the Bundis 90 which had emerged in the East in the aftermath of the fall of the Berlin Wall.

The subsequent experience of this Green party in the united Germany is a subject of controversy. Critics point to the emergence of the Greens in government in the two periods 1998–2002 and 2002–2005 as one of fateful compromise. The support given by the party to military inteventions in the former Yugoslavia and for the invasion of Afghanistan, as well as backtracking on anti-nuclear programmes, and a general move towards supporting the growing influence on neo-liberal economic policy are all cited as evidence of this. It is also argued that many of the Green political figures have themselves 'sold out' by accepting advisory policy roles with corporate groups or in pursuit of top ministerial positions. It is also argued that the party itself has now become too narrowly identified with more prosperous middle class voters.

For Jachnow these are all fair criticisms involving personality and tactics but fundamentally they stem from an existential problem: the failure to find a coherent common political ideology. With regard to the leftist influence in the party:

> While the gathering of so many currents under the Green umbrella seemed at first to have unified West Germany's shattered left, it arguably contributed further to the splintering and co-option of those elements.
>
> (Jachnow 2013: 101–2)

In Jachnow's analysis, the Greens in Germany had indeed become a refuge for different groups from both the defeated left movements of the 1960s and the 1970s in West Germany and the former eco-Marxists of East Germany from 1990 onwards. Far from being a strength of the party, he sees this as a fundamental weakness. Trying to forge common ground between eco-libertarians and radical ecologists is not possible because of 'their ideological antimonies'.

Gahrton (2015) takes a more optimistic view of the ability of Green parties to be politically effective. It would be wrong simply to focus on the experience of the German Greens as the definitive case study. From 1990 to 2015, Gahrton argues, Green participation in government has occurred in twenty-one (mainly European) countries.

For Gahrton, despite the compromises that coalitions bring and the danger of a disillusioned electorate turning against what it sees as the failed promises of an actual Green Party in power,

> [t]hat Green parties should try participation in government if given the opportunity and if the conditions are reasonable is obvious. At the same time there are limits to what can be done by a government in a democratic state. The necessary transformation into an ecological society can only be achieved through struggles on several levels: personal, local, regional, national and international. Greens in governments are an indispensable part of a Green future, but not the only one.
>
> (Gahrton 2015: 107)

A distinctive Green agenda?

There remains a big problem in relation to mapping out a distinctive Green approach to sustainable development. At its weakest, sustainable development is simply a vague and indeterminate vehicle by which businesses can assert their claim to being socially responsible whilst simply performing 'business as usual' (BAU) and using 'green washing' to show off their supposed eco-credentials. However, Porritt (2007) points out that there are further weaknesses. He is acutely aware that the term could simply be a contradiction in terms in a capitalist business environment and one which obscures the reality of potential ecological collapse. Furthermore, if seen simply as a need to tackle individual environmental issues, this will collapse into a narrow environmental policy agenda, but if it is bundled together with a range of leftish social, equity, and justice issues, it will deflect attention away from the core ecological base that he sees as being at the heart of the issue.

As Dryzek (2013) shows there are a range of discourses drawn from across the ideological spectrum that can be used to frame policy responses to environmental challenges. In recent years it has been the neo-liberal or Promethean approach that has been dominant. Of course Greens will dispute the effectiveness of these approaches but, as we have seen, there is a multiplicity of Green approaches. There is now no shortage of comprehensive blue-prints for a Green future (or should these be labelled Green-prints?).

For Green campaigners such as Lester Brown, the founder of the Earth Institute in the USA, BAU (or 'Plan A') models are simply inadequate and for 'true' sustainability there has to be a Plan B programme (Brown 2009). Porritt (2007) sketches his 'framework for sustainable capitalism' by outlining the changes that he thinks are both needed and possible in terms of sustaining the resources of the earth as defined by its natural, human, social, manufactured, and financial capital. Latouche (2009) and Daly (1997) are key figures in outlining how de-growth economics might be operationalized. There are also many detailed programmes emanating from bodies seeking to develop a 'green economics' agenda (New Economics Foundation 2015).

Translating Green ideas into policy

Gahrton (2015) argues that by 1990 the development of a wider Green consciousness gaining increasing political organization moved from thousands of local grassroots groups to the creation of a range of membership and pressure groups, attempts by people to create their own societies or 'Green alternative islands', and then the rise of political parties. The 1970s and 1980s witnessed the rapid growth of a number of activist groups that had emerged out of the counter-cultural currents of the 1960s. NGOs were formed such as Friends of the Earth (in 1961), the World Wildlife Fund for Nature (in 1969), and Greenpeace (in 1971) and these have attracted many members. In 1972 the oldest political party founded on a distinctive Green agenda was the Values Party in New Zealand and this was soon followed by the formation of the Ecology Party in the UK (now known simply as the Green Party) and other parties from the early 1980s onwards in Belgium, West Germany (see Case Study 10.4), Austria, Sweden, Ireland, Switzerland, Portugal, Luxemburg, Holland, and France (Gahrton 2015).

It could be argued that the true bearers of the Green flame are the wide range of activist groups that draw their inspiration from Deep Ecology. Popular slogans such as 'If you are not part of the solution, you are part of the problem', 'Resistance is fertile', and the sheer range and number of environmental activist groups bear witness to an emphasis in the wider Green movement on radical action. This may well stop short of being the type of eco-warrior envisaged by Foreman but he recognized that people could perform other roles to protect the environment. However, if a genuine radically new Green agenda were to be adopted, then this would have to involve broader civic society and so attention has to be paid to both the producers and consumers of resources as embodied in the commodities that are created in the economic system.

In the twenty-first century growing calls for ethical consumerism and ecological citizenship are reflective of this and the increase in the prevalence and use of social networking can prove a powerful tool in mobilizing campaigns against perceived environmental injustice and malpractice. However, to what extent is this a widespread concern amongst consumers in general? Porritt, for example, is a Green who is aware of the need to counter the claim that environmentalism is simply 'tree hugging escapism for the pampered middle classes'. To what extent might it be true that a post-materialist future is only conceived by those who are already materially secure?

Deeper Greens have an inherent scepticism about the degree to which consumers in general truly burn with a Green flame and there is an acceptance that the present reality is one of a rampant materialist culture in developed societies and an aspiration to create one in developing countries. This does present a challenge for how exactly a Deep Green agenda might be developed as we have seen a crucial part of the Deep Green hope is that a Green consciousness can be developed. There are a range of different explanations given for why this is not widespread, ranging from ignorance, a natural inclination to be materialistically orientated, or a tendency to

place the blame for this on the persuasive marketing techniques of business in affluent societies (Sheehan 2010).

Opinion remains divided about the precise role that the business community
can play in furthering a Green agenda. Business groups such as the World Business
Council for Sustainable Development (WBCSD) and the World Economic Forum
(WEF) are all active in promoting 'the business case' for sustainable development
(WEF 2009; WBCSD 2015) and argue that there is no inherent conflict between
long-term sustainability of profits and environmentally sustainable business practice. Deep Greens, though, remain convinced that in essence such developments
remain 'green washing' rather than the radical changes in business behaviour that
is required and, essentially, that such approaches are no more than the Promethean
responses to growth wrapped in Green language (Pierre-Lewis 2012).

It could be argued that while formal participation in the political process by
Green political parties has been limited, globally it is nevertheless clear that governments have been increasingly pressured into trying to be 'seen to be Green', but, as
Meadowcroft observes, there is generally a lack of a developed theory about how to
develop concerted state action to deliver Green policies. We have charted the development of the approaches to resource management and resource conservation in developed economies and we have seen that it is in some of the least developed countries
in the world that environmental issues are indeed seen to be a major problem. This
has recently been given formal global acceptance by the adoption in September 2015
of 17 Sustainable Development goals to form the basis of the post-2015 Development
Agenda (see http://www.un.org/sustainabledevelopment/sustainable-development-
goals/). Within the fastest growing developing economies, too, there is clear recognition that high rates of economic growth have come at an unsustainable cost in terms
of the environmental degradation. This recognition has often been the result of civil
protest from below. The formation of the BRICS bank (established by Brazil, Russia,
India, China, and South Africa) and its charter shows some acceptance of the fact
that sustainable development needs not only robust environmental protection but
also global cooperation between developing countries themselves (see http://ndb-
brics.org/agreement.html).

At the global level there has been a recognition that a number of global environmental
problems require international cooperation. Of all of these, it is the issue of global climate
change that has perhaps done more to force the environmental agenda to the fore at both
the national and global policy level (see Case Study 10.3), but it is clear that such developments do not provide evidence that thay are the result of a new radical Green agenda.

Green parties now exist across the globe and in 2001 the Global Greens association
was established as the global body to coordinate Green Party political programmes.
The association consists of four federations covering the African, European, Asia-
Pacific, and American regions and Green Party activities are guided by the Global
Greens Charter that sets out the core principles of 'ecological wisdom, social justice,

participatory democracy, nonviolence, sustainability and respect for diversity' as well as the 'political action plan' (see https://www.globalgreens.org/globalcharter).

However, there is a keen debate as to how effective Greens have been in government and fundamentally the extent to which Green Parties will attract widespread political support. For Porritt:

> [s]urvey after survey tells us that the majority of people are broadly content with our greed driven consumer society (even if it doesn't make them any happier) and election after election tells us that only a minority of people are prepared to vote for the only political party (the Greens) that has as yet honestly confronted those macro-trends.
>
> (Porritt 2012: 294)

Meadowcroft argues that while Green movements have grown and some Green parties have shared power

> [t]he relative disconnection from existing patterns of economics and politics and their lack of substantive engagement with the vast body of theoretical findings and accumulated experience which casts doubt on the viability of small scale, communistic and anarchistic social projects means that the current political salience of their approaches is strictly limited.
>
> (Meadowcroft 2001: 547)

For Ball,

> In sum it is probably fair to say that green economic thought at the end of the 20th century was more critical than constructive, more articulate about what is wrong with modern market thinking than about what alternative might be devised.
>
> (Ball 2015: 123)

Gahrton acknowledges that this pessimism exists but while

> [t]he world in 2015 may seem far from mature enough for the Green message; . . . the Greens must be the carriers of the true global mission to establish a democratic and ecological Green global governance in order to secure Mother Earth and create a life system in which quality, not quantity, is the guiding star.
>
> (Gahrton 2015)

Summary

- Modern environmental thinking emerged as a critique of the negative effects of industrialization on the ecological environment.
- The origins of Green thinking are located in developments in the natural sciences and political economy that see natural resource limits to economic growth.

- There is a debate concerning the extent to which Green ideology has emerged as a viable ideology in its own right. Many critics see environmental issues as being readily dealt with from within existing ideological frameworks and argue that attempts to define a distinctive core of Green thinking fail because of the multiplicity of different claims to be Green.

- The claim to the existence of a radical new Deep Green agenda is criticized in terms of having too vague a policy programme or because such a programme is unrealistic in not explaining clearly who will develop a new Green agenda.

- Green activists and thinkers assert that, despite differences in approach within the Green movement, there is a strong core of Green ideas and policies and that, in the face of growing evidence of ecological collapse, it is only Green ideology that analyses how we have got to this point and how we can best emerge from it.

- This claim from prominent Greens is that this strong core of Green ideas and policies can be seen as follows:
  Critique: It is only the Greens that have defined sustainable development in the way required to encompass all the political, social, and economic problems that emanate from ecological collapse.
  Ideal/Values: In order to address these problems, there is a need for a change to a new Green consciousness, and that 'clear Green water' separates the ecocentric approach of Green thinking from the anthropocentric policies of all other ideological approaches to environmental issues.
  Programme: The increasing scientific evidence that we are now exceeding the physical planetary boundaries requires a new holistic approach to policy making based on small-scale decentralzsed participatory decision-making. Green politics has already achieved much to build this 'Green Awakening'.

Review and discussion questions

1. Why is it difficult to define the term 'sustainable development' and to what extent do you think that there is a distinctive Green conception of it?

2. Critically evaluate the claim that there is a distinctive value system in Green thinking based on ecocentrism. To what extent do you think that this is a strength or weakness of the claim to a distinctive Green ideology?

3. Bookchin described Deep Ecology as being 'Eco la la'. To what extent could such a claim be applied to Green thinking in general?

4. In what ways should governance and the behaviour of citizens, consumers, and business change if a Green future is to be delivered? Do you think there is a realistic chance that such changes might occur?

Research exercises

1. Select a country in which there is a recognized Green Party and then compare and contrast the most recent party manifestos of the Green Party with those of two other leading political parties. Compile a report which compares and contrasts the three manifestos and assess the extent to which there is a distinctive Green policy programme in the Green Party manifesto.

2. There is optimistic talk amongst prominent Greens that we are on the brink of a 'Green Surge' of ecological consciousness and action. Using a country of your choice write a report that first outlines how we might measure such a rise in Green politics and assess the likelihood of this occurring in your chosen country.

Further reading

Dryzek (2013) uses a discourse approach to review the range of different approaches that have been taken to both analysing and then developing policies to address the environmental challenges.

Dryzek and Schlossberg (2007) collect together many of the key readings in relation to environmental politics and organize them in relation to the competing ideological schools of thought.

For what is regarded by many Greens as one of the most important texts that built the platform for the development of Green thinking, read Schumacher (1974).

Gahrton (2015) provides a useful guide written by a prominent Green activist outlining the prospects for effective Green political action.

References

ABBEY, E. (1975), *The Monkey Wrench Gang*, Philadelphia: Lippencott, Williams and Wilkins.

BALL T. (2010), 'Green Political Theory' in T. Ball and R. Bellamy, *The Cambridge History of Twentieth-Century Political Thought*, Cambridge: Cambridge University Press.

BOOKCHIN, M. (1987), 'Social Ecology versus Deep Ecology: A Challenge for the Ecological Movement, *Green Perspectives Newsletter of the Green Program Project nos 4-5*, Summer 1987.

BOOKCHIN, M. AND FOREMAN, D. (1991), *Defending the Earth—A Debate*, Montreal/NewYork: Black Rose Books.

BOULDING, K. E. (1966), 'The Economics of the Coming Spaceship Earth', in H. Jarrett, *Environmental Quality in a Growing Economy*, Baltimore, MD: Resources for the Future/John Hopkins University Press, pp. 3–14, http://arachnid.biosci.utexas.edu/courses/THOC/Readings/Boulding_SpaceshipEarth.pdf

BROWN L. (2009), *Plan B 4.0—Mobilizing to Save Civilization*, London: Norton W.W.

COYLE, D. (2011), *The Economics of Enough—How to Run the Economy as if the Future Matters*, Princeton, NJ, and Oxford: Princeton University Press.

DALY, H. (1991), *Steady State Economics*, Washington, DC: Island Press.

DALY, H. (1997), *Beyond Growth—The Economics of Sustainable Development*, Boston: Beacon Press.

DALY, M. (1978), *Gyn/ecology: The Metaethics of Radical Feminism*, Boston: Beacon Press.

DELINGPOLE, J. (2012), *Watermelons—How Environmentalists are Killing the Planet, Destroying the Economy and Stealing your Children's Future*, London: Biteback.

DIETZ, R. AND O'NEILL, D. (2013), *Enough is Enough*, London: Routledge.

DOBSON, A. (1991), *The Green Reader*, London: Andre Deutsch.

DRYZEK, J. S. (2013), *The Politics of the Earth*, Oxford: Oxford University Press.

DRYZEK, J. S. AND SCHLOSSBERG, D. (2007), *Debating the Earth—The Environment Politics Reader*, Oxford: Oxford University Press.

FREEDEN, M. (1996), *Ideologies and Political Theory—A Conceptual Approach*, Oxford: Oxford University Press.

FREEDEN, M. (2001), *Reassessing Political Ideologies—The Durability of Dissent*, London: Routledge.

GAHRTON, P. (2015), *Green Parties, Green Future*, London: Pluto Press.

GEORGESCU-ROEDEN, N. (1971), *The Entropy Law and the Economic Process*, Cambridge, MA: Harvard University Press.

GOLDSMITH, E., ALLEN, R., ALLABY, M., DAVOLL, J., AND LAWRENCE, S. (1972), 'Blueprint for Survival', *The Ecologist*, Vol. 2, No. 1.

GOODIN, R. E. (1992), *Green Political Theory*, Cambridge: Polity Press.

GORZ, A. (1989), *Critique of Economic Reason*, London: Verso.

HAQ, G. AND PAUL, H. (2012), *Environmentalism since 1945*, Abingdon: Routledge.

HARDIN, G. (1968), 'The Tragedy of the Commons', *Science* New Series, Vol. 162, No. 3859, pp. 1243–8.

HUMPHREY, M. (2013), 'Green Ideology', in M. Freeden and M. Stears, *The Oxford Book of Political Ideologies*, Oxford: Oxford University Press.

JACHNOW, J. (2013), 'What's Become of the German Greens?' *New Left Review*, Vol. 81, May–June.

JACKSON, T. (2009), *Prosperity Without Growth: Economics for a Finite Planet*, London: Earthscan: Princeton University Press.

KENNY, M. (2001), 'Ecologism', in R. Eccleshall, F. Finlayson, V. Geoghegan, M. Kenny, M. Lloyd, and W. Mackenzie, *Political Ideologies—An Introduction*, London: Routledge.

KOVEL, J. AND LOWY, M. (2001), *An Ecosocialist Manifesto*, http://ecosocialistnetwork.org/Wordpress/wp-content/uploads/2012/03/Manifesto-1-en.pdf

KUMAR, S. (2015), 'Small Country Big Dilemma', *Resurgence and Ecology*, July/August.

LATOUCHE, S. (2009), *Farewell to Growth*, Cambridge: Polity Press.

LOMBORG, B. (2001), *The Skeptical Environmentalist: Measuring the Real State of the World*, Cambridge: Cambridge University Press.

LOMBORG, B. (2007), *Cool It! The Skeptical Environmentalist's Guide to Global Warming*, New York: Knopf.

LOMBORG, B. (2010), *Smart Solutions to Climate Change: Comparing Costs and Benefits*, Cambridge: Cambridge University Press.

LOVELOCK, J. (1979), *Gaia—A New Look at Life on Earth*, Oxford: Oxford University Press.

LOVELOCK, J. (2014), *A Rough Guide to the Future*, London: Penguin.

LYTLE, M. H. (2007), *The Gentle Subversive: Rachel Carson, Silent Spring, and the Rise of the Environmental Movement*, New York: Oxford University Press.

MALTHUS, T. (1798), *An Essay on the Principle of Population*, Teddington, Middlesex: Echo Library.

MEADOWCROFT, J. (2001), 'Green Political Perspectives at the Dawn of the Twenty-first Century', in M. Freeden, *Reassessing Political Ideologies-The Durability of Dissent*, London: Routledge.

MEADOWS, D. H., MEADOWS, D. L., RANDERS, J., AND BEHRENS, W. W. (1972), *The Limits to Growth—A Report for the Club of Rome's Project on the Predicament of Mankind*, New York: Universe Books.

MEADOWS, D. H., MEADOWS, D. L., AND RANDERS, J. (1992), *Beyond the Limits: Global Collapse or a Sustainable Future*, London: Earthscan.

MERCHANT, C. (1980), *The Death of Nature: Women, Nature and the Scientific Revolution*, New York: First Harper and Row.

MIES, M. AND SHIVA, V. (1993), *Ecofeminism*, London: Zed Books.

MONBIOT, G. (2007), *Heat—How To Stop the Planet From Burning*, Toronto: Anchor.

NAESS, A. (1983), 'The Shallow and the Deep, Long Range Ecology Movement: A Summary', in J. S. Dryzek and D. Schlossberg, *Debating the Earth—The Environment Politics Reader* (2007), Oxford: Oxford University Press.

NAESS, A. (1989), *Ecology, Community and Lifestyle: An Outline of an Ecosophy*, Cambridge: Cambridge University Press.

NEW ECONOMICS FOUNDATION (2015), 'People, Power and Planet—Towards a New Social Settlement', http://www.neweconomics.org/publications/entry/people-planet-power-towards-a-new-social-settlement

O'CONNOR, J. (1988), 'Capitalism, Nature, Socialism: A Theoretical Introduction', *Capitalism, Nature, Socialism*, Vol. 1, No. 1, http://www.vedegylet.hu/okopolitika/O'Connor%20-%20Capitalism,%20Nature,%20Socialim.pdf

PIERRE-LOUIS, K. (2012), *Green Washed—Why We Can't Buy Our Way to a Green Planet*, Brooklyn, NY: IgPublishing.

PORRITT, J. (2012), *Capitalism As if the World Matters*, London: Earthscan.

ROCKSTRÖM, J., STEFFEN, W., NOONE, K., PERSSON, Å., CHAPIN, F. S. III, LAMBIN, E., LENTON, T. M., SCHEFFER, M., FOLKE, C., SCHELLNHUBER, H., NYKVIST, B., DE WIT, C. A., HUGHES, T., VAN DER LEEUW, S., RODHE, H., SÖRLIN, S., SNYDER, P. K., COSTANZA, R., SVEDIN, U., FALKENMARK, M., KARLBERG, L., CORELL, R. W., FABRY, V. J., HANSEN, J., WALKER, B., LIVERMAN, D., RICHARDSON, K., CRUTZEN, P., AND FOLEY, J. (2009), 'Planetary Boundaries: Exploring the Safe Operating Space for Humanity', *Ecology and Society*, Vol. 14, No. 2, pp. 32. http://www.ecologyandsociety.org/vol14/iss2/art32/

SCHUMACHER, E. F. (1974), *Small is Beautiful—A Study of Economics as if People Mattered*, London: Abacus.

SCRUTON, R. (2013), *Green Philosophy—How to Think Seriously About the Planet*, London: Atlantic.

SHEEHAN, B. (2010), *The Economics of Abundance—Affluent Consumption and the Global Economy*, Cheltenham: Edward Elgar.

SHIVA, V. (2014), *The Vandana Shiva Reader*, Lexington, KY: University Press of Kentucky.

SKIDELSKY, R. AND SKIDELSKY, E. (2013), *How Much is Enough?*, London: Penguin.

SPICHEN, B. (1989), 'Ecology's Family Feud: Murray Bookchin Turns Up Volume on a Noisy Debate', *Los Angeles Times*, 27 March, http://articles.latimes.com/1989-03-27/news/vw-425_1_deep-ecology

WORLD BUSINESS COUNCIL FOR SUSTAINABLE DEVELOPMENT (WBCSD) (2015), *Vision 2050—The New Agenda For Business*, Geneva: World Business Council for Sustainable Development, http://www.wbcsd.org/pages/edocument/edocumentdetails.aspx?id=219&nosearchcontextkey=true

WORLD COMMISSION FOR ECONOMIC DEVELOPMENT (WCED) (1987), *Our Common Future*, Oxford: Oxford University Press.

WORLD ECONOMIC FORUM (WEF) (2009), *The Business Case for Sustainability*, Geneva: World Economic Forum, http://www.weforum.org/pdf/ConsumerIndustries/BusSustainabilityExSum.pdf

11

Multiculturalism

Paul Wetherly

OBJECTIVES

- Examine the routes to cultural diversity within modern states, especially immigration into European societies in the period since the Second World War (i.e. post 1945)

- Discuss the linkages between the national and global dimensions of cultural diversity

- Analyse the attitudes of other ideological perspectives—liberalism, socialism, conservatism, nationalism, and feminism—to cultural diversity

- Consider whether multiculturalism is an ideology in its own right and identify variants of multiculturalism

- Examine how multiculturalist ideology has been expressed in political movements and shaped government policies

- Critically examine the nature of, and reasons for, the recent backlash against multiculturalism in European societies

Introduction

Cultural diversity is characteristic, to varying degrees, of societies in Europe and elsewhere in the world. However, each society has its own unique experience and pattern of diversity and has developed its own response to it, including whether it thinks of itself as 'multicultural' for official purposes or in public attitudes, and the policies it has developed to manage this diversity. It is this question of how a society *responds* to cultural diversity that is at stake in multiculturalist ideology, or multicultural*ism*. In this chapter we will sketch the origins and types of cultural diversity, examine multiculturalist ideology and policies, consider the relationship between multiculturalism and other ideologies, and finish by looking at the recent backlash against multiculturalism. The main focus will be on immigrant-origin ethnic minorities and what might be called immigration multiculturalism.

Migration and cultural diversity

Cultural diversity varies between states and regions of the world. Despite the political focus on cultural diversity in Europe, in global terms European countries are ethnically and culturally highly homogeneous, whereas African countries are the most diverse. This contrast largely reflects the formation of nation-states in Europe and the persistence of a multitude of tribal and language groups in Africa (Fisher 2013; Morin 2013). Is cultural diversity increasing or decreasing? From the point of view of individual immigrant-receiving societies such as the UK, the answer is that cultural diversity has increased. For example, in a very short space of time the UK has gone from a predominantly white British society to one in which, by 2011, non-white ethnic minorities made up 14 per cent, and non-British-white minorities a further 6 per cent, of the population (Figure 11.1). In numerical terms, the non-white population increased from around 100,000 in the early 1950s, mainly confined to dockland areas in cities such as London, Liverpool, Cardiff, and Bristol, to nearly 8 million half a century later (Lupton and Power 2004). Yet from a global perspective cultural diversity is decreasing, as indicated roughly by the accelerating decrease in the number of languages: it is estimated that about '95 per cent of the languages . . . [that have been spoken in the course of human history] will be extinct or moribund by the year 2100' (Diamond 2012: 370).

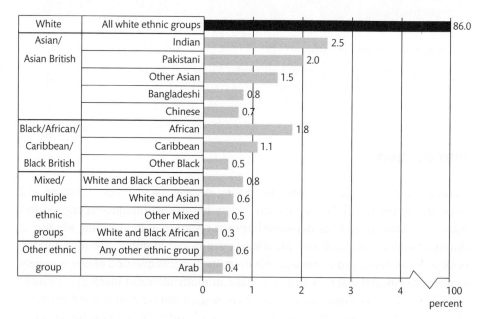

White	All white ethnic groups	86.0
Asian/	Indian	2.5
Asian British	Pakistani	2.0
	Other Asian	1.5
	Bangladeshi	0.8
	Chinese	0.7
Black/African/	African	1.8
Caribbean/	Caribbean	1.1
Black British	Other Black	0.5
Mixed/	White and Black Caribbean	0.8
multiple	White and Asian	0.6
ethnic	Other Mixed	0.5
groups	White and Black African	0.3
Other ethnic	Any other ethnic group	0.6
group	Arab	0.4

0   1   2   3   4   100 percent

Figure 11.1 Ethnic group of usually resident population, England and Wales, 2011
Source: Office for National Statistics (2012: 10, Figure 3)

Within nation-states we can identify three main types of ethnic minorities with different origins:

- immigrant-origin communities
- national minorities
- indigenous people

These communities ended up as minorities within their societies through different routes. In simple terms: indigenous peoples were conquered and subordinated by European colonizers, such as in the Americas and Australia (Diamond 2012: 22); national minorities were incorporated into unified 'nation-states' with a dominant nation and culture, such as the Scots and Welsh in the UK; and immigrant-origin communities established themselves as minorities within established nation-states through (mainly voluntary) migration, such as the migration of Europeans to the United Sates in the nineteenth century and of former colonial subjects to European states in the twentieth century (Castles et al. 2015).

Migration is not a new phenomenon and neither, therefore, is cultural mixing and diversity, but the scale and significance have increased in the modern era. In particular,

> migration took on a new character with the beginnings of European expansion from the sixteenth century and the Industrial Revolution from the nineteenth century . . . . A high point was the mass migrations from Europe to North America from the mid-nineteenth century until World War I.
>
> (Castles et al. 2015: 5)

Whereas in the nineteenth century migration was predominantly *from* Europe, in the second half of the twentieth century

> Europe has emerged as a major global migration destination. While migration of Europeans to the Americas and Oceania rapidly declined in the 1960s and 1970s, Western European countries started to attract increasing numbers of migrants, mainly from former colonies and countries located on the European periphery.
>
> (Castles et al. 2015: 102)

At the same time, migration became more globalized, in the sense of incorporating more regions and countries as source, transit, and destination countries.

In European countries political debate about cultural diversity resulting from immigration has largely been in response to migration from former colonies, involving 'the immigration from outside Europe of non-white peoples into predominantly white countries' (Modood 2007: 2). In addition, among other movements, migration within the member states of the European Union (formerly European Community) under free movement rules has been of significance, particularly in the UK as a result of immigration following the expansion of the EU to incorporate the A8 (i.e. eight accession countries) from central and eastern Europe in 2004.

When is a multicultural society multiculturalist?

In order to understand multiculturalism as an ideology, it is helpful to make two pre-liminary distinctions: first, between a society being multicultural and multicultural-ist, and, second, between multiculturalism and monoculturalism. In brief, a society is multiculturalist to the extent that it responds to its cultural diversity (i.e. its multi-cultural make-up) by rejecting monoculturalism.

Referring to societies as multicultural involves using a descriptive term which highlights the fact that its people are culturally diverse—there is a multiplicity or plurality of cultures rather than a single, homogeneous culture. Put simply, 'a multi-cultural society . . . is one that includes two or more cultural communities' (Parekh 2000: 6).

Multiculturalism can be seen as a normative or ideological response to the 'facts' of cultural diversity and related policies. It is concerned with the relations between the groups that make up a society and with questions such as: is a culturally diverse soci-ety a good society? How should this cultural diversity be managed? How are people with diverse cultures to live together? Behind these questions lies an assumption that cultural diversity *needs* to be managed, that living together successfully will not just happen spontaneously. There may be potential costs to society of cultural diversity that should be minimized or avoided, or potential benefits that ought to be encour-aged and facilitated.

According to Parekh (2000), there are basically two ways of responding to cultural diversity, monoculturalist or multiculturalist. Monoculturalism seeks to reinforce a single, homogeneous culture that is shared by all members of the society. Usually this is defined in terms of the dominant culture of the society, a culture that might be thought to have existed prior to the introduction of cultural diversity resulting from immigration. There are essentially two ways that such a shared culture might be pre-served. One way is immigration control: to severely restrict immigration (especially by people who are seen as culturally different), or to allow immigration only on a temporary basis and to encourage or require the return of immigrants to their coun-tries of origin ('repatriation'). The second way is to encourage or require immigrants to leave behind the cultures of their countries of origin and adopt the culture of the host society they have opted to join. This is a policy of '**assimilation**' and demands of immigrants that they become 'like us'(see Case Study 11.1).

In contrast, multiculturalism demands that immigration policy should not dis-criminate on the basis of cultural differences (which in practice largely means being '**race-blind**') and, in place of assimilation, the '**integration**' of immigrants and the 'accommodation' of cultural diversity is advocated. Thus a basic definition is that 'mul-ticulturalism . . . does not require immigrants to renounce their beliefs and practices as a condition of integration into . . . [the] society [they are joining]' (Callinicos 2008: 144). More than this, multiculturalism requires action on the part of the host society to secure 'the legal and political accommodation of ethnic diversity' (Kymlicka 2012: 1).

However, this is just a starting point, for once monoculturalism has been rejected, there remains a variety of understandings of what 'integration' and 'accommodation' of difference should entail—that is, there is a variety of multiculturalisms.

 Stop and Think

What are the meanings of these terms: multicultural society, monoculturalism, multiculturalism?

Case Study 11.1 Assimilation, integration, and the 'cricket test'

In simple terms, the difference between assimilation and integration, as these terms are usually used in debates about cultural diversity, is that integration means an ethnic minority becomes part of society without losing its ethnic identity, whereas being assimilated does involve relinquishing this identity. Both integration and assimilation should be seen as multi-dimensional processes which involve a time span of more than one generation. This means that assimilation or integration may be debated not just in relation to newly-arrived immigrants but also to second and subsequent generations who are born in the country of immigration, that is, immigrant-origin communities.

Assimilation suggests a one-way process in that the onus is on immigrants to become more 'like us' in order to 'fit in', with no onus on 'us' (the host society) to accommodate difference. Becoming alike includes being able to speak the language, but can also include adopting the values, customs, habits, and lifestyles of the host society. Assimilation may also involve a psychological and emotional dimension in terms of feeling of belonging and loyalty to the nation, its traditions, and institutions. For example, in 1990 the leading British Conservative politician Norman Tebbit proposed a 'cricket test' according to which it is reasonable to expect immigrants (and their descendants) to support the England cricket team rather than the team of their country of origin. Tebbit claimed that

> [a] large proportion of Britain's Asian population fail to pass the cricket test. Which side do they cheer for? It's an interesting test. Are you still harking back to where you came from or where you are?
>
> (Tebbit, in Carvel 2004)

Playing and supporting cricket was part of Asian (i.e. Indian and Pakistani) and West Indian culture that immigrants brought with them to Britain (having been taken to those countries through British colonialism), so in this respect the immigrants were easily assimilable into English sporting culture. But Tebbit was requiring more than this: not just a love of cricket but a love of country that would lead to support for the England team and the jettisoning of their prior sense of loyalty to the country of origin.

More recently Tebbit has stated that more Asians now pass his test, and this is because the presence in the England team of British Asian players 'encourages the generations of British-born Asians to feel part of the nation' (Tebbit, in Malnick 2014). It is also probable that 'British born Asians' are likely, in any case, to feel a weaker sense of identity with their country of heritage (from which they may be separated by two generations) and a stronger sense of identity with their country of birth. Whether or not Tebbit's test is reasonable, if his claim about more Asians now passing it is correct, it suggests that assimilation takes time and that it may be related to integration, here evidenced by British Asian cricket players making it into the England team.

> ⟴ **Stop and Think**
>
> Is Tebbit's test reasonable? Does it matter which cricket team Asians support?

Such a loyalty test as proposed by Tebbit might be justified on the basis of a conservative theory (see Chapter 3) that a deep sense of shared belonging and identity is a necessary condition for a society to be cohesive and to flourish. However, the theory is contentious, and there are objections to assimilation or monoculturalism in terms of both practicality and desirability. On practical grounds the difficulties are:

- immigrant-origin communities may be unwilling to relinquish all aspects of their cultural identity and this may be an unrealistic demand to make of them;

- it is questionable whether there is a homogeneous culture into which minorities can assimilate. 'Britishness', or any other national identity, is liable to mean different things to different people, and to matter to them to varying degrees.

In terms of desirability, the problems are that the preference of immigrants to retain their own cultures may be seen as reasonable, and the desirability of a homogeneous culture shared by all members of a society is questionable. On the contrary, it can be argued that diversity of values, beliefs, and lifestyles may bring substantial benefits to society as the source of advances in artistic, moral, political, and scientific thinking.

Integration is normally seen as a two-way process of mutual adjustment between minority immigrant-origin communities and the majority community. In the British context, a definition of integration was given in 1966 by the then Labour Home Secretary Roy Jenkins, as follows:

> I do not regard [integration] as meaning the loss, by immigrants, of their own national characteristics and culture. I do not think that we need in this country a 'melting pot', which will turn everybody out in a common mould, as one of a series of carbon copies of someone's misplaced vision of the stereotyped Englishman . . . . I define integration, therefore, not as a flattening process of assimilation but as equal opportunity, accompanied by cultural diversity, in an atmosphere of mutual tolerance. This is the goal.
>
> (Jenkins, in MacArthur 1999: 362–6)

This definition explicitly distinguishes integration from assimilation and, by the way, suggests that what it means to be an 'Englishman' is problematic so it would not be clear what immigrants were expected to assimilate into. Cultural diversity is accepted and the two-way adjustment is characterized in terms of 'mutual **tolerance**'—if we are to get along we must get used to difference. Finally, if immigrants are to be able to integrate, they must enjoy 'equal opportunity' in the labour market and other areas of life so that they can get on and contribute to society. On the basis that immigrants do face prejudice and discrimination, equal opportunity requires a change in attitudes and behaviour on the part of members of the majority backed up by anti-discrimination laws. Equal opportunity should, over time, enable minority immigration-origin communities to be represented throughout the occupational order rather than being confined to low-skilled and low-paid work, including British-born Asians being selected for the England cricket team. Thus we can conceive a 'cricket test' of integration.

In making the case for integration, Jenkins also argued that diversity is beneficial to society: 'To live apart, for a person, a city, a country, is to lead a life of declining intellectual stimulation' (1966, in MacArthur 1999: 364). In more general terms, it can be argued that diversity creates a more vibrant culture. However, cultural differences can also become sources of tension, as shown by the 'Danish cartoons' controversy (see Case Study 11.2).

Case Study 11.2 The 'Danish cartoons' controversy

The cartoons in question were originally published in the Danish newspaper *Jyllands-Posten* in 2005, following an invitation to illustrators to submit drawings 'depict[ing] Muhammad as they see him' (Klausen 2009; Wetherly 2012). Although diverse in their depictions of Muhammad, the cartoons were controversial on two grounds: (1) they contravened an injunction in Islam against depictions of the Prophet, and (2) some of the cartoons commented on the character of the Prophet (or, by extension, the nature of Islam as a religion, or members of the Muslim community) in ways that could be interpreted as being blasphemous or **Islamophobic**. The most controversial depicted the Prophet wearing a turban in the shape of a bomb with a burning fuse, apparently making a connection between the Prophet, Islam, or Muslims, and terrorism. For these reasons the cartoons were regarded by many Muslims as offensive and provocative.

Publication of the cartoons initially prompted protests in Denmark, but these soon spread to other European countries and beyond Europe to the 'Muslim world' where the cause was taken up by Arab governments and international organizations including the Arab League and the Organization of the Islamic Conference (OIC). The protests became a global phenomenon, affecting all continents except Latin America, and they were often violent in nature, resulting in many deaths.

Why did the newspaper publish the cartoons? Why did Muslims protest? What are the implications of the controversy for multiculturalism?

It might be argued that the cartoons need no justification since, in liberal societies, freedom of expression allows people to deal with religious issues in whatever way they choose, including ways that are likely (or even intended) to be perceived as offensive by the faithful. In this view, Muslims should be expected to put up with or tolerate the cartoons. This is just part of the normal give-and-take of a liberal society.

In this case the newspaper claimed that there is a problem in European societies of Muslim minorities that are intolerant and not prepared to accept free speech norms. The fear of a hostile reaction had led to a chilling effect on free speech, or 'self-censorship'. As evidence of this, and the pretext for the cartoons, the newspaper cited the case of an author who could not find an illustrator prepared to depict Muhammad for a children's book. Thus, in publishing the cartoons, the newspaper said it was making a stand for free speech that was under attack.

On the other side, some Muslim protestors demanded that the cartoons be banned on grounds that people should not be permitted to insult the Prophet. In other words, religion should be protected by a blasphemy law. Some protestors threatened violent reprisals against the newspaper and the cartoonists. Other critics, not all of them Muslims, saw the cartoons as 'branding . . . [all Muslims] . . . as dangerous or inferior with the likelihood of stirring up hatred. [In this view] such criticism is hate speech, and . . . should be penalized by law' on these grounds (Bleich, 2006). Without calling for a ban, others criticized the cartoons as racist or deliberately intended to cause offence and therefore as unreasonable.

Thus, while the newspaper defined the problem in terms of intolerant Muslims against whom it was necessary to defend free speech, critics saw the problem in terms of 'Islamophobia' as a pervasive form of racism directed at Muslims of which the cartoons were an expression. Each side saw themselves as the victims.

LESSONS OF THE CARTOONS

- All versions of multiculturalism express the importance of protecting ethnic minorities from racism. Therefore *if* the cartoons are interpreted as racist it was clearly wrong to publish them.

- Even if the cartoons were not racist they can be objected to on the grounds that they were likely to cause offence. However, against this it can be argued that free speech is too important to be constrained by a demand not to offend. We all have different ideas about what is offensive, some people might be too sensitive or be too ready to claim offence, and some people support the notion of a right to offend.

- The controversy shows that cultural diversity can create sharp conflicts where the beliefs and practices that are important to members of one community clash with those of members of a different community. Thus mutual tolerance is not a simple recipe for harmonious relations since people have different ideas about the limits of tolerance.

- This means that cultural diversity cannot simply be celebrated as an unqualified benefit for all members of a society but has to be negotiated. This is difficult, especially if people mark out positions they regard as non-negotiable.

- Although the controversy involved highly polarized positions, for and against the cartoons, it is too simplistic to interpret this as a conflict between Islam and Western liberal values, since there was divided opinion on both sides—many Muslims tolerated the cartoons and many non-Muslims saw them as unreasonable.

- The particular issue of the depiction of Muhammad is part of a more general and long-standing issue of the accommodation of religious beliefs and sensitivities in liberal societies committed to free speech. It is not only Muslims who have protested against representations of their faith in cartoons or other forms of expression.

- Issues raised by cultural diversity often transcend the borders of states—the offence felt by Muslims in Denmark could be felt by Muslims anywhere, and the need to take a stand against self-censorship proclaimed by the Danish newspaper could be supported by people who cherish freedom of speech anywhere.

This case study is adapted from and includes some extracts from Wetherly (2012).

Stop and Think

If multiculturalism stands for the accommodation of cultural differences, what form should this take in relation to the Danish cartoons controversy?

Multiculturalism as an ideology

There is some debate as to whether multiculturalism should be recognized as a distinctive ideology comparable to the long-standing classical ideologies that have dominated political understanding and commitment in the modern era. Multiculturalism is not comparable to 'classical' ideologies such as liberalism and socialism since it has a much narrower focus—whereas socialism and liberalism offer rival accounts of the good society that are comprehensive in scope, whether or not a society is multiculturalist concerns the specific question of how it responds to cultural diversity. For this reason multiculturalism might be regarded as a 'thin' ideology in comparison with the 'thick' ideologies of liberalism and socialism (Freeden 2003). However, multiculturalism still conforms to our understanding of what an ideology is—it constitutes a framework of political understanding and commitment incorporating the three elements of a vision of the good society, critique of the current society, and a programme of action.

If multiculturalism is a 'thin' ideology, in its narrow concern it can be seen, like other 'new' ideologies, as addressing an apparent gap in classical ideologies and therefore as providing a critique of them. To put this point slightly differently, it could be said that multiculturalism deals with a novel issue or problem—that of cultural diversity such as arises from postwar immigration. Although cultural diversity is not strictly a new phenomenon, it can be argued that it is the size and visibility of cultural minorities that is novel. This has been reflected in a new awareness within European and other societies that they have become multicultural, and this awareness has prompted reflection on how to respond to this diversity in the form of multiculturalism as an innovation in policy and in the field of ideology. '"Multiculturalism" entered public discourses in the 1960s and early 1970s, when both Australia and Canada began to declare their support for it', followed by European countries such as the Netherlands and the UK (Rattansi 2011: 7).

Like other ideologies, multiculturalism

- offers a vision of the good society;
- combines political understanding and commitment, theory and action (like feminism, its predominant political expression is through movements and as a current within mainstream political parties);
- involves a set of key values and concepts.

Vision of the good society

In the most basic terms, for multiculturalists a good society is a culturally diverse society, therefore one that 'accommodates' cultural diversity. This is advocated on the basis that it is the right thing to do in the interests of minority groups (that is, a question of justice), but also because it is good for the whole society.

In the British context, one of the most important attempts to formulate a multiculturalist vision was set out in the 2000 report of the 'Commission on the Future of Multi-Ethnic Britain' (often referred to as the 'Parekh Report' after the name of the chair of the commission). The commission's remit was, in part, to 'propose ways of . . . making Britain a confident and vibrant multicultural society at ease with its rich diversity' (Runnymede Trust 2000). The report also advocates as

> both possible and vitally necessary . . . a society in which all citizens and communities feel valued, enjoy equal opportunities . . . and help create a collective life in which the spirit of civic goodwill, shared identity and common sense of purpose goes hand in hand with love of diversity.
>
> (Runnymede Trust 2000)

In similar terms, Parekh characterizes a multiculturalist society as one whose response to cultural diversity is to 'welcome and cherish it, make it central to its self-understanding, and respect the cultural demands of its constituent communities' (Parekh 2000: 6).

These statements can be seen as going beyond the concept of integration set out in the speech by Roy Jenkins in 1966. For Jenkins the formula for integration in a culturally diverse society is 'equal opportunity + mutual tolerance'. For Parekh equal opportunities remain key, but 'tolerance', which can imply 'putting up with' the other, gives way to the more ambitious aspiration that diversity should be 'loved' or 'cherished' and the 'cultural demands' of the diverse communities should be respected (often referred to as '**recognition**').

The leading theorist of multiculturalism, Will Kymlicka, argues that the adoption of multiculturalist ideology and policies constitutes the third wave of a 'human rights revolution' that has advanced since the Second World War. In other words it represents an evolving vision of a good society based on human rights norms (Kymlicka 2010: 35, 2012). This means that, for Kymlicka, multiculturalism can be placed within the liberal tradition—as a liberal vision of the good society. The three waves, each of which carried forward the basic principle of 'the equality of races and peoples' (Kymlicka 2012: 6), have broken as follows:

(1) the struggle for decolonization, concentrated in the period 1948–1965;

(2) the struggle against racial **segregation** and discrimination, initiated and exemplified by the African American **civil rights** movement from 1955 to 1965; and

(3) the struggle for multiculturalism and minority rights, which emerged in the late 1960s (Kymlicka 2012: 6).

Thus multiculturalism builds on and goes beyond the demands and gains of the struggle for civil rights, which can be summed up as equal rights and non-discrimination. This form of equality is necessary but not sufficient. Multiculturalist policies are needed to address 'other forms of exclusion or stigmatization . . . [such as] economic inequalities, political underrepresentation, social stigmatization, or cultural invisibility' (2012: 6). Where Parekh refers to respecting the cultural demands of minorities, Kymlicka refers in similar terms to accommodating 'group-differentiated ethnopolitical claims' (2012: 6). In other words, as we will see later, in this view equality requires not treating all citizens the same but treating minorities differently in some respects. But the human rights revolution has a double role here in that it not only inspires the accommodation of minorities but also constrains their demands.

Key concepts and values

We can identify a number of inter-related concepts or values of multiculturalism:

- cultural diversity, or difference
- identity
- community
- citizenship and equality

Cultural diversity

The core concept of multiculturalism appears to be 'culture'—the ideology derives its name from its focus on the plurality or multiplicity of cultures that co-exist within society. Culture here means, roughly, a 'way of life' involving particular values, beliefs, and practices of various kinds. The concept of culture provides one way of thinking about the question of whether (or in what ways) people are basically the same everywhere or different. Culture is one of the key ways in which people can be said to differ from one another, but, beyond such cultural peculiarities, it can be claimed that people everywhere are essentially the same in the sense of a shared human nature—a sameness that is the foundation for universal morality such as expressed in support for universal human rights. If people are basically the same but, at the same time, different it is the difference to which multiculturalism draws attention and attaches significance.

Although *cultural* difference is what multiculturalism appears to be all about, to some extent this word acts as a catch-all that embraces a range of particular differences. This is evident in the Parekh Report (Runnymede 2000), which is based on an enquiry into multi-*ethnic* Britain, specifically highlights the problem of racial discrimination or racism, and mentions several communities of which individuals are members—religious, **ethnic**, cultural, and regional.

Identity

Multiculturalism is often referred to as a type of 'identity politics'. The 'politics of identity' is concerned with the sense that people have of who they are and how this sense has become an increased source of political contention, or 'politicization'. In other words, it is claimed that identity questions have increasingly become the basis for political demands and action. Immigration and the cultural diversity it has brought in its train is a key factor. Identity politics is also linked to a theory of oppression or injustice, on the grounds that people suffer harm when their identities, their sense of who they are, rooted in their cultures, are marginalized or denigrated within the society. The struggle against such oppression involves the assertion of a positive image of one's culture (e.g. 'gay pride') and the demand that it is valued by the wider society.

How are identities formed? One approach is to see individuals as authors of their own identities, making decisions as they go through life about who they want to be, and adopting values and lifestyles that make sense, or feel right, to them. On the other hand, an obvious response to this view is to point out that identities are shaped by our unchosen social backgrounds and the processes of 'socialization' that we experience. Thus an individualistic view (often associated with liberalism) that sees society as an aggregation of individuals and an outcome of their choices and actions can be contrasted with a sociological view in which we are born into a pre-existing society that shapes our characters. Of course, an in-between view might argue that our characters are always determined both by social background and our capacity for reflection and choice. And the way these influences combine can be seen as an empirical question, a relationship that varies historically and between societies. In other words, social institutions can promote or hinder conformity with tradition and dominant norms or the capacity for autonomy, reflection, and choice.

Multiculturalists come down on the sociological side of this argument, seeing individuals' identities as being inescapably shaped by their membership of particular groups or communities into which they are born.

Community

As expressed in the Parekh report,

> citizens are both individuals and members of particular religious, ethnic, cultural and regional communities. Britain is both a community of citizens and a community of communities, both a liberal and a multicultural society.
>
> (Runnymede Trust 2000)

This statement does not say that citizens should be seen as members of communities *rather* than as individuals, for they are both. But its purpose is to challenge the individualist approach of liberalism and, in effect, turn the spotlight on community, and thereby on difference.

The concept of community brings the idea of identity together with a specific notion of culture, exemplified by Parekh's notion of 'communal diversity', defined in terms of

> self-conscious and more or less well-organised communities entertaining and living by their own different systems of beliefs and practices. They include the newly arrived immigrants, such long-established communities as Jews, Gypsies and the Amish, various religious communities, and such territorially concentrated cultural groups as indigenous peoples, the Basques, the Catalans, the Scots, the Welsh and the Quebecois.
>
> (Parekh 2000: 3–4)

Thus it is communities of this type that make Britain, in common with 'most modern societies' (Parekh 2000: 3), a 'community of communities'. 'Communal diversity . . . springs from and is sustained by a plurality of long-established communities, each with its own long history and way of life which it wishes to preserve and transmit' (Parekh 2000: 4).

All the mentioned communities are minorities within the societies they inhabit— though they may originally have been the majority community (indigenous people) or still constitute the majority within specific territories (national minorities such as the Scots and Welsh). These communities are claimed to have 'systems of beliefs and practices' (i.e. ways of life, or cultures) that are different from each other, and different from the 'mainstream' or dominant culture within the society. The focus on minority communities and cultures is justified by the concern that they risk being dominated, marginalized, and treated unfairly by the majority—their preservation may be under threat. For multiculturalists, minority communities and their different cultures are valuable because they provide their members with their sense of identity, which matters deeply to them (individuals may be said to be 'culturally embedded'). As individuals derive their sense of who they are from their cultures, recognition of these cultures can be seen as an important ingredient of well-being (Taylor 1994; Parekh 2000).

Other than being minorities and exhibiting the communal characteristics that Parekh ascribes to them (self-consciousness or awareness of difference and distinctive identity, organization, and distinctive way of life) the communities listed by Parekh can also be classified into the different types identified earlier: immigrant-origin communities, national minorities, and indigenous people. The different origins have implications for how these communities might be accommodated by the wider society. For example, indigenous peoples typically have territorial claims and demands for autonomy, and national minorities may demand devolution within the nation-state or independence. Immigrants and their descendants, on the other hand, whether arriving as 'economic migrants' or seeking asylum, have no such historic territorial claims or grounds for self-government, and it might be argued that there is an onus on them to 'fit in'. But that sounds like assimilation, which multiculturalists reject. What then, in the case of immigrant-origin communities, does fair integration, allowing them to maintain their cultures and identities, look like?

 Stop and Think

How would you describe your own identity? To what extent is your identity something that you have chosen, or something that is given to you by your membership of a particular group, community, or society?

Citizenship

Citizenship involves a set of rights and duties, famously characterized by Marshall in terms of the evolution in the modern era of civil, political, and social rights (Marshall 1992; Pierson 2011). These are such rights as:

- freedom of expression, religious freedom (civil);
- rights to vote and stand for election (political);
- legal protections for employees such as maternity leave, and rights to benefits and public services (social).

In so far as all members of a society are citizens, it involves a form of equality—everybody enjoys the same rights and incurs the same duties. And citizenship can also be characterized in terms of full 'membership' of the community or nation. Should immigrants be admitted into citizenship on the same terms as members of the host community?

To take two contrasting postwar European examples: the UK 1948 Nationality Act granted unrestricted entry and citizenship to all people from the colonies and ex-colonies (i.e. India, Pakistan, and the West Indies) and the Dominions (i.e. Australia, Canada, New Zealand). In West Germany an ethnic conception of the nation denied citizenship to Turkish immigrants who were treated as 'guest-workers' (*Gastarbeiter*), meaning that they were allowed in as guests only when needed to supplement the workforce and were expected to return home when not needed. Considered more closely and over time, the contrast is less stark: the postwar Labour government did not expect the 1948 Act to encourage 'coloured' immigration and there were attempts to deter it. The initial immigrants from the Caribbean were thought of as guest workers who would not stay indefinitely. And from the early 1960s further 'coloured' immigration was restricted. On the other hand, since the

1990s Germany has moved towards 'an ever more explicit acceptance of guest workers as German' (Rattansi 2011: 36; Malik 2010; see also Kynaston 2007).

It may appear that granting citizenship is exactly the type of fair integration that multiculturalism calls for, accommodating immigrants as full 'members' of society on equal terms with the host community. For the denial of full citizenship amounts to the consignment of immigrants to second-class status. The contrast between the British and German cases would support this—the UK would be regarded as more multiculturalist than Germany.

However, it might not be enough simply to incorporate immigrants into the existing citizenship model as reforms might be needed to ensure equal treatment. We can see this is a number of areas.

Equal opportunity

The first difficulty can be considered in terms of Jenkins' call for equal opportunity and tolerance. One version of equality of opportunity (probably the version Jenkins had in mind) is that people should not be prevented by unfair discrimination from doing what they would otherwise do, for example in the labour and housing markets and in education. Fair discrimination in the jobs market includes choosing between candidates on the basis of their qualifications and experience, whereas unfair discrimination involves selection on the basis of an irrelevant criterion such as race or gender. Laws to prohibit such discrimination are an aspect of citizenship, and campaigns to enact such laws have been part of the historical struggle to extend citizenship. In the UK 'coloured' immigrants faced widespread 'racial' discrimination in the labour and housing markets and therefore did not enjoy equal citizenship. Thus the UK citizenship model had to be reformed (in response to political campaigns) by the introduction of anti-discrimination laws. Roy Jenkins was speaking a year after the introduction of the first such law in the UK, the 1965 Race Relations Act.

Tolerance

One concept of tolerance (again, probably what Jenkins had in mind) is expressed in the maxim 'live and let live', meaning that I leave you to live your life in your own way as long as you do not harm me, and you likewise leave me alone. Alongside the problem of discrimination, 'coloured' immigrants in the UK faced widespread 'racial' prejudice, hatred, and abuse, and such racism is inconsistent with the idea of tolerance and equal citizenship. A related phenomenon is religious intolerance. There is an important difference here since, while racism is irrational, there are reasonable grounds for criticizing, and not tolerating, religious beliefs and practices. This means that ensuring both freedom of religion and freedom to criticize and oppose religion can be a difficult balance (see Case Study 11.2). However, racism can manifest itself in a cultural or specifically religious form, such as in claims about the prevalence of

'Islamophobia' (strictly meaning 'fear of Islam' but in practice standing for 'hatred of Islam' and prejudice against Muslims). In that case, what is ostensibly an attack on Islam as a religion can veil racism directed against Muslims as a group. In response to these problems, the UK citizenship model has been reformed by laws prohibiting racial and religious hatred, notably the Racial and Religious Hatred Act 2006 (House of Commons Library 2009).

Blasphemy

Until 2008 a law of blasphemy in England made it an offence to insult Christianity. What is the purpose of such a law? On the face of it the purpose is to protect the faithful from being offended, but blasphemy laws are controversial because they restrict freedom of expression, specifically the right to criticize religion. This provided a strong argument for repeal of the law in the Criminal Justice and Immigration Act 2008, but a further reason was that in a multi-religious society the law was clearly discriminatory. Thus repeal of the law is a further example of reforming citizenship to ensure equal treatment. Now all religions are treated equally in that their adherents cannot appeal to a law of blasphemy to protect them from offence, but they are protected by the law on religious hatred (Beckford 2008).

Education

Education has been a major focus of multiculturalist policies and initiatives, and this is because education is a key site for cultural transmission. If minority communities wish, as Parekh says, to 'preserve and transmit' their ways of life or cultures, then they are going to want to see those cultures taken into account within schools, for example within the curriculum. Equally, if cultural diversity is, as multiculturalists affirm, of benefit to the wider society and a multiculturalist society is one which cherishes diversity, then school is a place for such cherishing to be nurtured. Thus learning about other cultures might also be expected to counter racial prejudice.

The idea of multicultural schooling for all was proposed in Britain in the 1982 Swann Report, which considered 'the contribution of schools in preparing all pupils for life in a society which is both multi-racial and culturally diverse' (Swann, in Farrar 2012: 11). The report set out a vision of a 'multicultural curriculum [that would] . . . draw on a diversity of cultural sources, and . . . incorporate a world perspective' (in Farrar 2012: 11). In other words the idea is that all children should learn about a range of cultures reflecting the reality of a multicultural society. This amounts to official, public recognition of cultural diversity.

A significant aspect of multicultural education, as endorsed by Swann and now mainstream, is that it can be seen as helping to create a multiculturalist society in which, to quote Parekh again, cultural diversity is 'central to its self-understanding'. In other words, 'preparing for life in a society which is culturally diverse' by learning about a range of cultures implies a revised conception of the British 'way of life' and Britishness.

Multicultural education for all pupils involves a universalist idea that all pupils should learn about diversity in the same way—it makes no special provision for children from minority backgrounds. However education is also the focus of multiculturalist demands that children from minority backgrounds ought, in some ways, to be treated differently, such as in relation to rules governing school uniforms. This takes us on to consideration of 'differentiated' rather than uniform citizenship.

Taking account of difference—'differentiated citizenship'

The idea of differentiated citizenship is sometimes referred to in terms of special rights accorded to specific groups or communities, or 'group rights'. These are rights conferred on members of a specific group that other groups do not enjoy, or exemptions from laws and rules that everybody else has to obey.

Kymlicka argues that multiculturalism involves 'the pursuit of new relations of democratic citizenship' (2012: 1) or 'democratic "citizenization"' (2012: 6), that is, extending citizenship to include minority groups. But this goes beyond the idea that 'the only way to engage in this process of citizenization was to impose a single undifferentiated model of citizenship on all individuals'. The history of lingering inequality after the second (civil rights) wave of the human rights revolution 'inevitably and appropriately generates group-differentiated ethnopolitical claims' to remedy these inequalities (Kymlicka 2012: 6).

The rationale for differentiated citizenship, as stated in the Parekh report, is that

> since citizens have differing needs, equal treatment requires full account to be taken of their differences. When equality ignores relevant differences and insists on uniformity of treatment, it leads to injustice and inequality . . . . Equality must be defined in a culturally sensitive way.

> (Runnymede Trust 2000)

The idea that 'equal treatment' requires difference to be taken into account contrasts with a 'difference-blind' approach in which differences are seen as irrelevant (see Case Study 11.3). The 'differing needs' that are at stake here are due specifically to *cultural* differences. In other words, the different 'ways of life' that exist in a society characterized by communal diversity give rise to different needs. It is in order to sustain these ways of life that specific groups or communities need to be treated differently—'in a culturally sensitive way'. In contrast, it is argued that 'uniformity of treatment' leads to injustice because it prevents some groups from following their preferred way of life or makes it harder. If they cannot live as they choose, they suffer harms that other groups do not suffer and this is a form of inequality. Differential, rather than uniform, treatment can prevent these harms and therefore ensure equality.

Case Study 11.3 To be or not to be . . . 'difference-blind'?

The idea of being 'difference-blind' can refer to a range of differences between people (including sex or gender, age, disability, sexuality, etc.) but for our purpose refers to those differences—especially ethnic, racial, and religious—that are captured by Parekh's conception of communal diversity.

Being difference-blind means ethnic, racial, or religious differences are not taken into account in the way a person is treated, on the basis that such differences are not relevant. This begs two questions: How are the concepts of ethnicity, race, and religion defined? How do we decide in what situations such differences are relevant or not relevant? These concepts are all hard to define, but 'race' is especially problematic. The idea that humanity can be divided into distinct races has long been discredited, so being race-blind involves not taking into account something that doesn't actually exist! Yet, even though there is no scientific basis for identifying distinct racial groups, this does not prevent people from seeing their own, and others', identities in racial terms and acting on these perceptions. For example, people might incite hatred of others on the base of their 'race', so if the law is to be used to prevent this behaviour, it is bound to be framed in terms of prohibiting 'racial hatred'. An unfortunate side-effect is to perpetuate the idea of race as though it really exists.

Although **racism** can assume a 'cultural' form (e.g. 'Islamophobia'), its predominant form has historically involved physical markers of difference, notably skin colour. To understand the demand to be treated in a race-blind manner, the civil rights struggle in the USA in the 1950s and 1960s provides an instructive example. In his 'I have a dream . . .' speech Martin Luther King saw the movement as a struggle to break 'the manacles of segregation and the chains of discrimination' and, in a famous line, proclaimed

> I have a dream that my four little children will one day live in a nation where they will not be judged by the colour of their skin but by the content of their character.

> (King 1963)

In other words, others will not judge, or 'see', them in terms of their skin colour but in terms of their character or personality. Thus being race-blind means non-discrimination in employment, education, and in the offer of services such as washrooms, swimming baths, public transport, hotels, theatres, and cafes. In other words, it is not relevant to take a person's race into account when determining the way they are treated in these situations. There is no good reason for an employer to favour a 'white' applicant over a 'black' candidate. Thus the framing and implementation of equal opportunity laws involves being 'race-aware' in order to enforce a duty to be 'race-blind'.

However, for multiculturalists being race-blind is not always appropriate, for race is sometimes relevant and should be taken into account in determining the way people are treated. Even if races do not exist, this has not prevented African Americans from celebrating their racial identity and advocating black pride, affirmed through such sentiments as 'black is beautiful'. This is, in effect, saying to 'white' society that, beyond equal rights, black people also demand that their distinctive way of life is given recognition and valued.

The idea of 'racial' identity is difficult to disentangle from 'ethnicity', and these terms are often conflated, as in the notion of black and minority ethnic (BME) communities. If racial and ethnic identities matter to people and they take pride in them, it may be expected that they will wish, as Parekh suggests, to 'preserve and transmit' them, which means passing them on to their children. Multiculturalists may then argue that, just as parents have an understandable desire to bring up their children within their own culture, for their part the children have a need, and perhaps even a right, to have their 'heritage' passed on to them. The implication is that they would suffer harm if their heritage were, in some way, denied them. This view is controversial since children do not literally inherit a culture (it is not transmitted genetically). It can be argued that although all children need cultural resources from which their sense of belonging and identity is constructed, it does not need to be the culture of their parents and ought to be something that they have the capacity to choose.

This debate has been conducted in relation to the rights and wrongs of 'inter-racial' adoption. Should adoption decisions be 'race-blind' or should race be taken into account? Is it necessary or desirable for there to be a racial 'fit' between the child and the adopter? Since 2014 UK law has adopted a race-blind stance, removing the previous requirement on adoption agencies to take a child's racial background into account. Against this, multiculturalists argue that racial or ethnic identity should be taken into account when children in care are placed with a family for adoption. Thus, if two potential adopters are alike in other relevant respects (e.g. able to offer material support, a loving environment, etc.) but only one provides a racial or ethnic 'fit', then it is in the best interests of the child to place it with that family as it can provide for the child's cultural needs. A white family is unable, in this view, to transmit to a black child its 'cultural heritage' which is the child's right and without which it will suffer harm.

⮕ Stop and Think

Is it important that children's cultural heritage is passed on to them? Should a child's 'racial' background be taken into account as a relevant factor in adoption decisions?

Multiculturalist policies

What does legal and political accommodation of cultural differences, recognizing 'differing needs' and 'group-differentiated ethnopolitical claims', mean in practice? There is no single prescription for multiculturalist policies and they differ between states. However, Kymlicka has identified eight policies or policy areas as the most 'common or emblematic' forms of immigrant multiculturalist policies. Together they constitute a 'Multiculturalism Policy Index' with which policies of particular states can be compared. The eight policy areas are:

- constitutional, legislative, or parliamentary affirmation of multiculturalism, at the central and/or regional and municipal levels
- the adoption of multiculturalism in school curricula
- the inclusion of ethnic representation/sensitivity in the mandate of public media or media licensing
- exemptions from dress codes, either by statute or by court cases

- the allowing of dual citizenship
- the funding of ethnic group organizations to support cultural activities
- the funding of bilingual education or mother-tongue instruction
- affirmative action for disadvantaged immigrant groups

(Kymlicka 2012: 7)

Diverse responses to diversity

The countries that took the lead in adopting multiculturalist policies were the settler societies of Australia, Canada, and the United States, and these have been joined by a number of European countries, largely in response to immigration. In the postwar period Europe became an important region of immigration, partly involving migration from former colonies, so that foreign-born people became significant proportions of the population in many European countries, creating large immigrant-origin minority communities through the addition of second and third generations, and creating new patters of cultural diversity. Thus

> Germany . . . [became] the world's second most popular immigrant destination, after the United States. In 2013, more than ten million people, or just over 12 percent of the population, were born abroad. In Austria, that figure was 16 percent; in Sweden, 15 percent; and in France and the United Kingdom, around 12 percent.

(Malik 2015a)

European countries that introduced multiculturalist policies include Sweden, the Netherlands, and the UK, while those that have not adopted multiculturalism, or have done so minimally, include France, Germany, Switzerland, and Denmark. In broad terms, multiculturalist approaches can be contrasted with two other types of response: assimilationism exemplified by France, and the *Gastarbeiter* (guest worker) system adopted by Germany (Rex and Singh 2003; Vertovec and Wessendorf 2010). Whereas multiculturalism is concerned with the relations between groups, recognizing diversity as a significant feature of the cultural, social, and political landscape, the non-multiculturalist responses ignore these relations and do not regard diversity as significant because the presence of immigrants in the country is expected to be temporary (Germany) or because immigrant-origin communities are expected to assimilate (France). It is worth noting, though, that multiculturalist countries have often moved onto multiculturalism after initially expecting that immigrants would either not settle or would assimilate. That is, multiculturalism stemmed in part from a realization that these expectations were unrealistic and perhaps unreasonable.

The USA, Canada, and Australia

In the United States a commitment to multiculturalism was a response to cultural diversity resulting from its history of European settlement and the subordination of native Americans, the legacy of slavery and racism, and its history as a country of immigration. Here 'U.S.-born African Americans, Asian Americans, Hispanics, and Native Americans made concerted calls for cultural recognition within schools and colleges starting in the 1960s' (Bloemraad 2011).

In Australia cultural diversity can be seen in terms of relations between descendants of the original British (involuntary) settlers, other white European settlers, indigenous (Aboriginal) people, and non-white immigrants from Asia. Canada was the first Western country to adopt an official policy of multiculturalism (in 1971), and became the only country in which multiculturalism was enshrined in the constitution (Bloemraad 2011; Kymlicka 2012). Cultural diversity stems from the co-existence of two settler nations—British and French—and the relation between them specifically concerns the rights of territorially concentrated French-speakers in Quebec, and more generally the concept of Canada as bilingual and bicultural. Additional dimensions of diversity have resulted from 'later European and Asian immigrants, as well as black and white immigrants from the United States and the Caribbean' plus 'the problem of the native peoples' (Koenig 2003: 11).

The Netherlands

The Netherlands and the UK constitute 'the classical European examples of long-established multicultural policy' (Vertovec and Wessendorf 2010: 23, 25). As in other European countries, Dutch multiculturalism developed in response to diversity resulting from immigration, from former colonies in Asia (Indonesia, Surinam) and North Africa (Morocco, Turkey), and from a realization that immigrants were not guest workers who would return to their countries of origin but who had settled and formed ethnic minorities. Prins and Saharso (2010) identify five stages in the development of Dutch policies towards immigrants from the 1950s: 'assimilation' until the early 1980s, followed by 'pillarization' and 'multiculturalism' in the 1980s and 1990s, and 'new realism' and 'civic integration' since 2002.

The template for multiculturalist policy was provided by the pre-existing approach for managing religious differences (between Catholics, Protestants, and Jews) involving separate cultural spheres, or 'pillarization', rather than promoting interaction. Thus multiculturalist policy allowed 'more formal institutional separation than in other countries, with the minorities being given greater freedom and resources to develop their own schools, newspapers, broadcasting facilities, and cultural associations' (Rattansi 2011: 19). From 1994 the stage identified by Prins and Saharso as multiculturalism involved a stronger emphasis on integration, with affirmation of Dutch culture and identity.

However, the election in 2002, involving the breakthrough of the right-wing, populist Lijst Pim Fortuyn (LPF) as a coalition partner, signalled 'the beginning of a serious backlash against multiculturalism' (Prins and Saharso 2010: 72). Since 2002, the 'new realism' became 'mainstream', criticizing multiculturalism for its emphasis on the acceptance of difference, and advocating instead shared citizenship based on acceptance of Dutch norms. It expressed a particular anxiety about Islam (Prins and Saharso 2010: 87). Thus, in the European context, the Netherlands provides an example of a distinctive multiculturalist policy—pillarization—but has experienced a similar pattern of the rise of multiculturalism followed by a backlash.

France

Cultural diversity in France has resulted mainly from postwar immigration from former colonies in North Africa, creating the largest Muslim community in Europe. In common with other European countries, these immigrants were treated as 'racially other' and regarded as temporary workers who would return to their countries of origin. Policy in relation to the Muslim minority has been framed within the tradition of republicanism although, as in other countries, there have been policy shifts and differing interpretations—'soft' or 'strict'—of republicanism (Rattansi 2011; Simon and Sala Pala 2010). Against a background of the republican tradition, Malik notes that policy has shifted from 'a relatively laid-back stance on multiculturalism, generally tolerating cultural and religious differences' in the 1970s and 1980s (expressed in François Mitterrand's slogan 'droit à la differénce'), to 'a more hardline assimilationist approach' (Malik 2015b).

In contrast with the Netherlands, where the tradition of pillarization was amenable to the development of multiculturalist policy, the French republican tradition has been inhospitable to multiculturalism, so that 'In France . . . republican anti-multiculturalism has always been the dominant position across the political spectrum' (Modood 2007: 13). Indeed, 'French "assimilationist" policies are generally seen as the polar opposite of British-style multiculturalism' (Malik 2015b).

In this context 'assimilation' does not mean that immigrants are expected to leave behind the cultures of their countries of origin and conform to an ethnic conception of Frenchness, but conformity with the republican conception of citizenship. This can be referred to as 'colour-blind republicanism' (where 'colour' encompasses ethnic, racial, and religious differences) and stands for a republic comprised of citizens who are not differentiated according to these traits. This does not mean that these traits do not exist but that they are not relevant to how people are treated as citizens, and have no place in the public sphere. In other words, they are left behind or confined to the private sphere. Thus there is a clash between republicanism, which refuses to recognize cultural differences, and multiculturalism, which does.

The republican tradition entails **secularism** or *laïcité* in which religion is privatized or kept out of the public sphere. 'This is particularly the case in state schools where the radical secularist idea of laïcité is interpreted as the production of future citizens in a religion-free zone, hence the popular banning of . . . headscarves worn by some Muslim girls' (Modood 2007: 75).

From the republican perspective multiculturalism, by treating individuals as members of particular racial or cultural groups, is inherently divisive. However, Malik claims that the two approaches are in fact comparable at a more fundamental level.

> In principle, the French authorities rejected the multiculturalist approach that Britain had adopted. In practice, however, they treated North African migrants and their descendents, in a very 'multicultural' way—as a single community, and primarily as a 'Muslim' community.
>
> (Malik 2015b)

Thus both approaches can be characterized in terms of the politics of identity, in both cases treating immigrants as different or 'other', and in both cases arguably fostering division.

Germany

In Germany, as in France, the political culture has been inhospitable to multiculturalism and, despite Angela Merkel's judgement that multiculturalism had failed, critics argue that it has not been tried. In this case the aspect of political culture that is relevant is the dominance of an ethnic conception of the nation, in contrast with France's civic republican tradition. This ethnic conception meant, until recently, that 'only those of proven German descent could really belong to the nation' (Rattansi 2011: 35), meaning that a person's parents had to be citizens, so that foreigners could not become citizens.

Like other European countries, postwar immigration responded to labour shortages in the growing German economy. Immigrants came from other European countries and, beyond Europe, notably from Turkey. While other countries at first thought of immigrants as temporary workers, in Germany treating them as guestworkers (*Gastarbeiter*) was official policy. Such a policy was inherently exclusionary and divisive. Indeed, 'Germany has encouraged immigrants to pursue separate lives in lieu of granting them citizenship' (Malik 2015a), maintaining their own language and way of life. This may make sense if people are not going to stay very long, but Germany had to come to terms with settlement and the establishment of an ethnic minority. Even though reform at the end of the 1990s provided a route for immigrants to acquire citizenship, the consequence of the guest-worker policy is that 'Out of the three million people of Turkish origin in Germany today, only some 800,000 have managed to acquire citizenship' (Malik 2015a).

Strong and weak multiculturalism

Figure 11.2 shows the strength of commitment to multiculturalist policies in a range of countries in 2010 (the horizontal axis) correlated with the proportion of the population who were foreign-born as a rough measure of ethnic/cultural diversity

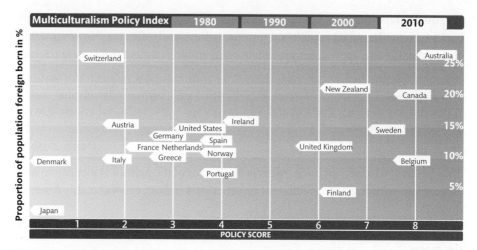

Figure 11.2 Multiculturalism Policy Index scores for selected countries in 2010
Source: Multiculturalism Policy Index, Queen's University, at http://www.queensu.ca/mcp/

(the vertical axis), based on the Multiculturalism Policy Index. The index shows the varying strength of commitment to multiculturalism among these countries, ranging from weak multiculturalist policies (Denmark, Japan) to strong policy responses (Belgium, Sweden, Canada, Australia). There does not appear to be a close relationship between ethnic diversity and multiculturalist policy strength. Figure 11.2 shows a 'snapshot', but the data for the whole period 1980–2010 show 'a recognizable "multiculturalist turn" across Western democracies in the last few decades of the twentieth century' (Kymlicka 2012: 8), and that the commitment to multiculturalism has increased in most of the countries and weakened in only two, including the Netherlands (Bloemraad 2011: Figure 1).

Communal diversity and the classical ideologies

At first glance there appears to be a left–right divide in relation to multiculturalism. On the right, conservatism, nationalism, and fascism place value on national and/ or racial identity and unity and this means that the response to cultural diversity is one of anxiety or hostility. Immigration and the resulting cultural diversity are seen to threaten the social cohesion that is believed to require a shared national or racial identity. Although these traditions on the right appear to stand in opposition to multiculturalism, there is a deeper level of philosophical agreement. Conservatives share with multiculturalists a view of culturally embedded individuals, but privilege the one-ness of the national community over the multiculturalists' notion of a 'community of communities'. In this view cultural diversity, and especially multiculturalism, is divisive.

This means that conservatism favours a monoculturalist response to cultural diversity with an onus on immigrants to assimilate (e.g. Tebbit's 'cricket test'). Some contemporary anti-immigrant movements and parties in Europe draw on more extreme nationalist and fascist ideas, and may see immigrants (particularly Muslims) as unassimilable and cultural diversity as a source of inevitable conflict. Movements such as the English Defence League (EDL) and Pegida in Germany often deny that they are racist and claim to oppose Islam and the supposed threat of the 'Islamization' of Europe rather than Muslims. However, they tend to 'racialize' or stereotype all Muslims as bearers of a backward culture and religion that is incompatible with Western civilization.

On the left, broadly conceived, liberalism and socialism may be seen as 'progressive' ideologies that are more comfortable with cultural diversity. For example, it has been argued that 'the traditional approach of the left has been . . . that diversity is good and that we should . . . embrace it by celebrating our differences' (Johnson 2006: 21), and that 'progressive' politics involves commitment to 'ideals of diversity, cosmopolitanism and anti-racism' (Seabeck et al. 2007: 215). Anti-racism, and opposition to ethnic nationalism, stem from the values of human equality and dignity that are shared by liberalism and socialism and can be seen as aspects of the Enlightenment tradition that the two ideologies inhabit. This standpoint emphasizes ideas of a universal human identity and equal moral worth—people everywhere are basically the same in terms of their needs and capacities and should be treated equally. However, this does not mean that cultural diversity poses no challenges for liberalism and socialism. In fact, in different ways, for liberals and socialists, as for conservatives, identity politics can be criticized as divisive.

Liberalism

On the face of it, there is a close affinity between liberalism and multiculturalism due to their shared commitment to diversity. In liberalism, diversity is closely bound up with the core value of liberty or freedom, defined by John Stuart Mill as each person pursuing their own conception of the good in their own way, subject only to the constraint of not harming others. Thus in the liberal good society freedom allows individuals to carry out diverse 'experiments in living'.

Autonomy

However, as we saw earlier, there appears to be a deep philosophical contrast between liberalism and multiculturalism relating to their foundational concepts of, respectively, the 'individual' and the 'community'. Liberals conceive society as made up of individuals—they are the basic units or 'building blocks' of society through their choices and actions, and it is the interests and needs of individual human beings that matter from a moral standpoint rather than collective entities such as communities or nations. In

contrast, multiculturalism conceives society as a 'community of communities'. This
is not to say that liberals neglect community, or that multiculturalists disregard individuals. After all, Parekh sees society as a 'community of communities' and a community of (individual) citizens. For multiculturalists community matters for individual
well-being, because individuals are 'rooted' or 'embedded' in communities. But it is
precisely this notion of embeddedness that is challenged by liberalism on the basis of
its view of individuals as capable of making choices for themselves about how they
live their lives. It is this capacity for autonomy that should be nurtured in a good
society so that individuals can, if they choose, 'uproot' themselves from the prevailing
way of life of a community. From a liberal point of view, the idea that individuals are
embedded in a communal way of life might involve unhealthy conformism, and the
challenge to it is similar to the challenge presented to the conservative attachment to
tradition. This does not mean that liberalism disregards community or fails to see its
importance in individuals' lives, but the key point is that membership of community
should be voluntary—individuals should opt in and be able to opt out.

The idea of a 'community of communities' each with its own distinctive way of life
is likely to be treated sceptically by liberals on the grounds that 'cultural needs' may be
defined by more traditional and 'conservative' elements within the community who
are in positions of authority, that there may be powerful pressures to conform within
the community, and that the idea of a homogeneous community may conceal internal debates, diversity, and oppositional voices. For example, the Muslim Women's
Network aims to provide a voice to the diverse experiences and needs of Muslim
women. Among its principles it states 'We are an Islamic feminist movement that uses
the Quran's spirit of equality and justice to challenge human interpretations (based
on culture and tradition) that discriminate against women and girls, to achieve equal
rights and opportunities for all' (http://www.mwnuk.co.uk/index.php).

Multiculturalists may respond that they share these concerns that adherence to the
way of life of a community should not be coerced and that internal debate and dissent
should be allowed. Parekh also favours 'interactive multiculturalism' in which cultural communities are open to outside influences and it is accepted that no culture is
above criticism. This suggests a more fluid notion of culture, but this does seem to be
in tension with the notion of distinctive ways of life. The idea of openness to external
influence also seems to be in tension with the idea that members of communities
wish to 'preserve and transmit' their culture, since a strong desire for preservation
is likely to lead to outside influences and criticisms being perceived as threats. The
desire to 'transmit' cultural beliefs and practices can also lead to pressure on children
to conform rather than nurturing their capacity for autonomy.

Illiberal practices

The main concern of liberals around cultural diversity relates to beliefs and practices
that violate liberal principles of freedom and equality. Barry advocates 'the classical

ideal of liberal citizenship' or 'unitary republican citizenship, in which all citizens share the identical set of common citizenship rights' (Barry 2001a: 7) based on universalist principles. This approach is compatible with 'appropriate acknowledgement of cultural differences' (Barry 2001b: 1) in the form of prohibiting indirect discrimination (e.g. 'making demands (as a condition of employment, for example) that are disproportionately burdensome to some people in virtue of their religious beliefs or norms, and cannot be justified as necessary for the conduct of the business' (Barry 2001b: 1)), and affirmative action (Barry 2001). But it is, in principle, 'fundamentally in conflict' (Barry 2001a:1) with the particularism of multiculturalism and group rights which Barry opposes: 'multiculturalist policies are not in general well designed to advance the values of liberty and equality, and . . . tend . . . to mark a retreat from both . . . . [G]roup differentiated rights . . . can [only] be supported pragmatically' (2001a: 12).

Barry is particularly concerned that accommodating the 'cultural needs' of minorities might open the door to illiberal practices that harm certain members of these communities, and has warned against 'the toxic consequences of multiculturalism in . . . reinforcing the traditional repression of women, children and nonconformists among immigrant minorities and indigenous peoples' (2005: ix). Barry criticizes Parekh's argument for accommodating the cultural needs of minorities because his retreat from universalism leaves him without a firm ground on which to reject such practices and means that he 'fails to make enough of the expectations that minority ethnic communities can be held to' (Barry 2001b: 4).

Liberal multiculturalism?

Liberal multiculturalists such as Kymlicka attempt to reconcile liberalism and multiculturalism, by emphasizing the importance of human rights as a constraint on the permissible range of cultural practices. Rattansi (2011: 3) states that 'supposedly traditional cultural practices cannot be allowed to override considerations of essential human rights', and Kymlicka argues that human rights set the expectations that minority ethnic communities can be held to that Barry seeks.

> [H]istorically excluded or stigmatized groups . . . have to renounce their own traditions of exclusion or oppression in the treatment of, say, women, gays, people of mixed race, religious dissenters, and so on. Human rights, and liberal-democratic constitutionalism more generally, provide the overarching framework within which these struggles are debated and addressed.
>
> (Kymlicka 2012: 6)

Kymlicka further argues that this principle has been carried through in the implementation of multiculturalist policies. 'No Western democracy has exempted immigrant groups from constitutional norms of human rights in order to maintain practices such as forced marriage, criminalization of apostasy, or cliterodectomy' (Kymlicka 2012: 9).

> **→ Stop and Think**
>
> Do you agree that an owner of a bed and breakfast business who believes, on the basis of religious conviction, that homosexuality is sinful should be prevented from turning away a gay couple? (For further information on a real case, see Davies 2012.)

Socialism

Liberalism is essentially difference-blind, conceiving individuals as born equal and equally entitled to the same set of human rights. Multiculturalism may be seen as divisive because it encourages us to view each other through the **particularist** lens of identity politics rather than the universalist lens of our common humanity. There are some similarities with socialism, which may also be seen as difference-blind and critical of multiculturalism for its particularist standpoint. However, unlike liberalism, socialism does not see society as a collection of individuals but as a class structure. In other words, individuals are seen first and foremost as members of distinct classes with conflicting interests. The central organizing principle of a capitalist society is the class relationship between workers and capitalists. This view is difference-blind in the sense that cultural differences are irrelevant to people's shared class interests. For example, workers' (predicted or actual) feelings of solidarity in the class struggle with capitalists arise from their shared experience of exploitation and are unaffected by irrelevant differences based on race, ethnicity, or religion. This does not mean that workers are not also individuals or that they do not also have diverse communal memberships, but that these are secondary considerations in the analysis of capitalist society.

This does not mean that socialists take no interest in disadvantage experienced by members of 'racial' and ethnic minorities, such as higher levels of unemployment and lower living standards. On the contrary, although the 'labour movement' has been far from free of racist beliefs, socialists have often been at the forefront of the struggle against racism and fascism. Sometimes this has included the defence of multiculturalism, as in campaigns by the group Unite Against Fascism (http://uaf.org.uk/; Mahamdallie 2011). However, in general the attitude to multiculturalism has been critical. One reason is that the strand of multiculturalism emphasizing a 'multicultural curriculum', 'learning about other cultures', and 'celebrating diversity' (parodied as the 'saris, samosas, and steel drums' approach) has been criticized for failing to address the deep-rooted nature of racism and disadvantage (Rattansi 2011: 27). Second, tackling racism and disadvantage has been seen as part of a wider struggle against social injustice requiring a wider unity with working class struggles. Identity politics is seen as divisive because it diverts attention away from this wider struggle and dissipates energy in a series of particularistic campaigns in which different communities compete with one another for political influence and resources. In other words, 'difference' has emerged as an alternative and competing basis of political mobilization to class interest.

Some left-wing critics see this particularism as, in part, an unintended consequence of misguided multiculturalist policies by political elites at local or national level which, by addressing people as members of particular racial, ethnic, or religious communities, have encouraged the rise of narrowly focused identity politics (Malik 2009). From a Marxist perspective, racism has been understood as a conscious 'divide and rule' strategy implemented by the capitalist class in order to benefit from a weakened working class and cheaper labour. Thus racism helps to keep capitalism going (Callinicos 1994). These views question the sociological reality of communal diversity, since the consciousness of difference that Parekh sees as a reflection of individuals' rootedness in communities may be driven largely by top-down policies implemented by political and economic elites.

Feminism

It is sometimes argued that multiculturalism is particularly bad for women, as well as for gay people (Okin 1999; Barry 2001a). This is because some ethnic minorities do not accept principles of equality in relation to women and members of the LGBT community, usually on the basis of religious teachings (although the distinction between 'religious' and 'cultural' reasons may be contested and hard to establish). Of course this is not just a problem of minorities—both Christianity and Islam have been criticized for harbouring sexist and homophobic beliefs and practices.

This can be seen, for example, in the long-running debate in the Church of England about opening the priesthood to women and gays, and in Catholic attitudes to homosexuality, divorce, and contraception.

It is important to avoid **essentialising** Islam as sexist as though all Muslims have the same beliefs and practices. Instead, as we have seen, there are Muslim voices and organizations which challenge sexist beliefs and practices, such as the Muslim Women's Network, and attempts to create an 'Islamic feminism' such as by the group Maslaha (http://www.maslaha.org/about). Multiculturalists may also argue that multiculturalism does not stand for an 'anything goes' attitude to minority cultures but for a critical engagement between cultures.

The feminist critique of Islam clearly overlaps with liberalism, to the extent that it is normally a liberal feminist position from which that critique is made. Thus we have seen that liberalism opposes practices that are harmful to women, such as forced marriage. We have also seen that supporters of a ban on the burqa may state their position in terms of a liberal feminist demand for sexual equality, on the grounds that Muslim women and girls are coerced within their communities. On the other hand, opposition to a ban is often expressed in terms of it being an illiberal measure that fails to recognize that Muslim women may choose freely to wear the burqa—see Case Study 11.4).

Case Study 11.4 Banning the burqa

Before 2011 Muslim women in France, as in all other European countries, were free to wear the niqab or burqa (which cover the face) in line with their religious beliefs, although relatively few adopted this form of dress. Wearing the burqa was a cultural or religious practice that Muslim women were not expected to renounce as a condition of integration into European societies. It could be said, then, that this freedom demonstrated a commitment to multiculturalism. In 2004 a law banning Muslim headscarves (the niqab) and other 'conspicuous' religious symbols specifically at state schools was introduced in France. However, in 2010 a law was enacted (coming into force in 2011) making it 'illegal for anyone to cover their face . . . anywhere in public in France'. Although the law was not restricted only to face veils it was widely perceived as intended to target Muslims. Indeed the law was justified as a 'defence of women's rights and secularism'—the veil being seen as a sign of the oppression of Muslim women who are perceived as coerced into wearing it, and as a challenge to the French tradition of secularism in which religion is a private matter to be kept out of the neutral public sphere. The law can be seen as a change of heart by the government in France and part of a more general 'backlash' against multiculturalism. The ban was upheld by the European Court of Human Rights (ECtHR) in 2014, ruling that 'the preservation of a certain idea of "living together" was the "legitimate aim" of the French authorities' (Willsher 2014).

The French ban was the first in Europe, closely followed by a similar law banning the veil in Belgium. Similar laws have been debated or introduced in other European countries, at national or local level including Barcelona in Spain, Switzerland (Ticino region), and Italy.

In Britain, there have been proposals for a law enforcing a 'burqa ban' but these have made little headway within the mainstream parties, despite evidence of persistent majority public support for such a ban. In a 2013 poll, 61 per cent of respondents agreed that 'the burka should be banned in Britain' with 32 per cent disagreeing. Reflecting ideological standpoints, clear majorities of UKIP (93 per cent) and Conservative (71 per cent) supporters favoured a ban, with lower levels of support among Labour (55 per cent) and Liberal Democrat voters (47 per cent) (YouGov 2013). In 2013 Conservative MP Philip Hollobone introduced a Private Member's bill—the Face Coverings (Prohibition) Bill—which would have created an offence of wearing a garment covering the face in a public place. The 'ban-the-burqa bill', which failed to make it into law, was modelled on the French ban introduced in 2011.

In the same year, a liberal democrat minister in the coalition government said that 'the government should consider banning young Muslim women from wearing the veil in public places . . . . The Home Office minister, Jeremy Browne, called for a national debate on whether the state should step in to prevent young women having the veil imposed upon them (Press Association 2013). However this suggestion did not materialize in a bill before Parliament.

➲ Stop and Think

Are you in favour of a law, such as in France, which prohibits wearing the burqa or niqab in public places? Should the French approach be adopted in other countries?

Has multiculturalism failed?

Multiculturalism is a 'new' ideology, originating around the 1960s, and yet it is already beset by accusations of failure. Of course, multiculturalist ideology and policies have always been contested, but from around 2000 it has become common to speak of a backlash (Vertovec and Wessendorf 2010). In this view, the story of multiculturalism is one of a rise followed by a rapid fall and even demise. The backlash is particularly associated with the 'revolt on the right'—the rise of nationalist, xenophobic, anti-immigration/anti-immigrant, and Islamophobic parties and movements in many European countries (although, despite their shared hostility to immigration and diversity, there are differences between these parties). This includes countries that have implemented multiculturalist policies such as the Netherlands (Party for Freedom) and Sweden (Sweden Democrats) as well as countries that have not been multiculturalist such as France (National Front) and Germany (Alternative for Germany) (Adler 2016; *New York Times* 2016). However, the backlash is not confined to far-right parties that were never sympathetic to immigration and diversity, but also includes mainstream parties and politicians of the centre-right (Christian democrats and conservatives) and centre-left (social democrats).

In 2016 both the UK referendum vote to leave the EU (Brexit) and the victory of Donald Trump in the US presidential election can be seen as manifestations of the revolt on the right, and in both cases hostility to immigration and diversity were prominent issues—immigration from eastern European EU states in the case of Brexit, and immigration from Mexico in the Trump campaign.

The backlash against multiculturalism is real enough. But does this mean that multiculturalist policies are being reversed or have failed? Against this backlash narrative, Kymlicka argues that, although there have been some notable retreats from multiculturalist policies (the Netherlands), the evidence shows that these policies have been strengthened or remained constant in most European countries between 2000 and 2010 (see Figure 11.2). Further, although evidence of the actual impacts of multiculturalist policies is limited, Kymlicka (2012: 21) argues that it does not support the claim that 'multiculturalism has failed and instead offers evidence that multiculturalist policies have had positive effects' in terms of political participation and social cohesion.

Since cultural diversity is a permanent characteristic of European societies (monoculturalism is not a realistic option), this diversity will need to be managed. This suggests that a rejection of multiculturalism flies in the face of the reality of these societies and, instead, the debate will necessarily be about the precise nature of the multiculturalist accommodation. Kymlicka argues that 'in the long term, the only viable response to the presence of large numbers of immigrants is some form of liberal multiculturalism' (2012: 24). Since these societies are *multicultural* they will have to be, in some form, *multiculturalist*.

Summary

- Although, in global terms, European societies are relatively homogeneous, increased cultural diversity, largely as a result of postwar immigration, has become the focus of increased political attention and controversy.

- Multiculturalism is a normative or ideological response to the 'facts' of cultural diversity. In contrast with 'monoculturalism', it does not require minorities to assimilate but aims to accommodate diversity.

- Integration is normally seen as a two-way process of mutual adjustment between minority immigrant-origin communities and the majority community, in contrast with assimilation or segregation.

- Multiculturalism can be viewed as a distinct, if thin, ideology as it constitutes a framework of political understanding and commitment incorporating the three elements of a vision of the good society, a critique of current society, and a programme of action.

- There is more than one version of multiculturalism. A key area of debate concerns the idea of differentiated citizenship. Multiculturalism has developed through a dialogue with existing ideologies.

- In recent years there has been a backlash against multiculturalism, partly fuelled by the 'revolt on the right'.

Review and discussion questions

1. Critically evaluate the characterization of British society as 'both a community of citizens and a community of communities'.

2. Discuss to what extent liberalism and multiculturalism are compatible.

3. Explain what is meant by a 'difference-blind' approach to cultural diversity and consider whether it is sufficient.

4. Explain the distinction between 'assimilation' and 'integration'.

Research exercises

1. Use BBC and newspaper archives to research three cases in which an exemption from a law or rule has been claimed on the basis of religious beliefs, summarize the cases, and reflect on the findings of your research in relation to the idea of multiculturalist accommodation.

2. Examine three recent speeches on immigration and/or multiculturalism from party leaders or spokespersons. Identify key areas of agreement and disagreement using 8–10 bullet points.

Further reading

Rattansi (2011) is an excellent short introduction to the multiculturalist debate. For particular approaches see Parekh (2000), Modood (2007), and Kymlicka (2012). Runnymede Trust (2000) is an important statement of multiculturalist principles, and Cantle (2001) provides a critique and argument for an alternative approach of 'interculturalism'. Barry (2001a) provides a critique of multiculturalism and defence of a left-liberal position. Malik (2009) is a left-wing critique, and Mahamdallie (2011) offers a defence from the left.

References

ADLER, K. (2016), 'Is Europe Lurching to the Far Right?' http://www.bbc.co.uk/news/world-europe-36150807

BARRY, B. (2001a), *Culture and Equality: An Egalitarian Critique of Multiculturalism*, Cambridge: Polity.

BARRY, B. (2001b), 'The Muddles of Multiculturalism', *New Left Review*, Vol. 8, March/April.

BARRY, B. (2005), *Why Social Justice Matters*, Cambridge: Polity.

BECKFORD, M. (2008), 'Blasphemy Laws are Lifted', *The Telegraph*, 10 May, http://www.telegraph.co.uk/news/1942668/Blasphemy-laws-are-lifted.html

BLEICH, E. (2006), 'On Democratic Integration and Free Speech: Response to Tariq Modood and Randall Hansen', *International Migration*, Vol. 44, No. 5 (this special issue of the journal has a number of articles on the cartoons controversy).

BLOEMRAAD, I. (2011), 'The Debate Over Multiculturalism: Philosophy, Politics, and Policy', *The Online Journal of the Migration Policy Institute*, http://www.migrationpolicy.org/article/debate-over-multiculturalism-philosophy-politics-and-policy

CALLINICOS, A. (1994), *Race and Class*, London: Bookmarks.

CANTLE, T. (2001), *Community Cohesion: A Report of the Independent Review Team*, London: Home Office.

CARVEL, J. (2004), 'Tebbit's Cricket Loyalty Test Hit for Six', *The Guardian*, 8 January, http://www.theguardian.com/uk/2004/jan/08/britishidentity.race

CASTLES, S., DE HAAS, H., AND MILLER, M. J. (2015), *The Age of Migration*, Basingstoke: Palgrave Macmillan.

DAVIES, L. (2012), 'Christian Who Refused to Let Gay Couple Stay at B&B Ordered to Pay Damages', *The Guardian*, 18 October, http://www.theguardian.com/world/2012/oct/18/christian-gay-couple-ordered-pay-damages

DIAMOND, J. (2012), *The World Until Yesterday*, Harmondsworth: Penguin Books.

FARRAR, M. (2012), 'Multiculturalism in the UK: A Contested Discourse', in M. Farrar, S. Robinson, Y. Valli, and P. Wetherly, *Islam in the West: Key Issues in Multiculturalism*, Basingstoke: Palgrave Macmillan.

FISHER, M. (2013), 'A Revealing Map of the World's Most and Least Ethnically Diverse Countries', *The Washington Post*, 16 May, https://www.washingtonpost.com/news/worldviews/wp/2013/05/16/a-revealing-map-of-the-worlds-most-and-least-ethnically-diverse-countries/

FREEDEN, M. (2003), *Ideology: A Very Short Introduction*, Oxford: Oxford University Press.

HOUSE OF COMMONS LIBRARY (2009), The Racial and Religious Hatred Act 2006, http://research-briefings.parliament.uk/ResearchBriefing/Summary/SN03768

JOHNSON, N. (2006), ' "We're All in This Together": The Challenges of Diversity, Equality and Solidarity', *Renewal*, Vol. 14, No. 4.

KING, M. L. (1963), 'I have a Dream' (speech), in B. MacArthur (1999), *The Penguin Book of Twentieth Century Speeches*, Harmondsworth: Penguin Books. Also available at http://news.bbc.co.uk/1/hi/world/americas/3170387.stm

KLAUSEN, J. (2009), *The Cartoons that Shook the World*, New Haven, CT: Yale University Press.

KOENIG, M. (2003), 'Editorial', *International Journal on Multicultural Societies*, Vol. 5, No. 1, UNESCO.

KYMLICKA, W. (2010), 'The Rise and Fall of Multiculturalism? New Debates on Inclusion and Accommodation in Diverse Societies', in S. Vertovec and S. Wessendorf, *The Multiculturalism Backlash. European Discourses, Policies and Practices*, Abingdon: Routledge.

KYMLICKA, W. (2012), *Multiculturalism: Success, Failure, and the Future*, Washington, DC: Migration Policy Institute.

KYNASTON, D. (2007), *The Smoke in the Valley*, London: Bloomsbury.

LUPTON, R. AND POWER, A. (2004) *Minority Ethnic Groups in Britain*, Center for Analysis of Social Exclusion (CASE), http://sticerd.lse.ac.uk/dps/case/CBCB/census2_part1.pdf

MACARTHUR, B. (1999), *The Penguin Book of Twentieth Century Speeches*, Harmondsworth: Penguin Books.

MAHAMDALLIE, H. (ed.) (2011), *Defending Multiculturalism: A Guide for the Movement*, London: Bookmarks.

MALIK, K. (2009), *From Fatwa to Jihad: The Rushdie Affair and its Legacy*, London: Atlantic Books.

MALIK, K. (2010), 'A Merkel Attack on Multiculturalism', http://www.kenanmalik.com/essays/expressen_merkel.html

MALIK, K. (2015a), 'The Failure of Multiculturalism: Community Versus Society in Europe', *Foreign Affairs*, March/April issue, https://www.foreignaffairs.com/articles/western-europe/failure-multiculturalism

MALIK, K. (2015b), 'Assimilationism vs Multiculturalism', https://kenanmalik.wordpress.com/2015/01/12/assimilationism-vs-multiculturalism/

MALNICK, E. (2014), 'Lord Tebbit Suggests more British Asians Now Pass his Cricket Test', *The Telegraph*, 30 September, http://www.telegraph.co.uk/news/politics/11131816/Lord-Tebbit-suggests-more-British-Asians-now-pass-his-cricket-test.html

MARSHALL, T. H. (1992), *Citizenship and Social Class*, London: Pluto.

MODOOD, T. (2007), *Multiculturalism*, Cambridge: Polity.

MORIN, R. (2013), 'The Most (and Least) Culturally Diverse Countries in the World', Pew Research Center, http://www.pewresearch.org/fact-tank/2013/07/18/the-most-and-least-culturally-diverse-countries-in-the-world/

NEW YORK TIMES (2016), 'Europe's Rising Far Right: A Guide to the Most Prominent Parties', 13 June, http://www.nytimes.com/interactive/2016/world/europe/europe-far-right-political-parties-listy.html?_r=0

OFFICE FOR NATIONAL STATISTICS (2012), *2011 Census: Key Statistics for England and Wales, March 2011*, http://webarchive.nationalarchives.gov.uk/20160105160709/http://www.ons.gov.uk/ons/dcp171778_290685.pdf

OKIN, S. (1999), *Is Multiculturalism Bad for Women?* Princeton, NJ: Princeton University Press.

PAREKH, B. (2000), *Rethinking Multiculturalism: Cultural Diversity and Political Theory*, Basingstoke: Macmillan Press.

PIERSON, C. (2011), *The Modern State*, Abingdon: Routledge.

PRESS ASSOCIATION (2013), 'Lib Dem Minister Calls for Debate on Islamic Veil', *The Guardian*, 16 September, http://www.theguardian.com/politics/2013/sep/16/debate-muslim-veil-lib-dem-minister

PRINS, B. AND SAHARSO, S. (2010), 'From Toleration to Repression—The Dutch Backlash against Multiculturalism', in S. Vertovec and S. Wessendorf, *The Multiculturalism Backlash. European Discourses, Policies and Practices*, Abingdon: Routledge.

RATTANSI, A. (2011), *Multiculturalism: A Very Short Introduction*, Oxford: Oxford University Press.

REX, J. AND SINGH, G. (2003), 'Multiculturalism and Political Integration in Modern Nation States: Thematic Introduction', *International Journal on Multicultural Societies*, Vol. 5, No. 1, UNESCO.

RUNNYMEDE TRUST (2000), *The Future of Multi-ethnic Britain: The Parekh Report*, London: Profile Books.

SEABECK, A., ROGERS, B., AND SRISKANDARAJAH, D. (2011), 'Living Together: Diversity and Identity in Contemporary Britain', in N. Pearce and J. Margo (eds), *Politics for a New Generation: The Progressive Moment*, Basingstoke: IPPR/Palgrave.

SIMON, P. AND SALA PALA, V. (2010), '"We're Not All Multiculturalists Yet". France Swings between Hard Integration and Soft Anti-discrimination', in S. Vertovec and S. Wessendorf, *The Multiculturalism Backlash. European Discourses, Policies and Practices*, Abingdon: Routledge.

TAYLOR, C. (1994), *Multiculturalism and the 'Politics of Recognition'*, Princeton, NJ: Princeton University Press.

VERTOVEC, S. AND WESSENDORF, S. (2010), *The Multiculturalism Backlash. European Discourses, Policies and Practices*, Abingdon: Routledge.

Wetherly, P. (2012), 'Freedom of Expression, Multiculturalism, and the "Danish cartoons"', in M. Farrar, S. Robinson, Y. Valli, and P. Wetherly (eds), *Islam in the West: Key Issues in Multiculturalism*, Basingstoke: Palgrave.

Willsher, K. (2014), 'France's Burqa Ban Upheld by Human Rights Court', *The Guardian*, 1 July, http://www.theguardian.com/world/2014/jul/01/france-burqa-ban-upheld-human-rights-court

YouGov (2013), 'Most Still Want to Ban the Burka in Britain', https://yougov.co.uk/news/2013/09/18/most-still-want-ban-burka-britain/

12

Religion, politics, and fundamentalism

Paul Wetherly

OBJECTIVES

- Define religion and examine the nature and extent of religious affiliation in the modern world—is religion in decline?

- Consider whether religion can be regarded as an ideology, and examine the relationship between religion and secular ideologies

- Critically examine arguments about the role of religion in politics—the separation of church and state, and 'religious talk' in politics

- Discuss the concept of fundamentalism as a form of political belief and the nature of religious fundamentalism

- Assess the nature and impact of movements based on religious fundamentalism in the modern world

Introduction

Mention 'religious fundamentalism' and most people will probably think of al Qaeda or so-called Islamic State (otherwise known as IS, ISIS, ISIL, or Daesh). But religious fundamentalism is not confined to Islam, and fundamentalism is not confined to religion. In addition, religious fundamentalism is only one way in which religion participates in the political arena. Therefore, this chapter approaches religious fundamentalism from wider angles, looking at both 'religion' and 'fundamentalism' in politics more generally.

In this chapter we will examine the nature of religion, consider the evidence concerning the religious 'landscape' in the modern world, and scrutinize the relationship between religion and politics. This relationship can be considered in two ways: empirically (involving evidence of what the relationship is), and normatively (involving arguments about what the relationship should be—the proper role of religion in relation to politics). We will consider how far religion can be understood as an ideology and, in particular, the phenomenon of 'religious fundamentalism'.

What is religion?

Religion is a contested concept. It is easy enough to *name* some of the major religions in the modern world, but harder to *define* what religion is in general terms.

The difficulty of defining religion satisfactorily is that definitions tend to be either too narrow and thus exclude some things that are accepted as religions, or else too broad and include things which are not recognized as religions. For example, if the definition includes belief in the existence of a personal God then it excludes Buddhism. One attempt to define religion that is probably as good as any other is as follows:

> Religion can be explained as a set of beliefs concerning the cause, nature, and purpose of the universe, especially when considered as the creation of a superhuman agency or agencies, usually involving devotional and ritual observances, and often containing a moral code governing the conduct of human affairs.
>
> (BBC no date, in Macey and Carling 2011: 2)

This definition incorporates the idea of 'transcendence' but omits what Parekh argues is a related idea of religion, which is 'faith'. Indeed the word faith is often used as if it is synonymous with religion. The transcendental principle is expressed in the idea that the 'cause, nature, and purpose of the universe' derive from an external source (particularly, God as the creator and ruler of the universe and therefore not bound by its laws). The second idea is connected: 'Since the nature of the transcendental source and its relation to the world are not a matter of empirical observation, religion involves faith' (Parekh 2008: 130). Thus beliefs grounded in faith are counter-posed to beliefs grounded in empirical observation or the method of scientific enquiry.

In the BBC definition, religion is a 'set of beliefs', usually including 'a moral code governing the conduct of human affairs'. This means that religion is concerned with the way humans live their lives and, therefore, the nature of the good society. To be, say, a good Christian or Muslim involves living your life according to a 'moral code' and, by extension, this code may encourage you to act in the world so as to make it a better place. In other words, religious beliefs can spill over into social and political action and so enter into the field in which secular ideologies compete by contesting visions of the good society. For example, Ruthven, in defining Islam, states that it 'may be both a religious faith [involving specific beliefs and practices] and a political ideology; it is also, in some contexts, a mark of personal and group identity' (Ruthven 1997: 2), but this is not peculiar to Islam—the same point could be made about other religions.

However, the relationship between religion as a faith and as an ideology is contested, and we should not assume that the ideology is reducible to, or a true expression of, the faith. Even though ideologists may make this claim, other adherents of the faith may dispute it. To take an obvious example, most Muslims would reject the claim by terrorist groups such as so-called Islamic State that they have a religious justification on the grounds that Islam is a religion of peace so those who commit terrorist acts cannot be true Muslims. In general, religions are not monolithic and there are disagreements on the set of beliefs that a religion holds, including the moral code. There are, it could be said, many ways to be, say, a good Christian or Muslim.

 Stop and Think

Why is religion difficult to define? In what way is religion, as defined by the BBC, similar to a political ideology?

Religiosity in the modern world–the resurgence of religion?

Religious belief is pervasive in the modern world, but there are large variations in religiosity between regions and states. According to a survey carried out in sixty-five countries in 2015, 63 per cent identify as a 'religious person', 22 per cent as 'not a religious person', and 11 per cent identify as a 'convinced **atheist**'. Western Europe has the lowest proportion of religious people (43 per cent) and is joined with Oceania as the only two regions in which the religious are a minority, whereas the most religious region is Africa (86 per cent). However, the two least religious countries are Japan (13 per cent religious) and China (7 per cent). Within western Europe the least religious countries are the Netherlands (26 per cent) and Sweden (19 per cent), with 26 per cent of the UK identifying as religious (see Case Study 12.1), while the most religious are Portugal (60 per cent) and highly religious Italy (74 per cent). The survey shows that the United States is notably more religious than western Europe (56 per cent compared to 43 per cent) (Akkoc 2015; WIN/Gallup 2015). Of course, just as religiosity varies between western European countries, so it varies between American states.

Christianity and Islam are the world's two largest religions and, according to the Pew Research Center (2012b), Christians (31.5 per cent) and Muslims (23.2 per cent) together made up more than half of the global population in 2010. It is estimated that Muslims are the fastest growing religious group, and will have increased to 30 per cent of the global population by 2050, almost equalling the share of Christians which is projected to remain stable at 31.5 per cent (Pew Research Center 2015b).

The proportion of people who are not affiliated to any religion is expected to increase in the United States and Europe, but to decrease on a global scale. Thus, on this measure, religiosity is growing in the modern world (Pew Research Center 2015b).

Case Study 12.1 Is Britain a 'Christian country'?

In his 2016 'Easter message' UK Prime Minister (at the time) David Cameron declared that we should have 'the confidence to say yes, we are a Christian country and we are proud of it'. Is there evidence to support this claim, or is it more accurate to describe Britain as a secular country?

There are three ways in which we might understand the claim that Britain is a Christian country: historical, official, and cultural. Two of these understandings are persuasive.

1. Historical: Britain is *historically* a Christian country or has a Christian *heritage*. Every Western country is religious in these terms since in the past religion was the universal basis of belief.

Therefore it is true that Christian values 'have helped to make our country what it is today'. This can be seen in the second persuasive understanding.

2. Official: Britain has an *official* or established Anglican church, with bishops in the legislature and the head of state as defender of the faith.

But Cameron suggested a third understanding, upon which the legitimacy of the official status of the Church arguably rests.

3. Cultural: Christianity plays a significant or pervasive role in British society, in terms of the way people think about their *identities*, beliefs and values

How persuasive is this understanding? What does the evidence tell us about the extent to which Britain is a Christian country in this sense or, more generally, a religious country?

RELIGIOUS IDENTITY

The report of the Commission on Religion and Belief in British Public Life (2015) identifies three trends as a result of which 'Britain's landscape in terms of religion and belief has been transformed beyond recognition':

- The first is the increase in the number of people with non-religious beliefs and identities. Almost a half of the population today describes itself as non-religious . . .

- The second is the general decline in Christian affiliation . . . Thirty years ago, two-thirds of the population would have identified as Christians. Today, that figure is four in ten . . .

- The third is the increased diversity amongst people who have a religious faith. Fifty years ago Judaism—at one in 150—was the largest non-Christian tradition in the UK. Now it is the fourth largest behind Islam, Hinduism, and Sikhism.

(Commission on Religion and Belief in British Public Life 2015)

In sum, as demonstrated by Figure 12.1, Britain is not a majority Christian country. It has been transformed from a majority Christian country in 1983 (67 per cent) to a minority Christian country in 2014 (42 per cent). While belonging to a religion other than Christianity has increased (from 2 per cent to 8 per cent) this has only partially offset the decline of Christianity so that overall religious belonging has declined (from 69 per cent to 50 per cent). The result is that the population is divided almost equally between those who profess a religious affiliation and those with none.

In fact these figures almost certainly overestimate the extent to which Britain remains a Christian country, as far lower proportions express central Christian beliefs (such as the existence of God) or engage in important practices (such as church attendance) (Wetherly 2016). This case study is an abbreviated version of Wetherly (2016).

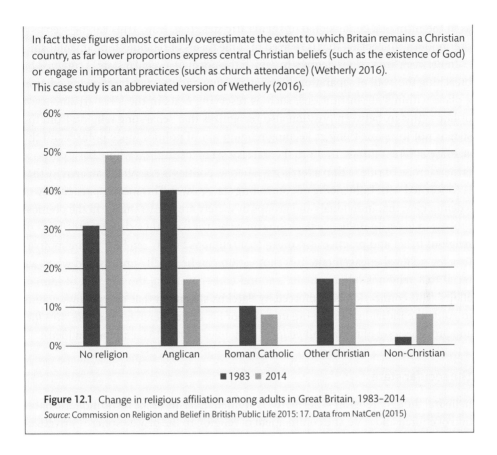

Figure 12.1 Change in religious affiliation among adults in Great Britain, 1983–2014
Source: Commission on Religion and Belief in British Public Life 2015: 17. Data from NatCen (2015)

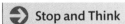 **Stop and Think**

How might Cameron have defended his characterization of Britain as a Christian country? What political motive might there be for talking about Britain in this way?

Religion and politics

It is possible to identify three positions concerning the relationship between religion and politics—both in terms of describing how that relationship does work in specific contexts and how it should work. The three positions are two opposite ends of a spectrum and a more broadly defined in-between view. At one end of the spectrum is the idea of a clear separation between religion and the state in the form of a **secular** state, in which the institutions that comprise the state are established on strictly non-religious or secular lines (e.g. the United States, France). This is a distinctly modern conception. At the other end of the spectrum is the idea of eradicating the distinction between religion and politics, so that politics is subsumed within religion, such as in the form of a confessional or **theocratic** state (e.g. Iran). This can be seen as a pre-modern conception that is revived in some forms of religious fundamentalism.

In between are various degrees by which the norm of a secular state is softened by breaching the 'wall of separation' between religion and the state by allowing religion a place within state institutions, such as reserving seats in the UK parliament for bishops. This in-between position also recognizes that separating religion from the state is not the same thing as keeping religion out of politics, since politics and the state are different things. In short, the state is a set of institutions whose basic purpose is the exercise of rule within a territory, whereas politics is essentially an activity that is concerned with influencing or controlling state power. This means, particularly in a democracy, that individuals and groups in society are free to engage in the political process in order to influence decisions on whatever basis they choose. Freedoms of religious belief and practice also mean that religious beliefs can be a prime motivation for political engagement. This motivation can be readily understood when we recall that religions often contain 'a moral code governing the conduct of human affairs'. This connection is reinforced by Parekh's statement that 'every religion aims to guide the individual in the organization of his or her personal and *collective life*, and provides a set of moral and *political* principles' (2008: 131, emphases added).

The secular state

In liberal thought religion is normatively framed in terms of the institutional separation of church and state, the confinement of religion to the private sphere ('privatization'), and the associated principles of religious freedom and tolerance. In this view separating religion from the state and allowing freedom of religion in civil society are two sides of the same coin. This is sometimes characterized in terms of a commitment to state **'neutrality'**, meaning that the state should be neutral between religions and between adherence to any religion or none. The principle of neutrality is expressed in the first amendment to the US constitution which declares:

> Congress shall make no law respecting an establishment of religion, or prohibiting the free exercise thereof . . .

This brief clause can be elaborated as follows:

> [it] not only forbids the government from establishing an official religion, but also prohibits government actions that unduly favor one religion over another. It also prohibits the government from unduly preferring religion over non-religion, or non-religion over religion. [It also] reserves the right of American citizens to accept any religious belief and engage in religious rituals.
>
> (Legal Information Institute, no date a)

Citizens having the right 'to accept any religious belief and engage in religious rituals' entails religious freedom and tolerance. There being no state religion which is imposed on everybody (which would violate neutrality between religions) or ban on religion (which would violate neutrality between religion and non-religion), religious beliefs are part of the freedom of conscience and belief, and people are free to practise their religion within a system of uniform laws that treat people equally. From a liberal perspective, as expressed by Mill, the law should only interfere in religious practice, as in any other aspects of citizens' lives, if it is necessary to prevent harm to others. Anything else must be tolerated.

Thus the strategy of privatization, on the one hand, restricts the claims of religion by keeping it away from political authority but, at the same time, it is a formula that liberates religion from state controls. Put simply, the faithful cannot have a theocracy and they have to accept secular laws, but by the same token they are protected against a theocracy based on a different religion, and are allowed to practise their own faith.

However, what freedom of religion in the private sphere means in practice, and the limits on permissible religious expression, are contestable and can be politically controversial. This is clear in the way in which secularism (*laïcité*) has been interpreted in France, including outlawing the wearing of the niqab (full face veil) in public. In 2016 the mayor of Cannes introduced a ban on the wearing of burkinis (swimsuits that cover the whole body) on public beaches, supported by the Socialist Prime Minister Manuel Valls (Chrisafis 2016). The justification is that the burkini is an ostentatious symbol of religion that violates secularism, but critics see the ban as a violation of the religious freedom that the separation of church and state is supposed to guarantee.

Religious freedom can be justified, along with freedom of belief more generally, on the universalist grounds that it is better for anyone to be able to 'to accept any religious belief and engage in religious rituals' (or none) than to be prevented from doing so. Religious freedom, tolerance, and diversity also benefit all individuals because the opportunity for dialogue enables individuals to reflect on their beliefs and whether there are good reasons for holding them. In so far as religion deals with important moral questions, it can be further argued that dialogue and the resultant possibility of revision of beliefs in the face of compelling reasons also benefits society through the potential for moral progress.

As well as freedom, the strategy of privatization is intended as a formula for peaceful co-existence. Indeed, Barry argues that this was the original purpose of the strategy:

> The liberal formula for the depoliticisation of differences first arose as a way of dealing with the strife between Protestants and Roman Catholics that the Reformation brought about. . . . The source of conflict . . . was the very attempt to create religious conformity [by the imposition of a state religion]. . . . Only if the state took no official line on religion would religious passions be calmed and peace assured.
>
> (Barry 2001: 25)

Thus privatization works as a strategy for peaceful co-existence if it is accepted by all sides, and this acceptance might not be without loss to religious groups. In particular it means all religious groups giving up any aspiration they might otherwise have to use state power to favour their religious beliefs or impose them on others.

 Stop and Think

What do you understand by the term 'secular state'? How is this idea related to the goals of peace and liberty?

Religion in the political sphere

As we have seen, a secular state can be characterized as a strategy of privatization (confining religion to the private sphere) or **depoliticization** (keeping religion out of politics), but it is debatable whether it is feasible or desirable to keep religion out of the political arena altogether. Indeed the freedom of religion guaranteed by a liberal secular state allows religion to thrive in society, and it might be expected that religion will spill over into the conduct of politics so that the idea of keeping religion out of politics is not feasible. However, this is a question not only of the religiosity (extent of religious belief and practice) in a society but also how individuals see the role of religion in their lives, and whether the political culture is welcoming or hostile to religion entering the political fray (i.e. whether it seen as desirable) (see Case Study 12.2). Here it is helpful to consider the idea of '**secularization**'.

Case Study 12.2 'Doing God'? UK versus USA

The USA and the UK (and western Europe more generally) offer contrasting cases of the relationship between politics and religion. The USA is a secular state (as enshrined in the first amendment) but a highly religious society. The constitution both separates religion from the state and at the same time guarantees religious freedom. The USA was founded largely by religious refugees from Europe but, unlike their European counterparts, Americans have retained a high level of religiosity (especially in the southern 'Bible belt'). And this religiosity spills over into the conduct of politics so that, although the state is neutral, politicians often make their religious affiliations central to their electoral strategies and political identities. Indeed, it is conventional wisdom that someone who is not religious could not be successful in a presidential election, and this wisdom is supported by evidence that two-thirds of Americans agree that 'It's important to me that a president have strong religious beliefs' (Pew Research Center 2012a).

The link between religion and political identity is particularly evident for Republican candidates with their highly religious electoral base, in contrast with the more secular (though still highly religious) Democrat base. Thus people with no religious affiliation make up 28 per cent of Democrat supporters, but only 14 per cent of Republicans. Evangelical Protestants are the largest religious group among Republican supporters (38 per cent) (Pew Research Center 2015a). Not only are Republican supporters more religious than Democrats, they also place greater importance on the religious identity of candidates. For example, in the 2016 presidential contest the Pew Research Center found that 'Roughly two-thirds of Republicans—as opposed to about four-in-ten Democrats—say it is important for a president to share their religious beliefs' (Pew Research Center 2016). The potential for politicians to use religion as a means of mobilizing support was illustrated by 'Republican presidential candidates' public obsession with creationism [in the 2016 contest, which aimed at] ... cementing their Christian credentials with the influential evangelical voting bloc' (Devi 2015).

In contrast, church and state are not sharply differentiated in the UK—there is no equivalent to the first amendment (in fact no codified constitution at all), and Britain has an established church (in fact there is a Church of England and separate Church of Scotland, based on different branches of Protestantism—Anglican and Presbyterian). However, the UK can still be described as a secular state 'in the sense that ... citizenship is not tied up with religious adherence [i.e. you don't have to be a member of the established church to be a citizen] and law and policy are controlled not by creed but by the legal-democratic process' (Joppke 2015: 5). Religious freedom is ensured and various legal protections for religion have been enacted. Unlike their American counterparts, Britons have not retained a high level of religiosity—Britain is a less religious (more secular) society—and religion does not loom large in electoral strategies and political identities. In other words, in the UK politicians rarely 'play the religious card' whereas in the USA they often do; and the American system encourages religious talk by politicians whereas the British system discourages it.

The UK political culture in respect of religion might be summed up in the phrase 'We don't do God', an injunction issued by Alistair Campbell, the Prime Minister's press secretary (or 'spin doctor'), when Tony Blair was asked a question about his religious beliefs in an interview. Campbell has explained that this reflected his 'view that in UK politics, it is always quite dangerous to mix religion and politics, not least because the electorate are not keen on it, and the media and politicians tend to misrepresent it whenever it happens' (Campbell 2010). However, this does not mean 'religious talk' is completely absent from British politics. David Cameron not only stated that the UK was a Christian country and that we should be proud of this fact but also emphasized his own commitment to Christianity (indeed his evangelism) and advocated a larger role for Christianity in politics. Still, these remarks were confined to Easter and Christmas messages and were not repeated on the campaign trail.

Table 12.1 summarizes the differences between the UK and the USA in this regard.

Table 12.1 'Doing God'? UK versus USA

United States	United Kingdom
Secular state	Established church
Highly religious society	Highly secular society
Religious talk common in politics	Religious talk rare in politics

 Stop and Think

Do you think that it is acceptable for politicians to 'do God', or should they stay away from religious talk?

The secularization thesis

To understand the idea of secularization it is necessary to distinguish between a secular state and a secular society, and to recognize that the two do not necessarily go together. Indeed the idea of a secular state can be seen as presuming a religious society, since it is a recipe for managing religious differences. But it presumes a society that is religious in a particular, modern, way, in which religion is an aspect of life rather than governing all of it and can therefore be differentiated from other aspects including the political. This is a modern conception since in pre-modern societies religion governed all aspects of life and, in particular, the 'fusion of religion and politics has been the norm through much of human history' (Joppke 2015: 5). You couldn't speak of someone being religious because there was no way of imagining someone being non-religious. Thus the idea of religion implies the idea of non-religion or the secular.

The secular state involves secularization in the form of institutional differentiation or separation, and in modern societies religion is not just differentiated from the institutions that make up the state but also from other institutional orders including the economy and science. Another idea of secularization refers to the decline of religious belief and practice in society: that is, that people will become steadily less religious. Whether this secularization thesis is true for all societies, for only some (e.g. some European societies), or for none is contested (but see Case Study 12.1 for evidence in relation to the UK). As a theory, secularization is associated with modernity, and particularly the idea that the unfolding of the Enlightenment with its commitment to reason and science would come into conflict with religion, and that the Enlightenment would win this conflict. People would relinquish religious ways of understanding the world and moral teaching in favour of science and reason because of the superiority of the latter. On the other hand, critics argue that things have not turned out as the modernists expected and religion has persisted and even revived. As we will see, religious fundamentalism can be viewed as a response to the threat to religion presented by modernity and as a manifestation of the revival of religion.

The expectation that reason and science would replace faith altogether has been a persistent trope of the modern era. Thus in the nineteenth century 'Thomas H Huxley, who popularised [Charles Darwin's] *Origin of Species*, insisted that people had to choose between faith and science; there could be no compromise: "One or the other would have to succumb after a struggle of unknown duration"' (Armstrong 2006). The expectation has continued through the last century, as

> it was generally taken for granted that secularism was an irreversible trend. . . . It was assumed that as human beings became more rational, they either would have no further need for religion or would be content to confine it to the immediately personal and private areas of their lives [i.e. they would be content to keep it out of the political arena].
>
> (Armstrong 2001: ix–x)

Thus the separation of church from state to manage religious differences in highly religious societies in the early modern period would be followed by the relentless progress of secularism (i.e. non-religious beliefs) and the decline of the church in civil society. In this scenario religion would no longer have to be 'kept out' of politics for it would simply retreat in the face of modernity's advance.

It is fair to say that faith has not entirely succumbed to reason. Britain may be characterized as a largely secular society but, as we have seen, the landscape of modern British society still has religious features. However, Britain is towards the secular end of the spectrum in international comparative terms, with higher levels of religiosity in some other developed countries (such as the United States or Italy) and throughout many of the less developed regions of the world. It can be argued that there has been a recent resurgence of religion in the form of religious fundamentalism, which we will examine later in the chapter. But before we do that it is important to note that even in the most advanced and secular countries religion has by no means become confined to 'the immediately personal and private areas' of people's lives. Thus we need to look at the ways in which religion remains part of the political life of these societies.

 Stop and Think

What do you understand by the 'secularization thesis'? Do faith and reason necessarily conflict? Is reason bound to triumph?

Mixing religion and politics

A secular state does not present any of the following: citizens voting on the basis of their religious beliefs; religious organizations lobbying political parties or politicians to influence specific policies in line with religious principles; the faithful going into politics in order to further a religious agenda; political parties being established with an explicit basis in faith, such as European Christian democratic parties; politicians using 'religious talk' to appeal to voters; or politicians voting on policies according to their religious beliefs or under the influence of religious lobbyists. These are all ways In which religion and politics can mix.

This mixing qualifies the extent of privatization and depoliticization of religion. Since religious beliefs contain 'a set of moral and political principles' people are not likely to leave their faith at home when they enter the public square and political fray. Religious freedom means freedom to practise religion but also to evangelize, spread the gospel, and seek converts (although it should be noted that not all religions are evangelical, e.g. Judaism). It is a logical extension of this to seek political influence to change laws and policies in line with religious values. Creating a more 'Godly' society can be achieved through conversions and/or political change. However, the extent of political engagement on the part of religion is clearly a matter of choice, ranging from quietism or disengagement at one end of a spectrum to militancy at the other.

Case Study 12.3 Do the faithful have a religious duty to get involved in politics?

The choice, or dilemma, of whether to get involved in politics is illustrated by the career of American evangelical preacher Jerry Falwell. In the 1960s, Falwell had chosen to keep out of politics and concentrate on 'preaching the pure saving Gospel of Jesus Christ', arguing that preachers 'are not called to be politicians, but to be soul-winners' (in Reynolds 2009: 491–2). However in 1979 Falwell went on to become one of the founders of the Moral Majority, a grassroots religious movement to challenge what he saw as the moral failings of politics, arguing that the 'mess' the country was in was due to Christians 'failing to show up for the fight' (in Reynolds 2009: 492) (see Case Study 12.2).

In the 1960s the civil rights movement, of which Falwell was not a supporter, was inspired and justified on explicitly religious lines. 'Martin Luther King . . . drew repeatedly on Biblical concepts and phrases to inspire blacks in the fight against discrimination—likening them to the children of Israel struggling from Egyptian bondage into the Promised Land' (Reynolds 2009: 583). King also articulated a theory of justice based on the law of God, arguing that

> there are two types of laws: there are just and there are unjust laws. . . . A just law is a man-made code that squares with the moral law or the law of God. An unjust law is a code that is out of harmony with the moral law.
>
> (King, from 'Letter From Birmingham City Jail,' in Rosen and Wolff 1999: 84–5)

In opposition to Falwell's initial view that the duty of preachers is limited to preaching the gospel, Pope Francis asserted that 'Getting involved in politics is a Christian duty' (in Fraser 2013; Tornielli 2013). This duty arises from Christianity's moral code, in just the same way that the commitment on the part of liberals to universal human rights or on the part of socialists to equality can be said to create a duty to act to remedy the harms caused by human rights abuses or poverty.

For example, the religious injunction to 'love thy neighbour' is evidently a moral and political principle that might be expressed in specific political demands and movements, such as the 'Refugees welcome here' movement in the context of the European migration crisis in 2015. Pope Francis made a political intervention during a visit to the Greek island of Lesbos which effectively aligned him with this movement, calling on

> European leaders to respond to the migrant crisis 'with courage and in a way that is worthy of our common humanity'. . . . Using The Parable of the Good Samaritan while addressing refugees and migrants, he called on Christians to show more mercy and understanding to those in need.
>
> (ITV 2016)

Francis put the principle of the Good Samaritan into practice by taking twelve Syrian refugees back to Rome (ITV 2016).

Stop and Think

Was Falwell right when he stuck to preaching the gospel or when he decided to 'turn up for the fight'?

Is it desirable to mix politics and religion?

The desirability of mixing religion and politics can be considered in terms of whether this contributes to some conception of a healthy functioning democracy and state. But there are two, contrasting, conceptions of politics that we might refer to: on the one hand, the idea of politics as concerned with formulating the common good or public interest; and, on the other hand, the idea of politics as a competition between rival interests in society. In the latter view, religious groups may enter the political arena in order to promote their particular interests, in order to preserve their own beliefs and lifestyles. This can be seen as part of the normal bargaining and negotiation of a healthy pluralist democracy in which the voices of all groups and interests within a diverse society should be heard. Against this, political mobilization on religious lines can be seen as a form of divisive identity politics which emphasizes difference at the expense of what people have in common (see Chapter 11 'Multiculturalism').

However, the political engagements by Falwell, King, and Francis involve the quest for the common good or the good society, as seen in the light of the moral codes contained within their (differing) religious beliefs. In this respect it is sometimes claimed that religious involvement in politics is not only desirable but essential, on the grounds that without belief in God there can be no morality. When King said that 'A just law is a man-made code that squares with the moral law or the law of God' he was saying that the word of God is the only basis for morality. Critics of this view argue that belief in God is not necessary for morality since we are capable of moral reasoning (i.e. that morality is a field in which we can apply reason), and that even those who believe in God have to interpret His laws and are bound to be selective in deciding to follow some and not others, and must use their capacity for reason in the interpretation and selection. Secular ideologies like liberalism and socialism contain moral codes and thus, it can be argued, demonstrate the capacity for moral reasoning.

However, even if we reject the indispensability of religion for morality, it can be argued that it is desirable that the religious voice be heard among others, a claim made in the *Catholic Herald* as follows:

> in order to have a healthy state, the secular arena (with its level playing field . . .) has
> got to host a wide and healthy conversation about the ideas that underpin the state and
> hold the national community together; and those ideas will be fed by beliefs of one sort
> or another, and many of those beliefs will be religious beliefs, though, in coming to

the conversation in the secular arena, these beliefs will be presented in rational terms accessible to all.

(Lucie-Smith 2014)

In this view religions should not be shut out of politics because, alongside secular ideologies, they can contribute to a 'healthy conversation' about the good society. The level playing field argues against any particular religion, or religion in general, having a privileged status in the conversation.

One of the potential difficulties concerns the language in which the conversation is conducted. When King referred to the 'laws of God' this argument is compelling for those who share his religion, but the justification of political positions on the basis of scripture cannot engage those of other faiths or none. Thus the requirement that the conversation be conducted 'in rational terms accessible to all'; that is, 'a non-sectarian idiom for public debate that is shared by all, above religious lines' (Taylor in Joppke 2015: 46). For example Pope Francis's demand that European leaders do more to assist asylum seekers was expressed in the non-sectarian, universalist appeal to 'our common humanity'.

Similarly, although religious motives helped to mobilize the faithful, the civil rights struggle was ultimately based on arguments expressed in rational terms. In his 1963 'I have a dream' speech, delivered on the 100th anniversary of the Emancipation Proclamation, King uses ringing Biblical tones, refers to all Americans as 'God's children', and speaks of

> a dream deeply rooted in the American dream. . . . a dream that one day this nation will rise up and live out the true meaning of its creed: 'We hold these truths to be self-evident; that all men are created equal' . . . [and] . . . a dream that one day . . . the glory of the Lord shall be revealed.

(King in MacArthur 1995: 487–91)

In this passage King appears to connect the demand for civil rights, the American dream as expressed in the Declaration of Independence, and the 'glory of the Lord' which seems to invoke the idea of 'the moral law or the law of God' as expressed in his letter from a Birmingham jail. In this way it could be argued that King is true to the original religious framing of the Declaration, the full version of the quoted passage being:

> We hold these Truths to be self-evident, that all Men are created equal, that they are *endowed, by their Creator, with certain unalienable Rights*, that among these are Life, Liberty, and the Pursuit of Happiness (emphasis added).

However, the speech also uses rational terms to deliver its demand for civil rights. King argues that the US constitution and Declaration make the promise that all men, black and white, would be guaranteed the rights set out, and this promise had been broken. In addition the speech uses the secular liberal concepts of justice, opportunity, freedom, and citizenship rights.

Religion and ideology

As we have seen, religions can be viewed as tantamount to ideologies as they contain moral and political codes or visions of the good society and can motivate political action. In addition it can be argued that the voice of religion should be heard alongside secular ideologies in the political conversation. However, if religions can be conceived as ideologies, they appear to differ in some important respects from secular ideologies such as liberalism and socialism. First, as we have seen (Chapter 1), ideologies are intrinsically action-oriented, meaning that their *essential* purpose is political engagement, whereas this is not true of religion. Getting involved in politics may be seen as a duty of the faithful, but Pope Francis would presumably not say that this is the primary purpose of Christianity.

Second, the grounding of religious beliefs in faith contrasts with the rational secular terms of ideological debate—a faith versus reason clash. This can be managed by acceptance that religious beliefs must be presented in rational terms accessible to all, thus playing by the rules of the secular realm. In addition, for Christianity at least, participation in the secular realm is facilitated by the tradition of 'natural law as a second source of law, alongside revealed law or religious law proper' since this emphasizes the human capacity for reason (Joppke 2015: 54–5). 'Divine natural law is given by God through His creation, and it is accessible through the faculties that every human being is endowed with' by God (Joppke 2015: 56). However religion has penetrated the political sphere more thoroughly: as well as being a distinct voice that is heard alongside other ideologies, it also speaks through them.

Relationship between religion and other ideologies

The Enlightenment and modernity, as manifested in the classic Enlightenment ideologies of liberalism and socialism, presented a challenge to inherited authority, tradition, and religion—a break with the past as expressed in the contrasts between 'traditional' and 'modern' societies, and between faith and reason. Religion was seen variously as a barrier to enlightenment or knowledge; as a consolation or (in Marx's phrase) 'opium of the people' that reconciled them to suffering in the here-and-now; or as a defence or legitimization of power and privilege.

However, the idea of a break is too simple as it conceals the more complicated story of both continuity and discontinuity, due to the influence of classical and medieval thought (Gamble 1981). European Enlightenment ideologies developed in a religious context, inherited religious (Christian) ideas, and articulated these ideas within a religious frame (e.g. the unalienable rights specified in the Declaration of Independence, that famous statement of liberal principle, are deemed to be given by God and justified on this basis). For example, Joppke (2015) emphasizes the Christian origins of the idea of the differentiation between church and state. Gamble highlights the

Christian roots of what might be thought of as the essential liberal conception of the individual. In fact Christianity contained ideas that are taken up within both liberalism and socialism.

> Christianity helped introduce the notion that all individuals, whatever their race or creed, were equal and should be equally valued. The Christian ideal was the community based on fraternity and the holding of goods in common, in which all individuals were entitled to equal respect, and in which human relations would be governed by altruism . . . rather than self-interest.
>
> (Gamble 1981: 10)

Of course, this does not mean that liberalism and socialism are inextricably bound up with Christianity. The progressive freeing of secular ideologies from the legacy of religious thought may be seen as part-and-parcel of the secularization process. Even if in 1776 life, liberty, and the pursuit of happiness were seen as unalienable rights with which men were endowed by God, today liberals can justify these rights in purely rational terms, and also reject the idea that the capacity for reason is God-given. God can be, and has been, removed from the picture.

However, as we know, secularization has not lead to the demise of religion, and it continues to have a voice in the political conversation partly as a variant or strand within secular ideologies, such as Christian socialism. Although the language of socialism is essentially rationalist and secular, some people find their way to socialist ideology through their religious beliefs because of perceived convergence or alignment between the moral codes of Christianity and socialism. Such people may feel not only a Christian duty to get involved in politics but that this duty compels them to get involved on the socialist side—being a socialist is a way of being a good Christian.

Christian socialism has been of particular importance in Britain where it formed part of the roots of the Labour Party, to the extent that it is often claimed the British Labour movement owes far more to Methodism that it does to Marx. The connection continues today as evidenced by groups such as 'Christians on the left' for whom 'a strong and active commitment to social justice and the alleviation of poverty' follows from 'a belief in equality; that we are all made in the image of God' (Beer 2013). It is also personified by recent leaders of the Labour Party—John Smith, Tony Blair, and Gordon Brown were all Christians who explicitly linked their faith to their politics (e.g. see Brown 2011).

Socialist principles can also be extracted from other religions. For example, 'social justice, egalitarianism and rejection of the unrestrained capitalist pursuit of profit . . . are central to (or can at least be shown to be a powerful strand within) Islam' (Parekh 2008: 146).

Christianity is not inherently socialist but can also be aligned with other ideologies and parties. In the British context, the historical connection with the Conservative Party is perhaps stronger than with Labour—in this case the equivalent saying is that the Church of England is the Tory Party at prayer. In ideological terms, religion can be seen as an important element of conservatism—seen as an ingredient of a shared national identity (i.e. Britain as a Christian country), and as the source of a common morality that holds society together.

Christianity has also been used to justify the neo-liberal ideological position that has taken over the Conservative Party (see Chapter 3) and was championed by Margaret Thatcher. If for Christian socialists Christianity leads to a commitment to the social justice and the alleviation of poverty through state action, 'For Thatcher personal responsibility and individual freedom of choice were the key religious ideals that led to and justified her commitment to minimal state intervention and her emphasis on the importance of wealth creation, self-help and philanthropy' (Theakston 2014). For Thatcher the lesson of the parable of the Good Samaritan, often used to support the socialist commitment to altruism and alleviation of poverty, is that 'Nobody would remember the Good Samaritan if he had only good intentions. He had money as well' (Thatcher in BBC 2013). In this view the parable lends support to the importance of wealth creation and the neo-liberal prescription of free markets driven by self-interest.

Fundamentalism

Having seen that religion has shaped modern political ideologies, that the secular state does not prevent religion entering the political arena, and that it continues to operate in this arena despite the secularization of society, we now can examine religious fundamentalism as a particular manifestation of religion in the political sphere. It is useful to start by considering the notion of fundamentalism in general before turning to its specifically religious form.

The nature of fundamentalism

Fundamentalism can be seen as a style of ideological argument and political action that emphasizes the fundamental (basic or essential) beliefs; that is, 'strict adherence to the fundamental principles of any set of beliefs' (*Collins English Dictionary*). Fundamentalism is not confined to religious beliefs but can be associated with any of the secular ideologies. Since all ideologies have fundamental or core beliefs—after all, if an ideology does not have any fundamental beliefs it is difficult to see how its distinctiveness could be asserted and defended—it would seem that adherence to these beliefs could be expected of any consistent advocate of the ideology in question.

Yet a fundamentalist attitude to ideology is often criticized as a defective style, or even refusal, of politics, as 'strict adherence' suggests that fundamental principles are non-negotiable, or that there is a refusal to allow these principles to be opened up to dialogue and criticism. This kind of inflexibility is based on the conviction that these principles are not only the fundamental ones but also that they are certainly true or right.

What to one person is seen as a necessary and commendable commitment to core beliefs or 'keeping the faith' is seen by another as an inflexible and dogmatic approach.

On the other hand, one person's betrayal of core beliefs can be another's necessary and desirable preparedness to reinterpret beliefs in the light of new circumstances. Thus whether fundamentalism is a good or bad thing depends on the attitude that is taken to the core beliefs of an ideology: what are they? how are they understood? are the original formulations still relevant?

Thus parties and movements are typically characterized by 'tensions between ideological purists who stick to the fundamentals of their cause without compromising their principles, and the **realists** who argue that real gains can be achieved through bargaining and compromise' (Ruthven 2007: 21–2).

In recent years free speech fundamentalism (a form of fundamentalist liberalism) has clashed with those, some of whom are religious fundamentalists, who wish to protect religious beliefs from some forms of criticism. Modood has argued that 'If people are to occupy the same political space without conflict, they mutually have to limit the extent to which they subject each others' fundamental beliefs to criticism' in order to avoid offence (Modood, in Malik 2012). This stance is most often taken in relation to religion, on the basis that religious beliefs are special in terms of how they matter deeply to people and are constitutive of identity. However, this view of religion is questionable both because for most people who affiliate with a religion it does not play a very important role in their lives, and because other systems of beliefs, including secular ideologies, can matter deeply to people and be important aspects of their identities. The beliefs of an ardent feminist can matter as deeply as those of a devout Christian. Therefore, we should treat all fundamental beliefs in the same way rather than affording special treatment to religion.

So what are we to make of Modood's stance that criticism of fundamental beliefs should be limited in order to avoid conflict? It can be argued, on the contrary, that each other's fundamental beliefs are precisely those that ought to be subject to rigorous criticism regardless of offence so that we can reflect on and revise our beliefs through mutual criticism. Limiting criticism as advocated by Modood would also limit the opportunities for false ideas to be exposed and for progress to be made. In this view, occupying the same political space (i.e. living together) without conflict is to be achieved not by limiting criticism but by everybody accepting the give-and-take of mutual criticism.

This is an argument for free speech or freedom of expression. Does this mean that people should be allowed to express any ideas or beliefs in whatever way they choose without limits? People who advocate a 'no holds barred' position, or support only very limited restrictions on freedom of expression, can be described as 'free speech fundamentalists' insofar as free speech is seen as a fundamental belief that should not be compromised. For example, some defenders of the 'Danish cartoons' which depicted the prophet Muhammad in a way that many Muslims found deeply offensive (see Chapter 11) have adopted this position. The culture editor of the Danish newspaper who commissioned the cartoons stated that he had 'definitely become a free speech fundamentalist' and argued that free speech means that everybody 'must be ready to put up with insults, mockery and ridicule' (in Malik 2012). According to Malik

Danish newspapers should be free to publish insulting cartoons about the prophet Muhammad [and] . . . Muslim demonstrators should be able to carry placards calling for the beheading of those who insult Islam; and . . . both the radical cleric Abu Hamza and British National Party leader Nick Griffin should be free to spout racist hatred.... [In a plural society] it is both inevitable and important that people offend the sensibilities of others. . . . What is . . . too costly is giving in to the demand not to cause offence. If we believe in free speech there can be no buts.

(Malik 2006)

 Stop and Think

Do you think that it is good for democracy if people adopt a position that certain fundamental beliefs are non-negotiable? Should criticism of such fundamental beliefs be limited to avoid offence?

Religious fundamentalism

In the public imagination, in the media, and in political debate the term 'religious fundamentalism' is today bound up with the series of terrorist attacks in recent decades undertaken by a range of movements in several different countries claiming allegiance to, and justification from, Islam, notably so-called Islamic State. More specifically, fundamentalism is associated with attacks on the West or on Western targets, the first of which to cement the idea of religious fundamentalism in the public mind and propel it up the political agenda was the attack on the twin towers of the World Trade Center in New York by al Qaeda on 11 September 2001 (generally referred to as '9/11') and, in the UK, the attacks in London on 7 July 2005 ('7/7'). However this understanding is flawed insofar as it sees religious fundamentalism as a recent phenomenon and associates it specifically with Islam and with terrorist methods.

In fact, fundamentalism is certainly not restricted to Islam. Parekh (2008: 148) claims it is primarily an aspect of Islam and Protestant Christianity, while others point to the emergence of fundamentalism 'within every major religious tradition' as 'one of the most startling developments of the late twentieth century' (Armstrong 2001: ix). But religious fundamentalism was not born in the late twentieth century, for its roots can be traced to the early twentieth century among Protestants in the United States who sought to distance themselves from 'liberal' Protestants through scriptural literalism: that is, a belief in the literal truth of scripture (see Case Study 12.4). Violence is certainly not confined to Islamic fundamentalists but has also been a feature of fundamentalisms of other faiths (Ruthven 2007: 3). Examples include violence directed against Muslims by Buddhists in Myanmar (Burma), against Muslims and Christians by Hindu nationalists in India, against abortion providers by Christians in the United States, and the racial violence of the Ku Klux Klan. But fundamentalism is not intrinsically violent; in fact terrorism is confined to a minority of fundamentalists (Armstrong 2001: ix). Thus fundamentalism is not recent (although there has been a recent resurgence), it is not peculiar to Islam (although 'Islamism' is its most prominent manifestation today), and it is not inherently violent (although it can be seen as containing a potential for violence).

Case Study 12.4 Christian (Protestant) fundamentalism

A century separates us from the emergence of the original form of fundamentalism 'in the very specific historical theological context of early twentieth-century Protestant America' (Ruthven 2007), although it is a form that persists today. Protestant fundamentalism was a movement to 'go back to basics and reemphasize the "fundamentals" of the Christian tradition, which they identified with a literal interpretation of Scripture' (Armstrong 2001: x). They sought to defend the literal truth of the Bible against a 'liberal' reinterpretation that questioned this view by showing, for example, that it was composed by many authors, and from the threat posed by science, particularly evolution which overturned the Biblical account of creation. Thus it was a reaction against a tendency within the religion as well as external threats (insofar as these can be distinguished—it might be argued that liberal Christians were influenced by the forces of modernity).

Fundamentalism took the form of a series of pamphlets setting out the fundamental beliefs of Christianity such as the literal truth of the Bible, God's creation of the Earth and human beings, the virgin birth of Jesus, and the End Times prophecies of the Old Testament: *The Fundamentals: A Testimony of Truth*. 'Expecting the world to end at any moment, [the publishers] saw it as their duty to save as many people as possible before the coming catastrophe, when sinners would perish horribly and the saved would be raptured into the presence of Christ' (Ruthven 2007: 8).

Evolution and its teaching in schools was, and remains, a key battleground for fundamentalists. In a famous case in 1925, a Tennessee state law banning the teaching of evolution was used in the successful prosecution of a teacher in the so-called 'monkey trial'. The outcome was to be expected before a fundamentalist jury some members of which claimed to read nothing but the Bible (Ruthven 2007: 12). According to Reynolds, the case can be seen as part of a wider 'cultural war' between rural and urban America that also encompassed issues such as prohibition, movies, and the general permissiveness of the 'jazz age'—a 'collision between new social freedoms ... and the traditional values of small-town Protestant America' (2009: 327). However, the victory was pyrrhic in the sense that the case discredited fundamentalism.

William Jennings Bryan, a prominent Democratic politician, opposed the teaching of evolution on religious grounds, claiming that Darwinism destroyed the faith of Christians and that the doctrine of the 'survival of the fittest' had created the conditions for the First World War (1914–18). Bryan also argued that schools should teach what the taxpayers want, meaning the Bible and not evolution. Thus he stirred 'a powerful cocktail of religion and democracy' which threatened, in the eyes of his opponents, free speech and scientific enquiry (Reynolds 2009: 331).

The trial involved the prosecution of a teacher, John Scopes, for breaking the law barring the teaching of evolution. Scopes was convicted (although the conviction was reversed on appeal), but the cause of fundamentalism was set back by the humiliation of Bryan who, called as an expert witness on the Bible, was pilloried by the defence for holding 'fool ideas that no intelligent Christian on Earth believes' (in Reynolds 2009: 332). The larger impact was that 'for the American public at large, fundamentalists were exposed as rural ignoramuses, rural hillbillies out of touch with modern thought' (Ruthven 2007: 15). The trial marked 'the end of the evangelicals' big public campaign' but fundamentalism was not dead—'fundamentalists imposed anti-evolution laws in many parts of the South and . . . created their own subculture of Bible colleges, camps, conferences and radio stations' (Reynolds 2009: 333).

That subculture persisted and re-emerged into public life in the 1960s and 1970s as 'evangelical Protestants were mobilized politically by what they saw as the Godless drift of American life' (Reynolds 2009: 492) manifested, for example, in Supreme Court rulings in the early 1960s on the basis of the first amendment (separating church and state) that banned Bible reading and recitals of the Lord's Prayer in schools. More generally campaigners sought to ensure that the curriculum and textbooks in schools embodied Christian values, for example in relation to sex, homosexuality, and creation. A difference from the early twentieth-century fundamentalism was that there was less concern with theological purity and literalism and more with political campaigning, and this was reflected in a political strategy of building alliances with non-fundamentalists on specific issues—including with Catholics on abortion (Reynolds 2009: 496). An important manifestation of this politicization of fundamentalist Christianity was the founding in 1979 by the prominent evangelical preacher Jerry Falwell of the Moral Majority (its opponents quipped that it was neither). The moral majority was conceived to be people from different denominational backgrounds (supposedly constituting a majority) who shared moral values which they derived from the Bible, notably the Ten Commandments.

Since the 1980s the 'culture wars'—in which conservative fundamentalist Christians have been mobilized on a range of moral issues, mainly through support for the Republican Party—have been a persistent feature of American politics. To a large extent, fundamentalists 'lobby for power and influence within the Republican Party' (Ruthven 2007: 17) and vote on religious lines, and Republican politicians seek power and win votes by emphasizing their deeply-held religious beliefs (or, more sceptically, 'playing the religion card'). This 'marriage' of religion and politics has had consequences at local, state, and federal levels, including the elections of Ronald Reagan (1981–89) and, especially, born-again Christian George W. Bush (2001–09). The religious right, 'ardent Reaganauts', influenced, or even swayed, the election in 1980, although the Reagan administration proved a disappointment as it distanced itself from the fundamentalist agenda (Reynolds 2009: 511). Armstrong states that 'Bush and his administration espouse[d] many of the ideals of the Christian right and rel[ied] on its support' and argues that this is reflected in attitudes to science (e.g. banning stem cell research and rejecting climate change science and the Kyoto protocol to tackle global warming), social policies, and foreign policy (e.g. uncritical support for Israel) (Armstrong 2006). The contest for the Republican nomination for the 2016 presidential election showed the continuing connection between the Republican Party and Protestant fundamentalists. Among the candidates, Jindal, as governor of Louisiana, passed a state law permitting the teaching of creationism in science classes in schools alongside evolution (the 2008 Louisiana Science Education Act) (Dart 2015). Other candidates, including Cruz, Carson, and Huckabee, sought to mobilize the evangelical Christian vote, in the last two cases publicly rejecting evolution and expressing their belief in creationism (Devi 2015). Thus Protestant fundamentalism, originating in the early part of the last century, continues to play an important part in American political life in this one.

➜ Stop and Think

1. Should Protestant fundamentalists confine their religious beliefs and practices to the private sphere, or campaign to preserve a Christian nation and save souls through political engagement?

2. Should the Biblical story of creation be taught in schools alongside (or even in place of) the scientific theory of evolution if that's what voters want?

It is difficult to pin down a concise definition of religious fundamentalism because it exists in all major religions and in a range of movements, and it can be argued that the best approach is to identify 'family resemblances' between these manifestations (Armstrong 2001; Ruthven 2007). Parekh defines fundamentalism in terms of two characteristics: it 'aims to reduce religion to its so-called fundamentals, and to use them to radically restructure and give a fundamentally new orientation to society'; that is, to regenerate a corrupt and Godless society by 'reconstituting it on religious foundations' (Parekh 2008: 141–2). This definition highlights the ideological character of religious fundamentalism, combining political understanding and commitment. The fundamental beliefs constitute a critique of existing society and motivate political engagement to realize a religious vision of the good society. Ruthven defines fundamentalism in broad terms as 'a religious way of being that manifests itself in a strategy by which beleaguered believers attempt to preserve their distinctive identities as individuals or groups in the face of modernity and secularization' (Ruthven 2007: 5–6). This definition pinpoints what is wrong with existing society from the fundamentalist point of view (critique) in terms specifically of modernity and secularization. Ruthven adds that fundamentalists not only oppose modernity but feel themselves to be beleaguered or under attack from it. Hence they fight back against modernity in order to preserve distinctive religious identities based on specific beliefs and practices. Similarly, Armstrong (2005) states that fundamentalism is 'essentially a revolt against modern secular society' and, in particular, the separation of religion and politics. Hence fundamentalists 'want to see religion reflected more prominently in public life' (Armstrong 2005). The family resemblances of religious fundamentalisms can be identified as outlined in the following five subsections.

The fundamentals and scriptural literalism

It seems obvious that, for the Abrahamic religions (Christianity, Islam, and Judaism), the fundamentals are to be found in scripture. Scriptural literalism means that, in extracting these fundamental beliefs, scripture is to be read literally and not subject to interpretation and to be regarded as true or inerrant. This was characteristic of the original Protestant fundamentalism in the USA (see Case Study 12.4). However Armstrong (2001) says this is a feature specifically of Protestant fundamentalism and not of Judaism or Islam. Ruthven (2007: 4) claims that scriptural literalism cannot be a defining feature of all fundamentalisms since 'all observant Muslims ... are committed to a doctrine of scriptural inerrancy' as the Quran is viewed as the 'unmediated word of God' (although it can be argued that this view downplays variants within Islam, including 'reformists' who allow for interpretation of the Quran—see Farrar 2012). If so, this means either that all Muslims are fundamentalists or that Islamic fundamentalism must be understood in other ways, particularly the aspiration to impose Islamic religious law (Sharia) on society.

Parekh distinguishes between 'scriptural literalism' and 'fundamentalism'. Both see scripture as inerrant and therefore non-negotiable; seek to live according to scripture and see this commitment and identity as overriding all others; see themselves as 'charged with the task of challenging and changing the corrupt [i.e. Godless] world' (Parekh 2008: 132); and are reactive, responding to a sense of threat or crisis. But beyond these similarities, the key difference is that literalists seek to 'be true to every scriptural utterance' (Parekh 2008: 137) (even if this makes impossible demands upon them), whereas fundamentalists are selective in identifying the fundamentals. Because fundamentalism seeks to regenerate society on religious foundations, the selective reading of the texts is geared towards mobilizing the faithful for struggle by extracting 'a moral and political programme . . . [which is] the religious equivalent of a secular political ideology' (Parekh 2008: 143). In contrast with literalism, the meaning of scripture is not uncovered through a scholarly reading but by an 'activist' one undertaken in the course of the struggle—the meaning 'is disclosed not to a contemplative scholar but to "God's humble soldier"' (Parekh 2008: 144). Parekh quotes the assertion of Ayatollah Khomeini (religious leader of Iran following the 1979 revolution) that 'a cleric who prefers fasting and prayerful reading to political struggle "will never know" his religion' (Parekh 2008: 144).

 Stop and Think

Scriptural literalism involves the idea that the words contained in scripture are true for all time. Can secular political ideologies also be prone to an approach that is equivalent to scriptural literalism?

Identity

Fundamentalism as a way of being religious is not just about being certain that fundamental beliefs of the religion are true but also about how those beliefs constitute the primary or even singular basis of identity. Thus Sen suggests that 'Islamic fundamentalism would like to suppress all other identities of Muslims in favour of being only Islamic' (Sen 2006: 14) so that the fundamentalist sees herself as 'nothing but a Muslim' (Parekh 2008: 138). Equally, a Christian fundamentalist may see his or her religious identity as everything. Sen defines this way of understanding identity as 'solitarist', meaning that human beings are seen 'as members of exactly one group' (e.g. religion) to the exclusion of other affiliations and aspects of multiple identities (Sen 2006: xii).

Reaction against modernity and the West

Religious fundamentalism is a reactive phenomenon, specifically 'a reaction against the scientific and secular culture that first appeared in the West' and has, as we have seen, spread beyond the West through trade, conquest, and the process of globalization (Armstrong 2001: xi). In this sense there is a parallel with other anti-enlightenment ideologies such as nationalism, which can in some circumstances also be seen as a reaction against globalization. Fundamentalists seem 'adamantly opposed to many of the most positive values of modern [liberal] society. Fundamentalists have no time for democracy, pluralism, religious toleration, . . . free speech, or the separation of church and state' (Armstrong 2001: ix).

This opposition to modernity may seem puzzling since, as a liberal might argue, the idea of a secular state is not an enemy of religion but, on the contrary, stands for religious freedom and tolerance. However, fundamentalists are not interested in tolerance, for tolerance and '**permissiveness**' are to blame for the moral degeneracy of modern societies. Tolerance involves the idea that, say, Christian values are merely one option but that other values and lifestyles are possible and acceptable. But fundamentalism does not accept plurality or being part of a conversation/dialogue involving give and take and compromise, and sees the fight against modernity as a 'war between the forces of good and evil' (Armstrong 2001: xi).

In any case, fundamentalists see modernity not as a guarantor of religion's continued place in society through religious freedom, rather fundamentalism is 'rooted in a deep fear of annihilation . . . [being] convinced that modern secular society wants to wipe out religion' (Armstrong 2005). It can be argued that other Enlightenment ideologies—notably socialism and anarchism, at least in some of their forms—have adopted explicitly anti-religious positions (see Chapter 5 on anarchism) on the basis that religion is oppressive and a barrier to human liberation. This standpoint has been carried into practice, notably in the 'actually existing socialism' of the Soviet Union. In many non-Western countries the modernization agenda has been pursued in a way that involves the suppression rather than tolerance of religion, so that 'modernization is often experienced not as a liberation but as an aggressive assault' (Armstrong 2001: xvi). In this connection Armstrong refers to the creation of modern Turkey as a secular state under Mustafa Kemal Atatürk, Iran during the rule of the shahs, or Egypt under the rule of Jamal Abdal al-Nasser (Armstrong 2005). And intervention has often contributed to a belief on the part of some Muslims that Western states are hostile to Islam or engaged in a modern crusade against it, as in the support for the shah in Iran before the revolution in 1979, the 'war on terrorism' following 9/11 (which was actually described by Bush as a crusade), and the subsequent war in Iraq. Even if liberalism is true to its promises of freedom and tolerance, it can be argued that it threatens religion because it sees no place for religion in modernity and looks down on it, sees religion as inferior to science and rational thought and expects the latter to displace the former, and advocates freedom of expression which is used to attack religion. The fear of annihilation can be seen as the obverse of the Enlightenment thinker's confidence in the triumph of modernity.

Religion as politics

The fundamentalists' rejection of modernity can involve either withdrawing from the world and, as far as possible, living in self-sustaining religious communities or political engagement to reconstitute or rejuvenate society on religious lines. However, the fear of annihilation that fundamentalists feel encourages a fightback against modernity, so fundamentalism appears in the guise of what Armstrong calls 'militant piety'. Through political engagement, fundamentalists 'strive to bring the sacred into the realm of politics and national struggle' (Armstrong 2001: ix).

Fundamentalist movements may operate within the parameters of liberal democracy, such as some American Protestant fundamentalists seeking to 'Christianize' society through political engagement within the system, especially through influence within the Republican Party, or Islamist parties such as the Muslim Brotherhood contesting elections. However, these might be seen as tactical manoeuvres since, as we have seen, fundamentalists reject democracy in principle. For example, Islamic fundamentalists reject democracy, secular politics, and man-made law and aim to replace it with religious law (Sharia). Instead of working within the system, they seek revolutionary transformation. In this view politics is subordinated to religion—in effect religion is politics because it is the basis of rule. Fundamentalist movements in Britain such as Hizb ut'Tahrir reject the nation-state and support the creation of an Islamic state or caliphate uniting all Muslim countries, which is the goal of so-called Islamic State (Hope Not Hate 2016).

Violence and terrorism

It can be argued that religious fundamentalism carries an inherent potential for violence, and this potential is clearly manifest in the world today. Parekh contends that the revolutionary ambition of fundamentalism to reshape society on religious lines 'obviously involves considerable violence' (Parekh 2008: 147). For Sen solitarism is not just an impoverished notion of identity but also carries with it the potential for violence because it heightens the sense of difference between people at the expense of what they have in common:

> many of the conflicts . . . in the world are sustained through the illusion of a unique and choiceless identity, . . . [a] predominant identity that drowns other affiliations.

> (Sen 2006: xv)

[For example,] theories of Islamic exclusiveness, combined with ignoring the relevance of all the other identities Muslims have . . . can be utilised to provide the conceptual basis for a violent version of jihad.

(Sen 2006: 179)

The World Economic Forum's 2016 report identifies 'large-scale terrorist attacks' within the category of geopolitical risks at a global level. Terrorism is 'caused by violent extremism' and engaged in by 'well organized, armed non-state actors' that 'position themselves as an alternative to traditional state-based governance structures, as a "non-state state", and . . . challenge the state monopoly of violence'. Of course, by no means all terrorist attacks are manifestations of religious fundamentalism (another important source is nationalist movements), just as not all religious fundamentalisms engage in terrorism—these are overlapping categories. However, the report specifically refers to manifestations of terrorism identified with Islam, particularly Daesh (ISIS), the Taliban, and al Qaeda (World Economic Forum 2016). Similarly, the UK government's Counter-Extremism Strategy states that the greatest challenge comes from 'the global rise of Islamist extremism' (HM Government 2015: 15).

Case Study 12.5 Islamism

In 2015 Abu Hamza (referred to earlier as a 'radical cleric' whom Malik argues 'should be free to spout racist hatred') was sentenced to life imprisonment in the United States following his conviction on terrorist charges, having been extradited from the UK.

> Hamza was convicted of 11 counts of criminal conduct related to the taking of 16 hostages in Yemen in 1998 that left three Britons and an Australian dead. He was also found guilty of advocating violent jihad in Afghanistan in 2001 and conspiring to establish a jihad training camp in Oregon between June 2000 and December 2001.
>
> (McVeigh 2014)

He had previously been convicted in the UK for inciting murder and racial hatred. According to the US charges, Hamza is a 'violent jihadist', and he would also commonly be referred to as an 'Islamist'. What is the relationship between a 'radical preacher' who incites murder and racial hatred and an 'Islamist' or 'violent jihadist'? This is a fraught question and relates to the distinction between religion and ideology (Islam and Islamism), and between words and actions.

Like the other major world religions, there are branches of Islam, notably the division between Sunni and Shi'ite Muslims. However, in general terms, Islam involves

> a number of fundamental convictions: belie[f] in the oneness of God; that the prophet Muhammad completes the tradition of Abrahamic monotheism; and that the divine word revealed to him is set out in the Koran. [There are] 'Five Pillars' of Islam: the duty to declare one's allegiance to the oneness of God and Muhammad as his messenger (shahada); praying five times a day (salat); almsgiving (zakat); fasting and exercising restraint during the holy month of Ramadan (sawm); and undertaking the pilgrimage to Mecca at least once in a lifetime (hajj).
>
> (European Parliament 2015)

Western politicians and governments are often at pains to distinguish between the religion and 'Islamist' ideology, and between the followers of each. The UK government's Counter-Extremism Strategy states that 'There is a clear distinction between Islam—a religion followed peacefully by millions—and the ideology promoted by Islamist extremists' (HM Government 2015: 21). David Cameron, as UK Prime Minister, similarly asserted that 'Islam is a religion observed peacefully and devoutly by over a billion people. Islamist extremism is a political ideology supported by a minority' (Cameron 2011). And former Prime Minister Tony Blair has argued that 'it is not Islam itself that gives rise to this ideology. It is an interpretation of Islam, actually a perversion of it which many Muslims abhor' (Blair 2014)

President Obama argued that 'extremist groups have perverted Islam to justify terrorism'. But Obama decided not to use the term Islamism at all (and received criticism for this refusal), arguing that whether or not so-called Islamic State was characterized as 'Islamist' was a 'distraction' and irrelevant to effectively opposing it. Obama also claimed that the term is counterproductive because it tends to create the impression that all Muslims are 'tarred with the same brush' and regarded with suspicion, and because it allows so-called Islamic State to make the (for Obama) false claim that it is engaged in a 'clash of civilizations' between Islam and the West (the term is associated with arguments put forward by Samuel Huntington) (Obama 2016).

It is, of course, important to distinguish between the supporters of 'Islamist extremism' and the vast majority of Muslims who 'abhor' the ideology and tactics of so-called Islamic State and al Qaeda, and to recognize that 'Islamist extremism' cannot be equated with, or reduced to, Islam. But this is not to say that the two are not at all connected. 'Islamists claim to base themselves entirely on the word of God as expressed in the Holy Qur'an, and in the words and deeds of . . . the prophet Mohammed' (Farrar 2012: 217). They claim to be the true believers. What are we to make of this claim? It could be argued that the religious justification for terrorism is no more than a cover for other motivations such as wealth and power, and that many supporters of the ideology are not particularly observant in terms of attendance at mosque and compliance with the five pillars. And even if Islamists are sincere in their profession of religious faith it can be argued that theirs is a 'perverted' interpretation of Islam. However, it seems implausible to argue that all Islamists are simply making up their identification with Islam. Even though most Muslims reject the extremists' interpretation of Islam it can be argued that the divine word of God as revealed to Muhammad and set out in the Quran is capable of being interpreted (through selective reading) to justify violence (although Harris (2005: 123) argues that a selective reading would be needed to 'not see a link between Muslim faith and Muslim violence'), and that there is no ultimate authority that can determine once and for all the true interpretation. Without attempting to resolve this debate here, we can at least acknowledge that the relation between the religion and the ideology is contested.

In political and media discussions, 'Islamism' is used in a specific and narrow sense to refer to 'violent jihadism' and to terrorist organizations such as so-called Islamic State and al Qaeda. This cannot be equated with Islam for two reasons. First, Islamism can also be used in a broader sense to include all manifestations of political Islam, referring to all 'those varieties of Islamic belief and practice which are explicitly political' (Farrar 2012: 217). In this sense Islamism includes a range of Islamic political ideologies, not only extremist or 'revolutionary' Islamism but also 'conservative' and 'moderate' variants (Browers 2013).

Second, as a political movement Islamism cannot be explained simply as an expression of religion since this would ignore the contextual factors that help to explain the rise of Islamist organizations (e.g. the historical sense of defeat and humiliation at the hands of non-Muslim Western powers through the Crusades and colonialism, the creation of the state of Israel and its illegal occupation of Palestinian land, Western support for corrupt and authoritarian governments in the region, and military intervention seen as a modern crusade against Muslims in the form of the Iraq war). Thus, Islamist extremism can be understood as one variant of political Islam, supported by a minority of Muslims, based on a selective (and arguably distorted) interpretation of Islam, and stimulated by a specific set of historical and contextual factors.

UNPACKING 'VIOLENT ISLAMIST EXTREMISM'

In order to understand the ideological character of Islamism in the narrow sense, as exemplified by organizations such as so-called Islamic State and al Qaeda and individuals such as Abu Hamza (while acknowledging divisions and rivalries between its various manifestations), the UK government's counter-extremism strategy (CES) can serve as a starting point. 'Violent Islamist extremism' is a compound of three elements that it is useful to unpack. Violent extremism can take forms other than Islamism (for example, the strategy refers to Islamophobia and neo-Nazi groups in the UK), and, as we have seen, Islamism is not reducible to violent extremism. In Figure 12.2 Islamism is presented, in line with the CES, as an over-arching category that includes extremism and, within that, violent extremism: not all Islamism is extremist, and not all Islamist extremism is violent.

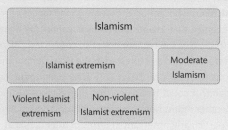

Figure 12.2 Islamism and categories of Islamism

In this approach extremism is defined, controversially, as 'the vocal or active opposition to our fundamental values, including democracy, the rule of law, individual liberty, and the mutual respect and tolerance of different faiths and beliefs' (HM Government 2015; see also HM Government 2013). This approach is controversial because fundamental British values are inherently contestable, so defining extremism in this way involves attempting to impose a particular conception of British values and restricting free speech. Many observant Muslims (like adherents of other faiths) find that their religious beliefs clash with how others interpret fundamental values, so the strategy raises the risk identified by Obama of all Muslims seemingly being 'tarred by the same brush'. Finally, it can be argued that beliefs and words need to be distinguished from violent actions, and incitement to violence should be permitted by free speech norms so that, as suggested by Malik (2006), 'Muslim demonstrators should be able to carry placards calling for the beheading of those who insult Islam'. In January 2017 criticisms of the government's definition of extremism were reported as holding back new counter-terrorism legislation (Townsend 2017).

Although 'most Islamists are not violent' (Farrar 2012: 218), violent Islamist extremists, such as so-called Islamic State, use violence and terrorism to achieve ideological goals, based on their interpretation of Islam. This commitment to violent struggle as 'the primary or even exclusive method for the pursuit of political change' is usually referred to by the term 'jihad' or 'violent jihad', and the terrorists as 'jihadists' (Mandaville in Farrar 2012: 217). Their acts of violence are based on a particular interpretation of jihad as 'struggle', giving priority to the 'outward' jihad of violent struggle against the enemies of Islam over the 'inward' jihad of struggle to live the life of an observant Muslim in accordance with the five pillars, so reversing the distinction in Islam between the greater and lesser jihad.

So-called Islamic State emerged in 2013 in the context of the civil war that followed the Arab spring in Syria. It explicitly presents an anti-Western ideology, sees this as a struggle between good and evil, and seeks to establish an Islamic state or caliphate uniting Muslim countries (centred in Iraq and Syria). The purpose of a caliphate is to enforce 'a "restoration" of Islamic law backed by the power of the state' (Ruthven 1997: 4). As a political programme, this involves aiming to 'replace the sovereignty of the people expressed through parliamentary legislation, with the "sovereignty of God" as revealed, in its perfection and finality, through the Shari'a' (Ruthven 1997: 5). Thus so-called Islamic State, as a particular manifestation of 'violent Islamist extremism', rejects central aspects of modernity: the nation-state as the framework for political rule, democracy, or popular sovereignty, secularism, pluralism, and religious tolerance.

Stop and Think

Why is the link between Islam and Islamism controversial?

Summary

- Religion is a contested concept with no agreed definition that captures its many forms.

- Religion can be likened to an ideology, particularly as it contains a moral code governing the conduct of human affairs.

- There is debate about whether religion is in decline as the secularization thesis predicts. However, there is strong evidence that Britain is becoming an increasingly secular society.

- The secular state involves the separation of church and state, but does not prevent religion entering into the political sphere, including through existing ideologies such as Christian socialism.

- Fundamentalism is not confined to religion but can be defined as strict adherence to fundamental principles or beliefs.

- Religious fundamentalism can be understood in terms of family resemblances between its various forms. It is linked to scriptural literalism, is opposed to modernity by which it feels threatened, and seeks to reconstitute society on religious lines.

- In the guise of radical Islam, its most significant form today, it is committed to violence as a means of achieving political change.

Review and discussion questions

1. What is the nature of religion? In what ways is religion comparable to ideology?

2. Examine the arguments for and against the separation of religion and politics.

3. To what extent is secularization an irreversible process?

4. Critically examine the nature of religious fundamentalism, and consider the extent to which it presents a threat to 'the West'.

Research exercises

1. Critically examine the arguments, methods, and goals of secularist organizations in the UK and the USA.

   Useful websites:

   National Secular Society http://www.secularism.org.uk/

   Secular Coalition for America https://www.secular.org/

2. Produce a report on 'Public attitudes to Islamic fundamentalism'. Your report should include:

   Definition of Islamic fundamentalism and related terms

   Examples of Islamic fundamentalist movements

   Analysis of public attitudes—levels of support or concern

   Useful reports from the Pew Research Center:

   Muslims and Islam: Key findings in the U.S. and around the world

   http://www.pewresearch.org/fact-tank/2015/12/07/muslims-and-islam-key-findings-in-the-u-s-and-around-the-world/

   The political divide on views toward Muslims and Islam

   http://www.pewresearch.org/fact-tank/2015/01/29/the-political-divide-on-views-toward-muslims-and-islam/

   Radical Islamist Movements: Jihadi Networks and Hizb ut-Tahrir

   http://www.pewforum.org/2010/09/15/muslim-networks-and-movements-in-western-europe-radical-islamist-movements-jihadi-networks-and-hizb-ut-tahrir/

Further reading

The Office for National Statistics provides data on religious belief in the UK based on the 2011 census—see ONS (2012), also NatCen (2015). On the USA see Pew Research Center (2015).

For analysis of the changing political landscape in Britain and the role of religion in public life see Commission on Religion and Belief in British Public Life (2015).

Brown (2011) sets out an argument about the relationship between religion and politics from the former UK Prime Minister Gordon Brown.

Good sources on religious fundamentalism are Armstrong (2001), Ruthven (2007), and Parekh (2008). Joppke (2015) analyses challenges to the secular state from the Christian right in the USA and Islam in Europe.

On Islamism see Farrar (2012) and Browers (2013).

References

Akkoc, R. (2015), 'Mapped: These are the World's Most Religious Countries', *The Telegraph*, 13 April, http://www.telegraph.co.uk/news/worldnews/11530382/Mapped-These-are-the-worlds-most-religious-countries.html

Armstrong, K. (2001), *The Battle for God: Fundamentalism in Judaism, Christianity and Islam*, London: HarperCollins.

Armstrong, K. (2005), 'What is Fundamentalism?', http://www.lse.ac.uk/publicEvents/pdf/20050126-Intolerance-Armstrong.pdf

Armstrong, K. (2006), 'Bush's Fondness for Fundamentalism is Courting Disaster at Home and Abroad', *The Guardian*, 31 July, http://www.theguardian.com/commentisfree/2006/jul/31/comment.usa

Barry, B. (2001), *Culture and Equality*, Cambridge: Polity Press.

BBC (2013), 'In Quotes: Margaret Thatcher', 8 April, http://www.bbc.co.uk/news/uk-politics-10377842

BBC (no date), Religions webpage, http://www.bbc.co.uk/religion/religions/

Beer, S. (2013), 'Still Christian, Still Socialist—But Starting Where The Voters Are', 15 October, http://www.christiansontheleft.org.uk/stephenbeer/still_christian_still_socialist_but_starting_where_the_voters_are

Blair, T. (2014), 'Full Text: Tony Blair's Speech on Why the Middle East Matters', *The Spectator*, 23 April, http://blogs.spectator.co.uk/2014/04/full-text-tony-blairs-speech-on-why-the-middle-east-matters/

Browers, M. (2013), 'Islamic Political Ideologies' in M. Freeden, L. T. Sargent, and M. Stears (eds), *The Oxford Handbook of Political Ideologies*, Oxford: Oxford University Press.

Brown, G. (2011), 'Faith in Politics? Lecture by Gordon Brown', http://rowanwilliams.archbishopofcanterbury.org/articles.php/903/faith-in-politics-lecture-by-gordon-brown

Cameron, D. (2011), 'PM's Speech at Munich Security Conference', February, http://webarchive.nationalarchives.gov.uk/20130109092234/http://number10.gov.uk/news/pms-speech-at-munich-security-conference/

Campbell, A. (2010), 'Baroness Warsi Misses Point of "We Don't Do God", Writes a Pro Faith Atheist', http://www.alastaircampbell.org/blog/2010/09/16/baroness-warsi-misses-point-of-we-dont-do-god-writes-a-pro-faith-atheist/

CHRISAFIS, A. (2016), 'French PM Supports Local Bans on Burkinis', *The Guardian*, 18 August, https://www.theguardian.com/world/2016/aug/17/french-pm-supports-local-bans-burkinis

COLLINS DICTIONARY OF THE ENGLISH LANGUAGE (1986), London: Collins.

COMMISSION ON RELIGION AND BELIEF IN BRITISH PUBLIC LIFE (2015), *Living With Difference: Community, Diversity and the Common Good*, The Woolf Institute, https://corablivingwithdifference.files.wordpress.com/2015/12/living-with-difference-online.pdf

DART, T. (2015), 'Bobby Jindal: Republican who Brought Creationism into Schools to Join Election', *The Guardian*, 24 June, http://www.theguardian.com/us-news/2015/jun/24/bobby-jindal-republican-creationism-2016-election

DEVI, G. (2015), 'Creationism Isn't Just an Ideology—it's a Weapon of Political Control', *The Guardian*, 22 November, http://www.theguardian.com/commentisfree/2015/nov/22/creationism-isnt-just-an-ideology-its-a-weapon-of-political-control

EUROPEAN PARLIAMENT (2015), *Understanding the Branches of Islam*, European Parliament Briefing, September, http://www.europarl.europa.eu/EPRS/EPRS-Briefing-568339-Understanding-branches-Islam-FINAL.pdf

FARRAR, M. (2012), 'Islamism and Terror: A Western Way of Doing Politics', in M. Farrar, S. Robinson, Y. Valli, and P. Wetherly (eds), *Islam in the West: Key Issues in Multiculturalism*, Basingstoke: Palgrave Macmillan.

FRASER, G. (2013), 'Far from Confining Itself to Matters Spiritual, the Church has a Duty to Get Involved in Politics', *The Guardian*, 2 August, https://www.theguardian.com/commentisfree/belief/2013/aug/02/confining-matters-spiritual-church-involved-politics

GAMBLE, A. (1981), *An Introduction to Modern Social and Political Thought*, Basingstoke: Macmillan.

HARRIS, S. (2005), *The End of Faith: Religion, Terror, and the Future of Reason*, Cambridge: The Free Press.

HM GOVERNMENT (2013), *Tackling extremism in the UK—Report from the Prime Minister's Task Force on Tackling Radicalisation and Extremism*, https://www.gov.uk/government/uploads/system/uploads/attachment_data/file/263181/ETF_FINAL.pdf

HM GOVERNMENT (2015), *Counter-Extremism Strategy*, https://www.gov.uk/government/uploads/system/uploads/attachment_data/file/470088/51859_Cm9148_Accessible.pdf.

HOPE NOT HATE (2016), 'Cheerleading for IS', http://www.hopenothate.org.uk/features/anjem-choudary/

ITV (2016), 'Syrian Refugee Pope Took to Rome "Overwhelmed"', http://www.itv.com/news/story/2016-04-17/syrian-refugee-pope-took-to-rome-overwhelmed/

JOPPKE, C. (2015), *The Secular State Under Siege: Religion and Politics in Europe and America*, Cambridge: Polity Press.

LEGAL INFORMATION INSTITUTE (no date a), 'First Amendment', Cornell Law School, Ithaca, NY, https://www.law.cornell.edu/constitution/first_amendment

LEGAL INFORMATION INSTITUTE (no date b), 'Free Exercise Clause'. Cornell Law School, Ithaca, NY, https://www.law.cornell.edu/wex/free_exercise_clause

LUCIE-SMITH, A. (2014), 'Christian Socialism has Always Been a Force in British Politics', *Catholic Herald*, 17 March, http://www.catholicherald.co.uk/commentandblogs/2014/03/17/as-tony-benn-showed-christian-socialism-has-always-been-a-force-in-british-politics/

MacArthur, B. (ed.) (1995), *The Penguin Book of Historic Speeches*. Harmondsworth: Penguin/ Viking.

Macey, M. and Carling, A. (2011), *Ethnic, Racial and religious Inequalities: The Perils of Subjectivity*. Basingstoke: Palgrave Macmillan.

McVeigh, K. (2014), 'Abu Hamza Found Guilty of 11 Terrorism Charges', *The Guardian*, 19 May, https://www.theguardian.com/world/2014/may/19/abu-hamza-found-guilty-terrorism-charges

Malik, K. (2006), 'Too Much Respect', http://www.kenanmalik.com/essays/cartoons_prospect.html

Malik, K. (2012), 'Enemies of Free Speech', *Index on Censorship*, Vol. 41, No. 1, http://www.kenanmalik.com/essays/index_enemies.html

NatCen (2015), 'NatCen's British Social Attitudes survey: Change in Religious Affiliation among Adults in Great Britain', https://www.natcen.ac.uk/media/893167/religious-affiliation-british-social-attitudes.pdf

Obama, B. (2016), 'President Obama's Speech Criticizing the Muslim Ban', *Time*, 14 June, http://time.com/4368733/barack-obama-donald-trump-muslim-ban-orlando-shooting/

Office for National Statistics (2012), Religion in England and Wales 2011, https://www.ons.gov.uk/peoplepopulationandcommunity/culturalidentity/religion/articles/religioninenglandandwales2011/2012-12-11

Parekh, B. (2008), *A New Politics of Identity: Political Principles for an Interdependent World*. Basingstoke: Palgrave-Macmillan.

Pew Research Center (2012a), 'Little Voter Discomfort with Romney's Mormon Religion', 26 July, http://www.pewforum.org/2012/07/26/2012-romney-mormonism-obamas-religion/

Pew Research Center (2012b), 'The Global Religious Landscape', http://www.pewforum.org/2012/12/18/global-religious-landscape-exec/

Pew Research Center (2015a), 'U.S. Public Becoming Less Religious', http://www.pewforum.org/2015/11/03/u-s-public-becoming-less-religious/

Pew Research Center (2015b), '7 Key Changes in the Global Religious Landscape', http://www.pewresearch.org/fact-tank/2015/04/02/7-key-changes-in-the-global-religious-landscape/

Pew Research Center (2016), '5 Key Findings about Faith and Politics in the 2016 Presidential Race', http://www.pewresearch.org/fact-tank/2016/01/27/key-findings-faith-and-politics-in-2016-presidential-race/

Reynolds, D. (2009), *America, Empire of Liberty: A New History*, Harmondsworth: Allen Lane.

Rosen, M. and Wolff, J. (eds) (1999), *Political Thought*, Oxford: Oxford University Press.

Ruthven, M. (1997), *Islam: A Very Short Introduction*. Oxford: Oxford University Press.

Ruthven, M. (2007), *Religious Fundamentalism: A Very Short Introduction*. Oxford: Oxford University Press.

Sen, A. (2006), *Identity and Violence: The Illusion of Destiny*, Harmondsworth: Allen Lane.

Theakston, K. (2014), '"Doing God" in Number 10: British Prime Ministers and Religion' https://www.psa.ac.uk/insight-plus/blog/%E2%80%98doing-god%E2%80%99-number-10-british-prime-ministers-and-religion

TORNIELLI, A. (2013), 'Francis on Not Wanting to be Pope and his Love of Having People Around him', *La Stampa*, 6 July, http://www.lastampa.it/2013/06/07/esteri/vatican-insider/en/francis-on-not-wanting-to-be-pope-and-his-love-of-having-people-around-him-eKhdUQeDBSvQuccWIeVwhP/pagina.html

TOWNSEND, M. (2017), 'Theresa May's Counter-terrorism Bill Close to "Sinking Without Trace"', *The Guardian*, 29 January, https://www.theguardian.com/politics/2017/jan/29/theresa-may-counter-terrorism-bill-sinking-without-trace-extremism-british-values

WETHERLY, P. (2016), 'Is Britain a "Christian Country"?' https://leedspage.wordpress.com/2016/04/03/is-britain-a-christian-country/

WIN/GALLUP (2015), 'Losing our Religion? Two Thirds of People Still Claim to be Religious', http://www.wingia.com/web/files/news/290/file/290.pdf

WORLD ECONOMIC FORUM (2016), *The Global Risks Report 2016*, World Economic Forum, http://www3.weforum.org/docs/Media/TheGlobalRisksReport2016.pdf

13

Beyond ideology?

Paul Wetherly

OBJECTIVES

- Review the different ideological conceptions of human nature
- Critically examine the implications of globalization for existing political ideologies
- Assess claims of the possibility and desirability of a post-ideological form of politics—can we move beyond ideology?

Introduction

In this book we have examined the nature of ideology as a contested concept (Chapter 1); surveyed the main ideologies which frame political debate today, setting out the core values and beliefs of each and noting internal variants; noted their historical, European origins, and subsequent global diffusion; and observed ideologies in practice as they are embodied in parties, movements, and political struggles.

In this concluding chapter we will draw together two key cross-cutting themes of the chapters—conceptions of human nature and ideological responses to globalization. We will then look at a range of arguments that suggest the possibility of resolving or ending ideological debate: the possibility (and difficulty) of showing the failure of a particular ideology; the final coming to an end of ideological debate and its replacement by consensus; and a form of non-ideological politics.

Ideology and human nature

If there is a universal human nature, defined in terms of needs and capacities, shared by everyone, this seems to suggest that we have shared interests—that what is good for one person is good for everyone else. For example, we all have an equal interest in being able to satisfy our needs and exercise our capacities. Surely, then, the good society is one which best meets these basic human interests. Does this mean that ideological disputes about the nature of the good society ought to be resolvable? We can understand the persistence of ideological dispute as arising from two reasons:

- Ideologies have different underlying views of human nature, and these different views continue to inspire competing visions of the good society consistent with this nature.

- Disagreement about the good society might be built into human nature, as suggested by Stoker's argument that it is because we are human that we disagree and want different things (see Chapter 1). In this vein it might be argued that we share certain basic interests such as human rights but beyond these minimum conditions for a good life we have different ideas of what constitutes the good life. For example, we all have an interest in freedom but want to do different things with that freedom.

As we saw in Chapter 1, humans are the 'raw ingredients' for constructing the good society, so ideas of human nature have implications for the feasibility and desirability of ideological visions of what the good society looks like, as discussed in the chapters of this book. Table 13.1 draws together some of the key ideas about human nature in ideological debates.

Table 13.1 Ideas of human nature

Ideology	Key ideas of human nature
Liberalism	Liberals hold a positive or optimistic view of human nature. '[All] people are born free and equal, and as such every person has a natural right to liberty . . . [T]he *Fundamental Liberal Principle* . . . asserts that freedom is the standard way of being for all humans' (Chapter 2). Society is seen as a collection of rational individuals who are generally the best judges of their own happiness.
Conservatism	In contrast with liberal optimism, 'human beings are flawed creatures . . . whose rationality is all too often overborne by passion, and whose passionate attachments are often misplaced' (Chapter 3). Individuals are mutually dependent members of a community rather than autonomous individuals, within an organic society that involves a natural hierarchy.
Socialism	Socialism shares an optimistic view of human nature with liberalism. In contrast with liberal individualism, socialists argue that 'humans are social animals and therefore the ideal form of social organization is one that emphasizes community and cooperation' (Chapter 4). Selfishness and competitiveness are products of society, not fixed elements of human nature. The belief that human nature can change and that a socialist society would bring out our cooperative nature 'gives socialism a uniquely optimistic edge' (Chapter 4).

Table 13.1 Continued

Ideology	Key ideas of human nature
Anarchism	Like socialists 'For the most part anarchists are not "essentialists"; that is they do not consider that there is a core and immutable character to human nature, not open to socialization' (Chapter 5). Human nature is compatible with a stateless society based on cooperation. In this sense they have a positive or optimistic view of human nature comparable to socialism.
Nationalism	In contrast with the universalism of liberalism and socialism, nationalism can be seen as a form of particularism in the sense that people have a feeling of belonging to their nation and sense of particular ties to fellow nationals. Humanity may be seen as naturally divided into nations, seen as ethnic communities sharing a common descent and distinctive way of life (ethnic nationalism).
Fascism	Fascism rejects liberal individualism. It exalts 'the nation, united on the basis of profound common ties that transcended class, political affiliation, or narrow self-interest' (Chapter 7). That is, fascism emphasizes the national interest over individual autonomy. Fascism envisages that 'a new kind of superior human being would emerge: a genuine "new fascist man" . . . that would be part committed citizen and part soldier ready to sacrifice themselves for the defence of the nation' (Chapter 7).
Feminism	Feminism poses the question of whether there is a universal human nature shared by men and women. The main thrust of feminism has been to challenge the ideas that men and women have different natures and that this explains or justifies the different positions occupied by men and women in society, and male dominance. Feminism has challenged these ideas by distinguishing between 'sex' and 'gender' and arguing that masculine and feminine gender roles are socially constructed rather than rooted in biological difference. Thus feminism points to the shaping of human behaviour by society. However, a different manifestation of feminism not only accepts natural differences between men and women but celebrates the qualities of womanhood. E.g. 'The link between women and peace is often based on an understanding of womanhood, as more humane, collaborative, inclusive, peaceful and nurturing . . . . Such understandings are framed by essentialist views of what constitutes the "essence" of womanhood' (Chapter 9). Further, 'the category of intersex has challenged the distinction between binaries of biologically assigned sex as either male or female' (Chapter 9).
Ecologism	Whereas liberalism and socialism may be seen as exalting humans, their capacities and needs, and their mastery over nature, 'there is a strong core in Green thinking that sees humans as not above or outside of nature and sees the need to assert our relationship with nature as one based on symbiosis, cooperation, and non-hierarchical forms of social and political organization' (Chapter 10). This also involves a challenge to the connection between materialism and human happiness.

Table 13.1 Continued

Ideology	Key ideas of human nature
Multiculturalism	Multiculturalism emphasizes the importance of culture in understanding human behaviour. Although humans everywhere are essentially the same in terms of their basic needs and capacities, they differ according to the cultures in which they are 'embedded'. Cultural diversity is manifested in differences in beliefs and lifestyles that people value and wish to preserve. Thus multiculturalism sees humans as essentially social creatures, shaped by their cultures and relations with others. 'If people are basically the same but, at the same time, different it is the difference to which multiculturalism draws attention and attaches significance' (Chapter 11).
Religious fundamentalism	Humans have a purpose that is not of their own choosing but divine. 'Religion [involves belief in the existence of] a superhuman agency [which is the source of] a moral code governing the conduct of human affairs' (Chapter 12). Belief in scriptural literalism and inerrancy trumps human capacity for reason, although natural law tradition emphasizes capacity for reason endowed by God. Religion can be understood as meeting a need for myth and meaning that cannot be supplied by science, i.e. humans are not purely rational.

 Stop and Think

Review your understanding of ideological conceptions of human nature, with reference to:

- Whether humans are naturally good or evil
- The distinctive capacities of human beings
- Whether human beings are naturally anything at all (have an essence) or are shaped by society—'nature versus nurture'

Globalization and ideology

The classical ideologies developed in the modern era, in what might be seen as the age of the nation-state—a period in which the nation-state has become the predominant form of political organization, creating a world of nation-states. The political movements and parties that embodied these ideologies were designed essentially to operate within national polities, most obviously to contest national elections and influence or control state power at a national level. However, the classical ideologies also had an international or global orientation and impact from the start, in several ways. Liberalism and socialism were Enlightenment ideologies and the

Enlightenment was itself a trans-national historical movement in which ideas were shared across borders in a series of linked national Enlightenments. Second, the classical ideologies which emerged in Europe spread beyond their European heartland as part of the expansion of the West. For example, liberal ideas moved across the Atlantic from Europe to North America with the colonists (as did religious beliefs). Third, the classical Enlightenment ideologies were internationalist and universalist in orientation, using the language of a common humanity which transcended national identities and borders, and seeing their visions of the good society as universally valid. Fourth, they inspired international movements, such as the International Working Men's Association which was established in 1864 (see Chapter 4). Finally, they provided intellectual frameworks for understanding the trends towards interdependence between nations: what today we refer to as globalization. Globalization can be defined as

> the process of integrating social, cultural, economic and possibly political systems into a single global system that extends across the boundaries of states. Interactions across the boundaries of states increase in frequency relative to interactions within states. So globalization is a process rather than an accomplishment.
>
> (Dryzek and Dunleavy 2009: 307)

As is clear from this definition, globalization is not 'one thing' but a multi-dimensional process and this means that, rather than seeing it as simply 'good' or 'bad', there can be different attitudes to different aspects, depending on ideological viewpoint. For example, global communication and access to information made possible by the internet may be welcomed while the enhanced power of global corporations, including the 'tech giants', may be a concern. Or people might welcome economic growth fostered by international trade but oppose large scale immigration.

Whether globalization is a novel phenomenon or an intrinsic aspect of modernity (as suggested by Marx and Engels in the *Communist Manifesto*) is debated. However, it is clear that today we live in a globalizing world, and the issue of globalization is certainly widely discussed. In this section we draw together some of the key ideological responses and claims in relation to globalization. What analyses do they offer of globalization? Are they pro- or anti-globalization? How does globalization fit into visions of the good society?

Liberalism

Liberalism is a universalist and **internationalist** ideology. It champions a liberal international economic order based on free trade which it argues drives prosperity and fosters interdependence and peace. In this way liberalism is closely associated with economic globalization, particularly in the guise of neo-liberalism or the '**Washington consensus**'. Thus economic globalization is not simply a manifestation of the inherent logic or dynamic of the market but a political project sponsored by neo-liberalism. At the same time neo-liberalism can be seen as a *response* to the pressures exerted on nation-states by processes of economic globalization, especially the **'race to the bottom'** to attract and retain investment by multinational corporations (MNCs). This argument assumes that deregulation and minimal states provide the most attractive environments for MNCs and that, therefore, all states are compelled to adopt the same neo-liberal policy mix—characterized as a shift from the welfare state to the **competition state**.

Politically, commitment to universal human rights requires the creation of international political and legal institutions to promote and safeguard them, and may justify states taking action up to and including military intervention to prevent abuses of human rights in authoritarian states (liberal or **humanitarian intervention**).

It can be argued that the triumph of liberalism—in economic and political terms—has taken place on a global scale with the defeat of communism as liberalism's only global challenger and rival (see the section 'The end of history' below).

Conservatism

Conservative parties and governments have often been at the forefront of promoting globalization, but this reflects the capture of these parties by neo-liberalism, especially the UK Conservative Party under Margaret Thatcher and the Republicans in the USA under Ronald Reagan. However, conservatism as ideology is troubled by economic globalization understood as opening up economies to market forces, since it magnifies the tension between the conservative emphasis on tradition and the corrosive effects of markets on all traditional beliefs and practices.

Globalization in the form of migration, and the cultural diversity it creates, also challenges the conservative idea of social cohesion based on shared values and sense of national identity. This tension has led some conservative parties in Europe, such as the Republican Party in France (Républicains) and the UK Conservative Party, to emphasize immigration and diversity as threats and the need for tougher control, often in response to the electoral threat posed by anti-immigration parties on the right. Thus the UK Conservative government held, and lost, a referendum in 2016 on membership of the European Union, which was framed mainly in terms of the need to control immigration from EU countries and was spurred by considerations of statecraft—internal party management and electoral competition from UKIP. Sarkozy, leader of the Républicains, seeking nomination for the 2017 presidential election, adopted 'an increasingly hardline stance on national identity and the place of Islam in France' (Chrisafis 2016).

Thus 'It would be tempting to argue . . . that the conservative world-view can only be a going concern in states which have contrived to insulate themselves to some extent from the unrelenting, transformative force of the globalized economy' (Chapter 3).

Socialism

Marx saw economic (or capitalist) globalization as the inexorable working out of the inherent laws of capitalist development, driven by the search for profits and markets. But it is also seen as a political project supported by the leading capitalist states and the intergovernmental organizations they dominate, such as the International Monetary Fund (IMF). At the same time, capitalist globalization may create tensions due to economic rivalries between national capitalist classes and consequent potential conflict between nation-states.

Capitalist globalization spreads capitalist class relationships and class struggle on a global scale, and the world market magnifies crisis tendencies and the risks of contagion (e.g. the global economic crisis beginning in 2008).

Reformist socialism or social democracy has been challenged by economic globalization because it has adopted a model of socialist progress within the framework of the nation-state, that is, by controlling state power at a national level by winning national elections. Social democracy sees economic globalization as increasing the power of MNCs in relation to governments and intensifying inequality. Thus, insofar as economic globalization has undermined the capacity of the state to manage the economy, it has undermined the social democratic project. However, social democrats have responded to globalization by arguing that it is not an inexorable force but the result of (neo-liberal) political choices and can thus be managed by arguing that states are not compelled to engage in a race to the bottom. This is evidenced by the variety of 'models of capitalism' and particularly the success of the highly developed and generous Scandinavian welfare states, such as Sweden. Social democrats may look to intergovernmental organizations such as the EU as having the potential to regulate capitalism on an international scale and avoid the race to the bottom. This was a prime reason for left-wing support for a Remain vote in the UK referendum on membership of the EU (although some on the left supported the Leave campaign due to their view of the EU as embodying neo-liberal principles).

The Third Way was presented by its advocates as a renewal of social democracy which involved embracing globalization and reforming the welfare state in order to assist people to 'navigate' the risks and opportunities that it brings. For example the socialist commitment to 'full employment' was replaced by 'full employability' and 'labour market flexibility', and 'equality' was redefined as 'social inclusion'. However, not surprisingly, critics saw the Third Way as a retreat from social democracy and acceptance of neo-liberalism.

Today, if socialism does not have clear answers to globalization, it can be argued that socialism is highly attuned to key problems engendered by capitalist globalization—unaccountable corporate power and growing inequality.

> **Stop and Think**
>
> What are the main disagreements between liberalism and socialism in their responses to globalization?

Anarchism

Historically the main thrust of anarchism has been opposition to the state, but in recent years, since the protests against the World Trade Organization (WTO) in Seattle in 1999, it has been a key ingredient, alongside socialism and environmentalism, of the anti-globalization movement. More specifically, this is a movement of protest against capitalist or neo-liberal globalization, which has itself been a global phenomenon.

Movements such as Occupy operate outside of conventional political party structures and reject the compromises involved in electoral politics, and this may be part of the appeal in an era of '**anti-politics**' and distrust of established parties and political elites. Occupy has been successful in raising issues such as global inequality—encapsulated in the slogan 'we are the 99 per cent', but it is questionable whether, beyond protest, the anti-globalization movement represents a revival of anarchism as an ideological alternative to global capitalism.

Nationalism

On the face of it, nationalism is the ideology that faces the most severe challenge from globalization, even to the extent that it may be seen as anachronistic. For the basic nationalist demand for self-determination or national sovereignty, that is, for political rule to be exercised within the territorial confines of the nation-state, seems to be swimming against the tide of economic globalization with increasing cross-border relations and processes. In particular, globalization makes it harder for national governments to manage their economies, and it might be expected that national identity will be weakened. This can occur to the extent that global communication and travel create a sense of connection with people in other parts of the world and extend the circle of empathy beyond particular ties to fellow nationals, and because migration creates multicultural societies which can lead to the formation of new hybrid identities through cultural mixing. 'Nevertheless, there is much evidence that processes of 'globalization'—particularly in terms of free market liberalization and increased migration flows—have re-energized nationalist sentiment, particularly in Western contexts' (Chapter 6).

Resurgent nationalism can be interpreted as a defensive reaction to the sense of globalization as a threat to economic security and identity. The 2016 referendum vote for the UK to leave the European Union ('Brexit') can be seen in these terms, particularly since national sovereignty ('take back control') and anxiety over net migration were the main issues in the Leave campaign. Thus a core element of support for the Leave campaign (and UKIP) has been characterized in terms of the 'left behind'— working class and poor voters who feel that globalization has not benefited them. However, there was a tension within the Leave campaign since, rather than being anti-globalization, leaving the EU was framed in terms of the UK being more 'open for business' with the rest of the world, suggesting a pro-globalization stance. It is interesting that support for Brexit was essentially an English and Welsh phenomenon—in Scotland nationalism (in the guise of the SNP campaign for an independent Scotland) is strongly aligned with support for EU membership. In the USA the successful campaign for the Presidency by Donald Trump played on the same anti-globalization sentiment, with its nationalist slogan to 'make America great again' and promise to shield Americans from global competition using protectionist measures.

Fascism

As an extreme form of nationalism, the resurgence of nationalist and anti-immigration parties and movements has involved some far-right and fascist elements, such as Golden Dawn (Greece) and Jobbik (Hungary), which 'share an extreme form of ethno-nationalism with a demonization of perceived national enemies, [and] a visceral opposition to globalization and internationalism' (Chapter 7). Given the emphasis of fascism on ethnic or racial identity and purity, it was to be expected that the era of globalization, particularly in the form of international migration, would produce a fascist response.

Feminism

Feminism identifies women's oppression as a global phenomenon in the sense that it is experienced by women throughout the world, and such practices are always harmful to women, regardless of cultural differences. In this sense, feminism is a universalist and global ideology. It rejects the relativism involved in claims that it is a specifically Western ideology reflecting Western values and therefore not relevant in other cultural contexts. For example, feminists believe that all women benefit from and have a right to education, and this right trumps local cultural practices that involve exclusion of girls from education. Globalization, particularly in the form of South–North international migration and the creation of multicultural societies, has brought some of these issues of cultural difference into political debate within Western societies, for example in relation to Muslim women wearing the veil (see Chapter 11). In fact it is misleading to see these issues in 'West versus non-West' terms since traditional ideas about the roles of women in the home as mothers and carers have been appealed to in opposition to feminism in Western societies.

Feminism has spread beyond its Western heartland to become a global movement. In part this has been facilitated by globalization, as part of the diffusion of Western ideas more generally. In particular, the increasing ease of global communication and the growth of global media have facilitated increased awareness of women's oppression throughout the world and the development of a 'global community of online activism and debate'—the fourth wave of feminism (Chapter 9). In addition feminism has achieved success in influencing the agendas and policies of international governmental organizations (IGOs), such as the 1979 UN Convention on the Elimination of All forms of Discrimination Against Women (CEDAW) and the UN's Sustainable Development Goals. However, in other ways globalization can be seen as double-edged. In particular, neo-liberal economic globalization has expanded employment opportunities for women, but this has often involved new forms of vulnerability and exploitation, with women concentrated in low-paid and low-skilled forms of work. In addition neo-liberal prescriptions for reduced public spending tend to adversely affect women (see Chapter 9).

Environmentalism

In some ways environmentalism is the most global ideology. This is because, although some environmental problems can be framed as local or national issues, the most pressing environmental challenge of our era is inherently global in scale—climate change or global warming.

Climate change is a global issue because the effects of CO_2 emissions are cross-border or transboundary (they affect everyone) and because individual nation-states have little incentive to reduce carbon emissions on their own and would have little effect if they did (collective action by all states is needed). Thus the ideology addresses the global community and demands political action at global level.

But, more than this, climate change is a global issue because it is bound up with economic globalization. The global trading system and movements of people around the world are major contributors to CO_2 emissions and, more generally, neo-liberal globalization is driving the global diffusion of materialism and consumerism. Because of this the anti-globalization movement has a strong environmentalist dimension (and environmentalism has a strong element of anti-globalization).

Environmentalism has developed as a global movement of parties, pressure groups, and NGOs. However it also retains a strong emphasis on local action, encapsulated in the injunction to 'think global, act local'.

Multiculturalism

As an ideology, multiculturalism can be seen as a response to one of the central aspects of globalization in the modern era—international migration and the creation of multicultural societies. Although multiculturalism essentially addresses the *effects* of migration, insofar as it welcomes and celebrates diversity, it takes a positive view of migration. In this way multiculturalism and some forms of resurgent nationalism represent opposite responses to globalization—open versus closed. Cultural diversity can also be seen as producing a kind of 'reverse globalization' in the sense that influences operate in the opposite direction to Westernization, from the Global South to the North.

Understood in terms of political action, the primary focus of multiculturalism has been the nation-state with different national 'models' of multiculturalism. However, globalization means that the society we live in together is not confined within national borders and therefore multiculturalism necessarily also has a global outlook. This is partly because, when people migrate, their sense of belonging to the receiving society may be coupled with an enduring sense of membership of a community (e.g. ethnic or religious) that connects them with their country of origin. When a Danish newspaper published cartoons depicting the prophet Muhammad, the controversy did not only engage Muslims in Denmark but in other European countries and in Muslim countries as well (see Chapter 11).

Religious fundamentalism

The world's two largest religions—Christianity and Islam—are world religions in the sense that they have adherents spread throughout the world and these adherents make up over half of the global population (projected to increase to 60 per cent by 2050) (Pew Research Center 2015a). They are also global and universalistic in the sense that, although many adherents are tolerant of other faiths and adopt a live-and-let-live attitude, they are in principle evangelical and claim to be the one true religion that is therefore right for everybody.

In the past the spread of religion has been facilitated by, and often provided justification for, colonial and imperial expansion. Thus the spread of Christianity was bound up with the expansion of Europe through trade, settlement, and conquest, such as through Christian missionaries in Africa and Asia in the late nineteenth and early twentieth centuries. In the recent era of globalization, by contrast, the revival of religion in the form of religious fundamentalism, such as Islamic fundamentalism, can be seen in part as a reaction against the West and modernity, perceived or experienced as presenting a threat of annihilation.

 Stop and Think

Is it possible to distinguish between ideologies as pro- or anti-globalization?

Beyond ideology?

Is ideology a ubiquitous and essential aspect of politics, or can there be a non-ideological way of doing politics? Could there be an end of ideology? Indeed, are we now living in a society that is post-ideological? It can be argued that society can never dispense with ideology since there will always be reflection, and disagreement, and therefore political struggle in relation to what constitutes the good society, that is, the best kind of society in which humans can live together. Such reflection could even be seen as part of human nature. However, there are three ways in which the end of ideology, or a non-ideological or post-ideological form of politics, might be understood:

- the failure of a particular ideology, which has been shown to be false or anachronistic and therefore consigned to the 'dustbin of history';
- the 'end of history' with the final realization of the good society and the defeat of all other rival ideologies;
- the rejection of or retreat from ideology in favour of a more limited style of politics.

The dustbin of history?

One way to think about ideological competition is in terms of a 'market place of ideas' in which, like products in a market, ideas are tested to see which ones work and which ones fail. Those that fail are rejected and consigned to the 'dustbin of history'. The liberal philosopher John Stuart Mill argued for freedom of expression on utilitarian grounds that it was conducive to scientific and moral progress. Free speech would allow moral and scientific ideas to be tested in argument and, Mill supposed, this would lead to error being exposed and the truth winning out.

To what extent can we understand ideological competition in terms of specific ideas or complete ideologies being rejected because they fail to stand the test of scrutiny and argument in a market place of ideas? Are there any examples of ideologies that have failed in this way? Can we think about ideological progress in these terms?

On the face of it, ideologies do not contain a separate category of beliefs and ideas, and they are just as amenable as any other ideas to being tested to see if they are true or false, right or wrong. Ideologies offer competing frameworks of understanding and political commitment, combining 'is' and 'ought' statements or claims: that is, statements about how the world works and how it can be changed, and statements of values about how the world ought to be changed to create the 'good society' (see Chapter 1). In this way, ideologies combine beliefs that come within the purview of political or social science, with those that are the subject of political or moral philosophy. 'Is' statements involve factual claims that can, in principle, be tested through empirical observation and shown to be either false or consistent with the evidence, thus enabling progress in understanding. 'Ought' statements can in principle be tested through moral or ethical reasoning, permitting progress in this field as well.

For example, liberalism and socialism both contain theories which make claims about how the 'free market' or capitalist economy works, how economic problems such as recessions, unemployment, or inequality are caused, and what interventions could solve these problems. They also contain commitments to specific values, defined in particular ways, such as liberty or equality, which the 'good society' is intended to realize. Environmentalism contains scientific theories about the anthropogenic causes of problems such as climate change, together with commitments to environmental ethics or values such as sustainability.

However, the market place of ideas does not always function effectively to eliminate error and ensure progress, and there are some specific difficulties when it comes to the market place for political ideas or ideologies. One of the problems for social sciences is that it is rarely, if ever, possible to subject their theories to the same standards of empirical observation and testing as applied in the natural or physical sciences (such as controlled experiments) and this means that knowledge in the social sciences is more contested and provisional. Put simply, it is much harder to falsify social science theories—to deliver a knock-out blow—and this may in part explain the persistence of ideological disputes. Critics of 'free market fundamentalism' and, in particular, the 'efficient markets hypothesis'—'the belief that the market accurately prices all trades at each moment in time, ruling out booms and slumps, manias and panics'—argue that it has been falsified by an event that contradicts it, the 2008 financial crisis (Skidelsky 2008; see also Chang 2014; Quiggin 2010). Yet the theory has not been discarded. Free market fundamentalism has come to the fore in the context of the proclaimed triumph of liberalism and death of socialism (see 'The collapse of communism and triumph of liberalism'). The failure of socialism is alleged to be demonstrated by the collapse of communism in the Soviet Union, yet socialism clearly still has advocates. In each case it can be argued that the evidence is not clear-cut and is susceptible to competing interpretations, and so it is not clear whether any empirical evidence could prove fatal to either of these ideologies. In addition, although the normative or 'ought' statements contained in ideologies can be tested through moral argument, they are intrinsically incapable of being tested empirically (except in the sense that 'ought' implies 'is'), and it may be the case that final 'once and for all' agreement on normative questions on the basis of moral reasoning is unattainable (Sandel 2009).

There are three specific aspects of the competition of political ideas that further complicate Mill's idea of progress through ideas being tested in debate: political ideologies compete for public support, the conduct of political argument rarely approximates a reasoned debate with careful scrutiny of arguments and evidence; and ideological struggle is bound up with interests and power.

Public understanding and support

Scientific ideas are tested, and progress is facilitated, by a process of peer review within a community of experts. This is also true of ideas in the fields of political science and political philosophy, with the qualifications already mentioned. Is Mill's optimism about the progress of ideas justified when we consider the wider context of public debate and understanding? The point about political ideas, particularly in a democracy, is that this is the ground on which they are tested, because their action orientation requires them to win public support in order to influence public policy. Being right is no good without such support, but is being right likely to lead to support?

A survey on American public attitudes to climate change conducted by the Pew Research Center found that

> When asked to pick among three choices, 50% of adults say that climate change is occurring mostly because of human activity, such as burning fossil fuels; 23% say that climate change is mostly because of natural patterns in the Earth's environment; and another 25% say there is no solid evidence the Earth is getting warmer (Pew Research Center 2015b).

These attitudes no doubt played some part in making it possible for Donald Trump, who has repudiated climate change science as a 'hoax', to be elected as President. Another Pew survey on the American public's views on evolution found that

> Only a minority of Americans fully accept evolution through natural selection. Roughly six-in-ten U.S. adults (62%) say humans have evolved over time . . . . But only a little more than half of them (33% of all Americans) express the belief that humans and other living things evolved *solely* due to natural processes. A quarter of U.S. adults (25%) say evolution was guided by a supreme being . . . . 34% of Americans reject evolution entirely, saying humans and other living things have existed in their present form since the beginning of time.

> (Pew Research Center 2016)

There is overwhelming scientific consensus that the theory of evolution is true and that climate change is mostly due to human activity, so these findings suggest Mill's optimism needs to be qualified. These attitudes to science are important politically because they feed into support, or lack of support, for political ideologies—such as religious fundamentalism and environmentalism—and therefore political action. So politics can go awry due to low levels of public understanding.

However, this is a one-sided view, for we should also ask about the reasons for low levels of public understanding. It could just as well be argued that dysfunctional politics helps, among other factors, to explain a not very well informed citizenry, as saying that poor public understanding explains dysfunctional politics. This brings us to the conduct of political argument and the role of interests and power.

The conduct of political argument

For 'ordinary citizens' to be able to make informed judgements on ideologically con-tested questions involves certain assumptions about the nature of political debate. Ideologies are used as resources in political struggles, so rather than thinking about politics in terms of a direct competition between ideologies, we should see this competition as mediated by, or filtered through, political actors such as campaigners, politicians, parties, and movements.

During the 'Brexit' referendum debate in 2016 on whether the UK should leave or remain in the EU, Michael Gove, a leading Leave campaigner, was challenged to name an economic expert who supported the Leave argument. He responded that 'I think people in this country have had enough of experts' (Gove in Deacon 2016). This denigration of expertise can hardly contribute to an informed public debate, any more than can unquestioning deferral to experts. Brexit can be taken as an example of a low point in political debate in the UK. In particular, the Leave campaign was accused of misinformation (or lying) in relation to the amount of money that would be saved by leaving the EU and that would be available to spend on the NHS, among other issues (Lewis 2016). However the more general point here is that political struggles are concerned with trying to win public support and this involves a style of argument that is calculated to win that support. This might involve misinformation, simplification, distortion, selective use of facts and expertise, 'truthiness', and **populist** appeal to prejudices.

 Stop and Think

To what extent can or should ideological debate be left to experts?

Interests and power

This relates to the role of interests and power in politics. As we have seen, ideologies may represent the interests of particular groups in society, and politics is fundamentally about groups in society with competing or conflicting interests seeking to mobilize power resources to influence public policies for their own ends. An obvious example here is the influence of money in politics, which may be linked to the evidence on public attitudes to climate change. Poole uses this example to ask:

> what happens when the world of ideas really does operate as a marketplace? It happens to be the case that many prominent climate sceptics have been secretly funded by oil companies. The idea that there is some scientific controversy over whether burning fossil fuels has contributed in large part to the present global warming (there isn't) is an idea that has been literally bought and sold, and remains extraordinarily successful.
>
> (Poole 2016).

This is an example of how freedom of speech in a capitalist society is unequal, and thus cannot deliver the open exchange of ideas and progress that Mill envisaged. Therefore, to achieve, as far as possible, healthy ideological debate, political reforms are needed.

Stop and Think

Do you think an ideology can be consigned to the dustbin of history on either of these grounds:

a) It has been falsified?

b) It lacks public support?

The end of history

End of history arguments generally involve the claim that one ideology has triumphed, or will do so someday, so that ideological dispute is replaced by ideological consensus. This does not involve the end of ideology as such but the final triumph of one ideology over all contenders. It is important that this triumph is understood as final, otherwise the condition would be one of a temporary lull in the ideological struggle. If the triumph is final, it is possible to speak of the end of history insofar as historical change is understood as driven by ideological struggles: no more ideological debate, no more history. This does not mean the end of politics, but it does mean politics will operate within more limited parameters. In this view humans will continue to disagree, but these disagreements will not bring into question the basic institutional structure of society, for there is agreement that the best institutional order for society—the good society—has been discovered. Here we will consider two opposing versions of the end of history, which argue that the historic clash within modernity between socialism and liberalism has been or will be definitively resolved one way or the other:

- communism and the end of 'pre-history'
- the triumph of liberalism

Communism and the end of pre-history

In the *Communist Manifesto*, Marx and Engels (1998: 34) asserted that 'The history of all hitherto existing society is the history of class struggles'. In this view, history comprises a series of modes of production or, roughly, economic systems, leading up to the development of capitalism in the modern era. Each mode of production was characterized by a certain level of development of technology (or 'productive forces') and by a particular pattern of ownership and control of the 'means of production' (things used in the production process such as tools, raw materials, and labour). In capitalism this involves a system in which workers are free (unlike in feudalism or slavery) but do not own any means of production and thus have to sell their labour power (ability to work) to capitalists who do own the means of production. This is where class struggle comes in. Marx saw capitalists and workers as the two basic classes of a capitalist society with conflicting or antagonistic interests. History was seen as a story of class struggles because previous economic systems were also characterized by class divisions and conflicting interests, and it was the struggle between these classes that Marx saw as the engine of historical change and progress. For example, the capitalist class or bourgeoisie developed within feudalism and acted as a revolutionary class to overthrow feudalism and establish a society that reflected its own economic interests—capitalism. This was a progressive change because capitalism was a more efficient or productive economic system than feudalism. In this way, history is a story of modes of production, technological progress, and class struggles.

Thus the *Communist Manifesto* describes and provides an explanation for the triumph of capitalism and the classical liberal ideas associated with it. But, for Marx, capitalism is a historical mode of production whose triumph is not final. Just as capitalism came about through class struggle, so its demise will come about in the same way. The class division between workers and capitalists cannot be healed within capitalism since it is rooted in the very structure of economic life. Class conflict arises from the exploitation of workers by capitalists in order to make profit. It can only be ended by the overthrow of capitalism through a working class revolution which will abolish private property.

But unlike previous revolutions which simply initiated a new historical stage, Marx believed this one will constitute the end of history in the specific sense of a series of modes of production. This is because 'all previous historical movements were movements of minorities', like the bourgeoisie, who sought to establish themselves as a new dominant class, whereas 'the proletarian movement is the . . . movement of the immense majority, in the interests of the immense majority' which will establish a classless society—communism (Marx and Engels 1998: 49). 'In place of the old bourgeois society, with its classes and class antagonisms, we shall have an association, in which the free development of each is the condition for the free development of all' (Marx and Engels 1998: 62). In other words, the interests of all members of society are harmonized. Since there are no class antagonisms or conflicts there is no class in society with an interest in establishing a new mode of production. Marx states that communism 'brings . . . the prehistory of human society to a close' (Marx 2000: 426).

Why does the end of history also entail the end of ideology? We can see this in two senses. First, in Marx's specific critical conception of ideology, it is bound up with the existence of a ruling class and seen as a mechanism for sustaining rule by presenting a distorted view of reality and manipulating the ideas that are prevalent in society (see Chapter 1). The prehistory of human society coming to a close would therefore entail the end of ideology in this sense. Second, we can think about the two principal Enlightenment ideologies—liberalism and socialism—as reflecting the basic class conflict within capitalist society—as class struggle fought out in ideological terms. In this sense, Marx's vision of communism as a classless society entails not the end of ideology but the final ideological triumph of communism and the establishment of ideological consensus. This does not mean the end of politics and the need for collective decisions involving disagreement, but it does suggest these disagreements would not touch on the basic structure of society.

The collapse of communism and triumph of liberalism

If Marx's end of history thesis has (so far) not worked out as expected, it has been not only rejected but has been turned on its head by the claim that liberal capitalism, the society communism was supposed to replace, is in fact the final destination of the historical journey. This claim is most strongly associated with Fukuyama in the context of the collapse of communism in Europe (1989–1991), ending the 'short twentieth century' which was characterized by the global rivalry, including in the form of the 'Cold War', between capitalism and communism (Fukuyama 1989). For Fukuyama, writing in 1989 during the era of reform undertaken by Gorbachev, the demise of communism, following the earlier defeat of fascism in the Second World War, demonstrates 'the total exhaustion of viable systematic alternatives to Western liberalism' and thus represents 'the triumph of the West, of the Western idea' (Fukuyama, in Hall et al. 1992: 48).

> What we may be witnessing is not just the end of the Cold War, or the passing of a particular period of post-war history, but the end of history as such; that is, the end point of mankind's ideological evolution and the universalization of Western liberal democracy as the final form of human government.
>
> (Fukuyama, in Hall et al. 1992: 48)

Fukuyama claimed that 'a remarkable consensus has developed in the world concerning the legitimacy and viability of liberal democracy' (Fukuyama, in Hall et al. 1992: 21). He saw evidence for this consensus in the discrediting of Marxism and turn towards liberalism in the world's two largest communist countries—China and the Soviet Union. In addition, contrary to Marx's claims and expectations, Fukuyama argued that 'the class issue has actually been successfully resolved in the West . . . . The egalitarianism of modern America represents the essential achievement of the classless society envisioned by Marx' (Fukuyama, in Hall et al. 1992: 48).

Despite their opposite conclusions, there are some striking similarities between the approaches of Marx and Fukuyama. Both see history in terms of an ideological struggle reflecting an underlying 'class issue', and both conceptualize the end of history in terms of the resolution of this issue (although Fukuyama's analysis is more 'idealist' in the sense that ideas drive history, whereas Marx's approach is 'materialist', seeing ideas as reflecting the material reality of society in terms of the way economic life is organized). The opposing conclusions stem from contrasting assessments of the nature of modern capitalism—in essence this is a replay of the long-running debate between liberalism and socialism. For liberals, egalitarianism means the idea that capitalism is compatible with equality of opportunity, whereas Marxists deny this and see inequality as built into the basic structure of a capitalist economy.

What has triumphed? Over what?

In assessing these two approaches, we might ask not only whether history has ended in the ways described, but also whether the very idea of an end of history is plausible. Marx's end of history vision clearly has not been realized and we no longer live in a world, as we did in the short twentieth century, in which communism presented a rival economic and political system to liberal capitalism on a global scale. In that sense liberalism has triumphed (Gamble 2009). But what has it triumphed over? One interpretation (Fukuyama's) is that communism has been tried and failed and there is no prospect of it being revived. However, an alternative interpretation (congenial to Marxists) is that neither China nor the Soviet Union constituted genuine experiments in communism, so that what liberalism has triumphed over is a distorted version of communism (which it is convenient for liberals and conservatives to present as the real thing). In this view it can be argued that Marx's vision of the end of history has not been realized yet but is still possible, in which case Fukuyama's declaration of the liberal end of history is premature. For example, Cohen argues that the main obstacle to socialism is that we have not yet designed what he calls the 'social technology' that we need in order to effectively harness the cooperative side of human nature; that is, the way of organizing the economy (Cohen 2009). Perhaps we will never be able to design this technology but, on the other hand, one day we might.

Whether Marx's vision of the end of history is possible (and how likely or unlikely) will depend a lot on the assessment that is made of the 'class issue' in capitalism today—has it been resolved or will class conflict continue to put a question mark against capitalism's future? For Marx the class struggle was bound up with the periodic economic crises to which capitalism is prone. It is fair to say that inequality has become a more, not less, salient political issue since the late 1980s, and in the last decade the global economic crisis triggered by problems in the financial system has posed the question of whether capitalism can secure economic prosperity and security for all its citizens. But capitalism's future is not just a question of whether class conflict and economic crises will continue as systemic problems but whether they will motivate a political movement that can be successful in challenging capitalism, or whether they can be managed within capitalism. Perhaps a middle way can be found in this debate by suggesting that while Marx certainly underestimated the longevity of capitalism, Fukuyama may have overestimated it. An in-between position would see the future of capitalism as more open and contingent than either of these two perspectives allows.

An alternative reading of history to the claimed triumph of liberalism and the potential triumph of communism is the view that 'the most successful ideology and movement of the twentieth century' was social democracy, understood as a 'full-fledged alternative to both Marxism and liberalism' that succeeded in providing a formula for combining a capitalist economic system and democratic polity (Berman 2006: 17 and 8). This argument has echoes of arguments put forward by Anthony Crosland in the postwar heyday of social democracy (see Chapter 8) and the contemporary 'end of ideology' thesis of Bell (Crosland 1964; Bell 1988). However, it would be difficult to argue that social democracy is thriving in the world today. Brexit and the election of Trump as US President, both drawing support from those who have been 'left behind' in economic terms, indicate the potential for economic crisis and class inequality to motivate a right-wing, rather than left-wing, 'revolt against elites'.

In any case there are other question marks against the end of history, arising from a range of problems facing liberal democratic capitalist societies and ideological challenges to liberalism. We can consider here the persistence of 'classical' ideologies, particularly the vitality of nationalism and the rise of far-right parties and movements in Europe. Add to this the challenges presented to liberalism by all the 'new' ideologies: environmental threats, particularly global warming; the continuing struggles to achieve sexual equality; the challenges presented by cultural diversity; and the resurgence of religion in the form of fundamentalism. In addition, liberal democracy is challenged by evidence of 'anti-politics', defined as 'negative feeling' amounting to 'unhealthy cynicism' towards the key institutions and processes of representative democracy 'including politicians, parties, councils, parliaments, and governments' (Clarke et al. 2016: 9). This hardly looks like the 'consensus' on the 'legitimacy and viability of liberal democracy' claimed by Fukuyama. However, the question is, like the 'class issue', whether these challenges can be resolved or managed within the political and economic framework of liberal democracy and capitalism and the ideological framework of liberalism, or whether they require 'systematic alternatives to Western liberalism'. This is Fukuyama's test. Within environmentalism and feminism there are variants that argue for marriage with liberalism and those that present systematic alternatives. Religious fundamentalism is clearly anti-liberal, and in its Islamic form has been seen as involving a 'clash of civilizations'. It certainly shows that the consensus that Fukuyama claims is not world-wide.

Variants of liberalism

Even if liberalism has triumphed, at least for now, it is important to note that this does not provide a precise idea or prescription for the future of Western liberalism or the 'Western idea'. This is because, as we saw in Chapter 2, liberalism is a broad tradition containing ideological variants and debates. Similarly there are variants of 'liberal democracy' and competing models of 'capitalism'. So the triumph of liberalism would still leave quite a lot to argue over in terms of the organization of economic and political life within the parameters of a liberal democratic polity and capitalist economic system.

For example, Europe may be viewed as a set of liberal democracies but some are more democratic than others, and European states display considerable variation in governing arrangements, such as different voting systems and differences between federal and unitary and presidential and parliamentary systems. Nationalist forces, pressure for devolution, and struggles over the aspiration to create an 'ever closer union' within the European Union are re-shaping the territorial basis of governance in the EU. This is clear in the UK where the 'Brexit' vote in 2016 to leave the EU immediately led to the assertion that a second referendum on independence for Scotland was now 'on the table' (BBC 2016a). Brexit has aroused fears of a possible 'domino effect' in the form of increased demands for a similar referendum being made by Euro-sceptic parties in other EU states, such as the Front National in France (ITV 2016). The aspiration for Scotland to become independent within the EU has also raised fears that this prospect may encourage secessionist movements elsewhere in Europe such as in Spain (BBC 2014). Further measures of devolution to the Scottish Parliament following the 2014 independence referendum prompted the introduction of an English Votes for English Laws (EVEL) procedure in the Westminster parliament (BBC 2016b), and demands for measures of devolution to English city-regions (Merrill 2014). The shift to a fully federal system in the UK remains a possibility.

The triumph of liberalism in economic terms, as a triumph of capitalism, does not entail the triumph of neo-liberalism. Although neo-liberalism has arguably remained dominant since the 1980s, even through the global economic crisis triggered by the financial crash, there is increasing questioning of this model and it does not provide the basis for a consensus. The struggles over neo-liberalism in Europe have been framed mainly in terms of arguments for and against the imposition of austerity, involving squeezing public sector deficits and debt. More generally, a basically capitalist economy is compatible with quite differing conceptions of the relationship between the state and the market, involving different ideas in the areas of regulation of the market, industrial policy, and the welfare state. In ideological terms three distinct positions can be identified: neo-liberalism, social liberalism, and social democracy (see Chapters 2, 4, and 8).

 Stop and Think

Do either Marx or Fukuyama provide a persuasive account of the end of history?

The retreat from ideology

Here we consider three types of argument which reject ideology as over-ambitious and possibly dangerous, in favour of a more limited style of politics:

- conservative scepticism—the limits of reason;
- the third way scepticism—'what counts is what works';
- post-modernist scepticism—the rejection of 'grand narratives'.

Conservative scepticism

Is it possible to make political decisions in a non-ideological way? What is the alternative to ideology? One answer to these questions is provided by conservatism, an ideology which cautions against ideological politics (see Chapter 3). This caution stems from an assessment of the limits of human reason—in this view ideologies such as liberalism and socialism embody an excessive confidence in the capacity of humans to understand the workings of society and reconstruct it from first principles in accordance with a rational plan or blueprint. For conservatives this is a leap in the dark that is likely to end badly, and we are better advised to stick with tradition and tried and tested institutions that embody the accumulated wisdom of previous generations. Thus, in this view, the alternative to ideology is cautious step-by-step reform when it has become unavoidable. However, this is not really an alternative to ideology as much as a cautious ideology.

The third way—'what counts is what works'

Conservatism is often associated with a pragmatic, as opposed to 'ideological', approach to politics. Pragmatism can be defined as 'action or policy dictated by consideration of the immediate practical consequences rather than by theory or dogma' (*Collins Dictionary*). In recent years, the idea of pragmatism as an alternative to ideology has been associated strongly with the global third way debate in the 1990s and the shift within the UK Labour Party from the 'old left' or 'old style social democracy' to New Labour (Blair 1998; Giddens 1998, 2001). In the Labour Party manifesto for the 1997 UK general election, Blair stated that 'New Labour is a party of ideas and ideals but not of outdated ideology. What counts is what works. The objectives are radical. The means will be modern' (Labour Party 1997).

Slightly adjusted, this closely mirrors the definition of pragmatism: action or policy dictated by consideration of *what works* rather than by *outdated ideology*. Obviously nobody would say that they stand for an ideology that is outdated, so the statement seems vacuous. Blair could be interpreted as saying that Labour rejects the outdated ideology of the old left specifically, but the statement does seem to suggest a dichotomy between what works and ideology in general. Can ideology be removed from the equation in this way? Is the dichotomy defensible?

Of course, practical consequences of policy matter. By 'what works' Blair means policy that is effective in achieving its stated objectives. Achieving policy objectives or goals can be seen as a key aspect of good governance and the main point of securing government power through an election. In this sense policy can be seen as a means to an end, and Blair states that the means will be 'modern' and the objectives (or ends) 'radical'. As well as pragmatic, this approach can be seen as technocratic in that political decisions involve selecting the most effective policy on the basis of the best knowledge and evidence available. Hence New Labour also characterized its approach in terms of 'evidence-based policy making'. On the face of it, selecting the best policy is not a task that ideology is going to be much help with.

However, ideology is involved in the selection of both ends and means. The first question is: how do we decide which objectives to pursue? And, given that limited resources mean that not all objectives can be achieved at once, how do we prioritize objectives? Similarly how do we resolve conflicts between policy objectives? These questions can only be answered on the basis of ideology since they concern values and ideas about the good society. Choosing objectives is what ideological debates are essentially about. In other words, ideologies contest the political agenda. Another way of saying this is that 'social problems' which public policies aim to tackle are 'socially constructed' in the sense that, although they really exist, they have to be defined as problems that merit political action, and this definition has to attract sufficient support to get the problem on to the political agenda. This involves the play of power but also values. For example, until quite recently, female genital mutilation (FGM) was 'under the radar' in political terms in the UK, before it was successfully placed on the political agenda by groups who identified it as an important social problem in light of their values. In the USA the 'black lives matter' movement has identified the shootings of black people by police as a social problem requiring urgent political attention.

The second question is: how do we select the means to achieve the desired ends? What works, or effectiveness, is critical here but this is also an ideological issue because ideologies offer competing accounts of how the world works, the causes of social problems, and therefore the policies that will be effective. For example, if poverty is seen as due to individual failings such as laziness it will be responded to by quite different policies than if it is seen as caused by the operation of the economic system. Similarly, different policies follow from the idea that criminals are responsible for their behaviour than if they are seen as victims of social conditions. In addition, the selection of means often raises ethical considerations, so values are relevant not only to what we are trying to achieve but to how we try to achieve it. For example, if we assume that a tough approach to crime (e.g. long prison sentences, a harsh prison regime) will be effective in reducing crime, there may be ethical objections to treating people in this way. Similarly, capital punishment and torturing terrorist suspects, even if they are effective, may be objected to on ethical grounds. In these cases it might be argued that the ends do not justify the means. They involve a conflict or trade-off between the goal of reducing crime or preventing terrorism, on the one hand, and the goal of upholding human rights, on the other, and deciding how to make this trade-off is an ideological question.

Thus the principle that 'what counts is what works' cannot be used to guide policy rather than ideology. Ideology also counts: it is inescapably involved in the selection of both ends and means.

 Stop and Think

Can pragmatism take the place of ideology? Is ideology enough, or is there always a place for pragmatism?

Post-modernism

A final form of retreat from ideology to be considered briefly here is post-modernism. What post-modernism stands for can be quite hard to pin down since the term only alludes to the idea that modernism is in the past and we are now, in some sense, beyond modernism. As we have seen in Chapters 1 and 8, modernism can be defined in terms of the transition to a distinctively modern *society*, characterized, in Gamble's formulation, as a combination of capitalist economy, democratic polity, and scientific rationalism (Gamble 1981). But it can also be defined in terms of a system of *ideas* that accompanied (both reflected and promoted) the transition to modern society. This is the 'scientific rationalism' dimension of Gamble's definition, and more broadly the Enlightenment commitment to reason and progress in human affairs, particularly expressed in the ideologies of liberalism and socialism.

Post-modernism is in part an argument about a shift from a modern to a post-modern form of society. This means that the social structures based on industrial societies with their distinctive occupational orders and class systems have broken down, and with them modern class positions and identities, being replaced by more fragmented social structures and more fluid identities. The consequence is that modern ideologies—liberalism and socialism—no longer have the same relevance or purchase on social reality and cannot guide political understanding and commitment. If identities, and therefore interests, have become more fluid and transient then ideologies no longer have anything solid or fixed that they can claim to represent.

More fundamentally, post-modernism is a theory of knowledge that rejects the very ambitions of modern ideologies to provide reliable knowledge of social reality, to find truth, and to guide progress based on reason. For example, Foucault, a key theorist of post-modernism, rejects the distinction drawn between ideology and science in Marxism (Foucault 1980). The distinction is rejected on the grounds that ideology is no more false than science, and science is no more truthful than ideology. It is the idea of truth that is problematic in the distinction.

The ambitions of modernism rely on a form of scientific rationalism applied to social reality—that methods of systematic empirical observation and reasoning can produce knowledge that is objective and universally valid. We can, for example, explain how modern societies work, diagnose the causes of social ills, and devise policies that remedy them. And we can identify universal values on the basis of understanding of human nature. Such objectivity and universalism enable progress. It is these claims to objectivity and universalism that post-modernism rejects, and with them the modern idea of progress. There are no foundations, such as objective facts, on which to base these claims. If there is no way, even in principle, to distinguish between what is right or wrong, true or false, this leads to the idea that all ways of understanding the world and all value positions are equally valid. There is, then, no way to formulate a universalist notion of progress, only many different and equally valid ideas of progress.

If post-modernism is correct, it clearly has devastating implications for ideological politics. It does not mean the end of politics, but the claims and ambitions of politics must be more modest, even conservative. However, there are three criticisms of post-modernism in defence of ideology.

- First, how do we know if post-modernism is indeed correct? In denying that any ideas have solid foundations it cuts the ground from under its own feet— why should we believe it is a plausible theory?

- Second, in rejecting foundationalism, post-modernism embraces relativism or even subjectivism, according to which all ideas of right and wrong are either only valid within particular cultural contexts or are merely subjective opinions. The argument against this is not to say that there are no values that are relative to cultural contexts, only that there are some which are universal. The issue to decide is which values fall into the universal category and which can differ between cultures. That there are some values which should be upheld universally to avoid serious harms to people seems hard to deny. Consider this: 'It is wrong to torture innocent children for pleasure'. Swift provides this as an example of a moral judgement that is true (Swift 2004: 142). Can it plausibly be claimed that this judgement, and the related idea that all children have a right to be protected against such treatment, is merely a cultural standard or subjective opinion?

- Third, it can be argued that post-modernism is undermined by evidence that can be adduced of real progress in human affairs, for example in the area of establishing and upholding the rights of children.

Summary

- All ideologies involve underlying, distinct but overlapping, conceptions of human nature.

- Ideologies offer contrasting responses to the process of globalization, understood as social, cultural, economic, and political integration across borders.

- It can be argued that we are all ideologists and society can never dispense with ideology since there will always be reflection, and disagreement, and therefore political struggle in relation to what constitutes the good society.

- However, there are three ways in which the end of ideology, or a non-ideological or post-ideological form of politics, might be understood: as the failure of a particular ideology; as the 'end of history' with the final realization of the good society and the defeat of all other rival ideologies; and as the rejection of or retreat from ideology in favour of a more limited style of politics.

Review and discussion questions

1. Is ideology a ubiquitous and essential aspect of politics, or can there be a non-ideological way of doing politics?

2. Critically assess the 'end of history' arguments put forward by Marx and Fukuyama.

3. To what extent can ideological competition be understood as involving a 'market place of ideas'?

4. What are the main strengths and weaknesses of the different ideological responses to globalization? In what ways do these responses converge or diverge?

Research exercises

1. Carry out an investigation into claims that we have entered an era of 'post-truth politics', with reference to either Donald Trump's campaign in the US 2016 presidential election or the Brexit campaign in the 2016 UK referendum on membership of the EU.

2. In relation to one of the following policy areas investigate the extent to which decisions are or should be guided by the principle 'what counts is what works', as opposed to ideology:

   - poverty
   - terrorism
   - gun crime/gun control

Further reading

Schumaker (2008) discusses conceptions of human nature in Chapter 6. For a full discussion of ideology in a global age see Soborski (2013). For the end of history debate on the failure of socialism and triumph of liberalism, read the original essay by Fukuyama (1989) and the discussion in Held (1992). See also Chapter 1 in Giddens (1998) and Gamble's (2009) discussion of 'The Western Ideology'. For short arguments for and against pragmatism see Harford (2011) and Worsnip (2012). Thompson (1992) provides a critical discussion of post-modernism.

References

BBC (2014), 'Scottish Independence: World Media Suggests "Domino Effect" ', http://www.bbc.co.uk/news/uk-scotland-29178438

BBC (2016a), 'Brexit: Nicola Sturgeon Says Second Scottish Independence Vote "Highly Likely" ', http://www.bbc.co.uk/news/uk-scotland-scotland-politics-36621030

BBC (2016b), ' "English Votes" Rules Used for First Time in House of Commons', http://www.bbc.co.uk/news/uk-politics-35295404

BELL, D. (1988), *The End of Ideology*, Cambridge, MA: Harvard University Press.

BERMAN, S. (2006), *The Primacy of Politics: Social Democracy and the Making of Europe's Twentieth Century*, Cambridge: Cambridge University Press.

BLAIR, T. (1998), *The Third Way: New Politics for the New Century*, London: Fabian Society.

CHANG, H.-J. (2014), 'Economics is Too Important to Leave to the Experts', *The Guardian*, 30 April, https://www.theguardian.com/commentisfree/2014/apr/30/economics-experts-economists

CHRISAFIS, A. (2016), 'Nicolas Sarkozy Declares Candidacy for French Presidential Election', *The Guardian*, 22 August, https://www.theguardian.com/world/2016/aug/22/nicolas-sarkozy-declares-candidacy-french-presidential-election

CLARKE, N., JENNINGS, W., MOSS, J., AND STOKER, G. (2016), 'Anti-Politics and the Left', *Renewal*, Vol. 24, No. 2, pp. 9–18.

COHEN, G. A. (2009), *Why Not Socialism?*, Princeton, NJ: Princeton University Press.

COLLINS DICTIONARY OF THE ENGLISH LANGUAGE (1986), London: Collins.

CROSLAND, A. (1964), *The Future of Socialism*, London: Cape.

DEACON, M. (2016), 'EU Referendum: Who Needs Experts when we've got Michael Gove?', *The Telegraph*, 6 June, http://www.telegraph.co.uk/news/2016/06/06/eu-referendum-who-needs-experts-when-weve-got-michael-gove/

DRYZEK, J. S. AND DUNLEAVY, P. (2009), *Theories of the Democratic State*, Basingstoke: Palgrave Macmillan.

FOUCAULT, M. (1980), 'Truth and Power', in C. Gordon (ed.), *Michel Foucault: Power/Knowledge. Selected Interviews and Other Writings 1972–77*, Brighton: Harvester Press.

FUKUYAMA, F. (1989), 'The End of History?', *The National Interest*, No. 16.

GAMBLE, A. (1981), *An Introduction to Modern Social and Political Thought*, London: Macmillan.

GAMBLE, A. (2009), 'The Western Ideology', *Government and Opposition*, Vol. 44, No. 1.

GIDDENS, A. (1998), *The Third Way: The Renewal of Social Democracy*, Cambridge: Polity.

GIDDENS, A. (2001), *The Global Third Way Debate*, Cambridge: Polity.

HALL, S., HELD, D., AND MCGREW, T. (eds) (1992), *Modernity and its Futures*, Cambridge: Polity Press.

HARFORD, T. (2011), 'In Praise of Pragmatism', *The Independent*, 6 June.

HELD, D. (1992), 'Liberalism, Marxism and Democracy', in S. Hall, D. Held, and T. McGrew (eds), *Modernity and its Futures*, Cambridge: Polity Press.

ITV (2016), 'UK Votes to Leave the EU in Historic Referendum', http://www.itv.com/news/update/2016-06-24/real-fear-in-brussels-of-domino-effect-if-leave-wins/

LABOUR PARTY (1997), *New Labour Because Britain Deserves Better, General Election Manifesto*, http://www.politicsresources.net/area/uk/man/lab97.htm

LEWIS, H. (2016), 'How the Brexit Campaign Lied to Us—and Got Away with it', *New Statesman*, 30 June, http://www.newstatesman.com/politics/uk/2016/06/how-brexit-campaign-lied-us-and-got-away-it

MARX, K. (2000 [1857]), 'Preface to *A Critique of Political Economy*', in D. McLellan, *Karl Marx: Selected Writings*, Oxford: Oxford University Press.

MARX, K. AND ENGELS, F. (1998 [1848]), *The Communist Manifesto: A Modern Edition*, London: Verso.

MERRILL, J. (2014), 'UK's Biggest Cities Demand Devolution "at Same Speed as Scotland"', *The Independent*, 24 September, http://www.independent.co.uk/news/uk/politics/uk-s-biggest-cities-demand-devolution-at-same-speed-as-scotland-9753752.html

PEW RESEARCH CENTER (2015a), *The Future of World Religions: Population Growth Projections, 2010–2050*, http://www.pewforum.org/2015/04/02/religious-projections-2010-2050/

PEW RESEARCH CENTER (2015b), *Americans, Politics and Science Issues, Chapter 2: Climate Change and Energy Issues*, http://www.pewinternet.org/2015/07/01/chapter-2-climate-change-and-energy-issues/

PEW RESEARCH CENTER (2016), 'On Darwin Day, 5 Facts about the Evolution Debate', http://www.pewresearch.org/fact-tank/2016/02/12/darwin-day/

POOLE, S. (2016), 'Why Bad Ideas Refuse to Die', *The Guardian*, 28 June, https://www.the-guardian.com/science/2016/jun/28/why-bad-ideas-refuse-die?utm_source=esp&utm_medium=Email&utm_campaign=Long+reads+base&utm_term=180064&subid=19145047&CMP=ema-1133

QUIGGIN, J. (2010), *Zombie Economics: How Dead Ideas Still Walk Among Us*, Princeton, NJ: Princeton University Press.

SANDEL, M. (2009), *Justice: What's the Right Thing To Do?*, Harmondsworth: Allen Lane.

SCHUMAKER, P. (2008) *From Ideologies to Public Philosophies*, Oxford: Blackwell.

SKIDELSKY, R. (2008), 'The Moral Dimension of Boom and Bust', *The Guardian*, 23 November, https://www.theguardian.com/commentisfree/2008/nov/23/economics-economy

SOBORSKI, R. (2013), *Ideology in a Global Age: Continuity and Change*, Basingstoke: Palgrave Macmillan.

SWIFT, A. (2004), 'Political Philosophy and Politics', in Leftwich, A. (ed.), *What is Politics?* Cambridge: Polity.

THOMPSON, K. (1992), 'Social Pluralism and Post-Modernity', in S. Hall, D. Held, and T. McGrew (eds), *Modernity and its Futures*, Cambridge: Polity Press.

WORSNIP, A. (2012), 'Against Pragmatism', *Prospect*, 29 December.

Glossary

ANARCHA-FEMINISM (also referred to as anarcho-feminism and anarchist feminism) is an approach which brings together key critical themes from anarchist thinking and feminism—the critique of coercive authority and patriarchy. State authority—the key critical focus of anarchist thinking—is embedded in patriarchal relations; the refusal of state authority must therefore simultaneously be a refusal of the exploitation and oppression of women. Thinkers associated with this approach include Emma Goldman and Mary Wollstonecraft.

ANARCHO-CAPITALISM an extreme form of individualist anarchism that is aligned directly with the support of capitalism. Where many anarchists regard capitalism as a barrier to freedom, anarcho-capitalists consider marketised property relations as a necessary condition for freedom. A key anarcho-capitalist thinker was Murray Rothbard (1926–1995).

ANARCHO-COMMUNISM like all anar-chists, anarcho-communists support the abolition of the state. However, anarcho-communists pay particular attention to the interconnection between the state form and private property relations. As with Marxists, anarcho-communists are concerned to abolish private property in the means of production, and bring about a society based not on production for profit, but rather on meeting human social needs. However, in contrast to Marxists, anarcho-communists argue that gaining state power is incompatible with achieving this goal. A key anarcho-communist was Peter Kropotkin (1842–1921).

ANARCHO-SYNDICALISM a form of anarchism which views **revolutionary** trade unionism as a mechanism through which workers could assume control of the economy in order to achieve wider anarchist social aims. Key anarcho-syndicalist tactics include direct action and workers' self-management. Anarcho-syndicalists believe that in adopting such strategies, workers should not cooperate with state bureaucracies; as with most anarchists, they are therefore anti-statist. The Confederación Nacional del Trabajo (CNT) in Spain was influenced by anarcho-syndicalist principles.

ANTI-IDEOLOGY an ideology defined more by its visceral opposition to established doctrines than by its positive vision for what it stands for and what society it aspires to.

ANTI-POLITICS refers to disengagement from and hostility towards mainstream politics, associated with **populism** and the feeling of being betrayed or abandoned by political elites.

ASSIMILATION the process through which immigrants adopt the culture of the society they are joining, losing their cultural distinctiveness. In contrast with **integration**, assimilation is normally seen as a one-way process in which the onus is on immigrants to 'fit in'.

ATHEISM belief that there is no God.

AUTHORITARIAN (AUTHORITARIANISM) a system of strong government in which obedience to authority is prioritized over personal freedom. Often counter-posed to democratic government and characterized as oppressive.

AUTHORITY legitimate **power**, power that is rightfully exercised.

AUTONOMISM is an anti-**authoritarian** form of politics which emerged from the anti-statist and 'workerist' left-wing movements of 1970s Italy. Autonomists challenge the Marxist–Leninist approach to **revolutionary** politics, an approach which argued first that the vanguard party was the organization best fitted to bring consciousness to the masses, and second, that a key historical goal of this party was to establish the 'dictatorship of the proletariat'. In place of centralization, autonomists emphasize democracy and working class self-organization. The criticisms of Marxism–Leninism made by autonomists have significant resonance with anarchist thinking. Key autonomist thinkers are Mario Tronti, Paolo Virno, and Antonio Negri.

BAU ('business as usual') refers to the belief that while environmental concerns are in evidence they can essentially be dealt with without fundamentally altering current consumption and production processes and that we can still have 'business as usual'.

BOLSHEVIKS co-founded by Lenin in 1898, the Bolsheviks (meaning 'majority') were a faction of the Russian Social Democratic Labour Party who came to power in Russia after the October revolution of 1917. The Bolshevik Party became the Russian Communist Party in 1918.

BOURGEOISIE in Marxist terms, one of the two classes (along with the proletariat or working class) specific to capitalist society. The term bourgeoisie (or capitalist class) generally refers to those that 'rule' in capitalist society and are specifically in conflict with the working class.

CAPITALISM an economic system based upon private property rights, free trade, and profit accumulation.

CHARISMATIC LEADERSHIP a form of authority resting on the recognition of the leader's extraordinary qualities that may generate faith and devotion among a large group of adherents willing to follow the leader.

CIS someone who has a gender identity that is the same as the sex they were assigned at birth.

CIVILIZATION can refer to an entity, as in the idea that the world is made up of a number of more-or-less distinct civilizations, or a process of becoming civilized. Pinker uses the term in the second sense when he refers to the 'emergence of civilization some five thousand years ago' (2011: 42) as a crucial aspect of the historical decline of violence. Pinker refers particularly to the development of government or the **state** capable of monopolizing the use of force as the key attribute of civilization. In the first sense, civilization refers roughly to a distinctive culture or way of life, such as in the idea of 'European' or 'Western' civilization. This involves a contrast with other civilizations, such as 'Chinese', 'Asian', or 'Muslim'. But the concept is problematic as it may tend to overstate both the homogeneity of cultures and their distinctiveness from each other, whereas they are internally diverse and overlapping. For example, if we define 'Western' civilization in terms of liberalism or Christianity, it is apparent that these features, though historically important, are contested.

CIVIL RIGHTS an aspect of citizenship referring to civil liberties including free speech. The civil rights movement demanded an end to racial **segregation** and the guarantee of equal rights.

COLLECTIVISM in contrast with **individualism**, refers to action undertaken by a group or collective, based on an idea of shared interests or responsibility on the part of the group to protect the interests of members. It can involve the idea that collective interests take precedence over individual interests. In social democracy and social liberalism, collectivism is expressed in commitment to the **welfare state**. However **collectivist anarchism** involves an anti-statist form.

COLLECTIVIST ANARCHISM is associated with the work of Mikhail Bakunin (1814–1876). As with **anarcho-communists**, collectivist anarchists advocate the abolition of both the state and the private ownership of the means of production. The means of production should be controlled by producers themselves. Collectivist anarchists maintain that such a goal cannot be achieved by gaining state **power**. There is perhaps little difference between anarcho-communism and collectivist anarchism, other than the fact that Bakunin refused the label 'communist' in part because of his opposition to Marx.

COMINTERN abbreviation of (third) Communist International, was an international organization of communist parties and movements, founded in the wake of the **Russian Revolution**, and united in their common pursuit of a world socialist revolution.

COMMUNITARIAN(ISM) (COMMUNITY) the position that major importance should be placed on the role of community in the political life and in the identity of that community's members, in contrast with the individualism of liberalism.

COMPETITION STATE in contrast with the **welfare state**, a form of state that prioritizes competitiveness and the imperative of providing favourable conditions for businesses to operate and compete.

CONFUCIAN a Chinese cultural system in which the needs of the individual are balanced with (and sometimes subordinated to) the wider needs of society at large.

CONTESTED CONCEPT according to Freeden, ideologies are made up of, or 'assembled' from, political concepts such as equality, freedom, and so on. In other words, *concepts* are the basic building blocks of ideologies. A concept can be defined simply as a word or term that refers to some aspect of the real world and helps us to understand its nature. For example 'freedom' gives us a word to describe and understand an aspect of the condition that people are in—that they are (or are not) free. These concepts are *contested* in the sense that there is deep controversy about their meanings: people have different ideas about what it means to be truly free. These disagreements are the stuff of ideological disputes. They might never be resolved once and for all.

CORPORATISM a model of economic and political organization of state and social institutions made up of large interest-based groupings. Although its origins may be located in Christian Catholic thought, it became an integral part of the critique of liberalism in the twentieth century.

COSMOPOLITANISM an attitude of willingness to embrace humanity as a single international group, casting aside artificial divisions but also respectful of differences between different groups.

CRISIS a juncture in time when a current system (structure, institution, way of life) can no longer continue without either fundamental transformation or its replacement by a new system. This means that a crisis can be in a system and of a system, the latter far more serious and destabilising than the former. Crisis has been presented as an objective category (e.g. economic indices highlighting the extent of the impact of the 1929 financial crash); but it can also be understood as a subjective perception, whereby people can exaggerate what they perceive as crisis in the face of factual information or expert view.

CULTURAL DIFFERENTIALISM the idea that different cultures are bound by their specific geographic and historic locations. Similar meaning to 'ethnopluralism' (see Chapter 7).

DEPOLITICIZATION the removal of certain issues, e.g. religion, from political decision-making.

DIGGERS a **radical** religious group during the English Civil War. Seen as a precursor to both anarchism and socialism, the Diggers saw themselves as the 'true **Levellers**' and advocated egalitarianism through economic equality and the common ownership of land.

DIVISION OF LABOUR the breaking down of the labour process into ever more specific tasks in the name of efficiency. The worker performs menial, boring tasks, becoming increasingly less skilled and less developed. Marx argues this process is specific to capitalism while, within a communist society, labour would be much more creative and fulfilling.

DOGMA can have a specifically religious meaning as beliefs that are authoritatively held to be true, but in ideological debates it is usually used in a pejorative sense to refer to beliefs that are not reasoned or open to scrutiny or debate. To be described as being dogmatic is not generally thought to be complimentary.

ECOLOGICAL ANARCHISM like all anarchists, ecological anarchists support the abolition of the state. Ecological anarchists on the whole are concerned to challenge exploitation and domination in all its forms. However, ecological anarchists extend anarchist thinking to provide a critique of the way in which human beings have come to dominate and exploit the natural environment. Thus, ecological anarchist politics combines a focus on human liberation with that of ecological liberation. A key ecological anarchist is Murray Bookchin (1921–2006).

EGALITARIAN in general, advocacy of equality, though specifically it can involve different answers to the question 'equality of what?'

ENLIGHTENMENT bound up with the idea of 'modernization', the Enlightenment refers to an intellectual movement that highlighted the role of reason and science in understanding the natural and social worlds and hence the potential for progress in human affairs.

ESSENTIALIST an approach that claims to identify the essence or essential characteristics of a thing, e.g. a system of beliefs or a group. The danger is that it can involve negative stereotyping.

ETHNICITY a contested term, sometimes used synonymously with 'race'. For example, the UK census question on ethnicity distinguishes between 'white' and 'non-white' groups. Can also be used to refer to cultural characteristics shared by members of a group, such as language, religion, and/or customs.

EXTREMIST extremist views are those that are held to be beyond what is considered reasonable or acceptable, such as in relation to the left–right spectrum—extreme left or extreme right. But views that are characterized as extreme are not normally seen this way by those who hold them, and 'extremism' can be used as a term of abuse. The UK government has controversially defined extremism as views that run counter to 'British values'.

FEUDALISM a structured social system organized around the holding of land, in which peasants would be tied to the land and required to work for wealthy landowners, rather than workers who enjoy freedom in a labour market.

FIRST INTERNATIONAL see **International Workingmen's Association.**

FUNDAMENTALISM associated with religious belief, but any ideology can give rise to fundamentalism as strict adherence to the fundamental (basic or essential) beliefs of the ideology. Because of the strict adherence to these beliefs, fundamentalism is often seen as a defective style of politics as it seems to involve a refusal of dialogue or debate (see also **dogma**).

GENERAL WILL an idea within democratic thinking that a particular decision can express the wishes of the people as a whole.

GLOBALIZATION process of increased interconnectedness and interdependence through which nations and communities are brought closer together, for instance in terms of culture, economics, and/or politics.

HEGEMONIC MASCULINITY practices, ideas, and structures that promote and maintain the dominant social position of men and the subordination of women. A form of social organization in which men hold, produce, and reproduce their **power** and dominance.

HEGEMONY particularly associated with the Marxist theorist Antonio Gramsci, refers to the capacity of the capitalist class to sustain its domination of society by securing the consent of the working class through the exercise of ideological **power**.

HETERONORMATIVE a world view that promotes heterosexuality as the norm.

HIERARCHY a system which embodies an unequal structure of status, **power**, and/or wealth—an arrangement of levels from top to bottom.

HISTORICAL MATERIALISM a theory of history developed from the ideas of Karl Marx. At the core of historical materialism is the belief that it is how human beings produce and reproduce their existence that shapes how a society is organized and how it develops. Understanding the mode of production (e.g. capitalism) is crucial to understanding how the rest of society is organized.

HUMANISM broadly, the prioritization of human interests, values, and flourishing. More specifically, humanism contests religious understandings of the world. For example, morality is based on the human capacity for reason and does not depend on the word of God or the teachings of religion.

HUMAN NATURE all ideologies contain ideas of human nature, which refer to characteristics of humans—capacities and needs—that are rooted in nature (as opposed to nurture) and therefore fixed (as opposed to being open to change). Conceptions of human nature differ in relation to the balance between nature and nurture; whether all humans share the same nature; and tendencies to 'good' and 'evil'.

HUMANITARIAN INTERVENTION the justification of military intervention in order to achieve humanitarian objectives such as preventing crimes against humanity.

IDEOLOGIST (OR IDEOLOGUE) these terms are used by Krugman and Freeden to refer to anybody who has ideological views, and they argue that we are all ideologues or ideologists in this sense even though some people might not describe themselves in this way. The term 'ideologue' is sometimes used in a pejorative sense or to convey opprobrium, just as 'ideology' can be used negatively, e.g. to refer to extremist or dogmatic views.

IDEOLOGUE see **ideologist**.

IMAGINED COMMUNITY referring to the nation as **socially constructed**, as imagined by its citizenry.

INDIGENOUS refers to peoples or ethnic groups who identify as the original inhabitants (or first peoples) of a particular territory or region. Some forms of multiculturalism focus on the rights of indigenous people.

INDIVIDUALISM associated with liberalism and some forms of anarchism, individualism involves a number of ideas in contrast with **collectivism**: that society should be seen as a collection of individuals whose choices and actions explain social outcomes; that the interests of individuals are what matter in moral terms, and take precedence over ideas about collective interests; that individuals are the best judges of their own welfare; and that individuals should be self-reliant.

INDIVIDUALIST / EGOIST ANARCHISM individualist anarchism is in part influenced by the egoist anarchism of Max Stirner, who regarded all collective concepts—including the state—as 'spooks'. A key individualist anarchist was the American thinker Benjamin R. Tucker (1854–1939), who argued that 'if the individual has the right to govern himself, all external government is tyranny' (Tucker 1888). For Tucker, a key individual right was the right of property ownership, a right with which states ought not to interfere. Tucker's work had a significant influence on **anarcho-capitalism**.

INTEGRATION involves immigrants participating in and becoming part of the society they join but without losing their cultural distinctiveness. In contrast with **assimilation**, integration is normally seen as a two-way process in which the host society has to adjust to the immigrants.

INTER-GENERATIONAL EQUITY OR JUSTICE the concept of fair dealing and fair treatment between those of different generations. In the context of the environment, refers to the possibility that resource use in the present generation might undermine the potential of future generations to enjoy the same levels of prosperity currently enjoyed. Considerations of equity or justice should take account of the interests and needs of future generations.

INTERNATIONAL WORKINGMEN'S ASSOCIATION (ALSO KNOWN AS THE FIRST INTERNATIONAL) an international organization of socialists and anarchists, in existence from 1864 to 1876, which

aimed to unite working class struggles. The organization brought together a variety of leftist strands of thought and included key figures such as Karl Marx, Mikhail Bakunin, and Pierre-Joseph Proudhon. The conflict between socialists and anarchists eventually lead to its dissolution.

INTERNATIONALIST an outlook that, in contrast with some forms of nationalism, emphasizes affinities and ties of solidarity and cooperation between people of different nations.

INTERSECTIONALITY the multiple and overlapping identities (such as race, sexuality, and class) and associated arenas of oppression and subordination that women, and those identifying as women, experience.

INTRA-GENERATIONAL EQUITY OR JUSTICE in the context of the environment, refers to the possibility that at the present time different groups have vastly differential access to resources and that the prosperity of the resource rich may be undermined and be at the expense of the resource poor.

ISLAMOPHOBIA ostensibly 'fear of Islam' but in practice a form of racism directed at Muslims.

JINGOISM a **populist** form of patriotism in which citizens are expected to give unthinking loyalty, often in times of war.

KEYNES/BEVERIDGE WELFARE CONSENSUS Keynes and Beveridge were key liberal architects of the postwar **welfare state** in the UK, combining commitment to the maintenance of full employment through government economic policy and entitlement to a comprehensive range of social provision.

KHMER ROUGE the ruling Communist Party of Cambodia 1975–1979 which came to power in the aftermath of the

Vietnam War. One of the most extreme regimes ever to exist, the Khmer Rouge aimed to develop a completely agricultural and classless society that rejected industrialism and technology. This involved evacuating the cities and attempting to turn the entire population into peasants, killing anyone who stood in their way. Estimates vary, but between one-quarter and one-third of the population of Cambodia died as a result.

LAISSEZ-FAIRE (French: 'allow to do') a policy in which a government will aim to avoid interference in the economic affairs of individuals and society—allowing markets to operate freely.

LEVELLERS a political movement during the English Civil War. Less **radical** than their **Digger** contemporaries, the Levellers are nevertheless regarded by some as an early form of socialism, espousing ideas of democracy and equality which were quite radical for the period.

MARKET FAILURE refers to inherent limitations of markets due to which they cannot be relied upon to deliver socially desirable outcomes if left to their own devices (**laissez-faire**), and this therefore justifies some forms of state intervention. There can be disagreement about the form and extent of market failures, based on different views of the operation of markets and different conceptions of socially desirable outcomes. This means that 'market failure' is a political rather than a purely technical term.

MARXISM–LENINISM based loosely around the ideas of Marx and Lenin, Marxism–Leninism is closely associated with Stalinism from the 1920s onwards. Contemporary states who still adhere to Marxism–Leninism—at least in name—include China, Laos, and Vietnam. It is historically associated with a strong, one-party state and the controversial notion of

socialism in one country and is often seen as highly oppressive.

MERCANTILISM a system of political economy in which a country tries to advance its own wealth by restraining imports and encouraging exports.

MERITOCRATIC the idea that positions or goods should be distributed to the candidate viewed as being most worthy, associated with a liberal conception of equality of opportunity.

MODERNITY (MODERNIZATION) can be used to refer to a commitment to reason and scientific understanding associated with the Enlightenment, and to the emergence of distinctly modern societies characterized by industrialization, capitalism, and democracy.

MOMENTUM a left-wing UK political organization that was founded in 2015 shortly after the election of Jeremy Corbyn to the position of leader of the Labour Party. Although not part of the Labour Party, it requires its members to support the aims, values, and ideological vision of the Labour Party.

MONETARISM an economic school of thought that aims to stabilize the economy via control of the supply of money.

MONKEY WRENCHING refers to the need for environmental activists to stir public attention to environmental issues by organizing forms of direct action.

MUTUAL AID a theory of social cooperation developed by Peter Kropotkin to challenge the key assumptions of socio-biology, particularly as embodied in the theory of the 'survival of the fittest'. Kropotkin argued that human beings had proved adaptable to their natural environment not because of the way in which they pursue egoistic self-interest, but because of their cooperative capacities. Individual egoism undermines the possibility of survival. Social cooperation for the purpose of survival, Kropotkin terms 'mutual aid'.

MUTUALIST ANARCHISM maintains that a just society is one in which each individual or group of individuals possess their means of production and therefore can trade the products of their labour freely in the market place. Marx was critical of the way in which mutualism failed to challenge the idea of individual property rights. However, Marx shared a view with mutualists that the value of an object—and therefore that with which it can be equally exchanged in the market place—was determined by the amount of human labour embodied in it. A key mutualist anarchist thinker was Pierre-Joseph Proudhon (1809–1865).

NATIVISM a perspective favouring an **indigenous** group over individuals and groups that are not. It is a form of nationalism and ethnocentrism that leads to belief in human inequality, as well as discrimination against, or even persecution of, non-native groups.

NEO-FASCISM a set of organizations, movements, and parties that appeared after 1945 and sought to revive and adapt the core ideological principles of interwar fascism (which they still held to be sound) for a new, very different era.

NEUTRALITY (OF THE STATE) especially in the context of religious belief, the state is neutral between religions and between religion and non-religion. More generally, the state may be neutral between beliefs and lifestyles that its citizens may choose (as long as they do not harm others).

NEW DEAL in some ways the US equivalent of the postwar UK **welfare state**, the policies introduced by Roosevelt in the 1930s in the context of the Great Depression, including welfare provision and investment in infrastructure projects.

NEW RIGHT particularly associated with President Reagan (US) and Prime Minister

Thatcher (UK) in the 1980s, this approach can be defined as an attempt to blend neo-liberal free market principles with conservatism, or as a combination of neo-liberalism and neo-conservatism. The combination creates inherent tensions and, in practice, the neo-liberal element has been dominant.

OCCUPY first coming to prominence in 2011, Occupy is an international political movement that campaigns against inequality and champions new forms of democracy. It campaigns against financial corruption and a global system that works for the few at the expense of the many. Its targets are often multinational corporations and the global financial system more generally.

ORGANIC in social and political thought, an analogy between society and a living organism, normally used not only to justify a clearly-defined structure of authority but also to emphasize that individuals are interdependent rather than autonomous.

PALINGENETIC referring to the rebirth or regeneration of something primordial. It is often linked to the metaphor of the phoenix rising from its ashes.

PARLIAMENTARY SOVEREIGNTY the idea that the **power** to define and amend laws should rest with a parliament, rather than with a single individual or government; parliament as the highest source of authority.

PARTICULARIST (PARTICULARISM) in contrast with **universalism**, emphasizes particularity and difference, e.g. the focus on the distinct cultural needs of different groups in multiculturalist thought (see also **relativism**).

PARTY MANAGEMENT political parties in liberal democracies have the primary goal of winning government **power** through electoral victory. However, as parties are typically broad churches with rival factions their unity is not automatic but has to be managed successfully.

PATERNALISM an approach to politics in which those in authority act in what they believe to be the best interests of the governed, without allowing the latter any effective means of expressing their views.

PATRIARCHY the term traditionally refers to the rule of the father and male leadership of the family, however within feminism it means more generally the all-pervasive dominance of male rule and/or superiority in the home, the community and society as a whole.

PATRIOTISM feelings of loyalty and belonging to the nation.

PERMISSIVENESS associated with freedom, permitting behaviours that were previously seen as taboo or unacceptable, the loosening of moral constraints or the re-framing of issues from 'morality' to 'personal choice', e.g. sexuality or sexual preferences.

POPULIST (POPULISM) can refer to an individual, or a policy platform, whose main consideration is the accumulation of public support, or an anti-status quo discourse that is based on hostility to elites and an over simplified division of people into 'us' and 'them'.

POST-DEVELOPMENT this school of thinking about the problems and policy solutions facing the developing world arose as a direct rejection of 'Western' dominated development models.

POST-FEMINISM the idea that society has moved beyond concern for gender equality to a new phase beyond feminism.

POWER can refer to 'power to' or 'power over'—the capacity to achieve desired outcomes or power over the behaviour of other actors, to be able to get them to do what they would otherwise not have done. The idea of 'ideological power' is power in the second sense, exercised by influencing people's beliefs. Ideology is also related to power in the first sense, particularly controlling state power.

PRAGMATIC (PRAGMATISM) concerns the relationship between theory and action, and the idea that ideological commitments may need to be tempered by practical constraints or what can realistically be achieved in current circumstances.

PREFERENCE ACCOMMODATING refers to the attempt by political parties to win **power** by adapting to or accommodating the preferences of voters, as distinct from **preference shaping**.

PREFERENCE SHAPING refers to the attempt by political parties to win **power** by shaping or influencing the preferences of voters to bring them into line with the ideology and goals of the party, as distinct from **preference accommodating**.

PRE-FIGURATION anarchists tend to be characterized as adopting 'pre-figurative' politics. Such politics, in the words of Carl Boggs, should embody 'within the ongoing political practice of a movement . . . those forms of social relations, decision making, culture, and human experience that are the ultimate goal' (see Boggs 1977). Pre-figurative politics is at its core social; it is concerned with generating the form of collective arrangement beyond the state through which a better society can be possible.

PRESCRIPTION the notion that a practice, institution, etc. enjoys authority because it has lasted a long time.

RACE TO THE BOTTOM the process of states reducing social protections and removing tax and regulatory 'burdens' on corporations in order to attract inward investment and remain competitive in the global economy.

RACE-BLIND a commitment to not take account of (be blind to) racial differences in order to treat people equally (i.e. equal opportunity or non-discrimination). The point is that race is not a relevant characteristic in, for example, choosing between candidates for employment.

RACISM involves the idea that humanity is comprised of distinct races and therefore regards people from racial groups different to one's own as 'other'. This may involve ideas of racial hierarchy, prejudice, and hostility, and opposition to racial mixing and integration. Races may be defined in biological terms but racism can take a cultural form, e.g. **Islamophobia.**

RADICAL (RADICALISM) an approach that seeks to deal with the root or fundamental causes of problems rather than the symptoms or appearances. Can be used as an umbrella term for a diverse series of ideologies (ranging from communism to feminism to the **populist** right). See also **revolution**.

REACTIONARY someone who is antagonistic to the process of change, to the extent of either hoping for or trying to promote a return to previous conditions.

REALISTS in contrast with 'ideological purists' who are not willing to compromise their principles, willing to compromise in order to make gains in the real world.

RECOGNITION beyond mere **tolerance**, requires that minority cultures are afforded public recognition, e.g. in school curricula.

REFORMIST (REFORMISM) commitment to improvement through a (usually gradual) process of reform designed to remedy identifiable problems. Associated particularly with social liberalism and social democracy, and contrasted with **reactionary** thought and **revolution**.

REFUSAL the political idea of refusal was initially used by anarchists and some Marxists specifically to refer to the tactic of the 'refusal of work'—that is the adoption of practices which in refusing to adapt to the capitalist wage system, deny the legitimacy of that system. Refusal in the broader sense refers to the adoption of practices which refuse the adoption of forms of exploitative behaviour, and as such deny the legitimacy of those practices. The tactic of refusal is not entirely negative, to the extent that it may also point to forms of non-exploitative practice.

REGULATORY CAPTURE occurs when regulatory bodies established by the state to ensure that economic agents comply with government regulations become too close to the bodies that they are supposed to be supervising so that they are effectively 'captured' by them.

RELATIVISM a view of the status of ideas and knowledge which rejects the idea that universal or objective 'truth' is attainable (see **universalism**). For example, values or moral judgements are related to particular historical and cultural contexts and cannot be generalized to other contexts. Clearly some ideas of what behaviour is acceptable or unacceptable are culture-specific, but the question is whether any values are universal and how to draw the line (e.g. universal human rights) (see also **particularist**).

REPUBLICAN referring to a system of government in which the citizenry rule themselves, often contrasted with monarchical regimes.

REVOLUTION (REVOLUTIONARY) in contrast with **reformist** views, advocates the need for wholesale transformation of society, which might involve the use of force (but can be non-violent). Particularly associated with anarchism and communism.

RUSSIAN REVOLUTION the February and October revolutions (1917) in Russia led to the abdication and eventual execution of Tsar Nicholas and the overthrow of the Tsarist regime. The (communist) **Bolsheviks**, led by Lenin, ended Russia's involvement in the First World War and established what would become the Soviet Union in 1922 after defeating their socialist rivals and various counter-revolutionaries.

SCEPTICAL difficult to convince; unwilling to make judgements until a range of views has been explored; in extreme cases, opposed to the view that certain knowledge-claims can be valid. Not to be confused with 'Euro-sceptics', who by sharp contrast are very willing to be convinced by any evidence suggestive of imperfections in the institutions and policies of the European Union.

SCIENTIFIC SOCIALISM associated with Marx and Engels and often in opposition to **utopian socialism**. Scientific socialism claimed to be based on a scientific analysis of society and history that could predict and understand social and economic phenomena.

SECOND INTERNATIONAL an international organization of socialists, in existence from 1889 to 1916. Supporting workers' struggles as the First International had done (see **International Workingmen's Association**, the movement generally excluded anarchists. The Second International fell apart during the First World War when socialists reverted to nationalism and supported their national governments over international workers' struggles. A notable member who vehemently opposed such nationalism was Vladimir Lenin.

SECTARIAN adherence to the doctrines of a particular (religious) sect or group, refusal to engage in dialogue with other sects, lack of tolerance towards other sects.

SECULAR (STATE) non-religious or separate from the church; in a secular state, state institutions are formally separate from the church.

SECULARISM (SECULARIZATION) an empirical tendency for the role of religion in society to weaken, or an argument in favour of such weakening, particularly the separation of church and state. More generally, the decline of religious belief in society.

SECULARIZATION see **secularism**.

SEGREGATION (RACIAL) as an official policy of exclusion, racial segregation in the southern states of the USA was challenged by the **civil rights** movement. Segregation can also be used to refer to the phenomenon of minority communities being concentrated in spatially separate areas and living 'parallel lives', but there are disagreements both about the reality of this phenomenon and its causes which can be understood in terms of both discrimination and voluntary segregation.

SELF-DETERMINATION referring to the self-government and self-rule of the 'people' or nation.

SOCIAL CONTRACT a voluntary agreement in which individuals consent to found a system of government to regulate relations between themselves for their mutual benefit. The idea of a social contract (rather than the existence of an actual contract) is used to justify the need for government in society.

SOCIAL REPRODUCTION the biological reproduction of human life and the reproduction of labour, which brings the focus on to the household and family in the analysis of capitalist development.

SOCIALLY CONSTRUCTED something which is not 'natural' but that is created or 'constructed' through social interpretation and inter-subjective understanding rooted in social norms e.g. gender or 'race'.

SOVEREIGN referring to legitimate power and authority at its highest level e.g. a monarch or nation, **parliamentary sovereignty**.

THE STATE often used interchangeably with 'government', the term 'state' is better understood to refer to the set of institutions over which government presides. Following Weber, it can be defined in terms of its essential capacity to exercise rule within a definite territory on the basis of a monopoly of the use of force. However, the modern state has expanded to take on a range of other tasks, notably the provision of services to meet collective needs (**welfare state**).

STATE OF NATURE an imagined situation in which people live without any form of political organization ruling over them.

THATCHERISM the political outlook associated with British Prime Minister Margaret Thatcher and her governments (1979–1990), combining a fervent belief in free-market economics with a less tenacious attachment to traditional moral norms.

THEOCRATIC (STATE) religion and politics are fused, religious leaders control the state.

THIRD-WAY IDEOLOGY an ideology that is based on a rejection of both liberalism and socialism, seeking an alternative path to a better future society organized according to different economic, social, and/or political principles. More often than not, third-way ideologies borrow selectively from existing left- and right-wing doctrines but produce a novel synthesis that is more difficult to classify on the left-right spectrum.

TOLERANCE (TOLERATION) putting up with opinions and behaviours of which you disapprove or that you find offensive—can be expressed in the maxim 'live and let live', e.g. religious tolerance.

TOTALITARIAN associated with authoritarianism, totalitarianism is a form of government that establishes control over all aspects of life, i.e. the reach of political authority is total. It thus breaks down the liberal distinction between the public and private spheres and the protection of the latter.

TRANS-BOUNDARY many environmental problems are global in the sense that they are not confined within the national boundaries of any one country.

TRANSFEMINISM a transwomen movement that views the liberation of transwomen as being intrinsically linked to the liberation of all women.

TRANSGENDER someone who has a gender identity or expression that is different to the sex they were assigned at birth.

TRANS-INCLUSION the inclusion of **transgender** and transsexual people into the feminist movement.

TRANSNATIONAL denoting interaction across, above, beyond, and typically regardless of national lines. Unlike 'international' (which refers to relations between entities continuing to identify primarily along national lines), 'transnational' indicates the waning of national lines and the emergence of new collective subjects with diverse, supra-national loyalties.

TYRANNY OF THE MAJORITY a tyranny is a form of despotic or oppressive government, to which democracy may be seen as an antidote. However, a tyranny of the majority occurs when a minority group finds itself oppressed by the rule of a democratic majority.

ULTRA-NATIONALISM an extreme form of devotion to the nation, based on a full rejection of liberal principles and usually manifesting itself through the aggressive pursuit of a narrow national interest at the expense of all other perceived competitors.

UNIVERSALISM a view of the status of ideas and knowledge which, as opposed to **relativism**, holds that universal or objective 'truth' is attainable—that some values are universally valid or applicable to everyone (e.g. universal human rights). In contrast with **particularism**, emphasizes what all people share in common.

UTILITARIANISM particularly associated with the nineteenth-century liberal thinker Jeremy Bentham, utilitarianism is a philosophy or political doctrine which promotes the promotion of happiness as a guide for public policy and, more specifically, 'the greatest happiness of the greatest number'.

UTOPIAN a project or political vision arising from an excessively positive evaluation of human potential (following the ideal state described by St Thomas More, 1478–1535). See also **utopian socialism**.

UTOPIAN SOCIALISM a collective term associated with early modern socialists such as Fourier, Saint-Simon, and Owen. Utopian socialists envisaged a more just and ethical future society but were criticized by rival forms of socialism, such as Marxism, for being idealistic, unrealistic, and unscientific in their analysis of society.

VALUES those things that we hold to be good or have reason to value. E.g. freedom is a concept, and a value when a certain understanding of freedom is valued or felt to be desirable.

WASHINGTON CONSENSUS the claim that the major Washington-based international organizations (World Bank, IMF) were committed to a neo-liberal world view and policy agenda.

WELFARE STATE a form of state involving **collective** responsibility for a comprehensive range of public services that can be seen as enhancing the well-being or welfare of citizens, including healthcare and cash benefits.

THE WEST / WESTERNIZATION becoming more like 'the West' in the sense of adopting characteristic Western ideas and institutions, i.e. those that are associated with **modernization** and first appeared in the West.

WESTPHALIAN referring to the international system based upon the **sovereignty** of its constituent nation-states.

WOMEN'S SUFFRAGE the idea that the suffrage (the right to vote) should not just be restricted to men, but also extended to women.

XENOPHOBIA feelings of hatred, disgust, or fear towards people of another ethnic, national, or cultural background.

Index